# Diaries and Correspondence of James Harris, First Earl of Malmesbury

## Volume III

Elibron Classics
www.elibron.com

Elibron Classics series.

© 2005 Adamant Media Corporation.

ISBN 1-4021-7333-4 (paperback)
ISBN 1-4212-8471-5 (hardcover)

This Elibron Classics Replica Edition is an unabridged facsimile
of the edition published in 1845 by Richard Bentley, London.

Elibron and Elibron Classics are trademarks of
Adamant Media Corporation. All rights reserved.

This book is an accurate reproduction of the original. Any marks, names, colophons, imprints, logos or other symbols or identifiers that appear on or in this book, except for those of Adamant Media Corporation and BookSurge, LLC, are used only for historical reference and accuracy and are not meant to designate origin or imply any sponsorship by or license from any third party.

# DIARIES

AND

# CORRESPONDENCE

OF

# THE EARL OF MALMESBURY.

---

VOL. III.

Sir Thos. Lawrence pinxt.   John Cook sculpt.

*James Harris*

FIRST EARL OF MALMESBURY.

London, Published by Richard Bentley, New Burlington St. 1844.

# DIARIES AND CORRESPONDENCE

OF

# JAMES HARRIS,

# FIRST EARL OF MALMESBURY;

CONTAINING AN ACCOUNT OF
HIS MISSIONS AT THE COURT OF MADRID, TO
FREDERICK THE GREAT, CATHERINE THE SECOND,
AND AT THE HAGUE;

AND OF HIS SPECIAL MISSIONS TO
BERLIN, BRUNSWICK, AND THE FRENCH REPUBLIC.

EDITED BY HIS GRANDSON,

THE THIRD EARL.

SECOND EDITION.

VOL. III.

LONDON:
RICHARD BENTLEY, NEW BURLINGTON STREET,
Publisher in Ordinary to Her Majesty.
1845.

LONDON:
Printed by S. & J. BENTLEY, WILSON, and FLEY,
Bangor House, Shoe Lane.

# DIARIES AND CORRESPONDENCE.

## BERLIN.

EXTRACTS FROM A DESPATCH FROM LORD GRENVILLE TO
LORD MALMESBURY.

Whitehall, 20th Nov., 1793.

His Majesty having been pleased to charge your Lordship with an Extraordinary Mission at the Court of Berlin, I am now to convey to your Lordship His Majesty's instructions respecting the objects of that Mission, and the conduct to be observed by your Lordship.

You are already informed of all the transactions which have taken place between the two Courts respecting the present war with France, and particularly the Memorial delivered by M. Lucchesini to Lord Yarmouth, and of the note which was lately presented at Berlin in His Majesty's name, claiming the succours stipulated by the defensive Treaty;[*] of the verbal answer which was given to me on that subject by Mons. Jacobi,[†] and of my refusal to report to His Majesty any such communication, unless it was made in writing. That Minister has since communicated to me the copy of a despatch from his Court, directing him to notify the King of Prussia's peremptory determination, with respect to his conduct in the present conjuncture of affairs. I enclose a copy of this communication, with the paper accompanying it, for your Lordship's information. You will observe that the principal points there stated as rea-

[*] Of 1787, subsequent to the Provisional Treaty of Loo made by Lord Malmesbury.
[†] Prussian Minister at London.

sons for not furnishing the stipulated succours now demanded by His Majesty are the same which were brought forward in conversation by Mons. Jacobi. These are—

"1st. That before the demand of those succours can be made, it is necessary for His Majesty to fulfil the stipulations of the secret article respecting the number of troops to be actually employed against the enemy at the time when the requisition is made.

"2dly. That the King of Prussia not having claimed the benefit of the alliance, when attacked (as it is alleged, by France), ought not now to be called upon to furnish the succours to His Majesty, in consequence of an attack from the enemy.

"3dly. That the Convention recently concluded supersedes the former alliance, as with respect to this war, and renders the King of Prussia's co-operation in the war dependent on circumstances."

I think it superfluous to enter further into the discussion of Mons. Jacobi's communication, or of the other groundless arguments alleged by his Court, as pretences to justify a direct violation of the subsisting Treaty. If the King of Prussia's determination cannot be altered, it will then become necessary to examine and refute these pretexts in a formal memorial to be delivered by your Lordship in His Majesty's name, which shall expressly declare the Treaty of Alliance to be annulled by the refusal of the King of Prussia to fulfil its obligations.

The object of your Lordship's Mission is, however, to endeavour if possible still to bring the King of Prussia to a just sense of what he owes to his engagements with His Majesty, and to the steady and uniform good-faith which he has experienced from this Court, than to terminate the connexion hitherto subsisting by a declaration, which, however justified by the Court of Prussia, would nevertheless, in the present circumstances, be productive of inconvenience to the cause in which His Majesty is engaged.

Your Lordship will, for that purpose, as soon as you can after your arrival at Berlin, endeavour to obtain an interview with the King of Prussia himself, from whose sense of his engagements more may, perhaps, be expected than from the principles or policy of those by whom he is advised. You will urge in the strongest manner the *impolicy*, as well as the *injustice* of his present measures. You will state in the most explicit and unreserved terms, that His Majesty never will submit to purchase by a *subsidy* that assistance to which he is entitled by *Treaty*. You will avail yourself as far as possible of the strong and just animosity which the King of Prussia is supposed to entertain against the Republican faction in France, and of the apprehension with which he looks to the effects of their principles; and, above all, you will endeavour to impress his mind with a true sense of the consequences which would arise to the most material interests of Prussia from an open breach of the alliance between that country and the maritime Powers. It is, indeed, obvious that the effect of this must be the throwing Prussia entirely into a state of dependence on Russia; and the jealousy which has always been felt at Berlin respecting the latter power, will probably be sufficiently alive to such an apprehension. In making, however, any representations on this last point, your Lordship will be particularly attentive to say nothing which could, if repeated at Petersburg, give just grounds of offence or uneasiness to the Empress, whose interference with the King of Prussia His Majesty has thought proper to request on this occasion, and whose friendship he is disposed to cultivate.

The late communication from Baron Jacobi renders it necessary that your Lordship, after urging these several points with earnestness and energy, should in every case insist on the King of Prussia's acknowledging the *casus fœderis*, as an indispensable preliminary to all further discussion, as it must be understood that His Majesty cannot suffer the express provisions of the alliance to be called in question in a ministerial communication from his ally, without receiving on that head the most ample and satisfactory explanations; and this is a point from which your Lordship is not to consider yourself as at liberty to depart, under any circumstances which may arise.

With respect to the possibility of adopting any arrangement by which the views of His Majesty and the King of Prussia might yet be conciliated, supposing the *casus fœderis* to be distinctly and formally acknowledged by the Court of Berlin, much must depend on the real state of the Prussian finances. I trust that on the spot your Lordship will have little difficulty in ascertaining this point with some degree of certainty. If the *alleged distress* of the King of Prussia's *treasury* is wholly *feigned*, it will in that case be evident that the determination of the King of Prussia is taken rather to break his alliance with the maritime Powers, and to risk the dangers which may result from the final establishment of the Jacobin principles in France, than to contribute to the indemnification which Austria has in view; in that case all attempts at other arrangements must be useless, and nothing will remain to be done, except to insist on the succours being furnished, and, in case of non-compliance with that demand, to prepare the declaration necessary to be given in for the purpose of annulling the defensive treaty.

If, on the other hand, the pecuniary difficulties which are stated have a real existence, the disposition to co-operate further in the war may still exist; and in that case some advantage might be derived from the adoption of such arrangements as might enable His Majesty to contribute towards removing those difficulties, and securing the King of Prussia's co-operation in the war, but without departing from the just claims resulting from the existing treaty.

Before I enter into the consideration of any of the general ideas on which such plans might be grounded, I must observe to your Lordship that they are all of a nature which require their being concerted with Austria and Holland, and adopted with respect to those countries, as well as with respect to Great Britain. In passing through the Hague you will have the fullest opportunity of explaining these points, as well as the other subjects of this despatch, to the Dutch Ministers; and your Lordship's intimate knowledge of that country makes it unnecessary for me to add anything on that head. With respect to Austria, I must observe to your Lordship, that the utmost jealousy prevails between the two Courts of Vienna and Berlin; that the former has certainly been deceived by the extent given to the late acquisitions of Prussia in Poland, and that the latter is unquestionably desirous of checking, at least by indirect means, the plans of indemnity which the Emperor is now pursuing against France. Your Lordship is apprized that M. Lehrbach is to be sent to Berlin,* on a commission in some degree similar to that which your Lordship has undertaken, and he will probably arrive there about the same time. It will be very necessary that your Lordship should maintain with him an intimate and confidential communication and concert, so as that all the steps which either of you may separately take may be directed to the same common object.

---

On Wednesday morning I saw Mr. Pitt; he repeated nearly what Lord Grenville had said—was obliged to me for accepting it—said it was but fair to tell me there was no Embassy vacant, or likely to be, in case that was my object. I replied, It was not my object; that I could not, from family reasons, stay long abroad; and that I accepted the present commission under the idea that it would be a *special* one and a *short one*. That I was indifferent both as to diplomatic rank and appointments, and begged he would make both the most conformable to his own notions of what he thought right and becoming.

From him I went to the levée—King gracious. Dined with Dundas—the Cabinet there and Lord Darnley, who was to go with me as my friend.

---

Thursday, Nov. 14.—At the office, reading. Appointed Mr. Ross my secretary. Read Lord Yarmouth's correspondence, and Ewart's, at the time of the Russian armament,† and its going off. Dined with the Chancellor‡— no one there but Parnell, Chancellor of the Exchequer in Ireland. When he went, I staid some time with the Chancellor—much confidential talk;—*he* for giving a large subsidy to the King of Prussia, but Pitt and Grenville think otherwise.

* As Envoy from Vienna.
† Vide Vol. ii., page 406.     ‡ Lord Loughborough.

Friday, Nov. 15.—Reading at the office in the morning—conversation with Lord Grenville; dined at the Chancellor's.

Saturday, Nov. 16.—At the office; saw Nagel, the Dutch Minister—told him of my Mission—that I should go through Holland; desired him to write to Princess of Orange. Dined at Douglas's, and to the play.

Monday, Nov. 18.—At the office; saw Lord Grenville—conversation on foreign politics of all sorts. Dined with Elliot, of Wells, at the Star and Garter.

Tuesday, Nov. 19.—Went to Windsor to see the Duchess of York. Jacobi, Prussian Minister, gave in a kind of Memorial, expressive of His Prussian Majesty's intention not to grant the succours we had asked for, and declining all general interference in the war, without being largely paid. Dined with the Chancellor, with Lord and Lady Darnley. Went to Devonshire House—Duchess much interested about Lafayette—begged me to get him some comforts in his prison, &c.* T. Pelham† much approved my accepting; so did, in answer to my letters, Lord Bute and Windham, of Norfolk.

Wednesday, Nov. 20.—At the levée. Took leave of the King—afterwards with him in the closet (for the first time since the Regency Bill‡). He began by saying something complimentary on my accepting the Prussian Mission; then went on by saying, "A few clear words are better perhaps than long instructions. I believe that the King of Prussia is an honest man at the bottom, although a weak one. You must first represent to him, that if he allows his moral character the same latitude in his explanation of the force of treaties, as he has allowed it in other still more sacred

* Lafayette had been taken by the Austrians and imprisoned at Wesel.
† Afterwards Lord Chichester.
‡ Lord Malmesbury had voted against Government on this Bill in 1788.

ties" (referring to his marriage) "all good faith is at an end, and no engagement can be binding.* You must then state to him how much his honour is engaged in joining in this business, in not giving up a cause in which he had begun so nobly. Then you should apply to his interest, that the event of the war must either fail or succeed ; that if he withdrew himself from the number of coalesced Powers, in either case he would suffer from leaving them. In the first case (the failure of the war) he perhaps would be the first to feel the consequence of suffering this *Tartarian horde* to overrun Europe. In the second, if we succeed, he certainly might be sure that, not having contributed his share to the success, would put him in respect to the other powers in a situation of contempt and want of consequence, and that he would not be consulted or referred to in the general system of Europe, when that became a matter of discussion. That if you fail on referring him to these three great points—his *integrity*, his *honour*, and his *interest*—it will be certain nothing can be done; and although I have the greatest confidence in your skill and abilities, yet I shall rest assured in that case that *no* skill or any ability would be equal to success."

After having said this, which the King did with great perspicuity and correctness, he said the King of Prussia was an "*illuminé*," so was the Queen—that he understood from what he had heard that these "*illuminés*"† were a sect invented by the Jesuits to overthrow all governments and all order. That this scheme was only known to *a very few* at the head of the sect, and instructed in its mysteries, and that all the followers were kept in ignorance, and taught to consider it as innocent, and more moral than Free Masonry.

* A curious preamble for an ambassador to make! but the events of Lord Malmesbury's mission proved that George the Third knew well the King of Prussia's character.

† The Illuminés were republican in their principles, and advocated perfect equality. If they had sincere and honest brethren amongst them, they also numbered countless adventurers and roués, who worked upon the imagination of vain and handsome women, and silly rich men, to obtain from both what they desired. They had spies at most of the Courts, who, in return, had informers among them; but it is difficult, from the accounts we have of these secret societies, to ascertain if they really had the influence that some attribute to them over the opinions of their generation, or whether they were not, on the whole, more profitable to swindlers than to reforming politicians.

His Majesty then conversed on the Prussian Court, and confessed he could not guess who now governed the King, but he believed Manstein had much influence with him. On dismissing me he was very civil, and took evident pains to impress me with the idea that he bore no malice or recollection of what passed at the time of his illness. I dined with Lord Grenville; much talk with him and Pitt—conversed over my instructions.

THURSDAY, NOV. 21.—Breakfasted with Batt—at the office—took leave of the Queen—she civil, but stiff—King uncommonly attentive, as was also the Prince of Wales. Dined with Elliot, of Wales, at the Star and Garter.

FRIDAY, NOV. 22.—Left London at a quarter past nine, rode to Cobham; dined there; got to Dover by ten with Lord Darnley.

SATURDAY, NOV. 23.—Left Dover at 1 P.M. on board one of the packet-boats under convoy of the Savage sloop-of-war; was 53 hours on the passage, and did not get to Ostend till the evening of Monday the 25th. General Stuart, the commander, Colonel Vyse his Secretary, called on me. Wrote to Duke of York,* at Tournay.

TUESDAY, NOV. 26.—Left Ostend at 5 o'clock, got to Brussels at 1 in the morning—dined at Ghent, and staid three hours with Colonels St. Leger† and Fox—Conversation about the army; both wish me to see the Duke—Col. Fox spoke most highly of him as a man, and able general—

---

\* The Duke of York was commanding the British army. He had laid siege to Dunkirk in the previous August, and had been obliged to raise it with the loss of his battering trains. The French then attempted to break into the Netherlands, but were repulsed at Morent, Ypres, &c. On the 15th and 16th of October, Jourdan attacked the Prince of Cobourg, and drove him across the Sambre; and from this time the French armies, which had previously been worsted on this frontier, were almost always victorious.

† Lieutenant-Colonel of the Guards then in Flanders.

Both think Sir James Murray* an unfit man for his station. I declined going to head-quarters, but appointed St. Leger to meet me at Brussels.

WEDNESDAY, Nov. 27.—Saw Lord Elgin† at 10.—Some general discourse with him. At 1 went to Antwerp—slept there, left it at 4 A.M. On Thursday, was on the other side of the More Dyke by 3 P.M., and at the Hague by 1 in the morning. Met Larrey‡ (the Colonel) near the More Dyke.

FRIDAY, Nov. 29.—Called on Elliot; he communicated to me his last letter from Berlin—rather better than the former accounts. Went to Court, and dined there—Pensionary§ and Greffier|| and Count Welderen¶ were asked to meet me. Pensionary on seeing me said, " Voilà Ulysse revenu à Ithaque." He was everything that private friendship and public confidence could wish. Prince and Princess not at all forgetful of past times, and a general sort of kindness and attention from everybody which flattered me very much. I visited many old acquaintances (Mad. de Welderen among others), and wrote letters and supped with Kalitcheff.** The society very little altered. Archibald Hope and his wife there; he is now in the " Magistrature."

SATURDAY, Nov. 30.—Count Rhoon Bentinck†† early—blames the Hereditary Prince of Orange—praises Duke of York. At ten with the Pensionary—he glad I am going to Berlin—reasons admirably on my mission. Suggests various ideas (they appear in my correspondence)—rather prejudiced against Austria when we began, but I gradually brought him to be less so. Prince *still* untractable,—re-

---
\* Adjutant-General to the Duke of York. He commanded afterwards the expedition which made the attempt on Ferrol in 1800.
† English Minister at Brussels. ‡ In the Dutch Service.
§ Mons. Vander Spiegel. || Baron Fagel.
¶ Count Welderen was long Dutch Envoy in London, and married the sister of Lord Howard de Walden.
\*\* Russian Envoy at the Hague.
†† Head of the younger branch of the Bentinck family. His seat was near the Hague, and he had independent possessions in Lower Germany.

commends me to talk to him.—From Vander Spiegel to the Greffier's at 12. He quite, as usual, diffident to advance his opinion, but quite right—Talked to him about the Frontiers the Dutch wished to recover. He pointed them out to me from the tenth volume of Lamberti, specified in the Treaties of 1704.

---

EXTRACTS OF A DESPATCH FROM LORD MALMESBURY TO LORD GRENVILLE.

*Brussels, Tuesday, 3rd Dec., 1793. Private and confidential.*

I SHALL confine myself in this despatch to what the Great Pensionary said to me, on several points, not immediately belonging to the main object of my Mission, but which are closely connected with it, and on which, from my habits of intimacy with him, I have every reason to believe he spoke with the utmost sincerity, and most unreserved confidence.

As they take in a very extensive field, I shall endeavour to compress them as much as possible. They may be divided into two heads—his opinion on the general system to be observed by Europe in the present crisis, and as to that more particularly applicable to the Republic, of which he is one of the leading Ministers, and its allies.

On the first, he thinks that one common object unites *all* the different Powers, but he conceives the *four governing* ones, and which ought to direct the others, are Great Britain, Austria, Prussia, and Holland; their object is the resisting the progress and destroying the source of those execrable principles which have lately manifested themselves in France.

That this purpose, in the pursuit of which no one can have a distinct interest from another, ought to supersede all other consideration: that all references to past jealousies, as well as all future apprehensions, should be forgotten, since, while this is under contest, an apprehension infinitely superior to any other *actually exists*.

That therefore a plan of union should be formed expressive of the end in view, and explanatory of the means by which this end is to be attained.

That the end spoke for itself; it was the preservation of the *rights of all property* as well *national* as *individual*, and the destruction of a system that aimed at the overthrow of *all social order*, and *every social and religious virtue*. The means he stated to be reducible to four.

1. To decide what was to be done with the Interior Government of France; how it was to be so settled as to give it sufficient energy to prevent the contagion from breaking out again, and at the same time not enough to enable it to be the perpetual disturber of the peace of Europe, as it has been for a century and a half under its three last monarchs.

2. A clear and distinct understanding, as well on the military operations as on the political measures requisite to secure this object.

3. A correct, and not overrated statement of the force each power can, and means *bonâ fide* to furnish, and also to what extent they can reciprocally assist each other with pecuniary aids, or credit if required.

4. An arrangement (necessarily subservient to events) of what each of the Powers is to take from France, by way of defraying the expenses and risks of the war.

On these four cardinal points being precisely and speedily settled, he considered the fate of the war, and with it the fate of Europe, to rest. It was on similar principles that the Grand Alliance in 1701 was framed, and history furnishes us with many examples that all leagues, without such a previous accord, have constantly failed.

That *separate conventions* between each Power will not answer the end, and such necessarily will create *separate operations*, and in the result perhaps *separate interests;* they must all be circled by one strong and common political chain for one common and distinct cause; that for this purpose the four Courts should, without loss of time, appoint a place for the meeting of their respective Plenipotentiaries, —in this meeting all these points should be settled and methodized; and that it should be afterwards considered as the centre, on which all the operations should turn, and to which all doubts and dilemmas should be referred.

On the fourth and last point (the subject of indemnification) the Pensionary thought that all the acquisitions

France had made since the peace of Munster* were very fair objects of reprisal.

At two, with the Princess of Orange. Told her my commission—she very civil about it, but could give me no information—was shy about condemning her brother, yet could not approve what he did—suggests the idea of our taking 30,000 Prussians into our pay, instead of increasing our own army. At three, with the Stadtholder—he very talkative, but not on the point. Events of the campaign†—incidents during my embassy—reflections on his own conduct *then*, and proving to me from events he was right at times when I thought him wrong. Talked admirably on the temper of the times—said the two words "democracy" and "aristocracy" were not new in Holland. His friends were of the first description, and he feared lest they should be tainted by Jacobinism—strong advocate for a respectable aristocracy.

Dined at the Hereditary Princess's—she very pleasing—came late with the Stadtholder, who kept me till half-past four. Her son (an infant, a fine child). More conversation with the Princess; nothing remarkable—I recommended strongly to the Prince energy and vigour. Took leave of him. Counts Rhoon and Welderen, "Frondeurs;"—all Dutchmen are, but they are only so in *words*. Rhoon grown more steady—wants a Congress, and to be employed at it. Called on Lady Athlone and Madame Slane. The first told me a story of Lady ———, who has run away with a ———. The other low and melancholy. Saw Keller, Prussian Minister, at his own house—he seemed to know nothing, but wished to have the appearance of having talked with me—a heavy dull man—his wife prettyish but "*mauvais ton*"—supped with Schanbart (the Dane).

* In 1748 the Treaty of Munster terminated the Thirty Years' war.
† On the 29th the Duke of Brunswick had beaten the French at Landau, and on the same day, Wurmser, commanding the Imperial army, defeated them on their whole line, and drove them beyond Strasbourg; but his success was short, as he was in his turn pushed back over the Rhine by Hoche and Pichegru. Prince Hohenlohe, who was besieging Landau, and who was covered by the Duke of Brunswick's Prussians, was then obliged to raise the siege, whilst the Duke himself retired on Mentz, and on the 6th of January, 1794, resigned the command of the army.

SUNDAY, DEC. 1.—General Bentinck called—read me a letter from Fischer to engage him to prevail on the Stadtholder to pay early attention to the army. I advised him to show it to the Pensionary. Bentinck communicated to me a Memorial of Angely* on La Vendée (I took an extract of it)—a very curious piece if true. At twelve with the Pensionary—he read me a memorial he had drawn up on the times†—much reasoning with him; he, as he is always, very clear, clever and acute. Great complaints, and very justly, at the Hague, of being left without an Ambassador from England for so long. Left the Hague at seven in a yacht, and Rotterdam at twelve, in the yacht of the Gecomitteerderaden—got to the More Dyke by ten A.M., and to Antwerp by seven—wrote letters, and slept there on Monday, Dec. 2.

TUESDAY, DEC. 3.—Got to Brussels by two—writing for the post. St. Leger came to see me. Dined at Elgin's—returned home to write. Despatched Brooks at midnight.

WEDNESDAY, DEC. 4.—Captain Cook returning to Toulon—news from Lord Howe—visits to Mesdames Balbi and Caumont — to Merci‡ at three — his manner slow and rather pedantic, his figure that of a Minister de la *vieille Cour*—apparently open and frank, but I should doubt his being so.

Conference with Count Merci.—Genoa, its arrangements, &c.—all the little states of Italy, in alarm, had applied to the Emperor; he no troops but 10,000 men in the Milanese—Sardinia behaves ill; danger of an incursion on the side of Nice.

On my Mission, which I opened to him, he told me what had passed between his Court and that of Berlin—very

* Sent by the Royalists to La Vendée as an agent.
† A very clever document, in which he argues that the French have a great advantage over their enemies by paying their army by assignats, whilst the latter pay in gold; and advocates a quadruple alliance between England, Austria, Prussia, and the States, who shall give security to a paper currency, the French to pay *all loss* when beaten.
‡ Merci was Minister to the Austrian Viceregal Government at Brussels, under the Archduke.

different from what it said to us—Lehrbach's mission;*—
talked of his own principles and feelings on the French
Revolution; he had been twenty-five years in Paris, as a
mentor to the Queen.† Was "*intime* at the French Court."
Saw the "*pourriture*" of it long ago—that if the conviction
of the cause did not operate, nothing could. It was not
possible for any power to discontinue war, without risking
its ruin—thought this consideration must operate on King
of Prussia; said he did not know who his Ministers were.
Asked about Schulenburg and Hertzberg, described Haugwitz as a man new in business—talked of England and
Austria as the two Courts on whose shoulders everything
rested—they were united "*sous tous les rapports*"—praised
our Cabinet; said his own was composed of "*de très honnêtes gens.*" Talked much in favour of the old system—
praised Duke of York, and our troops—said, "*la bonne
cause lui devoit les plus grandes obligations;*" urged the
necessity of an immediate plan of co-operation — that
although great valour had been displayed, the last was
"*une campagne chétive.*" Said Paris must be pressed.
Intimated whether the King of Prussia could not be prevailed on to act as defender of the frontiers of Germany on
the Rhine, and leave us to act in Flanders.—Dined with
Elgin.—St. Leger called on me—states Sir J. Murray as
unpopular, and this makes the Duke of York so.—Much
general talk about the army, which he says is ill-provided.—
In the evening at Madame de Matignon—she pleasant, but
thoroughly *French*.—Frugal, but cheerful supper. Afterwards at Lord Elgin's.

THURSDAY, DEC. 5.—Sent Estafette to Duke of York to
say, I would meet him at Ath, as His Royal Highness had
suggested, on Friday. At one, to the Archduke—well man-
nered and speaking to the purpose. Breteuil‡ in bed—
very pompous, and still *the Minister*. Dined at Merci's—

---

\* Austrian special Minister at Berlin.      † Marie Antoinette.
‡ Mons. de Breteuil was ambassador at Petersburg under Louis XV. Afterwards his Minister for the Home Department; he kept this post till the Revolution of 1789, when he emigrated. He returned to France under the Empire,
and died there in 1808.—*Biog. Univ.*

formal company. Lord Yarmouth come*—called on him—found him angry beyond expression at my going to Berlin—quite overcome by passion; would not listen, but begging his own questions—went on accusing me with breach of confidence, friendship, &c.—a perfect angry child, who vents his passion on the first object he meets. But his real anger was with Ministers, which he did not dare show, for fear of their displeasure; he therefore vented it on me, who he knew would take more from him than any other person in the world. There was not an unpleasant thing he did not say, or an unpleasant reference he did not make. He glanced more than once at a challenge, and if I had not known him so well, and felt it right on every account to bear with him, I must have lost my temper. I was forced to stay, as I had sent away my carriage, expecting to meet Lord Yarmouth in the most cordial and confidential way. Supped at Elgin's—chiefly French—Mesdames Matignon, Balbi, Caumont, la Baronne de Montmorenci, Richelieu, &c.—Merci d'Argenteau also there. Conversation with him about Dutch Frontiers. I thought their demand reasonable, as what they want is important to them by way of safety and defence, and no real value to the House of Austria. Merci thinks otherwise—values the district wanted by the Republic high. These districts are Lillo and Liefenshock, and their territories, to join the Generality with Dutch Flanders; and the space between Ecluse, or Sluys, and the sea, and that mouth of the Scheldt called the Swyn. The first is necessary to prevent a reincursion on the side of Antwerp, the other to protect the land. Besides this (but that I did not mention) the Dutch want to join Maestricht to the Republic. This very difficult. Necessary to get Roermunde, or at least all the country round it; in order to give them the complete sovereignty of Maestricht, an exchange must take place with the Bishop of Liège. All this difficult, and I disapproved it when the Pensionary and Greffier mentioned it, because their ideas seemed to go to

* Afterwards Marquis of Hertford. He had been sent to the King of Prussia; and Lucchesini, not accustomed to the frankness which it appears he met with in this Minister, said of him, " Ce Milord est un homme d'une probité bien aimable, car il vous dit d'abord tout ce qu'il sait, et tout ce qu'il peut faire."

the secularizing ecclesiastical dominions, which in *these times* I am very much against. After, however, talking a good deal with Merci on the first of these points, we agreed with him, if the war ended as we hoped it would, the Dutch would evidently be entitled to their share of indemnity. That they deserved it, and if they had not done quite as much as the other Powers, yet it was wise and more candid to praise than to blame them.

At one in the morning Lord Yarmouth wrote me a note, to say he wished to see me the next morning; Lord Elgin had been to call on him (but was not received) to speak about the Hessian Troops, which had positively refused to embark under Lord Moira,\* pretending that it was against the Treaty, which ran " *de ne pas servir sur la flotte.*" This we mean as Marines, and they construe *to embark, or under any pretence whatever to go on shipboard.* Two separate Treaties, verbatim the same, and both after old precedents in the office, were signed, one by Lord Elgin, the other by Lord Yarmouth. The first about a year ago, the second (that in question) in this summer; and it was on this point Elgin wished to see him, and instead of seeing him, Lord Yarmouth (conscious perhaps that he had really supplanted him in his Prussian mission) expressed a wish to see me. I appointed him early, as I was to go to Ath to meet the Duke of York. He called on me at half-past nine; was rather less violent, yet still wrong-headed; I tried to explain to him, and in some degree succeeded; I found his aim was still to come to Berlin. He was embarrassed when I told him I knew he had *accepted* Spain, and had even *asked* for Switzerland; that I was ready to give way to him at Berlin if Ministers thought it useful for the King's service. He had said the preceding evening, in a moment of passion, that I should be ill received, and gave for reason my having signed the Treaty of Loo. This he unsaid this morning, and, in coupling the two conversations, exhibited his character—selfish, intemperate, cunning, and nervous, and with a fear to displease—which occurs to him (from its attendant inconveniences) always on recollection.

\* The 4000 Hessians subsidized by his (Lord Elgin's) Treaty, did receive afterwards orders to join Lord Moira.—*Original Note.*

We parted on tolerable terms, but I was forced to write to Lord Grenville on the subject, and to request him to explain how, and why, I had the Prussian Mission, to convince Lord Yarmouth that I had never a thought of supplanting him, or even could guess I was in his way.

FRIDAY, DEC. 6.—At twelve went to Ath, Lord Elgin with me to Halle, and got to Ath by half-past six; roads very bad, full of soldiers and waggons, it being those to both the head-quarters of Prince Cobourg and Duke of York. Duke brought Sir J. Murray with him, but he left us often alone. He said his army was ill provided. Condemned the whole measure of Dunkirk and separation of the armies; spoke slightingly of the Dutch, and still more of the Hereditary Prince of Orange, whom he called " *Young Hopeful.*"

On my hinting a possibility or rather a certainty that Grey would make *Dunkirk* the first object on the opening of the Session, the Duke said he trusted none of *his* friends would be so over-zealous as to think it necessary to defend him at the expense of others. That whatever he might feel or think as to himself, and the *usage* he had met with, yet, that this consideration was a very secondary one indeed, if the obtaining it stood in the way of the great cause for which we were contending; and he should be very sorry indeed that any blame should be thrown on any particular measure, or any particular Minister, as it certainly would go to censure the principle of the War and produce the worst consequences. The Duke of York (Sir J. Murray being absent) went into a detail of his own situation, which he said was unpleasant; he had *nobody* about him, no Secretary to write for him as the old Duke of Cumberland had; no *really experienced* officer. He had written to the King; had been forced to say, Sir James was unpopular. The Duke read me the King's Answer, which was that of a most affectionate Father to a favourite Son. His Majesty entered into all he said, proposed giving Murray rank and a Scotch brigade, to appoint Craggs in his stead, and, in answer to a request of the Duke's to return home, advises him not to ask it, in order to keep his officers abroad, but that he will send for him to England soon. This was an excellent and most affectionate letter; and the Duke's answer, which he read me, was equally so—all respect and proper attention.

The conversation confirmed me in the opinion, that the Duke of York has a very good understanding; but he *talks* too much, and is careless to whom. I ventured to tell him so, and took an opportunity of recommending him to ask the superior officers to dinner; and, as he could not prevent their writing home, to try at least to furnish them, by *his* conversation there, with *materials* which would do *no harm.* Now they, and particularly the Guards, write nonsense, almost equal to mutiny. To this he attended with great good-humour. I staid till one in the morning, and then returned to Tournay. I remained at Ath all night—wrote on the morning of Saturday, Dec. 7. Lord Herbert* came to me, and we returned together to Brussels. He was very glad to see me—complained very much of the insubordination of the army, that it was greater than could be believed; that the Guards were so beyond measure; that the Duke of York was most unjustly unpopular, and he believed the worst used man in the world, as all his foibles were cried out against, and none of his good qualities, which were many, noticed. The French, he said, fought well, and had every appearance of disciplined soldiers. That he had seen them run away,—so had English, Austrians, and Germans; praised the Hanoverians for *fighting*, but not their *activity*—Marshal Freytag an old woman†—Prince Cobourg rather a "*bon homme.*" He expressed himself sick of the profession, but could not leave it. Condemned the conduct of Gage, who had resigned on being refused leave of absence. Got a late dinner at Lord Elgin's. Went home to write—despatched Brooke.

---

Sunday, Dec. 8.—Lord Herbert with me till twelve, when I left Brussels—Lord Darnley to follow the next day.

---

\* Eldest son to the Earl of Pembroke.

† Freytag in his youth bore the character of a good officer, but his day was past; and, like most of the German Generals at this period, he had become inefficient.

Dined at Louvain (Lord Elgin went with me); at Fernan Nuñez, Spanish Ambassador at Paris, who has been living there ever since the revolution. He the same good pleasant man, but low and vexed at having lost a great succession (that of Rohan, by the troubles in France, near three millions of livres). His politics seem right; his wife good-humoured; he has seven children—none well-looking.

Elgin returned to Brussels; I went on and slept at St. Trond, at *l'Homme Sauvage*—moderate inn. Left St. Trond Monday, Dec. 9, at five—dined at Aix la Chapelle—slept at Juliers. At Liege (Dutch head-quarters) saw several officers of my acquaintance. Nineteen hours on the road.

TUESDAY, DEC. 10.—To Bonne—delightful day—ten hours on the road.

WEDNESDAY, DEC. 11.—To Coblentz—eleven hours on the road—roads spoilt, and worse than I ever saw them.

THURSDAY, DEC. 12.—Lord Darnley joined me. Left Coblentz at nine. Passed through * * * * and Limburg to * * * *, where we got by nine, having dined on the road.

FRIDAY, DEC. 13.—Left * * * * — (moderate inn) — at half-past seven passed through Koenigstein, which is quite destroyed, and got to Frankfort by half-past three. Road bad. Found Kinckel at *La maison rouge*. Lucchesini not likely to succeed at Vienna. His wife (a sister of Bishopswerder) † clever and meddling. Had written to Stein—said the Court of Vienna was stiff—would not listen to a subsidy, or to an indemnity, and that (qu'il ne valoit

---

\* Names illegible in the original manuscript.

† Bishopswerder (properly spelt Bischoffwerder) was a Saxon who entered the Prussian service with the rank of Colonel. He had at the beginning of the reign, great political as well as personal influence with the King. The latter he retained. A private wrong became on his part a cause of national dislike towards England.

pas la peine de s'être meublé) for she foresaw they should not remain long there. Lehrbach, an overbearing man, and used to dictatorial language, from having always been employed at *small courts*. Kinckel* did not know his present instructions, but those he had when with the army were not conciliating. Lucchesini, anti-Austrian, very Russian, an enemy to England, had by his intrigues removed everybody from the King of Prussia's ear and confidence, who were either English or Austrian, (a very different description of men, however, at Berlin,) and seemed to favour no system but a Russian alliance. He had deceived Lord Yarmouth entirely. Sir James Murray sent first (in March, 1793) to talk over Dumouriez's† intended interview with Lord Auckland and Vander Spiegel. This failing, he remained there, and was doing very well, when Lord Elgin was sent, who did well, but was too frank and "*loyal*" to be a match for Lucchesini's cunning, which he found out and reproved too loudly. Lord Yarmouth succeeded him, and was Lucchesini's dupe. Lord Yarmouth did, however, well with the Duke of Brunswick, whom he kept up to act at a time (in October) when it was feared he was going back with his army.

Mad$^{lle}$. Bethman very artful and ambitious. Had made the King of Prussia believe she really loved him for *his* sake, and that no other woman ever had; this had disposed him to go all lengths—even that of a left-handed marriage‡, but it was stopped by an anonymous letter her cousin (little Bethman) sent to Ma$^{de}$. Lucchesini, to state the character and views of his relation; and Lucchesini finding from this she would not answer his purpose, and *be tractable*, was now doing his utmost to overset her. He, Kinckel, believed he had succeeded, and that a young woman of rank at Berlin, whose name he did not know, but whom I suspect

---

* Admiral in the Dutch Service, and acting with Lord Malmesbury for the States, in the present negotiation. He was a German gentleman by birth, clever, honest, and zealous; he was also well acquainted with the parties with whom he had to deal. He died at a very advanced age at Munich, where he was Dutch Envoy.

† Commander-in-Chief of the French Republican army on the N.E. frontier, who conquered Austrian Flanders in 1792, and lost it again in 1793.

‡ This could only be in the event of the death of the Queen, a Princess of Hesse Darmstadt, who was still living.

to be Mad[lle]. Vienck, was now nearly declared favourite. Yet that since this week two chasseurs had come from Potzdam to Mad[lle]. Bethman ; she is well-made, but not handsome.

King of Prussia found in his treasure seventy-six millions of crowns. He expended ten in the Dutch campaign, twenty in that of Reihenbach (this large sum was necessary, as all his army was then to be put in order for motion), fifteen in his preparations against Russia, and fifteen in the last two—remain then sixteen millions from his original treasure, to which must be added, according to Kinckel's calculation, three and a half millions, which are supposed to be saved each year. Of course the whole remaining treasure may be forty-one or forty-two millions of dollars.

Prince de Nassau\* very well with the King, and the instrument the Empress of Russia employs—he also well with Lucchesini. Kinckel observed, that, as the King of Prussia would not allow us to reckon Hanoverians, he could not reckon the Saxons—there were 6,000, and if taken from his army would leave it 42,000 men; that is, 10,000 more only than his contingent to the House of Austria, and quote part to the empire, and for these 10,000 he asked twenty-two millions of crowns. Kinckel said that Bishopswerder told him, that Lord Elgin, when in Italy, would have succeeded in making a triple alliance for the purpose of general peace and tranquillity when he was with the Emperor Leopold at Florence, if he had not run too much after Mad[me]. Lamberti (Leopold's mistress), and by that means displeased and soured him. Bishopswerder he thinks an honest man, and of strict integrity—certainly for an Austrian connexion, and might *perhaps* be made very useful. Lucchesini venal, and bought he believes by Russia. Stein (once a favourite, and his minister at Mayence) now disgraced. Alopeus not noticed by the King on his return. King displeased with Treaty of Alliance between Russia and Poland.

Kinckel said Mad[me]. de Lucchesini was very averse to live

\* Spurious Prince, a sort of bettermost adventurer, employed by Empress Catherine. (*Original Note*.) He was born and bred up in France ; had commanded the Russian fleet in the Black Sea, against the Turks and the King of Sweden. He was sent in 1793, by Catherine, on a special Mission to Berlin.

at Berlin, and would object strongly to her husband's return
—Mad^me. Bishopswerder and Mad^me. Lucchesini sisters. The
first was a Mad^me. Pinto, and Bishopswerder was divorced
from his first wife, who is still living, and by whom his
daughters are. Lucchesini relies much on the influence of
Mad^me. Bishopswerder over her husband. She is a vain talking woman, not to be trusted, but may be made useful by
discreet management.

It is believed the King of Prussia left the army with
reluctance, and was intrigued and cajoled into it by Lucchesini. He staid two days at Frankfort, not merely to see
Mad^lle. Bethman, but because he was doubtful whether he
should not rejoin the army, and was low and ashamed of
what he had done. At the army his return is considered as
sure. He has left his equipage at Anspach; and his two
sons theirs, at Mentz. His connexion with Mad^lle. Bethman
is one of sentiment. She is too artful to let it go further.
Her cousin and relations want her to marry a Mons. Jeannot,
a merchant at Frankfort; she declines this, and has *certainly*
in view a left-handed marriage with the King. Manstein[*]
not in high favour, but belonging to the "Conseil de Guerre"
—an empty good-for-nothing fellow—French to a degree,
was overheard talking to the French Commissaries at Worms,
in the most abject and flattering way. Reede[†] (Dutch
Minister) gets his intelligence through his wife's mother—
from Minister Schulenburg. Reede ill at Court—Lucchesini
called him, Ewart, and Hertzberg, the *triumvirate*. "Ewart
avait l'esprit, Hertzberg la plume, and Reede les poumons."
Prince Louis, son to Prince Ferdinand of Brunswick, has
democratical leanings; very brave but "étourdi;" wants to
raise 500,000 florins by subscription to form a kind of inde-

---

[*] Manstein was a Prussian Colonel on the Duke of Brunswick's Staff, during the campaign of 1792, in Champagne. He held negotiations on the part of the Duke with the French, which were followed by the retreat of the Allied army from France. In their correspondence Dumouriez addressed him as "le vertueux Manstein," a designation which did not appear sufficiently appropriate to prevent its being used facetiously as coupled with his name.

[†] Baron de Reede was clever, but he was more naturalized at Berlin than it is desirable that a Foreign Minister should be; and he became extremely jealous of Kinckel, and, as Lord Malmesbury thought, thwarted him during this Mission. He had a most acute jackal in his Secretary, M. Bourdereaux.

pendent legion to be given afterwards to the best bidder. Hompesch,* the hussar, deep in this.

From many circumstances it seems likely that Lucchesini is bought by France through Merlin.

---

LORD MALMESBURY TO THE HONOURABLE THOMAS PELHAM.

Frankfort, Dec. 13th, 1793.

My dear Pelham,—I had a great deal of interesting and confidential conversation with the Duke of York (at Alost on the 6th instant), too much so to be trusted on paper to the common post; the result, as far as it related to himself, went to confirm me in the good opinion I always was disposed to have of him, and in general not to alter that I had of many mistakes which had defeated the effects of his exertions and abilities, and rendered the end of the campaign less brilliant than its beginning. He was not insensible to these, but he expressed a very earnest and anxious desire, that if any of the more violent Members of Opposition (and he named Grey) should in their attempt to distress and criminate Government affect any solicitude about him and his situation, or even if they should join him in the common blame and censure about Dunkirk, or any other military operation, I say, that in either of these cases, the Duke of York expressed his earnest and anxious desire, that none of his friends, out of regard and attachment to him, should say anything *which might raise a cry against Ministers, or weaken their measures by defending him at their expense.* That such a defence, however gratifying it might be to him, would necessarily go to weaken Government, and in its effect militate directly against a cause—the support of which he considered as a duty before which every personal consideration whatsoever ought to give way. That it would be impossible to separate in the minds *of the many* partial blame of any one specific measure, in the course of the war, from a general disapprobation of the principle on which it was

* Hompesch was afterwards a General in our service.

begun and continued, and that the very worst of consequences would attend such an idea being attributed to those whom he was happy to think his best friends. He named you and Mr. Windham, and expressly directed me to write to you both, and which I have done in his own words, as nearly as I can recollect them; I am sure I have not altered them. The only case in which he hoped to be defended was, if any gross and obviously abusive attack should be made upon him; and then he wished (as this would be evidently made to provoke), that the defence should rest on general grounds, and all particular details and personalities be avoided.

I am the more anxious to write to you on this subject, as I knew it was one you were desirous of being informed on. I intimated this to the Duke, and I am sure you will love and esteem him the more for this manly and liberal behaviour. I have written this nearly verbatim to Windham also at his request; and I wish you would concert with him, and with such other persons as you have confidence in, in order that they may observe the line of conduct the Duke wishes; as, although his sentiments on this occasion must add to the zeal and ardour of his friends, yet he is most certainly as right and judicious in what he advises, as he is moderate and forbearing in his feelings; for it is undoubtedly of the last importance, that Parliament should open with the greatest appearance of unanimity, and that England should give the impression to Europe, that all private animosities and party feuds are lost in the *great cause* for which we are struggling, and be assured that all good and great impressions can come from England alone.

My dear Pelham, be convinced that it is not because I am in a sort of employment that I hold this language—I would hold it even if Lord Lansdowne was Minister; and every step I move on the Continent convinces me that to hold any other, or to express a different sentiment, would be committing a decided act of Jacobinism. You must give me credit for this, and upon assertion, for I have neither time nor opportunity to prove it, which if you were sitting with me I could and would do in an hour.

I am, &c.   MALMESBURY.

SATURDAY, DEC. 14.—Rode with Kinckel—went to a bookseller, by name Elsinger—excellent one—walked afterwards round the whole town, and dined with Bethman; various people at dinner—good, in the German style. His mother well-mannered; and his sisters, one married to a Swiss, M. Levi, the other a widow. Bethman (the young man) quite right, alarmed.—Told Lord Darnley, Lucchesini was gone to treat with the Court of Vienna—that he was to propose their giving back Galicia for Alsace and Lorraine (this I do not believe); I settled a correspondence with him. Wrote to Windham and Pelham.

SUNDAY, DEC. 15.—Breakfasted with Kinckel. Left Frankfort at nine—got to Schotten in twelve hours—roads indifferent.

MONDAY, DEC. 16.—Left Schotten at six—got to Bergen by nine—roads very good to Vacha—bad and hilly from thence to Bergen. Dined very well at the post.

TUESDAY, DEC. 17.—Left Bergen at half-past seven—arrived at Gotha at three—forced to stop there, as the Princesses of Mecklenburg had taken all the horses. Lord Darnley left me at Bergen, intending to go round by Dresden to Berlin. Gotha, a town of a middling size, in a very open country, on the north side of a hill; running water in most of the streets, or "trottoirs." The palace on an eminence finely placed—commands the town and adjacent country. Apparently large; bad, or rather no architecture; pleasant drive round the town on the outside. No symptoms of trade—Almanacs famous.

WEDNESDAY, DEC. 18.—Left Gotha at twelve—got to Erfurt by four—still stopped by the Princesses. Erfurt, an academy with only eighty students. An ill-looking town; belongs to Elector of Mentz—the Coadjutor resides here.

THURSDAY, DEC. 19.—Left Erfurt at seven—got to Naumberg at six. I never saw such fine weather in December; no rain, no wind, no frost during any part of my journey, but mild sunshine. Good inns at the post at Erfurt, at Naumberg, and civil landlords.

FRIDAY, DEC. 20.—Slater, the messenger, overtook me at four in the morning with despatches. Lord Grenville approves the idea of *Les Billets de Confiance*. Lord Howe returned empty-handed. Left Naumberg at half-past seven —at Leipsic by five—sent Slater on to Berlin.

SATURDAY, DEC. 21.—Left Leipsic at seven—Wittenburg by nine—dined in my carriage.

SUNDAY, DEC. 22.—Left Wittenburg at a quarter before four—got to Berlin by one in the morning—dined in my carriage—Lord Darnley just got there before me; lodged at the Ville de Paris, where rooms were taken for me.

MONDAY, DEC. 23.— Rose,* Secretary of Legation, and Chargé des Affaires, came to me—desired him to announce my arrival to Count Finckenstein,† according to usual form. Baron Reede, Dutch Minister, called on me—his information similar to that I had heard from the Pensionary, as to the situation and disposition of the Court—assured me that I might lead it—that I had been expected with great impatience—that the treasure was exhausted—pressed very much that the plan of the next campaign should be settled here—offered me his best services and assistance. Walked

---

* Afterwards Sir George Rose, and for many years M.P. for Christchurch. I am indebted to him for much of the explanatory information contained in my notes relating to Lord Malmesbury's Mission to Berlin. His long residence at that Court makes it most authentic.

† Count Finckenstein was the senior of the Prussian Ministers: old in years and ancient in office. He was a mere formalist; and under Frederick the Great had been nominally his Foreign Secretary.

—dined at home—went to Count Finckenstein—left him a copy of my credentials—told him the substance of my commission—mentioned no details. He said the King would see me as soon as possible.

TUESDAY, DEC. 24.—Count Finckenstein, by a note, informed me the King would see me at a quarter past four next day. Wrote—dined with Reede; Count Lehrbach, who is here on the same errand as myself from the Court of Vienna, and Prince Reuss,* dined there. At half-past four I had my audience, being introduced by Count Finckenstein; King altered in his looks—has lost his upper teeth. I observed to him that I had no diplomatic rank—that I had declined it purposely to avoid subjecting myself to the etiquette and privation belonging to it—that I hoped His Majesty would receive me with his usual goodness, and admit me to his society, as he had done before. From him to the Queens, reigning and dowager, both very civil to me—from them to the wedding of the Prince Royal—the ceremony as usual (this the sixth wedding I have been present at, at Berlin). Supped at Count Finckenstein's table—Madame de Haugwitz, wife to the Acting Minister for Foreign Affairs. Finckenstein appointed me to meet him and his two colleagues, Alvensleben and Haugwitz, at eleven the next morning.

WEDNESDAY, DEC. 25.—At eleven to the conference—dined at the Prince Royal's—at five to a Court of Compliment to the Princess Royal, and from thence to a supper at the King's—played with the Princess Royal at Cassino—many old acquaintances. On return home found Hislop from Petersburg—letters from Whitworth† announce the Empress's good disposition, and that she was going to send Prince Nassau to enforce them—sorry for it—re-despatched Hislop.

THURSDAY, DEC. 26.—Began writing my despatches;

* Prince Reuss was Austrian Envoy at Berlin.
† Sir Charles Whitworth, English Minister at St. Petersburg.

called on Rose; at 11, at a second conference as the day before, the *casus fœderis* avowed, poverty pleaded, goodwill promised, &c. &c. Called on Reede, and on Lehrbach—this last very talkative and prolix, but right and well-inclined; stated his commission, &c.—observed the difference of conduct held by King of Prussia at Vienna and at London. Seemed full of suspicions about this Court. I spoke very openly to him. Dined at Arnim's. Marriage of Prince Louis; the two brothers marry two sisters, daughters to Prince Charles of Mecklenburg, and nieces to the Queen of England. This evening the same as Tuesday—dined with Madame Haugwitz. Wrote letters till a late hour.

FRIDAY, DEC. 27.—Writing till one o'clock. Despatched Wiffin. Dined with the Queen's Court at Princess Louise's.* Ball and supper in the Great Apartments as at Court—told the King of Prince Nassau's appointment.

EXTRACT OF A DESPATCH FROM LORD MALMESBURY TO LORD GRENVILLE.

Berlin, 26th Dec., 1793.

I AM happy that the result of my audience with His Prussian Majesty, and that the conferences I have had since with his Ministers, enable me to send away the messenger Wiffin sooner than I thought it would be in my power to do, when I wrote to your Lordship on Tuesday last.

I was introduced on the evening of that day to the King of Prussia by Count Finckenstein, and I remained alone with His Prussian Majesty for half an hour, after delivering, in the usual form and with the usual compliments, my credentials, and receiving from His Prussian Majesty the usual answer. I asked leave to enter with him on business, saying, that experience had left a very lasting and agreeable

* Daughter of Prince Ferdinand of Russia, youngest brother of Frederick the Great. She married Prince Anthony Radziwill. She was distinguished by talent and great amenity of manners, and enjoyed an unblemished reputation.

impression on my mind; that he had before admitted me to that honour, and that very essential advantages had been derived from it. On His Majesty acquiescing readily in my request, I stated to him in very respectful terms the first point of my instructions, and declared that till it was distinctly acknowledged that the treaty of alliance of August 13, 1788, existed in its full force, and that the present war was admitted as a *casus fœderis*, my hands were tied from proceeding a step further; and that I was ordered to obtain this avowal previous to any other discussion whatever.

The King of Prussia expressed a surprise that a possible idea could exist of his departing from the principles of the Treaty, or of his intention to observe its stipulations being doubted; but, without breaking into what I intended to say by dwelling on this point, at this period of the conversation, I went on by observing, that His Prussian Majesty's good faith never could be called in question—that the King, my master, had the strongest confidence in it, and the utmost reliance on the strict integrity and high honour of his character; that besides this motive for adhering to his engagements, the glory of his arms and military reputation rested on his not giving up a cause, the defence of which he had begun so nobly and maintained so bravely; that his political interests and consideration, and even safety, were also intimately connected with his not withdrawing himself from the number of the coalesced Powers; and that to these three strong incentives of good faith, honour, and interest, a still more imperious one might be added—that of necessity. For it was impossible for His Prussian Majesty to say that the war should cease, or to stop that horde of barbarians, whose steps were to be traced by anarchy and cruelty wherever they came, from overrunning his dominions, and effecting ultimately the destruction of his monarchy.

Your Lordship will naturally suppose that I repeat only the substance of what I said, not the words in which I spoke; these I endeavoured to make the most suitable to the great personage to whom I was addressing myself; but I also endeavoured that my meaning should not be lost in too much attention to ceremony. His Prussian Majesty, as

I went on, acquiesced in everything I advanced; and from the manner with which he listened to me, I was induced to hope (and I expressed this hope), that the unpleasant impressions the two Memorials of the 23d September and 19th November had given, would be done away, and that His Prussian Majesty would order his Ministers to reconsider them, and empower them, when I should meet them to discuss on these points, to say to me, what I had begun by stating as an indispensable preliminary to all further discussion—viz., that His Prussian Majesty considered the Treaty of 1788 to exist in its full force, and all its stipulations as binding.

His Prussian Majesty declared in the strongest manner that he never had the most remote idea of departing from the Treaty of Alliance. That if he had expressed doubts as to the *sense* in which its stipulations were to be understood at this moment, it was not from any alteration either in his sentiments of cordial and sincere friendship for His Majesty, or in those of his abhorrence and detestation of the ruling party in France; that he continued to set the highest value on His Majesty's alliance; that he considered it as the one the most conformable to the interests of the kingdom, and a perfect co-operation with His Majesty as the most likely to put a short and successful end to the present war; that it was from the peculiar circumstances of this war, that these doubts had originally arisen; but that he was fully disposed to dismiss them, and acknowledge, fairly and candidly, that the real reason which made it equally impossible for him to begin another campaign with the same force as the last, and to grant the succours we required, was *the want of money.* He then said, "You will, I am sure, believe me when I tell you, *on the faith of an honest man,* and for being one, I hope the King, your master, will give me credit, I have not in my treasury enough to pay the expenses of a third campaign. Those I have incurred since my accession are not unknown to you. You also know that the late King strained the resources to their highest pitch; that I cannot raise a new tax on my subjects, and to attempt it would drive them to the worst consequences, without its producing anything; and that the nature of the Prussian monarchy is such that it cannot bear a loan. In short, that without my allies come to my assistance, and afford me pecuniary support, I shall be compelled to stop short in the war, and leave only a small portion of my army on the Rhine; and I feel," added His Majesty, "the importance of its not being lessened, and the consequences of it, in as strong a manner as any of the coalesced Powers, for they affect me as much as they do them."

"I have no difficulty," continued the King of Prussia, "in stating this embarrassed situation of my finances to you, openly, and without fear; I have not exhausted my treasure in idle or useless expenses, and, although perhaps at times the most exact economy has not been observed, yet it has been employed in forwarding measures which related to the general interests of Europe, as well as to the particular ones of Prussia. It cannot be those of England to see me degraded and sunk; and this certainty, joined to my high notion of your national character, leaves me without apprehension as to the consequences of the declaration I make, which I repeat to be the sole and real cause for my apparent backwardness in continuing the war." His Prussian Majesty then spoke on a subject I had avoided mentioning, and said suspicions and jealousies had been entertained of him; that it was but too natural that ill-wishers to him and to the cause should be industrious to give such reports the air of veracity, but that they were in fact the grossest impositions on truth and common sense; and that, far from objecting to any indemnities the Court of Vienna might wish to have (arising from France), he not only thought such indemnities perfectly reasonable, but should see them carried into execution with the greatest pleasure.

This is nearly what His Prussian Majesty said. I ended the Conference by asking his permission to address myself *directly* to him, when I should have anything material to say; and that he has allowed me to do; and I took my leave, by expressing my hopes that I should find his Ministers prepared for what I had to say to them.

EXTRACT OF A LETTER FROM LORD MALMESBURY TO MADAME LA
COMTESSE DE BALBI.

> Berlin, 27 Decembre, 1793.

Le peu de momens que j'ai passé avec vous à Bruxelles, Madame la Comtesse, ne m'a laissé que des regrets de ce que je n'ai pas pu vous voir, pendant plus long tems ; d'y suppléer par des lettres est une manière bien peu satisfaisante. Mille choses se disent mutuellement, qui prennent une autre forme dès qu'elles se trouvent placées dans une lettre, quand même, comme celle-ci, elle ne sera pas exposée à l'inspection des maîtres de postes. J'ai regretté surtout d'avoir passé si superficiellement sur ce que vous m'avez dit du voyage eventuel de Monsieur à Toulon.* Je ne sais pas à présent comment rattraper cette occasion, sans avoir l'air de faire l'officieux, ou bien le Ministre. Cependant je ne suis motivé que par un attachement aussi zélé que sincère, et respectueux pour Monsieur, ce qui, joint à une counoissance légère, mais assez certaine des affaires du moment, me fait désirer, et m'engage même, à hazarder de vous exprimer ce désir que Monsieur n'entreprenne pas le voyage qu'on l'a invité à faire. Il est difficile, mais très difficile, qu'il en resulte gloire ou avantage pour lui, ou pour sa cause, et son éloignement de ce côté-ci de l'Europe dans les circonstances actuelles peut avoir des inconvéniens réels pour l'un et pour l'autre. Je suis sûr, Madame la Comtesse, que votre esprit pénétrant les saisit d'abord ; si vous les envisagez comme moi, votre opinion sera conforme à la mienne, et votre opinion (comme de raison) peut beaucoup.† Elle sera selon moi employée bien heureusement, si elle sert à déterminer Monsieur à revenir dans ces parages.

A moins que les affaires prennent une tournure bien heureuse, il ne peut rien à Toulon. Et si ceci arrive, comme j'aime à croire, un Régent de France fera cent fois plus

---

* Toulon had, early in this year, been given up to Lord Hood, on condition that it should be returned to the Bourbons at their restoration. We held it till the end of the year, when we abandoned it to the Republican armies, having first brought off our troops and destroyed the shipping.

† Madame Balbi had great personal influence with Monsieur, afterwards Louis XVIII.

d'effêt de ce côté-ci, qu'enfermé dans une place assiégée, où sa présence ne fera que redoubler les efforts des assiégeants. Leur surcroît d'acharnement contre la ville peut même occasionner en addition, et s'il y a des malveillants parmi les habitans, ils peuvent dégoûter les autres, et avec un tel ôtage entre leurs mains, les persuader à marchander un accommodement, et il n'est pas besoin de vous mettre sous les yeux tout ce qui resulteroit d'affreux si Monsieur se trouvoit au pouvoir des Patriotes.

"Je sais la juste déférence qui est due à la Cour de Madrid, qu'elle a agi depuis la Guerre avec toute la loyauté possible, mais peut-être n'a-t-elle pas calculé les inconvéniens que je viens de citer, et je les crois si réels, que je ne doute nullement que s'ils furent représentés en Espagne, elle ne voudroit plus que Monsieur entreprisse de se jetter dans Toulon.

"Je suis si accoutumé de vous parler avec toute la confiance possible, Madame la Comtesse, que je ne crains pas de penser haut avec vous, sur que de telle manière que vous envisagiez mes sentimens, vous n'en ferez jamais un mauvais usage."

---

SATURDAY, DEC. 28.—Prince Ferdinand presented to the King.—Visit to Lehrbach—shewed me his memorials on arrival here—those which had passed between Lucchesini and the Austrian ministers.—Lucchesini's style harsh, and not cordial—evidently with a view to get the Court of Vienna into a promise of pecuniary succours before England, in order to facilitate their project.—Italian and shabby. Dined with the Prince Louis. Opera. Supper at Prince Royal's. King told me of bad news from Würmser's army*—that he had lost two battalions and twenty-one pieces of cannon. He seemed rather pleased with this bad news,†

---

* Würmser commanded the Austrian army on the Upper Rhine. He had acquired reputation as a partisan in the French service during the Seven years' war.

† This feeling of hatred towards Austria was shared by every Minister at Berlin, and every officer in the Prussian army, and rendered all our efforts to combine efficiently the two nations against France unavailing. This went to such an extent, that, after the campaign was over, the French General Desaix (killed at Marengo) told M. Barthelemi, the French Minister at Berne, that

but admitted that it would do harm by raising the spirits of the Jacobins.—Talked of Nassau's coming. I said I hoped his commission would *now* be useless. Madame de Reuss, niece to Prince Sacken.*

SUNDAY, DEC. 29.—With Colonel Manstein by appointment at 11. He pressed much for a plan of campaign—condemned the last—said the first should have been made against Lorraine, not against Alsace—this was against the course of the Rhine, and of course the country rose—that it carried the two armies from each other—urged the necessity of money; that it was important that it should be known if it was to be given, that measures may be taken—said it would require three months and a half to put the army in readiness to begin the campaign—talked of recruiting magazines, &c. &c.—he seems heavy, but not without parts. Walked for the first time. Dined at Hertzberg's—found him shewing three Poles, on a map, how *he* would have divided Poland, if he had been consulted. Great and moderate dinner. The Minister Blumenthal preaching peace. Ball and supper at the Queen's—played with Prince Sacken and Prince Ch. of Mecklenburg.

MONDAY, DEC. 30.—Walked—dined at Nesselrode's—immense dinner—opera buffa. Bad news from Würmser confirmed. Lehrbach came to me dejected and alarmed—said Würmser's letter to the Duke of Brunswick was that of a man "au désespoir," that he seemed to have lost his head—represented his whole army as ruined, &c. The Duke of Brunswick's "rapport" and observations tending to enforce this. advises the keeping beyond the Rhine.

TUESDAY, DEC. 31.—Walked to upholsterer's and cabinetmaker's. Lehrbach—he read me all the unfavourable ac-

occasionally the *Prussian* officers came over at night to apprize them of movements which the *Austrians* proposed to make the next day.

* Prince Sacken was made Great Chamberlain by Frederick II., as an inducement to him to spend his large income at Berlin.

counts from the Rhine, as they were communicated to him to shew me, by Colonel Manstein.—The Austrian army was attacked and beaten by the French near Trischweiler on the 22nd — lost two battalions and twenty-five cannons — French approach Landau, which must be saved—Würmser retreating—Duke of Brunswick advises a battle—Würmser declines it—writes a desponding letter to the Duke of Brunswick, dated Frenckenfeldt, 26th December, 1793— describes his army as ruined, not in a state to be kept together—relates the position he has taken, but says he cannot keep it, but must retire beyond the Rhine to save his army from utter annihilation—Duke's answer to this is, to advise an immediate concert of measures, to attempt to save the hospitals, magazines, &c. ; to keep his position till the 28th, and then retire beyond the river Leich, and canton from Hambach to Germersheim ; if Würmser cannot keep beyond the Rhine, at least to secure Manheim, and keep up the communication between the two armies ; that on this the safety of Germany depended.

The Duke of Brunswick, in the report he makes of this defeat to the King, says, " *que l'Armée Impériale est entièrement renversée, et se trouve dans un état d'épuisement et de mécontentement ;*" that by his movement he had prevented its being cut off from Weissenberg ; that he had proposed to attack the French, but that Würmser's army was not in a state for it ; that on the 26th he had repulsed the French. The Duke then describes his position to the King ; apprehends that the Austrians must repass the Rhine, and that, by this means, the " blocus" of Landau must be raised, and nothing to be done but to canton the army near Mentz.

Duke of Brunswick, in a letter to Manstein, described the Austrian army as without head, without money, and *without discipline*—recommends the King to write to Prince Cobourg, to attempt a diversion in the Low Countries, to reinforce his army near Treves, and to cover Coblentz.

All these accounts, though true in great part, are probably *exaggerated*, and sent with a view to *depress the Court of Vienna*, and facilitate the demands made here for money. Dined at home—supper at Queen Dowager's—tea with Madlle. Bishopswerder—Prince Nassau arrived in the evening late.

WEDNESDAY, JAN. 1, 1794. — Visits — King's levée— dined with Queen Dowager—Prince Nassau came home with me—said he brought a long letter of six pages from the Empress Catherine to the King—he had seen the King after the Levée—he said to Nassau nearly what he had said to me; was to see him again—he read to me what he said was the *précis* of his conversations with the Empress, written down herself, and afterwards copied by him—begins by referring to " the treaties concluded between Russia and England, and Russia and Holland"—states the " necessity of fulfilling his engagements"—mentions the Convention of 1793 " as strengthening these engagements"—refers to the Treaty of Alliance and agreement with the Emperor, also the Convention of January 1793, and dwells on " the partition of Poland and the engagements he contracted for his share—that all these oblige him to continue the war;" and his own declarations and manifestos from the first, by his own confession, make him to be a principal in it. The Empress then, in the strongest terms, points out the risks he runs of the French principles getting into his country— " that he encourages them by weakness—that by his listening to timid councillors, and by going from *foiblesse à foiblesse*, Louis XVI. first lost his throne, then his life—if the King of Prussia fears a revolt, his irresolution and wavering will provoke, not prevent it."

Describes the *épuisement* of her Treasury, and avoids touching upon pecuniary succours—talks of her impartiality, and desirous of preserving an equal power between Austria and Prussia. Prince of Nassau said he intended to read this to the King of Prussia. His conversation very right, and in general sensible. He called himself *habitant du monde*, and that he was taxed with being Prussian; that he was of no country—said Alopeus was a Prussian agent; he had orders not to trust him—lamented Lucchesini's absence as a man of sense *très fin;* but added, that his being so, or not, in the present case was of no consequence.

I approved his reading this paper to the King, and to say, if an opportunity offered, that the sum required was out of all proportion to the succours offered; that the one must be diminished, or the other very much increased, before anything could be agreed. Talking of the army, Nassau said he was sure the command of it would be taken from the Duke of Brunswick, who would retire of his own accord, and that he believed Möllendorff would have it. Opera—supper at Prince Louis'—King expressed great anxiety that I should go on with the negotiation; said " qu'il ne désiroit rien que de retourner à l'armée." I said I had no powers to *conclude*, but that I was ready to suggest such ideas as I had, and thought were conformable to the wishes and means of my Court, and to listen to any His Majesty had to propose. I requested him to name *with whom* he chose I should talk; he hesitated as to naming anybody, but went on by urging the necessity of no time being lost—mentioned the Prince of Nassau—said he was to see him again the next day.

TUESDAY, JAN. 2.—Walking in the morning. To Reede, learnt nothing from him.— No letters from England; now three weeks without any.—Dined at home.—At 5, Nassau. He said he had read that paper to the King (I rather doubted it)—expressed himself satisfied with what had passed; asserted that he was quite sure of the King's good disposition, and also want of money. I observed, the sum was too great, or the number of men to be given too small—Nassau proposed an increase of the latter, the indemnity to be paid by France. I approved it, desired him to see the King again. Agreed to it. Lehrbach came in—stated his mission to Nassau—prolix and *ardent*. Nassau went away. I then opened myself to Lehrbach on the different means suggested to supply the King of Prussia with money; appointed him next morning.—Ball and supper at Alvensleben's.

FRIDAY, JAN. 3.—Lehrbach, and then Nassau, with me. First uneasy—approved my idea of taking some step which might prepare the way, and advance the business—expected his messenger from Vienna back.—Nassau keen and sanguine—said the King of Prussia was eager to take the field—that he would see me at half-past ten next day—said he had read to him the paper he had shewn me, that it had great effect (talked rather *en aventurier*).

Walked in the Park—dined with Rose—called on Madame Haugwitz—Dull supper at Princess Henri's, Loto.—Lehrbach came home with me, stayed till near two in the morning. His messenger returned—ordered to give in a note, to say his Court referred the arrangement to Russia—was tedious and prolix to a degree, full of suspicions and doubts about this Court, and not clear on any subject. Just after he went, I received an estafette from Lord Elgin, to inform me of the bad news of Toulon being retaken by the French on the 18th December.

SATURDAY, JAN. 4.—Up early, called on Lehrbach and Nassau.—At half-past ten to the King.

---

EXTRACT OF A DESPATCH FROM LORD MALMESBURY TO LORD GRENVILLE.

Berlin, 5th Jan., 1794.

THE necessity of pecuniary relief which I must suppose to exist is, indeed, still the constant theme of the Prussian Ministers; but they no longer seem to demand it (if I may be forgiven the expression) like sturdy beggars, but to be disposed to put their demands into the common course of negotiation.

I might unfortunately add, that the unpleasant events on the Rhine, and the still more unpleasant accounts from Toulon, struck me as forcible though uncomfortable motives for pressing forwards; and I was finally determined to do so, from the repeated anxiety His Prussian Majesty has expressed to me almost every day, that, if I had not authority to go on, I would at least take some measures to prepare the way, and which might tend to facilitate future discussions when they were to take place.

On the 1st of January he took me aside before supper, and pressed this point so very strongly to me, that, impressed as my mind was with the consideration I have just stated, I replied, that although I could not enter ministerially into the subject, yet, if His Prussian Majesty would allow me, I was perfectly ready to hear everything he might be disposed to say, and afterwards to submit to his consideration such ideas as appeared to me the most practicable, and the most conformable to the means and interests of the parties concerned. That I would, if he desired it, confer with any confidential persons he might appoint; but that it would be infinitely more satisfactory if I might be allowed to see him. In consequence of this conversation His Prussian Majesty sent for me to come to him yesterday at half-past ten, and my motive for despatching Slater is to inform your Lordship what has passed in this, and in another interview I have since had with him.

The King of Prussia began his conversation by repeating to me the expediency he felt to continue the war, his invariable abhorrence of the French principles, and his thorough conviction that, if they were not checked, all government and all order would be overthrown; and that if impressions had been attempted to have been made, either at London or Vienna, that he had in any degree altered his sentiments on these points, it was either the work of ill-disposed or bad-intentioned people, or the consequence of his principles being mis-stated or mis-understood. That it was necessity, and necessity alone, that governed his conduct; and that if he was not certain that another campaign would completely exhaust his treasure, and leave him without the means of providing for any future extra expense, he should not hesitate a moment as to the line of conduct he should observe. He said, he trusted I would give him full credit for this, and that the fidelity of my reports would leave no doubt on His Majesty's mind of the sincerity of his professions or truth of his assertions; that he was eager and anxious on every account to return to his army, which (and it was for this reason he was so desirous of explaining himself to me) he was so far from wishing to lessen or withdraw from its present situation, that he would increase it to the amount of 100,000 men, if it were possible he could be supplied with the means of supporting them in the field.

He paused here, as if he expected I should say something relative to these means. I told His Prussian Majesty, and I believe with great truth, that the idea had gone forth so generally, and was so generally believed, that it was from a change of system, and not from any other reason, that he was about to withdraw himself from the number of the Coalesced Powers, that all the attention had not been bestowed on the different ways of raising those means that would have been done, had the real reason been alleged in the first instance, and not a great deal of time lost, and suspicions raised, by unnecessary Memorials. That it was not in England alone this apprehension existed, but also at Vienna; and His Majesty had a very recent and convincing proof from all he had heard from the Prince of Nassau in a still stronger degree at St. Petersburg. That, when what His Majesty now said was known, there could be no doubt that these false and unfortunate impressions would be done away, and every possible attention paid to what he said. That if, in the meanwhile, he would condescend to explain himself, and state to me something like a plan on which so responsible an army as that of 100,000 men might be formed, I should hold it my duty to transmit what he said to my Court in any way he might direct, either as a confidential or as a ministerial communication. That I only wished it to be understood by His Majesty that I had no authority to proceed, much less power to conclude; that my positive orders were to wait till the return of the messenger I despatched on the 26th ult.; and that he would be pleased to consider what I had ventured to say, and my undertaking to repeat what I heard, as an effect of the high confidence I reposed in him, and of my perhaps too forward zeal to determine an object the importance of which was so strongly felt. I repeatedly urged this at different moments of the conversation, and it was distinctly admitted by the King of Prussia. If, therefore, it should be thought that I have observed an improper conduct, I have at least carefully avoided committing my Court: I have spoken all along as *from myself;* and everything which I have said or done may be disavowed without the possibility of an accusation of inconsistency or retracting being fixed on the declarations and measures adopted by His Majesty on this occasion towards this Court.

Having stated this circumstance as clearly, I hope, to your Lordship as I did to His Prussian Majesty, I shall now proceed to relate what he went on by saying, which he desired might be considered as a confidential communication to serve as the basis of a future arrangement. His Prussian Majesty declared he was ready to bring into the field the number of men stipulated by his treaty of alliance with the Emperor, and his contingent to the Empire; this he said would amount to about 28,000 men (for he rated his contingent at only 7,500): and that he would by the opening of the campaign increase his army to 100,000 men, if the Coalesced Powers could supply him with the means of defraying the expenses of this additional number. He thought this might be done by each of them taking a quota part of the whole expense; and that the money might be raised by a loan, for the security of which, part or the whole of France should be engaged: that he had understood also that the idea of creating a paper currency had been suggested, (I found this had been intimated to him by the Dutch Minister here), and that, though he was by no means experienced in finance, he thought this might greatly facilitate the operation; but as he had not the remotest view of enriching himself, but only to prevent his being involved in complete ruin, he was ready that the expense requisite for the maintaining this corps (72,000 men), with their necessary dependences in the field, should be regulated by two commissaries, the one on his part, the other on that of the Coalesced Powers.

That at the head of this army he would begin the campaign, by acting in such a manner as he trusted would leave no doubt of his sentiments on the present war, or of his invariable wish to fulfil his engagement to the utmost of his power.

---

SUNDAY, JAN. 5.—Writing. Haugwitz at twelve: his manner gentle and pleasant, but not easy. Dwelt on *total* emptiness of the treasury—said the King could contribute *nothing*—Empire should contribute. With Nassau: he shewed me his intended report, good and correctly stated.

Dined at Marshal Möllendorff's; long but good: he very right and satisfactory. Supped at Queen's.

Monday, Jan. 6.—Writing. Despatched Slater at one. Baron Leuthe, Hanoverian Minister; talked with him about the means of the Empire; alarmed lest an exchange should take place, and Mecklenburg Schwerin be given to the King of Prussia in lieu of the Margraviates. Short walk; dinner at Nesselrode's; wrote to Whitworth by Nassau's messenger. Opera; supped with the King; he very anxious still to go to the army—talked to me of nothing else.

Tuesday, Jan. 7.—Walked—dined with Queen—supped at Arnim's; sat next the Princess Louisa, pleasant, amiable, and well educated. Ridotto – quadrille—Reede as Godfrey of Bouillon—ridiculous!

Wednesday, Jan. 8.—Writing all day. Dined tête-à-tête with Darnley. Lehrbach, late in the evening, brought me the answer to his note. King of Prussia refuses the mediation of Russia—insists on having his army supplied, or threatens to withdraw it by 1st of February. Lehrbach angry—states a mistake in the answer—is to get it altered.

Thursday, Jan. 9.—Writing in the morning. Darnley went away at two. Dined with Prince Sacken—great dinner. Supped with Queen Dow$^r$. Played with Princesses Louisa and Augusta. Got into my new house.

LETTER FROM LORD MALMESBURY TO LORD GRENVILLE.

Berlin, Thursday, 9th January, 1794.

My dear Lord,—The inside of this Court is really a subject fit only for a private letter: unfortunately it is so closely connected with its public conduct, and influences it so much, that I wish to give you every information relative to it in my power. I have been here so short a time, and so constantly employed, that my account will be naturally very imperfect; but Lord Darnley, who has had more leisure and opportunity than myself to investigate it, will supply the defect.

The female in actual possession of favour is of no higher degree than a servant-maid. She is known by the name of Mickie, or Mary Doz; and her principal merit is youth and a warm constitution. She has acquired a certain degree of ascendency, and is supported by some of the most inferior class of favourites; but, as she is considered as holding her office only during pleasure, she is not courted, though far from neglected, by the persons of a higher rank.

The two candidates for a more substantial degree of favour are Madlle. Vienk and Madlle. Bethman. The first (I really believe, extremely against her will and her principles) is forced forward by a party who want to acquire consequence; and I am told she has the good wishes of Lucchesini, who thinks he shall be able to lead her. Madlle. Bethman plays a deeper game: she acts from, and for, herself; she professes to love the King, but that her principles prevent her giving way to it; she is all sentiment and passion; her aim is to be what his first mistress was, and to turn to her account all the licentious latitude it is said the *illuminés* allow themselves. Madlle. Bethman is cousin to the wealthy banker of that name at Frankfort, and, from what I have learnt there, is perfectly qualified to act the part she has undertaken. The King of Prussia inclines to believe all she says, and calls her "*une fille bonne et précise.*"

Lucchesini is still certainly a very governing man here. Why he went to Vienna on a commission which required no superior talents, or was likely to produce any great applause, and why he stays on there, I cannot learn; unless we are to suppose him acting in complaisance to his wife, who is at daggers drawn with her sister, Madame Bishopswerder, and who I am told dislikes Berlin.

Bishopswerder is undoubtedly restored to great personal

favour, but hitherto is neither consulted nor trusted in any matter of business, foreign or domestic. He is now living at Potzdam. The King of Prussia visited him there on Monday, and writes to him, as I hear, every day.

Manstein is his great opponent, and very unlike him in character: he is rough, active, and interested. He has no system of his own: depends on Lucchesini, and pays the most assiduous court to Haugwitz, who is the only person amongst the Ministers of State at all in possession of the King's favour or confidence. Haugwitz has gentle and pleasing manners; without knowledge and experience, but with capacity sufficient to understand an unpleasant commission, and temper enough to acquit himself of it with great moderation. He is supposed also to be an *illuminé*, and it was as such he was first noticed by the King.

Count Finck and Alvensleben, the other two Ministers for the Foreign Department, are perfectly insignificant. Finck is respected for his age; Alvensleben is the fine gentleman of Berlin, and takes the lead in all the balls and suppers. Among the other Ministers of State none are worth mentioning but Struenzee, who is said to be an able financier, although no proof of his ability in this branch is to be found.

The first man, undoubtedly, here in every respect is the Marshal Möllendorff; he possesses character and integrity. He thinks and reasons most judiciously on the part this country ought to take. It is of the last consequence that he should command the army, if the Prussian army is to act.

In regard to the Foreign Ministers, either by forming connexions here, or from a deficiency of understanding, they are all much more like *agents* of this Court, than like men of rank sent to attend to the interests of their own. Prince Reuss from Vienna, Count Zinzendorf from Saxony, Mons. Alopeus from Russia, and, above all, Baron Reede from Holland, come so entirely under this description, that it is impossible to derive any other advantage from a connexion with them, except to learn what the Prussian Ministers wish you to do.

I am at a loss what to say of the Prince de Nassau. I am well aware of the French proverb, that says, "Nothing is so like an honest man as a clever rogue," but I really do not know whether it might be applied to him. I have as yet discovered no deceit or duplicity in his conduct, and his vanity and indiscretion have rather given me an advantage over him in our conversations. He is uncommonly well received by the King, who likes his manners, which are very pleasant.

I am exceedingly well satisfied with Count Lehrbach : he is open, confiding, and active ; his only fault is the betraying too strongly his feelings at the manner in which this Court does business, and his suspicions of its insincerity. The answer he has just received to his last note, though it is drawn up in the usual style of their official papers here, yet does not make any material difference as to the main object ; and I think the King of Prussia, having declined the mediation of the Empress of Russia, may by displeasing her produce rather a good effect. This measure I believe to have been advised by Lucchesini from Vienna, since, when I first mentioned it to the King of Prussia (on Saturday morning), he seemed rather pleased with it.    I am, &c.

MALMESBURY.

FRIDAY, JAN. 10.—Lehrbach with me early—consulted what he was to say at this appointed conference—Nassau eager and sanguine—Reede more communicative in consequence of a letter from the Pensionary—offers to act in concert. Lehrbach again ; relates before Reede the result of his conference—Alopeus (Russian Minister) at it—I recommend that Lehrbach, Reede, and myself should act in concert. To the Opera—conversation with Haugwitz—mentioned to him *all* my letters from England having been stopped. To Count Reuss, thence to the King's supper, and then returned with Madlle. Bishopswerder to Reuss's—she in the carriage told me her father was coming here—that he believed, for both our sakes, and that of the cause, it was better I should not appear to be much with him—that he had as yet acquired no political favour, although it perhaps might come.

SATURDAY, JAN. 11. — Writing—short walk—pleasant

dinner at Prince Reuss's—assembly at Marshal Möllendorff's crowded—King and Royal Family all there—supper tedious and long.

SUNDAY, JAN. 12.—Wrote to Vienna—King's levée—Möllendorff appointed to the command of the army in room of Duke of Brunswick—Court and supper at the Queen's.

MONDAY, JAN. 13.—Nassau with me early—reasoned on Möllendorff's going—Thiel and the Minister Schulenburg to go with him. Walked—dined with Reede—Opera—supped with the King—he still anxious for news from England.

TUESDAY, JAN. 14.—Wrote—called on Rose, Madame Reuss. Supper at Arnim's with two Princesses—sat next Princess Louisa at supper—very pleasant and accomplished—Ridotto.

WEDNESDAY, JAN. 15.—Walked to several gardeners, and afterwards dined with Prince Nassau—ball and supper at the King's.

THURSDAY, JAN. 16.—Alopeus—visited Madame Schulenburg—Queen Dowager at supper—played with the Princess Royal—afterwards Alvensleben's—singing—small party.

FRIDAY, JAN. 17.—Conference with Marshal Möllendorff —his ideas right, and intentions excellent—his plan of campaign, to leave the Prussians the defence of the Rhine, and to increase the Austrian army in Flanders—the Prussians to attack by Lorraine, the Austrians by Picardy—said two or three millions might be advanced from home. Dined with Count Finckenstein—Opera—supper at Reede's.

SATURDAY, JAN. 18.—Walked—dined at Arnim's—assembly at the Minister Haugwitz's.

SUNDAY, JAN. 19.—King's levée—walked with Haugwitz in the Park—he suspicious lest we should make a separate peace—afraid of the opening of Parliament; in other respects right and well-spoken. Dined at home—supped at the Queen's.

MONDAY, JAN. 20.—Wrote—walked. Dined at home; Lehrbach dined with me. Opera.

TUESDAY, JAN. 21.—Wrote—dined at Queen's—supper at Arnim's; ridotto.

WEDNESDAY, JAN. 22.—Walked to Charlottenburg. Dined at Nesselrode's. Visited Madame Schulenburg. Conversation with him—same language as the other Minister; he more clever. Supper and ball at the King's.

THURSDAY, Jan. 23.—With Madlle. E. Bishopswerder; said that her father's enemies (Manstein and Haugwitz) had contrived to interrupt her sister's match with Gurowski, a Pole—thought her father's influence was nearly over—said Madame Dienhoff was at Augermunde. Walked with her—advised to observe and take care of Reede, the Dutch Minister*—to find out if there was no French intrigue going on, &c.—Dined with Count Reuss—fifty-one persons. Concert at Countess Maurice Bruhl. Supper at the Queen's.

SUNDAY, JAN. 26.—King's levée. Dined at home. Supper at Queen Dowager's.

TUESDAY, JAN. 28.—Dined at Queen's, on Marianne Bishopswerder's marriage with Count Gurowski, a Pole. Supper at Arnim's. Ridotto—the last.

* Reede was decidedly French by inclination and interest, and jealous of Kinckel, the Pensionary, and others of his countrymen more distinguished by the Stadtholder than himself.—*Harris Papers.*

WEDNESDAY, JAN. 29.—Dinner at Nesselrode's. Ball at Court—the last—danced.

FRIDAY, JAN. 31.—Dinner at Minister Struensee's *—Chevalier Bouffleurs there.

SATURDAY, FEB. 1.—Dinner at Zinzendorff's.† First assembly at Count Finckenstein's.

EXTRACT OF A DESPATCH FROM LORD MALMESBURY TO LORD GRENVILLE.

Berlin, 1st Feb., 1794.

I AM sorry to say that suspicion and mistrust increase every day between this Court and that of Vienna. It is as difficult as it is useless to decide where the blame lies. M. Lucchesini has undoubtedly behaved with the most unjustifiable petulance; and the peevish method the Prussian Cabinet has of doing business has worked very sensibly on the frank but irritable temper of Count Lehrbach, and possibly contributed to sour his reports. My only wish is, to keep everything even until some decisive measure is agreed upon; this once determined, it will be very easily discovered from the conduct of this Court whether it is playing false or not; and if it is, it requires no instructions either to Count Lehrbach or me, to know what we ought to do. In the meantime, although it would be highly censurable to act on a principle of implicit confidence, yet the manifesting a direct contrary opinion, prematurely, prepares us for a negotiation, every step of which will be marked by cavil, mistrust, and ill-humour.

Your Lordship will undoubtedly have heard from different quarters that this Court has agents at work to negotiate either a truce or *separate peace* with the *Convention*.‡

---

\* A Dane by birth, and brother to the Struensee who was executed in 1772, as compromised in the affair of the Queen of Denmark.
† Saxon Envoy at Berlin.
‡ The National Convention at Paris.

This idea has, I have reason to believe, found a place in the correspondence of most of the Foreign Ministers here, and certainly would not have been omitted in mine could I have grounded it on any positive data. It rests principally on the departure of a person of the name of Settan (formerly with Count Goltz at Paris), who left Berlin a fortnight ago, and who it is supposed is gone either to Geneva or Deux Ponts (it is doubtful which) to meet an agent from the Convention; and it is added that he received his instructions from Baron Alvensleben, and set out from the house of this Minister in the night. I cannot even ascertain the matter-of-fact part of this report; and if it could be done, unless we were sure of the rest, it would only lead to a conjectural conclusion which would be in such direct contradiction to the positive assurances I hear daily from the King of Prussia, that although I am very far from being credulously confident, and disposed to make great allowances for instability of character, yet I confess I should think I acted unfairly, if on such loose ground I suffered my mind to suspect a duplicity of conduct so very disgraceful when coming from so high a quarter.

SUNDAY, FEB. 2.—Court.

MONDAY, FEB. 3.—Breakfast at Fredericksfeldt with Meden.* Went with Count Reuss—dined with me at home, and Prince Reuss. Supper at Prince Henry's— played with Princess Royal.

TUESDAY, FEB. 4.—At home—supper for the wedding— afterwards at Madame Gurowska.

WEDNESDAY, FEB. 5.—Called on Madame Reuss and Madame Gurowska. Walked. Dined at home. Supped with Queen Dowager. Went with Landgrave George of Darm-

* In the Prussian service, and brother to the Duchess of Courland.

stadt into her apartment—she and Queen very much pleased with King's speech. Timms (messenger) arrived with full powers for me.*

THURSDAY, FEB. 6.—Called on Lehrbach and Reede. Went into the park to meet the King. Walked with him and Haugwitz. Dined at Nassau's. Supped at Bellevue—went with the Reusses.

FRIDAY, FEB. 7.—With the King—Lehrbach had a Ministerial conference. Dined with Nassau—he said he would go to Vienna. Ball at Finckenstein's—Nassau and Lehrbach there—very hot.

SATURDAY, FEB. 8.—*Death of Kivilicki.*† To Prince Reuss. Assembly at Arnim's. King eager for Nassau's going to Vienna—presses the business.

EXTRACT OF A LETTER FROM LORD MALMESBURY TO SIR MORTON EDEN.‡

Berlin, 8th February, 1794.

WE are engaged, my dear Sir Morton, in one of the most material negotiations that ever existed, and on our success depends the fate of Europe. I am happy in having you for my fellow-labourer. Our situations, however, differ materially—you are at a Court, all sincerity, confidence, and system. I need not say how different our position is, but it is of the utmost importance for me to conceal all I feel and mistrust: to betray my suspicions would destroy every means I have here of getting on. I consider all we are

* The despatch here alluded to contains Lord Grenville's scheme. It was that 2,000,000*l.* should be given to the King of Prussia to bring 100,000 men into the field. That England should furnish two-fifths, or 800,000*l.*, Austria one-fifth, the Republic of Holland one-fifth, and the other fifth should remain as an advance from Prussia, to be reimbursed by France at the restoration of peace. Lord Grenville suggests an invitation to Russia to join in the subsidy.

† Kivilicki was Polish Minister at Berlin—and the last.

‡ English Minister at Vienna, and brother of Lord Auckland, and subsequently created Lord Henley.

now about, as leading ultimately to that wise and natural union between England and Austria which lasted for their mutual advantage and benefit for so many years. But, to attain this, we must get successfully through this war; and, to ensure success, we must employ every means in our power, as well of exertion within ourselves, as to induce others to act with us efficaciously and vigorously. This principle is the clue of all we are about here.

---

SUNDAY, FEB. 9.—Haugwitz. Dinner at Nesselrode's, Wrote to Vienna by Heckel. Conference—refuse *note verbale*. Supper at the Queen's.

---

DESPATCH FROM LORD MALMESBURY TO LORD GRENVILLE.

Berlin, Sunday, Feb. 16th, 1794.

MY LORD,—I am now to give your Lordship an account of the manner in which I have obeyed the instructions contained in your despatch of the 28th of January, delivered to me by Timms late on Wednesday the 5th inst.

If I have deferred sending this account longer than perhaps was expected by your Lordship, it has arisen from my feeling the extreme importance of coming to a clear and explicit understanding here on the several points I had it in command to discuss; and of not re-despatching a messenger till I had it in my power to state to your Lordship so distinctly the result of what I had done, that it might lead, if possible, at once to a decision, and not bring on fresh and doubtful deliberations, which from the time they must consume would defeat the end which the measure itself was intended to produce.

I am well aware that I have not done this in so complete a manner as may be wished; but I trust some allowances will be made, as well for the complicated nature of the subject itself, as for the particular character of the Court at which I am employed.

My first object, after I had made myself master of the

spirit of your Lordship's very able despatch, was to see the King of Prussia. I found him walking in the park near this town on Thursday morning (the day after Timms' arrival). The publicity of the place, and the number of persons round us, made it impossible to enter minutely into the business; but he appeared well pleased with the hasty communication I made him of the outlines of my instructions. He appointed me to come to him the next morning, and desired me in the meanwhile to see Count Haugwitz: this I had an immediate opportunity of doing, as he was also walking. The King of Prussia joined us in a more retired part of the park; and on my then, at his request, explaining myself more fully, he, in the presence of his confidential Minister, expressed such an eagerness for the business to go on, that I began to hope I should find fewer difficulties in the course of my negotiation than I had reason to expect.

In this first conference with Count Haugwitz, I confined myself to the general purport of my instructions, without entering into details, or coming to any specific proposition. I contented myself with stating succinctly to him His Majesty's favourable disposition to assist the King of Prussia, jointly with the other coalesced Powers, with pecuniary support, provided that for such assistance a Prussian army, to the amount which had been named, should be brought into the field; and I, on this (as I have done on every preceding occasion), expressed His Majesty's invariable expectation that the stipulations of this Treaty of Alliance with His Prussian Majesty should be acknowledged, and if possible complied with. I found Count Haugwitz disposed to listen to everything I said with attention; he expressed much satisfaction at the cordial and liberal manner in which His Majesty had entered into the situation of this Court, and seemed inclined (as indeed I have since found him to be) to facilitate, as far as lay in his power, the success of the measure with which I was charged. He expressed, however, a wish, that in the first instance I should open myself to his colleagues in a conference according to the usual forms, but undertook afterwards to obtain from the King, his master, orders for going through the rest of the business with me himself.

I was with His Prussian Majesty on Friday morning, the 7th instant, at ten o'clock. His Prussian Majesty, before he gave me an opportunity to speak, shewed so much eagerness to act, lamented so feelingly the inability of the finances, and expressed such satisfaction at what I had told him of His Majesty's sentiments and intentions the day before, that I felt I should only incur all the inconveniences belonging to an appearance of art and cunning, and drive His Prussian Majesty back again into a system of reserve and suspicion, if I did not speak out fairly. I said, therefore, at once to His Prussian Majesty, that if he would be pleased to declare to me, without reserve, the amount of the army he would undertake to have on the Rhine, and the lowest calculation of the means necessary for providing for such an army, I would on my side with freedom and openness tell His Majesty how far it was within the bounds of my instructions to meet his idea, and come up to his demands.

The King of Prussia without any hesitation replied, that it was his wish to bring 100,000 men into the field, comprising in this number 6000 Saxons, and 2000 or 3000 troops of the Palatinate; that, as this subject had employed his mind constantly since the departure of my second messenger (Slater), he had given orders to his War Department to make out the most exact account, what such an army, with every contingent expense attendant on a campaign which was not to be a *defensive*, but an *offensive* one, and carried on at a great distance from his frontiers, would cost; that he had particularly ordered it should not be exaggerated; that he would direct this account to be laid before me; and that I was at liberty to compare it with any other I could obtain, or to make any inquiries or animadversion on it I pleased, as it was his sincere and honest wish that it should be as true and as accurate as possible.

I replied that on the amount of this sum the whole depended, since, if it was wide of that His Majesty conceived to be within the possibility of the united Powers to grant, the negotiation must at once fall to the ground. His Prussian Majesty, with great warmth, said, he trusted this would not be the case; and, taking out a pocket-book, said, from a paper in his hand, that the lowest expense of such an army as we proposed to assemble, acting in the way and in the country where it was to act, would amount to twenty millions of dollars, without reckoning the bread and forage.

I replied, that this sum was so much beyond what my powers authorised me to comply with, that it was almost useless to mention them. "Remember," says the King of Prussia, "that I am ready to go to the whole extent of my resources; explain to me yours. Let us act up to the magnitude of the cause we are defending; and not, when we both wish and intend the same end, be afraid who shall first commit himself by proposing the means."

I assured His Prussian Majesty no such apprehension could exist in my mind when I had the advantage of speaking to him, and that I would give him an immediate proof of it by obeying his orders.

I then, my Lord, (I trust I shall not be considered as having acted either injudiciously or inconsiderately,) stated to His Prussian Majesty the particulars of my instructions. I mentioned the two millions sterling, as the first and last sum I had to propose; and as this was to be raised by different quotas, paid by other Powers, I observed it was necessary, before any final arrangement could take place, to have the concurrence of the Emperor and of Holland. I confined myself simply to the sum of two millions offered, and to the 100,000 men required in return. To agree on these two leading points seemed to me to be the great object I had to obtain from the King of Prussia himself; and that, these once settled with him, the detail part of the business would go on much more smoothly with his Ministers.

His Prussian Majesty, after a pause, said; Short as the sum was of the expenses he must incur, he would agree to the terms, providing the Empire would contribute bread and forage, and provided he might be alleviated in some shape or other from his quota, which he declared he was utterly unable to pay, in addition to the sums he must expend over and above that he was to receive for the maintenance of the army we required.

I observed, that the recurring to the Empire for bread and forage, was a point to which I had no authority to speak, but which I conceived belonged more properly to the great

Powers in Germany to determine on ; that I presumed, however, that my Royal Master would not think it unfair that the Empire should contribute in a degree adequate to its ability to the carrying on a war so intimately connected with its safety and defence; but at the same time I was quite sure, and happy to have an opportunity given me of expressing it clearly and strongly to His Prussian Majesty, that His Majesty never would concur in any arrangement grounded on the plans of *sequestration* or *secularization*, because His Majesty considered them as founded on unjust principles, and as extremely dangerous to the tranquillity of Europe ; that, in regard to the quota at which His Prussian Majesty was rated, I was extremely sorry to find he objected to it, because I was fearful this objection would raise an insurmountable obstacle to the conclusion of the business ; and even that if it did not, if such a Treaty of Union as this now under negotiation was to be laid before the public, (as it necessarily must be,) and His Prussian Majesty appear in it, not as a contracting party to the joint expense, but merely as one subsidized, it would not only lessen his consideration amongst the Powers of Europe, but also appear as if his concurrence in the cause was not so cordial or disinterested as that of the three other Powers.

I entreated him, therefore, to consider the subject, and not, for the sake of avoiding a temporary inconvenience, reject a proposal, the acceptance of which appeared to me as closely connected with both his dignity and interest.

Although His Prussian Majesty combated but feebly what I said, yet I perceived he had been prepared to hold out on this particular point. He referred me to his Ministers on it, and said he would recommend me to be as practicable on this and on every other I had to treat as possible.

From the King of Prussia I went to Count Haugwitz, and from this Minister to a conference with him and his two colleagues. Count Haugwitz, who had seen the King at an earlier hour in the morning than myself, was prepared for all I had to say to him in consequence of my audience. In our conversation, which from the time of my appointment at Count Finck's was very short, he stated, that the only two points on which we could at all disagree was, that the Empire, in addition to the sum of two millions sterling, should supply bread and forage, and that the quota allotted to the King his master should be arranged differently.

In the conference, which was composed of the same persons I had before met on the same occasion, I stated that it had given my Royal Master great pleasure to receive from His Prussian Majesty the most positive assurances, that he considered the Treaty of Alliance which united them as subsisting in its full force, at the same time that His Majesty had to regret that the efforts His Prussian Majesty had made during the two last years had so considerably exhausted his treasury. But as the continuing the war was not a measure of *choice*, but one of *necessity*, and as the pressure of the moment called every day more and more for a plan of vigorous and decided operations, His Majesty observed with extreme satisfaction that the sentiments of His Prussian Majesty were perfectly conformable to his own ; and that, with this conviction on his mind, and feeling the importance of His Prussian Majesty taking a leading part in the next campaign, it was his wish to see the Prussian army augmented to a much greater force, and his desire, as far as circumstances would allow him, to contribute jointly with the other Powers to this augmentation ; that His Majesty having maturely weighed these important considerations in his mind, had come to a resolution, subject to the consent of the other coalesced Powers, of furnishing His Prussian Majesty with a very considerable sum of money, (and I then mentioned the sum and the allotments with the same reserve I had used before towards His Prussian Majesty and Count Haugwitz,) on condition that he would have an army of 100,000 men on the Rhine ; that in this number I required in His Majesty's name that 16,000 infantry and 4000 cavalry should be supplied by His Prussian Majesty, as the succours stipulated by the Treaty of Alliance subsisting between the Courts of Great Britain and Berlin. I intimated that it was His Majesty's wish that these 100,000 men should be a separate army, and under the command and direction of the King of Prussia. I ended by recalling again to the minds of the Prussian Ministry, that the whole of this arrangement was subservient to the consent of the Court of Vienna, and to that of the States-General, to whom His Majesty has communicated this projected arrangement, but with whose decision he could not as yet be acquainted.

The Prussian Ministers, after minuting what I said, took it for reference, in order to report to the King of Prussia; and very little passed on their part except a few vague expressions from Count Finck, signifying the insurmountable difficulty he foresaw in furnishing his fifth part. I made only a general reply, reserving all I had to say on this point till I was alone with Count Haugwitz.

I was prevented by various reasons from seeing him on Saturday; the evening of that day, however, I had a short conversation with His Prussian Majesty, and had the pleasure to hear that he was perfectly satisfied with what I had said to his Ministers.

On Sunday evening I was invited by them to another conference, when, after reading to me the minute or *protocole* of what had passed in that of Friday, Count Finck put into my hands a *note verbale*, which he told me was drawn up in consequence of the King's orders. On reading it over, I immediately felt, that if I received it *ministerially*, and transmitted it to your Lordship, that it would from its style and tenour certainly puzzle and protract, if not entirely defeat the negotiation. I therefore begged leave to be allowed to take it home with me to peruse at my leisure, and to decline receiving it from them officially, till such time as I could put into some order, and be able to state to them for their consideration, the many objections I had to make to it. Some of these I mentioned directly, and on the whole represented it to them so forcibly as being likely to impede the success of the negotiation, that they would have withdrawn it before I left the conference, if I had insisted on it. I wished, however, to have it in my power to send your Lordship a copy of it (which I here enclose). You will be pleased, my Lord, to recollect it is a paper absolutely suppressed; that no part of it is in force; that it is even scarce fair towards the Prussian Ministers to communicate it; and that my only reason for wishing you to see it is, that you may the better understand what has since passed between Count Haugwitz and me.

I saw him on Monday morning early, when I told him very freely I was convinced our negotiation would never end pleasantly if it was to be carried on by *des notes verbales:* that they had in the course of the autumn gone near to set the two Courts at variance,* and that several parts of that delivered to me yesterday were of the same nature as those I referred to. I then read it over with him, and made my objections as I went along.

I objected strongly to the idea of His Prussian Majesty refusing to pay his fifth part, and still more to the proposal of dividing it amongst the other three powers.

I objected to the increase of 16,000 men as insufficient; and, although I could not speak as to the propriety of the Saxon and other troops of the Empire serving with this army, I could not possibly admit the idea of these corps being counted to complete the number of 100,000 Prussians we were agreeing for.

I resisted decidedly the proposal that His Majesty should become a guarantee that bread and forage should be supplied for the maintenance of the Prussian army by the Empire, supposing this measure should be adopted.

I objected to the date to be fixed to the Treaty, particularly if in addition to the giving it this retro-active force, an advance of two millions of crowns, as appeared from the note, was to be required. I told him I disliked the fixing *a precise term* for the completion of a measure, the utility of which was evident to all the parties; and that, if these once agreed, they would for their own sakes bring it to a conclusion as soon as possible. In short, after going through the whole note, I said, that as I was quite certain His Prussian Majesty earnestly wished success to the negotiation, and that I was speaking to a minister who partook of the sentiments of his Sovereign, I believe I might venture, without any disrespect either towards His Prussian Majesty or his ministers, to desire him (Count Haugwitz) to take back this *note verbale*, and to adopt some different mode of pursuing our business.

Count Haugwitz, after a good deal of argument, but

* When His Prussian Majesty attempted to escape from his engagements made by the Treaty of 1787, denying the present war to be a *casus fœderis.*

carried on with the greatest good temper on both sides, gave up the idea of reckoning the Saxons and other troops amongst the 100,000 men, and also that of His Majesty's becoming a guarantee for the Empire supplying the army with bread and forage; but he made a stand on the impossibility of the King of Prussia paying his quota, and on the date fixed for giving effect to the Treaty. He asserted to me, and made use of the expression "*foi de gentilhomme*," that, notwithstanding the very liberal supply we were disposed to afford His Prussian Majesty, that over and above the two millions sterling His Prussian Majesty would be obliged to disburse at least seven millions of crowns; and that if, in addition to those seven millions, he was called upon to furnish his fifth quota, which would amount to upwards of two millions and a half more, it would not only entirely empty his treasury to the last penny, but force him to have recourse to a loan. That it was from the same principle that the year 1794, from its beginning to its end, was taken as the term for the duration of the Treaty; since, by making the first day of the year the date of the Treaty, His Prussian Majesty would receive about the two millions which was necessary for him to complete the army on the Rhine, and put in motion (*en état de mobilité*) the number of troops necessary to raise it to 100,000 men. And that if this date was admitted, the advances required would cease of course.

I employed uselessly every argument in my power to make him give up these two points; he opposed to every one I used, the invincible one, that it was not in the King of Prussia's power to act otherwise than he did.

He then adverted to what I had said relative to the *notes verbales*, which he was ever ready to admit was quite true, but asked what mode I wished to adopt in their stead? I replied, that nothing could forward the business so much, and lead to a decision one way or other so quickly, as to draw up a *projêt* of a treaty. That in addition to this he should give a correct and true state of the number of fighting-men to be employed, which I said I required should be all Prussians, and not mixed with any troops of the Empire, and also a faithful and minute account of the expenses of such an army in the field; that the being in possession of these three papers, which I should transmit to your Lordship, the business might at once be brought to a point, for they would serve to shew what His Prussian Majesty intended to do, what he expected the other Powers to do, and the conditions by which the performance of these reciprocal engagements were to be ensured. That I saw no other possible way of bringing the business to an early determination. And that in the present situation of affairs, it certainly had better be broken off at once, than die away in a lingering negotiation; as, while any hopes of its success were kept alive, other measures that might be adopted for pursuing the war with equal vigour would be suspended.

Count Haugwitz approved very much this method of proceeding; he took back the *note verbale,* which he observed I was now to consider as null and void, and said he would immediately mention to the King my motives for not receiving it, as well as the way I had traced out for forwarding the negotiation.

On Tuesday morning the 11th instant Hislop delivered me your Lordship's despatch. I was happy to find from its contents that I had in some points forestalled your Lordship's orders, and in none acted contrary to them. What your Lordship mentions of the reluctance of the Court of Vienna to contribute any pecuniary assistance to the King of Prussia, and of its jealousy of the effect which might be produced by placing him at the head of so large and separate an army, was evident from the conduct of Count Lehrbach towards me for the last three weeks. I do not mean to say that it has been at all unfriendly or disagreeable, but his language has been one perpetual abuse of the character and conduct of this Court, without ever mentioning his own, from whence he declares he has not received a line for nearly a month. I endeavour to conceal from him that I observe this alteration in his manner, and am still more careful to conceal it from the ministers here, who would be too ready to catch at anything which could gratify their never-ceasing animosity against the Court of Vienna.

I passed several hours with Count Haugwitz, both in the morning and evening of Tuesday. Our great object was to hit on some temperament which might make it practicable for His Prussian Majesty to contribute his fifth part; but we could devise none on which we could agree. Count Haugwitz proposed as ultimatum, that the sum to be given should be two millions and a half sterling, rated in the same manner as the two millions already offered; and that, if this were agreed to, His Prussian Majesty would then consent to furnish 500,000*l.* as one-fifth part of the whole, without any stipulation for a reimbursement at the peace, and put himself in this arrangement precisely on the same footing with the other subscribing Powers.

I told him my instructions were so binding as to the utmost extent of the sum to which I was to go, that I could not give him the smallest hopes that this increase would be admitted, but that I would mention it to your Lordship. The expedient he proposed for easing the King of Prussia of his quota will appear in the *projêt*. It scarce deserves that name, and I send it because I could not gain any ground on this point.

Count Haugwitz said the King had commanded him to conform to the three points I had proposed; that he had orders from His Prussian Majesty to draw up, without loss of time, the project of a treaty; and also to give me the most exact account of the names of the regiments which were to compose the army we required, and the amount of its expenses for one campaign; that it would require two days to have these papers in readiness, particularly that relative to the choice of the regiments, which was a point the King settled himself, without allowing anybody to interfere.

Wednesday and Thursday I had no communication with the Prussian Ministry. I employed these days in endeavouring to collect the most accurate information I could obtain of the expenses of a large army in the field: such as I have been able to acquire, I shall send in a separate despatch.

Count Lehrbach could afford me no assistance; he is no military man himself, and has nobody with him at all versed in military concerns.

On Friday morning I received a message from Count Finck, desiring me to attend a conference at twelve o'clock, when I received from the Prussian Minister the enclosed *projêt* of a convention. They also gave me a list of the army His Prussian Majesty intends to have on the Rhine, if this Convention is agreed to, and a statement of what such an army thus employed would cost. I enclose both these papers.

In regard to the Convention itself, it is such a one as, after what I have written, your Lordship will be prepared to receive. I had, in my conversations with Count Haugwitz, prevailed upon him to alter several parts of it, particularly an insertion they had made, requiring that the interest on the loan to be raised by His Prussian Majesty, and considered as his quota, should be paid in equal shares by the coalesced Powers, in addition to their being security for the reimbursement of the principal sum borrowed. In this original *projêt* also, the first of January stood as the day from which we should commence the payment of bread and forage for the 20,000 men furnished to us by treaty. This I of course could not hear of, and it remains in blank to be filled up.

I could not by any possible suggestions obtain any other mode of regulating His Prussian Majesty's fifth part; every one which tended to lay the charge more directly on him, was resisted from the plea I have already mentioned. The alternative the Prussian Ministers have proposed under the title of *Premier Cas*, would certainly get rid of this difficulty; and in the choice of these two articles (supposing they are not both treated as inadmissible) it is perhaps a point for consideration, whether in the event the several Powers are not equally bound by both of them to pay ultimately the fifth share allotted to His Prussian Majesty, and if this is the case, the first would not be the most preferable, as His Prussian Majesty offers to contribute 500,000*l.*: 400,000*l.* would be the sum wanted to complete the two millions and a half, which 400,000*l.* is also the amount of the reimbursement to be secured. If we take the second case, Count Haugwitz suggested that France should be engaged eventually at the peace for the repayment of this 400,000*l.* to the three Powers, on the same conditions we had proposed it should be repaid to the King of Prussia. But

I declined entering into any deliberation on the subject, repeating to him that my instructions were positive, and that I could not listen to any proposal which required our supplying a larger sum than that I have mentioned.

In regard to the term of this present year being fixed for the duration of the Treaty, notwithstanding I represented it as likely to be found liable to great objections, I could not prevail upon the Prussian Minister to alter it.

I discussed all these points again, after the conference with Count Haugwitz, and with the same effect.

The list and amount of the army speaks for itself. It is, I believe, on the whole correct, and is certainly composed of the choicest troops the King of Prussia has. Count Haugwitz observed to me, that, if the reinforcement to be sent appeared inferior in number to that necessary to raise the army now on the Rhine to the amount we required, it was from His Prussian Majesty intending to put on the full war establishment the regiments which were there : and Count Haugwitz took upon himself to pledge his word that the whole number stated should take the field ; and that I might be sure His Prussian Majesty, as well for the sake of his military glory, as out of a regard to his engagements, would take care it never should be less.

As to the calculation for the expenses, I have closely questioned General Gnesau and Colonel Manstein, who are at the head of the War Department, on that point. I represented to them how essential it was for their Master's honour, and for the success of a negotiation to which they were so cordially well-wishers, that the account should be as fair and as clear as possible. They both assured me they felt this, and had never lost sight of it while they were drawing it up. Yesterday morning (Saturday) the King sent for me to come to him. His Majesty kept me with him some time. He recapitulated everything that had been done, which he hoped (whatever might be the fate of the negotiation) would give His Majesty a convincing proof of his earnest wish to co-operate in a cause on which their feelings and sentiments were so perfectly similar : that he most assuredly should not have applied for pecuniary assistance, if he had any means left within his kingdom for continuing the war in an effectual manner without it: that he felt in the strongest degree the confidential, liberal, and open manner in which His Majesty had acted on this occasion towards him; and that it gave him the greatest satisfaction to see that the two Courts were now placed again on a footing of mutual confidence and cordiality: that it had given him great pain to observe that this had been for a while interrupted, and that doubts had been entertained that he intended to abandon the cause abruptly; and, what hurt him still more, that he could *degrade* himself so much as to enter into a negotiation with the Convention (which he qualified with the most injurious epithet). He authorized me, in the strongest expressions, to declare the contrary; and finished a longer speech than I ever heard him make, by desiring me to express from him to His Majesty every possible sentiment of personal friendship and regard, and every wish to unite the two Courts by a system of the closest political union.

I made a suitable reply to what I heard, (which I do not exaggerate in the report I have just made,) and I took this opportunity of saying to His Prussian Majesty, that if, from an impossibility of concurrence on the part of the other Powers concerned, the transaction with which I was charged should not be found practicable, that from the readiness His Majesty had shewn to comply with His Prussian Majesty's request, and from the manner in which he entered into his situation, I hoped that His Prussian Majesty would consider his engagement with His Majesty by treaty as binding, in preference to any other; and that, as the necessity for continuing the war would still remain, he would, in concert with His Majesty, take the most efficacious measures for pursuing it with vigour.

His Prussian Majesty did not hesitate a moment to say he would. The rest of what passed was relative to the *projêt* I had received, which His Prussian Majesty sincerely hoped would be adopted, and assured me that the negotiation never should fail by his refusing any concession which may be required of him, and which it was in his power to make. He spoke out of humour of the Court of Vienna, which he said was losing time and creating delays at the moment when the pressure was so great that too much expedition could not be employed. He seemed to have hopes of the good effect of the Prince de Nassau's journey there, and calculated that he would arrive nearly about the same time that Sir M. Eden would receive your Lordship's instructions. His Prussian Majesty mentioned, as he had often done before, the Austrian indemnity, and wished to know where they would be. On my saying, probably in Alsatia, Lorraine, and Flanders, he said he should be perfectly ready to agree to this, if the Court of Vienna would come to a fair explanation on the subject.

I was with Count Haugwitz again yesterday and this morning, and we again went over the whole business; but I do not recollect that any new matter arose, or that anything passed worth relating, except that the Count assured me, that from the different letters they had received, and from the language of the Electoral Ministers here, there was every reason to expect that the Empire would very readily consent to contribute bread and forage to the Prussian army, if the measure was recommended and supported by the Emperor.

I shall now no longer delay sending away my messenger: I could have wished some information had been received from Vienna relative to the intentions of that Court before I despatched him, but this is not likely to come as yet for several days; and as it will, when it does arrive, lead probably to long discussions and Ministerial conferences, I thought it most advisable (and in this Count Lehrbach agreed with me) not to wait, but to transmit you the steps I had taken here, and the form into which I had put the business, in order that it might go on, at least as far as related to England. To save time was my principal motive, and for this reason I have been as circumstantial and minute as possible. Yet I still fear I have omitted many points to which your Lordship will think it necessary to recur before any final arrangement can be taken. With the materials you have now in your possession you will be the best judge whether some "provisional convention" might not be proposed and signed while the "main treaty" is under deliberation. Had my colleagues of Austria and Holland been prepared, I felt myself empowered by my instructions to have done it now; but without them it was useless for me to propose it, even if any one could have been drawn up which would have satisfied the views of this Court without pledging too far the other powers.

The first point of any provisionary arrangement must be the consenting to advance two or three millions of dollars to His Prussian Majesty, as they persist here in declaring that without this advance it is impossible for them to put the army in motion. I have, &c.

MALMESBURY.

Right Hon. Lord Grenville, &c.

---

MONDAY, FEB. 10.—Breakfast at Frederickstadt with Meden—went with the Reusses, and stayed till five—at Haugwitz's till seven—at home to write.

---

FRIDAY, FEB. 14.—Writing. Conference.—Received, &c. *Projêt* of convention from Haugwitz.

---

SATURDAY, FEB. 15.—Writing. Haugwitz called on me. With the King. Assembly at Court—supper at Meden's—elegant apartments.

---

LETTER FROM THE DUKE OF PORTLAND TO LORD MALMESBURY.

London, Sunday, 16th Feb., 1794.

MY DEAR LORD,—My good friend and neighbour, Mr. Mellish, is very anxious that I should request your countenance and protection for the young gentleman who will have the honour of delivering you this letter; his name is Lawrence, and I understand that the object of his ambition is to qualify himself for the diplomatic line, for which I most heartily wish we had a *supply of fit and able persons*, because we can't divide you into one quarter of the situations where your services would be of importance to the common cause, and where I know they are wished for as much as ever they are in Holland, from whence I never receive a letter without lamentations for the want of you, and representations of the necessity of your return there, or of some person as like Lord Malmesbury as possible being sent there. General Bentinck writes me word, that by the end of the week after next the Hereditary Prince of Orange *will be* at his head-quarters at Namur, at the head of an army of about 25,000 effective men, rank and file, by which I hope he means exclusive of officers. I know you will be glad to hear that I have got a majority for my son William,* and that I am not without hopes of getting him a lieut.-colonelcy before the opening of the campaign, and that in such a way as will enable him to gratify himself in serving again under the Duke of York, who will return to the army the latter end of next week. But I cannot help saying, that unless the licentious, not to say mutinous, spirit against the Duke of York, which prevails among our troops, and which originated in, I am sorry to say, and is even cultivated in, the Guards, is not subdued and extinguished, there is an end of the army, and that of the country cannot be very far distant; and, when I cannot deceive myself with respect to the quarters from whence this infernal spirit is encouraged, I cannot consider it but with equal astonishment and horror. I wish this intimation, but which I think cannot be new to you, may enable you to be of some service; and yet I can have no great confidence in the influence you possess either at *Carlton House*, or the *Queen's Lodge*. I am, &c.

PORTLAND.

SUNDAY, FEB. 16.—At Court—writing at home—re-despatched messenger.

* Lord William Bentinck, who afterwards commanded our army in Sicily, and was Governor-General of India in 1831.

EXTRACTS OF A DESPATCH FROM LORD MALMESBURY TO
LORD GRENVILLE.

Berlin, 16th Feb., 1794.

I LOST no time in acquainting both Count Lehrbach and the Baron de Reede with the substance of the instructions brought me by Timms.

I explained to both of them the sum His Majesty had supposed requisite to empower His Prussian Majesty to bring 100,000 men into the field, and the manner in which His Majesty proposed this sum should be raised.

They applauded and approved the idea, but informed me that they were without any specific instructions on the subject.

The Dutch Minister, indeed, expressed a readiness to subscribe to any eventual arrangement I might make; but Count Lehrbach declared himself to be absolutely without any powers, and that he could not take upon himself to act without them.

As I perceived these symptoms of jealousy and apprehension, your Lordship's despatch has since confirmed to me, growing very fast in the mind of the Austrian Plenipotentiary, I made it my particular object to be as open and confidential to him as possible; and I spared no pains to impress his mind with the importance of the object, and that it was such that all collateral and ordinary considerations ought to disappear before it.

After delaying Timms from Wednesday till Saturday, and hesitating what I should do, I determined at last to send him to Petersburg. Sir Charles Whitworth will be the best judge of the steps he is to take in consequence of what I wrote, which was stating to him the turn I by that time saw the negotiation was likely to take here. I fear we must expect nothing from the Empress but fair words, but it would be contrary to my duty to act solely on this idea.

---

MONDAY, FEB. 17.— Lehrbach with me. Dined with King—called on Nesselrode—wrote to Petersburg—supped and played ombre with Prince Henry.

Tuesday, Feb. 18.—King went to Potzdam. Wrote to Vienna—called on Madame Reuss—supper at Count Finckenstein's.

Thursday, Feb. 20.—Walked. Ball at Prince Royal's. King returned from Potzdam.

Friday, Feb. 21.—Walked with Haugwitz—dined at home—Haugwitz very friendly and communicative—if Vienna does not agree to our plan, proposed to form a new one between England and Russia. Alvensleben in the evening.

Sunday, Feb. 23.—Walked—dined at home—ball at King's. King talked about Vienna, expressed his doubts of that Court acceding to the convention.

Monday, Feb. 24.—Walked and breakfasted with Princess Royal and Louis—dined at home—supper at Princess Henry's.

Tuesday, Feb. 25.—At home till evening—Bellevue—pleasant style of supper—played deep whist with Princess Ferdinand.

Wednesday, Feb. 26.—Letters from Vienna—that Court disinclined to accede; Lucchesini's description of it to Haugwitz. With him in the morning—long conversation on the subject—great acrimony and prejudice against the Court of Vienna—I endeavour to soften it. Dine at home—sup at Queen Dowager's.

EXTRACTS OF A DESPATCH FROM LORD MALMESBURY TO
LORD GRENVILLE.

Berlin, 1st March, 1794.

WEDNESDAY morning a messenger brought letters from the Marquis de Lucchesini, to say that the Court of Vienna was by no means inclined to come into the terms proposed. I had letters to the same effect from Sir M. Eden, and Prince Nassau gave similar information to the King of Prussia.

Count Haugwitz, whom I saw soon after these letters were received, expressed himself in very severe terms on this behaviour of the Court of Vienna, which he called tergiversation. He said, the King his Master partook strongly of the same feelings, and was determined to insist on an early and decisive answer. He said to me the greater part of M. Lucchesini's letter, which appears to be written with less virulence than I expected to find in his style. After mentioning the disinclination in the Court of Vienna to accede to the terms of the Convention, he enters into a description of its Ministry; he states the whole power as being in the hands of Baron Thugut and M. Rollin, and that they are the great opposers to the plan of coalition; that Prince Colloredo and Marshal Lascy are not unfavourable to it; that the Elector of Cologne is decidedly for it.

In the evening of Wednesday I saw His Prussian Majesty, who spoke of the intelligence he had received from Vienna as his Ministers had done; and he added, that he was extremely concerned to perceive that the jealousy and suspicion there, were likely to defeat the whole negotiation—that everything, however, ought to be done to prevent this. Thursday morning, Count Haugwitz told me the substance of the instructions they intended to send to Lucchesini by a messenger that evening. The style of this letter, which was communicated to me, is less cordial than I could have desired; but it is that of the underlings in the Prussian offices, who are left to draw up all these papers, and who think they increase their master's importance by making him talk a high and even uncivil language.

I felt it of such infinite importance that His Majesty's Minister at Vienna should be exactly informed of what was going on here, and as I am sure, from the way in which Lucchesini mentions Sir Morton Eden in his despatches, he would not be so from him, that I determined to send one of my servants to Vienna with an account of what had been done; and this servant (on whose fidelity and expedition I can depend) left Berlin on Thursday evening, nearly at the same time as the messenger despatched by the Prussian Ministry.

I hope, my Lord, that I have not exceeded my duty in saying this much. The most difficult and hopeless part of the important measure now under negotiation is, to keep the two Courts of Berlin and Vienna on anything like even terms: extreme suspicion and envy pervade them both; and their mutual prejudices are so strong, that it is impossible to *believe* them when *speaking of each other*. This unfortunate principle supersedes every other consideration, whether it be one of common danger or of mutual advantage; and I much fear we shall feel the bad effects of it during every period of the negotiation, and even after its conclusion, let it terminate how it will.

---

FRIDAY, FEB. 28.—Walked. Dinner at Reede's. Visits. Tea at Alvensleben's—Duke of Brunswick came.

---

SATURDAY, MARCH 1.—Called on Madame L. Reuss.— Dinner at King's with Duke of Brunswick—great dinner —King very civil, but formal with the Duke. Supper at Queen's—Duke of Brunswick told me he was glad Möllendorff had the command; he would do better politically than he could—Duke appeared sour—said he was *moralement malade*, and that he would come and tell me his whole story.

Sunday, March 2.— Court in the morning. Walked. Dined at home. Ball at King's—Princess Louis's birthday.

Monday, March 3.—Dinner with the King—small dinner—Duke of Brunswick silent and obsequious. Supper with Prince Henry.

### EXTRACTS OF A DESPATCH FROM LORD MALMESBURY TO LORD GRENVILLE.

Berlin, 8th March, 1794.

Although I am preparing letters for your Lordship, to go by a Dutch messenger who is to leave Berlin this evening, yet, as it is most likely he will travel slower than the post, I think it necessary to write a few lines to say, that in consequence of Marquis Lucchesini's letters, and of the reports made by Prince Nassau, who returned on Thursday night, the dissatisfaction of this Court towards that of Vienna is at its height. The civil terms in which Count Lehrbach conveyed the refusal of the Emperor to accede to the arrangement proposed, and the friendly professions with which he qualified this refusal, have been of no service; neither has any effort of mine as yet been able to soften the King of Prussia's feelings, or to alter his opinion on the conduct of the Emperor.

In proportion, however, as his resentment against the Court of Vienna is great, his assurances of remaining inviolably attached to His Majesty and to his system are strong.

Count Haugwitz repeats this to me every day, and has expressed his earnest desire that some new plan may be immediately formed for establishing a military co-operation between His Majesty, and the King of Prussia, and the States-General.

I, however, have desired Count Haugwitz to wait a few days before any new *projêt* is drawn, as I have reason to expect in a short time an answer from your Lordship to my despatches by Hislop, and also my servant sent back from Vienna.

The Prussian Minister acquiesced in the propriety of waiting till these messengers arrived, but intimated at the same time that it would be impossible (from the want of provisions and magazines) for the Prussian army to remain on the Rhine in its present position later than the 1st of April. I replied, I could not suppose it possible that the King of Prussia would give any orders for it to move as long as any negotiation was pending; as such a step, besides being perhaps in the event contrary to the conditions which would finally be agreed on, would produce the worst and most dangerous effect. I shall persist in urging this, and have little doubt but I shall be listened to.

WEDNESDAY, MARCH 5.—With Count Haugwitz. Walked. New *projêt* in contemplation.

THURSDAY, MARCH 6.—Walked. Dined at Reede's. With Haugwitz in evening—very right in his ideas. Supped at Princess Royal's.

SATURDAY, MARCH 8.—Walked. Dined at Arnim's. Assembly at Minister Haugwitz's.

SUNDAY, MARCH 9.*—Dinner at Prince Reuss's. Queen's supper and ball.

MONDAY, MARCH 10.—Princess Royal's birth-day. Dinner at Prince Reuss's. Ball at King's. Haugwitz called on me to propose to remove the negotiation to the Hague†— I accept it.

* Lord Malmesbury writes a despatch of this date, describing the increasing jealousy and acrimony between the Courts of Vienna and Berlin, greatly to be attributed, either to Lucchesini's meanness, or to his French leanings.

† It appears from Lord Malmesbury's papers, that, finding his projects constantly thwarted by the French party at Berlin, who were working on Haugwitz against us, he determined, if possible, to remove the negotiation to the Hague, and cleverly induced that Minister to originate the idea himself, by hinting that at the Hague he would be rid of all Austrian annoyances, and of the interference of his rivals at Court.

LETTER FROM LORD MALMESBURY TO LORD GRENVILLE.

Berlin, 11th March, 1794.

MY LORD,—As your Lordship may be surprised at not hearing from me at so very interesting a moment, I write to say that the return of my servant from Vienna last night, and some very interesting conversations I have since had with His Prussian Majesty and Count Haugwitz, make it expedient for me to send a messenger in a day or two. In the meanwhile the Emperor persists in the most decided refusal, without alleging any other reason whatever than that of money; and although I am authorized by Baron Thugut to make a kind of indirect proposition, so much mistrust is expressed at Vienna towards this Court, that I despair of a possibility of ever deriving the smallest advantage from any plan in which their military operations are dependent on each other, and my object is, if possible, to hit upon one in which by acting separately they may act usefully. It is on this point I shall have the honour to write by the messenger.

I have, &c. (Signed) MALMESBURY.

---

WEDNESDAY, MARCH 12.—Dinner at Sacken's. Count and Countess Reuss left Berlin. Supped at Queen Dowager's.

---

THURSDAY, MARCH 13.—At home. Ball at Prince Royal's.

---

TUESDAY, MARCH 18.—At home. Announced in the morning my going to the Hague to Finckenstein and Alvensleben—*to no one else.*

---

THURSDAY, MARCH 20.—Went at eight o'clock with Count Haugwitz to Potzdam. Dined with only four persons with the King in his new palace—audience before dinner, and settled the plan—the King promises more fairly, expresses his desire to act, and detestation of the French—blames Austria.

### EXTRACTS OF A DESPATCH FROM LORD MALMESBURY TO LORD GRENVILLE.

Berlin, 13th March, 1794.

THE failure of this negotiation has thrown us back to where we were three months ago, and we are on the eve of seeing the campaign open without any determined measures being taken to ensure the co-operation of this Court.

I trust, therefore, I shall be forgiven if I have ventured to go beyond the limits of my instructions, and taken upon myself to deliberate with His Prussian Majesty and his Ministers on some other means of ensuring his co-operation, even before I have received His Majesty's final orders on the *projêt de convention* I transmitted to your Lordship in mine of the 16th February by Hislop : but I have not committed myself in any one specific point ; everything is to be submitted to the determination of my Court. The great end I have had in view is to save time, by preparing the business in order to accelerate that determination.

I have acted on the supposition that a powerful and cordial co-operation of the King of Prussia is a most desirable object, and the primary one of my Mission ; that the Court of Vienna is irrevocably decided not to contribute to it in the manner proposed, and that this Court is as determined not to consent to the plan, the Court of Vienna being left out of it. I also venture to suppose that, if this co-operation is still attainable nearly with equal effect, and on nearly equal terms as those before stated, it will not be rejected by His Majesty.

These are the data I have taken for the ground-work of my conduct ; and, on their being admitted, the whole of its merit rests. As soon as it became evident to me that the Court of Vienna would not subscribe to the *projêt de Convention*, I immediately employed my mind in seeking the means to substitute, if possible, some other measure in its stead, which might in a degree compensate for its failure.

I was encouraged in this from the very great eagerness His Prussian Majesty constantly expressed to act; from the concern he shewed at the Emperor's refusal; and from the confidential manner in which he conversed with me himself, and with which he directed Count Haugwitz (the favourite and only acting Minister) to treat me.

I found both the King and his Minister disposed to listen to anything I had to suggest, and very ready to enter into any engagements with Great Britain and Holland.

I had, however, in the course of these conversations a very difficult part to support; as, although I had to agree with them that we were not to reckon any longer on the Court of Vienna as on a *contributing party* in the particular measure on which we were debating, yet it was not for me to lose sight of the immediate interests of that Court; and that, although I could not but admit it was separated from us in this distinct point, I was not to forget, for an instant, that it was intimately connected with us on all others; that it made a very important, very sincere, and very powerful branch of the Coalition, and that the same regard and care were to be maintained for its safety, honour, and interests, as if it had acquiesced cordially in the Convention.

By perpetually repeating to the King of Prussia that there could not, in the nature of things, exist any secret or dangerous designs on the part of that Court, that there was nothing offensive in its conduct towards him, and that the very worst interpretation that could be given to it was a timid jealousy which ought rather to flatter than anger him, I brought him gradually to be in tolerable temper; and I should not do His Prussian Majesty justice if I did not say, that, when I stated to him how intimately connected the general welfare of Europe was with his not appearing to be at open variance with the Emperor, he did not fully admit the consideration. It also was as fully admitted by Count Haugwitz, who talked judiciously and reasonably on the subject, and whom I brought at last to listen to me with patience and good-humour when I remonstrated with him on the bad policy, as well as impropriety, of mixing up passion and personal resentment with the conduct of public business, and observed that the gratifying the one was highly pernicious to the other.

In the engagements which were to be made with the Maritime Powers His Prussian Majesty proposed that the force he should bring into the field should consist of 80,000 men; that of these, 20,000 should be in garrison at Mentz, under the command of General Kalckreuth, to defend that place and cover the Empire; and that the remainder should be employed in the way the most advantageous to the general cause, and the most conformable to the views and interests of Great Britain and Holland.

After various conferences on this subject, some with His Prussian Majesty himself, and others with Count Haugwitz, the detail of which would swell this despatch to a most unreasonable size without conveying any material intelligence to your Lordship, I have prevailed upon them to draw up two *projêts;* the one stating the subsidy required from England and Holland, the other the manner in which they conceive their army may be employed the most usefully.

In regard to the new *projêt de Convention* to be concluded between the Maritime Powers and this Court, I have laboured as much as possible to lower their terms. That I now send is very different from what was first given me, which went to require, on our part, bread and forage for the whole army, and not even a semblance of the expense allotted to the King of Prussia.

I am just returned from a conversation with Count Haugwitz on this subject, in which I went over the whole ground again, and the very best terms I can obtain are those as they now appear in the *projêt.*

In regard to the paper,* which contains a reasoning on the operations of the war,—for it cannot in its present shape be called anything else,—it is grounded on the principle, that, as the defence of the Empire is now to be left to a force which is to arise from within itself, the offensive part of the campaign naturally will be carried on on the side of the Low Countries.

The King of Prussia has talked to me very much on this

* Inclosed, and to the effect here described by Lord M. himself.

subject, and expressed his readiness to undertake any plan of attack on that side we should think proper to recommend.

The King of Prussia, on my dwelling repeatedly in the most forcible manner on the necessity that his army should not quit its present station till further notice was given to the Austrian General of its intended removal, assured me positively that no part of it should stir till the first week in April.

It certainly would have been more desirable that no alteration whatever should have taken place in the situation of the Prussian army till such time as I received an answer to this letter, but it was not in my power to effect this; and what I have effected, and what may yet be done, will, I trust, prevent any very great evil arising from the orders the King of Prussia has given.

The result of all I have written is, that from the inability of Austria to comply with the plan proposed, a new one is brought forward, to be agreed to between Great Britain and Holland on one part, and the King of Prussia on the other, by which the number of men to be given will be reduced one-fifth (from 100,000 to 80,000 men),—I do not speak of rank or file in either case,—and one-fourth abated of the sum originally required. Of these 80,000 men, 20,000 men are for the present to remain as the succours due to the Court of Vienna by treaty; and the rest to be at the disposition of the Maritime Powers, to act on the side of the Low Countries.

In this new arrangement, the proportion of the force to be given to that of the subsidy required, is somewhat more advantageous than in the first plan, as we shall have 750,000*l.* to pay, instead of 800,000*l.* The 20,000 men making the Austrian succours were always reckoned in the number the King of Prussia was to supply; and although this corps for the moment is to remain at Mentz (and it is highly essential that it should), yet I should suppose that if required, the Court of Vienna would not refuse to let it (as a body of auxiliaries belonging to them, and for which they were to supply bread and forage) act with the other 60,000 men, and by that means keep the Imperial and Prussian armies entirely distinct from each other, which experience has taught is a circumstance on which the event of the campaign will probably depend.

The bread and forage to be supplied by us and the Dutch, I should by all means recommend to be paid for in money, and not furnished in kind. If the latter method was adopted, endless confusion and dispute would inevitably ensue.

The King of Prussia himself will be with this army, although the direction of it would be left to Marshal Möllendorff.

It may be, perhaps, said in favour of this plan, as preferable to the other, that, by bringing the greater force nearer us, it will ensure not only the safety of Holland and the Austrian Netherlands, but also open a very fair and reasonable prospect of success and conquests on that side.

The protection of these countries is certainly more material to us, and would be better understood by the nation, than that of the empire on the side of Suabia and Franconia; and any conquests made in French Flanders would certainly give greater pleasure, and be considered as more for our purpose, than on the distant provinces of Lorraine and Alsatia.

These advantages, however, and every possible benefit which could arise from this measure, depend entirely on its being concluded on in time.

It required no arguments of mine to make these felt by His Prussian Majesty; but I was much, and, I must say, agreeably surprised, when on Friday last he sent me word from Potzdam, that, with this impression strong on his mind, he had come to a resolution (provided I was ready to subscribe to it) to order Count Haugwitz to go with me to the Hague, and to give him full powers to negotiate and terminate the transaction there. His Prussian Majesty added, that the treating with this minister would be the same as if I treated with him; and that from the proximity of Holland to England, as well as to the route his army was taking, much very valuable time would be saved in the execution of the orders by the Hague being made the seat of the negotiation and decision.

I am free to confess, my Lord, that I did not hesitate a moment in acceding to this proposal, which, while it carried with it so pleasing a proof of His Prussian Majesty's sincerity, is attended with so many circumstances favourable to the business itself.

It is a most advantageous consideration the having to do with Count Haugwitz alone. I have acquired the habits of doing business with this Minister, and he is certainly a character more to be depended on than either of the other two. Count Finckenstein is superannuated, and Baron d'Alvensleben, though with little or no influence, is as adverse as possible to the war, and I am told his leanings and opinions are very different from those that ought to belong to the minister of a great Sovereign; and it is impossible for Count Haugwitz, while he is here, to carry any measure through, without previously communicating it to them.

I am also well pleased to be relieved myself from my colleagues on this occasion, for although I certainly have not any reason to complain either of the zeal or abilities of Count Lehrbach or Baron de Reede, yet I by no means receive from them that satisfactory and judicious support I am certain of finding in the assistance and advice of Mons. Vander Spiegel. To this may be added the not being exposed to the great and active curiosity of all the Foreign Ministers here, and the effects of their idle reports, in consequence of what they collect, either from the corruption or extreme carelessness of the different offices, which render it next to impossible for any secret to be kept.

In short, my Lord, in every point of view the negotiation will certainly go on with more safety and expedition at the Hague than here.

Our departure is to be a profound secret; we are to join the King at Potzdam, and begin our journey from thence. It is not to be told to any of the King's Ministers; and, to prevent any suspicion, Count Haugwitz's full powers will be made out after he is gone, and sent after him.

---

FRIDAY, MARCH 21.—Our departure postponed. Dined with Bishopswerder. Supped with Manstein.

1794.]  BERLIN.  81

SATURDAY, MARCH 22.—Craig* with the King. King refused to lend any of his troops.† Dinner with Haugwitz. East the messenger arrives. Fresh proposals‡—rejected. Our journey fixed for the next day.

SUNDAY, MARCH 23.—Re-despatched East. Col. Craig departs. We set out at one P.M.—reach Rathenan, eight miles in ten hours.

* MONDAY, MARCH 24.—To * * * *—twelve miles in eighteen hours.

TUESDAY, MARCH 25.—To Burgsdorff—nine miles in fourteen hours.

WEDNESDAY, MARCH 26.—To Salingen, eleven miles and a half in fourteen hours—pass through Hanover—much improved.

THURSDAY, MARCH 27.—To Osnabruck, nine miles and a half—thirteen hours.

FRIDAY, MARCH 28.—To Delden—twelve miles in nineteen hours and a half.

SATURDAY, MARCH 29.—To Voorthingen—eight miles and a half in fifteen hours.

SUNDAY, MARCH 30.—The Hague—ten miles and a half in sixteen hours. We found the roads excellent everywhere, very decent inns, and good treatment. We had twenty-two

---

\* Afterwards General Sir James Craig.
† The Duke of York had asked, through Col. Craig, as a personal favour, for 4000 light troops.
‡ By a despatch which crossed Lord Malmesbury's containing his *projêt* of the 13th, Lord Grenville offers that England shall take into her service 30,000 Prussian troops for a subsidy of one million per annum, and instructs Lord Malmesbury to make this the ultimatum; but, although the King of Prussia rejects the proposal, Lord Malmesbury, hoping to carry his *projêt* of the 13th, leaves the negotiation still open.

horses at each post. I lodged at the "Heeren Logement," at the Hague.

MONDAY, MARCH 31.—Grand Pensionary—opened the business to him—told him that I had prevailed on Haugwitz to stop the return of the Prussian troops till further orders.* Dined at Court—most graciously received by everybody—much conversation with Princess and Prince of Orange.

EXTRACTS OF A DESPATCH FROM LORD GRENVILLE TO LORD MALMESBURY.

Downing Street, 28th March, 1794.

YOUR Lordship's despatch of the 13th March, with its enclosures, was received here on the 22nd instant, and has since been under the most serious consideration of His Majesty's confidential servants.

Nothing can have been more proper than your Lordship's having entered, as far as could be done without committing your Court, into the discussion of the means of securing the limited co-operation of Prussia, after the more extensive plan had failed; and you will since have perceived how much your ideas accorded with those adopted here on that occasion, particularly with respect to the conciliating as far as possible the views and dispositions of the two great German Powers, although the uniting them in one plan in the manner proposed from hence was found impracticable. The interest which all Europe has in the union of the principal Powers engaged against France, is certainly such as to make it desirable that much should be passed over, and much conceded to so important a point; and the impressing the King of Prussia with this sentiment, is perhaps of all others the most important object in the present moment.

The King's servants entertain some hope, from the circumstance of His Prussian Majesty having proposed to remove the negotiation to the Hague, that the present impression of His Prussian Majesty's mind may not be un-

* On pain of breaking off all further negotiations.

favourable to His Majesty's views; but they cannot conceal from themselves that there are still many circumstances of a suspicious nature, and that, on the whole, great caution must be had as to any reliance which is to be placed on the present assurances. Your Lordship's conduct in assenting to the proposal for this removal, is entirely approved; and it is highly satisfactory to me that this circumstance will so much facilitate the means of my communicating with your Lordship on this interesting business. I trust that I shall hear by the next mail of your Lordship's arrival at the Hague, where your business will also be facilitated by the presence of the King's ambassador to their High Mightinesses, with whom I had, before receiving your Lordship's letter, taken the necessary steps for his immediate departure.

To the pecuniary part of the *projêt*, stated to you by Count Haugwitz, no objection will therefore be made on His Majesty's part; and I trust it will not be found impracticable to induce the Republic to accede, on the consideration which I shall have occasion to state in the course of this despatch, particularly as any considerable reduction in the expense of bread and forage would bring their contribution down to very little more than the sum to which they have already shown a willingness to accede.

But, with respect to the form of the transaction, two points occur which appear material.

The paying by retrospect for three months, which have already elapsed, and for another month, which may possibly elapse before the business can, even in its present shape, be brought to produce its full effect, and during all which time the Prussian troops have been in no respect at the disposition of the Maritime Powers, or even employed in concert with them, appears very objectionable.

With respect to the Military Paper, no considerable objection is felt here to the destination there proposed for the Prussian army; but, as this point cannot of course be matter of public treaty, it may be sufficient to express in the Convention, that the troops furnished as the contingent, or *subsidized by the Maritime Powers, are to act in the Low Countries*, and that a Concert shall immediately be entered into on that subject respecting the most effectual mode of carrying on operations against the common enemy. As a part of such secret Concert, His Majesty would be quite content to abandon the idea of requiring the Prussian troops actually to join his army in Flanders, provided that the arrangement is adopted for their acting in one army on the side of Namur. If you find that it would facilitate the conclusion of this business, that it should be understood that His Prussian Majesty should himself be at the head of that army, no objection could arise to this idea from hence; and you will of course express to His Prussian Majesty, in proper terms, the just sense which the King entertains of the advantage which the cause would derive from His Prussian Majesty's presence and personal exertions. It is, however, evident, that the precise regulation of the operations and destination of the Prussian force must require concert with the Austrian Generals, and this is greatly facilitated by the removal of the negotiation to the Hague. It is therefore material that no time should be lost in bringing to a conclusion the other parts of the negotiation, which, from these instructions, I flatter myself you will be enabled to do, with no other delay than must arise from the share the Dutch Ministers are to have in it; but in this point of view also I am not ignorant of the great advantage which the business will derive from your Lordship's knowledge of the persons and Government with whom this matter is to be settled at the Hague, and from your long experience of the manner of doing business there.

It is, however, likely, that the necessity of the concurrence of the Republic in these measures, and the delay which must arise on this account, may give sufficient time for your transmitting here for approbation, previous to actual signature, any *projêt* on which you may ultimately agree with Count Haugwitz; and on an occasion of such extreme delicacy and importance, this, if it can be done without incurring the mischief of delay, would certainly be more satisfactory to your Lordship, as well as to the King's servants. But, if you are of opinion that any hazard would arise from this, the King would rely with confidence on your Lordship's known abilities and experience, and you are at full liberty to conclude, on the principle of these instructions, without further reference home.

TUESDAY, APRIL 1.—Writing. Visits. Dined at Keller's.* Pensionary and Haugwitz after dinner.

WEDNESDAY, APRIL 2.—Walked. Dined at Alva's.

THURSDAY, APRIL 3.—Pensionary and Greffier—*projêt de Traité*. Dined with Elliot—circle. Little supper at Court.

SATURDAY, APRIL 5.—I send *projêt de Traité* to England. Walk. Dinner and supper with the Hereditary Princess†— she handsome and pleasant, but pale—her Court well served —she inhabits la Vieille Cour.

SUNDAY, APRIL 6.—Pensionary at twelve. Dine at home alone. Visit concert at Court—some Emigrés sing—much talk at supper with the Princess.

MONDAY, APRIL 7.—Walk with Haugwitz. Dine at Archibald Hope's. Supper at Keller's—bad society—Jacobin style—she prettyish.

TUESDAY, APRIL 8.—Greffier. *Projêt* of separate convention with Holland. Greffier calls on me—dine with him— a family dinner. Concert at Lady M. Reede's‡—court there —stay late.

* Prussian Envoy at the Hague.
† Daughter to the reigning King of Prussia.
‡ Lady Mary Reede was daughter of the Earl of Athlone, who was descended from General Von Ginckel, a Dutchman whom William III. raised to the English Peerage for his successes in Ireland. His family name was originally Von Reede.

EXTRACT OF A DESPATCH FROM LORD MALMESBURY TO
LORD GRENVILLE.

Hague, 8th April, 1794.

The alarms at Manheim, Mentz, Frankfort, and all along the Rhine, on the idea that the King of Prussia was either going to separate entirely from the confederacy, or to remove his army from that neighbourhood, pass all description.

I have no doubt of the reality of the fears of the inhabitants in general, and it would be unreasonable to say they are wholly groundless; but I am satisfied that there is a description of men in the three towns I have mentioned above, who make it their business to raise and increase these fears by every possible exaggeration of the danger. I do not mean to include the Marshal Möllendorff in this number. He is a man of an honourable, open, and upright character, but is of an easy temper; and most of those who surround him have their particular interests and designs in view in impressing his mind with opinions, which would be very different if it was left to its own natural operation.

The persons I particularly allude to (besides many inferior ones whose names would be unknown to your Lordship) are *Count Schulenburg* and *General Kalckreuth*, who I know oppose to the utmost all we are doing here, and who are attempting to make the Marshal Möllendorff, and through him the King of Prussia, believe that his army is averse to serve in the Low Countries.

Count Haugwitz, confident of his own strength, and secure of the King his master's favour, apprehends no danger, nor even inconvenience, from this quarter. I am not quite so easy about it, and wait with great impatience an answer to the letters he has written on this subject to Potzdam.

The chasseur despatched by Count Haugwitz on the 31st March, with orders to stop the retreat of the Prussian army, returned here to-day; the order appears to have given great pleasure to Marshal Möllendorff, who writes word that everything is now quiet and safe, and that he will be responsible that no impression shall be made by the enemy on the side of the Rhine, as long as his army holds its present post. He presses, however, the necessity of losing no time.

Thursday, April 10.—Dined at Kalitcheff's. Supped at Lady Athlone's—the Court and the Princess of Hesse Homburg there.

On the 17th I received the *projêt* of the two Treaties approved ; and although the 18th was Good Friday, and the 19th Saturday in Passion week, I had influence enough to assemble the States General, and get them to approve the treaties, and to give full powers to the Pensionary and Greffier, and we signed them on the afternoon of Saturday the 19th April, in the apartment where the " Besogne Secrète" meets. I despatched the same evening a messenger with them to England. I remained at the Hague till Friday, April 25th, when, in consequence of instructions from Lord Grenville, I went through Brussels and Flushing to England.

EXTRACT OF A DESPATCH FROM LORD MALMESBURY TO LORD GRENVILLE.

Hague, 19th April, 1794.

Shaw delivered me your Lordship's despatches of the 14th instant on Wednesday the 16th at noon, and I now redespatch him with the Treaty between His Majesty and the States General on the one part, and the King of Prussia on the other, as well as with the Convention between His Majesty and the States General, duly signed and executed by the several contracting parties. I transmit, at the same time, the separate Article signed between His Majesty and the King of Prussia, which relates to the renewal of the Treaty; and also copies of notes which have passed between me and Count Haugwitz, and between me and the Pensionary and Greffier, on these subjects.

All these instruments were signed about an hour ago, in the apartment where the Secret Committee of the States General usually meet.

It was a matter of no small ·difficulty to get this business through so fast, not only from the forms of this Government, but from its being the Holy Week ; but, the moment Shaw had delivered me your Lordship's despatches, I waited on the Prince of Orange, and made a point with him that he should assemble the States General yesterday and to-day ; yesterday for the "Besogne Secrète," to lay the Treaties before their High Mightinesses; and to-day, in order that their High Mightinesses should return the Treaties with their approbation, and with full powers for their Plenipotentiaries to sign them.

Had I not insisted on these two extra meetings (which it was no easy matter to obtain), nothing could have been done till the middle of next week, as their High Mightinesses had adjourned over till then.

I trust there is no alteration either in the wording or measures of the treaties I have signed, which will be objected to by your Lordship.

---

[This Treaty obliged His Prussian Majesty to furnish an army of 62,000 men, under a Prussian commander-in-chief, to be subsidized by England and Holland, and to serve against their common enemies. This army to be in the field by the 24th of May. The Maritime Powers to pay His Prussian Majesty 50,000*l*. per month to the end of the year, and 300,000*l*. to put his army in motion, also 100,000*l*. on its return home. All conquests made to be at the disposal of the Maritime Powers.

A separate article was added, to extend the engagements of this Treaty as long as the war lasted, on the same conditions ]

EXTRACT FROM A LETTER FROM LORD MALMESBURY TO THE
DUKE OF YORK.

Hague, 19th April, 1794.

I HAVE delayed till now acknowledging your Royal Highness's letter of the 3rd from St. Armand, in order to have it in my power to send you some positive intelligence relative to the event of the negotiation with which I am charged.

I held it my duty to be silent while its event was uncertain, lest, in the very important situation your Royal Highness holds, I should perplex and perhaps mislead you by acquainting you with all the doubts and difficulties which have attended its progress.

I have now the honour to inform you that about an hour ago I signed a treaty with His Prussian Majesty, (to which the States General are a party,) by which he stipulates to furnish 62,400 men to act in support of the cause, exclusive of the 20,000 men he is bound by treaty to give to the Emperor.

I have not time to have this engagement transcribed at length, but it states in substance that an army to the amount above-mentioned should act together, jointly with a corps in our or in the Dutch pay, and under a Prussian commander, (by which is understood the King himself,) where, and in a manner which shall be deemed most conformable to the interests of the *Maritime Powers;* that this army is to be at the place of its destination by the 24th of May; that it is to be supplied with everything necessary to take out and remain in the field *except battering cannon;* that all the conquests it may make shall be in the name and at the disposal of the Maritime Powers, as well during the war as at the peace; and that as far as possible its force shall be effective.

For these conditions, we and the Dutch agree to pay to His Prussian Majesty a subsidy of 50,000*l.* a-month, and bread and forage for the whole army at the rate of 1*l.* 12*s.* a mouth per month. We give 300,000*l.* for the *mobilification* and *rétablissement,* and 100,000*l.* for its return.

The Treaty is to last till the end of the year; but in a separate article I have stipulated that it is to be renewed at the end of the year, on the same conditions *and for the duration of the war.* This was not done now, because the nature of the Dutch Government is such as not to allow them to come to any *new* resolution under several weeks, and every hour now is precious.

Your Royal Highness will naturally suppose Great Britain takes the largest share of the payment. The Dutch, however, contribute handsomely; and I hope it will not be thought that they contributed too little, or that the King of Prussia has been allowed too much. I am prepared, however, to be hauled over the coals by my old friends;* but they have departed so widely from their former principles, that I never expect that they and I can ever again think alike on any public subject.

I am despatching a messenger this moment to England, with the Treaty executed. The moment it is ratified I probably shall remove from hence, and I rather hope to Brussels; and I need not say, in that case, my first wish shall be to pay my duty to your Royal Highness.

Nothing remarkable either in private or public life occurred while I remained at the Hague. I lived principally at Court, or with the Greffier—I found him extremely aged; the Pensionary growing infirm, but with the same strong and clear head; the Stadtholder vastly improved; and the Princess nearly the same.

---

[Lord Grenville ordered Lord Malmesbury to England to give the Government "general information" respecting the best means of employing Prussian troops in concert with those of Austria and the English army under the Duke of York. It appears that this ill-judged recall contributed much to the success with which the French party, taking advantage of treachery and national prejudices, contrived through Lucchesini to stultify the Treaty. It is difficult to know whether Haugwitz was really honest or not, (Lord Malmesbury thought him so at the time,) but it is clear that, when once freed from the influence Lord Malmesbury had gained over him, he shunned meeting him again, and joined in the disgraceful conduct adopted by the Prussian Court at the instigation of Lucchesini. This corrupt Italian Frederick the Great had taken as his *reader;* and at that King's death he was employed by his successor, who found among his subjects a complete dearth of all those moral and intellectual qualities which should belong to a State servant.]

* The Fox Whigs.

## BERLIN.

ON FRIDAY, 25TH APRIL, I left the Hague at half-past one, and travelling all night got to Brussels the next day, Saturday the 26th, at three o'clock—passed that day with Bruce—Lord Elgin absent.

SUNDAY, APRIL 27.—At eleven with Merci—right, but *fin* and cautious—said he could only give his *own* opinion—lamented the disunion with Prussia—blamed Lucchesini. On my observing, the Court of Vienna did wrong not to flatter him, he said, "It was a Court that was not *captante*." He was, however, clearly for the Prussian succours. From him to Thugut—his figure mean, like Pollock—his manner complimentary, but not communicative—railed against Prussia—talked quite officially and very insufficiently. In the evening at Madame Metternich's—a conversation with General Liekendorff—his ideas the same about the placing the Prussian army as those I afterwards had from Mack.*

MONDAY, APRIL 28.—To Valenciennes—lodged at a Mr. Rigan's—excellent house—Mrs. Johnstone there. Lord Elgin arrived soon after me. Victory on the 26th. Sir W. Erskine passing through with the succours for Clairfayt.

TUESDAY, APRIL 29.—Early to Cateau and Fôret Cateau Cambresis,† where the famous Treaty was signed and Telemachus written—is the Duke of York's head-quarters—he was out on an *alerte* when I came—long conversation with him. He was very confidential—said Lord Cornwallis had been thought of to replace him—King first mentioned it to him, afterwards Pitt. He said he would do anything for the service, but he could not act under Lord Cornwallis. Lord Grenville strongly for Lord Cornwallis. After dinner to

---

\* Mack was at the head of the Staff of the Austrian army in 1794. He became afterwards too well known from his defeats by Napoleon, and his capitulation of Ulm.

† The Treaty of Cateau Cambresis was signed in 1559 between France and Spain.

Emperor's head-quarters—for an account of what passed see despatches—strange inconsistency the next day. Called on Prince of Orange.

WEDNESDAY, APRIL 30.—Bad news in the morning early from Clairfayt*—good at noon from Landrecy—it surrendered at four—lost my way in going there—got to Valenciennes very late—lodged again at Rigan's.

THURSDAY, MAY 1.—Dined at Tongres—Slept at Brussels. Alarm—French broke in on Courtray. Road through Ghent not sure.

FRIDAY, MAY 2.—Left Brussels. Expected the Prince of Orange at Antwerp—he did not come.

SATURDAY, MAY 3.—Left Antwerp early. Breakfasted and dined at Bergen op Zoom. From thence by water to Tervecre.—Slept in a bad inn—got there late.

SUNDAY, MAY 4.—Early to Middleburg.—Dined tête-à-tête with Lynden de Blytterswyk—much good sense in his talk. In the evening to Flushing, and, at the very moment I arrived here, the vessel sent round to convey me arrived—also the French Captain Nerval. Flushing a neat town, and all Zealand a fine country.

MONDAY, MAY 5.—Sailed at five o'clock, and got to Margate at eight, and to Sittingbourne at half-past one.—Slept there.

TUESDAY, MAY 6.—Got to London at twelve o'clock, and remained in England till Saturday, May 24.

During the time I was in England, although Ministers had

* General Clerfayt had succeeded the Prince of Saxe-Coburg in the command of the Austrians in Flanders.

*sent for me over*, they were so fully employed in their discoveries and examinations of seditious and treasonable practices, that I had very short and very few conversations with them; and, although I *constantly pressed their sending me back, I neither could obtain any final instructions from Lord Grenville, nor put the subsidy in a way of being paid till the 23rd of May.* I left London on the 24th.

I was twice with the King in the closet, and found him talking the wisest and most spirited language possible. He said *he*[*] thought the war ought to last, as people's minds were not yet thoroughly up to the danger; and that a premature peace would only conceal, not cure, the evil. He recommended the bringing on the Prussians immediately. Talked much with the Duke of Portland, Windham, and Pelham—impossible to be more right than they are. A likelihood of their *all* coming in.[†] I proposed to Pelham to succeed me, as I meant to stay a very short time.—He not averse to it, but desirous to wait to see whether his friends would not also come in. I expressly told both Mr. Pitt and Lord Grenville that I would stay no longer on the Continent than was necessary to complete what I had begun; and that as soon as the Prussian army was at the place where it was to act, I should expect to be allowed to return. To this they both assented.

I passed a week in the country, and found Mr. Hooper very much broken indeed. Durnford[‡] improved, and improving. Opposition going all lengths, even to resist every measure proposed to discover and punish the seditious.

---

[Lord Malmesbury's instructions now were, to accelerate as much as possible the march of the Prussian army towards Liege and Hanover, and on no account to allow them to be employed more to the *left* than the country of the Meuse. Lord Cornwallis to co-operate with an English Force. The

---

[*] It appears from the Harris Papers that Lord Grenville was ever for prosecuting the war against France, and opposed to all the negotiations for peace which Pitt proposed at different periods subsequent to these events.
[†] They took office on the 11th of July.
[‡] Lord Malmesbury's place in Wiltshire.

first instalment of the subsidy, (300,000*l.*,) was remitted from the Treasury, May 27.]

---

SATURDAY, MAY 24, 1794.—At five I left London, and got to Harwich by half-past twelve. I found Madme. Nagel and Madlle. Hompesch waiting to pass over with me for the sake of my convoy (the Lark, Capt. Rowley). He did not sail till Sunday at nine, and our passage was bad, as it was three o'clock A. M. on Wednesday the 28th before we got to Helveot Sluys. The packet we crossed in was called the Diana, Capt. Deane.

I got to the Hague by 10, and called immediately on the Greffier; then on Lord St. Helens, our Ambassador. I saw the Prince of Orange at three o'clock—the Princesses all absent. I dined with Lord St. Helens, and afterwards had a meeting with the Pensionary and Greffier at the countryhouse of the first.—I supped at Lord St. Helens'.

---

THURSDAY, MAY 29.—I dined with the Prince, who gave a very fine dinner. He invited all the principal members of the States, and not one foreigner but myself.—Supped with Madame Keller.

---

FRIDAY, MAY 30.—With the Prince in the morning.— Greffier called on me—dined with him in the country— supped with Madame Ricci, and wrote to England.

The result of my conference with the Dutch Ministers was, their agreeing to the propriety of the Prussian troops being employed in the Low Countries, which the Prince of Orange at first opposed; the nomination of Kinckel to reside at the Prussian army; and the deciding the Stadtholder himself to assist, on the part of the Republic, at our conferences to be held at Maestricht.

I found Lord St. Helens very friendly, but *insouciant* as to business, and not attentive enough for his post. The Pensionary was unwell, and crabbed from illness, which Lord St. Helens does not allow for. The Prince of Orange was uncommonly right, and I learnt from Count Keller that

Count Haugwitz expected me at Maestricht on the 30th; I therefore left the Hague on Saturday the 31st, early; slept that night at Eindhoven, and got to Maestricht on Sunday, June 1, about 4 o'clock.—Count Haugwitz had arrived the day before—I called on him at 8 o'clock, and found him very uneasy about the money not being yet paid; and although he consented to have the army where we decided, yet he said it was in want of so many articles to be purchased by this subsidy, that it could not move till the money was received. This delay highly blamable—Ministers knew that this money would be wanted in three months, and yet had provided no means of remitting it. I immediately despatched Timms (on Monday, June 2nd, at 3 o'clock) to London with strong letters on this subject.

Lord Elgin, whom I found at the Hague, came with me to Maestricht, and returned to Brussels on Monday, to give an account to the Duke of York and Lord Cornwallis of what had passed. I dined at home, and was in the evening with the Prince and Princess of Hesse, where I supped.—He an alarmist and complainer, Governor of the town.

---

EXTRACT OF A DESPATCH FROM LORD MALMESBURY TO LORD GRENVILLE.

Maestricht, 2nd June, 1794.

I GOT here yesterday between six and seven P.M.; Count Haugwitz had arrived the preceding evening. Dressins, with your Lordship's despatch of the 28th ult., and its several enclosures, overtook me about twenty miles from this place. I did not lose a moment in entering with the Prussian Minister on the important business with which I am entrusted, become even more important than it was when I left England from what has since passed in Flanders, and from the sudden resolution taken by the Emperor of returning to Vienna.

I found Count Haugwitz apparently in the same sentiments and same dispositions I had left him in; I thought, however, I observed in him a wish that the Prussian army should *remain on the Rhine;* and, in order to put an end to every possible discussion at once on that point, I set out by telling him in express terms, that it was His Majesty's *declared and decided intention not to listen to any proposal of employing the Prussians in any other place than on some point to be fixed upon between the Meuse and the sea.*

Count Haugwitz declared in the most positive manner His Prussian Majesty's readiness to bring this army wherever the Maritime Powers thought it could be employed the most usefully, and he gave me the strongest assurances that his eagerness and zeal in the cause were invariably the same: that therefore he could assure me that the army should be brought as soon as possible to the point I had mentioned; but that the money not having been received at Berlin on the day it was agreed to be paid by the Treaty, necessarily would cause inevitable delays; since the army, though in the highest order, and completely effective, was without magazines, without a sufficient quantity of ammunition and pontoons, and particularly without artillery and boat-horses; and that these articles, from the state of His Prussian Majesty's treasury, which he assured me in the most strong terms could not supply a single dollar, could only be purchased by the subsidy to be paid by us and the Dutch.

Count Haugwitz told me he had no doubt but that His Prussian Majesty would in a very short time leave Poland, and join his army now on the Rhine.

---

TUESDAY, JUNE 3.—Letters from the Bishop of Liège, and from the Prince of Wurtemburg, from Madame La Coste. —Haugwitz.—Received an account from Jacobi of no money being yet paid. He quite soured, re-despatched his messenger immediately, and I wrote very strongly to Mr. Pitt and Lord Grenville on this subject. Dined at home. Wrote— walked in the evening round the ramparts—very pleasant. I had a very good lodging at the Rue Petits Fossés, at a Jew's named Meyer Solomon.

WEDNESDAY, JUNE 4.—News received of Charleroi being relieved, and the French driven across the Sambre.*

THURSDAY, JUNE 5.—With Prince of Hesse—examined the environs of Maestricht on a map, and concerted the means of joining the town to the Generality. About ten leagues belonging to the Bishop of Liège requisite; from * * * * * to Falkenburg; in this district no farm but Bree (a small one) and a village called Az, the rest heath. Walked with Haugwitz. He said that the Minister was with Bishopswerder doing great mischief at Berlin, by introducing new theological doctrines. That they had availed themselves of his absence, and it was necessary he should return as soon as possible, in order to suppress these *abominable* attempts. He meant, I believe, the doctrines of the *Illuminés*. Dined with Prince de Hesse,† and sent away messenger in the evening.

---

EXTRACTS OF A DESPATCH FROM LORD MALMESBURY
TO LORD GRENVILLE.

Maestricht, 5th June, 1794.

I HAVE not been honoured with any commands from your Lordship since I last wrote.

The Prince Stadtholder is expected here to-morrow, and we shall then only wait for the arrival of Lord Cornwallis, in order to proceed on the business which assembles us in this place.

I have nothing more to say to your Lordship on that subject. Count Haugwitz has written to the Marshal Möl-

---

\* On the 14th of May, by the Hereditary Prince of Orange, after a bloody battle. The French, undaunted, soon re-crossed the river and recommenced the siege. On the 26th of June, the Allies attacked them at Fleury, but were completely routed and pursued to Halle. This battle established the reputation of General Jourdain, and settled the fate of the Netherlands. It lasted thirteen hours. In Flanders, Moreau defeated Clairfait on the 17th, and took Ypres. General Walmoden evacuated Bruges. The Duke of York was obliged to abandon Tournay and Oudenarde to their fate, and retired upon Antwerp on the 3rd of July.

† The Prince of Hesse was brother to the Elector, a General in the Dutch service, and Governor of Maestricht.

lendorff to the effect he promised; but we must not look for any advantage from what he writes, till such time as Mons. Jacobi sends word that the first payments are actually made. It is to no purpose that I endeavour to convince Mons. de Haugwitz that the money due is as much at this moment the King of Prussia's, as if it was actually in his treasury. He remains inflexible, and persists in assuring me in the most positive manner that the army has not the means of moving without this supply. He adds, however, at the same time, that, when it is received, we may depend on finding them ready to act where and how we please; and that the King of Prussia is more eager than ever to crush the progress of French anarchy. I have had several conversations with him on the present situation of his own Court, of what had passed and is passing since his absence, and on the effect Mons. Lucchesini's arrival at Posen is likely to produce.

He adverted to the principles of the Illuminés, whom (rather to my surprise) he spoke of with great abhorrence,—said they went to destroy all good order and subordination, and were one of the great instruments of the Jacobins. He would not say explicitly that he feared these impressions might reach the King of Prussia, but he evidently intimates that it was possible they would, if he remained longer absent.

I confess I apprehend much less of the effects of this attempt than of the presence of Mons. Lucchesini, whose art and cunning are, I fear, more than a match for any influence Count Haugwitz may have acquired, and I shall not be easy as long as he is near His Prussian Majesty.

FRIDAY, JUNE 6.—Chevalier Puysegur called on me—a very sensible Frenchman. From the beginning he saw right, and still appears to see right. His brother, the Marquis de Puysegur, and his wife and family, at Maestricht.—Good people.

JUNE 7 and 8.—Prince of Orange does not come.—

Sends me his opinion;* for the Prussians *remaining on the Rhine!* Lord Cornwallis arrives on the 9th.—Conference with Haugwitz the 10th. — Difficulties about magazines on the march, obviated by Brook Watson.† Major Pfuhl did not assist in these conferences. On the 12th Kinckel arrived at Maestricht, and on the 14th we left it. It was understood by myself, and also by Lord Cornwallis, that there was *no difficulty* as to the march of the Prussians towards the Low Countries, and for this purpose Lord Cornwallis went to Mentz.

SUNDAY, JUNE 15.—Through Cologne, where we overtook Lord Cornwallis, to Bonn.

MONDAY, JUNE 16.—At home till four P. M.—Conversation with Walstein, favourite of the Elector of Cologne—explains and blames conduct of Austria. Slept at Andernach; 17th June to Limberg, 18th to Frankfort; fine weather and good roads the whole way. Hochstetter gives me a letter from Haugwitz, to excuse his meeting me. I receive an estafette from Lord Cornwallis at Mayence, desiring me to come to him immediately, and attend him to Prussian head-quarters. He encloses one from Marshal Möllendorff, which announces clearly his intention of not moving from the Rhine. King of Prussia in Poland—his Minister at Berlin. Our negotiation becomes difficult—*no one to treat with.*

·JUNE 19.—At Mentz. Lord Cornwallis dispirited. I send to Frankfort for Kinckel to come, and go with us to Prussian head-quarters.

FRIDAY, JUNE 20.—We go to Kirckheim, where Marshal

* An elaborately written and weak statement, and also a very strange one, since he helped to subsidize the Prussians, with the understanding that they were to act in the Low Countries. How impossible that any plan should succeed with men who, when honest, could not see their own interest, and, when interested, lost sight of their honour!

† Brook Watson was Commissary General to the Duke of York in Flanders, and remarkable for his integrity and accuracy. In his youth he had his leg bitten off by a shark off the Havannah.

Möllendorff was—our conference unpleasant and angry—Lord Cornwallis quite silent—leaves all the *military reasons*, alleged by Marshal Möllendorff against marching, *without a word of reply*. Kinckel of little use, not having been at Maestricht. The whole fell on me, and I had some sharp words with the Marshal and Schulenburg. The result, to wait for orders, or return to Mentz. Letters from Pensionary, to state to Kinckel the increasing danger of the Dutch, and the necessity of having the Prussians.

EXTRACTS OF A DESPATCH FROM LORD MALMESBURY TO LORD GRENVILLE.

Mentz, 21st June, 1794

On Lord Cornwallis opening the conversation, by saying he was come to regulate with the Field Marshal the most expeditious and convenient manner of marching the Prussian army towards Flanders, the Marshal entered at once into a long enumeration of all the bad consequences which would result to the cause if his army was to be removed from the spot where it was now acting. On my intimating that this point was fully decided on, he expressed his surprise and resentment that before and during the conferences at Maestricht he had been kept in profound ignorance of what was passing, and never received the most distant hint that an intention of carrying his army into the Low Countries had ever existed. He enlarged very much on the impropriety of this conduct, spoke of the hardship it was for a military man of his rank to be called upon on a sudden to carry into execution plans on which he never had been consulted. He declaimed with vehemence and bitterness against Count Haugwitz, and was disposed (in which he was supported by Count Schulenburg and Baron Hardenberg*) to deny the right the Maritime Powers had to dispose of the army, and to insist that the Treaty was one of

---

* Count Hardenberg was a Hanoverian by birth, but left that service on a matter of personal feeling, and hated the English. He became Minister of the Duke of Brunswick, and held several high offices with the title of Prince.

union and reciprocity between the three Powers, and that the King of Prussia had the same rights of opinion as to the disposal of the troops, as either of the other two.

I immediately silenced this unjustifiable assertion by proposing to them to read the first article, which conveyed so distinctly and precisely to the Maritime Powers the *sole right* to dispose of the troops, and left to His Prussian Majesty no other than that to concert with them on the means of carrying their resolution into execution; so that the Prussian Ministers, notwithstanding their inclination and ability to cavil, were forced to give up this point.

Marshal Möllendorff spoke like a man hurt and angry. Count Schulenburg, who had worked him up to this pitch, and who supported him in all he said, affected to be high, and at times sarcastic. Baron Hardenberg said very little. I suffered them to go on without any interruption till they had concluded all they had to say. I then observed, that, for everything which related to the *military objections*, I referred them to the Marquis of Cornwallis, who would well know how to appreciate what he had heard, and to distinguish between real and imaginary difficulties; that in regard to the *Treaty*, and to the sense of its stipulations, I must begin by saying, that these in the most unequivocal and clear terms proved that we, Ministers of the Maritime Powers, came there not to *consult* on measures which were to be taken, but to *regulate* the best mode of carrying into execution a measure already definitively agreed on by us and by the Minister who acted in the name, and with the fullest authority any Minister ever enjoyed, of the King his Master; that therefore it was impossible for me not to observe that the conversation had rather gone beyond its proper limits; that, however, I had too much respect and esteem for Marshal Möllendorff, not to explain myself to him freely and confidentially; and that, although it was not for me to examine the motives which might have induced His Prussian Majesty not to have kept them regularly acquainted with the course of the negotiation, I was willing to relate to him the substance of what had passed. I then went through a succinct but very faithful account of the Treaty, from the time Count Haugwitz and myself removed to the Hague, to the end of our conferences at Maestricht. I made it clearly appear, by quoting dates, and referring to conversations I had had at Berlin with the King himself, that the very basis on which the Treaty rested, was that *the troops should be employed in the Low Countries.*

While I was addressing myself to the Marshal, Baron Kinckel (from whom I feel I shall derive the most influential services) took Count Schulenburg aside.

Baron Kinckel then asked him, if, whether as one of the most ancient, and certainly most enlightened Prussian Ministers of State, he should wish, merely from motives of etiquette and personal pique, to be responsible for the consequences of such a conduct. This language had its full effect on Count Schulenburg; and, when he joined the conversation, I should have been surprised at the alteration both in his language and manner, if I had not observed that my very active colleague had been talking to him. He was no longer arrogant and sneering, but affected to be biassed by the account I had been giving; he confined his objections to the single point of marching the army through the County of Luxembourg; argued with great eagerness on the necessity of protecting Holland, if either the Emperor was unequal or unwilling to defend it; and seemed ready to acquiesce in the idea of moving that way, as soon as the army could be put in a state to march, which they still contend cannot be till towards the end of July. Our conversation having now lasted from eleven till two, we were called off to dinner. This finished, it was resumed again with more temper and good-humour than in the morning, and the result of it was, that we should each of us write to our respective Courts; that in the meanwhile preparations should be immediately taken for making the army *mobile;* and, as to do this would require more time than would be necessary for us to receive our answers, none would in fact be lost by waiting for them.

This is nearly the substance of our conference; and, if your Lordship adds to it what Lord Cornwallis has written to Mr. Dundas, you will be in full possession of all that passed.

The result of this conference is extremely disagreeable

and unsatisfactory; and it would lead to very alarming reflections indeed, if, instead of coming from piqued and prejudiced minds, and from persons who, acquainted with their Royal Master's easy temper, presume a great deal upon it, it should, in the end, appear that it was carried on from secret but positive instructions, or even from any well-grounded reasons that it would be supported at Berlin. But this would be such an outrageous, and, at the same time, such a dangerous violation of every principle of good faith and political integrity, that I cannot believe that any man, even there, is weak or wicked enough to advise it, or bold enough to undertake it.

I despatched Wiffen as early as I could this morning with a letter to Count Haugwitz, with orders to find him wherever he is. I enclose a copy of it; I could not have spoken a stronger language than I write.

I intend myself removing to Manheim this evening, there to wait for the answers to the letter I have written to Count Haugwitz, and to this despatch.

I shall employ the intermediate time in combating all the idle difficulties the Prussians attempt to throw in the way of their march; and, as I feel the greatest anxiety on this occasion, your Lordship may rest assured nothing within the reach of my means shall be neglected.

---

EXTRACT OF A LETTER FROM LORD MALMESBURY TO COUNT HAUGWITZ.

A Mayence, ce 21 Juin, 1794.

MONSIEUR LE COMTE,—C'est avec beaucoup de peine que j'ai appris par la lettre que Votre Excellence m'a fait l'honneur de m'envoyer par estafette de Montebaüer en date du 15 courant, et qui m'a été remis par Mons. de Hochstetter le 18, au moment de mon arrivée à Francfort-sur-le-Main, que des affaires pressantes vous appellaient à Berlin, et vous empêchaient pour le moment de venir me rejoindre selon de ce que nous sommes convenus lors votre départ de Maestricht. J'ai prévu, Mons. le Comte, l'extrême importance de ce que vous fussiez présent à l'entrevue qui devroit se tenir entre Milord Marquis Cornwallis, et Mons. le Maréchal Möllendorff, et vous vous rappellerez avec combien de force j'ai appuyé sur la nécessité absolue que nous ne nous séparerions pas avant que toutes les dispositions nécessaires pour accélérer la marche des troupes Prussiennes vers les Pays Bas ne fussent déterminées, de manière à ne laisser aucun doute que les résolutions prises à ce sujet dans nos conférences à Maestricht ne fussent effectuées avec promptitude, et conformes à l'opinion unanime de tous ceux qui y ont assistés.

Le résultat n'a que trop prouvé combien j'avais raison. Milord Cornwallis, Mons. le Baron Kinckel et moi, nous nous sommes rendus à Kirckheim, où Mons. le Maréchal avait eu la bonté de venir au devant de nous. Il fut accompagné de Son Excellence Mons. le Comte de Schulenburg et de Son Excellence Mons. le Baron de Hardenberg.

Il n'est pas besoin de vous dire, Mons. le Comte, que le but de notre abouchement était de nous concerter sur les moyens les plus propres pour mettre en activité des mesures déjà arrêtées, et pas pour délibérer sur des mesures à prendre. Vous jugerez donc de notre surprise lorsque nous apprîmes par Mons. le Maréchal qu'il ignorait absolument le résultat de ce qui s'était passé à Maestricht, qu'il n'avait jamais appris qu'il fut question de déplacer l'Armée qu'il avait l'honneur de commander, et que quand nous lui fîmes part que les Ministres des Puissances Maritimes de concert avec Votre Excellence, avaient, en vertu des pouvoirs dont ils furent revêtus definitivement conclus que cette Armée devroit se passer avec la plus grande promptitude vers les Pays Bas, que Mons. le Maréchal nous a témoigné un éloignement si marqué pour entreprendre cette marche, et nous opposoit tant de difficultés, que cela nous paraissoit équivaloir un refus.

Quoique je n'aye osé compromettre l'opinion de Sa Majesté le Roi de Prusse, lorsque Mons. le Comte de Schulenburg disait qu'on ignoroit à l'Armée qu'il avait jamais été question de placer l'Armée Prussienne dans les Pays Bas, il m'était impossible de ne pas répondre, que depuis la fin du mois de Janvier et dès le premier moment qu'il s'agissait de conclure un Traité Subsidiaire entre les Puissances Maritimes et le Roi de Prusse, il n'avait jamais été question d'employer les troupes Prussiennes ailleurs, et je n'ai pu m'empêcher d'ajouter ce que j'avais à plusieurs reprises eu l'honneur d'entendre de la bouche du Roi lui-même, que Sa Majesté approuvait entièrement cet emplacement pour son armée.

Mais il est inutile, Mons. le Comte, de me reposer sur des faits qui non seulement sont connus de vous, mais que sans vous je n'aurais jamais été à même de faire valoir. C'est simplement pour vous mettre dans le cas de savoir avec la plus grande précision ce qui s'est passé hier à Kirckheim, et de vous supplier très instamment d'employer vos lumières et votre crédit à concilier la conduite de l'armée avec le parti que nous avons pris à Maestricht, et de veiller à l'exécution d'un Traité qui est votre ouvrage, et dont depend peut-être le bonheur de l'Europe entière. Je suis, &c.

SATURDAY, JUNE 21.—I despatch a messenger with strong remonstrances to Berlin, and another to England.

EXTRACTS OF A DESPATCH FROM LORD MALMESBURY TO LORD GRENVILLE.

Manheim, 27th June, 1794.

IN speaking to Baron Hardenberg, I expressed not only my surprise, but my indignation at the very extraordinary resistance we had experienced on the 20th inst. from Marshal Möllendorff, and those who surround him, to carry into execution a measure which had already received the approbation of His Prussian Majesty, through his principal Minister Count Haugwitz. I observed, he could not expect that I should listen for a moment to the plea of ignorance that Marshal and Count Schulenburg affected on this occasion; for although it was just possible that they were without an official communication of the result of our conferences at Maestricht, yet it was notorious they must have learnt them from Major Pfuhl, who was present; that, besides, I knew beyond a doubt that they had been kept acquainted with the progress of the Treaty from the beginning; that they *knew* its meaning and object as well as we who signed it, and were, in their own minds, as fully satisfied that the army was to march into the Low Countries six weeks ago, as at the moment I called upon them to effect it; and that, if I had not this moral certificate of their knowing it, the ingenuity and studied manner with which they opposed this march, would be an indisputable proof that the proposal did not take them by surprise, or unprepared; that, in regard to the military difficulties and dilemma thrown in the way, they were brought forward in a shape to leave me no doubt that they were the effect, not of conviction, but of repugnance and opposition to the measure, and such as the Marshal would be ashamed to allege in a cool and dispassionate discussion with a professional man; that this was too serious a concern, and one where, in addition to the great public moment, I considered my own personal reputation as so deeply committed, not to be clear and explicit; and I applied to him, as to a man of honour and of experience in business, whether it was possible to consider what had passed at Kirckheim in any other light than as the most artful, daring, and dangerous opposition to the King of Prussia's authority, arising partly from jealousy and envy of Count Haugwitz's favour, and partly from a strong predilection which prevailed in the army, from no very military motives, to remain where it is; that I must be supposed to be equally void of common discernment and common sagacity, if I did not see through all these motives, and know exactly how to appreciate them in my own mind, and how to state them in my reports; that I therefore addressed myself to him as to the only ministerial person to whom I could speak here, and requested him, as his duty, to write immediately to the King of Prussia, (wherever he was,) to urge in my name, speaking under the direct commands of my Royal Master, an immediate compliance with the stipulations of the Treaty, and conformable to the result of the conferences at Maestricht; and to state to His Prussian Majesty, if he should allow his good faith to be surprised by the artful counsels and reports which he would receive from the head-quarters at Keyserslautern, the immediate consequences must be a suspension of the Treaty, which being a subsidiary one, to be made by monthly payments, it would be folly in the extreme for the Maritime Powers to continue making good their engagements, while it was in doubt whether His Prussian Majesty intended to act up to his. I told Baron Hardenberg, that I need not observe, besides the political coolness which it would inevitably create, what a disgrace it would be for His Prussian Majesty to have received such immense sums as those already in his possession, and afterwards to hesitate as to the part he was to act ; that I could not suppose this possible, and that I must consider the whole as the effect of an intrigue and cabal going on in this neighbourhood ; and as I had no reason to suppose the abettors of it made any part of His Prussian Majesty's Councils, or acted with any degree of authority from him, I felt no scruple in speaking of them in the terms I had done.

Just as he was making up this letter, (on Wednesday morning, the 25th instant,) he received one from Marshal Möllendorff, informing him that General Blanckenstein had sent an officer to him, pressing him very eagerly to occupy the post of Treves, which he, in consequence of orders he had had from Prince Cobourg, was obliged to quit ; and the Marshal desired Baron Hardenberg to make Baron Kinckel and myself acquainted with this request, and to ask our opinion on it, dwelling at the same time very much on the extreme importance of this post, and of the fatal consequences which would attend its being neglected.

As I recollected that he had been frequently solicited in the course of this campaign to take charge of this post, and that he had constantly declined it, I immediately perceived the drift of this letter at this particular moment, and did not hesitate to say (and Baron Kinckel agreed completely with me) that I protested against any step which went to separate the Prussian army, or to employ them in a way likely to retard or hinder their going to the destination we had given it ; but as I was well aware of the importance of preserving the post of Treves, and also (from the situation of the war in the Low Countries) of the necessity of General Blanckenstein moving forward with his corps, the Marshal might, if he judged proper, (but that I left it entirely for his own decision,) employ the corps under General Kalckreuth, which I understood was that destined to be given as auxiliaries to the Austrians for this purpose ; but that it was not in my power to consent that a single man should be detached from the 62,400 which, according to a treaty, were at the disposal of the Maritime Powers. Baron Hardenberg sent this answer, and I have since learned that General Kalckreuth with 6000 men has actually been ordered to draw nearer Treves, and had yesterday got as far as Ottweiler.

It appeared to me highly essential, before I met Marshal Möllendorff again, that I should go to the Austrian army. As soon therefore as I had settled the points I have been just relating, Baron Kinckel and myself went to the Austrian head-quarters: there was no time for conversation before dinner, but in the evening Duke Albert took Baron Kinckel and myself into his closet and called in General Brown.

Being thus in possession of the sentiments of the Austrian generals, with whom I had every reason to be perfectly satisfied, both as to the manner in which they spoke, and the result of their conversation, I yesterday went to Keyserslautern (to which place Marshal Möllendorff had removed his head-quarters) ; Barons Hardenberg and Kinckel accompanied me.

I told the Marshal that I did not come to hold a ministerial conference with him ; that everything I could say in that capacity had been already said on the 20th ; and that it was impossible, circumstanced as I was, to enter with him again on the discussion of a point I considered as definitely settled ; but I thought it right he should be informed of what had passed the preceding day at the Austrian head-quarters, and be told that there was no opposition there to the immediate departure of his army from the Rhine, provided that the corps of Auxiliary Prussians and the Saxon Contingent remained. On the Marshal saying this would be done, I observed, in that case, all the difficulties which we had been taught to believe would come from the Austrian army, were done away ; and the arguments so often brought forward and so strongly insisted upon, that the Empire would be lost if the Prussians changed their position, fell to the ground ; that, therefore, none remained but those which came from him; and that, as in answer to these I had to oppose a clear and specific engagement taken between the two Courts, I hoped he would not consider it as an inattention towards him, or a want of due regard to his opinion, if I waived entering into discussion with him on this subject, since, if it were possible for him to impress my mind as strongly as his own of his being in the right, it could make no difference in my conduct, which was regulated by positive instructions from which I could not deviate; that all therefore I had to say was, that, as certain advice had now been received of the arrival of the 600,000*l.* at Hamburgh, I trusted no time would be lost for putting his army into a state of mobilification, or afterwards in making it march towards the Low Countries; and that unless His Prussian Majesty had entirely changed his own opinion, and wished to do away the whole effects of the Treaty he had concluded with the King my master, he (the Marshal) would in a very short time receive orders to this effect.

Marshal Möllendorff being alone with me, and not worked upon by Count Schulenburg, and a tribe of ill-disposed persons who compose the Prussian head-quarters, answered me with great temper and moderation. He persisted in his opinion that greater advantages, even for the defence of Flanders and Holland, would be derived from diversions he should make by his moving forwards into Lorraine, than by his acting in the Netherlands; but he did it mildly, and not with that harshness and petulance he assumed in his conference with Lord Cornwallis. He repeated his surprise and dissatisfaction that he had never been consulted or kept informed of what was passing; and he would not conceal from me, that he had thought it his duty to state his reasons, as a military man, against the removal of the army into the Low Countries; that in doing this he had acquitted his conscience, and that it now remained with the King to give him his final orders.

I also requested Baron Hardenberg, whose conduct on this occasion has been the most honourable, the most manly, and I hope will be the most useful, to state to the Marshal and Count Schulenburg, in a private letter, that if, from the opposition they have thought proper to make to our requisition, they should be able so far to influence the King's judgment as to induce him to swerve from his original opinion, and refuse to comply with what he stands so solemnly pledged to do, first by treaty, and since through his principal Minister, that all the responsibility for the many disagreeable and serious consequences which would inevitably follow, would fall on *them;* that if their Master should incur in the eyes of Europe the disgrace of having received nearly half the subsidy he was entitled to, and afterwards not performing any part of his engagements, this disgrace would be owing to *them;* that if he drove the Maritime Powers into a contrary system, and His Prussian Majesty should find himself placed in an isolated situation, without an ally,* or without any prospect (after what had passed) of having one, and if he was to lose all consideration during the war, and all weight at the peace, the fault would be *theirs,* since, from my certain and intimate knowledge both of the King's sentiments and intentions, and those of his Ministers, I was sure this change of conduct could not be attributed either to His Prussian Majesty or his Minister, but would be owing solely to their representations and to their intrigues; and on this I entreated Baron Hardenberg to request them seriously to reflect. He has written nearly word for word what I have said, and, however little effect it may produce immediately, it will certainly be remembered by them hereafter.

I have now, my Lord, stated to you, I fear in a tedious, but I believe in a very accurate manner, everything which has passed since my arrival here; and I can most conscientiously say, not a single moment of my time or thoughts has been employed on any other subject than that of my commission.

The conclusion to be drawn from it is, that from the weakness or negligence of the Prussian government, the army here is become an *imperium in imperio;* that the Prussian head-quarters, composed of a set of men, some of whom are still the creatures of the Duke of Brunswick,† and others

---

* This is exactly what happened to Prussia afterwards; and till it did happen, and she was in consequence crushed by Napoleon, she followed the same disgraceful course here reprobated by Lord Malmesbury.

† Who had thrown up the command of the army in a moment of pique.

corrupted by the little Princes who have their possessions in the Upper Palatinate, are all interested to keep the army on the Rhine, and, being uncontrolled by any superior authority, dare to speak their opinions, and support them by every act in their power.

Count Schulenburg, a disappointed, bilious man, has a double motive for opposing; namely, the satisfaction of gratifying his personal spleen and ill-humour by injuring Count Haugwitz, whom he detests, and the chance, (though it is but a poor one,) if he can arrive at disgracing him, of getting his place; and he is artful enough, at the same time, to get popularity by affecting to be the *patriotic Prussian Minister*, treating Haugwitz, Hardenberg, and Lucchesini, all as strangers.

Marshal Möllendorff, against the integrity of whose character there is not a word to say, but whose abilities never were great but in the line of his profession, is now near seventy; his mind has lost its energy, and, standing single, he is overruled and led by the crowd of advisers who surround him. Besides his being totally unequal to combat with them on political grounds, he is influenced by the most paltry military considerations. His army is still in cantonments, and not a regiment encamped; by these means the tents are saved, provisions are spared, and the troops preserved, as if they were in one of their own garrisons; and, in fact, it is impossible to see men in finer order, or who have less the appearance of being harassed by war; this is the real state of the case.

Whether we are to expect firmness enough on the part of the King of Prussia to resist this scandalous opposition, or whether we are to suppose he will give way to it, will very shortly be known, since the messenger I sent to Count Haugwitz will be returned in a day or two. My letters to him, and the strong representation I have made from hence through Baron Hardenberg, will, I am certain, have had as much effect as anything I could have said had I been with His Prussian Majesty; and, on the other side, if I had not been here to check and resist the spirit of opposition, there is not the smallest doubt that it would have gone all lengths and overthrown our Treaty completely. As it is, much harm is done, and I fear, at all events, we shall never derive the advantage we reckon upon from the Prussians in the Low Countries. They will go there *unwillingly*, and never afford a hearty and sincere co-operation.

I should feel myself undeserving of any indulgence, if I could impute to myself the failure of this great measure, if it is to fail; but no experience or habits of business, no prudence or care can read so deep into the human mind as to foresee that a great Sovereign and his confidential Ministers would be so regardless of their *personal honour*, and so forgetful of their *public interests and glory*, as to refuse to be bound in *June* by the stipulations of a Treaty ratified with their full consent and approbation in *May*.

SUNDAY, JUNE 22.—At Mentz—Lord Cornwallis declines staying any longer, and returns to the Low Countries. His presence certainly did no good, as he was perfectly silent, and it gave umbrage to the Marshal.

JUNE 23.—To Manheim. Conversation on the ramparts with Hardenberg. (N.B.—He, in his despatches to the King of Prussia, made this conversation official, whereas it was in fact only private.) I however wished him to write strongly.

JUNE 25.—Kinckel and myself go to Schwetzingen, head-quarters of Duke Albert. Satisfactory conversation with General Brown and Duke Albert—settle everything as far as depends on them.

JUNE 26.—To Keyserslautern, Prussian head-quarters—repetition of the same language—great, but shabby art and cunning—ill-will, jealousy, and every sort of dirty passion. The Marshal proposes a Memorial to us, which we decline receiving; and he despatches his first aid-de-camp, Meyerinck, to the King of Prussia, with his account of what we had said. (N.B.—It appears that these were exaggerated, and calculated to do mischief and embroil the negotiation.)

JUNE 28.—Hardenberg returns to Ansbach—we accompany him to Heidelberg. From this day to the 2nd July no event except extreme heat. Manheim dull—dined with Prince Max†—called on the Duc de Deuxponts, both civil. —Abbé * * * *, Minister, (a French Abbé, pimp to the Duke)—not unclever, but importunate: I was forced to cut him very short, and stop his questions, which were most indiscreet.

JULY 3.—Some trifling successes greatly increased by Prussian accounts. Kinckel receives fresh instructions to press the march of the Prussians, or at least a detachment—these carry him the next day (July 4) to Keyserslautern; he sees the Marshal, who is less vehement, but still refusing to march.

JULY 6.—Despatch a messenger to Berlin with a very detailed and strong remonstrance to Haugwitz, in reply to his answer to mine of the 21st June. His answer was unsatisfactory and weak. Received a letter from Hardenberg to say he was ordered to return immediately, and was empowered to treat with us—he entreats us not to take any steps till he arrives, but this we do not attend to.

EXTRACT OF A LETTER FROM LORD MALMESBURY TO COUNT HAUGWITZ.

A Manheim, le 6 Juillet, 1794.

IL ne me reste, Mons. le Comte, que d'observer, que si malheureusement nous nous sommes mésentendus sur le sens ou le but de notre Traité, ou bien que nous croyons que nos vues et nos intérêts ne cadrent plus; hatons nous de le déclarer. Dans le choix des maux c'est le moindre; la nature de ce Traité, moins que tout autre, ne souffre que l'accomplissement de ses stipulations soit unilatéral—et Dieu ne plaise que ce moment arrive quand nous devons nous embarquer dans des altercations sur la signification des

† Afterwards King of Bavaria.

phrases ! moment qui nous réduira à nous glorifier de l'affligeant calcul des maux que notre désunion nous causera reciproquement, et nous fera oublier celui du bien général que nous pouvons faire en travaillant de concert contre l'ennemi commun avec les grands mais différens moyens qu'il a plu à la Providence de nous donner.

Il ne me reste, Mons. le Comte, que de vous dire deux mots sur le payement des subsides. Il est impossible que vous avez pu croire pour un moment qu'il a pu exister de notre côté autre motif de delai dans ces payemens que ceux qui nécessairement étaient attachés à trouver les moyens les plus sûrs pour faire passer des remises si fortes dans une ville, avec laquelle il n'y avoit point de change directe, ni un commerce d'argent considérable.

La lettre cy-incluse vous fera voir, Mons. le Comte, l'empressement avec lequel nous cherchions ces moyens, et notre désir de remplir nos engagemens de la manière la plus libérale.

Cependant, Mons. le Comte, je dois ajouter, que je présume que ma Cour jugera qu'il convient de *suspendre* ses payemens mensuels, tant qu'il existe des doutes sur le sens du Traité, ou sur l'accomplissement de ses stipulations.

(Signé) MALMESBURY.

---

MONDAY, JULY 7.—Bad news by a messenger from Low Countries.—Kinckel writes to Marshal Möllendorff, but without effect. Nothing remarkable for several days.—Count Walmoden with us.

On the 12th and 13th July, Prussians driven from their posts—evacuate Keyserslautern—their reports of their defeat as exaggerated as those of their successes.* Write to Marshal Möllendorff to know the truth—his answer and that from Schulenburg quite absurd and wild.

---

* This defeat could not be "exaggerated," although Lord Malmesbury's sanguine temper refused to believe it. The battle lasted four days, and gave the French a considerable territory, which the allies abandoned by crossing the Rhine.

### LETTER FROM MARSHAL MOLLENDORFF TO LORD MALMESBURY AND BARON KINCKEL.

Kaiserslautern, le 15 Juillet, 1794.

MESSIEURS,—Depuis huit jours je suis continuellement à cheval sans avoir dormi une nuit. L'ennemi fort de plus de 150,000 hommes m'a attaqué sans relâche et avec furie. Il a été repoussé d'abord de tout côté avec valeur ; les malheureuses circonstances cependant qui m'ont obligé de rester sur la défensive tandis que j'avois occupé des pointes de montagne nécessaires pour entrer dans l'offensive, mais très difficiles à soutenir en présence d'un ennemi si supérieur en nombre, ont occasionné que ces mêmes pointes dans les montagnes ont été emporté par les Français. Ceci m'oblige à quitter ma position actuelle et à en prendre une retrograde. Je compte donc encore cette nuit faire défiler l'armée. Les affaires de ces jours ci ont été extrémement meurtrières, nous y avons perdu passé 500 hommes, et du canon ; la perte de l'ennemi est certainement de plus de 5000 hommes. La proportion trop inégale du nombre a seule décidé du succès. Voilà, Messieurs, ce qu'à la hâte je puis avoir l'honneur de vous mander : de mon côté je ne crains pas d'être suivi par l'ennemi, il n'y a que le Prince de Hohenlohe qui pourroit risquer une attaque générale.

C'est avec des sentimens très distingués que j'ai l'honneur d'être,

Messieurs,<br>Votre très humble et très obéissant serviteur,<br>MÖLLENDORFF.

---

### LETTER FROM COUNT SCHULENBURG TO LORD MALMESBURY AND BARON KINCKEL.

Au Quartier Général de Kayserslautern, le 15 Juillet, 1794.

Nous sommes sans équipage, descendant de cheval, pour y remonter, sans papier, sans plumes, j'ai prété l'un et l'autre. L'armée ennemie est augmentée à un point incroyable. Comme nous n'osions avancer, il a pris les postes que nous pouvions prendre sans coup férir. Notre position étendue a empêché de mettre à chaque poste autant de troupes qu'il aurait fallu contre une attaque furieuse de gens ivres. Malgré cela, ils ont été repoussés partout jusqu'à trois fois, mais revenant toujours à la charge avec des troupes fraiches ils ont forcé enfin deux postes, celui de Schenzel et celui de Johannis ———.* Ses bataillons qui y étaient, ayant repoussés trois fois l'assaut et ayant diminué à proportion, furent incapables de résister au quatrième. L'ennemi a prodigieusement perdu, au moins cinq milles hommes, dans tous ces différens combats. Je ne connais pas encore notre perte exacte, mais elle est sensible, quoique sans proportion, peut-être six cents, et *seizes* pièces. Le poste de Johannis ——— fut repris la baionnette au bout du fusil, mais la communication étant interrompue avec le corps de Hohenlohe, dont l'aile droite avait occupé le Schenzel, qui étoit forcé par un corps de vingt mille hommes contre quelques bataillons. Le Maréchal va quitter dans ce moment les montagnes et prendre sa position près de Kirckheim, rétablira sa communication directe avec le Prince de Hohenlohe, et attendra l'ennemi dans un endroit, où les troupes peuvent se soutenir, et où chaque poste n'est pas éparpillé et coupé pas des défiles, sans pouvoir être soutenu, comme c'est le cas des Vosges. Tout le monde peut se tranquilliser, car certes il n'ira pas plus loin sans être battu, ce qui n'est pas probable, car je doute que l'ennemi, tout fort qu'il est, entame une affaire générale. Si cependant les Autrichiens passoient le Rhin, je ne sais pas si nous pourrions seuls nous soutenir contre cent cinquante ou cent soixante mille hommes. Toutes les troupes de la Vendée, quelque chose de l'armée du Nord et des Ardennes, la plus grande partie de l'armée d'Italie est ici, même beaucoup de cavallerie ; Dieu sait où ils ont pris les chevaux !

Mons. de Meyerinck est de retour, dès que nos combats auront fini il arrivera à Manheim, où Mons. de Hardenberg se rendra également par ordre du Roi ; je crois qu'il arrivera Vendredi dix-huitième, au soir.

Vous voudrez bien excuser mon griffonnage ; après plu-

* Illegible in the MS., which, as much as the style of this letter, shews the writer to be at his wit's end.

sieurs nuits blanches presque toujours à cheval, la main tremble d'échauffement.

Nous avons perdu beaucoup d'officiers à proportion des soldats : le Général Pfau, qui commandait au Schenzel, est blessé et prisonnier ; le Général Kleist, qui commandait au Johannis —— est blessé ; le Général —— est également blessé. Le régiment de Romberg a perdu au Schenzel onze officiers.

Monsieur le Baron, nous avons été surpris des ménagemens visibles qu'a eu l'ennemi pour nos voisins,* il nous a fait l'honneur de porter toutes ses forces contre nous.

Votre très humble et très obéissant serviteur,<br>SCHULENBURG.

JULY 15.—Sent an estafette to Hardenberg, to inform him of our intention to remove to Frankfort—the Austrians pass the Rhine. Major Pfühl—his language absurd to a degree—desponding or treacherous—write by him to the Marshal. We leave Manheim, and sleep at Darmstadt—arrive at Frankfort on the 18th.

JULY 20.—I take a country-house. Hardenberg arrives. Call on Prince Reuss at Offenbach. Conference in evening with Hardenberg. He has no full powers—his intention good—his means *null*—his capacity moderate. Meyerinck arrives from the Marshal, and is sent by him to us.

MONDAY, JULY 21.—Dinner at my house—Hardenberg Meyerinck, Kinckel—long conference.

TUESDAY, JULY 22.—Despatch a messenger—Hardenberg and Meyerinck go to the head-quarters.

JULY 23.—Learn that the King of Prussia wishes to

---

\* The Austrians : this remark is a specimen of the vile feeling existing between the allied armies.

combine the defence of Holland with that of Germany—is betrayed by his army, and deceived by his Ministers, particularly Lucchesini.

THURSDAY, JULY 24.—Hardenberg returns—reads us a long Memorial,* and wants us to take two others, dated 22d of June, and to give him a retrospect—this we decline on the 25th of July.

SATURDAY, JULY 26.—Agree to go to Head-quarters.

EXTRACT OF A DESPATCH FROM LORD MALMESBURY TO LORD GRENVILLE.

Frankfort, 29th July, 1794.

ON the 26th, Baron Kinckel, myself, and Baron Hardenberg, went to the Prussian head-quarters, where Prince Reuss had arrived a few hours before us. Prince Reuss had come the preceding day with a commission from the Prince de Cobourg to Marshal Möllendorff; had been sent by him, accompanied by Major Gravent, to the Duke de Saxe Teschen, from whom they were just returned when we got to Mentzenheim.

The inclosed paper will inform your Lordship to what this commission relates,† better than anything I can say on the subject; it is nearly the plan M. de Hardenberg mentioned to us, and I am well pleased that it was settled between the different commanders without any interference on the part of the Dutch Minister and myself, and that we were at liberty to take it simply as a communication for reference, and at the same time to declare (which we both did) that although we did not object to it, we did not consider it as having anything to do with the stipulations of

---

* This contains Möllendorff's military reasons for not marching to the Low Countries, stated at immense length. He concludes by saying, that this movement would be "à n'en pas douter des plus funestes pour nous, et pour la cause commune."

† This relates to military movements concerted between Prince Cobourg and Möllendorff, tending to approach the Low Countries.

our Treaty, which remained precisely in the same situation they did before.

This, my Lord, is all that I can report of a very long visit we made at the Prussian head-quarters. It would be painful for me to attempt to transmit the conversation of Marshal Möllendorff, whose faculties are evidently impaired, either by age, by fatigue, or by passion; he was extremely agitated and incoherent. He talked at one moment on the immense number of the enemy, then on his own great achievements, and his language was a mixture of apprehension and boasting, very unlike his natural character. It was literally *impossible to enter into business with him;* and as the plan now agreed to be taken between the armies brings the business for a moment to a period, and will, I hope, be attended with good consequences, I thought it as well to suspend all fresh discussions till I hear from your Lordship.

JULY 27.—To Mentzenheim—on the 29th concert signed between the Marshals.

JULY 30.—Lord Spencer and Tom Grenville on Special Mission to Vienna—their object to save the garrisons in Valenciennes and other towns, and to persuade the Emperor to make a forward movement on the Netherlands. Cobourg promises him to remain on the Meuse—much conversation with him—they set out in the afternoon. Alarm from Hamburg about the subsidy being stopped—it was false, but proves how much the Prussians feared it by the great uneasiness they expressed.

JULY 31.—Hardenberg returns to the charge with his Memorials—we agree to accept the *military* one, but decline the other.

FRIDAY, AUGUST 1.—Frankfort. Short Memorial to Hardenberg, to press the co-operation as agreed to in the Concert of 26th July.

August 3.—Schulenburg proposes our coming to live at Guntersblum—evident disinclination to move to the right, and to fulfil the Concert.

August 7.—Timms on return home—Lord Spencer writes by him to England and to Duke of York—brings me letter from Duke of Portland—despatch Vansheick to Vienna, with account that Marshal Möllendorff is disposed to fulfil his engagement, though slowly and ungraciously. Report of French moving towards Treves.

DUKE OF PORTLAND TO LORD MALMESBURY.

Wednesday Morning, 23rd July, 1794.

It may not be amiss to inform you that Mr. Pitt and I were the most averse of any of the King's servants from withholding the mensual payments, and coming to a rupture with the Court of Berlin, as long even as any *negative* good could be derived from our *apparent* connexion.

Your's ever,   P.

EXTRACT OF A LETTER FROM LORD MALMESBURY TO T. GRENVILLE, ESQ.

Frankfort, 7th Aug., 1794.

There are rumours here of a conspiracy having been discovered at Vienna of many people of various descriptions having been arrested, and that the spirit of the people inclines to insurrection. I do not believe a word of all this, but I should be glad to hear from you that it is not true. I have been reading, with all the attention I am capable of, *Le Journal Politique de France* from the 26th July to the 30th. I fear the overthrow of Robespierre is only to make room for a new set of tyrants, who for a few months will govern as despotically and as furiously as he has done. I think, however, even with all the art that Tallien and Collet d'Herbois have told their story, that there was a more marked party, and a more powerful resistance now, than in any of the antecedent changes of government, and I would willingly hope that it is not all over.

One comfortable reflection arises from these scenes of horror, that no successes, no conquests, can give union and concord; that under every circumstance there is a perpetual struggle for power: and if we add to this, the total impossibility that mankind can long continue to be led by such prancing nonsense as is talked in the Convention, we may safely conclude, that if we persevere with courage and patience, we shall carry our point; and on the other side, the very short time which power remains with any one faction, leaves us no choice what we are to do, and ought to convince all those who recommend *peace*, that they are recommending what it is *impossible* to effect.

---

EXTRACT OF A LETTER FROM LORD MALMESBURY TO THE DUKE OF PORTLAND.

Frankfort, 7th Aug., 1794.

HERE I have to do with knavery and dotage, but you have enough of this in my public correspondence, without my introducing it in a private letter. My great aim is to endeavour to obtain as much as is practicable from the Prussian army under the present circumstances, without committing, either by official acquiescence or official approbation, our indisputable right to claim and insist on the full performance of the Treaty whenever we may judge proper so to do.

The events of the 27th ultimo at Paris, and the overthrow of Robespierre, are too recent, and the details belonging to them too imperfectly known to me, for me to be able to conjecture to what they may lead; one very comfortable inference, however, may be drawn from them, viz. that their Government is one of perpetual discord and disunion, and that all their brilliant successes of late cannot give it even temporary security or stability: and another still more comfortable conclusion in my mind follows *logically*, that if we persevere with courage, firmness, and patience, we shall infallibly succeed; but if we relax, or if we listen prematurely to the strong inclination that prevails on the Continent to overtures for peace, we shall fix the evil, and render it incurable.

(Confidential.)

I must thank you on a separate sheet for your few confidential lines. If we listened only to our *feelings*, it would be difficult to keep any measure with Prussia. But your opinion, and that of Mr. Pitt, is one of sound political wisdom, and I am well pleased it has prevailed. We must consider it as an alliance with the Algerines, whom it is no disgrace to pay, or any impeachment of good sense to be cheated by.

SUNDAY, AUG. 10.—Gravinus (Hardenberg's friend and assistant) calls on me to say Treves is taken by the French—evident ill-will and wilful carelessness on the part of Kalckreuth. Call on Prince Reuss at Offenbach—Dinner at Bethman's.

AUG. 12.—Confirmation of Treves being taken comes to Hardenberg; yet is doubted by all the principal people of Frankfort.

AUG. 14.—Nothing material. Rode with *Sophy Bethman*—King of Prussia in love with her—she is not pretty, but a good countenance—clever, artful, well-informed, and takes great pains with herself—well-made—said to be very charitable, and to do a great deal of good—talks English very well, and Italian.

AUG. 15.—Writing. Treves taken beyond a doubt. Sir Robert Ainslie\* and Mr. Walker in the evening. Sir Robert assures me the Turks were not democratically inclined nor French, nor disposed to quarrel with Russia. Paget, in the

\* English Ambassador to the Porte.

Romney of fifty, has taken La Sibylle of forty-four; and Sir Robert says our trade has suffered very little, but many ships taken under Russian and Austrian colours.

AUG. 16.—Letter from Meyerinck to Hardenberg, complaining of Möllendorff—he will not move towards the Netherlands. Kinckel determines to go to Mentz to see Schulenburg.—Courvoisier, messenger from Vienna, in the evening.—Lord Spencer mentions his having opened the Conference, but made no progress.

EXTRACT OF A LETTER FROM LORD MALMESBURY TO THE HON. A PAGET.[*]

Frankfort, 16th Aug., 1794.

You are perfectly right in your information. Haugwitz is nobody—Lucchesini rules despotically; and, as he did not make the Subsidiary Treaty, he opposes it in every part. Möllendorff is a dotard; his parts and mind are gone, and nothing remains but his vanity and malice. The army is in as high order as possible, but we never shall derive any real benefit from it. All the leading officers are ill-disposed, and many of them with decided Jacobin leanings. The loss of Treves is to be attributed solely to wilful negligence on the part of *Kalckreuth*. I have pressed Möllendorff strongly to make an attempt to retake it, but I am certain without effect, although there is little doubt but the measure would succeed. Reede is a bilious, proud, disappointed man: he is particularly angry with me,[†] but without a shadow of reason: he is also led by his secretary, *Bourdereaux*, who is a notorious democrat. I cannot guess how long I am likely to remain on the Continent—it depends on events.

[*] English Chargé des Affaires at Berlin.
[†] For having removed the negotiation from Berlin, where he was Dutch Minister, to the Hague.—*Harris Papers*.

Aug. 21.—At Offenbach with Kinckel. T. Grenville writes me word that Cobourg and Prince Waldeck are to be removed from the command—it devolves on Clairfayt. Send Major on—write to Duke of York—dinner at Goutard's—news of a successful sally made by Marshal Benden on the French near Treves.

---

EXTRACTS OF A DESPATCH FROM LORD MALMESBURY TO LORD GRENVILLE.

Frankfort, Aug. 21st, 1794.

Baron Kinckel returned from Mentz on the evening of Sunday the 17th. The result of his conversation with Count Schulenburg went evidently to prove that there has been, to use the gentlest term, great misconduct on the part of the Prussians in not making a forward movement, and Count Schulenburg did not scruple to blame very strongly the hesitation of M. Möllendorff on this occasion. He asserted that he himself had done everything in his power to press this measure, but that he was overruled by officers at the head-quarters, to whose opinions the Marshal listens; and particularly by the influence of General Kalckreuth, who, when it was proposed to him to advance, represented his corps as having done everything in their power, and as extremely harassed by the forced marches it had already made, in order, although without success, to arrive in time to support the Austrians in the defence of the lines of Pottingen, on which the safety of Treves depended. Count Schulenburg lamented the situation of the army, confessed that the Marshal was no longer possessed of those eminent qualities he once had, and which were so very essential in such a command; that he had lost that steadiness of character and decision of mind; that he consulted his adjutants and aides-de-camp, and generally took the opinion of the last adviser. Of this we have most uncomfortable proofs; and I wish I could say that there was not also the strongest appearances that these advisers, with whose names your Lordship is not unacquainted, are not wrought upon by the most unbecoming means.

This language will appear to your Lordship singular in the mouth of Count Schulenburg; but his passion sometimes gets the better of his cunning, and it is to be accounted for on his being piqued at those persons having acquired a superior ascendancy to his over Marshal Möllendorff. But although he was very free in his expressions, he very carefully avoided committing himself beyond words; and when my colleagues proposed to him, as a duty in a manner incumbent on him, to use his endeavours to prevent the Marshal from being led by such pernicious counsels, and that he ought to write to the King his Master on this occasion, Count Schulenburg declined it positively, saying, that his duties were circumscribed by his office of Commissary-General, and that it would be highly dangerous for him to attempt to move officially out of their sphere. My colleague very wisely did not bring to his recollection, that the whole of his conduct from the conference at Kirckheim on the 20th June, to this day, had been in constant contradiction to what he now said. Such a reflection, however natural, would only have served to irritate Count Schulenburg uselessly, at a moment when he was disposed to be communicative, and to concur, at least in appearance, with our opinions and wishes.

Baron Kinckel pressed, however, on the expediency of an immediate attempt to recover Treves. He pointed out the many military reasons drawn from the inferior force of the enemy, and from the nature of the country occupied by the Prussians, which seemed to ensure the success of such an enterprise; the immediate good harmony it would re-establish between the Austrian and Prussian armies (which the loss of this place had occasionally interrupted); and, above all, what ought to have the most weight with him (Count Schulenburg) as a Prussian Minister, the lustre it would give, or rather restore, to the Prussian arms, which had not during the whole of this campaign distinguished themselves by any one memorable action. Count Schulenburg was ready enough to admit these reasons, but he declined taking any active part on this occasion; and the only good effect derived from this visit of my colleague was, to ascertain what we had so much reason to suspect, and to convince us that if we can succeed in keeping the Prussians to maintain the line they have undertaken by the Convention of the 26th, it will be *all* we can expect.

The latest accounts from Warsaw* are far from satisfactory. It should appear that the success of the attempt on that town is very doubtful, and that His Prussian Majesty finds himself in a situation of difficulty and possible disgrace he by no means expected. It would be very fortunate if this should serve to open his eyes on the character of Mons. Lucchesini, by whose advice he was placed in this situation, and to whose influence solely are to be attributed the whole of the conduct which has been observed here, and the little attention paid to the engagements they entered into on the 19th of April.

---

EXTRACT OF A DESPATCH FROM LORD GRENVILLE TO LORD MALMESBURY.

Downing Street, 16th Aug., 1794.

I HAVE the honour to enclose to your Lordship the copy of a despatch sent by this mail *en clair* to Mr. Paget at Berlin. It contains the substance of all that I have to communicate to your Lordship with respect to the question of the employment of the Prussian troops, and the continuance of the subsidy. It was not till I had received from your Lordship the account of the arrangement made between the Austrian and Prussian Generals, that it was possible for me to add anything to the instructions contained in the despatch delivered to your Lordship by Lord Spencer and Mr. Grenville ; and, indeed, a part of the policy of the Prussians on this occasion has evidently been to embarrass the business by repeated deceit, as well as to delay the adoption of any decisive measure in this country as long as possible. The necessity of affairs, as resulting from

---

* In 1793, after the Russian garrison had been expelled by the Poles, Kosciusko took possession of Warsaw, and defended it successfully against the King of Prussia. But, in 1795, the Russians, under Suwarow, retook it, and the final partition of Poland followed.

the late ill-successes in Flanders, makes it perhaps now a fortunate circumstance that these delays have intervened; and in the present moment, the distribution of force is such as to leave nothing to be wished for in that respect, except a juster ground of confidence in the punctual execution even of that engagement by the Prussians.

This messenger will pass through the Hague, and will bring to your Lordship the information of the sentiments of the Dutch Government as to the present state of this business; but I imagine there can be little doubt of their concurring with His Majesty in wishing to keep the Prussian troops in their present position under the now existing circumstances, and to consider their acting there as being for the present an execution of the Treaty.

The conduct of the Court of Berlin is, however, so little veiled in all this business, that it seems neither wise nor dignified to affect to be deceived by it. No language that we could hold could impose upon them so far as to make them believe that we adopt the present resolution from any other consideration than that of an immediate and pressing interest, or that His Majesty is or can be insensible to the manner in which the Court of Berlin has acted on this occasion.

All, therefore, that remains for your Lordship to do is, to be careful in signifying to Mons. Hardenberg the King's acceptance of the engagement above mentioned, as a present fulfilment of the Treaty; to restrain that acceptance to the present circumstances; and to declare expressly, that the King does not, and will not, renounce the right of disposing of the future movements of those troops, according to the express unquestionable meaning of the Treaty.

---

EXTRACTS OF A DESPATCH FROM LORD GRENVILLE TO THE HON. ARTHUR PAGET.

Downing Street, 15th Aug., 1794.

I THINK it right to acquaint you that Mr. Jacobi yesterday, at the usual conferences, took upon himself to complain of the manner in which the late Treaty had hitherto been executed on His Majesty's part, and to ask what were His Majesty's intentions with respect to the future. To the first part of this communication it was impossible to give any other answer than that, if the Treaty had not hitherto been punctually executed, it was notorious to all Europe that the failure had not been on His Majesty's part. With respect to what was to come, he was told explicitly, that the same exact and punctual execution of the Treaty on His Majesty's part would nevertheless be continued, provided that it was for the future more punctually fulfilled on the other side by His Prussian Majesty.

After this answer, which so extraordinary a demand on his part rendered indispensable, he was told that, wishing to refer to the just ground of complaint which past transactions had given to this part, it seems sufficient now to say, that under the circumstances which recent events had occasioned, His Majesty regarded the disposal of the Prussian army, such as it had been settled in the agreement made between Duke Albert and Marshal Möllendorff, as being for the present the best which could be made for the common cause.

You will, of course, regulate your language in exact conformity to what I have above stated, and you will plainly give it to be understood by the Court of Berlin, that the continuance of the liberal subsidy granted by His Majesty will depend solely on the faithful execution of the engagement taken by Marshal Möllendorff, and on the efficient service of the Prussian army under his command.

SATURDAY, AUGUST 23.—Ride to Bergen—delightful. Dine with Kinckel.—News of an advantage obtained by Prince Cobourg near Tongres on the 19th. Sup at Madame Bethman's.

AUGUST 27.—Hardenberg returns from army—well pleased with his visit—answers our Memorial. Dinner at Metzler's, at Offenbach. In the evening at half-past eleven, I despatch Courvoisier (messenger) to England.

EXTRACT OF A DESPATCH FROM LORD MALMESBURY TO LORD GRENVILLE.

Frankfort, 27th Aug., 1794.

THE manner in which your Lordship sees the conduct and designs of the Court of Berlin, is, as far as my judgment and information go, strictly the truth.

It is particularly painful to me, to whom so considerable a share of this business has fallen, to have met with so little good faith; but it required more suspicion than I ever wish to possess, and more penetration than I have any claim to, to suppose there could exist in a great Court such a total disregard to public character and to sound policy; and I hope I shall stand acquitted of every other charge on this occasion, but that of having been induced to believe, that, when these two considerations unite, they are in general tolerably good securities for the performance of engagements.

The present case has been, unfortunately, an exception to this rule; I have, however, little doubt that His Prussian Majesty, from the insulated position in which (in consequence of what has now passed) he must sooner or later be placed, will have to lament much greater inconveniences from his having abandoned this principle, than we feel from his defection.

I lost no time in obeying your Lordship's instructions on the 22nd instant; in the evening I presented, jointly with my colleague, the enclosed note to Baron Hardenberg; and, while I remain here, I shall persist in my endeavours to keep M. Möllendorff fast to the agreement he entered into on the 26th July with the Austrian commanders. It is a matter of some comfort, although it arises from incidents, that, if we can now obtain a faithful execution of this agreement, it would be, perhaps, as advantageous an employment of the Prussian troops as any we could have derived from our Treaty.

In giving in the note to Baron Hardenberg, I employed the words with which your Lordship ends your last despatch, and signified very distinctly that the King's acceptance of this engagement as a present fulfilment of the Treaty was restrained to the present circumstances only ; and I declared expressly, that "*His Majesty does not and will not renounce the right of disposing of the future movement of the Prussian army, according to the express and unquestionable meaning of the Treaty.*"

THURSDAY, AUG. 28.—Dined at Goulard's with Baron and Madame Vreden. Good news from Italy in the evening.

AUG. 29.—No public event. Ride on the left side of the Maine—very pleasant.

AUG. 31.—English post arrives—nothing material. Great dinner at Gozel's—old hock at a guinea the pint. Supper at Goulard's.

MONDAY, SEPT. 1.—Letters by Austrian messenger—Merci's death.* Dinner at *Vorst Hause* Wood—pleasant drives. Count de Saleyn. "Fat manqué."

SEPT. 2.—Pleasant ride in the woods near Isenberg. Dine at home. Hardenberg returns from head-quarters. Möllendorff determines to take charge of the left side of the Moselle. Bad news from Poland ; Warsaw holds out. Insurrection in South Prussia, near Silesia—riots at Berlin.— King of Prussia, through Haugwitz, affects to draw towards the Maritime Powers, partly from these commotions, and partly because the *subsidy* is ending.

WEDNESDAY, SEPT. 3.—Nothing. Dinner at Kinckel's. Count Schlik, Imperial Minister at Mentz—vain—not deep —ill-informed.

SEPT. 6, 7, 8, 9.—Nothing. Gravinus returns—has been

* Merci was Austrian Minister at Brussels, and had been much at the old French Court, where he was supposed to have possessed considerable personal influence.

through Berlin—says the King of Prussia never meant to break Treaty—wishes to be well with the Maritime Powers, and talks a language calculated to induce a renewal of the subsidy. Hardenberg the same—he called on me on the 9th, and seemed very uneasy on my being likely to leave Frankfort—he assured me, when Warsaw was taken, the King would come to Berlin, and from thence here—he also *dwelt very much* on the *absolute necessity* England was under to keep the Prussian army.

I replied to all this, that the mischief was done, and that if the King had the sentiments he said he had, why did he not shew them?—that my Mission was to him, and never to the head-quarters—that I was willing to do anything I could to keep up a system of harmony and friendship, but that it was impossible for me to expose myself to be duped a second time.

Valenciennes and Condé are lost—also Sluys. Slater passes through on Sunday the 7th, on his way from Bois le Duc, where he left Windham, (Secretary at War,) to Vienna.

Letters from Lord Grenville on the 9th, to announce the speedy return of Dressins, and to desire me to stay till he comes.

---

SEPT. 10.—Hardenberg with me in the morning—he gave strong assurances of the King of Prussia's wishes and intentions to keep well with the Maritime Powers; that he had been deceived by a *cabale;* that the moment the Polish war was over he would return to Berlin; that then Haugwitz would resume his influence, and everything go right: he therefore pressed my going to Berlin, and continuing my Mission there. All this he supported by saying he had sent Gravinus to Berlin, and that he had seen Haugwitz, and explained to him all the intrigues at the head-quarters here, and their consequence; and that Haugwitz was convinced, and so was the King, that they had been misled.

This was said to Kinckel and me with a clear and evident view to prevail on us to renew the Subsidy Treaty, as the term of its expiration draws near, and as the Court of Berlin is uneasy at our negotiations at Vienna, and apprehensive of the event of an attack on Warsaw : it was too thinly veiled not to be seen through. I therefore answered, that I was fearful " *the evil was done;*" that if the King and his Ministers had acted up to the sentiments M. Hardenberg now mentioned, or even if I saw a sincere disposition of doing it now by Möllendorff's army *really acting*, it certainly would be good grounds to hope ; but that this was not the case. That what he (Hardenberg) said to me at present, Haugwitz had said word for word to me last year, and that it had been confirmed to me by the King himself. That, however, this was of no avail, and a conduct was observed by His Prussian Majesty in direct contradiction to the assurances and to the plain sense of the Treaty ; that, therefore, I certainly could not, *nor would not*, take upon myself to engage in a fresh negotiation, or to go to Berlin. That, when I said this, I was at the same time so sincerely in earnest in the cause, and so desirous to do everything in my power to serve it, that I would not hesitate to enforce all he said to me *at home;* and that if His Prussian Majesty really and *bonâ fide* wished systematically, and not *subsidiarily*, to unite himself with the Maritime Powers, the only way I could point out was, to send a Minister of high rank and confidence to London ; that we should have one in a short time under that description (Lord H. Spencer) at Berlin ; and that certainly some one would be named to reside near the Prussian army on the Rhine.

Hardenberg employed every argument and every *trick* within the narrow compass of his means to persuade me they were earnestly anxious to unite with us, and disposed to rectify their past behaviour ; but I remained firm, and absolutely declined giving in to a belief of it.

This led him to say that we could not *do without the Prussians*, and that we *must* continue the subsidy ; that therefore it was wisest and best to do it in the manner the most useful and most conciliatory.

I replied, that, without deciding on this strong question of•*necessity*, I could not but observe that, by stating it as an argument, he brought his Court on a level with the lowest German prince, and supposed it to be actuated by principles like those of the Dey of Algiers ; and that, if *necessity* was to decide the measure, it required no negotiation, it would do itself, and I felt myself by no means in a rank to conduct *such* a business.—As he had let slip the word *necessity* from awkwardness, he was eager to retract it, and then said the whole would depend on our not forming a system with the Court of Vienna. He asked me, by a straightforward question, what our conduct towards that Court was? I told him it depended on that which his Court *would* observe, and *had* observed; and that from this he might be sure to draw a safe conclusion.—He replied, If it is yet *res integra*, all may yet do well. He then again repeated his *concerted* assurances about the King of Prussia's dispositions and sentiments, and again urged my staying on, and going to Berlin. I at last told him very fairly, that, having been the dupe *once*, it was impossible for me to expose myself a second time; that I would very sincerely and willingly do my best to forward any measure His Prussian Majesty might propose at *London*, if I saw such proposition come forward with an air of truth and sincerity; that more I neither could nor would undertake.

Gravinus, who dined with me, repeated (but with more judgment and art) all Hardenberg had said. He urged the necessity of a new Commander, and mentioned the Duke of Brunswick; and it was evident, from all he said, that his journey to Berlin was undertaken to get full powers for Hardenberg; and, as Hardenberg formerly was in the Duke's service, to replace him in the command, with a hope that then the main direction of the whole business might fall into his hands. All that was said to us was only an accessory to this principle; and perhaps it would be very fortunate was it to take place, although I certainly will not be mixed up in the arrangement.

SEPT. 11.—General Zinzendorff—explained the shameful conduct of the Prussians in the affair of Treves. Dined at Hardenberg's—play—Madame de Spec—handsome.

SEPT. 12.—Zinzendorff dined with me—long desultory

conversation—he abuses the Prussians, yet denies the possibility of doing without them. His nephew, Count Poppenheim, with him—he wants to raise a corps for our service—man of high rank, and good reputation as a soldier.

From hence to the end of the month, Frankfort fair.—Madame ———, sister to Hatzfeldt, at Berlin—clever, well-mannered, handsome—presses me to come to Aschaffenberg—expresses Elector's wish to see me.—No letters from Lord Grenville. Defeat of La Tour* on the Ourt, just as we induced Möllendorff, *in appearance*, to support Clairfayt's left. Hardenberg, (not the Minister, but a relation, in the Hanoverian service,) from Duke of York, presses this point. I send him to Möllendorff, and Duke Albert; and this journey, with our representations, produces *an appearance* in Möllendorff to act as we wish. I say *appearance*, because it looks as if he foresaw La Tour would be beaten, and he not called upon to fulfil his promise.

Sept. 20.—Write by Dressins, and on the 26th by a messenger I got from Bethman. Press eagerly to get the Prussians to the assistance of Clairfayt, but without success.

EXTRACT OF A DESPATCH FROM LORD MALMESBURY TO LORD GRENVILLE.

Frankfort, 20th Sept., 1794.

The enclosed extract of a letter from Paris comes to me from good authority, and I believe and hope it to be a true picture of the present situation of that capital.

Paris, du 12 Septembre, 1794.

Il parait que les choses vont changer de face à Paris. Tallien tombé en disgrace chez les Jacobins fut dans la nuit attaqué par un meurtrier, et il fut, quoique pas dangereuscment, blessé d'un coup de pistolet. Après cela, Mer-

* An Austrian general, defeated by Jourdan.

lin de Thionville prit la parole dans la Convention, et lui parla fortement contre les Jacobins, et d'une manière courageuse leur impute l'attentat contre Tallien, les appela tyrans sanguinaires, élèves de Robespierre, brigands; enfin il demande à la Convention si elle continuera de souffrir à côté d'elle une autorité rivale, laquelle proscrit les membres pour leurs opinions. Cette société trop fameuse, dit-il, a sans doute rendu de grands services à la Révolution, mais n'ayant plus de trône à renverser, elle veut renverser la Convention. C'est en ce ton qu'il parla longtemps; on applaudissait très fort, et il fut soutenu de plusieurs membres. Tout ceci, de même que l'adresse des Jacobins, fut renvoyé au comité, qui doit dans peu rendre compte de la situation actuelle de la République. Quand cela paraitra, il en résultera de nouveaux débats.

OCT. 1.—Clairfayt driven from the Roer on the 4th— he crosses the Rhine. Renew my instances. Hardenberg returns on the 7th. Send Duke of York copies of all my Notes and Memorials. An extra messenger arrives on Friday, 10th October, with instructions to suspend subsidy.

EXTRACTS OF A LETTER FROM LORD MALMESBURY TO LORD GRENVILLE.

Frankfort, 2nd Oct., 1794.

I HAVE written to Lord Spencer all I have to write officially. I have, I fear, mixed up a little bile with my intelligence; but the times are bilious, and it is beyond the compass of my patience to see the great stake we are playing for lost by imbecility, treachery, and neglect. It is really deplorable that we should be the only nation in Europe who are up to the danger of the moment, and that the minds of all the other Cabinets are either so tainted with false principles, or are so benumbed, that it is impossible to work upon them. It is manifest, from the most undoubted information, that the interior of France is in a state of the greatest disorder and confusion; that the successes of the armies* are the only cause of this confusion not breaking out in the shape of a civil war; and that, if we could at this moment obtain any one brilliant success, the whole fabric would fall to pieces.

SATURDAY, OCT. 11.—Gave a Note to suspend subsidy—the measure taken precipitately, but, as it was communicated to Jacobi by Mr. Pitt, impossible to suppress it—I soften it as much as possible—likely to produce great anger and resentment. Hardenberg, on the 12th October, gives me an answer, saying he must take the King's orders.

WEDNESDAY, OCT. 15.—Lord Spencer and Grenville from Vienna—*re infectâ*. Great promises—strong assurances—no effect, nothing done—advise with him as to my going to Berlin—they against it—I write word so on the 17th by Wiffen (messenger) to Lord Grenville—they go away on the 18th. Rumours of proposals for peace to be made at the Diet by Elector of Mentz.

OCT. 19.—Coadjutor of Mentz, Baron d'Alberg,† confirms this intention—says that when he was at Constance, of which bishoprick he has the reversion, the Senate of Zurich opened to him the views they had collected from Barthelemi. These go to restore the Netherlands and Holland, if we gave back the Islands, but to keep the Rhine as their frontiers. Elector of Mentz to propose peace on the terms of that of Munster, or to continue the war with more vigour. *I disapprove every measure which, at this moment, can put peace*

* The successes of the French armies against the Austrians continued almost without a check. After La Tour's defeat, Jourdan attacked Clairfayt between the Meuse and Lower Rhine, near Ruremonde, on the 29th of September, and nearly destroyed his army after four days' fighting. Cologne, Venloo, and Bonn submitted to the Republican arms. Coblentz surrendered, as well as Worms, without firing a shot, and the Austrians crossed the Rhine. Pichegru's whole attention was now turned to the reduction of Holland, and the expulsion of the Duke of York's army.

† Head of that great family. He afterwards went over to Napoleon, from whom he received additional territory, and other favours, with employment.

*into people's heads.* The terms of France inadmissible—the proposition of the Elector useless and dangerous—Sweden to be solicited to come forward as the only guarantee of the peace of Munster. Coadjutor recommends that the Elector of Hanover should vote always with the Emperor, and that the Emperor should put the whole conduct of the war into Marshal Lang's hands. Germany vastly rich—equal in men and money to France.

---

EXTRACTS OF A DESPATCH FROM LORD MALMESBURY TO LORD GRENVILLE.

Frankfort, 21st Oct., 1794.

As the Coadjutor and myself were not talking officially, and as my object was much more to get information from him than to convince him, I did not hold it necessary to enter into a regular discussion with him on this occasion; it is equally unnecessary for me to make any comment upon what I heard to your Lordship; it will, I presume, strike you in the same light it does me, particularly should it correspond with the intelligence you may receive from other quarters; I must, however, subjoin as a further motive for suspicion, that it is supposed the Coadjutor is a little infected with the principles of the *Rose-croix* and *Illuminés*.

The reflections to which this gives rise, naturally lead me to a subject which has long since struck me as one of the most alarming circumstances attending this very critical juncture, viz., the progress of the French opinions in Germany: I do not mean precisely the exaggerated ones which now prevail in France, but those which first began the Revolution there; which, perhaps, even *originated* amongst those who call themselves men of letters in this country; which have long since been instilled into the minds of the rising generation here, most insidiously and plausibly, by the professors of the different Universities, and which, if they once get head, would soon overthrow a fabric so tottering and so complicated, but at the same time so important to be preserved, as that of the German Constitution.

The nobility, the gentry, and large capitalists in this town and neighbourhood, the most populous and most independent in Germany, cannot be made to understand the danger with which they are threatened, and which is at their very gates.

They are all clamorous for peace, and, by the most fatal error which ever perverted the human understanding, attribute the evils of war and its duration, not to the enemy, who is endeavouring so strenuously to destroy them, but to the very powers who are endeavouring to rescue them from destruction.

They are, in a manner, stunned into security, and it is as impossible to awaken them to a sense of their danger, as it is to rouse in them a due spirit of resistance and indignation.

To every attempt of this kind which I have made, I receive for answer, "England finds its account in the war, and only wants to engage us to continue from views of ambition and conquest."

It is useless to argue against such miserable reasoning, as it would be childish to resent it; but it is impossible not to be deeply affected when we see an immense country like this, abounding at this moment with wealth, and possessing within itself alone means sufficient to resist and repel all the efforts of France, poisoned with doctrines and prejudices which falsify all its faculties, and make those very powers which ought to ensure its safety, act as instruments to forward its destruction.

This must be attributed to what I said above, to the influence of a few artful but clever men, to whom the education of the younger part of the country is entrusted, who have acquired a footing and ascendancy in all the great and rich families. These act slowly, but surely and systematically, on uninformed and indolent minds. They divert and govern all their operations; they never lose sight of their object; they turn every incident, and apply every event, to their final purpose, which is the establishing universally a new order of things, which, though they may think it safer and wiser if it is brought about less rapidly and more humanely than by the French Revolution, has for its object the same levelling and destructive principle.

This sentiment, I am sure, prevails in the Prussian army. A spirit of party and perhaps corruption may influence the conduct of some of its principal commanders; but there is, besides this, a strong taint of democracy amongst the body of officers and men, and a dislike to the cause for which they ought to be fighting.

I am told something very nearly of the same sort is to be found in the Austrian army; and, if this is the case, we must never look for resistance in them, much less expect victory. We may (if we admit this disagreeable consideration) account for a retreat of an hundred leagues, for the surrender of so many towns on the first summons, and for all our misfortunes since the 22nd of May, and consider the situation in which the Maritime Powers stand as one into which they have been drawn in order to effect the most fatal of all purposes.

OCTOBER, 17, 18, 19.—Romanzoff. Much talk—he right, but all for French Princes—agrees with, but not *au fait*, or trusted by his Court—supposes deep plans long since concerted to force the Maritime Powers to peace—that all the ill-successes have been contrivances. Great Jacobin party in Germany, particularly about Ham, and in Westphalia.

OCT. 20.—In the evening, Lieut.-Colonel Don from the Duke of York with letters to Möllendorff—his wish that the Prussian army should defend the right side of the Rhine as far as Bonn, and he to Gorcum.*

OCT. 21.—Colonel Don goes to Prussian head-quarters near Mayence—returns on the 22nd. Marshal Möllendorff crusty before dinner, better tempered after it.

* Lord Grenville had sent fresh instructions that the subsidy should continue, if Möllendorff agreed to the Duke of York's plan.

EXTRACTS OF A DESPATCH FROM LORD MALMESBURY TO
LORD GRENVILLE.

Frankfort, 23rd Oct., 1794.

I WAS on the point of sending Courvoisier away with my despatch of the 21st, which I thought of sufficient importance to be communicated by a messenger, when Lieut.-Colonel Don arrived from the Duke of York, and brought me letters from His Royal Highness and your Lordship's of the 10th instant.

No answer was then or has yet been given by Baron Hardenberg to the note of the 11th, and this Minister continues to declare that his hands are tied up till he receives orders from the King; and on the other side Marshal Möllendorff (without waiting for those orders) has not ceased to declare, from the moment he received Baron Jacobi's account of his conference with Mr. Pitt, that he considered the Subsidiary Treaty as at an end, and no further connection as subsisting between him and the Ministers of the Maritime Powers.

It was, therefore, without any prospect of success that Baron Kinckel and myself could take any step here in virtue of these new instructions, neither could we entertain any hopes that any representations of ours (circumstanced as we now are) would engage the Prussian commander to afford any attention to the very reasonable proposal made by the Duke of York, although it rested on grounds of the most urgent necessity, and regarded as closely the interests of His Prussian Majesty as those of England and Holland.

After making Lieutenant-Colonel Don acquainted with the outlines of what had passed here, and giving him such general lights on the character of Marshal Möllendorff, and of those who surround him, as might make him acquainted with their characters, I advised him to go to the Prussian head-quarters, a league beyond Mentz; I recommended him not to refer to the Treaty, but to ground his proposal on military expediency, and particularly on the Military Convention of 26th July,* in which the existing case is provided

* Between Prince Albert and Möllendorff.

for in the way we wish ; and I desired him, if the Marshal should consider that Convention also as annulled, to bring to his recollection his own secret article, the strict performance of which would go still nearer our wishes than that of the Convention itself.

Lieutenant-Colonel Don acquitted himself with great address of his commission. He found Marshal Möllendorff harsh and unguarded in his expressions, precisely as I have ever found him. He was told by him abruptly that the Treaty was at an end ; that he had nothing to do with any plan of coöperation either with the Duke of York or General Clairfayt ; that his army was going to pass the Rhine, and that he had orders from the King what he was to do. It is probable that he has replied nearly to this effect, and not in very civil terms, to the letters Colonel Don brought him from His Royal Highness and General Clairfayt, as he wrote those answers immediately after he had read the letters, and gave them to Colonel Don sealed up.

On the Colonel's mentioning to him the Convention of the 26th, the Marshal declared that also to be void ; neither would he admit its being still in force, although it is manifestly an engagement made between *him* and the *Austrian* commanders, and relates no further to the Maritime Powers, than from its having received their sanction through myself and Baron Kinckel. He was rather embarrassed on Colonel Don's bringing forward the secret article,* with which he did not suppose him acquainted, and which your Lordship will recollect was one of his own drawing up, contrary to all custom and rule; and he endeavoured by every kind of means to give the conversation another turn. After dinner the Marshal softened his manners, and of his own accord renewed the subject with much more temper and more practicability than he had treated it before. He admitted the necessity of doing something for the defence of the Dutch Republic, and went so far as to tell Colonel Don the general disposition he was ordered to make of his army : 20,000 men, he

* Extending the period of time contained in the main plan of the Military Concert, and relating to the treatment of expected acquisitions.

said, were to leave the Rhine and move towards Southern Prussia, and 15,000 men under General Kalckreuth were to march to Westphalia, and the remainder to continue in this neighbourhood. The body of men destined for Westphalia goes so very near to meet our wishes, that Lieutenant-Colonel Don heard it with satisfaction, and pressed its immediate march. The Marshal, however, replied, that it would be *ten days* before this corps could be put in motion; and I own I fear this is not from any real difficulty in doing it sooner, but in order to receive an answer from the King of Prussia to letters the Marshal wrote to him on Sunday last. I do not exactly know the contents of these letters, but they are certainly not friendly to the cause.

Oct. 24.—Prussians cross the Rhine, and come to Hockheim. Mayence defended by Austrians.

EXTRACTS OF A DESPATCH FROM LORD MALMESBURY TO LORD GRENVILLE.

Frankfort, 26th Oct., 1794.

I do not lose a moment in transmitting to your Lordship by a special messenger the enclosed Note, which Baron Hardenberg delivered yesterday to Baron Kinckel and myself as an answer to that we gave him on the 11th instant.

This town is now completely under military Prussian government, and the authority of governor is exercised by Count Schulenburg in a most arbitrary and unjustifiable manner.

I shall take the greatest pains to avoid every kind of disagreeable discussion with him; and I have requested several officers belonging to the corps to be raised for His Majesty's service by Count Viomenil, to remove beyond the jurisdiction of this town, in order that they may not be sent out of it by a Prussian mandate, which it would be extremely improper for me to pass over in silence, and highly disagreeable to remonstrate against without effect, which most certainly would be the case.

The whole Prussian army have now passed the Rhine, and I expect to-morrow or next day to hear that the French have shewn themselves near Mentz. The Austrians evacuated the town of Coblentz on the 21st, and retired to the fortress of Ehrenbreitstein on the opposite side of the river.

ENCLOSURE.

A Francfort S. M., le 25 Oct., 1794.

Le soussigné, Ministre d'Etat et du Cabinet de Sa Majesté le Roi de Prusse, ayant reçu les ordres de son Souverain au sujet de la Note que Messieurs les Plénipotentiaires de Sa Majesté Britannique et de Leurs Hautes Puissances les Seigneurs Etats-Généraux des Provinces Unies, le Lord Malmesbury et le Baron de Kinckel, lui ont remise le onzième du courant, se voit en état de leur répondre : qu'on aurait été prêt de se concerter sur l'exécution de tous les plans possibles d'après les circonstances ; mais que depuis la suspension du payement des subsides stipulés, il ne pouvait plus en être question du tout, Sa Majesté regardant cette suspension comme une rupture du Traité de la Haye ; que du reste le Baron de Jacobi était chargé de s'expliquer sur cette affaire à Londres, et d'y faire connaître les résolutions du Roi.   (Signé)   Hardenberg.

[This impudent note from Hardenberg crowns the folly and dishonesty of the Prussian Government. There can scarcely be found in history a breach of faith so quickly following a political engagement, and so manifestly fatal to the criminal himself. In the dishonour and degradation which fell afterwards upon Prussia and her Royal Family, England received a melancholy atonement for the baseness of her ally. Lord Malmesbury had succeeded in obtaining a formal Treaty with Prussia. That Prussia immediately broke it, was no fault of his ; and he fairly stated the case to Lord Grenville in his letter of the 27th of June, in which he wrote, "I should feel myself undeserving of any indulgence, if I could impute to myself the failure of this great measure ; but no experience nor habits of business, no prudence nor care, can read so deep into the human mind as to foresee that a great Sovereign and his Ministers would be so regardless of their personal honour, and so forgetful of their public interests and glory, as to refuse to be bound in *June* by a Treaty ratified with their full consent and approbation in *May*."]

Oct. 29 and 30.—Don goes to see Prince Hohenlohe and to Darmstadt.

Nov. 2.—Slater brings me my recall.

EXTRACT OF A DESPATCH FROM LORD GRENVILLE TO LORD MALMESBURY.

24th Oct., 1794.

I have the honour to transmit to your Lordship the minute of a conference which I had yesterday with Baron Jacobi, in which that Minister made to me a verbal communication of the orders actually given by the King his master to *withdraw his army from the Rhine*. It is wholly unnecessary for me to enter upon the discussion of the different arguments by which this resolution is attempted to be defended by the Court of Berlin. You are sufficiently acquainted with all that has passed to be able to shew unanswerably, that the King has on his part gone far beyond what good faith would have required in the performance of the Convention of the Hague, and that the conduct of Prussia has been such as to evince the most settled determination to elude all its engagements.

In the present state of things His Majesty does not think it necessary that your Lordship should remain on the Rhine; and I have the King's commands to convey to you His Majesty's most gracious permission to return home, first delivering to Baron Hardenberg a formal Memorial, stating the grounds which prove the justice and good faith of His Majesty's conduct in the whole of this transaction, and the evident bad faith of Prussia, particularly as evinced in this last determination.

I have at the same time the satisfaction of being permitted to assure your Lordship, that however unsuccessful your endeavours have been, in execution of His Majesty's commands, to procure a more cordial coöperation of the Prussian army, and to induce Marshal Möllendorff to execute with more exactness the different engagements entered into by his Court, the King is entirely satisfied that the failure is in no degree to be imputed to any omission on your Lordship's part, but that the same zeal and talents have been exerted by your Lordship on this occasion, as have so often before been employed so beneficially to His Majesty's service.

---

MONDAY, Nov. 3.—I give in my Memorial—redespatch Slater on Tuesday, 4. Hardenberg, who returned on the day he said, hurt and dejected. Prussians evidently tampering with France. Meyerinck going to Basle.

---

FRIDAY, Nov. 7.—At one o'clock P.M. leave Frankfort—Crauford rides with me part of the way to Friedberg. Roads good for four leagues—two last detestable. Leave Friedberg at 7—get to Marburg at 7—in twelve hours, although only seven miles—first stage execrable—rest better—country fine.

---

SUNDAY, Nov. 9.—Leave Marburg at 6. Get to Cassel at 9—roads tolerable, but ill driven. Monday at Cassel—hear that the Duke of Brunswick has declined the command—see his letter to the King—he rests it on the want of unanimity amongst the Combined Powers.

---

Nov. 11.—Leave Cassel at 10. Get to Gottingen by 6—roads good—beautiful view on the hill beyond Cassel. Pass through Münden—charming situation. The Fulde falls into the Weser. Hanover begins at three English miles from Cassel. Gottingen large town.

Nov. 12.—Left Gottingen at 9—Slept short at Eimbeck—only four miles—roads very good—five hours going it—passed through Nordheim—a moderate town. Left Eimbeck on Thursday, November 13—seven miles and a half to Hanover—got there at five. Sir W. Boothby called on me. Madame de Croquenbourg, dame d'honneur to the Archduchess Christine, told me that the Archduchess said to her, on looking at the light and close-sitting breeches the men wear, "Ce sont ces maudites culottes qui ont perdues ma pauvre sœur la Reine de France."

[I here insert the following remarks, made by Sir George Rose after reading the first edition of this work. The reader will recollect that he was employed officially at Berlin during the transactions lately described.

"There was a moral stagnation in Prussia, caused by the long reign of a cynical, selfish despot, who affected gross immorality, and was an open and bitter enemy to the religion of his people. His internal administration of finance was conducted on the narrowest principles. A very long peace had abated materially the vigour of an army in which promotion was slow, for want of purchase and of foreign service. The very Captains had become inapt for war by age and habits, as their external appearance testified. The mischief was increased by the feebleness and misrule of a King, nowise devoid of good intentions, and personally brave, but bewildered and led astray by intrigues of every sort; without the consideration of his people, governed by women of various descriptions, the dupe of strange superstitions, and always influenced by the last opinion given to him. Let there be added to this state of things the hatred to Austria pervading the nation, and especially the army, and a Cabinet so composed as is accurately described by Lord Malmesbury, and it is easy to determine what chance of success that Minister could have in his negotiation. Haugwitz was in good faith with him until he returned to Berlin from the Hague; but there he found his difficulties increased, and only thought of maintaining his office, and the influence which his absence had shaken."]

# BRUNSWICK.

[Lord Malmesbury now received His Majesty's commands to demand the Princess Caroline of Brunswick for the Prince of Wales. He had them from the King himself, with no discretionary power to give advice or information to His Majesty or the Government on the principal subject of this mission. It will be seen, therefore, that publicly he confined himself strictly to its execution, although in private he did all he could to prepare his eccentric charge for her high elevation.]

NOVEMBER 14.—Count Kielmansegge* with me—he the first of the Regency, now composed of six members—Alvensleben, Kielmansegge, Ende, Beulwitz, Arnshaldt, and Steinberg. The Secretary *Rudloff* supposed to be the efficient man. Count Kielmansegge very anxious to know when demand of the Princess to take place—very civil.

I receive my nomination to ask the Princess Caroline of Brunswick for Prince of Wales in form by the post—dine at Court—ladies in their diamonds—very fine dinner—pages wait. Write—return to Court and cards—sup with Madame Waggenheim, Madame de Walmoden—Madame de Beaulieu, &c. Madame Walmoden† quick and sensible, but rather manly—Madame Waggenheim full of questions—disagreeable, but vastly attentive. Elliot arrives from Brunswick.

SATURDAY, Nov. 15.—Walk round the ramparts with Sir B. Boothby and Elliot—pleasant and well kept. Elliot gives me an account of the Duke's motives for declining the com-

---

\* Minister of State and of the Regency.
† General Walmoden commanded the army in the retreat from Holland in 1794.

mand, evidently arising from an apprehension of displeasing Prussia. Dinner at Count Kielmansegge's—the same as at Court—cards in the evening. Beulwitz there—an ill-favoured man—said to be clever and industrious—very fond of Hertzberg, and not unlike him in his manners—his wife dull. Marshal Reden eighty.

SUNDAY, Nov. 16.—Walk to Herenhausen with Elliot—dinner at home. Assembly at Madame * * * *, wife to the Grand Chambellan—very large woman—*bonne amie* to Kielmansegge. Whist—supper at Madame de Waggenheim's—pleasant.

MONDAY, Nov. 17.—Elliot returned early to Brunswick. I desired him to prepare the way for my coming there *before* I got my credentials—always the same society—cards. Supper at Madame Walmoden's.

TUESDAY, Nov. 18.—Long walk out of the town. Great dinner at Beulwitz's—cards afterwards—he enters into a discussion with me on what is passing at Ratisbonne,—asks my opinion and advice.

WEDNESDAY, Nov. 10.—Leave Hanover at ten — get to Peine, five miles, at five in the evening—sleep there—decent inn at the post.

THURSDAY, Nov. 28. — Leave Peine at eight — get to Brunswick at half-past eleven—three miles—roads bad—hard frost. Grand Maréchal Münchausen calls upon me immediately—offers an apartment in the palace—servants, carriage, &c. Invitation from the Duchess to dine—she receives me most kindly—all good-nature, and he, as usual, civil, but reserved and stiff.—The Princess Caroline (Princess of Wales) much embarrassed on my first being presented to her—pretty face—not expressive of softness—her figure not graceful—fine eyes—good hand—tolerable teeth, but going—fair hair and light eyebrows, good bust—short, with what the French call " des épaules impertinentes." *Vastly happy with her future expectations.* The Duchess full of nothing else—talks incessantly. Home for an hour, then return to Court—ball—danced with the Princesse Héréditaire and Princess Caroline—the first not at all altered—very amiable and pleasant—ombre with the Duchess and Mons. de Preene, her Grand Maître. Supper at round tables—Duke did not stay—retire at eleven.

---

FRIDAY, Nov. 21.—The Landgravine (dowager) of Cassel arrived. I take possession of the palace destined for me by the Court—a valet-de-chambre, a concierge, three footmen, and carriage—two sentinels at the door—the palace, that occupied by the late Duke Ferdinand—very spacious and well furnished. Called on Madame de Merode—driven here from the Low Countries—all their property (not less than forty estates) in possession of the French—they have brought away some money. Dined at Court in the great apartments; all the family there—Duchess Dowager, now seventy-eight, not much altered from what I remember her twenty years ago—Princess Augusta, now Abbess of Gandersheim, very much altered—immense dinner—conversation with the Duke, on whose right hand I sat—he against peace—rails at Prussia and Austria—keeps to general terms, and although apparently agreeing with me in opinion, yet cautiously avoiding to commit himself—supper at Duchess Dowager's—whist with her, and the Landgravine.

---

SATURDAY, Nov. 22.—With Stampfort[*]—he informs me of his commission—he was first to offer the command to the Duke—this being declined, now to propose his going to Holland—he reads me several letters from the Duke to him, and says the Duke is afraid of Prussia; and unless he has a letter or message from His Prussian Majesty desiring him to go, that he will not stir—that he (Stampfort), to endeavour to promote such a letter on the part of the King of Prussia,

---

[*] Stampfort, a general in the Dutch service, preceptor to the young Prince of Orange; a very able man and an excellent writer.—*Original Note.*

had met Reede† at Magdebourg, and that he expected to hear the effect of their negotiation on Monday—he despaired of success. Stampfort blamed without reserve their conduct at Nimeguen, which, he asserted, there was no good reason for evacuating—he disapproved of Bentinck having been sent here. (N.B.—This is a personal feeling.)

On my return from him, and just as I was going to send away Courvoisier, Fabian arrived with instructions for me to come on here, (I had already obeyed them,) and to propose to the Duke to accept the command, or else go to Holland to give his advice and assistance. Previous to the receiving these instructions, I had written to the Duke of York, to endeavour to get at his *real* wishes and intentions; I had also written to the Prince of Wales; but both these letters, which were to have gone by Courvoisier, were now detained for a day or two.

Dinner at the Duchess Dowager's‡—great anxiety and curiosity to know whether my messenger brought me my full powers, and great disappointment at hearing he had not. I took an opportunity of mentioning to the Duke that I wished to speak with him, and he appointed me at my own house the following day.—Duchess very inquisitive—against his taking the command, not for his going to Holland—said she knew his refusal had hurt the Prince very much—she talked of *Edward* Duke of York as her favourite brother— said she recollected he liked my father—praised the Duke of Gloucester—abused the Queen, who, she said, was an envious and intriguing spirit—told several anecdotes to this effect on her first coming over—that she disliked her mother (the Princess of Wales) and herself—was extremely jealous of them—took an opportunity while the Princess of Wales was dying to alter the rank of her ladies of the bed-chamber. —King very good, but not liable to deep impressions— talked slightingly of the Duke of York—said he behaved badly here to his Duchess—I defended him—she reprobated his conduct at Hanover, and particularly that towards his old flame, Madame de * * * * to whom, on his return to England with the Duchess, he did not speak—the Duchess of York, she said, behaved vastly well on this occasion. She

† Dutch Minister at Berlin.   ‡ Sister to George the Third.

obtaining any effective succours from Berlin. I then told him that we were much more likely to draw it from Austria; and I informed him of the great probability of an immediate relief to the amount of 25,000 men coming to the Duke of York, and the appearance of measures being taken this winter for concerting a larger support from that country.

The Duke expressed a disinclination to take the command of the Austrians: he said the men were good, but the officers jacobinically inclined; that the Emperor was weak, Rollin corrupted, Ferrari a democrat; and that he feared that nonsensical sect of Illuminés, which were laughed at and treated too lightly in the beginning, had now taken such a root, and had acquired so many followers, that they governed everywhere. He said, however, he would think over what I said—read my papers at his leisure—that he expected an answer from Berlin to-morrow: in short, his conversation was preparatory either to an acceptance, or to a refusal. He told me Schulenburg was to retire on a pension, and that Prince Henry had re-appeared at Potzdam, and was paying his court to Haugwitz and Bishopswerder.

Dined this day at Court with the Landgravine, and returned there in the evening. Duchess, as usual, very communicative—vastly anxious I should be satisfied.

MONDAY, Nov. 24.—General Stampfort with me. Duke had had a meeting in August (the 14th, I believe,) with the Bishop of Hildesheim, in which it was proposed to him to take the command of the Austrian army in the room of Prince Cobourg, and be "Gouverneur Civil" of the Low Countries during the war. Duke, from his answer, inclined to accept; but his resolution fails, and the proposal is not renewed. Duke influenced by Feronce,* who is governed by his wife, who is a democrat. Dine with Hereditary Prince at three o'clock—prepare my letters—with the Duke at five, in his own apartment—he declines both the proposals—shews me his answers from King of Prussia and Bishopswerder—strange and unaccountable, but making it evidently appear that the Duke, instead of soliciting the

* Count Feronce, Minister of State of the Duke of Brunswick at Brunswick.

King of Prussia's consent, as he said he would, had expressed in very clear terms his disinclination to take the command; and this the King of Prussia approves strongly. Bishopswerder's letter very short, and talks of "intrigues et illusions," and such a one as he should not write to the Duke. I pressed the Duke with every argument that suggested itself to me, but in vain; he seemed struggling between an inclination to accept an offer which gratified his ambition, and the fear of Prussia: the last prevailed. He said he could not go alone and unsupported. I told him he would have the support of the country he was in, and of England; and that *I* was ready to attend him, and, provided he would advise, would take all the responsibility on myself. This struck him, and he appeared wavering; he, however, ended by remaining fixed in his determination. I proposed to him to accompany Princess of Wales to England; to this he gave no answer. I left him at seven to sup at the Duchess Dowager's, and at ten he wrote me a letter, lest I should have mistaken his intention. In the conversation he employed the grossest flattery towards me—said *I alone* could do more in Holland than he and a large army; and this was the answer he always came round to when I pressed him—warm in his professions of right principles. Despatched Fabian (messenger) at three in the morning.

---

TUESDAY, Nov. 25.—Dine at General Riederel's—very good people. He tells me that Hohenlohe's corps is ordered to the Rhine—that Warsaw is taken, and Prince Joseph Poniatowski and his corps have surrendered. In the evening to a meeting called Cassino—cards and dancing—sup at the Hereditary Princess's—quite alone, no one but myself and the family—she all kindness and good-humour.

---

WEDNESDAY, Nov. 26.—Walk to Richmond—pleasant house, in good taste—about one mile from the town—dine there. Duke keeps at a distance from me. Assenberg, Russian Minister at Ratisbonne there—married to a daughter of Count Schulenburg of Welsburg. To the opera in the evening—in the Duchess's box—long conversation with Princess Augusta—clever in the Beatrix way—Princess Caroline improves on acquaintance—is gay and cheerful, with good sense. Supped at Hereditary Princess's—very pleasant conversable supper.

Thursday, Nov. 27.—Write to Frankfort. Walk on the ramparts with Merode and Princess Augusta. Merode gives me a very good paper of his writing to justify the behaviour of the Brabançons. Dine with the Duchess late. Concert in the evening.

Friday, Nov. 28th.—General Stampfort—shews me letters from the Duke, all proving his restless ambition to act, yet withheld by his fear of Prussia. Mentions Prince Henry's visit to him in October—called it "une visite démocrate en manteau royal."—Assures me that Dumouriez* was not bribed. Dinner at the Duchess's. Much conversation with the Duke—all to the same effect. He did not like Ewart.†—Abuses Kalckreuth. Letters from Kinckel and Crauford at Frankfort. Meyerinck returned "avec un pied de nez." Schulenburg and Möllendorff frightened. Supper and ball in honour of the Princesse Héréditaire's birthday. I dance till one. At all these meetings I play with the Duchess at ombre.—She said that Queen Charlotte was very much hurt at the very fine diamond ring the King gave her (the Duchess) as a "bague de mariage," in 1764.—That she wanted it back, and was quite peevish about it. This ring, and a pair of bracelets, the only diamonds she brought with her from England. Declared she never would allow *Caroline* to have her brothers with her—that it would make her unpopular—that the Queen did it to get them money—that it was shabby, &c. Said the King offered her a Princess for her son, if she would let him first come over and be seen. The Duchess replied, that *Charles* was a very good-humoured, harmless boy—would certainly make a good husband; but she would not send him over, as she was quite

---

* Commander-in-chief of the army of the French Republic.
† Formerly English Minister at Berlin.

sure if he was to shew himself, none of the Princesses would have him.

SATURDAY, NOV. 29.—More letters from Frankfort and Paris. Overthrow of the Jacobins on the 13th November. Great re-appearance of luxury, &c.—carriages and dress there. Walk round the ramparts—dine at Duchess-Dowager's—dinner for me—she vastly attentive—talk about the late King of Prussia and old times. Supper at Feronce's—like all large suppers.

SUNDAY, NOV. 30th.—Walk to Richmond. Dinner and supper with the Duchess in great apartments—nothing material.—Puysegur (the Marquis) very right on French affairs—Stampfort told me that Assenbourg had an idea of the Duke's going to Petersburg—nothing can be more absurd.

MONDAY, DEC. 1st.—East (the messenger) arrives at eight o'clock—brings my instructions and credentials.—With the Duchess at nine—she delighted—anxious to know which route we are to take—wishes for Stade.—With Feronce—settled that on Wednesday I should have my audience. No difficulty about the Treaty. - He enters on politics—artful and insincere—talks of what is passing at the diet at Ratisbonne—thinks the Duke's going could *now* do no good. The Duchess told me she was sure he felt himself unequal to it—that he was grown nervous, and had lost a great deal of his former energy.—She said, when he returned from Holland in 1787, he was so shaken, and his nerves so worn out, that he did not recover for a long time. She confirmed what I long since knew, that the Duke wants decision of character, and resolution. Went to porcelain manufactory—pretty and cheap.—Dined at the Hereditary Princess's.—Talked over Holland.—Sent Estafette to Hanover, with a letter to Kielmansegge. Cassino. Stampfort at the Cassino—relates me the note he had received from the Duke, in which the Duke says that he had learnt underhand (through Feronce, probably,) that I intended to see him again on his going to Holland.—Stampfort with him for two hours—found him use, which were those inserted in my own letter to the Prince. Wrote and despatched Fabian (messenger) at two. Dinner as usual. Duke conversable to-day—enters into general politics—recommends trying to do something through Russia—tells me King of Prussia is attempting to make a forced loan in Germany—that he has written to Duke of Saxe Gotha—Duke of Brunswick condemns the measure. On my touching on Berlin, and hinting the good he might do if he was to write to the King, his answer was quite in character, " Voulez-vous, my Lord, que je vous parle *avec franchise?* Il n'y a que *vous*, my Lord, qui puissiez quelque chose. Je sais qu'on vous craint à Berlin, et on redoute votre arrivée." Thus does this very clever, but cautious, suspicious, and cunning man, evade every proposition made him, and sully all his merits by art and tricking. As a proof, however, that his mind is *full* of our proposal, he wrote of his own accord to Stampfort, to say to him he was of Mons. Puisieux's opinion, who, in his "Caractères," says, "Il ne faut pas s'embarquer de propos délibéré dans aucune de ces entreprises dont on ne peut sortir que couvert de gloire, ou couvert de ridicule." A foolish saying, a mere jingle of words, quite French, and not at all applicable to his situation.

After dinner he held a very long and very sensible discourse with me about the Princess Caroline ; and here, where he was not on his guard, and where he laid aside his "*finesse*" and suspicion, he appeared in all his lustre. He (the Duke) entered fully into her future situation—was perfectly aware of the character of the Prince, and of the inconveniences that would result, almost with equal ill effect, either from his liking the Princess too much or too little. He also touched on the Queen's character, with which he is perfectly acquainted. He was rather severe on the Duchess of York—he never mentioned the King. He said of his daughter, " Elle *n'est pas bête*, mais elle n'a pas de jugement—elle a été élevée sévèrement *et il le falloit.*" The Duke requested me to recommend to her discretion not to *ask questions,* and, above all, not to be free in giving opinions of persons and things aloud ; and he hinted, delicately, but very pointedly, at the free and unreserved manners of the Duchess, who at times is certainly apt to forget her audience. He desired me to advise her never to shew any jealousy of the Prince; and that, if he had any *goûts*, not to notice them. He said he had written her all this *in German*, but that, enforced by me, it would come with double effect.—Grand opera in the evening—good theatre and decorations—Princess Caroline much applauded on coming in. Supper with the Duchess—Sir M. Eden arrives.

SATURDAY, DEC. 6.—Sir Moreton with me from nine—he left London the 29th, and was three days on the sea to Hamburgh. Lord Hertford, after much *shilly-shally*, declined Vienna. Visited the Princess Augusta—clever, artful, and rather *coming*—she gave me an excellent picture of Duke Ferdinand. Dinner at Court—ball and ombre. Madlle. Hertzfeldt repeats to me what the Duke had before said—stated the necessity of being very *strict* with the Princess Caroline—that she was not clever or ill-disposed, but of a temper easily wrought on, and had *no tact*. She said my advice would do more good than the Duke's, as, although she respected him, she also feared him, and considered him as a severe rather than an affectionate father—that she had *no* respect for her mother, and was inattentive to her when she dared.—I led the Princess Caroline to supper, and am placed between her and the Duchess—her conversation very right: she entreats me also to guide and direct her. I recommend perfect silence on *all* subjects for six months after her arrival.

SUNDAY, DEC. 7.—With Stampfort. Shews me a letter from Princess of Orange, in which she deprecates the idea of peace—condemns the Duke's refusal, but can propose nothing to induce him to retract it—Prince of Orange and she not well together, but, as usual, reciprocally jealous. Stampfort " au bout de son Latin." We agree to remain quiet till fresh orders or fresh events, and are both perfectly of accord on the Duke's character, which is all suspicion, cunning, and irresolution, whenever he is talking on business. He owns this himself, and says that " cela est plus fort que lui."

[1794.]

| Left column (partial) | Margin | Right column (partial) |
|---|---|---|

Walk to Richn... /0.3  .y Elizabeth Eden arrives. Dine
at Court. Cal    C   ly Elizabeth—she goes to Court.
Concert and sv       ore the concert another long conversation with       about his daughter: he extremely
anxious about        right; said he had been with her
for two hours        :ning—that he wished to make her
feel that the        tion in which she was going to be
placed was r         one of amusement and enjoyment;
that it had ?        nd those perhaps difficult and hard
to fulfil. F         rnestly entreated me to be her adviser—not 1          ier when in England; that he was
more afraid          uld happen there than here; that he
dreaded th           bits. He said the Princess had not
taken amis           d to her; she had repeated it to him,
and he th            or it. Lady Elizabeth Eden, whom I
carried he   M^s µ   irt, said that Lady —— was very well
with the      C      t she went frequently to Windsor, and
appeared             favourite. This, if true, most strange,
and bode   P.B       Sat next Princess Caroline at supper; I
advise h             familiarity, to have no *confidantes*, to
avoid gi             nion; to approve, but not to admire ex-
cessivel             fectly silent on politics and party; to be
very at              respectful to the Queen; to endeavour, at
all eve)     C       ll with her. She takes all this well; she
was at               rs, but on account of having taken leave
of son               acquaintance. Sir B. Boothby arrives.

---

M                    8.—Walk with Sir Brook to Richmond;
see t                the form of a lozenge—not very good, but
com                  ounds pretty—great marsh before it. Sir
Bro                  d pleasant—democratic leanings, but by no
mea                  : jacobinical. Dinner at Duchess Dowager's.
Du                   me a letter from the Duke of Gloucester,
dat                  in which he says, the squadron to convoy us
wi                   der a fortnight, and that it will be the middle
of                   fore we reach England. He also says, Lord
M                    ; on an expedition with 15,000 men. Old
I                    civil—talks of *very old times*—of her father,
i                    els with George II. The Waggenheims from

Hanover there. Opera in the evening, and supper at Duchess's—next to Princess Caroline at table—she improves very much on closer acquaintance—cheerful, and loves laughing. Count Kielmansegge from Hanover.

TUESDAY, DEC. 9.—Write to England. Breakfast at Grand Maréchal Münchausen's—conversation with him and Count Kielmansegge about our journey—could settle nothing from want of orders. Dinner at Duchess's. Supper at Duchess Dowager's—no material incident. Princess Caroline recommends ———'s son. I take this opportunity of requesting her not to make any promise, or to attend to any request made her; to refer them all, if she pleased, to *me*, but to say to all invariably, that she had laid it down as a rule to ask for nothing on her arrival in England; and never on any account to meddle with the distribution of offices, or interfere on any account in anything which bore reference to public affairs. She approved what I said; to which I added, that if amongst the number of applications made to her, there was any one she felt really and sincerely interested about, if she would mention it to me, I would make a point of recommending it when in England; but that this should not be told to the requiring person, and the event, when it happened, not furnish an example for further application. This, to which she acquiesced most readily, gave me an opportunity to recommend her to make no distinction of party, except that made by the King and Queen; never to talk politics, or allow them to be talked to her; and never on any account to give any other opinion on public and political subjects but such as was expressive of her anxiety for the public good. She asked me about Lady ****, appeared to suppose her an *intriguante*, but not to know of any partiality or connection between her and the Prince. I said, that, in regard to Lady ****, she and all her other ladies would frame their conduct towards her by hers towards them; that I humbly advised that this should not be familiar or too easy, but that it might be affable without forgetting she was Princess of Wales; that she should never listen to them whenever they attempted anything like a *commerage*, and never allow them to appear to influence her opinion by theirs. She said she wished to be popular, and was afraid I recommended too much reserve; that probably I thought her too prone *à se livrer*. I made a bow. She said, " Tell me freely." I said, " I did;" that it was an amiable quality, but one which could not in her high situation be given way to without great risk; that, as to popularity, it never was attained by *familiarity;* that it could only belong to respect, and was to be acquired by a just mixture of dignity and affability: I quoted the Queen as a model in this respect. The Princess said she was afraid of the Queen—she was sure she would be jealous of her and do her harm. I replied, that, for this reason, it was of the last consequence to be attentive towards her, to be always on her guard, and never to fail in any exterior mark of respect towards her, or to let drop an inconsiderate word before her. She took all this in good part, and desired me to continue to be her *mentor* after she got to England, as well as now. She said of her own accord, " I am determined never to appear jealous. I know the Prince is *léger*, and am prepared on this point." I said I did not believe she would have any occasion to exercise this very wise resolution, which I commended highly; and entreated her if she saw any symptoms of a *goût* in the Prince, or if any of the women about her should, under the love of fishing in troubled waters, endeavour to excite a jealousy in her mind, on no account to allow it to manifest itself; that reproaches and sourness never reclaimed anybody; that it only served as an advantageous contrast to the contrary qualities in the rival; and that the surest way of recovering a tottering affection was softness, enduring, and caresses; that I knew enough of the Prince to be quite sure he could not withstand such a conduct, while a contrary one would *probably* make him disagreeable and peevish, and certainly force him to be false and dissembling.

---

WEDNESDAY, DEC. 10.—Breakfast and concert at Madame Münchausen's—she and her mother sung duets.—Conversation with Kielmansegge on public affairs—shallow, but good-humoured. Walk with Abbesse and Madame Constant.

Note from Hereditary Princess to say Duke of York went to England on the 4th—unexpected—tell it the Duke at dinner; it strikes him, as it did the day before, that Prince Nassau was coming with a high rank into the Prussian service: he, however, was less *thinking* this day than usual; he was conversable with the ladies at dinner—said that his famous Manifesto was drawn up by a *Brabançon* of the name of Himon (now here); that it was approved by Count Schulenburg and Spielman, and forced upon him to sign; that he had not even a *veto* on this occasion. After dinner he had a long conversation with Count Kielmansegge, the object of which was to persuade him nothing could be done for carrying on the war with any effect, without the assistance of Prussia, in order that Kielmansegge might repeat it to me; this Kielmansegge did, without seeing through the Duke's design, and I did not think it necessary to point it out to him.

Concert at Court—Madlle. Hertzfeldt takes me aside, and says nearly these words: "Je vous conjure, faites que le Prince fasse mener, au commencement, une vie retirée à la Princesse. Elle a toujours été très gênée et très observée, et il le falloit ainsi. Si elle se trouve tout à coup dans le monde sans restriction aucune, elle ne marchera pas *à pas égaux*. Elle n'a pas le cœur dépravé—elle n'a jamais rien fait de mauvais, mais la parole en elle devance toujours la pensée; elle se livre à ceux à qui elle parle sans réserve, et de là il s'ensuit (même dans cette petite Cour) qu'on lui prête des sens et des intentions qui ne lui ont jamais appartenus—que ne sera-t-il pas en Angleterre—où elle sera entourée de femmes adroites et intrigantes (à ce qu'on dit) auxquelles elle se livrera à corps perdu (si le Prince permet qu'elle mène la vie dissipée de Londres), et qui placeront dans sa bouche tel propos qu'elles voudront, puisqu'elle parlera elle-même sans savoir ce qu'elle dit. De plus, elle a beaucoup de vanité, et quoique pas sans esprit, *avec peu de fond*—la tête lui tournera si on la caresse et la flatte trop, si le Prince la gâte; et il est tout aussi essentiel qu'elle le craigne que qu'elle l'aime. Il faut absolument qu'il la tienne *serrée*, qu'il se fasse respecter, sans quoi *elle s'égarera*. Je sais (continuat-elle) que vous ne me compromettrez pas, je vous parle

comme à mon vieux ami. Je suis attachée cœur et âme ⟨à⟩
Duc. Je me suis dévouée à lui, je me suis perdue pour lu⟨i⟩
C'est le bien de sa famille que je veux. Il sera le plus ma⟨l⟩
heureux des hommes si cette fille ne réussit pas mieux q⟨ue⟩
son ainée. Je vous répète, elle n'a jamais rien fait ⟨de⟩
mauvais, mais elle est sans jugement, et on l'a jugée
l'avenant. Je crains (dit Madlle. Hertzfeldt) la Reine. ⟨La⟩
Duchesse ici qui passe sa vie à penser tout haut, ou à ⟨ne⟩
jamais penser du tout, n'aime pas la Reine, et elle en a tr⟨op⟩
parlé à sa fille. Cependant son bonheur depend d'être bie⟨n⟩
avec elle, et pour Dieu répétez lui toujours cette maxim⟨e⟩
que vous avez déjà plus d'une fois recommandée. Elle vo⟨us⟩
écoute. Elle trouve que vous parlez raison d'une manièr⟨e⟩
gaie, et vous ferez bien plus d'impression sur elle que so⟨n⟩
père, qu'elle craint trop, ou sa mère, qu'elle ne craint p⟨as⟩
du tout." I had not time to reply to this, as I was call⟨ed⟩
away to cards with the Duchess. Masquerade—I walke⟨d⟩
with the Princess Caroline, and had a very long conversatio⟨n⟩
with her. I endeavour not to mix up much serious matter ⟨at⟩
such a place; but whenever I found her inclined to giv⟨e⟩
way too much to the temper of the entertainment, and to g⟨et⟩
over-cheerful and *too mixing*, I endeavoured to bring he⟨r⟩
back by becoming serious and respectful.

When we returned to the "Balcon," (the masquerade wa⟨s⟩
in the Opera House,) she entered, of her own accord, int⟨o⟩
the kind of life she was to lead in England, and was ver⟨y⟩
inquisitive about it. I said it would depend very much o⟨n⟩
her; that I could have no share in settling it, but that m⟨y⟩
wish was, that in private she might enjoy every ease an⟨d⟩
comfort belonging to domestic happiness; but that when sh⟨e⟩
appeared abroad, she should always appear as Princess o⟨f⟩
Wales, surrounded by all that "appareil and etiquette" du⟨e⟩
to her elevated situation. She asked me what were th⟨e⟩
Queen's drawing-room days? I said Thursday, and Sunda⟨y⟩
after church, which the King and Queen never missed; an⟨d⟩
I added, that I hoped most ardently she would follow thei⟨r⟩
example, and never, on any account, miss Divine Service on
that day. "Does the Prince go to church?" she asked me.
I replied, she would make him go; it was one of many advantages he would derive from changing his situation. "But

if he does not like it?" "Why, then, your Royal Highness must go without him, and tell him that the fulfilling regularly and exactly this duty can alone enable you to perform exactly and regularly those you owe him—this cannot but please him, and will, in the end, induce him also to go to church." The Princess said mine was a very serious remark for a masquerade. I begged her pardon, and said it was in fact a more cheerful one than the most dissipated one I could have made, since it contained nothing *triste* in itself, and would infallibly lead to everything that was pleasant. She caught my idea with great quickness; and the last part of our conversation was very satisfactory, as I felt I had done what I wished, and set her mind on thinking of the *drawbacks* of her situation, as well as of its " *agrémens*," and impressed it with the idea that, in the order of society, those of a very high rank have a price to pay for it, and that the life of a Princess of Wales is not to be one of all pleasure, dissipation, and enjoyment; that the great and conspicuous advantages belonging to it must necessarily be purchased by considerable sacrifices, and can only be preserved and kept up by a continual repetition of these sacrifices.

Madame Waggenheim absurd, ridiculous, ill-mannered, and *méchante*. She asked me, in speaking of the Princess, "Comment j'ai trouvé *la petite;*" and added, " Quoique assez agée, son éducation n'est pas encore *finie.*" I replied, " Que je voyois qu'à un age bien plus avancé que celui de *Son Altesse Royale*, la bonne éducation dont elle parloit n'étoit pas toujours *commencée.*"

———

THURSDAY, DEC. 11.—Long walk round the town. Dinner, concert, and supper at Court—Duke disposed to converse at dinner—his mind full of the idea we had proposed to him, but always harping on the same string, Prussia. On my observing that it appeared that Prussia was actuated by principles in direct opposition to ours, and had formed a system perfectly French—and if Prussia was thus *systematically* against us, it would be useless and even dangerous to make any attempts there: he replied, " Prussia has *no* system, nor ever will while this reign lasts;" he then went into the vices and weaknesses of the Prussian Cabinet. I said they had reached the army, and the politics the Generals mixed up with their command had reached the officers, and even soldiers, "Une armée ne doit être qu'une machine, me répondit le Duc; dès qu'elle est autre chose, elle sert à la destruction et non pas à la protection d'un état. Feu le Roi savoit changer cela d'un regard." The Duke then talked on the necessity of subordination on all occasions and everywhere; he said in business as in a battle, " Celui qui a le dernier bataillon en ordre la gagnera toujours." Wrote to Prince of Wales, and sent letter by estafette to Hanover.

FRIDAY, DEC. 12.—Stampfort with me in the morning—he " au bout de son Latin"—thinks Duke of York might do good at Berlin. Duke tells him Hugh Elliot might be of some service. I reprobate both these suggestions—the persons unfit: it would be a humiliating measure to send the Duke of York, and Hugh Elliot is a *crane*. " Le Roi l'a goûté," Stampfort replied, " and he is well with some of his alentours." He desired me to write to Lord St. Helens, to desire the Princess of Orange (in case she passed through the Hague) not to put herself or family to any expense. She had sent her diamonds here, and was now going to send for them back, in order to appear *en gala*. I undertook this commission.

Duke comes to me at one, full of anxiety, perplexed and alarmed at what is passing at Berlin—cannot explain it.\* It cannot be the real interest of the King of Prussia to act as he does; it must be his vanity which is worked upon, or corruption of those who surround him. He proposes that it should be stated to him the dangerous position in which he would stand, if he was separated from his old allies, the Maritime Powers; that France, under its present form of Government, *could* not be considered as a safe ally; and that, even supposing it to be re-become a monarchy, it must be under a constitutional king, whose powers would be limited and disputed, and the country weak and exhausted; that the two Imperial Courts would unite against him; that the very peace of which he seemed ambitious to be mediator, would work his own ruin; that therefore it should be required of

\* Prussia was now treating with the French Convention.

him to say what he wished, to which measures he inclined, that by knowing them, some joint plan of concert might be adopted; that if it was peace, a general peace, to be brought about by a course of measures, and, above all, by an immediate preparation for a vigorous campaign; that if to carry on this, he said he wanted supplies, to say these should be furnished him, *provided* it was certain that *they were employed for the purpose they were given;* that the leaving his army (*le nez contre Mayence*) on the Upper Rhine, while the enemy were invading and even in possession of his territories on the Lower Rhine, and when his ancient Westphalian dominions had no other protection but an *Austrian* army, unequal in number for their defence, and, according to his own accounts, *ill organized*, was a measure equally dangerous to his interests as disgraceful to his honour; that, therefore, *if* he, as we and all the Powers at war, only looked forward to a safe and honourable peace, and felt, as reason and common sense must point out, that this could only be brought about by assuming the countenance of war, that he should say so, that he should agree and settle where his force might be usefully and efficaciously employed; that if he would bring his army to defend the Republic of Holland, and the Lower Rhine, means might be found for supplying them. The Duke added, as an additional *lure,* that it might be held out that the King should command this army in person; but then, added he, it must be *intrigue contre intrigue,* and you and the Dutch must employ *fit* persons to counteract those about the King. He ended by proposing Stampfort for this commission; said he might go to Berlin as coming from the Hague, and as having seen me here; and that we should then have tried the only possible means of getting at truth, without which nothing could be done. He said he was so deeply interested in all this, and considered the separation of England from the Northern Powers as so destructive to them all, (and in which destruction his small patrimony would undoubtedly be enveloped), that he saw no other means of preservation left, if this could not be prevented. He said Prince Henry was, he believed, our greatest and most dangerous adversary. When here in August, he had distinguished this war from others by saying, that in the seven years' and other wars, England had considered her alliances on the Continent as a diversion to favour her conquests and interests elsewhere; that now her conquests of the Islands, &c., should be considered as a diversion in favour of the interests of the Continent, and England be called upon to restore them for this purpose. He told me Prince Nassau had his *congé*, and was going to retire to Venice with a pension of 12,000 roubles from the Empress of Russia—the Duke was *full of his subject;* I admitted his idea, but doubted its effects, as it had under another shape been repeatedly tried; and that if *the King of Prussia was not systematically acting against us, and systematically* led into it by France, it was impossible things should be where they were, and that, against a *parti pris* and formed, no reason or argument could act with effect. I shewed to the Duke Paget's proposal of the 25th, and the negative answer. All this struck him, and he left me; his anxiety and uneasiness increased, and I endeavoured, I confess, to work them up to the highest pitch. At dinner he expressed these feelings very strongly, but said nothing new; he got back to my mission in Spain in 1768, and talked over the business of the Falkland Islands. Whimsical conversation, and curious questions of the Duchess about Empress of Russia and her favourites. Opera—*cosa rara*—pretty music—in the Duchess's box. The Princess Abbess, who staid the last, on going out was disposed to slight the Duchess, and to complain of her under the title of *La Princesse d'Albion;* I put on a very grave face, and made no reply. Supper at round tables—Princess Caroline in great good-humour, and very naturally pleasant : we staid till late.

SATURDAY, DEC. 13.—With Stampfort—communicate to him the Duke's wish that he should go to Berlin—his reasons for declining; that he had no official commission—that he would be suspected and not believed. I admit these reasons—settle that it would be perhaps better to write to Haugwitz, and take measures for the King seeing the letter; at all events, to wait for the return of Dressins from Berlin. Long walk—dinner at Court—assembly at Madame Luttichau's—

good house—whist—the Princess Caroline asked me, with an apology as for *une question indiscrete,* whether I was to be *her lord-chamberlain?* On my saying, I knew nothing of it, she was very gracious, and expressed a strong wish it should be; and added, she feared it would not be good enough for me, and that I should decline it. I told her any situation which placed me near her would be flattering to me, but that these situations were sought for by many persons who had better claims than myself; and that besides I never solicited anything, and could not expect that such an office would be offered me without my asking for it. She again (and apparently in earnest) expressed her wish it should be, and said it would be of infinite use to her to have a person near her she was used to, and whom she had confidence in. Supper at Court—cheerful—talking of ugly children; and on my saying, when this happened, and they were like their father, it did honour to their mother's virtue,—" Not at all," said our Duchess; " on the contrary, when a wife has done a wrong thing, and she is afraid of her husband, and if she sees him when she is breeding, she takes fright, and the child *is marked* with the husband, as it would with a spider, or cat, or anything she saw which frightened her during her pregnancy."

---

SUNDAY, DEC. 14.—Write to Vangoens, Cunningham, &c. Walk.—Great dinner at Court—Beulwitz and Amswerdt from Hanover. Beulwitz told me at dinner that Hertzberg was dying—that Prince Henry was coming into play—that this would produce great evil. He would recommend treating with Germany and Poland—would be for taking Pomerania, Mecklenburg, and the counties of Bremen and Verden—he cared no more for a title to what he claims than Alexander or Cæsar. Mons. de Meilhan, author of " Les deux Cousins"—a talking man, with parts; said to be dangerous and intriguing; a thin figure, and shallow look. Prince Nassau disgraced and dismissed (as he says), because he asked for the command of the Russian army in Poland.* The Empress refused him. He asks his dismission—she grants it—gives him 12,000 roubles pension, and calls him *un*

* Name illegible in MS.

*ingrat.* He going to Venice.—Duke said that he remembered the present Empress fifty years ago at Brunswick, *un très petit personnage*, with her mother. That she was dressed in red damask, with satin brocade—was then very pretty, " mais ne promettoit rien :" he then made a remark, which evidently meant to express his feelings at such a woman having made such a progress in the world, while *he* remained nearly where he set out.—Concert.—Duchess said that Duke Louis of Brunswick \* was a vile man—he had belied her, and made the late Duke believe that she prevented the Prince of Orange from marrying the Princess Augusta (now l'Abbesse). It was a lie, and she never spoke to him afterwards. (N.B.— This the occasion, probably, of the dislike of the Abbesse towards her.) She said Duke Louis wrote all sort of ill-natured things here about the present Princess of Orange— accused her of infidelity, &c. Duke praises exceedingly the Hereditary Princess to me—says, " que dans une position très difficile, et *sans agrêmens*, elle n'a jamais donné prise sur elle"—that she has the best head possible—writes admirably—" C'est un trésor pour moi," added he. I was the more pleased with this, as I think the same of the Princess, and have thought so from her earliest infancy. Beulwitz and Amswerdt return to Hanover after supper—they and all the Hanoverians sore at not having had any notice from the King of this match. Princess Caroline very talkative at supper. Told anecdotes of the late Duke Ferdinand, who before his death was *tombé en enfance*. Great and natural impatience to get away.

Monday, Dec. 15.—With Elliot to De Lolme, jeweller— buy watches for the two pages. Walk. Dinner at Court. Much conversation before dinner with Princess Caroline.— She very inquisitive about what she is to do to please—my constant answer, to *commune with herself*, to be very cir-

---

\* Duke Louis of Brunswick had been invited to command the Dutch army by the Stadtholder, William the Fourth, and quitted the service of the Empress Queen (in which he was at that time engaged) for that purpose. When the Stadtholder died, the Princess Regent, Anne, sister of George the Second, continued him in her service; and at her death in 1759, Duke Louis took the oaths to the States as guardian and representative of the young Prince of Orange, whose majority took place in 1766.

cumspect, and to think always before she speaks. Duke in good-humour—communicates to me a letter from Berlin—his mind full of nothing else.—Approves my writing to Haugwitz—entreats me to do it—says he will give a paper to Stampfort—and ends a rather long conversation, in which he had betrayed the greatest anxiety and *interest*, by saying, " Pardon, my Lord, si j'abuse de votre patience en vous parlant de choses que vous savez mieux que moi, et qui ne me regardent pas." Thus does his character always appear—timidity and cunning. Ball. Stampfort receives an estafette from Princess of Orange. Hereditary Princess delivers me a message from Princess Louisa Ferdinand to recommend a Doctor M'Cagan.—Supper at round tables.

TUESDAY, DEC. 16.—With Stampfort—he reads his letter from the Princess, which is a statement of what had passed in Holland, relative to a separate peace. About the 7th or 8th November, Van Breugel, secretary to the town of Bois le Duc, comes to the Hague. He assures the Pensionary, that the Convention is disposed to listen to terms of accommodation, and that an honourable peace may be had. He speaks in the name of La Combe, *représentant du peuple* at Bois le Duc, whom he describes as well-intentioned; but he cautioned him against his colleague Bellegarde, who is a *Dutch* aristocrat, and in correspondence with the Patriots in Holland.—The Pensionary considers Van Breugel as a person who had always acted a friendly part, and listens to him. His intelligence is communicated to several of the leading members of the Government in the different provinces, and from their eager desire for peace, and, as the Princess writes, from their despondency being increased by the Duke of Brunswick's refusal, is caught at by them. The Pensionary also sends Van Breugel to Lord St. Helens, (the English Ambassador at the Hague,) who gives no positive opinion, but takes what he hears for reference. It never becomes a matter of public deliberation in any of the Colleges; but in consequence of the opinion of some of the principal people, and of the Prince (not the Princess) Rysselaer, commissary at the Dutch army, receives instructions to go to Bois le Duc, and speak with La Combe. On his approaching the town, he is, from various frivolous reasons, refused admittance, and he never sees La Combe, who goes in the meanwhile to Antwerp; but Van Breugel, who now assumes the title of *Agent du Représentant*, comes to him at a village near the town, remains with Rysselaer half an hour, and assumes the language of a Carmagnol, talking of the risk he runs, and that if he is discovered he shall be " mis hors de la loi," &c. The whole ends by Rysselaer giving in a paper to be transmitted to La Combe, stating, that the Dutch are ready to acknowledge the French Republic; and that, if all conquests are restored, and an engagement entered into not to interfere with the internal government of the country, they will sign a peace, and remain neuter; this to be preceded by an immediate armistice. This paper was sent to La Combe on the 16th November, and on the 10th December no answer was received, nor any notice taken of it, and the armistice, or even a suspension of hostilities till an answer came, positively declined. From this the Princess naturally concludes that the whole is a trick meant to lure and gain time.—Stampfort and I concert about a letter to Haugwitz, and the best means that the King of Prussia should get a sight of it. I propose sending with much publicity a courier to Potzdam, to inquire for Haugwitz there, and to leave the letter with *Ritz*, the King's favourite valet-de-chambre. — Duke very eager it should be written.—Stampfort reads me a paper he has received from him—goes to the idea of renewing our pecuniary engagements with Prussia—cautiously and *not ably* drawn up—agree to wait the return of Dressins, and to prepare the letter in the meanwhile.—At dinner next Princess Caroline; she says it is wished here that her brother William should marry the Princess Sophia of Gloucester; I advise her not to meddle in it. She talks about the Duke of Clarence, whom she prefers to the Duke of York; and it struck me to-day for the first time, that he originally put her into the Prince's head, and that with a view to plague the Duke and Duchess of York, whom he hates, and whom the Prince no longer likes; well knowing that the Princess Caroline and Duchess of York dislike each other, and that this match would be particularly unpleasant to her and the Duke. I praise the Duke of York to her, and speak with great applause of the behaviour of the Duchess, who by her discretion and conduct has conciliated to herself the good-will of the whole nation. I did this to pique her, and to make her anxious to do the same.—She has no *fond*, no fixed character, a light and flighty mind, but meaning well, and well-disposed; and my eternal theme to her is, *to think before she speaks, to recollect herself*. She says she wishes to be *loved* by the people; this, I assure her, can only be obtained by making herself respected and *rare*—that the sentiment of being *loved* by the people is a mistaken one—that sentiment can only be given to a few, to a narrow circle of those we see every day—that a nation at large can only respect and honour a great Princess, and it is, in fact, these feelings that are falsely denominated *the love of a nation:* they are not to be procured as the goodwill of individuals is, by pleasant openness and free communication, but by a strict attention to appearances—by never going below the high rank in which a Princess is placed, either in language or manners—by mixing dignity with affability, which, without it, becomes familiarity, and levels all distinction.

. After dinner the Duke and Duchess thanked me for what I had said; the more, they added, since I run the risk of getting into a scrape with the Prince on my return, to whom their daughter, in a moment of fondness, would tell all I said, and he certainly would not approve such serious advice. I replied, I luckily was in a situation not to want the Prince's favour; that it was of infinitely more consequence to the public, and even to me (in the rank I filled in its service), that the Princess of Wales should honour and become her high situtation, recover the dignity and respect due to our Princes and Royal Family, which had of late been so much and so dangerously let down by their mixing so indiscriminately with their inferiors, than that I should have the advantages and emoluments of a favourite at Carlton House; and that idea was so impressed on my mind, that I should certainly say to the Prince everything that I said to the Princess Caroline.

Duke enters on Berlin politics—tells me he has a letter from Prince Henry, but not its contents. Supper at Dowager Duchess's.

WEDNESDAY, DEC. 17.—Letters from England and Holland, and answered them. Accounts from Arnheim that the French attempted to cross the Waal at several points on the 11th, and were repulsed—General Busche killed. Duke at dinner—says he has answered Prince Henry's letter—that it looked as if he expected to get into power, and contained very dangerous doctrines.—Concert in the evening. —Princess Caroline talks very much—quite at her ease—too much so.

THURSDAY, DEC. 18.—Stampfort with me. We communicate what we had prepared for Berlin, and out of both compose a letter for Haugwitz, to be sent eventually, and according to what Dressins brings back—much talk about the Duke—nothing to be done with him—about the Prince of Orange, who, besides the perilous situation of his Stadtholderate, is completely ruined, so much so as to be obliged, in order to pay the interest of his debts, to employ the whole of his own family income, and to add even a part of that he receives from the States. Hereditary Prince of Orange disposed to be avaricious. Duke at dinner, and at the opera—very conversable, but on common subjects—idea of King of Prussia being threatened with a dropsy—mentions Chamberand (a French general) to me. Opera—pretty music—cold excessive. At supper Princess Caroline tells me of a kind of admonitory conversation the *Abbesse* had held to her—it went to exhort her to trust not *in men*, that they were not to be depended on, and that the Prince would certainly deceive her, &c., and all the nonsense of an envious and *desiring* old maid. The Princess was made uneasy by this, particularly as her aunt added, that she was sure she would not be happy. I desired the next time the Abbesse held this language to her, to ask her whether, if she (Princess Caroline) was to propose to exchange with her, and to take the Abbey of Gandersheim, and give her the Prince of Wales, she would then think *men* to be such monsters, and whether she would not expose herself to all the dangers and misfortunes of such a marriage. I told the Princess that through life she might be sure that people's advice was always tainted by their situations and particular circumstances, and that it was ever expedient to advert to these before we gave implicit faith to their counsels and opinions. She again urges me to accept a place about her Court at my return. I avoid an explicit answer, but earnestly entreat her not to solicit anything on my behalf; I had the Duke of Suffolk and Queen Margaret in my thoughts. Steinberg from Hanover—says King of Prussia is borrowing four millions of crowns on the interior circles, and raising money at home by a paper currency.

FRIDAY, DEC. 19.—Nothing remarkable. At Court as usual. Princess Caroline plagued to carry over a Frenchwoman, sister to Duchess of Cumberland's chambermaid, by Parson Macaulay—I oppose it, and again urge strongly the absolute necessity of her receiving *no* petitions, and making *no* promises—myself plagued and importuned by Mons. Chamberand. Duke of Brunswick communicates to me the Elector of Treves' answer at the Diet, about peace— a very good one.

SATURDAY, DEC. 20.—Walk with Sir B. Boothby. We regret the apparent facility of the Princess Caroline's character—her want of reflection and *substance*—agree that with a *steady* man she would do vastly well, but with one of a different description there are great risks. Duke at dinner—mentioned an anonymous letter he has received— conjectured to be from Sir J. M'Pherson[*]—its object to induce him to take the command, although the means employed do not appear at all to promote it. Assembly at Madame Riederel's—she recommends a *fiddling émigré* to me, by name Chevalier Monveau. Supper at Court. Duke recommends to Princess Caroline to make an eventual

[*] Sir John MacPherson had been for a short time Governor-General of India *ad interim;* he was in 1794 acting as a sort of volunteer Councillor to the Continental Sovereigns in the concert in which they were engaged.

engagement with Maddle. Rosenzweig (her *lectrice,*) and if she does not please, to send her back with 600 crowns pension. Preached my constant theme ; discretion, reserve, no familiarity, and less talking—all this she *still* takes well, but at the long run it must displease.

---

SUNDAY, DEC. 21.—Write to England. Breakfast at Madame Luttichau's country house—cold—tiresome—she a Dane, he nothing—been in England—talks of Oxford, Blenheim, and all the commonplace stuff of foreigners who think themselves English. Walk with Major Hislop—he at Toulon as Deputy Adjutant-general under J. St. Clair— intelligent and modest—gives due praise to O'Hara*—says the first thing he said on coming to Toulon was, that it was not to be kept if attacked seriously, and with sufficient numbers ; he was quite at his duty when taken. He does not admire Lord Hood—praises Sir G. Elliot—doubts that more than eight ships were burnt at Toulon. At dinner next to Puysegur—talk about Spain, &c.—after dinner Duke takes me aside, and enters into conversation about his daughter—begs me to continue to advise her—that she listens to me, and thanks me for the freedom and sincerity of my advice—desires me to correspond with him —great concert and supper—cassino with Princess and Duchess. At supper Princess unusually at her ease, quite *un laisser aller*—asks me (ushering it in with an apology) which I think would make the best Princess of Wales, herself, or her sister-in-law, the Hereditary Princess ; I avoid the answer by saying which I was sure would be the Prince's choice. She presses me farther ; I said she possesses by nature what the Hereditary Princess has not, or ever can acquire,—beauty and grace, and that all the essential qualities the Hereditary Princess has, she may attain— prudence, discretion, attention, and *tact.*—" Do I want them ?"—" You cannot have too much of them."—" How comes my sister-in-law, who is younger than myself, to have them more than I ?"—" Because at a very early

* General O'Hara commanded the English forces, and was wounded and made prisoner in the last action at Toulon in the previous year.

period of her life, her family was in danger—she was brought up to exertion of the mind, and she *now* derives the benefit, '*d'avoir mangé son pain bis le premier.*'"— " I shall never learn this; I am too open, too idle (*trop légère*)."—" When you are in a different situation, you will; you do not want these forbearing virtues here—only *commune with yourself*, question *yourself*, and you will always act up to your situation." This was well taken, though I expressed myself strongly, and with more freedom than usual. She talked of her aunt the Abbesse—said she had endeavoured to inspire her with a diffidence and mistrust of me—had represented me as *un homme dangereux*. I tried to get rid of this sort of conversation, but the Princess stuck by it, and I was forced to say that I believed her aunt had forgotten that twenty years had elapsed since she had seen me, or heard of me; and that, besides, such an insinuation was a tacit accusation of my being very *foolishly* unprincipled. She said she meant well, that she perhaps thought too partially of me herself, and was afraid for her. It was in vain to attempt to turn the subject—she went on during the whole supper—was in high spirits, and laughed unmercifully at her aunt, and her supposed partiality for me.

MONDAY, DEC. 22.—Wrote to Berlin—long walk—Duke at dinner desires me to see Stampfort in the evening—he gives me information the Duke has received of the state of the negotiation between France and Prussia.—Concert, and small supper.

TUESDAY, DEC. 23.—Dressins from Berlin—Paget writes to Lord Grenville that he did not make any distinct proposal to King of Prussia, as to the continuation of his coöperation in the war, because he was afraid of receiving a flat refusal; that he confined himself to endeavour to sound in what terms this could be accomplished, and to bring a proposal from them; that to this Haugwitz replied, that all proposals must originate with England; and that none would be listened to till the whole subsidy was paid; that the King of Prussia's dignity would not admit of it, particularly on so just a claim; that, therefore, this must be *condition, sine quâ non.* Paget notices the unreasonableness of this language, but without effect, and gets nothing more, *ministerially,* from Haugwitz—*unministerially* he intimates to him that if the subsidies are paid and the Hague Convention renewed, the King will not be averse to detach 20,000 men towards Holland, and leave the remainder of his army where it is, or on any given point; and that he would endeavour to prevail on the Duke of Brunswick to take the command of those 20,000 men. Paget argues that from the pressure of the moment these hard conditions may, perhaps, be considered as admissible, and that if they are, he urges *immediate* decision, as the army wants magazines. (N.B. This despatch remarkably well drawn up.) Another from Gardiner, who states that he thinks a farther division of Poland likely.

I write to the Duke; he comes to me—long conversation with him. I communicate to him the substance of Paget's despatch; I compare it with what the Duke sent me through Stampfort; and the Duke agrees with me that nothing can be so abominably false and foolish as the conduct of Berlin; he launches out against that Court in the strongest terms. "J'ai été," dit-il, "leur mannequin l'année passée, le mannequin de gens que je méprise. Je ne veux avoir rien à faire avec eux, à moins qu'il n'y ait un revers de la médaille —(he meant another King). Ils sont pires que la Convention, et s'ils ne font pas le même mal, c'est qu'ils n'ont pas les mêmes moyens. J'aimerois mieux vivre dans un bois, que de les servir, &c." He then said it was Bishopswerder and Prince Henry who did all this; that it would not last; that Bishopswerder would desert Prince Henry if there was any appearance of things going ill, or of a change in the King's disposition, and lay the whole blame on him. The Duke then said, he had written to Gravent a letter he was sure would be shewn, and he promised to give me every possible information. I never before saw him so apparently open and sincere, or so disposed to be confiding. I, however, held it not *yet* time to renew my idea as to his taking the command or going to Holland. With Stampfort. Send on Dressins. Dinner at Court, as usual. Supper at Duchess Dowager's—nothing remarkable.

WEDNESDAY, DEC. 24.—Write to Haugwitz—Stampfort sends me a letter from the Princess of Orange, dated 19th. ———* and Rysselaer going to Bois le Duc on an answer being come from the Convention that they are disposed to listen to terms of peace, and agree to an armistice under certain conditions. ———* and Rysselaer wait for their passport—Princess thinks it will end in nothing. "Nous serons les dupes de leur finesse, et je vois cette négociation avec une répugnance extrême," are her words. She says the English do better since the Duke of York's departure—that Harcourt and Walmoden agree very well, and that Alvinzi seems well disposed: 6000 Austrians at or near Arnheim— French in want of provisions; they had formed no magazines. Duke after dinner talks of the year 1793 and the campaign —that it was a misfortune such a man as Lord Beauchamp was sent in such a critical moment—that he was lost and bewildered. "Il ne s'orientait pas." Lucchesini overreached him. Lucchesini gave at this moment a new turn to the King of Prussia's ideas, by making him believe he was *not a principal* but an auxiliary in the war—that to this referred the famous words in Lord Beauchamp's Convention "Autant que les circonstances permettent"—that under this idea the King of Prussia affected to be always waiting for a plan of campaign from the Emperor, and left him, the Duke of Brunswick, under this dilemma. "*Dans une situation incroyable,*" says the Duke. He added that during the siege of Mentz, Lucchesini said to him, "When this is over we must do as little as possible, and leave the rest to the Austrians;" that, however, it was the moment for acting; that the German armies were of 60,000 men each, and the French under Houchard on the Saar, not more than 70,000 altogether; that if the Prussians and Austrians had then advanced, the campaign would have been a glorious one, but Lucchesini's cunning or corruption, and Lord Beauchamp's inability, prevented it. The Duchess, before whom all this was said, observed, "You are doubtless disgusted with Prussia." "To be sure," said he, "never was a man so ill-used as I have been; they treat me with civility in public in order to *m'écraser* in private." He told me Bishopswerder

* Name illegible in MS.

had certainly consented to the House of Austria having Bavaria, but that Lucchesini had declared to him (Duke of Brunswick) that this never should be as long as he had any influence.

Supper at Münchausen's (*Grand Maréchal.*) Court—played, but did not sup. Conversation with Prince about Macaulay—Madame Münchausen joined in it—gossiping and missy—good supper. Madame Riederel talkative, good-humoured, her daughter handsome.

THURSDAY, DEC. 25.—Dutch messenger despatched to Berlin—brings letter to the Duke from Prince of Orange, with an account of the opening a negotiation for peace, and one to Reede on the same subject. I write to Paget and Haugwitz. Duke approves my letters. Count Westphalin, Imperial Minister to the circles of the lower Rhine—*un fat.* Concert. Princess Caroline asks about the Duke of Clarence—says she believes he was the person who first mentioned her to the Prince.—(N.B.—My own private ideas and feelings on this remark.)

FRIDAY, DEC. 26.—Timms arrives at two in the morning. Orders to set out. Fleet comes to Texel. Ratification of Treaty. Present to Feronce. Letter from Prince—well satisfied and approves what I have done—positively refuses to let Madlle. *Rosenzweit* come over. She was to be a sort of *reader.* King writes on the subject to the Duchess; both she and the Duke press it. I insist upon it; and it is settled that she is not to accompany the Princess. Duke takes me aside, and says that the only reason why he wished her to be with the Princess was, that his daughter writes very ill, and spells ill, and he was desirous this should not appear. Affected to be indifferent about this refusal, but at the bottom hurt and angry. Suspects the Queen, whom he and the Duchess hate. Settle everything for the journey, and despatch East to England in the evening. Princess Caroline much affected, very naturally and very rightly so. Duke very anxious about his daughter—again and again recommends her to me—says she *cannot go alone*—she must be guided and directed.

SATURDAY, DEC. 27.—Stampfort—agree to try to bring Duke to a point as to the taking the command of the army. Grand Maréchal Münchausen about the journey—great fuss—" beaucoup de bruit, peu de besogne." Count Westphalin calls upon her—shallow and vain—silly enough to tell the Duke that the Austrian army was in a state of great disorder, and the generals diagreeing amongst themselves. Make visits of congé—tormented with requests and petitions—reject them all.

SUNDAY, DEC. 28.—Major Hislop with me—give him instructions about his journey; to keep before us and give notice in case of danger from the enemy. Parson Macaulay and Captain Farquhar—engaged to take them over with me. Mr. Burnaby, Archdeacon, and Burnaby's son, come to Brunswick. Audience of congé—Duchess Dowager takes me into her closet—says she considers me as one of her family—makes me sit down—vastly kind and obliging—recommends her granddaughter—hints about Lady * * * *. Duke extremely attentive—requests me earnestly again not to forget my promise of taking care of his daughter. " Ma gloire," said he, " à part de mes sentimens paternels, est intéressée à son succès." He was much moved, and betrayed sentiments of feeling I scarce thought to be in him—usual compliments to the King, for whom, as well as the Queen and Prince, he gave me letters. I mentioned the idea of his taking the command, and asked him *straightforward*, whether, if he could get a large body of Austrians, he would consent to it?—he was much more complying than before, and ended by giving me a paper.—Hereditary Prince and Princess vastly friendly—she a most admirable character, all sense and good judgment; he little of either, but very harmless and good-natured. At dinner I found the Duchess and Princess alarmed, agitated, and uneasy at an anonymous letter from England, abusing the Prince, and warning them in the most exaggerated terms against Lady ———, who is represented as the worst and most dangerous of profligate women. The Duchess, with her usual indiscretion, had shown this to the Princess, and mentioned it to everybody. I was quite angry with her, and could not avoid expressing my concern, first at paying *any* attention to an anonymous letter, and, secondly, at being so very imprudent as to bruit about its contents. The Princess soon recovered it, but the Duchess harped on it all day. The Duke, on being acquainted with it, thought as I did, but was more uneasy about it than he ought. On his examining the letter, he assured me it came from England,— (I suspected it the work of some of the partisans of *Madlle. Rosenzweit*, on her being refused,)—and that the person who wrote it wrote in the character of a man, not a woman, and said he was in the daily society of Carlton House. Madlle. Hertzfeldt again talks to me as before about the Princess Caroline—" Il faut la gouverner par la peur, *par la terreur même*. Elle s'émancipera si on n'y prend pas garde—mais si on la veille soigneusement et sévèrement elle se conduira bien." The King of England, in a letter to the Duchess, says, " Qu'il espère que sa nièce n'aura pas trop de vivacité, et qu'elle menera une vie sédentaire et retirée." These words shock Princess Caroline, to whom the Duchess very foolishly reads the letter. Princesse Abbesse importunately civil and *coming*, and plagues me with her attentions and affectation of wit and cleverness, and concern at our departure. Princess Caroline shews me the anonymous letter about Lady ——, evidently written by some disappointed milliner or angry maid-servant, and deserving no attention ; I am surprised the Duke afforded it any. Aimed at Lady —— ; its object to frighten the Princess with the idea that she would lead her into an affair of gallantry, and be ready to be convenient on such an occasion. This did *not* frighten the Princess, although it did the Duke and Duchess; and on my perceiving this, I told her Lady —— would be more cautious than to risk such an audacious measure ; and that, besides, it was *death* to presume to approach a Princess of Wales, and no man would be daring enough to think of it. She asked me whether I was in earnest. I said such was our law ; that anybody who presumed to *love* her was guilty of *high trea son*, and punished with *death*, if she was weak enough to listen to him : so also would *she*. This startled her.

---

Monday, Dec. 29.—My secretary Ross and a servant set out early. Stampfort with me—settle correspondence with him. At twelve breakfast at Court. At two we depart—Duke affected—recommends again and again his daughter—says I must be *her second father*—desires me to write to him. Great crowd as we pass through the streets—cannon fire from the ramparts—escort of horse till near Peine. At Peine the Princess lodged at a Mr. ——— ;* we at the post.

---

Tuesday, Dec. 30.—Set out at eight.—At Herenhausen great dinner—all Hanover—quite a Court. Left it at four—got to Neustadt by six—sleep in the bailliage or château—large house, well situated on the river, which passes by Hanover. Ombre with the Duchess.

---

Wednesday, Dec. 31.—To Diepholz, through Vieuburg and Sulingen. At Vieuburg a triumphal arch—people in the streets—guards—God save the King, &c. Diepholz illuminated. Severe cold. Lodged again at the bailliage. Roads in good order—Princess wanted me to be in the same coach with her—I resisted it as impossible, from its being improper—she disposed to laugh at the matter—I discountenance it.

---

Thursday, Jan. 1, 1795.— To Osnabruck,† through Bohmte—got there by four—conducted through the town to the palace—streets filled—guards, &c.—palace fine—due attention, &c. I receive at five a courier to say the French had driven the Dutch from the Bommelwaert, taken several battalions, and made lodgement at Zuil, opposite Bommel. Our journey retarded—great uneasiness. At seven, news comes of the French being driven back by General Dundas and Lord Cathcart. Joy as excessive as

* Illegible in MS.     † A Bishopric held by the Duke of York.

disappointment. I however refuse to go on, the frost being very severe.* No news of the arrival of the fleet, and the enemy still in possession of Bommel, &c. ; agree, therefore, to write to Holland and head-quarters, and to wait for news. *Mons. le Chambellan de Sc hele*very civil and attentive ; his daughters, particularly Madame Ledebur, pretty and well-looking.

Friday, Jan. 2.—Despatch East (messenger) to head-quarters, and an estafette to Brunswick to mention our delay. Walk—town large. Dinner and supper as at Brunswick. Converse with Madame —— about *émigrés*—desire her to distribute what I intend to give them—their situation deplorable, as they are exactly those who, from their penury and want, cannot get farther on, and are dying of hunger, and through want. I persuade the Princess Caroline to be munificent towards them—she disposed to be, but not knowing *how* to set about it. I tell her, liberality and generosity is an enjoyment, not a severe virtue. She gives a louis for some lottery tickets, *I* give ten, and say the Princess ordered me—she surprised ; I said I was sure she did not mean to give for the ticket its *precise* value, and that I forestalled her intention. Next day a French *émigré*, with a pretty child, draws near the table—The Princess Caroline *immediately*, of her own accord, puts ten louis in a paper, and gives it the child ; the Duchess observes it, and enquires of me (I was dining between them) what it was. I tell her a *demand on her purse.* She embarrassed—" Je n'ai que mes beaux doubles louis de Brunswick." I answer, " Qu'ils deviendront plus beaux entre les mains de cet enfant que dans sa poche." She ashamed, and gives three of them. In the evening, Princess Caroline, to whom these sort of virtues were never preached, on my praising the coin of the money at Brunswick, offers *me very seriously* eight or ten double louis, saying, " Cela ne me fait rien—je ne m'en soucie pas—je vous prie de les prendre." I mention these facts to shew her character : it could not distin-

* The frost prevented our ships getting into Helvoetsluys to embark the Princess, and Lord M. was afraid of being taken by the French in their absence.

guish between *giving* as a benevolence, and flinging away the money like a child. She thought that the act of getting rid of the money, and not seeming to care about it, constituted the merit. I took an opportunity at supper of defining to her what real benevolence was, and I recommended it to her as a quality that would, if rightly employed, make her more admirers, and give her more true satisfaction, than any that human nature could possess. The idea was, I was sorry to see, new to her, but she felt the truth of it; and she certainly is not fond of money, which both her parents are.

SATURDAY, JAN. 3.—Dusseldorff Gallery was brought to Osnabruck to be secure—some of its finest pictures spoilt—some famous Vanderveldts, and a Gerard Dow—" And who is Gerard Dow?" says the Duchess, "*was he of Dusseldorff?*" "Sénèque étoit-il de Paris?" Visit all the town—severe cold—great uneasiness about Holland, &c. Court well served—good dinner, good wine, &c. I receive by Captain Farquhar a very foolish coming letter from the Princess Abbess of Brunswick—take no notice of it.

SUNDAY, JAN. 4.—At six o'clock letters from Lord St. Helens and Count Harcourt arrive from the General Harcourt; both recommend our going on, but Count Harcourt describes the situation of Holland as so critical on the side of Williamstadt, and the frost so hard, that I demur, particularly as I am without accounts of the fleet being at the Texel—anxious day—one of doubt and thinking. I tell Madame Ledebur that I will send her 150 louis to be distributed by her amongst the French *émigrés*—she astonished at the sum. Baron Freytag, Grand Marshal, arrives—takes Schele's place, but does not fit it so well. In the evening I write and despatch Vanscheick to the Hague to say, unless there is a thaw, I shall not set out—assign my reasons, &c. Many petitions from *émigrés*—reject all of them—desire those who want me to *see* them to say, that I never saw or heard a *Frenchman*, that my inclination to assist him did not go off—that I would give them money, *but nothing else*.

Princess Caroline very *gauche* at cards—speaks without thinking—gets too easy—calls the ladies (she never saw) " Mon cœur, ma chère, ma petite." I notice this, and reprove it strongly. The Princess, for the first time, disposed to take it amiss; I do not pretend to observe it. Duchess wants to return to Brunswick, and leave us to go on by ourselves; this I oppose, and suppose it impossible. " If I am taken," says she, " I am sure the King will be angry." —" He will be very sorry," I reply; " but your Royal Highness must *not* leave your daughter till she is in the hands of her attendants." She argues, but *I* will not give way, and *she* does.

Monday, Jan. 5.—Wind changes to S.W. Dutch messenger from Berlin—bad there—all rogues and fools. Letters from Duke of Brunswick and Hereditary Princess. Decide to set off on Thursday if weather remains mild. See Münchausen on this point.

Tuesday, Jan. 6.—Thaw. Hold my resolution of going. Despatch East at eleven with letters to England, to Lord St. Helens and General Harcourt. French women, with their children, attend now every day at dinner in order to get something from the Princess. I make her observe it, and advise her not to give, as this is a trick—to inquire who is the most in want, and send it to them through her ladies. I send Mr. Ross with 150 louis to Madame Ledebur, desiring her to conceal my name, and not to distribute it till I have left Osnabruck. Count Harcourt returns to the headquarters. Conversation after dinner with Mons. Busch, Duke of York's Minister, a well-informed, sensible, strongheaded man.

Wednesday, Jan. 7.—Hunter (messenger) arrives from Major Hislop—brings accounts that everything is apparently quiet. Thaw ceases—but I hold my intention of going, and of trying to pass through Holland—my secretary and young Fitzgerald set out. Dinner and supper as usual. Previous to our going, arrangements were taken about proper gratifications and presents. Princess of Wales (at my instigation) directs me to say to Messrs. Freytag and Schele that she has nothing with her, but that she will send them marks of her recollection from England. I tell her before several people, " Que je me suis acquitté *de ses ordres.*" " C'est bien à moi," says she, " de vous donner des ordres."—It put me in mind of — " *A glass of small beer, good Mr. Butler.*" I prevail on the Duchess to be liberal on going away—to give 50 louis to the house, &c.—much against her inclination.

THURSDAY, JAN. 8.—Leave Osnabruck at seven, Mons. Freytag attending. Cannon fire from the ramparts. Arrive at Bentheim at five—roads good—frost sharp—lodged at the President's, Mr. Fonk—odd figure—but Count Bentheim de Steinfort, who comes to pay his duties to the Princess, much more so—the most exaggerated macaroni in their day not equal to his dress, and his manners apparently correspond ; yet he is no fool, and has the reputation of a very domestic man and good master. It was with great difficulty I kept the Princess from laughing out—the Duchess did, but it was not perceived. I slept in the Judge's house. Note from Mrs. Parkhurst.

FRIDAY, JAN. 9.—Leave Bentheim at seven—Delden at twelve ; about four leagues further on, Vanscheick, whom I had sent on, on Sunday the 4th, met me with letters from Lord St. Helens, dated the same morning, saying the French had passed the Waal—that they were near Baren, and that there had been fighting all day ; he recommends our turning back, and says General Harcourt also advises it. I mentioned this to the Princesses, and I must in justice say that the Princess Caroline bore this disappointment with more good temper, good-humour, and patience, than could be expected, particularly as she felt it very much. We return to Delden, where we slept in the inn. I despatched letters to the head-quarters, to the Hague, and to England ; and Elliot, who had been with me till now, undertook to go to the Texel (where I expected the fleet would be), and to tell Commodore Payne the reasons which prevented me from joining it. Bad night, and bad room. A heavy cannonade was heard all night at no great distance. The Princess in the morning seemed sorry not to go on towards the fleet. I mentioned this cannonade. "Cela ne fait rien," says she, "je n'ai pas peur des canons."—"Mais, Madame, le danger d'être pris." "Vous ne m'y exposerez pas?" said she. I told her the story of the Queen of France (St. Louis's wife) during the siege of Damiette, and le Sieur de Joinville—I said, "Qu'elle valoit mieux que celle là, que les François seroient pires que les Sarrazins, et que moi j'ai pensé comme le Chevalier." The story pleased. "J'aurois fait et désiré comme elle," said she.

JAN. 10.—Leave Delden at nine—get to Bentheim by two—castle fine—situation striking. Fonk as before, but instead of blue and gold, grey and gold. He tells our fortunes by examining the hand. Call on Mrs. Parkhurst—very handsome—in distress. A desire from a Madame Beaucorps to see me—I wish her to write—call on her, find her with two nieces, daughters of a Mons. Lancloski, in great distress—these children, the one fourteen, the other twelve—I relieve them. Return to the Duchess and play at ombre—she observes I am low-spirited—I tell her the situation of the people I have been seeing—she does not comprehend *this* can affect the spirits, and persists in taxing me with being *bored*, and so pertinaciously, that I am forced to say I am very *near it*. Strange mixture—much goodness, but all her feelings like her understanding, jumbled together and confused. She does much good at Brunswick, but it is mechanically; her charity is not up to a surprise, and if misfortune takes her unexpectedly, she shuts the door against it. I clearly perceived she, and much more her suite, disapproved exceedingly my instigating the Princess Caroline to be *very* profuse in her acts of benevolence; they considered it as so much taken from *them*. I, however, continued to preach this doctrine, and I was glad to find the Princess admit it most readily; this, and her behaviour on being obliged to retrograde, pleased me very much; if her education had been *what it ought*, she might have turned out excellent; but it was that very nonsensical one that most women receive—one of privation, injunction, and menace;

to believe no man, and never to express what they feel, or say what they think, *for all* men are inclined to entrap them, and all feelings are improper ; this vitiates or *abrutit* all women,—few escape. On summing up Princess Caroline's character to-day, it came out to my mind to be, that she has quick parts, without a sound or distinguishing understanding; that she has a ready conception but no judgment ; caught by the first impression, led by the first impulse ; turned away by appearances or *enjouement;* loving to talk, and prone to confide and make missish friendships that last twenty-four hours. Some natural, but no acquired morality, and no strong innate notions of its value and necessity ; warm feelings and nothing to counterbalance them ; great good-humour and much good-nature—no appearance of caprice—rather quick and *vive,* but not a grain of rancour. From her habits, from the life she was allowed and even compelled to live, forced to dissemble ; fond of gossiping, and this strengthened greatly by the example of her good mother, who is all curiosity and inquisitiveness, and who has no notion of not gratifying this desire at any price. In short, the Princess in the hands of a steady and sensible man would probably turn out well, but where it is likely she will find faults perfectly analogous to her own, she will fail. She has no governing powers, although her mind is *physically* strong. She has her father's courage, but it is to her (as to him) of no avail. *He* wants mental decision ; *she* character and *tact.*

---

SUNDAY, JAN. 11.—On leaving Bentheim, it was thought expedient to give something to Fonk, who would not take money. Duchess (speaking, I am sure, after the Duke, who is a servile imitation of the late King of Prussia) talks of sending him some porcelain from Brunswick. Prene, who is her *grand maître,* and very liberal, objects and comes to me—I speak to Princess Caroline ; she immediately recollects a diamond ring she has—sends for it, and gives it to Madame Fonk ; this pleases me. A messenger (Sir M. Eden's *maître d'hôtel*) passes through Bentheim—write by him to Lord St. Helens. Leave about seven—get to Osnabruck at six P.M.—settle with Baron Freytag (*grand maré-*

*chal)* about the expenses—agree that they should be at the expense of the Duke of York. Small dinners four times a week—servants on board wages. I engage for the King to repay Duke of York. At supper Princess Caroline very cheerful, and pleasantly so—understands a joke, and can make one. Freytag, Schele, and Busche; no ladies.

---

MONDAY, JAN. 12.—Hunter from Hislop—(Hunter talks and tells stories; I reprove him very sharply)—no material alteration. Call on Comtesse Walmoden, amiable and pleasant—her daughter-in-law very much so. Walk—thaw. At dinner Princess uneasy about a Mr. Strafford Smith, who formerly was well, "*au mieux*," with the Abbesse, her aunt (as she tells me), and who threatens that if he is not placed about the Prince's new Court, he will publish the correspondence between them. Duke writes to her about him— says he has a cold, which the Duchess affects to be uneasy about. Duchess has a *hankering* to leave her daughter, and return to Brunswick—very evident from her manner: *I* wont hear of it. She told me at dinner that the Duke was in love with Duchess of G * * * *, Lady O * * * *, and Lady D. B. * * * *; that he kept at the same time an Italian girl. All this in 1766, when he was in England; she knew it all—it made her uneasy, but she held her tongue.

Presidente Walmoden—Princess Caroline affects to dislike her, to call her a bore, &c. I say she ought to ask her to play with her; she does it, but reluctantly, and during the party whispers and giggles with some of the young women. I notice this to her afterwards, as what I could not approve; I do it as gently, but as strongly as I dare. She at first disposed to contend the point with me, but at last confesses I am right, and promises to correct herself. My freedom at first discomposed her, but finding me seem very indifferent as to her liking or not liking what I said, she became herself soon again, and ended by taking it very right, and was in perfect good-humour during the supper. The Duchess delighted with the Presidente, who is a clever talkative woman. They told stories all supper, and amongst others (strange as it may appear), the Duchess told me that when they were quite children, she and her brother the King slept in the same bed—that he was as disagreeable a bedfellow as any royal or plebeian infant could be, but that her father (the late Prince of Wales) cured him of his fault by making him wear the blue ribbon with a piece of china attached to it, which was *not* the George.

TUESDAY, JAN. 13.—Hard frost—streets slippery. Freytag proposes a concert, *providing* somebody will pay for it. As *I* think that whenever a great Princess is in a little town she should make a strong impression, I assure him the Princess Caroline will. Dinner in small apartment. Visit Mesdames de Schele and Walmoden—last amiable and sensible. Supper as usual.

WEDNESDAY, JAN. 14.—Timms (messenger) returns with answer to my letters from Delden. Holland in the last stage of danger. Send Hunter on to Hanover. Write to Kielmansegge. My design of bringing the Princesses there. Call on Madame Ledebur, and appoint Madame Lamberty to meet me.—N.B. I saw her at Bentheim, and wish to settle something for them. Paget arrives from Berlin and Brunswick. Prussian Monarch remains the same. Stampfort proposes that Duke should go to Berlin, with ample means and full powers. Princess Caroline foolish about Paget— uncivil to him—I remonstrate—she says she disliked him at first sight—I reprove this sort of hasty judgment—read a lecture upon it—she argues—is inwardly angry, but conceals it. Write to the Hague and to England, by Timms and Paget, who go away at twelve. Paget clever, and *growing* industrious and pains-taking. Walk. Princess *coldish* at dinner—I do not remark it, and she comes round. Concert—Princess pays twenty louis for it. Vanscheick returns—bad news continues. The Dutch on the point of giving in. Lord St. Helens talks of flying. Frost severer than ever. Lieutenant-Colonel *Gun* comes in his way to Brunswick to fetch the troops—old and odd soldier—amuses the Duchess.

FRIDAY, JAN. 16.—At Madame Ledebur, to meet Mesdames Lamberty and Beaucorps—inquire into their situation and those of their nieces—resolved to relieve them. Abbé Dillon and L. Pierrepont arrive. Call on Comtesse Walmoden—sensible, good, and interesting—proposes me to stand godfather to her child with Prince Adolphus, Duke of York, and Mrs. Harcourt. No event. Duchess takes to, and talks to Dillon—he overwhelms Pierrepont. Never let a Frenchman and an Abbé travel with a young Englishman.

SATURDAY, JAN. 17.—Dillon is brother to the Beau Dillon and Madame d'Osmond. Hunter returns from Hanover. Count Kielmansegge writes me word that the Château is at our service. Settle to go away on Thursday the 22nd. Duchess makes difficulties about receiving the proper honours there. I insist on the Princess of Wales taking them. Christening of the Comtesse Walmoden's child—he is named *James*—all the principal people there. The chief families here (les familles chapitrales) are Busche, Weitz, Ledebur, Hammerstein, and Schele. Chapter composed of twenty-one, reckoning le Grand Prevôt and Grand Doyen. Presidente Walmoden still here—sensible, but not *suave*. Madlle. Frederica Walmoden very pretty; her sister, Madame L———n, separated from her husband, on account of young A———m. Supper as usual. Princess too apt to joke about the Duchess; I constantly *frown* at it; she remarks it, and corrects herself. I preach to her about circumspection, &c., while at Hanover.

SUNDAY, JAN. 18.—Despatch at eleven Vanscheick to Hanover, to announce our near arrival; and at twelve Hunter to the head-quarters, to mention our departure. Queen's birthday—gala—great dinner—all the clergy. Duchess shams sick, in order not to go to the sermon, to avoid *paying* for it. Princess gives fifteen louis. Mr. and Mrs. Parkhurst arrive. Princess Caroline very *missish* at supper. I much fear these habits are irrecoverably rooted in her: she is naturally curious, and a gossip—she is quick and observing, and she has a silly pride of finding out everything—she thinks herself particularly acute in discovering *likings*, and this leads her at times to the most improper remarks and conversation. I am determined to take an opportunity of correcting her, *coute qu'il coute.*

Monday, Jan. 19.—At Madame Schele's, to meet Mesdames Lamberty and Beaucorps, and Mrs Parkhurst. Courier passes from the Hague—difficulty in getting through. French at Arnheim. Princess of Orange's escape doubtful—Lord St. Helens' and Elliot's still more so. Harold and another, apparently adventurers—say they have lost a letter from Sir B. Boothby.

Tuesday, Jan. 20.—Madame Walmoden. Mrs. Parkhurst—she interesting, but not disposed to open. Madame la Presidente Walmoden—sensible—well-disposed—rather gossiping, and somewhat *méchante*—but does much good—talks to me of Madame L——n, and her adventure with Fritz A——m— of Madame la Générale Walmoden, and all sorts of subjects, but listens to none. Dinner as usual. After dinner, Vinck, the Grand Ecuyer, makes me a strange proposal about giving the Low Countries to the Landgrave of Hesse Cassel—tells me of a Prussian army in Westphalia, and of the King of Prussia's being at the head of it—and such stuff. Visit Madame Walmoden—Burgomestre Overskye there—she very amiable and good. Captain ——,[*] from the Duke of Brunswick. Duke writes very *nervously* to the Duchess and Princess—betrays his *real* character. Duchess and Princess vastly alarmed—I endeavoured to quiet them—difficult, because I can find no very valid reason.

Wednesday, Jan. 21.—Things in Holland very bad. Major Hislop arrives safe—uneasy about Macaulay and Farquhar. Timms and Hunter from head-quarters—news deplorable—Holland lost—Paget safe—boats established at Embden. Princess Caroline has a tooth drawn—she sends it down to me by her page—nasty and indelicate. Visit Madame Le-

[*] Name illegible in MS.

debur and Walmoden, and Commander Münster—he shows me a letter from Golowkin, Governor of Amsterdam, which begins, "*Notre histoire est finie.*" The French expected at Amsterdam on the 19th. Constant and six others gone as deputies from Amsterdam. Royer and ——[*] from the Hague —all lost. Madame Walmoden's submission, goodness, and good sense very great—B. Watson about magazines, and King of Prussia's prohibition—send his letter to Lord H. Spencer. Busche, conseiller privé and Minister to the Duke of York, tells me that the Duke is the best master and best sovereign possible; that although the wealth and means of the Bishoprick are increased, he requires less from them as *don gratuit* than any of his Protestant predecessors. They received a hundred years ago from 100,000 to 130,000 crowns. The Duke receives only 90,000 (the demesnes, which are small, not included); that *he* keeps an expensive court, (besides paying for a regiment,) that *they* kept none; that *he* is benevolent and gives pensions, *they* gave none; that, in short, *he* gives more and receives less than any of his predecessors; that he never is at law with the States, who from being priests and Catholics, always wish to wrangle with their Sovereign when a Protestant. Busche quotes several *traits* of the Duke's kindness, and says with great candour and spirit, "*if anybody complains that this country is harshly and unfairly governed, let them lay the blame on* ME *for not executing properly the Duke's orders, which are all calculated for the ease or good of the subject, and not on the Duke himself, who means they should all be happy and comfortable.*" I was much pleased with this assertion. He and Freytag sorry to hear Count d'Artois[†] was coming here. I advise them to treat him with great civility, but not give him the château. Osnabruck manages its own police—makes its own bye-laws—taxes itself—administers its own justice —the Sovereign only an appeal in last resort. Yet, notwithstanding all these circumstances, which contribute to make it the freest town in Germany, people are disaffected and jacobinically inclined.

[*] Name illegible in MS.
[†] Afterwards Charles X. of France, and dethroned by the revolution of 1830.

THURSDAY, JAN. 22.—Left Osnabruck at 9. Hislop with me in my carriage. Cold intense—17 degrees below zero, Reaumur's scale. Pass through Bohmte and get to Diepholz by 4—seven miles—lodge as before at the ———. Duchess overcome with the cold. Play at ombre—servants on the outside quite frozen.

FRIDAY, JAN. 23.—Leave Diepholz at a quarter before 8. Cold increased. Pass through Sulingen and Vienburg to Neustadt—roads good—arrive there at a quarter past 6—nine miles and a half. Duchess sleepy and quite benumbed with the excessive cold, which is greater than I ever felt out of Russia. She retires early. I have a long and serious conversation with the Princess about her conduct at Hanover, about the Prince, about herself and her character. She much disposed to listen to me, and to take nothing wrong. I tell her, and I tell her truly, that the impression she gives at Hanover will be that on which she will be received by the King and Queen in England. I recommend great attention and reserve—to try to please the graver men and elderly women. I told her she was *Zemire* and Hanover *Azor*, and that if she behaved right the monster would be metamorphosed into a beauty; that *Beulwitz* (at the head of the Regency, the most ugly and most disagreeable man possible,) would change into the Prince of Wales; that the habit of *proper, princely* behaviour was natural to her; that it would come of itself; that acquired by this (in that respect) fortunate delay in our journey, it would belong to her, and be familiar to her on her coming to England, where it would be of infinite advantage. She expresses uneasiness about the Prince; talked of his being *unlike*, quite opposite to the King and Queen in his *ideas and habits;* that he had contracted them from the *vuide* in his situation; that she was made to fill this up; she would domesticate him—give him a relish for all the private and home virtues; that he would then be happier than ever; that the nation expected this at her hands; that *I knew* she was capable of doing, and that she would do it.—She hesitated.—I said, that I had seen enough of her to be quite sure her mind and understanding were equal to any exertions; that, therefore, if she did not do *quite* right, and come up to *everything* that was expected from her, she would have no excuse. I added, I was so sure of this, that it would be the *first* thing I should tell the *King and Queen,* and that therefore she must be prepared; that they would know her as well, and judge her as favourably, and at the same time as *severely* as I did. I saw this had the effect I meant; it put a curb on her desire of amusement; a drawback on her situation, and made her feel that it was not to be all one of roses. She ended on retiring by saying, she hoped the Prince would let her see me, since she never could expect any one would give her such good and such free advice as myself; and, added she, " I confess I could not hear it from any one but you."

SATURDAY, JAN. 24.—Left Neustadt at a quarter past 10. ——* and his sister good people, everything clean and comfortable—she makes excellent *pot-pourri.* Get to Hanover at 1. Escort at Herenhausen to meet the Princess. Duchess on her arrival very disagreeable about the cold, peevish, and ill-mannered. Princess Caroline much otherwise. Duchess troublesome about choosing her apartment —complains vulgarly of the cold. Maréchal Reden at supper. Mesdames Waggenheim and Steinbergen at dinner. I call on Kielmansegge. Great uneasiness about the army. Plan of defence.

SUNDAY, JAN. 25.—Waggenheim (Grand Marshal) with me —settle about the order of the Court, and way of living. He a *butor*—no head—drinks. His wife not a *butor,* but also drinks. Ministers of the Regency dine with us. Visit in the evening as usual—Court, and great supper.

MONDAY, JAN. 26.—Münchausen goes to Brunswick. Write to the Duke—Duke's alarms puerile and feminine—excessive —writes them to his wife and daughter—he never can be fit for a commission of difficulty, or a trust where there is doubt

* Name illegible in MS.

and dilemma. Theatre in the evening. I write, and visit Mrs. Parkhurst.

TUESDAY, JAN. 27.—Hunter from the army early. Sad fate of the House of Orange—courage of the Stadtholder. Count Kielmansegge with me. Their ideas of defence combined with the Landgrave of Hesse, and to be assisted by the Duke of Brunswick. Despatch Timms by Embden. Dinner as usual. Visit theatre. Duchess declines a Court day on Wednesday—I insist upon it, and carry my point. Queen's brother, Prince Ernest, not unclever, well-behaved, and gentlemanlike—rather effeminate Duchess told me he was not fond of women—he to command the Cordon, and be at Diepholz.

WEDNESDAY, JAN. 28.—Long walk. General Veynhausen from Cassel—going to England—tells me that the Landgrave is disposed to do everything—give him an order for a boat. Letters from Duke of Brunswick.

THURSDAY, JAN. 29.—Hinuber, Hanoverian resident, arrives from the Hague. Write to Count Walmoden, through Marshal Freyberg. Hinuber with me—gives me an account of what passed at the Hague up to the 18th—all lost—Despatch an estafette to Brunswick with this account to be shewn to the Hereditary Princess. Assembly at Madame de Reden's. Sup at Court. Receive an estafette from Lord H. Spencer, with information that he has obtained leave for the giving out of grain and forage from East Friesland.

FRIDAY, JAN. 30th.—Count Kielmansegge with me—talk over the situation of the Electorate—the danger of a French invasion, &c. I send Hunter to the head-quarters at two. Dinner at Arnsweldt. Marriage of his son. Write to Duke of Brunswick by Count Montjoye. Return to Arnsweldt's assembly.

SATURDAY, JAN. 31.—Write to Prince Salm, Van Goens, &c.

With Princess of Wales to choose presents for this Court—tedious and disagreeable office. No event.

SUNDAY, FEB. 1.—Estafette from Duke of Brunswick. Letter from Stampfort. Kielmansegge with me at half past 11. Settle about means of writing to England. Münchausen. Court in evening.

MONDAY, FEB. 2.—Lady ——* presented Bagwell and Cailey, Irish. Timms returns from Embden. Rivers frozen—no getting away. Letters from Paget and Captain Popham.† Prince Ernest of Strelitz offers to go to Berlin to speak to the King of Prussia—eager and zealous. Letters from Leuthe to say King of Prussia is determined to defend Westphalia. Write to Duke of Brunswick, Hereditary Princess, and Stampfort by Colonel Richardson. Tea at Madame Busche's. Visit President Walmoden.

TUESDAY, FEB. 3.—Long walk. Austrian couriers in the evening—write by them to England through Embden. Prince Ernest hesitates about going in consequence of my letters, which announce the Treaty at Basle‡ at an end—Princess too childish, and over merry at supper.

WEDNESDAY, FEB. 4.—With Münchausen to various jewellers. No event. Prince Ernest goes to Brunswick and Berlin. Count d'Alberg presented.

FEB. 5, 6, 7, 8.—No event—usual life. Several letters from Duke of Brunswick.

---

* Name illegible in MS.
† Captain Popham, afterwards Sir Home Popham, was actively engaged in facilitating the retreat of our army in Holland, especially in passing the Waal.
‡ Then going on with the French Convention.

MONDAY, FEB. 9.—Dinner at Court. Kielmansegge and Steinberg with me in the afternoon—explain to them my fears as to sincerity of Prussia. Write to General Harcourt—entreat him not to suffer the Austrians to move from his left, under the reliance that the Prussians would supply their place. Steinberg writes the same to General Walmoden.

---

WEDNESDAY, FEB. 11.—Dinner at Marshal Reden's. At 11, Court and drawing-room.

---

THURSDAY, FEB. 12.—Despatch Timms to Embden. Servant from Lord H. Spencer. Despatch Vanscheick to overtake Timms. Grand Marshal Waggenheim drunk generally after dinner—his manners and conversation odd.

---

SATURDAY, FEB. 14.—Hunter returns from army. Harcourt and Walmoden not well together.

---

SUNDAY, FEB. 15.—Regency inform me of their intention to send to Basle. Kalitcheff arrives—his account of Holland.

---

MONDAY, FEB. 16.—My letter of the 16th to the Hereditary Princess of Brunswick. Prince Ernest of Strelitz returns from Berlin; he saw the King once alone. His Prussian Majesty as usual *speaks* fairly—*promises* well—talks *war*. Prince Henry, whom he saw afterwards, talks *peace*—says that the whole plan is his; that it meets with rubs and difficulties, but that it will answer. Prince Ernest praises Prince Royal. On the whole he appeared to have done well, and not to have been taken in at Berlin.

---

TUESDAY, FEB. 17.—Walk with Kalitcheff. Re-despatch Lord H. Spencer's servant. Write to Brunswick. Cassino in the evening—dullish and ordinary.

WEDNESDAY, FEB. 18.—Hinuber with me. News of ships from England—Princess and Prince of Orange got safe. Send Vanscheick with this intelligence to Brunswick at 11 P.M. Argument with the Princess about her toilette. She piques herself on dressing quick; I disapprove this. She maintains her point; I however desire Madame Busche to explain to her that the Prince is very delicate, and that he expects a long and very careful *toilette de propreté*, of which she has no idea. On the contrary, she neglects it sadly, and is offensive from this neglect. Madame Busche executes her commission well, and the Princess comes out the next day well washed *all over*.

THURSDAY, FEB. 19.—Dinner at Court. Assembly at Beulwitz's. Supper at Madame Walmoden's. Letters from England by Cuxhaven. We are to go by Stade. My conduct approved at home.

FRIDAY, FEB. 20.—Despatch estafette to Hereditary Princess of Brunswick. Dinner and concert at Court. Princess out of humour. Very nonsensical confidence about Prince of Orange—cannot be committed to writing—must recollect it, as well as my answer and advice. Duchess unwell—retires before supper.

MONDAY, FEB. 23.—Stampfort from Brunswick. Prussia consents to peace on the terms proposed by France—infamous and incredible—Prince Henry's doing. Stampfort wants to go to England.

TUESDAY, FEB. 24.—Long conversation with Stampfort on the times. He very right. Reede wrong and a Jacobin. The Croys all arrive—call upon them.

WEDNESDAY, FEB. 25.—Bad news from the Ems and headquarters—enemy advance. Despatch Hunter to Osnabruck at 7.

THURSDAY, FEB. 26.—Despatch Sparrow to England by Cuxhaven—let Count Martange's son go with him. Enemy attack our outposts near Bentheim. General Vandamme to attempt to land with 6000 men at the mouth of the Ems—alarm and uneasiness here. Assembly at Madame Arnsweldt's.

FRIDAY, FEB. 27.—Count Kessels called on me. Sat for picture. Visited Mrs. Parkhurst. Dull dinner at Court. Concert. The Croys all there. The Princess pretty and pleasant. No event. Letter from Duke.

SATURDAY, FEB. 28.—Counts Westphalia and Kissels with me—the first full of questions—ignorant of what is passing. Comes from Hildesheim. Bishop wants to be included in the peace. Bishop of Wurtzburg dead. At Court to finish my picture. After dinner long and serious conversation with the Princess, on her manner of calling women by their plain name—of saying, " ma chère," " mon cœur," &c., and of *tutoying* when talking to them in German. She takes it right—prepare her for a still more serious conversation on the subject of Hereditary Prince of Orange. Kalitcheff comes home with me—he inquisitive, and as close as usual. Visit the Croys. Pleasant supper at Court.

SUNDAY, MARCH 1.—Duke de Croy with me—his misfortunes—his resources—his wishes—his politics—his desire to have Condé restored, &c.—a very good man, but helpless. At dinner Count Kielmansegge communicates to me a letter he received in the night from Münchausen, Grand Marshal of Brunswick, *written by the Duke's order* by him in the capacity of *Ministre d'état*—in which note it is said that Pichegru has orders from the Convention to pass the Ems and Weser, and take possession of this country. It goes on by recommending this Electorate to stipulate for a " neutrality," or put itself under the " protection" of the King of Prussia, the only Power that *can* protect it—as director of the circle of Westphalia, and as having weight with the French. Kielmansegge greatly alarmed. I tell him, that although I admit the information to be not void of foundation, and in itself very important, yet the immediate object of the note is *a trick* invented by Prussia, and supported by the Duke. That it certainly is wise for them here to be very much on their guard against the progress of the enemy, but also that it behoves them to be almost equally so against His Prussian Majesty, and those who are from habit, interest, or opinion, influenced by his Cabinet. That, therefore, before they take any decisive step, I beg them to consider it well over, particularly as they act without any advice from the King, which is not without its risk. From this day to that of our departure from Hanover, nothing passed to make a *diary* necessary. Our life was uniformly the same—the same company, same manners, same conversation. I had frequent opportunity of confirming what I have already said of the Princess Caroline. If she can get the better of a gossiping habit, of a desire to appear *très fine*, and of knowing what passes in the minds of those around, and of overhearing and understanding their secrets, and of *talking* about them, she will do very well; but this is very difficult. I make it the daily object of my conversation to urge upon her never to *stoop* to *private* concerns, *de vivre et laisser vivre*, to avoid remarks, and not to care what passes in society and in her neighbour's house—" Uno tonto sabe mas en su casa, que uno sabio en la de ageno"—a very excellent Spanish proverb. —I also took frequent opportunities of speaking very *seriously* to the Princess Caroline on her not showing due respect to the Duchess her mother, of her sneering and slighting her; and on this point I went perhaps beyond the bounds of *decorum*, as it appeared to me of the last consequence to make her feel, in the most strong manner, the necessity of her attending to *these sort of duties*. She *at first* took it amiss, but very soon after admitted the truth of what I said and observed.

On politics I had frequent conferences with the Regency, and two with Marshal Freyberg. They are without news or orders from England—are under the alternative of being overrun by France, or *protected* by Prussia. The Duke of Brunswick also writes to me daily almost on the times. He urges me in the strongest way possible to go to Berlin— spares no flattery or pains to make me feel the *impossibility* of anything being done without Prussia. He, *perhaps*, may be right; but *I* cannot consent to be engaged afresh in such a negotiation. The Duke sends me an account of what Hardenberg says, and I also receive nearly a similar one from Crawford at Frankfort. Hardenberg undertakes to lengthen out the negotiation at Basle till he hears from me, and eagerly recommends England to offer a subsidy to Prussia. I reply that I believe *him sincere*, but not his Court.

---

MARCH 6.—I receive letters from home, to say that the fleet to escort us is to go to Stade, and on the 9th it arrives. Mrs. Harcourt to attend the Princess—the former comes to Hanover from Osnabruck on the 16th. Sillily attended by two light-horsemen. She puts herself *professedly*, and I believe really *sincerely*, under my protection, and promises to follow my advice. I immediately see the Princess does not like her. Mrs. Harcourt gossips too much with the Duchess, who is with her all the morning.—Latter days at Hanover fair with the Princess—see the gardens belonging to General Walmoden, and to Mr. Hinuber at Marienwerder.

I had two conversations with the Princess Caroline. One on the toilette, on cleanliness, and on delicacy of speaking. On these points I endeavoured, as far as was possible for a *man*, to inculcate the necessity of great and nice attention to every part of dress, as well as to what was hid, as to what was seen. (I knew she wore coarse petticoats, coarse shifts, and thread stockings, and these never well washed, or changed often enough.) I observed that a long toilette was necessary, and gave her no credit for boasting that hers was a "*short*" one. What I could not say myself on this point, I got said through women; through Madame Busche, and afterwards through Mrs. Harcourt. It is remarkable how amazingly on this point her education has been neglected, and how much her mother, although an Englishwoman, was inattentive to it. My other conversation was on the Princess's speaking slightingly of the Duchess, being peevish towards her, and often laughing at her, or about her. On this point I talked *very seriously* indeed—said that nothing was so extremely improper, so *radically* wrong; that it was impossible, if she reflected a moment, that she should not be sorry for every thing of the kind which escaped, and I assured her it was the more improper from the tender affection the Duchess had for her. The Princess felt all this, and it made a temporary impression; but in this as on all other subjects, I have had but too many opportunities to observe that her heart is very, *very* light, unsusceptible of strong or lasting feelings. In some respects this may make her happier, but certainly not better. I however must say, that, on the idea being suggested to her by her father that I should remain on business in Germany, and not be allowed to attend her to England, she was most extremely afflicted even to tears, and spoke to me with a kindness and feeling I was highly gratified to find in her. Both she and the Duchess made very handsome presents on leaving Hanover. I supplied the Princess with 800 frederics d'or for this purpose, and took her receipt for them.

MARCH 24.—We leave Hanover—Duchess *very much afflicted*—Princess keeps up her spirits, takes leave of the ladies with grace and propriety. Pass through Möllendorff to Walsrode—eight hours on the road — first part bad—last better. Duke of Brunswick meets us there—two long political conferences with him; he communicates to me a letter of the 20th from Bishopswerder — civil, but mysterious. Another from the King of Prussia to him of the same date—very civil, and thanking him for his letters and memorials, and engaging him to continue giving his advice and opinion on public affairs. " Car quoique j'aie encore l'espoir (says the King) de donner la paix à mes sujets, il ne faut pas moins agir avec prudence et vigueur." Bishopswerder says in his letter, " Il est juste qu'on sache les sentiments de l'Angleterre, et j'en ferai mention au Roi." From all this, and from other information the Duke has received, he infers that, if England pleases, the negotiations at Basle may be broken off, and the Court of Berlin be had. The Duke strongly urges the wisdom of this measure, and its necessity, if we mean to have any success in carrying on the war.* He

* A report of this conversation Lord Malmesbury sent to Lord Grenville in a despatch.

does not take up the defence of Prussia,—on the contrary, he condemns and reprobates its conduct ; but he observes, and very truly, that it is a power which has 200,000 men, and worth *managing*. I admit the truth of this, but allege the little dependence which can be placed on the King of Prussia after what has passed. The difference between what he tells me, and what is said to Lord H. Spencer, and particularly in a ministerial Note drawn up in the most hostile manner and imperious tone ; the very harsh and overbearing conduct of the Prussian army in Westphalia towards ours, and the extreme insolence and misrepresentations of the civil officers in East Friesland, &c., as to our behaviour,—*all* this seems to me to denote such a strong and systematic intention to close with France, and break with England, that even, although I was ready to admit the King, and perhaps a few thinking and *uncorrupted* individuals, were inclined to renew with us, yet their weight would be insufficient to resist the general opinion. The Duke replied, that if any able and experienced English Minister was at Berlin, he would certainly succeed. Money, he said, must be employed, because he knew money would be taken. That in regard to the harsh tone in which the note I alluded to was drawn up, he would mention it to Bishopswerder; and he again pressed me on my return to state what he said, at least that England might not decide on false principles.

I asked him what *he* himself would do, and whether *he* would take the command. " Not if the King goes ; c'est impossible que je m'expose de nouveau à toutes les avanies que j'ai eues sur le Rhin ; le Roi perd la moitié de la journée à la parole et à ses repas ; il ne sait pas *qu'à la guerre*—il ne faut donner qu'un moment à chaque chose." I never saw the Duke so open, so decidedly eager, or so ready to give a clear and distinct opinion. He said *he* was ready to do anything, and authorized me to say so. He added, he wished I would return to Berlin, or come with him if he was employed ; and he said every possible flattering thing to me he could. On talking about his daughter, he said, " All his domestic happiness depended on her doing well; that he was infinitely obliged to me for what I had done, and entreated me not to forsake her when in England." The Duke then thanked me for having promised to print in England an account General Stampfort had drawn up under *his eye*, and with *his* approbation, of his campaigns in Champagne. It was a kind of answer to Dumouriez. *He* said much more could have been added, but he only wished to defend himself, not to criminate *others*,—and by *others* he meant the King of Prussia. I received this work from General Stampfort on the 21st of March, with directions how it should be printed.

Wednesday, March 25.—At half-past eight, got through Rottenberg to Closterseven at seven—slept at the curate's.

Thursday, March 26.—Left Closterseven at nine. Timms arrived from the army. Got to Stade at four. Burghers under arms. Magistrates at the gates. Mr. Ende the Minister at the door of his house. Many presentations—Commodore Payne, Captains Lechmere, Stopford, and Legge. I lodged at First Counsellor's—good, but dampish house. Conversation with Payne.[*] Fixed our departure for the 28th.

Friday, March 27.—Walked round the ramparts—very pleasant. Stade like a Dutch town—large. Calonne[†]—great dinner and supper.

Saturday, March 28.—Leave Stade at seven. Streets lined by the burghers under arms. Embark on the Schwinde in Hanoverian boats—by nine reach the Fly cutter—sail towards the mouth of the river till half-past twelve—beyond Gluckstadt (Danish town) on the right—wind slackens—obliged to get into the boat—row for three hours—cutter overtakes us—get on board again—about two miles from the squadron get into man-of-war's barge. Royal salute at a distance—yards manned—royal standard hoisted on the

[*] Commonly called Jack Payne, and a favourite companion of the Prince of Wales.  [†] The Ex-Bourbon Minister, then in exile.

barge. At seven got on board the Jupiter, fifty-gun ship—
royal salute from the Jupiter returned by the fleet. Very
fine evening, and fine sight. Dinner. Officers presented.
(Madame Waggenheim, Grand Marshal, and Münchausen,
attend the Princess to Cuxhaven—they leave us at eight.)
Petition from Lady Gilford—Stopford good enough to take
her;—from Colonel Richardson and various French—refuse
Duchess of Fitzjames, also Mrs. Parkhurst. Kinckel on
board the Jupiter—Mrs. Fitzgerald, Sir B. Boothby, and
Hislop, on board other different ships in the fleet. Impossible to be more cheerful, more *accommodante*, more
everything that is pleasant, than the Princess—no difficulty,
no childish fears—all good-humour.

SUNDAY, MARCH 29.—Despatch Hunter and Scott (messengers) to England. Got under weigh at nine with a S.E.
wind—sea smooth—got clear of the Elbe by three—at
seven off Heligoland, the only land to mark the mouths of
the Elbe and Weser. Weather charming. Princess delighted
with the ships, and the officers greatly pleased with her
manners and good-humour.

MONDAY, MARCH 30.—Wind still fair—sea smooth. Nobody sick. Off the Texel by four.

TUESDAY, MARCH 31.—From the noon of the preceding
day to noon to-day, we ran 122 miles west, and 66 south,
without any motion, and living precisely as in a good house.
Two or three French privateers were discovered this morning
and chased—it became foggy.

WEDNESDAY, APRIL 1.—Still foggy. Cast anchor in the
night at about eight leagues from Orfordness, between that
and Yarmouth. Wind fair, but the mist so thick as to make
it impossible to proceed, for fear of the flats. Long and
frequent conversations with Jack Payne about the Prince

and Lady ——. He against her—and her behaviour, by
his account, very far from proper—his account of her tricks
to get aboard the yachts—her behaviour at Rochester.—
Prince's weakness.—Talk to Princess about delicacy in her
language. English more nice than foreigners. Never to
talk of being sick, &c. With Mrs. Harcourt on various
subjects—she good and very right, but a very mean courtier,
to a fulsome degree.

THURSDAY, APRIL 2.—Fog still—no moving. The Amphion
passes by with the convoy from Embden with the sick—she
salutes. Payne and I go on board the Phaeton, Captain
Stopford. Lady Gilford very sick—her clothes left behind.
Princess and Mrs. Harcourt send her linen, &c. Phaeton
about 300 yards from the Jupiter. Sea smooth. Stopford
returns our visit in the evening. Lieutenant ——,* on
board the Jupiter, has been seventeen years lieutenant! Fog
continues. Princess unwell—*malaise*. Conversation with
Mrs. Harcourt after supper about the Regency—she *exaltée*
—servile courtier, &c.

APRIL 3.—GOOD FRIDAY.—Weather clears at four in the
morning—get under weigh—fine wind, E.S.E.—land at five
leagues distant—sail at nine knots an hour—pass Harwich
at eleven. Send Timms in a cutter to announce our arrival.
All the ships up—charming sight. Anchored and passed
the night at the Nore.

SATURDAY, APRIL 4.—Sail early—enter the Thames—
anchor off Gravesend at two P.M.—each shore of the Thames
lined with spectators. The day fine, and the whole prospect
most beautiful.

SUNDAY, APRIL 5.—At eight the Princess got into the
royal yacht (Augusta)—pleasant and prosperous sail to
Greenwich, where we arrive at twelve o'clock. The king's
coaches not yet arrived, owing, as I have since heard, to

---

* Name illegible in MS. It is to be hoped that if a long and *hot* war could
not obtain promotion for this gentleman, his approximation to *Royalty* now procured it for him.

Lady —— not being ready; she, Mrs. Aston, and Lord Claremont, came to meet the Princess. We waited at least an hour for the carriages, and were very attentively but awkwardly received by Sir W. Pattison, Governor of the Hospital, and his two sisters. Lady —— very much dissatisfied with the Princess's mode of dress, though Mrs. Harcourt had taken great pains about it, and expressed herself in a way which induced me to speak rather sharply to her. She also said she could not set backwards in a coach, and hoped she might be allowed to sit *forward:* this (though Mrs. Harcourt was servile enough to admit as a reason), as it was strictly forbidden by the King, I most decidedly opposed, and told Lady —— that, as she must have known that riding backward in a coach disagreed with her, she ought never to have accepted the situation of a Lady of the Bedchamber, who never ought to sit forward; and that if she *really* was likely to be sick, I would put Mrs. Aston into the coach with the Princess, and have, by that means, the pleasure of Lady ——'s company in the carriage allotted to me and Lord Claremont. This of course settled the business; she and Mrs. Harcourt, according to the King's direction, sat backward, and the Princess sat by herself forward. There was very little crowd, and still less applause on the road to London, where we arrived and were set down at St. James's (the Duke of Cumberland's apartments, Cleveland Row) about half-past two.

I immediately notified the arrival to the King and Prince of Wales; the last came immediately. I, according to the established etiquette, introduced (no one else being in the room) the Princess Caroline to him. She very properly, in consequence of my saying to her it was the right mode of proceeding, attempted to kneel to him. He raised her (gracefully enough) and embraced her, said barely one word, turned round, retired to a distant part of the apartment, and calling me to him, said, "Harris, I am not well; pray get me a glass of brandy." I said, "Sir, had you not better have a glass of water?"—upon which he, much out of humour, said, with an oath, "*No;* I will go directly to the Queen;" and away he went. The Princess, left during this short moment alone, was in a state of astonishment; and, on my joining her, said, "Mon Dieu! est ce que le Prince est toujours comme cela ? Je le trouve très gros, et nullement aussi beau que son portrait." I said His Royal Highness was naturally a good deal affected and flurried at this first interview, but she certainly would find him different at dinner. She was disposed to farther criticisms on this occasion, which would have embarrassed me very much to answer, if luckily the King had not ordered me to attend him.

The drawing-room was just over. His Majesty's conversation turned wholly on Prussian and French politics; and the only question about the Princess was, " Is she good-humoured?" I said, and very truly, that in very trying moments, I had never seen her otherwise. The King said, "I am glad of it ;" and it was manifest, from his silence, he had seen the Queen *since* she had seen the Prince, and that the Prince had made a very unfavourable report of the Princess to her. At dinner, at which all those who attended the Princess from Greenwich assisted, and the honours of which were done by Lord Stopford as Vice-Chamberlain, I was far from satisfied with the Princess's behaviour; it was flippant, rattling, affecting raillery and wit, and throwing out coarse vulgar hints about Lady ———, who was present, and though mute, *le diable n'en perdait rien.* The Prince was evidently disgusted; and this unfortunate dinner fixed his dislike, which, when left to herself, the Princess had not the talent to remove; but, by still observing the same giddy manners and attempts at cleverness and coarse sarcasm, increased it till it became positive hatred.

From this time, though I dined frequently during the first three weeks after the marriage at Carlton House, nothing material occurred ; but the sum of what I saw there led me to draw the inferences I have just expressed. After one of these dinners, where the Prince of Orange was present, and at which the Princess had behaved very lightly, and even improperly, the Prince took me into his closet, and asked me how I liked this sort of manners. I could not conceal my disapprobation of them, and took this opportunity of repeating to him the substance of what the Duke of Brunswick had so often said to me—that it was expedient *de la tenir serrée;* that she had been brought up very strictly, and if she was not strictly kept, would, from high spirits and little thought, certainly emancipate too much. To this the Prince said, "I see it but too plainly ; but why, Harris, did not you tell me so before, or write it to me from Brunswick ?" I replied, that I did not consider what the Duke (a severe father himself towards his children) said of sufficient consequence—that it affected neither the Princess's moral character nor conduct, and was intended solely as an intimation which I conceived it only proper to notice to His Royal Highness at a proper occasion, at such a one as now had offered, and that I humbly hoped His Royal Highness would not consider it as casting any *real* slur or aspersion on the Princess ; that as to not writing to His Royal Highness from Brunswick, I begged him to recollect I was not sent on a *discretionary* commission, but with the *most positive commands to ask Princess Caroline in marriage, and nothing more;* that to this sole point, respecting the marriage, and no other, those commands went ; any reflection or remarks that I had presumed to make would (whether in praise of, or injurious to Her Royal Highness) have been a direct and positive deviation from those His Majesty's commands. They were as *limited* as they were *imperative.* That still, had I discovered notorious or glaring defects, or such as were of a nature to render the union unseemly, I should have felt it as a bounden duty to have stated them ; but it must have been *directly to the King,* and to no one else. To this the Prince appeared to acquiesce ; but I saw it did not please, and left a *rankle* in his mind.

I should have said, that the marriage ceremony took place late on the evening of Wednesday, the 8th of April, at St. James's Chapel Royal. The ceremony was performed by the Archbishop of Canterbury (Moore). The usual etiquette observed — we had assembled in the Queen's apartment ; from thence to the usual drawing-rooms (very dark). The procession, preceded by the heralds and great officers of the Court (amongst which I was ordered to attend)—walked to the chapel—very crowded—Prince of Wales gave his hat, with a rich diamond button and loop, to Lord Harcourt to hold, and made him a present of it. After the marriage we returned to the Queen's apartment. The King told me to wear the Windsor uniform, and have the *entrées*. The Prince very civil and gracious; but I thought I could perceive he was not quite sincere, and certainly unhappy; and, as a proof of it, he had manifestly had recourse to wine or spirits.

It is impossible to conceive or foresee any comfort from this connection, in which I lament very much having taken any share, purely *passive* as it was.

[It appears from many private passages in the Harris papers that Lord Malmesbury had more than once been on the point of expressing his opinion to Lord Grenville or Mr. Pitt of the probable unsuitableness of the Princess Caroline's personal habits and manners with the tastes of the Prince of Wales; but that the circumstances of his mission, and his belief that her faults were of a remediable character, determined him to execute his instructions implicitly. He had received these whilst he was still abroad from the *King himself*, without any interview with Ministers, or any discretionary power. He had no confidential friend at Brunswick by whom he could convey *verbally* to any person in England the doubts he entertained. When, added to this, he found the proposal of marriage had been privately broken to the Duke of Brunswick *before* he was sent there, and that the faults of the Princess did not (as far as he knew) affect her fame, he decided on declining the responsibility of an advice, that must (if followed) have raised a host of enemies against him at both Courts and in this country, and which being a mere matter of taste and opinion, he could only have maintained as such.]

[The following letters are extracted from Lord Malmesbury's correspondence at Brunswick. I have preferred subjoining them to interrupting the foregoing narrative by inserting them according to their date.]

LETTER FROM HIS ROYAL HIGHNESS THE PRINCE OF WALES TO
LORD MALMESBURY.

My dear Lord,—I have sent Major Hislop back again to Brunswick, which I judged to be an advisable measure on many accounts, as more particularly, I think, he may prove, from his knowledge of the country, a very useful *avant courier* to you and your fair charge in your journey to the water's side. I have charged him with letters for the Duke, Duchess, and Princess, which I will beg of you to present to their different destinations, with every proper expression on my part, and to which no one can give so agreeable a *tournure* as yourself.

I have likewise desired Major Hislop to give you an ample and thorough account of the steps I have taken towards the expediting everything on this side of the water, as well as with my brother the Duke of York, to whom I have written also by Hislop ; and as to what is now necessary to forward the completing everything at Brunswick, I must leave that to you, hoping that you will make every exertion possible to put the Princess in possession of her own home as near the 20th of the ensuing month as possible, for everything that can create delay at the present moment is bad on every account, but particularly so to the public, whose expectations have now been raised for some months, and would be quite outrageous, were it possible for them to perceive any impediment arising to what they have had their attention drawn to for so long a time, besides the suspense, and the naturally unpleasant feelings attendant upon suspense, which I myself must be subject to, and the very honourable, fair, and handsome manner in which the Duke and Duchess have both conducted themselves to me in this transaction ; their having also in their last letters, both to the King and me, said that the Princess was ready to set off instantly ; in short, all these reasons make it necessary for me, my dear Lord, to desire you to press your departure from Brunswick at as short a date as possible from the receipt of this letter. I have written fully to the Duchess upon the subject, and I doubt not but she will acquaint you with the contents of her letters, as I desire that you will have the goodness to do so by her, by shewing her, or acquainting her nearly of the purport of this letter.

I should think the travelling through Holland still practicable and safe, and if so, certainly preferable on every account; but if not, we then must have recourse to the Elbe, which is certainly a very disagreeable alternative; however, whichever way the Princess is to come, I am clear it should be determined upon instantly by you. I wish most certainly, if possible, that she should pass through Holland, if it is still upon the cards; therefore desire you to determine, if you can, upon that. We cannot tell on this side the water as well as you can, or rather as Hislop can, after his communication with the Duke of York; and you will then be able, when you have seen the Major, and know what has passed between him and the Duke, to fix your plan *immediately, and so immediately put it into execution.* According to our calculation, Hislop ought to be at Brunswick the 8th; I therefore trust that by the 16th I shall from you, my dear Lord, receive an account of your having fixed the day of your departure, and not only of the probability, but indeed of the certainty of your being many miles on your journey. There are some other particular circumstances which might not be so proper or so safe to commit to paper, which I have entrusted Major Hislop with, and which he will communicate by word of mouth to you. I will not detain you, my dear Lord, any longer, except to assure you how happy I was in having this opportunity of testifying the very sincere regard I entertain for you, as well as those sentiments with which I remain, &c. GEORGE P.

Carlton House, 23rd Nov., 1794.

---

LETTER FROM LORD MALMESBURY TO LORD ST. HELENS.

Brunswick, 25th Nov., 1794.

I AGREE most entirely with you, my dear Lord, that the instructions brought me by Fabiani[*] were nearly unexe-

[*] Lord Malmesbury was instructed to use every means to induce the Duke of Brunswick to accept the command of the allied armies.

cutable, and the result of my attempt to carry them into effect justifies very fully our apprehensions. I found the business prepared, and indeed almost done, by Elliot and Stampford; and the Duke has from the beginning invariably rested his consent on the certainty of being at the head of a large body of Prussians. This cannot be obtained or asked; neither was such a measure practicable, should I advise the trying of it, as it would put the whole direction into the hands of the Court of Berlin, and place us in a situation of still stricter dependence on it than we have been this year; but I will not repeat what I have written in my official letters, the substance of which I beg you to communicate to the Prince and Princess, and Pensionary. I am *now* in favour of Reede's plan; it is like all those of his invention, made in the closet, without any knowledge of what is passing beyond and out of it, and without any reference to it; he collects his military notions through his brother-in-law Kreusemark,* who is with Möllendorff, and his political ones from his secretary Bordeaux, who is much better qualified from his principles to be Secretary to the Convention, than to be a Minister from their High Mightinesses. If, however, he could induce Holland to subsidize singly 30,000 Prussians, I should be well content, as it will leave us at liberty to dabble with Austria.

I fear before we can do anything, or take any provisional step for the present security of your republic, that the pusillanimity of our friends, and the activity of our adversaries within it, joined to the dissensions and discouragement which prevail in our army, will produce the catastrophe, and that the scene will close by a shameful accommodation, a conquest, or what is precisely the same, a forced surrender. The Duke insists that with common prudence, and with the smallest military knowledge, it is impossible for the enemy to penetrate any farther; but whether it be *his real* opinion, or only given in order to make it appear that his refusal to go to Holland is not so important from his presence not being so necessary, I cannot pretend to say. Nor, indeed, *do I ever know whether he is sincere or not.* I am only sure that his passion is to be at the head of an

* Afterwards Prussian Envoy at Napoleon's Court.

army, and that the declining it in the way he does, must be produced by some more powerful reason (at least to his mind) than what he thinks proper to allege. We hear the Silesian division, which were under march from the Rhine towards Gotha, are ordered to return. This gives pleasure here, but I conceive (if it means anything) it is only to have the more powerful means at hand to force the Austrians to make peace, and that we shall see Prussia appear as an armed Mediator, and *my* utmost wish is to see all the Prussians back and quiet in their own territories.

I feel for your situation in Holland; I know how helpless and cold our friends are in times of danger and difficulty. Try to make them brush through the winter, and to give us the chance of what may happen in France, where there are an hundred indications of the disgust of the war, of the Government becoming feeble, and of internal divisions. I am in daily expectation of my credentials and full powers from England; in the meanwhile I have all the honours of my Mission, and am lodged at Court, and with Court attendants. I think our future Princess will do vastly well. I am uncertain the route we are to take. Is it safe to bring her through Holland? pray write to me on this point, on which you probably will also be consulted from home. May I trouble you to tell Bentinck, that the 100 bottles of old hock I purchased from him should be sent to Mr. Crawford, who will take charge of them for me, and send them on to England.

Adieu, my dear Lord. I hope Ministers have now given the *last* commission they mean to charge me with, and that I may be allowed to return to the only quiet spot in Europe, though at *this* moment, that is not very quiet.

I am, &c.   MALMESBURY.

---

LETTER FROM LORD MALMESBURY TO THE DUKE OF YORK.

Brunswick, Friday, Dec. 5, 1794.

SIR,—I beg leave to thank your Royal Highness most respectfully for your letters of the 28th by Major Hislop. Your sentiments and expressions relative to the Duke of

Brunswick's taking the command, are such as I have ever been accustomed to find in your Royal Highness's character. There is no chance, I believe, of moving the Duke from hence. He does not think differently about Prussia from your Royal Highness and myself, but he is under an habitual fear of the Court of Berlin, and will not take any step not promoted as well as authorized by it.

If I receive any positive and certain information, that the ships destined to escort the Princess of Brunswick to England are ordered to Helvoet before the 11th of this month, we shall set out on that day from hence; but of this I will give your Royal Highness timely information by a messenger. It is impossible for me to take my departure before I receive this information, as I am tied down by the most precise instructions, and as from a letter from Mr. Burgess, there seems an appearance that *Stade* will be the port fixed on by the King.  I am, &c.  MALMESBURY.

---

LETTER FROM LORD MALMESBURY TO THE DUKE OF PORTLAND.

Brunswick, 5th Dec., 1794.

MY DEAR LORD,—Allow me to write to you in the double capacity of a Cabinet Minister and confidential friend. I cannot better explain to you the motive for my applying to you under these titles, than by enclosing you a letter I received from the Prince, and my answer. This letter was brought by a Major Hislop, (with whom I am unacquainted,) and this officer, in addition to what the Prince writes, strongly urged in his name my immediate departure from hence with the Princess, and that I should proceed with her without loss of time through Holland. I have resisted this proposition from the reasons I have assigned. I am here under the *King's* immediate command, and cannot act but by his special order. Everybody will, I am confident, feel this but the Prince; and nobody, I believe, but the Prince would have placed me in the predicament in which I now stand, by conveying to me his wishes, or rather his orders, without having previously communicated with His Majesty's Ministers, and having it in his power to say to me he wrote under their sanction. If he should be displeased with me for a non-compliance with these wishes, I only have to entreat your Grace to justify me, when any justification may be necessary. I have in my official letters mentioned the substance, or rather outlines, of this business, but I did not think them a proper mode for entering fully into it. I most heartily join with the Prince in his earnest desire to see the Princess at Carlton House, but sincere and strong as this desire is on my part, I cannot stir from hence but by the King's order.

I am sure you will enter into my feelings on this occasion, which puts me in mind of several other situations in which I have been placed of a similar nature from the same quarter, and that you will excuse my communicating them to you. I trust by Christmas to pay my respects to you at Burlington House. I am, &c. MALMESBURY.

LETTER FROM LORD MALMESBURY TO LORD GRENVILLE.

Brunswick, 23rd Dec., 1794.

MY DEAR LORD,—I can venture to say that you may depend on the authenticity of the information I have enclosed in my official letter.* It proves at once as many bad political qualities in Prussia as can possibly exist at the same time in the same Power,—weakness, perfidy, insolence, avarice, and folly, and all of these come forward in their turn and appear in Haugwitz's conversations with Paget. I cannot resist the desire of writing him one more strong letter before I leave the Continent. I expect no good whatever from it, but it is some sort of satisfaction in return for their conduct, that its duplicity and folly should stand upon record in a manner not to be contested.

I need only say how impatient we all are here to get away, nor how many puzzling and distressing questions I am asked on this side of the water, and how many pressing instances I receive from the other.† It *ought* to be felt that I can-

* The substance of this despatch may be gathered from the foregoing Diary.
† The Prince of Wales continued to press Lord Malmesbury to bring over

not stir without His Majesty's commands, and that the negotiation with which I am now charged is as much a State affair as any Treaty whatever. I fear, however, this is not the case, and that on my return I shall be exposed to a little ill-humour for not having obeyed a summons it was against my duty to listen to. I am, &c. MALMESBURY.

---

LETTER FROM LORD MALMESBURY TO THE PRINCE OF WALES.

Brunswick, Tuesday, 23rd Dec., 1794.

SIR,—I was in great hopes that my letter of the 17th would have been the last I should have had the honour of writing to your Royal Highness from hence; but although I am in daily expectation of orders, none are yet arrived, and the sharp frost and easterly wind, now set in, may prevent my receiving them for some time. I can only repeat, Sir, that on this side of the water no delay has arisen or will arise, and that not an hour shall be lost, whenever it shall please His Majesty's Ministers to inform me to what place I am to conduct the Princess, a point which was certainly not determined on the 9th instant, the date of my last letters from England.

The impatience of the Princess to get away is evidently her governing feeling; but it is tempered with so much good-humour and cheerfulness, that it is impossible not to consider her behaviour on this occasion as the most amiable possible.

I am myself so very anxious that your Royal Highness should find every principle of happiness, that my judgment may be a little warped by my wishes; but I am sure I must have lost every power of discernment, if there does not exist in the mind of the Princess the most fixed intention to make your happiness the study of her life, and in her heart every affection to promote it.

I am, &c. MALMESBURY.

---

the Princess; but as he had the King's command not to move until he received positive instructions to that effect, he refused to do so.

## EXTRACTS OF A LETTER FROM LORD MALMESBURY TO THE HON. A. PAGET.

Brunswick, 25th Dec., 1794.

A DUTCH messenger charged with letters from the Prince of Orange to Baron Reede, gives me an early opportunity of thanking you for your letter by Dressins, who passed through here on Tuesday. I detained him only a few hours. Your despatch to Lord Grenville cannot fail of doing you credit; you have done everything that prudence and ability could devise, and you have stated it in the clearest and fairest manner possible. The Court of Berlin is working its *own* destruction, and all we have to do is to avoid being buried under its ruins. The enclosed paper* (on the veracity of which you may rely) will perhaps give you more accurate information on the state of the negotiation, and the manner in which it is conducted, than you will have it in your power to collect at Berlin. The Dutch, who are panic-struck, have on their side been also weak enough to enter into *pour-parlers* with the French, and two persons of the name of Branken (formerly Ambassador at Paris) and Rysselaer, are going to Bois-le-Duc to have a conference with La Combe for a separate peace. There is little doubt that both these disgraceful overtures will end in nothing but to expose the iniquity and folly of those who have made them; and that the only reason for their being listened to on the part of the French, is in order to gain time for their own hostile preparations, and to prevent those of the Combined Powers, by amusing them with the prospect of pacification they neither can, nor mean to give them. The Stadtholder and Princess of Orange see all this with extreme repugnance; but I fancy that Reede (who is generally actuated by confined and selfish motives) has gone very warmly into the idea; and, from

---

* Containing an account of the secret negotiation opened by Prussia with the French Convention. Lord Malmesbury never lost an opportunity of sending to official persons any information which could possibly be useful to them, either in their military or civil capacity. I have no room to print these letters, which, perhaps, show as much activity and patriotism as any of his more public services; they doubtless tended much to obtain the reputation he enjoyed among his contemporaries.

what I learn, the principal reason for sending him this messenger, is to repress his ardour on this occasion, and to entreat him not to move faster in a matter of such magnitude than his instructions authorize him to do.

I am myself so convinced that peace is, first of all, impossible; and, secondly, (that if it were possible) that it would be the most fatal and ruinous measure which could be adopted; that although I am fully persuaded, that nothing which can be said or done by me, is at all likely to produce the smallest effect at Berlin; yet, in order to liberate my own conscience, and to acquit myself of my last political duty before I return to England, I have written the enclosed letter* and reflections to Haugwitz. You will be good enough to fasten the seal, and either send or give them to him. It is my wish they should get to the King, as I cannot but believe many official papers I gave in at Frankfort have been suppressed, and that His Majesty is not fairly and fully kept informed of what has passed and is passing. I say I cannot but believe this, because his present conduct is in direct contradiction to what, not ten months ago, he assured me *ten times a day* to be his invariable principles, founded on what he considered the welfare, dignity, and safety of his Monarchy to rest. If, therefore, you can, by any indirect channel, convey to the King that such a letter is in Haugwitz's possession, it will probably move in him a curiosity to see it; and, indeed, unless Haugwitz is as much altered in his opinions as I suspect he is, he would be the first to show it to him.

In regard to the Duke of Brunswick, it certainly is not likely that he will be prevailed on to take the command, without being sure that such a measure would not expose him to the anger and resentment of Prussia; this, which is but a poor excuse for a great man, is, I am satisfied, his only motive; for he sees the conduct of that Court in the same light we do, and rails at it still more.

If you have a safe opportunity, pray write to me; these easterly winds may detain us here many days longer. You must not think, my dear Paget, of quitting the line. I am sure Lord Grenville will not allow you, as, without a com-

* A copy of this letter is not extant.

pliment, I believe your despatches to be much the best he receives from the Continent.

Is Nassau gone? Why and where? Two lines in *juice*\* to acknowledge this will greatly oblige me.

---

LETTER FROM LORD MALMESBURY TO LORD GRENVILLE.

Osnabruck, 4th Jan., 1795.

MY DEAR LORD,—I have acted on the present very anxious and distressing occasion, to the best of my judgment; were I travelling with my wife and children, I should have acted as I have now done. The frost is so intense, and wears every appearance of being so permanent, that I cannot but consider Holland as in the most imminent danger.† It would be blamable in the extreme were I to conduct the Princess into that country at such a moment, and without the certainty of having a fleet to convey her out of it. I hope all the circumstances will be taken into consideration, and not the single one of the road being safe as far as Utrecht. I have no doubt about this, but my doubts are on the risks and uneasiness to which the Princess will be exposed when she is there, and during the remainder of her stay and journey in that country. If we have a thaw, or if I was sure Commodore Payne was at the Texel, I should not demur; but neither is likely, and I cannot but fear that it will be found that the only safe and secure mode of conveying the Princess to England is by Stade, and that to do this, we must wait till the mouth of the Elbe is free from ice.

On any other occasion I should certainly not make *extreme* prudence and precaution the governing principle of my conduct; but on this, I ought not to have any other. My duty is to arrive *safe*, and not to sacrifice this circumstance to the wish of arriving *soon*. I hope this will be admitted and understood as the only rule by which I ought to act.

I am, &c. MALMESBURY.

\* Invisible until held before a fire.
† It need scarcely be mentioned that the inundations, which are Holland's safeguard against an enemy in open weather, become bridges to carry them over during a frost.

LETTER FROM LORD MALMESBURY TO THE PRINCE OF WALES.

Osnabruck, 4th Jan., 1795.

SIR,—In order to lose no time in despatching the messenger who is charged with this letter for your Royal Highness, I take the liberty of enclosing a copy of the despatch I have written by him this day to Lord Grenville, in which I have stated fully and distinctly the different motives on which I have grounded my conduct. I am most anxious that it should have your Royal Highness's approbation in a measure where the trust was so very important, and where so much was left to my own judgment. I could not conceive a safer rule to go by, than to place myself in a similar situation to that in which I now stand with my children and family, and had this been the case, I certainly should have acted as I now have done. My apprehensions for Holland are very great, and the same easterly wind that produces the frost also keeps the fleet from arriving at the Texel; and were I to undertake to recommend their Royal Highnesses to go as far as Utrecht, I should expose them to all the uneasiness and disquietude attendant on an invaded country, probably to insult, and possibly to danger in the extreme, since it would almost be as difficult to retrograde, or regain a place of security on this side, as to attempt to cross the sea.

Till, therefore, I can be satisfied that the fleet is at the Texel, and that the attempts of the enemy to penetrate into Holland on the side of Goree or by the Moerdyk (should it be frozen, as it probably is,) have failed, I shall not feel myself justified in my own mind, or acting up to the sense of the very high duty reposed on me, were I to move forward. The Princess Caroline and the Duchess of Brunswick, whose pleasure and commands I have taken on this point, agree in this decision. The first is too anxious to get safe to England, and expects too much happiness there to wish to leave anything to chance, and this consideration supersedes her extreme impatience to be at her journey's end.

I expect to-morrow or next day to receive fresh intelligence from Lord St. Helens; and your Royal Highness may be assured that not a minute shall be lost, and nothing of any kind delay our journey, but the considerations I have already mentioned, which are of a nature that cannot be too much attended to. I trust, by making them the rule of my conduct, I shall have acted in conformity to your Royal Highness's pleasure. I have, &c. MALMESBURY.

LETTER FROM LORD MALMESBURY TO THE PRINCE OF WALES.

Delden, Friday, Jan. 9th, 1795.

SIR,—Their Royal Highnesses were within a few leagues of Deventer when I was met by one of the messengers I had sent forward, who brought me a letter from Lord St. Helens written from the head-quarters this morning, saying that the French had again crossed the Waal in considerable force; that there had been an affair yesterday in which they had *not* been driven back, and that it was expected they would renew the attack to-day with increased numbers. He gave it me as his decided opinion, and as one in which General Harcourt concurs, that I must on *no account come into Holland*, but return immediately with the Princess to Osnabruck. This, Sir, as soon as I could read the letter, I directly recommended to them to do; and on Sunday we shall again be at that town, where I have written to Lord Grenville word that I shall remain till I know His Majesty's pleasure. I hope your Royal Highness will not disapprove my having come to this resolution. Nothing short of a miracle can save Holland; it will either be conquered or capitulate, and in either case it would be impossible to think of exposing the Princess to pass through it. I have as yet, too, no account whatever of the arrival of the squadron at Texel; and, without that certainty, nothing could justify my attempting to continue the route in the way originally proposed.

Osnabruck is as near Stade as it is to the Texel; and in case that port should be chosen, which I much fear must be the case, we cannot remain at a better or more becoming place.

It is impossible for me to describe to your Royal Highness how much I am hurt and vexed at these very unpleasant delays; but it is a great alleviation to my feelings to observe the great good-humour with which the Princess submits to them; at the same time that I can assure you, Sir, she feels them as strongly as if she had already the pleasure of knowing your Royal Highness.

I shall write again very soon, but I am at present so hurried to get away my messenger, whilst he can yet pass with impunity through Holland, that I fear what I write to-day will be very incorrect.

I am most anxious to know that your Royal Highness does not disapprove my conduct. I have left nothing untried to bring the Princess both *soon and safe* to England; but, when one of the two is to be given up, I should be very unfit for the high trust confided in me if I hesitated.

Mr. Elliot is so good as to promise me to go to the Texel, under chance of finding Commodore Payne arrived, and to explain to him our situation. I have likewise desired him to send on Mr. Anthony St. Leger* to me through Holland, which for a single man is a practicable road, as I shall want very much his aid and assistance. I hope this will not be blamed by your Royal Highness.

I am, &c.    MALMESBURY.

---

EXTRACTS OF A LETTER FROM LORD MALMESBURY TO THE DUKE OF PORTLAND.

Hanover, 27th Jan., 1795.

As it is very difficult for me to be *quite* explicit in an official letter as to *all* the reasons which determined me to bring the Princess Caroline back as far as this place, and to advise Her Royal Highness to remain at it till such time as I can receive His Majesty's further orders, allow me to mention them to you more fully in a private letter, and to entreat your Grace to make such use of them as your kind-

---

* Brother to the Prince's companion, Col. St. Leger; he was a great beau of his time, and remarkable as a good *dancer*.

ness for me will, I am sure, prompt you to do, in case my conduct on this occasion may seem reprehensible, and not sufficiently justified by what I have mentioned in my despatch of to-day. The proximity and character of the enemy, the probability of their coming on towards Westphalia, the establishment of the hospital, and the certainty that our army would soon fall back behind the Ems, would, of themselves, I trust, be considered sufficient reasons for removing the Princess from Osnabruck; but, in addition to these, the arrival of Count D'Artois, who, when we left it, was already as far as Bentheim on the road with his suite, operated very decidedly on my opinion; for, although I am very far from attributing either to him, or those who attend him, all those vices and dangerous follies which it was said belonged to them in their days of prosperity, yet I felt it highly improper that the Princess of Wales, and a fugitive French Prince, should remain in the same place; and I am sure the inconveniences which would have resulted from it cannot escape your observation.

I confess, also, I had a repugnance at putting His Royal Highness the Duke of York to so considerable an expense as that of maintaining, for any length of time, so numerous a Court as we formed; for although nothing could be more attentive than the conduct of his household and ministers there, and although I know enough of the Duke's liberal temper of mind to be sure this would not a moment weigh with him, yet it *did* not become me to forget it, and it ought to and *did* influence my conduct. These reasons for leaving Osnabruck will, I hope, be considered as valid ones. Two places only remained to which I could conduct the Princess, either Brunswick or this. In regard to the first, I have, in my public letter, only stated that (considered as a measure) I knew it would be unpleasant to the Duke; and the carrying a Princess, circumstanced as the Princess Caroline is, back to her own Court, after the ceremonies which had passed, and she had formally taken leave of it, appeared to me one which would be liable to many disagreeable animadversions and remarks. Writing to your Grace confidentially, I can add that many other very powerful objections occurred to me against placing

Her Royal Highness again in the situation in which she stood at Brunswick. It was one perfectly dissimilar to that she is about to fill; it was a subordinate one and of great restraint, and where her mind had not fair play; where it never could act for itself, where it was governed severely, not guided gently; where she had formed and contracted habits and manners; and where the ladies, never expecting to see the Princess called up to the high station she is now going to assume, had allowed themselves towards her habits of familiarity and easy intimacy always pernicious in their effects from the gossiping to which they lead, and very different from that respectful and distant attention she is entitled to, which certainly will be shewn her in England, and to which I have it very much at heart she should get accustomed, and feel as right and indispensable before she arrives there.

Everything that I have taken the liberty to say has gone to this point, as the one which has been the least attended to in her education; for, in my judgment, the happiness of the Prince, as well as her own, I will even add, that of the country, rest in a great measure, in times like these, in her feeling properly the dignity of her high situation and acting up to it, and in understanding that, if this is painful to her, it is the price she is to pay for its pre-eminence. Her own good sense, of which she really and truly has a considerable share, has induced her to listen to this advice, and to feel its consequence; and, since we have left Brunswick, the manner in which she has conducted herself towards those who have come to pay their court to her has been the most becoming possible. To carry her back there would be to place Her Royal Highness in a position where she could not follow it up, and where she necessarily must resume her former customs and behaviour, which, although perfectly unexceptionable and innocent, are by no means those calculated for the rank of a Princess of Wales. Hanover is the contrary of all this. The manners of the Court are uncommonly proper and decorous; those who compose it are of a most respectable character; and, before I brought the Princess here, I was certain she would be received in a way she never yet had been used to, and one which would give those impressions I so anxiously wish her to receive. My expectations have been fully justified. The Princess Caroline is here received and treated exactly as a Princess of Wales Elect ought to be treated ; and I am convinced that, all things considered, the delay in our arrival is a most fortunate circumstance, and that the two months or more which will elapse from the time of our leaving Brunswick till that of our landing in England will form and shape the Princess's mind and manners to her situation, and give her a more exact sense of it than if the journey from the Palace at Brunswick to Carlton House had been performed with all the expedition we originally wished for.

I have been insensibly led to say more on the subject than was my intention when I began my letter, which was simply to explain the motives of my own conduct.

LETTER FROM LORD MALMESBURY TO THE COUNT DE WALMODEN.

Hanovre, ce 29 Janvier, 1795.

MONS. LE COMTE,—J'ai eu l'honneur de recevoir par le courier Hunter, votre lettre en date le 24ᵉ, le 27ᵉ, à sept heures du matin. J'ai expédié sur l'heure celle que vous avez insérée pour le Duc de Bronswic par un exprès, et j'ai envoyé d'abord les autres à leur adresse. Je pense que Votre Excellence aura déjà reçu la réponse du Duc ; il a eu la bonté de me la communiquer. Je la crois parfaite quant aux arrangemens militaires qu'il propose ; mais le ton de *Low Spirits* qui y règne me peine très sensiblement, et son idée de vouloir se transporter avec la famille au delà de l'Elbe n'est propre qu'à répandre de la consternation en cas qu'elle transpire, et d'ajouter aux embarras du jour déjà presqu'insupportables. Je viens de lui écrire une longue lettre, dans laquelle je cherche à le rassurer. Le silence du côté de Berlin devrait le fâcher et non pas l'abattre ; peut-être aussi sera-t-il rompu, dès que le Roi de Prusse soit informé de la manière dont la Convention a reçu ses ouvertures pour une pacification. Le Sieur Barthelemi a fait à Bâle à M. Goltze des propositions les plus insolentes et moins admissibles ; elles sont arrivées à Francfort par un chasseur le

23ᵉ, et le 26ᵉ à Berlin. Je vous supplie, Mons. le Comte, de vouloir bien disposer de moi dans toutes les occasions où je puis vous être utile, et surtout quand je pourrai vous prouver la haute considération et estime avec laquelle j'ai l'honneur, etc. MALMESBURY.

---

LETTER FROM LORD MALMESBURY TO THE DUKE OF BRUNSWICK.

Hanovre, ce 29 Janvier, 1795.

MONSEIGNEUR,—Mons. le Comte de Montjoye ayant remis son départ jusqu'après demain, et Mons. Hinuber, Ministre de l'Electeur de Hanovre en Hollande venant d'arriver de la Haye avec des informations qui pourraient intéresser Votre Altesse Sérénissime, et surtout Madame La Princesse Héréditaire, j'ai l'honneur de vous faire parvenir ces lettres par estafette.

Mons. Hinuber a quitté la Haye Dimanche le 18ᵉ courant : il a voyagé avec Mons. de Keller ; ils ont allongé les Dunes jusqu'à la Hollande. Ils sont restés à Enckhuysen jusqu'au 22ᵉ. et alors ont passé le Zuyder Zee *sur la glace* jusqu'à Steveren. Les deux Princesses d'Orange avec le Prince enfant, accompagné de M. Larrey fils et (à ce que Mons. Hinuber croit) l'Amiral Kinsbergen, sont embarquées à huit heures le matin du 18ᵉ à Scheveningue sur un *pink* arrangé exprès pour les recevoir, et avec un équipage choisi parmi les matelots de l'amirauté d'Amsterdam. Le vent était favorable sans être trop fort, et il y a toute raison de croire que Leurs Altesses Royales sont arrivées Lundi de bonne heure *en Angleterre*, car il n'était pas question de joindre un vaisseau de guerre. Ils étaient tous enfermés par les glaces dans le Helder, et à Vlessingue. A midi du même jour (le 18ᵉ) le Prince Stadthouder et les Princes ses fils se sont démis de tous leurs emplois, et à trois heures Leurs Altesses sont également partis de Scheveningue dans un *pink*. Il s'agissait un moment de gagner la Frise, et de faire un rassemblement des amis du parti d'Orange à Lewarden ; mais à mesure que les Français approchaient les amis diminuaient, et on craignait d'être livré au lieu d'être soutenu d'abord après que le Stadthouder a donné sa dismission. Les Sieurs Kalhoen et Boertzlaer de Kyefoet ont été députés aux Français, pour dire que la République ne leur opposait plus de résistance, et avec ordre à leurs propres troupes de ne plus en faire.

À cinq heures le 18ᵉ, cinquante houssards Français, ayant à leur tête les nommés Dandils et Kreinoff, deux célèbres Patriotes, sont entrés à Amsterdam. Lundi de grand matin la régence de la ville a été changée, et Fischer nommé *Grand Officier*.

Il est à présumer que les Français furent à la Haye le 19ᵉ. Woerden s'est rendu le 17ᵉ.

Mons. Rougers s'est offert pour accompagner Leurs Altesses Royales; mais Mᵈᵉ. la Princesse n'a pas voulu le lui permettre, vû qu'il avait sa femme et ses enfans en Hollande.

Le Grand Pensionnaire était malade à la mort, accablé également d'infirmités et de chagrin; les Ministres de Russie et de Portugal n'ont pas pu s'évader. Le Comte de Welderen est très malade, mais la Comtesse se soutient à merveille. Mons. et Madame d'Aigloa sont à la Haye, et y restent: Mons. de Rhoon est allé à Amsterdam pour faire à ce qu'on dit ses conditions avec les Français. Haerlem a changé ses magistrats Dimanche le 18ᵉ le soir, et toutes les villes en Hollande allaient faire la même chose: il n'y avait cependant point de Français dans ces parages le 22ᵉ. Voilà à peu près tout ce que j'ai pu apprendre de M. Hinuber. Votre Altesse Sérénissime aura la bonté de le communiquer avec le ménagement qu'elle croit convenable, à Mᵈᵉ. la Princesse Héréditaire. Je participe trop sensiblement à tous ces malheurs pour oser lui écrire directement, mais je connais la force de son caractère, et sa soumission aux volontés de la Providence. J'espère que l'heure de la vengeance arrivera, et que le règne de l'anarchie aura son terme. Vous voudrez bien pardonner, Monseigneur, le peu de méthode avec laquelle cette lettre est écrite, mais je suis vivement ému de tous ces détails, et je désire qu'ils vous arrivent sans délai aucun.

J'ai l'honneur, &c.  MALMESBURY.

EXTRACT OF A LETTER FROM LORD MALMESBURY TO LORD
GRENVILLE.

Hanover, 3rd Feb., 1795.

SEVERAL private letters I have received from Berlin mention that in consequence of the treatment le Sieur Harnier has met with at Paris, and of the strange and inadmissible conditions proposed by Barthelemi to Count Goltze at Bâle, His Prussian Majesty has come to a determination to pursue the war with vigour and in earnest; that he has given orders to Möllendorff to march towards Westphalia with his whole army; and that great preparations are making for the defence of that country and East Friesland. The Regency here have received similar accounts from Baron Lenthe, their Minister at Berlin, and the Duke of Brunswick hints the same in a letter I had from him yesterday; several I have received within an hour from Frankfort (dated the 27th) leave no doubt as to what has passed at Paris and Bâle, and they speak of the effect it has had on the Prussians there in very strong terms. All those who promoted and advised this measure are dismayed; and Marshal Möllendorff declared to Baron Hardenberg, "that he had been egregiously deceived; that all negotiations with the French should immediately be abandoned, and the greatest exertions made for opening the campaign." An officer of the name of Massenbach, the Prince of Hohenlohe's principal Aide-de-camp, was to be sent on the 28th to Berlin with this opinion and advice. It would appear that the head-quarters at Hochheim are confounded at the magnitude of the disasters to which they have so greatly contributed; and Lord H. Spencer will certainly write to you the effect this produces. I trust it will be a good one. If the King of Prussia does nothing on this side, the dismay is so great, and the means of defence so small, that everything is to be apprehended, and the enemy may make themselves masters of the mouths of the Ems and Weser, and even of the Elbe. The Regency, however, is taking every precaution in their power. Prince Ernest, of Mecklenburg Strelitz, is to command their cordon; and he has just informed me, in great confidence, that he is going to-morrow to Brunswick to concert with the Duke, and from thence to Berlin—he intends to see the King, and, if he says to him what he said to me, I think he may do good. If you wish to have more Brunswick troops, I believe 2500 may be had on the same terms as the last.

I hope we shall lose no time in taking possession of the Cape and Trinidad, and of all the principal *Dutch* settlements in India. It is an act of political duty to keep them, as a deposit until the Government of the United States of Holland is restored.

Möllendorff went so far as to say that he disliked the part he had acted, and expressed a desire to resign the command to the Duke of Brunswick, and a readiness to act under him.

EXTRACT OF A LETTER FROM LORD MALMESBURY TO GENERAL HARCOURT.

Hanover, 8th Feb., 1795.

In a short and hasty letter I wrote to you on Thursday last through ———, * I informed you of what it is said are His Prussian Majesty's intentions,† in consequence of the manner in which the overtures for peace have been received by the Convention. These intentions have been communicated officially both to the Hanoverian and to the English Minister at Berlin; but through a private channel, and one on which I can rely: I am very much afraid that we must not look upon them as sincere, or in their event as likely to be favourable to us. I am assured that those who direct the King of Prussia (and he is always directed) are bent on peace on any terms; and that the measures now taken, in appearance, for the defence of Westphalia, and which look so like real anger, are calculated to counteract our negotiations with Austria, and to force the troops under Clairfayt to move from their present ground, and occupy that Möllendorff will leave vacant on the Upper Rhine. My information even goes so far as to say that orders are eventually given to M. Möllendorff *not to expose his army*, but to

* Name illegible in MS.  † Described in the preceding letter.

fall back behind the Weser in case the enemy should come forward in force; certain it is, that all the arrangements proposed to this country for magazines, &c., carry this appearance. They are also calculated to lay on this Electorate the whole charge of forming and furnishing them; and it should seem, that after having devoured, like a swarm of locusts, the inferior members of the Empire, the Prussians are now coming to feed on the upper ones. In the mean time there can be no doubt that the negotiation for peace between them and the Convention is not broken off. The Duke of Brunswick (I must entreat you not to mention this circumstance) has been called upon officially by the Prussian Cabinet to give in a ministerial Note that his Duchy may be included in the Treaty; and it is supposed that this Electorate, and the possessions of the Electors of Cologne and Treves, on the right of the Rhine, are not to be inserted, or, at least, not to be insisted on as comprised in the pacification, if the French should make a difficulty to admit them, as they most assuredly will.

I may, perhaps, be incorrect as to the smaller points, but, in general, I think I can venture to take upon myself to say that my intelligence is sufficiently true to make it highly essential for us to be on our guard not to confide in Prussian assistance, or rely on Prussian faith, and, above all, not to allow ourselves to suffer on any account Clairfayt's army to stir an inch to the left, under the assurance that the Prussians will defend Westphalia. In the plan proposed by the Cabinet of Berlin, the line of defence was to extend from Hanover to the Dollard; and, in the disposition of the troops, the defence of East Friesland, and of the country from Osnabruck to Embden, was allotted to us.

You will be so good as to consider what I write as confidential. I believe Baron Steinberg (one of the principal members of this Regency) will, in consequence of what I have said to him, write nearly to the same effect to General Walmoden. It is of the last importance that persons in your very important and difficult situation should be regularly and accurately informed of such events as are so nearly connected with the operations of the troops under your command; and it is from feeling this conviction very strongly impressed on my mind, that I have troubled you with so long a letter.

EXTRACT OF A LETTER FROM LORD MALMESBURY TO LORD H. SPENCER.

Hanover, 16th Feb., 1795.

THE correspondence between the Duke of Brunswick and myself is too long to have copied, and indeed it is not worth your reading; it is more curious than important, as it goes to shew that, with all his personal courage, his mind is timid and wavering, and that his nerves are very ill braced. I found this to be the case when we acted together in Holland, but it has grown strangely on him since.

After what I have experienced, you will not be surprised that I should be cautious myself, and recommend caution to others before they trust to the performance of promises or execution of plans proposed by Prussia. I certainly am well pleased to see Möllendorff's army move towards Westphalia; but I cannot look upon it as a measure on which we can venture to build, much less to act, as long as the *pourparlers* at Bâle are open, and when a stroke of the pen may at once destroy its whole effect. I am not without hopes, as I said to Lord Grenville, that the extreme insolence of the Convention may predominate; particularly, as after I had written to him, and Timms was gone, I received by estafette, from Frankfort, the Moniteur of the 1st of February, which has in it a report made by *Boissy d'Anglas*, from the Committee of Public Safety; which, although it is more particularly pointed against us and Russia, is conceived in terms so injurious and offensive to all the Kings and Governments of Europe, and at the same time pledges so positively the Convention to the people of France never to make peace but on such extraordinary conditions, and in so extraordinary a manner, that even Goltze and Hernier would be forced to consider them as inadmissible. In addition to this proof of their being intoxicated by their successes, I hear (also from Frankfort, my letters from thence dated the 9th,) that Barthelemi has signified that the Convention will insist on the *status quo* in Poland as in 1792 as a *sine quâ non*. *If* this be true, it ought to put an end to the dangerous disputes between the co-dividing Powers, to anger them all equally, and induce them to lay aside all idea of a pacification, general or separate, by mediation, or through principals.

In the mean while, and as long as all those very essential points remain in suspension, we all must be governed by the very imperious nature of the circumstances of the moment: danger presses us on every side, and it is not a time to betray misgivings, or enter into minute discussions. We must take things as they are, and make the best of them. I, however, should be very sorry to see a single regiment of Clairfayt's army move to the right, even supposing the enemy had views on that side, (which they have not,) and were they then in force, (which they are not—their whole army, from Bâle to Mentz, not exceeding 40,000 men). It is of a very inferior consideration what passes on the Upper Rhine, and towards Franconia and Suabia: but if Prussia makes a separate peace, and if the Austrians are gone from the Lower Rhine, and nothing remains but the fragment of our army, all this Electorate, all the upper circles, and all the coast of Germany, from Embden to Hamburgh (inclusively), will be at the mercy of the French.

It is for this reason that I have written to General Harcourt and General Walmoden to entreat them to prevail on General Clairfayt not to quit his present position till they hear from England, or till he has positive orders from his Court. Besides the evident danger I have just stated, I believe such a movement is in direct contradiction to our plan, which (although I know it only by inference) I take to be not such a tame defensive war, as you will observe the King of Prussia proposes behind the Weser, but to try to pass the Rhine, drive the enemy behind the Meuse, and make an attempt to deliver Holland and the Low Countries; no other can be worth the expense we shall be at, or in any degree answer our purpose.

Besides General Reidesal, you will have had Prince Ernest, of Strelitz, at Berlin. General Reidesal is accompanied by a private secretary of the Duke of Brunswick, (who is a clever man, though suspected to be jacobinically inclined,) and who is the acting minister. The object of his mission was to be very careful that the duchy of Brunswick should be included in the peace, if peace is made. That of Prince Ernest to discover the real intentions of the Cabinet of Berlin, and to settle a plan of campaign. Reidesal may be successful in his object; but I much doubt whether His Serene Highness will be up to the difficulty of that he is charged with. He however has quick parts, and is extremely zealous.

I return your Lordship the decyphers of Whitworth's despatches, with many thanks. Russia is playing the same game with us now, she has been playing these twenty years; and, when I read what Sir Charles writes, it appears to me that I am carried back fifteen years, and treating myself with Ostermann and Besberodko; it is literally the same phrases, same arguments, same intention to deceive us on the part of the Empress, and same inclination to believe on ours.

EXTRACT OF A LETTER FROM LORD MALMESBURY TO THE
DUCHESS OF BRUNSWICK.

Hanover, 17 Feb., 1795.

J'AI l'honneur d'accuser la réception de la lettre que Votre Altesse Sérénissime m'a écrite en date d'avant hier. J'aurai tout le soin possible de celle qui s'y trouve incluse.

Les nouvelles que M. de Constant mande de Hollande sont une suite naturelle de l'irruption des Carmagnols, et de la restoration des Patriotes. Les maux qui en résulteront serviront peut-être plus efficacement à faire sentir aux Hollandais leurs vrais intérêts et leurs vrais amis que toute autre chose. Nous ne sommes pas peut-être à la dernière révolution que nous verrons dans ce pays dans ce siècle; et tout ce qui se passe à présent servira, à ce que je crois, à effectuer une guérison radicale. C'est le Sieur Paulus qui dirige la barque; il va tenter de réaliser le changement dans la Constitution qu'il a voulu, avec ses associés, adopter en 1786 ; et s'il faut croire à la Gazette de Hambourg, il y va d'une manière nullement propre à concilier les esprits.

J'ai l'honneur d'informer Votre Altesse Sérénissime que M. de Kalicheff est ici depuis Dimanche ; il a quitté la Haye le 28 Janvier avec des passeports Français. Il paraît très rassuré sur le sort de votre auguste famille, et n'a pas une doute sur leur heureuse arrivée en Angleterre. C'est M. ——, et le jeune ——,* qui ont accompagné les Princesses dans leur pink, et M. Vaillant qui a été avec les Princes. M. de Wassenau Staremberg est parti en même temps.

Sa sœur et Mde. de Reede étaient dans une autre pink destinée à suivre celles qui conduisaient Leurs Altesses Royales, ainsi que Madame Münchausen. Les nouvelles publiques que nous donnent Mons. de Kalicheff, ne sont pas d'une date bien fraîche. A son départ Leurs Hautes Puissances ainsi que Leurs Nobles Puissances furent en fonctions. Mons. de Rhoon travaillait avec les Commissaires Français pour conserver la tranquillité à la Haye. Mons. Vander Spiegel fesoit des expéditions avec eux, et on allait envoyer un ordre au Greffier Fagel de revenir. Ses deux frères à ce que leur sœur Agnès écrit à Madame Goden (qui est ici) en date du 5$^e$, sont de retour depuis le 3$^e$. Depuis, on a changé tout ceci, et on a introduit un nouveau régime. Le Grand Pensionnaire doit être renvoyé.

Mons. de Kalicheff dit que Pichegru se comporte très bien, mais que les quatre Commissaires sont des rustres et des insolens. Il n'y a guère au-delà de deux cent Housards à la Haye ; le tout est tranquille, mais d'un triste inconcevable. Le Comte Welderen est très abattu ; sa femme se soutient à merveille. Madame d'Ablaing n'a pas pu se sauver ; elle se porte bien. Deux Housards sont billetés chez elle, mais ne la molestent pas. Les Ministres de Suède et de Danemarc se comportent en vrais Carmagnols, ainsi que Mons. Arango, à qui j'espère cette conduite vaudra une disgrace. On a respecté l'hôtel de Lord St. Helens ; la grande garde est dans la maison de Mons. Lynden.

* Names illegible in MS., but not those mentioned in Lord Malmesbury's letter to the Duke of Brunswick in page 230.

EXTRACT OF A LETTER FROM LORD MALMESBURY TO GENERAL WALMODEN.

Hanover, 25 Feb., 1795.

JE vous ai bien des obligations des deux lettres que vous m'avez fait la grâce de m'écrire de Münster et d'Osnabruck. J'apprends avec bien de la peine que vous êtes incommodé : *à chaque jour suffit son mal*, et assurément dans celui d'aujourd'hui ceci est doublement vrai.

Les nouvelles qui me sont entrées ce matin de Berlin sont d'une nature à confirmer toutes mes craintes sur le peu de fonds à faire sur la conduite de cette cour, soit politique soit militaire. Le Roi, influé par le Prince Henri, a consenti aux conditions infiniment outrageantes que la Convention avait osée proposer comme son ultimatum. Le Roi de Prusse abandonne aux Français toute la rive gauche du Rhin, y *compris ses propres états dans le pays de Clèves:* rien n'est stipulé en sa faveur, ou en faveur de ses alliés. On prétend que le Duché de Bronsvic doit être compris, et il y a un bruit qui se répand que le Landgrave de Hesse Cassel désire la même chose. Il est peu nécessaire, M. le Comte, que je fâsse un commentaire sur une mesure pareille, également contraire aux intérêts comme à la dignité du Souvérain qui l'adopte. Il est douloureux de voir qu'il ne sera ni le premier ni le seul à sentir tous les maux qui en resulteront, et c'est une faible consolation de prévoir qu'il sappe les fondemens de son trône et entraîne sa propre chute.

---

LETTER FROM HIS ROYAL HIGHNESS THE PRINCE OF WALES TO LORD MALMESBURY.

Carlton House, 21st Feb., 1795.

MY DEAR LORD,—I do myself the pleasure of acknowledging the receipt of three letters I received on the 19th from your Lordship, two dated the 15th and 18th January, the other, I suppose, written on a subsequent day, but bearing no date. Accept my best thanks for every step that you have taken, as, to the best of my judgment, nothing can have been more consistent in point of prudence and propriety, and, indeed, more consonant to my wishes, than your conduct appears to me to have been throughout this very tedious and trying Embassy. The accounts you are so good as to give me of the temper and resignation with which the Princess is so good as to bear with the interruptions in her journey, is more than I fancy any one would venture to say for me from hence; as I assure you, all the mismanagement, procrastinations, and difficulties that I have met with in the conduct of this business on this side of the water have totally put patience (a virtue you well know that our family in general are not much endowed with) out of the question. On account of the unfortunate position of affairs on the Continent, I have judged it necessary, in order to bring the Princess over in the most expeditious, as well as the safest mode, to contrive she should be in a manner *smuggled* over into this country ; this meets entirely with His Majesty's approbation, and the plan to be pursued is this. The yachts, as well as the ladies and gentlemen who were to have had the honour of attending the Princess, to remain under expectation of receiving sailing orders hourly. The convoy destined originally to attend upon the Princess, to proceed to sea with the rest of the fleet and transports going to fetch the remains of our army from the Continent. By which means they will endeavour to make Stade, having detached themselves from the rest of the fleet at a certain latitude. Finding themselves there, to take you and your charge aboard, before it is suspected even on this side of the water that such a plan is in agitation. Not thinking it proper that the Princess should come without a lady, Mrs. Harcourt is ordered to attend her ; and her own ladies, Lady Jersey and Mrs. Aston, who were to have sailed in the yachts to have fetched her over, will be ready to receive her at the water-side on her landing, together with Clermont and the rest of her suite. The general and universal mortification occasioned by the fleet's being obliged to put back, made us doubly anxious by every means that human foresight can devise to prevent a similar unpleasant *contretemps* happening again ; and we therefore think, in addition to this motive, that by retaining the yachts and attendants here, we shall prevent entirely our enemies from having the smallest intimation of our having in present and immediate contemplation the scheme of the Princess's crossing.

I hope you will make this plan acceptable to the Princess as well as the Duchess, as you must be well acquainted with my impatience; and I beg you will assure them both, that there is no sort of respect, state, and attention, that shall not be shown the Princess, the moment she sets her foot on our dear little island. I am convinced you will heartily concur with me in my anxious endeavours through this, or even any other means, to bring your voyage to as expeditious and happy a termination as possible. I write to the Duchess of Brunswick by the same courier, which letters you will have the goodness to deliver into her hands yourself. I cannot help once more reiterating my thanks to you, my dear Lord, for your judgment and caution through all these late occurrences, &c. I remain with great truth, &c.,

GEORGE P.

P.S.—Pray say everything that is kind from me to Hislop.

---

EXTRACT OF A LETTER FROM LORD MALMESBURY TO LORD GRENVILLE.

Hanover, Thursday, Feb. 26th, 1795.

THE apprehension that the King of Prussia has consented to the extravagant conditions proposed by France, and that he is on the eve of signing a separate peace, has naturally produced a great degree of alarm here; this apprehension, your Lordship will perceive from Lord H. Spencer's Despatch, is but too well founded. For a few days, it is said, His Prussian Majesty appeared determined not to submit to so disgraceful a cession as that of his own territories on the left bank of the Rhine, and in this moment he declared *his* intention that M. Möllendorff's army should immediately march to the defence of the lower Rhine, and that he would put himself at the head of it. But it was never the intention of those who surround and lead him, that this should take place in the way he intended; and if they did not oppose the march of the troops from the Upper Rhine, it was because the removing them from thence, and bringing them home through Westphalia, answered their purpose in every respect.

Prince Henry of Prussia prides himself upon having managed and managing the whole of this disgraceful measure. How he acquired this ascendancy, and how he maintains it, I neither can conjecture nor learn; he is probably brought forward as the temporary instrument of that mass of corruption and treachery which surround the King of Prussia, and will be sacrificed whenever their work is complete.

It is difficult to understand how His Prussian Majesty can dispose of countries not his own, and from their constitution, inalienable from the German Empire, unless he means to unite with France hostilely against those to whom they belong, and to guarantee them to France, under all circumstances. The Treaty, then, instead of one of a shameful and ignominious peace, may be considered as one of a predatory alliance; and such a league between two such powers may have very serious consequences. It is impossible that this consideration should escape the minds of people here, and it augments very materially their anxiety. It is indeed very reasonable to suspect that the Court of Berlin has in view some equivalent for the loss of the Duchy of Cleves, Prussian Guelders, and the County of Maes.

The Duke of Brunswick has, I understand, received assurances from the King that his Duchy shall be included in the negotiation; I have not heard it from himself, but there is, I believe, no doubt of the fact. It is also said that the Landgrave of Hesse has solicited to be comprised in it. The condition that the French will undoubtedly attach, as a *sine quâ non* to their admission, will be an immediate withdrawing of their troops in our pay from the combined army.

I have written the substance of what I hear on this subject to Generals Harcourt and Walmoden. They probably have no other channel of information at this moment, and it appears to me of the last importance, that they should not, in the disposition of their army, reckon on any real and effectual assistance from that under M. Möllendorff, which is marching towards them; its arrival on its ground, instead of assistance and utility, will only add to the difficulty and distress of their situation by the quarters it will fill, the provisions it will consume, and the pernicious doctrines its officers will spread amongst our troops.

---

EXTRACT OF A LETTER FROM LORD MALMESBURY TO COMMODORE PAYNE.

Hanover, 13th March, 1795.

MAJOR HISLOP will tell you more in five minutes than I could write to you in as many pages. I should be extremely sorry that the weather should force you to put to sea again; for although I am satisfied you would soon return, yet the idea would give great pain and anxiety to the Princess.

I apprehend that as our infantry is to return to England, the enemy will be able to force our cordon; and as they are particularly bent on destroying our troops, endeavour to cut off their retreat, and follow their heels to the water side. If this happens (and we are not safe), we shall be involved in the same difficulty, and become an additional motive for the adopting this measure; and it is in consequence of this apprehension that I determined to prevail on Major Hislop to go to Cuxhaven, as he can speak much more positively on it than I can. Whatever you and he decide, I will venture, —*only decide.*

I thank you for the several letters you enclosed to me. I send you one I received from Mr. Burgess; in addition to this, Lord and Lady Gilford are here (you knew her at Lady Payne's under the name of Caroline de Thunn), and are most anxious to get to England safe and soon; to them, as to all others, I have given the same answer, that I cannot dispose of any place on board of any of the ships, and that I conceive your hands are tied by Admiralty orders. I feel, however, very much disposed to plead the cause of Lady Gilford: she is daughter to a very old friend of mine; she is a very amiable woman, and she is far gone with child: but all these circumstances must give way before duty and orders; I write them merely to interest your feelings, if you are at liberty to give way to them.

EXTRACTS OF A LETTER FROM LORD MALMESBURY TO GENERAL
HARCOURT.

Hanover, 16th March, 1795.

I MOST sincerely wish I had not the merit of being a true prophet, but my apprehensions went but upon too solid grounds. Since I wrote to you on the 14th, I have received indirect intimation from Baron Hardenberg in his way through Frankfort to Bâle, which confirms everything I then said, both as to the nature of his instructions, and the extent of his full powers. He insinuates, however, in expressions nearly tantamount to a promise, that he will temporise and protract the final determination of his negotiation till he is quite sure we do not intend to come forward with any proposals to renew our Subsidiary Treaty with Prussia, either in the same shape as last year, or under any other more applicable to the present time; and as he conceives that this will not be *irrevocably* settled till after my arrival in England, he seems to fix some weeks beyond that day for the conclusion of his work. I have replied to him *also indirectly*, " that I will make an exact report of what he has conveyed to me from Brunswick and from Frankfort; that I have no doubt of his sincerity, and *his* political principles, and that as far as these can influence the conduct of his Court, I am confident all will go well; that, however, he must be aware that the Ministerial reports from Lord H. Spencer at Berlin, must be those on which His Majesty's Ministers must rest their conduct, and that I wish, more than I expect, that they may coincide with what he said to me, and what I am sure *he* thought; in the meanwhile I much approved his idea of prolonging his negotiation."

The longer the French are in the dark as to the way in which they are to consider the Prussian army, the better. This doubt is, I fear, the only advantage we are likely to derive from its presence in Westphalia.

I mentioned to you in my last the uneasiness felt here, and at Brunswick, in the removal of the British infantry from the army. The members of this Regency and Marshal Freytag (to both of whom, in consequence of orders from home, I had communicated this intended measure, previous to the reception of yours of the 12th) have pressed me to entreat of you, if possible, to delay their departure for a few days; till such time as the gap made by their being withdrawn can be filled up either by Prussians or Austrians;, for, as to the corps under Prince Ernest, they declare (and I believe very truly) that it is not fit to take the field, and utterly disqualified for that purpose.

LETTER FROM LORD MALMESBURY TO L. CRAWFORD, ESQ.

Secretary of State's Office, London, 10th April, 1795.

MY DEAR SIR,—I send you, enclosed, a letter for our friend at Bâle, which I wish you to get conveyed to him by a safe channel. It is impossible for me to enter with you into a long detail of the measures likely to be taken here, because hitherto the outlines of them only are formed, but with a sufficient degree of certainty as to the result to authorize me to say, without hesitation, to Hardenberg what I have said. I could wish you, on your side, to add a letter to Gravinus, to keep him up tight to the collar, and to urge, in the strongest manner, the extreme necessity of Hardenberg's keeping faith with us, and not finally concluding his Mission till he hears from Berlin, and from the King himself. You will do a very essential service to the two Courts and to Europe by enforcing this measure. I am happy to have been able to have brought it so soon to a point, and particularly at a moment when there is so much business of another nature going on, and which engages almost entirely our whole attention.

The marriage was celebrated on Wednesday; and if they go on as well as they have begun, all will do well.

I write in haste, as the person who is to take charge of this as far as Brunswick is waiting. Compliments to everybody at the Red House. I am, &c. MALMESBURY.

P.S. Make Hardenberg and Gravinus feel no time has been lost. I got to England only on Sunday night, and it is now only Friday morning.

[Prussia made a separate Treaty with France, April 5th, in which she ceded to the latter her territories on the left bank of the Rhine.

The campaign of 1795 closed in favour of the Austrians, who retook Manheim, and drove the French across the Rhine.]

LETTER FROM LORD MALMESBURY TO THE DUKE OF YORK.

London, 5th Dec., 1795.

Sir,—No foreign mail is come in, neither have I heard since yesterday any event worthy your Royal Highness's notice.

The debate on the Bill for the Suppression of Seditious Meetings will come on, on the Second reading of it, on Wednesday next in the House of Lords. I am sorry to say, that almost everybody who ever votes in Opposition, means to attend and vote against it. The Duke of Leeds, whose member (Abbott) spoke so forcibly in the House of Commons in its favour, has been wrought upon by some of the enemies to the bill, and, I apprehend, will be against it. The Duke of Grafton and Lord Lansdowne are in town; and I should not be surprised if the minority on Wednesday should be from eighteen to twenty. The original day intended for the debate was Tuesday, but it was postponed at Lord Lauderdale's request; the Whig Club being to meet on that day.

I am, &c.      Malmesbury.

LETTER FROM LORD MALMESBURY TO THE DUKE OF YORK.

London, 7th Dec., 1795.

Sir,—Your Royal Highness will be pleased to accept my most respectful thanks for your letter of yesterday.

There was a very considerable meeting of the different factious societies to-day in Marylebone Fields, and it is not yet (4 P.M.) dispersed. Their object appears solely to be to keep the cause alive and the spirits of their followers up, in order to act whenever they may think it safe and prudent. Jones was the principal speaker, and his language was chiefly to this effect. A resolution of thanks was voted to Mr. Fox, for some of the late declarations he has made in Parliament. I cannot but be glad of this, as, whatever explanation he may think proper to give them, it is very clear how they are understood by these societies. There is no doubt but this meeting will break up without coming to any riot, or committing any excesses, which I am sorry for, as at the present moment every preparation is made to subdue them, which may not be the case some time hence. Your Royal Highness will forgive my writing in haste, as I am going down to the House of Commons to hear the budget, of which, if it ends before the post goes out, I will have the honour to send an account.

I am, &c.     MALMESBURY.

P.S.—The Austrians, so far from having received any check, have on one side gained a considerable advantage over the French on the ——*, and on the other, have advanced as far as Deux-ponts and Saarbrüch: this appears from the last French papers received yesterday.

---

LETTER FROM LORD MALMESBURY TO THE DUKE OF YORK.

London, 10th Dec., 1795.

SIR,—The expectation I was under of news from the Continent every moment, and no mail coming in till a very late hour, was the reason of my not writing to your Royal Highness.

The debate† in the House of Lords began at five, and did not end till a quarter past three. The speakers against the Bill (and usually in Opposition) were those your Royal Highness noticed in your last letter. Lord Thurlow was artfully and cautiously factious; Lord Moira (I am very sorry to say) loudly and violently so; and I think I never

---

\* Name illegible in MS.
† On the Bill for the Suppression of Seditious Meetings.

heard a speech with so much unfair and unprovoked invective against Ministers, with so much misrepresentation and misstatement, nor with such inflammable materials for raising discontent and the worst of suspicions in the minds of the people. It was evident to me from the manner of these new partisans of the Opposition, and from the part they had allotted to themselves on this occasion, that they have it in their expectations the present Ministry will not last; that Fox and his party will not be chosen to succeed them; and that *they* shall be the persons to fill their offices. Lord Lansdowne's speech had clearly this in view; he was neither violent nor very mischievous—at least for him, and neither he nor Lauderdale, nor any on that side of the House, hinted at the word *resistance*. In speaking confidentially to your Royal Highness, I must say that I do not think the measure was ably or judiciously supported by Ministers. Lord Grenville, who opened the business, was prolix and heavy. Lords Westmoreland and Mulgrave did tolerably well; but the Chancellor, who replied to Lord Thurlow, was below himself. He made a speech of no effect as to the measure, and which drew upon him abuse and sarcasm from Lauderdale, whom he left unanswered. Lauderdale's speech was addressed to the bar, and Lord Mansfield very justly compared him to Cleon haranguing an Athenian democracy, except that his language was not elegant Greek, but very vulgar English. Lord Boringdon did extremely well in support of the bill, and spoke more to the purpose than any one. The Duke of Leeds did not speak, and I believe went away without voting. Lord Moira went into the closet on Thursday last, to deliver his intentions to His Majesty, of voting against this Bill; his audience was made very short. Yesterday he was an hour at Carlton House, and it is to be remarked that neither Lords Cholmondeley nor Jersey attended. The Duke of Bedford did not speak; the division was sixty-three to fifteen, and forty-six proxies to six. I enclose a list of the minority, which is the largest one in the House of Lords for a long time. To-day we are to receive the King's message; and although it should seem to convey a disposition perfectly consonant to that expressed by Opposition at the opening of the session, yet I find it is to be strongly reprobated, and Ministers to be abused to-day for doing what they have been abused for not doing, for these last two years. The bill is to go into committee to-morrow, and to be read a third time, I hope, on Monday. It seems doubtful whether Opposition will *all* attend the Committee. Thurlow most certainly will, with an endeavour to pull it to pieces in every sense of the word.

Your Royal Highness will, I take it for granted, have received letters from Crawford, with a more circumstantial account of the retaking of Manheim, than any which have come to my knowledge. I had a letter from Baron Kinckel, who was present on this occasion; he says nothing could equal the patience, the perseverance, and bravery of the Austrians. In speaking of their generals, he says, "*L'appétit leur vient en mangeant, et ils ne parlent de rien moins à présent que de chasser les Français des Pays Bas avant de prendre leurs quartiers d'hiver.*"

Lord Grenville told me that Clairfayt had detached a very considerable corps towards Treves; and he added, that the desertion, or rather dispersion, of the French army was so great, that if the number of battalions which only made up the 10,000 captured in Manheim had been complete, their amount would have been 30,000.* The town has suffered a great deal. The Prince de Condé's army has crossed the Rhine, high up the river, with a view to penetrate into Franche Compté. General * * *,† it is said, is marching towards Coblentz. I am, &c.

(Signed) MALMESBURY.

| NOT-CONTENTS. | | PROXIES. |
|---|---|---|
| Norfolk. | Besborough | Northumberland. |
| Bedford. | Abingdon. | Shaftesbury. |
| Derby. | Egmont. | Thanet. |
| Suffolk. | Thurlow. | Grafton. |
| Albemarle. | Say and Sele. | Guilford. |
| Moira. | Chedworth. | Teignham. |
| Lauderdale. | St. John. | |
| Lansdowne. | | |

* These prisoners were restored afterwards to the French, on condition of not again serving against the Austrians. They were sent to La Vendée, where they decided the fate of the war, being the best troops the French had at that time. † Name illegible in MS.

# PARIS.

[In the autumn of 1796, the successes of the Archduke Charles over Jourdan, induced Mr. Pitt to believe this a favourable moment for an attempt to put an end to the war. He made the first overture to the Directory,* through Mr. Roenemann, the Danish Minister at Paris. This was rudely rejected; but the intimation given, that passports would be granted to a negotiator officially appointed. In announcing this event to the Council, the Directory openly denounced the English Government as insincere in its intention, and this overture as a mere contrivance of Pitt to delude the people and obtain fresh supplies; and under such almost hopeless circumstances, Lord Malmesbury was sent to Paris in October. Revolutionized France was a new world to the English, and much curiosity is evinced in all the letters of Lord Malmesbury's correspondents to learn every particular of a country and people which had overturned all the moral,

---

\* The Directory was at this time composed of Barras, Rewbell, La Réveillère-Lépeaux, Carnot, and Letourneur.

Paul Barras—Nourri dans un rang élevé, grand et beau de sa personne, mais son regard avoit quelque chose de sinistre. Plus emporté que méchant. Il avait une justesse et pénétration d'esprit ; mais paresseux et ignorant. Du reste dissolu et cynique—républicain par sentiment et par position, mais homme sans foi—(Thiers, tom. v.) He died 1829, aged 74.

Rewbell.—Ancien avocat. A la pénétration, au discernement les plus rares, il joignoit une instruction étendue, une mémoire fort vaste, une rare opiniâtreté au travail. Républicain chaud, sincère, et ferme.—(Id.)

Carnot.—Ex-Montagnard. On voyoit en lui l'union d'un grand génie militaire à un caractère stoïque—(Id.) He shared in the cruelties of the Revolution. Napoleon recognised his talents, but found him too inflexible for his purposes. He died 1823, aged 70.

La Réveillère-Lépeaux.—Homme simple et modeste, peu propre au maniement des affaires et des hommes. Parlant bien et d'une fermeté rare, il servoit beaucoup le Directoire par sa considération personnelle.—(Id.) He died 1824, aged 71.

Letourneur.—Bon homme, mais vaniteux. Il étoit prompt à donner son avis et aussi prompt à le retirer. Sa voix dans toutes les occasions appartenoit à Carnot.—(Id.)

social, and political principles by which Europe had for centuries been ruled. In this year, and in their *first* diplomatic intercourse with England, the Directors appear to have sometimes studiously and purposely tried to affront any aristocratical prejudices they might believe innate in our Ambassador, even to the childish omission of the usual and technical expression of courtesy with which all letters are concluded; but in 1797 they became more humanized.

Lord Malmesbury's instructions were, to go to Paris, and express to the French Government " our anxious desire to terminate the war by a just and honourable peace ;" then to proceed to state " that this peace must be negotiated and concluded with the consent of, and conjointly with, our ally the Emperor of Austria, and this condition to be a *sine quâ non*. That, therefore, reference to the Court of Vienna must be permitted, until that Court had sent a Negotiator to Paris. Not to sign any agreement between himself (Lord Malmesbury) and the French Republic, without previous reference to the Secretary of State in London. To be particularly careful to insist upon enjoying in France all the rights, prerogatives, &c., belonging to a public Minister ; and to insist on being treated in the same manner as public Ministers are treated, according to the law and custom of nations as *generally received in Europe*. To act as much as possible in concert with our allies, the King of Naples and Queen of Portugal, (at that time negotiating for themselves a peace with France,) and to give a watchful attention to the conduct of the Spanish Ambassador."]

MEMORIAL TO THE FRENCH DIRECTORY.

Sa Majesté Britannique, désirant, comme elle a déjà déclaré, de contribuer en autant que cela pourra dépendre d'elle, à rétablir la tranquillité publique, et à assurer par des conditions de paix, justes, honorables, et solides, le repos futur de l'Europe, Sa Majesté pense, que le meilleur moyen de parvenir le plutôt possible à ce but salutaire, sera de convenir dès le commencement de la négociation du principe général qui devra servir de base aux arrangemens définitifs.

Le premier objet des Négociations de la Paix se rapporte ordinairement aux restitutions et aux cessions que les parties respectives ont à se demander mutuellement en conséquence des évènemens de la guerre.

La Grande Brétagne, d'après le succès non interrompu de sa guerre maritime, se voit dans le cas de n'avoir aucune restitution à demander à la France ; sur laquelle, au contraire, elle a conquis des établissemens et des colonies de la plus haute importance, et d'une valeur presque incalculable.

Mais, en revanche, cette dernière a fait sur le Continent de l'Europe des conquêtes auxquelles Sa Majesté peut d'autant moins être indifférente, que les intérêts les plus importans de ses peuples et les engagemens les plus sacrés de sa couronne s'y trouvent essentiellement impliqués.*

La magnanimité du Roi, sa bonne foi inviolable, et son désir de rendre le repos à tant de nations, lui font envisager dans cet état des choses le moyen d'arriver à des conditions de paix justes et équitables pour toutes les Parties Belligérantes, et propres à assurer pour l'avenir la tranquillité générale.

C'est donc sur ce pied qu'elle propose de négocier, en offrant de *compenser* à la France par des restitutions proportionnelles les arrangemens auxquels cette Puissance sera appelée à consentir pour satisfaire aux justes demandes des Alliés du Roi, et pour conserver la balance politique de l'Europe. En faisant cette première ouverture Sa Majesté se réserve à s'expliquer dans la suite d'une manière plus étendue sur l'application de ce principe aux différens objets, dont il pourra être question entre les parties respectives.

---

* At this period the Belligerent Powers were, Great Britain and Austria on one side ; France, Holland, and Spain on the other. Great Britain had wrested from France and Holland almost all their colonies, and maintained her naval superiority in every quarter ; and the Archduke Charles had compelled Jourdan and Moreau to retreat from the heart of Germany to the banks of the Rhine. On the other hand, France had annexed Belgium to her territory by conquest. Holland was revolutionized, and entirely under her influence. In Italy, Buonaparte had conquered Piedmont and the Milanese, blockaded Wurmser in Mantua, and had taken up a position to intercept the Austrian army marching to his relief from the Tyrol, under General Alvinzi.

C'est cette application qui sera la matière des discussions, dans lesquelles elle a autorizé son Ministre d'entrer dès que l'on sera convenu du principe à adopter pour Base Générale de la Négociation.

Mais Sa Majesté ne peut se dispenser de déclarer que si cet offre généreux et équitable n'étoit pas accepté, ou si malheureusement les discussions qui s'en suivroient venoient à manquer de l'effet désiré, ni cette proposition générale, ni celles plus détaillées qui en seroient résultées, ne pourront plus être regardées dans aucun cas comme des points convenus ou accordés par Sa Majesté.

---

NOTE FROM LORD GRENVILLE TO M. DELACROIX.[*]

à Westminster, 13 Octobre, 1796.

Le Lord Malmesbury, nommé par le Roi pour traiter avec le Gouvernement François d'une paix juste et équitable, propre à rendre le repos à l'Europe, et à assurer pour l'avenir la tranquillité publique, aura l'honneur de remettre cette lettre de ma part à Mons. Delacroix.

Le rang et le mérite éminent du Ministre que Sa Majesté a choisi dans cette occasion me dispense de rien dire à son sujet, en même tems qu'il fournit une nouvelle preuve du désir de Sa Majesté de contribuer à la réussite de cette négociation, objet pour lequel je fais les vœux les plus sincères.

Monsieur Delacroix voudra bien agréer de ma part l'assurance de la considération la plus parfaite.

(Signé)     GRENVILLE.

Au Ministre des Relations
   Extérieures à Paris.

---

[*] Delacroix (French Minister for Foreign Affairs) capable d'être bon administrateur, mais du reste mauvais diplomate, trop pédant et trop rude dans ses rapports avec les ministres des Puissances.—Thiers, tom. v. page 319.

## DESPATCH FROM LORD GRENVILLE TO LORD MALMESBURY.

Downing Street, 14th Oct., 1796.

My Lord,—I have His Majesty's commands to desire, that immediately on your arrival at Paris, you should make inquiries respecting the situation and treatment of Captain Sir William Sydney Smith,* who, as it has been represented to His Majesty, has been confined in a manner highly injurious to him and utterly repugnant, both to the established maxims of war among civilized nations, and particularly to the humane and generous treatment which the French officers, who have been made prisoners of war, have uniformly experienced in this kingdom during the present war.

I enclose to your Lordship a copy of a note which I have received on this subject from the Swedish Minister. The certainty which this official paper conveys to His Majesty's Government of the rigorous confinement of Captain Sir W. S. Smith, made it absolutely necessary that orders should be given for observing a similar conduct towards all the French officers prisoners of war in England. But you will acquaint the French Government that these orders have not yet been carried into execution, and that His Majesty's great reluctance to take any step that may aggravate the calamities of war, has induced him previously to avail himself of the opportunity of your Lordship's mission, to direct your Lordship to make the strongest representations to obtain for Sir S. Smith a treatment suited to his rank and situation, and to prevent the necessity of retaliations here, to which nothing but the indispensable obligation of protecting his own officers from unmerited rigour and indignity could induce His Majesty to have recourse.

If any attempt is made to distinguish the case of Sir

---

\* Sir Sidney Smith had been taken prisoner in the preceding month of April, in the attempt to cut out a privateer from Havre. The French Government affected to consider him as a spy, and kept him in rigorous confinement in the Temple. He escaped in May, 1798, and the year following conducted the heroic defence of Acre, compelling Buonaparte to raise a siege which had lasted sixty days, with the loss of 2,500 men, and his battering train.

S. Smith from that of any other officer prisoner of war, you must firmly and invariably declare, that as there are not the smallest grounds for such a pretext, so His Majesty is resolved not to suffer it to be made for a moment matter of discussion. Sir S. Smith, in the exercise of his duty as an officer, and in the conduct of a spirited military enterprise, surrendered to a superior force as prisoner of war, he was accepted as such, and so recognised in the letter which the Governor of Havre wrote the next day, in answer to the application which had been made by the officer next in command to know his fate.

You will endeavour in speaking on this subject to avoid in the first instance all unnecessary irritation, and to obtain by a conciliatory, but dignified representation, a change of measures which disgrace the Government by whom they are adopted; but if this mode should be found ineffectual, you will notify formally to the French Government, that until Sir S. Smith is suffered to go at large upon his parole, in the manner usually practised with respect to officers of his rank in wars between Great Britain and France, no French officer will be allowed a similar liberty.

I am, &c.    GRENVILLE.

LETTER FROM LORD MALMESBURY TO LORD GRENVILLE.

(Private.)           Spring Gardens, Oct. 14th, 1796.

MY DEAR LORD,—I have to apologize for not mentioning to you this morning, that I had it much in my wishes to take with me a *confidential friend* to Paris; but I was far from being sure when I had the pleasure of seeing you then, that Mr. George Ellis, the only person in whom I could place in every respect entire confidence, and who has been so often with me on similar occasions, would have it in his power to accompany me; he has very kindly consented to do it, and I lose not a moment in intreating your permission to be allowed to instruct him so far with the general object of my Mission, as to enable me to have recourse to his opinion and judgment on those numberless points of difficulty and dilemma which must inevitably arise in the course of it, and upon which I should be obliged to act without any reference. It would be of such infinite, and I really must say, necessary comfort to me to have a person of such tried judgment and ability to recur to, and at the same time add so much to my power of acting in a manner conformable to the spirit of the instructions you have given me, that I am sure you will not think my feelings as an individual extraordinary, or my request as a servant of the public unreasonable.

I have seen Mr. Pitt since I saw your Lordship, and since I had hopes of Mr. Ellis's consenting to attend me. He has entered very kindly into my wishes, at the same time that he entirely approved the choice I had made, and was good enough to authorize me to say as much to you.

After what I have written, it will be perhaps unnecessary to observe, that Mr. Ellis, by going with me, neither intends now, or at any time, to be considered as having any claims on Government, or as in any degree standing in the way of the many persons who are advancing in the Foreign Line. He goes entirely and solely as my private friend, and every degree of public responsibility which may attach to the situation of confidence in which he will be placed will rest on me, and it is running very little risk in saying, that I shall be most ready to be accountable for it.

LETTER FROM LORD GRENVILLE TO LORD MALMESBURY.

Dropmore, 16th Oct., 1796. 8 A.M.

MY DEAR LORD.—As I think that this may probably still overtake you at Dover, I write to say, that we have received despatches from Vienna, the tenor of which, though not unsatisfactory as to the spirit of union and concert with His Majesty which prevails there, still leaves us in much uncertainty with respect to the objects which that Court may preferably urge in case of detailed negotiations for peace. In this state I do not think it useful to add anything to your instructions, but I would not leave you unapprized of the circumstance, as the knowledge of it will naturally induce you to use, if possible, still more care than you would otherwise have done, not to let any hint or insinuation drop from you that may have the remotest tendency to commit us in this respect. It is perhaps unnecessary for me to recall to your recollection that, by the Convention signed with the Court of Vienna in the beginning of the war, the King is bound not to make peace without the *consent* of Austria, except on the terms of procuring for that Power the restitution of *all* it may have *lost* in the war. I mention this to you, merely as a thing to be kept in your own mind; the effect or application of this stipulation to the present state of things must be matter of detailed instruction to you if the negotiation proceeds.

Ever, &c.    G.

LETTER FROM LORD MALMESBURY TO MR. PITT.

Dover, Monday, 9 A.M., 1796.

MY DEAR SIR.—I am greatly obliged to you for the few lines you were so good as to write to me yesterday evening from Beckenham; I hope to sail in about an hour, and to reach Calais early this evening. I am sorry Austria does not heartily concur in the measure we have adopted; but I trust, when it is perceived in how fair and honourable a manner we shall act by her, that in the end it will rather confirm than weaken the union now subsisting between us.

Good news will enable me to execute my orders much better than any means I have within myself; I hope all our fair prospects will be confirmed. I cannot sufficiently express my thanks to you for the confidence and kindness with which you have treated me on this occasion.

I am, &c.    MALMESBURY.

OCT. 15, 1796.—Left London at one. Rode to Cobham.

OCT. 16.—Dover. Dine with Mrs. Knatchbull, General Greenfield, Lord Downe, Trevanion, Mr. and Mrs. Beering.

OCT. 17.—Dover. Kept by contrary wind. Our flag of truce Captain Ratcliff.

OCT. 18.—Left Dover at ten. Three cheers. 27th Vendémiaire—at Calais by three—most attentively received. Municipality—what they said—give them the list of my suite. Directeur de la Douane, Pigot Monbaillard. Commissaire du Pouvoir Exécutif—his speech. L'Etat Major de la place—headed by their commandant, Trontines—his civility. Directeur de la Douane again. All equally civil and full of *égards*, giving me the highest titles, and all praying for peace. Sent on six persons.

OCT. 19.—Calais.—Returned Pigot Monbaillard's and Trontines' visits. First expecting us—very affectedly civil—second a plain soldier. Report of an intended invasion. Bill dear at Calais. Lion d'Argent—Landlord du Crocq—very republican, yet very civil. Left Calais at twelve—got to Boulogne by five. Passport examined. Women and children follow. Several persons on the road cry for peace. I mentioned at Calais that my title on the passport was Envoy Extraordinary; it ought to have been Minister Plenipotentiary. I asked whether any order had been given to let my couriers pass. He said, None, but that he thought they should. Doubts still about the departure of the flag of truce. I foresee they will not let it go. Got to Boulogne at half-past four.

OCT. 20.—Inn at Boulogne—kept by a Mrs. Knowles and Parker, but they in the Conciergerie eighteen months—maid and granddaughter left in charge of the house. Good town and decent people—town more populous than Calais. I had a cordial harangue from a very fat *poissarde*. Troops at St.Valery. Gun-boats on a new construction in Boulogne. Twenty-five men, two twenty-four pounders, and two horses —to slip out on rollers. Roads good—many women and children,—no men. Lands well cultivated. Asses used in the plough. Abbeville deserted—many houses shut. Cathedral destroyed. Postilions quiet, neither talking nor asking for money. Got in ten hours from Boulogne to Abbeville—nine posts and a half. Inn, *Tête de Bœuf.* Visit from the *Commandant du Civil,* Citoyen Plaidant ; his speech. Came while at dinner, accompanied by *Commandant Militaire,* a little man, and *Commandant du Génie,*—le seul qui paroissoit en avoir.

Oct. 21.—Left Abbeville at a quarter before seven—got to Clermont at a quarter after seven. Dined at Breteuil, à l'Ange—moderate inn. Amiens less deserted than Abbeville.

Quarrel between two women about begging. Children's songs on the road disapproved by the post-boys. Met more carriages to-day than the two others, but still an appearance of decreased population. People all civil, and more decorous than before. Cultivation nowhere neglected. Woods cut down but apparently regularly, except that the poor people seem to cut green underwood at will. The *post* gives way to *waggons* and *carts.* Churches everywhere in part, or in the whole destroyed. Also some châteaux, but not all. Small children and women at work in the fields. An evident scarcity of men. Inn at Claremont le Cygne—moderate—good beds.

Saturday, Oct. 22.—Left Clermont at a quarter to eight—got to Paris before three. At Evreux, (a post on the English side of St. Denis,) a deputation from the Poissardes, and another from the *Musique et Tambours du Directoire* (as they styled themselves). They opened the carriage doors ; the Poissards made a speech in their way, gave me nosegays "*en attendant des lauriers,*" as they said, and ended by embracing me and my companion. The musicians were equally violent, but both ended by asking for money. Found at St. Denis a note from Perregaux*—he has taken lodgings at l'Hôtel de Chatillon. Nothing particular on coming into Paris. All quiet. Good dinner. Saw Perregaux. Sent Ross to Delacroix.

* The banker ; his house once belonged to the famous dancer and courtezan, La Guimard.

## LETTER FROM LORD MALMESBURY TO LORD GRENVILLE.

*Paris, 23rd Oct., 1796. Sunday, 9 P.M.*

MY DEAR LORD,—I hope that I have proceeded thus far on my Mission without mistake or blunder; but I confess I have the feeling of an unsteady head on the edge of a high precipice.

I must entreat of you not to be disappointed if I do not send you *early* intelligence as to the state and temper of this country. You may rely on my being most assiduous to obtain safe and accurate information, but without being on the spot it is difficult to form an idea how impossible it is to select the true from the false. If I was absolutely compelled to give an opinion, I should say the negotiation would go on, but I should be sorry to be bound by such an opinion.

The wearing of the national cockade is so universal in the streets, and so unpleasantly enforced by the populace, that it is impossible to appear in them without it; the Government by no means insists upon it, and certainly it never shall be worn by any persons belonging to me, when I am acting in an *official* capacity; but it would inevitably make them and me liable to the most disagreeable species of insult were they not to put it on when they walk out in a morning.

The weakness of this Government, when opposed to the temper of the people, is such, that were such an event to happen, it would not be in their power to give me satisfactory redress; and I trust I do not judge wrong in supposing that, by exposing myself to it, much more serious and degrading consequences might be produced, than by the simply conforming to a general usage, prescribed by popular custom, and not at all dictated by the Government.

From my receiving so early an answer from M. Delacroix, it is evident they are in a hurry either to begin the negotiation, or to send me from Paris.

I have, &c. MALMESBURY.

DESPATCH FROM LORD MALMESBURY TO LORD GRENVILLE.

Paris, 23rd Oct., 1796.

My Lord,—I had the honour of informing your Lordship on Wednesday last of my landing at Calais, and that my reception there was in every respect one with which I had reason to be satisfied. Immediately on my arrival there, I was waited upon by the principal officers of the Municipality, by the Commissary of the Executive Power, by the Commandant of the place, and the *Etat Major* of the garrison, and by the Director of the Customs. They were all equally civil, none of them using any of the new modes of address, and all of them very strongly expressing their earnest wishes for the restoration of peace.

I left Calais on Wednesday at noon, and arrived here yesterday at three P.M. I could indeed have got here on Friday evening, but in that case I should have found no apartments provided for me. I slept at Boulogne, at Abbeville, and at Clermont. At Abbeville, the *Commandant du Civil*, (as he termed himself,) with the military commanders, waited upon me, and in a very laboured speech expressed every civility he could devise, and his hopes that my Mission would terminate successfully. Such also, as far as could be collected from the few words I heard casually drop from the people as I passed through the towns and villages, seemed to be the general sentiment; but whether it is or not, no conclusion whatever should be drawn from it. At Ecouen, a deputation from the Poissardes of Paris, and another from the National Music (to use their own method of styling themselves) met me. The first opened the carriage doors while I was changing horses, got into the coach, made me an harangue in their style, presented me with nosegays, and insisted on embracing me and my companions. They and the musical deputation vied with each other in their wishes for my success, but as they both ended by asking for money, their sincerity may justly be called in question.

My coming into Paris was attended with nothing remarkable; I was suffered to drive very quietly through the streets to my hotel, and have been allowed to remain very quietly in it since my arrival.

The roads were, the whole of the way, in tolerably good repair; the country from Calais hither appeared to be in a state of high cultivation, and every part of the farming business belonging to this season was either completed or going on. Most of the ploughs had horses to them, but some were drawn by asses, several of them were driven by women, and nearly all of them by old men or boys. It was indeed evident that the male population is diminished, as the number of women we saw on the road certainly exceeded that of the men in the proportion of four to one. The most striking change to me was the silence which seemed to prevail. No noise at the post-houses on changing horses; none by the post-boys while they were driving, and an universal stillness seemed to pervade the whole country; but it did not seem to be the placid quiet arising from content and repose, but the effect which terror and perpetual fear had produced on their minds.

These are the only remarks I can venture to make in so short a view of France; and when, as your Lordship will perceive from my other despatch, every moment of my time since my arrival has been filled by attending to the duties of the very important Mission with which His Majesty has been pleased to intrust me.

There were very few troops in any of the towns through which we passed, not even in Calais, neither during the whole route did we meet with any soldiers on the march.

Nothing but the walls were remaining of the churches in most of the villages, and those of the Cathedral at Amiens, and the principal church at Abbeville, were nearly destroyed. Over the door of several of them was written, *Temple de la Raison*, and afterwards " *Le Peuple Français reconnait L'Etre Suprême et l'Immortalité de l'Ame;*" and at the entrance of the small towns near Paris, was written, in large characters on the walls, " *Citoyens, respectez les propriétés et les biens d'autrui; ils sont le fruit de ses travaux et de son industrie.*"

I have, &c.     MALMESBURY.

LETTER FROM LORD MALMESBURY TO LORD GRENVILLE.

Paris, 23rd Oct., 1796.

My Lord,—About an hour after my arrival at Paris yesterday, I sent, according to your Lordship's directions, my secretary, Mr. Ross, to notify my arrival to M. Delacroix, Minister for Foreign Affairs. Although I had the fullest confidence that Mr. Ross would execute this commission with the greatest exactness and propriety, yet, as it was one of the last importance that not the smallest deviation should be made from the spirit of my instructions, and that it should be distinctly ascertained in what manner this first step in my Mission had been taken, I gave to Mr. Ross the enclosed note (A) for M. Delacroix. Mr. Ross was received in every respect (according to his report, on which I can thoroughly depend,) in the same way as he has been before received by the Ministers for Foreign Affairs at other Courts to whom I have frequently been obliged to send him on similar occasions. Mr. Ross, in about half an hour, brought me the answer (B), to which I immediately sent the answer (C).\*

I myself went to M. Delacroix at the hour appointed this morning. He received me, also, as I had always been received under the same circumstances; gave me the upper place in the room, and affected neither to use nor require any of the terms introduced into the French language since the Revolution.

I began by putting into his hands your Lordship's letter,† desiring him to read it, which he did. I then claimed the enjoyment of all the rights, prerogatives, franchises, and liberties, belonging to persons invested with a public character, according to the usual practice, and also the right of receiving and despatching messengers. All this was assented to without difficulty; but some arose on my mentioning to him, that I had found an embargo laid on at Calais, which, I apprehended, was not yet taken off. After representing to

---

\* These inclosures are merely formal notes to ask for and appoint a meeting between the Plenipotentiaries.

† Vide page 253.

him that it was perfectly useless to send my messenger from hence if he was to be stopped at the ports, and it being impossible for him not to admit this, he said he would speak to the Directory; and if any demur should arise on that point, your Lordship shall hear of it in a separate despatch.

After having gone through these points, I gave him a copy of my full powers, which he immediately read; the only observation he made on them was, that he perceived they were not addressed to the Directory. I explained to him the reason, and what had been the uniform practice on similar occasions; with this he seemed satisfied, but said he must lay them before the Directory, adding, however, that he could promise that no objection with respect to form or etiquette would arise on their part to prevent the opening of a negotiation.

I then said the only thing which could be said at this early period of the business, viz., that His Majesty was most sincere in his wish for the restoration of a general peace; to this M. Delacroix replied in precisely these words: "*Je peux aussi vous assurer, Milord, que moi, et tous ceux qui composent le Gouvernement Français, désirons bien sincèrement de rendre la tranquillité à notre trop malheureuse patrie, qui a tant souffert par ses ennemis, tant du dehors que du dedans.*"

I ended my conference by asking him whether I could hope that I should soon receive from him a copy of the full powers given to the person appointed to treat with me. He replied he could not with any degree of authority answer me as to the time, till he had taken the orders of the Directory. He said, "You know we have *our Allies*," and seemed to infer that it would be necessary to consult with their Ministers. I was not displeased to hear this word in his mouth, and I immediately added, "His Majesty also had his Allies, towards whom His Majesty intended most religiously to fulfil all his engagements." To this no reply was made; I took leave, and M. Delacroix, as is usual, conducted me to the door of the first ante-chamber.

It is, I am sure, unnecessary to premise to your Lordship, that it is not safe to form any judgment whatever as to the probable progress, much less as to the event of the Negotiation, from what passed in this conference, as the French Minister reserved the approbation of the Directory as a condition which attached to almost every word he said. His only positive assurance was that which I have written in French; there cannot, however, be a doubt but that he was ordered to receive and treat me in the manner he did, which I must in justice repeat (and I was most watchful it should be so) was unexceptionable, and precisely the same as I have experienced so many times at the opening of negotiations with which I have been charged.

I am the more certain that he acted from directions, as his common behaviour is reputed to be coarse and repelling; whereas, towards me it was grave indeed, and serious, but perfectly civil and well-bred.

I went to him dressed in His Majesty's uniform; he appeared to have taken as much pains to be well dressed as a man at his time of life, and in the present fashion of this country, could do.

M. Delacroix appears to be about fifty-five, of a very grave look, speaking rather slow and very little, listening with attention and answering correctly.

I should not, at any other time, have introduced these trifling remarks into a public despatch, but the particular circumstances of my Mission authorize me to do it.

I shall, in a very few days, despatch another messenger; but some time must yet pass before I can presume to say anything as to what I may suppose to be the real disposition and true situation of this country and its present Government, which appears to me to be so complicated, both as to the description of the different parties, as to their temper, power, and designs, that I ever shall speak of it with diffidence, and under the greatest apprehension of misleading your Lordship.

I have this moment (11 P.M.) received a passport for Wiffen, and an order that the embargo should be taken off at Calais for a vessel to carry him over to Dover.

I have at the same time received a note from M. Delacroix, a copy of which I enclose together with my answer. The title of *Commissioner* given me appears to be a literal translation from the Latin word used in my full powers;

and, although I have not adopted it in my answer, yet, as it is a word by no means novel in diplomatic language, I do not see any reason for its being objected to.

I am happy to have received this answer before Wiffen sets out, as your Lordship may now nearly guess to a certainty when to expect another messenger from me.

I am, &c.    MALMESBURY.

INCLOSURE.

Le Ministre des Relations Extérieures a l'honneur de prévenir le Lord Malmesbury, Commissaire Plénipotentiaire de Sa Majesté Britannique, qu'il a reçu du Directoire Exécutif les pouvoirs nécessaires pour négocier et conclure la paix entre la République et Sa Majesté. Dès demain, si le Lord Malmesbury le désire, les pouvoirs respectifs seront échangés. Le Ministre des Relations Extérieures sera prêt ensuite à recevoir les propositions que le Lord Malmesbury est chargé de faire à la République de la part de Sa Majesté Britannique.

Le Ministre des Relations Extérieures prie le Lord Malmesbury d'agréer les assurances de sa haute considération.

(Signé)    CH. DELACROIX.

Ce 2 Brumaire, an 5.

SUNDAY, OCT. 23.—At 11 with Delacroix, by appointment—no deficiency on his part in point of civility or etiquette. Poissardes again at my carriage-door as I went out of the hotel. Wrote the rest of the day, and despatched Wiffen at midnight.

MONDAY, OCT. 24.—With Delacroix—began our conferences, &c. Walked from two till four. Paris little altered, except fewer carriages and fewer well-dressed men—the women, on the contrary, much dressed, and all on foot with dark-coloured stockings. Called on Perregaux, and on the Portuguese Minister. He and the Neapolitan Prince,

Belmonte Pignatelli, called on me in the evening. Portuguese a philosopher and republican. The Neapolitan a clever and apparently well-intentioned man. He communicated to me his Treaty, which he said he had brought to bear by seeing Carnot, Rewbel, and Reveillière De la Peaux in private, and particularly Carnot. He recommended me to call on them. A Mr. Potter called on me in the morning—*avec des projets insensés.*

Tuesday, Oct. 25.—Writing. Walk. Play in the evening. Le Glorieux, and le Bourru bienfaisant. Milot acted. Theatre tolerably pretty—boxes good. "Citoyens ne faites pas des compliments," said the sentinel on our getting into the carriage.

EXTRACTS OF A DESPATCH FROM LORD MALMESBURY TO LORD GRENVILLE.

Paris, Oct. 27th, 1796, at midnight.

I informed your Lordship in my last that, at the moment when I was closing my despatches for Wiffen to carry to England, I received a note from M. Delacroix, saying, that he was authorized by the Executive Directory to treat with me as His Majesty's Minister Plenipotentiary, and would be ready to see me the next morning.

I went to him by my own appointment at half-past eleven on Monday, October 24. He immediately communicated to me the original of his full powers, a copy of which I enclose. I read them with the utmost attention; and, notwithstanding they appeared to me quite unexceptionable, yet I thought it right to remark to him, that although the words *Commissaire et Plénipotentiaire* were a literal translation of *Commissarium et Plenipotentiarum,* yet the character and title I intended to assume here was that of Minister Plenipotentiary. He said it was undoubtedly understood so by the Directory, and that nothing was meant by the word *Commissaire,* but to conform strictly to the Latin title given me in my full powers. And I could not indeed pretend to say that this expression would admit of any other construction. I, however, laid in the strongest protest against its being considered as at all inferior to that of Minister, and to this M. Delacroix assented in the fullest extent.

I then gave him a copy of my full powers certified by me to be a true copy, and asked from him one of his certified in the like manner ; and we reserved to ourselves, as is the usual practice, the formal exchange, till such time as the articles of the treaty shall be agreed on and ready for signature.

I had brought my secretary with me in order to produce the original full power, but M. Delacroix did not require to see it.

This ceremony performed, in which I hope nothing has been omitted or allowed which can at all commit His Majesty's dignity, or the character with which I am invested, I opened the conference by referring to the words I had used the preceding day, and said that I should now be able to prove that I had not asserted too much, when I had affirmed that my Royal Master was most sincere in his wishes to restore the present tranquillity of Europe, and to insure its stability by a general pacification. I expatiated on this point some time before I gave him the Memorial I received from your Lordship ; and I endeavoured not to forget any circumstance which could tend to show the just and equitable nature of the proposal there made, or impress his mind with the conviction that its adoption on the part of all the Belligerent Powers (France not excepted) would be the simplest and most advantageous method of attaining what must necessarily be the ultimate object of their wishes.

M. Delacroix, after reading the Memorial aloud, said it was of so important a nature, that he could not take upon himself to give me an official answer to it before it had been communicated to the Executive Directory. He could not, however, conceal from me that it did not appear to contain any proposal sufficiently distinct or specific ; that it was too vague in its expressions ; and that he thought the answer given to Mr. Wickham's* note of the 8th of May last, would apply perfectly to it.

* British Minister at Switzerland. He had been directed to sound the dis-

I begged him to read again and reconsider the Memorial, and to call correctly to his recollection the paper to which he referred, and I was persuaded that he would then perceive how little justified he was in both his observations.

Mr. Wickham's note went simply to inquire, what were at that time the sentiments of France, relative to a pacific negotiation. This Memorial, he must allow me to say, made a direct proposal of the general basis of a negotiation, and it was impossible not to perceive that a positive assurance was conveyed in it, to enter into more specific terms whenever the principle there laid down should be admitted by France. That although the future application of this principle was of course left open and indefinite, yet it was distinct and specific in itself; and it appeared beyond a possibility of misconstruction in what mode His Majesty was disposed to restore peace, and to secure by it the interests of his own kingdoms, of his allies, and of Europe in general.

M. Delacroix said, rather abruptly, " Do you mean the *status quo ante bellum*, or the *uti possidetis?*" I said it was too soon to reply to this question; but probably neither would be admitted, but under modifications. He desired me to define what I meant by the word *modifications*. I answered, the sense it conveyed was not equivocal, and I meant by using it, only to repeat what was stated in the Memorial as to His Majesty's intentions of employing the effects of his successes during this war, in *compensating* France for restitutions of such of her conquests on the Continent, as may be necessary to satisfy the just claims of His Majesty's allies, and to preserve the political balance of Europe.

M. Delacroix, after a little further argument, carried on, however, in a very civil and cordial manner, admitted in some degree the truth of what I said; but on turning again to the Memorial, and reading the words " *Le succès, non interrompu*,"\* &c., he broke out in what I really can express in no other words, but a republican rant. His object seemed to be, to overcome me by declamation, and by a string of

position of the French Government through their Minister, Mons. Barthelemi, and to suggest a European Congress for the purpose of effecting a general pacification. The Directory rejected the proposal, and published the correspondence. \* Vide Memorial, page 251.

pompous and prepared phrases, to prove that France was the most powerful nation in the world, and disposed to be the most moderate in the use of its power. But though his voice was loud, and his manner theatrical, yet as he said nothing offensive, either to my Court or to my public character, I heard him with the greatest composure and patience ; and when he had finished, contented myself by saying, he talked his own language so eloquently, and so much better than I could be expected to do, that it was not in my power to reply to him in the same style. That I, however, by no means disapproved his using this style, as it was the substance of what he spoke, and not the words in which it was conveyed, which it was my duty to report ; that every country knew how to appreciate its own power, and to compare it with that of other nations. But I conceived this point to be perfectly foreign to the main object of our conference, and one on which it was neither probable nor essential that our ideas should meet.

M. Delacroix (who, although he spoke with eagerness, had never lost his temper,) immediately resumed the subject. He said that any further observations on his part would be perfectly useless till he had laid the Memorial before the Directory, unless I was prepared on my part to be more explicit, and to tell him, whether we meant the French Republic should annul any of the treaties of peace it had already made with several of the German Princes, or give up the conquests it had by an act of the Constitution united to its territory, because the proposal in the Memorial seemed to go to both these points. I told him that my instructions went no further than to say, that His Majesty was ready to enter into a negotiation for peace, in the mode stated in the Memorial, provided that this principle be first admitted, viz., that this peace should be combined with that of Europe in general, and of His Majesty's allies in particular ; and that in every period of the negotiation, constant reference should be had to the manner in which the affairs and interests of the Continent were to be arranged, and especially the fullest attention paid to those of His Majesty's good and faithful ally the Emperor. This naturally led M. Delacroix to inquire whether the Court of Vienna concurred in this measure.

I replied, No part of it was concealed from that Court, and that I should demand a passport for a messenger to go to Vienna, as soon as I knew the manner in which His Majesty's proposals were received by the Executive Directory. M. Delacroix said, " How are we to expect a general peace, when we hear every day that the Emperor is determined to carry on the war; and when it is to be inferred from dates, that he must be unacquainted with your Mission here?" I replied that this was a remark which, although it was very natural for him to make, was so irrelevant to the question before us, that I was sure he would not expect me to enter into any discussion upon it. That it was sufficient for every present purpose to know that His Majesty's intention was to combine the interests of his allies, and the future security of Europe in general with those of his own kingdoms; and that the end His Majesty so seriously wished to obtain could not be produced, if any other mode of negotiation were required.

M. Delacroix here said, what he appeared to have been watching during the whole of our conference for an opportunity to bring in, and observed to me, that he believed it would be much easier to make a *separate* peace between England and France, than to undertake at once a general pacification. Without entering into the merits of this question, I replied, that I was perfectly sure no such proposal would be listened to by His Majesty; and that he (M. Delacroix) himself had pronounced on the impropriety of it, by mentioning in his conversation of yesterday the allies of France, and the intentions of the Directory to support them.

M. Delacroix pressed this point no further, and although in speaking of the allies of France, he manifestly had alluded to Spain as well as to Holland, yet he did not choose to particularize it. I thought it premature to attempt drawing from him any of his views with respect to that Power, being fully persuaded that a more advantageous opportunity must offer in the course of the negotiation for obeying my instructions on this head. He ended the conference by repeating that he would lay the Memorial before the Directory, and let me know whenever they authorized him to make an answer; that he was much afraid that what struck him on this cursory view, would strike them more forcibly on an attentive perusal of it, and consequently that it would not lead to the restoration of that general tranquillity which was so much the object of our joint wishes.

Yesterday (Wednesday), at about ten in the evening, M. Guiraudet, Secretary-General to the Foreign Department, called upon me, with a letter from M. Delacroix, directed to me as His Majesty's Minister Plenipotentiary.

M. Guiraudet informed me, that he had M. Delacroix's orders to bring me the resolution of the Executive Directory in answer to the Memorial I had left with him on Monday.

I had nothing to say to M. Guiraudet, but to desire him to thank M. Delacroix for the attentive manner in which he had conveyed to me this answer, and that I would wait upon him this morning; but it was not till four P.M. that he was at leisure to receive me.

I am just returned from him: our conference was very short. I told him that although there was much to observe on several parts of the answer that the French Government had thought proper to make to the Memorial I had given in; yet, as I considered it as my primary duty to suppress every remark I could consistently with my duty suppress, which was at all likely to impede the progress and completion of a measure of such high importance as that now pending between the two countries, I would abstain from every reflection whatever; and as the last sentence in the answer did express a readiness on the part of the French Republic to consent to enter into a combined negotiation with my Royal Master for a general pacification, I would pass over in silence all the extraneous matter introduced in it, which certainly, were I disposed to animadvert, would admit of much and just animadversion. I should content myself by submitting it to my Court, without troubling him with any other observations at present; and in order neither to mislead my own Court, nor that of Vienna, to which I should of course communicate the whole of what had passed, I should now content myself with asking him whether by the words, "*faire apparoître les pouvoirs suffisants des Puissances Alliés de la Grande Brétagne,*" anything else was meant than that they should either send ministers here themselves, or empower the ministers of their allies to act for them. He said, Certainly not; the Directory by no means pretends to trace out a mode of negotiation to other Powers; its only wish is to avoid unnecessary delay, and particularly that which would arise from a *congress*. I observed to him, I had never mentioned the word *congress*, which generally was understood to be a meeting of ministers in a town belonging to some Neutral Power; and that everything I had by order of my Court proposed, was evidently proposed with a view to negotiate at Paris, and to determine the great question of peace or war as soon as possible; and that he might be assured himself, and in the fullest confidence assure the Executive Directory, my Royal Master's most anxious wish was to bring this point to a speedy and clear decision.

M. Delacroix in reply said, this would have been effected much sooner if I would have consented to treat for a separate peace. I told him I could only repeat what I had already so often enforced, that a general pacification, and one in which the interests of Europe and those of His Majesty's allies were to be attended to, equally with his own, was the only one His Majesty ever would consent to listen to; because the conciliation of many and various interests was evidently necessary to restore universal tranquillity, and ensure the political balance of power in Europe.

It remains for me only to say, that, in conformity to His Majesty's order, I shall despatch Dressins to Vienna, at the same moment that I despatch Silvester for England; that I have written fully to Sir M. Eden,* and enclosed to him a copy of my principal despatch of this day to your Lordship, leaving out of it only such parts as relate to the ceremonial of my reception. I have also transmitted to him a copy of the Resolution of the Directory, in answer to the Memorial; and have, I trust, omitted nothing that may tend to prove to His Imperial Majesty that on this occasion I am acting as becomes the Minister of a Court in strict and faithful alliance.

* Sir Morton Eden, Ambassador at the Court of Vienna.

EXTRAIT DES REGISTRES DES DÉLIBÉRATIONS DU DIRECTOIRE
EXÉCUTIF.

Paris, le cinq Brumaire, l'an cinq de la République Française
une et indivisible.

Le Directoire Exécutif charge le Ministre des Relations Extérieures de faire au Lord Malmesbury la réponse suivante.

Le Directoire Exécutif voit avec peine qu'au moment où il avoit lieu d'espérer le très prochain retour de la paix entre la République Française et Sa Majesté Brittannique, la proposition du Lord Malmesbury n'offre que des moyens dilatoires ou très éloignés d'en amener la conclusion.

Le Directoire observe que si le Lord Malmesbury eut voulu traiter séparément, ainsi qu'il y est formellement autorisé par la teneur de ses Lettres de Créance, les négociations eussent pû être considérablement abrégées ; que la nécessité de balancer avec les intérêts des deux Puissances, ceux des Alliés de la Grande Brétagne, multiplie les combinaisons, complique les difficultés, tend à la formation d'un Congrès, dont on sait que les formes sont toujours lentes, et exige l'accession de Puissances qui jusqu'ici n'ont témoigné aucun désir de rapprochement, et n'ont donné au Lord Malmesbury lui-même d'après sa déclaration aucun pouvoir de stipuler pour elles. Ainsi sans rien préjuger contre les intentions du Lord Malmesbury, sans rien conclure de ce que sa déclaration ne paroît point s'accorder avec les pouvoirs qui lui sont délégués par ses Lettres de Créance, sans supposer qu'il ait reçu des instructions secrèttes qui détruiroient l'effet de ses pouvoirs ostensibles, sans prétendre enfin que le double but du Gouvernement Brittannique ait été d'écarter par des propositions générales les propositions partielles des autres puissances, et d'obtenir du peuple Anglois les moyens de continuer la guerre, en rejetant sur la République l'odieux d'un retard qu'il auroit nécessité lui-même, le Directoire Exécutif ne peut se dissimuler que la proposition du Lord Malmesbury n'est autre chose, et seulement sous des formes plus amicales, que le renouvellement de celles qui furent faites l'année dernière par

M. Wickham, et qu'elle ne présente qu'un espoir éloigné de la paix.

Le Directoire Exécutif observe encore à l'égard du principe des Rétrocessions mis en avant par le Lord Malmesbury, que ce principe vaguement et isolement présenté ne peut servir de base à des négociations ; que l'on doit considérer avant tout le besoin commun d'une paix juste et solide, l'équilibre politique que des Rétrocessions absolues pourroient rompre, et ensuite les moyens que peuvent avoir les Puissances Belligérantes, l'une de soutenir des conquêtes faites lorsqu'elle étoit appuyée par un grand nombre d'alliés aujourd'hui détachés de la Coalition, l'autre de les céder lorsque celles qui avoient été d'abord ses ennemis sont devenues presques toutes ou ses propres alliés ou au moins neutres.

Cependant le Directoire Exécutif, animé du désir ardent de faire cesser le fléau de la guerre, et pour prouver qu'il ne se refuse à aucune voie de conciliation, déclare qu'aussitôt que le Lord Malmesbury fera apparoître au Ministre des Relations Extérieures les pouvoirs suffisans des Puissances Alliés de la Grande Brétagne à l'effet de stipuler pour leurs intérêts respectifs, et leur promesse de souscrire à ce qui aura été conclu en leur nom, le Directoire Exécutif s'empressera de répondre aux propositions précises qui lui seront faites, et que les difficultés s'applaniront autant que peuvent le comporter la sûreté et la dignité de la République.

Pour expédition conforme,
 (Signé)  L. M. RÉVEILLIERE LÉPAUX, Président.
Par le Directoire Exécutif le Sécrétaire Général,
     (Signé)  LAGARDE.
Pour copie conforme,
    Le Ministre des Relations Extérieures,
     (Signé)  CH. DELACROIX.
  Par le Ministre le Sécrétaire Général,
     (Signé)  T. GUIRAUDET.

### LETTER FROM LORD MALMESBURY TO LORD GRENVILLE.

(Private.) Paris, Thursday, Oct. 27th, 1796, at midnight.

MY DEAR LORD,—I should not have troubled you with a private letter by this messenger, if I did not wish to say that I probably shall have no plausible pretence for sending away another before a week hence; neither, unless I should have anything very essential to write, shall I think it necessary to send one away sooner. I still am doubtful whether it will become a negotiation; but I hope you will not disapprove my not having noticed in stronger terms than I did the exceptionable surmises in the answer. Any remarks will not only come with more effect from you, but also be so expressed as to accord with your future intentions; whereas, if I had once given way to my feelings, the words could not have been recalled, and they might have done us hurt. I am, &c. MALMESBURY.

---

### DESPATCH FROM LORD MALMESBURY TO LORD GRENVILLE.

Paris, 27th Oct., 1796.

MY LORD,—I have already had the honour to represent to your Lordship that I must, for some time to come, continue to speak with great diffidence on every point that relates to the interior government and policy of this country; and, although I have lost no opportunity of obtaining the most exact information it was in my power to procure on this complicated subject, I must again repeat, that you will consider what I now offer to your Lordship as a mere sketch which will probably require much future correction.

It appears that the several descriptions of men who compose the Directory, and the two great Councils of the nation, may be classed under three general divisions (for they cannot with propriety be called parties); the individuals of each reserving to themselves their separate opinions, not only in matters of detail, but often on the most fundamental points of the constitution, which they all equally profess to support, and generally aiming at the acquisition of preeminence in power or popularity, without any concert or common principle of action.

The most powerful and numerous of these divisions is that which may, perhaps without much impropriety, be called the faction of the Conventionalists, or those who are attached to the present constitution, under the modifications which were annexed to it by the last Convention, at the close of their session, with a view to preserve as long as possible in their own hands the power which they had wrested from the partisans of Robespierre. These, though they are admitted to be the most moderate of the Jacobins, are in some measure implicated in the odium that now attaches to every remnant of that once formidable club. They are violently censured for having assumed to themselves so great a preponderance in the constitution which they gave to the nation, instead of leaving that preponderance to the primary assemblies ; for having defended their usurpation by force of arms ; and for having refused to crush the faction of the Mountain, who are the objects of general execration. It was owing to the unpopularity arising from these causes, that, at the last election for one third of the Council, the primary assemblies took care to reject all candidates of this description; and it seems to be generally supposed, (though I do not know whether justly or not,) that the approaching elections in the month of March will be no less unfavourable to them.

The second party is that of the Mountain, whose principles (which they still continue to avow) are sufficiently known to your Lordship. As their numbers are so much diminished, and their persons so universally odious, it is generally supposed that they are only tolerated by the party now in power, as engines who may be employed on any occasion, where the Government may wish to have recourse to such measures of violence as are incompatible with the freedom of the present constitution.

The third party, or *Modérés*, who call themselves *les Honnêtes Gens*, and who are stigmatised by their enemies as *la Faction des Anciennes Limites*, are those who were chosen at the last election, and consequently form the minority, consisting of one third of the Council. They profess to be pure republicans, and intimate the warmest attachment to the present constitution ; the spirit of which, however, they interpret very differently from the majority, affecting the greatest deference for the opinions of the people at large, which, indeed, they in a great measure direct, declaring war only against the partisans of the system of terror, and endeavouring to conciliate the friends of every other party by principles of liberality and universal toleration. They have lately, on several occasions, very nearly extorted from the majority of the Council their assent to measures which in secret they greatly disapproved, and which, indeed, have a direct tendency to transfer into other hands the direction and government of the country. There are two very important laws, on which the two parties are at this moment at issue. The first relates to the priests, of whom about 20,000 are at present confined in the different prisons in France: the minority strongly protest against their further detention, and have very lately endeavoured to repeal the law of the Convention by which it was commanded; and, though they have ultimately failed of success, their defeat is attributed solely to a temporary manœuvre of the Directory. In the mean time their popularity has been greatly increased by the abilities they displayed on this occasion. The other measure, on which the Council has not yet decided, is the repeal of a law of the Convention called "La Loi du troisième Brumaire," which excludes from all places of public trust and confidence any person who is related to, or in any way connected with, any of the several classes of emigrants. In their opposition to this law, which is almost universally considered as equally repugnant to all ideas of justice, and to the spirit of the constitution, the minority are strongly supported by the public opinion; and although, notwithstanding the superiority in point of argument, they may possibly fail of success in the present Council, it is universally supposed, and indeed with great appearance of probability, that both the above-mentioned laws will be repealed soon after the change which will be made in the Council by means of the next elections.

From this state of things your Lordship will not be surprised to hear that many persons look forward with great confidence to an early and very considerable revolution in the Government of France. It certainly appears that the memory of their late unhappy monarch is no longer regarded with disgust, but rather with sentiments of compassion and remorse;* that, the principle of separating the executive from the legislative authority being admitted, the fondness for an oligarchy is not likely for any length of time to preponderate over the known advantages of a mixed monarchy; and that experience having shewn the compatibility of Republicanism and the most savage tyranny, and the animosity of the different parties—who have alternately prevailed under what is called the *new order of things*—having produced nothing but domestic misery, the nation begins to wish for the oblivion of party distinctions, the cessation of civil discord, and perhaps an ultimate return to some mode of government founded on the solid basis of experience. I must observe, however, that the present Government has been long in the possession of power and influence; that they are active and vigilant, and apparently very well served by their inferior agents; and that it cannot be supposed, either that they are ignorant of the views of their adversaries, and of the measures by which it may be proposed to carry those views into effect, or that they are unprovided with formidable means of defence.

Although, for the reasons just given, I am not yet able to form any decided opinion with respect to the probable stability of the existing Government, there can be no doubt of its present efficacy in all matters of internal regulation. The police of Paris, which is in the hands of Cochon, a man apparently much respected by all parties, is unquestionably as perfect in all its parts as it ever was under the direction of M. Le Noir, or even under that of M. de Sartines; the inferior officers employed by those Ministers having been lately restored to their places, and armed with every power that can be necessary to secure the public tranquillity.

I have already had the honour of mentioning to your

* The truth of this opinion was proved in the following year, when the Royalist and Moderate party nearly obtained the victory over the Ultra-republicans.

Lordship, that I had been much struck with the general appearance of plenty and excellent cultivation in all that part of the country through which I passed on my road from Calais; and I am assured that the same description would apply to almost every province of the Republic: in fact, the peasants and small landed proprietors, though exposed to frequent requisitions and other revolutionary vexations, appear to have been among the principal gainers by the new order of things; having from the beginning refused to accept of assignats in return for the produce of their industry, and that produce consisting of articles of the first necessity, they gradually accumulated and constantly secreted a very large proportion of the whole mass of coin in circulation. With this, which they had the art and courage to defend against all the violence of the revolutionary Government, they contrived, during the progressive depression of assignats, to make purchases of land to such advantage as appears almost incredible. By the annihilation of paper money all this mass of coin is now returned into circulation, and it certainly appears in as great abundance as it ever did during the old *régime*. This plenty, however, is only apparent, since it is admitted on all sides that the quantity of coin now existing in France does not amount to much more than two-thirds of what this country formerly contained: and, as this position has not been denied or contested, it is argued as demonstrable, without entering into the labyrinth of French finance, that there does not and cannot exist any fund capable of furnishing the enormous supplies which would be necessary for another campaign; that the collection of the arrears of taxes is evidently impossible; that the emission of new paper would only drive the money of the country again into concealment; and that the produce of taxes, whether direct or indirect, could evidently amount only to a small proportion of the coin in circulation, and must consequently prove a very inadequate resource. To this it might be answered, that at this moment the army of Moreau is recruited and supplied by requisitions and arbitrary levies raised on the departments in its neighbourhood; that the same revolutionary methods might, and must, in a case of necessity, be employed throughout the kingdom; and that, admitting all the ruinous consequences of such measures, they certainly would not occasion, in the course of one or two campaigns, the total destruction of the country.

It is undeniable, however, that the distresses of the Directory are extreme, that the cry for peace is universal, that a total disregard for the general wish might be fatal to them, that the speedy restoration of peace would probably be their strongest recommendation to national favour at the next election, which is now rapidly approaching; and, consequently, that the expression of their wishes on this head may be presumed to be tolerably sincere. The greatest obstacles to the attainment of this point will probably arise from the exaggerated promises of assistance and aggrandizement which they are supposed to have made to their Allies, and to the fraternized departments in the moment of their unexampled prosperity. I have, &c. MALMESBURY.

---

LETTER FROM LORD MALMESBURY TO MR. CANNING.*

Paris, Thursday, Oct. 27th, 1796.

MY DEAR CANNING,—If we have escaped the guillotine here, how shall we escape the Tower in England?

I need not tell *you*, who know his style, that although the despatch on the " state of parties" in this country is the result of our *combined* observations and information, yet the putting it together in the clear and orderly method in which it appears, is the separate work of George Ellis. *Render unto*

* Mr. Canning was at this time Under-Secretary at the Foreign Office. From his earliest entrance into life Lord Malmesbury appreciated and cherished his great qualities and talents, and Mr. Canning appears to have returned this partiality with the most sincere regard. His letters to Lord Malmesbury are often like those of an affectionate son, and would prove that a warm and enthusiastic heart is not to be chilled even by the selfish atmosphere of politics. He and his friend George Ellis were Lord Malmesbury's constant guests, and were certainly not the least brilliant amongst the many clever visitors whom he collected at his house.

Mr. Canning was placed in his office by Pitt, who at this time had his own proud temper constantly ruffled by the still haughtier and much colder nature of Lord Grenville. Canning had a difficult part to play between Pitt, to whom he was devoted, and his immediate chief, who (if I may judge from various letters in the Harris collection) could never elicit the personal regard from his subalterns which they were obliged to grant to his fine understanding.

*Cæsar that which is Cæsar's*, is or will be in my instructions; and I had almost as soon keep Belgium from the Emperor, as the merit of this letter to myself. Pray therefore tell Pitt and Lord Grenville *who wrote it*, that through them it may be known in the Closet and Cabinet.

Pray, pray take care that the puzzle and embarrassments, which I foresee with so much certainty must arise from the manner in which we have conducted this business at Vienna, be not made over to me in its puzzled and twisted state to unravel. Besides the injustice of visiting this sin upon me, let it be considered that I have a sufficient number of knots to untie, and ends to pick out, without the addition of this most confused one. I am sure your opposite neighbour* will be kind to me on this occasion, and to him you will apply in my behalf.

We go on delightfully among ourselves, and you would be astonished how very soon Talbot found out what I wished him to be, and how exactly he is become so. I anxiously hope *nobody* whatever will be sent over to me yet. We already give umbrage from our numbers and *reputed* cleverness, and *any* increase of *suite* would (till the negotiation is fairly opened) be pernicious; and then let Morpeth,† *and Morpeth alone* be the person. I am really in earnest in this request, and that not from any feelings of my own, but because I am quite sure of the bad effect it would produce.

I scarce know how I am to pass the interval which now must elapse before I can resume the business on which I am sent. I have nothing but Sir Sidney Smith to play with, and he is an edged tool. Adieu, &c. MALMESBURY.

---

SUNDAY, OCT. 30.—To the Museum in the Louvre. Robert shewed it us—pictures not hung up. Saw Puget play—" Surprise de l'Amour" and " Marriage Secret."

---

MONDAY, OCT. 31.—Baron de Schenck called.‡ Walked—wrote in the evening.

---

\* Mr. Pitt. † The present Lord Carlisle.
‡ He was attached to the Prince of Orange, and took Lord Malmesbury's

TUESDAY, NOV. 1.—Went to Maison Grange Batelière. Good apartments—saw the Library—national now, formerly King's — 60,000 MSS. (quere) — well kept. Louis XIV. *heures*—those of *Anne d'Autriche* finer. No fund now to support it. Went to *Les Italiens*—" Pauvre Femme"—remarkable play—acted by Madame Dugazon.

WEDNESDAY, NOV. 2. — Hardenberg — Ross and Champs Elysées. Visited Naples and Portugal.* Nothing new. Naples with me in the evening.

THURSDAY, NOV. 3.—Madme. de Noailles† from Versailles. Champs Elysées. Wurtemburg minister comes to pump. Went with Lord G. Leveson to the Pantheon—very fine. Walked back through the Cité. Play in the evening. Dugazon superiorly excellent in Mariamne—the finest acting I ever saw. Letters from Sir S. Smith.

Letters to England. The Directory at this period of the Negotiation published in the " Redacteur" the memorial presented by Lord Malmesbury, and their answer to it, with comments upon them. When Lord Malmesbury remonstrated against this unfair and unjustifiable appeal to the passions of the people during a transaction of this nature, it was defended by M. Delacroix " as indispensable in the present responsible situation of the Directory." Some personally libellous articles against our Ambassador and the gentlemen of his suite were voluntarily reprobated and condemned by the French authorities.

* The Ambassadors, Pignatelli and Sandoz.

† The following account relative to one of the most amiable and talented members of this family is from an original memoir in the Harris Papers. "Lord Malmesbury was at Brighton at the period of the bitter and sanguinary persecution of the French nobility and clergy during the Revolution. As he was walking on the pier, a French fishing-boat approached it, and one of its crew jumped out with a baby in his arms, which a lady, he said, had thrown into the boat, entreating them to save its life, and land it on the British shore, whither, if she were spared, she would follow it. The lady was known to these poor fishermen, and beloved by them. They immediately stood over to Brighton with their innocent charge, unconscious of the bloody republican hand that had threatened its frail existence. Lord Malmesbury took it under his care, and had it conveyed to Lady Malmesbury at his house. Within a month arrived, after a multitude of hair-breadth escapes, the harassed mother, who had learnt the spot where the child had been landed, soon discovered its place of refuge, and was again in possession of the darling object of so many days' anxiety. Her gratitude was unbounded. This baby became a handsome and fascinating woman, and a leader in the first circles in Paris. She always signed herself in her communications to Lord Malmesbury, ' Leontine Harris.'"

FRIDAY, Nov. 4.—Las Heras, late Spanish Consul in England, to pry. Wrote to Sir S. Smith. Walk to the Bastille. Perregaux dined with me. Opera—moderate, not so good as formerly. Not full, and bad-looking company. Ballet moderate—dresses fine—orchestra good. Received from M. Thurot through Perregaux a translation of "Hermes."*

SATURDAY, Nov. 5.—Walk before breakfast. Wrote to Thurot. Walk with Ellis to Lignereux—beautiful furniture. No. 2, Rue Christine, to Vignon, who sells maps in la Rue Dauphine—apparently honest. To Pillons—he died in the morning. To Magimel, bookseller—sensible man. To Rondonneau's, who published all the acts and laws—very talkative, but clever—10,000 laws published since 1789, only *seventy* in force.

LETTER FROM MR. PITT TO LORD MALMESBURY.

Wimbledon, Nov. 5th, 1796.

MY DEAR LORD,—Although I have nothing material to trouble you with, in addition to what you will receive from the office, I do not like to let the messenger go without thanking you for your letter, or without telling you how glad I was to receive the interesting information of different kinds which you had in so short a time collected. The reference to Vienna, which was indispensably necessary, of course renders your negotiation for the present not very active. We have thought, however, that we have a fair opportunity of urging again discussions *on the basis*, as the best way to abridge subsequent details. If you find a disposition in the French Government to entertain any discussion on the basis we have proposed, we may fairly expect that we may very soon receive from Austria such communications as may enable us to furnish you with more particular instructions, and enable you to enter on more precise

* M. Thurot had, by order of the Convention, translated "Hermes," the philosophical work written by Lord Malmesbury's father. This accidental compliment was curious, considering the times and the respective parties.

explanations. I think it, however, not improbable, though I much wish the contrary, that the French Government may take some line, in consequence of the Note which you are by this messenger instructed to present, which, instead of advancing the negotiation, will only shew more clearly the desire to evade it. All this is, however, very vague conjecture; and I own I am quite at a loss to judge whether they feel most the *necessity of peace*, (of which I think there are strong indications in what has already passed,) or the impossibility of maintaining their power after peace shall have been made. I have been much struck with an idea accidentally suggested to me in the course of this day. It is founded (I know not how accurately) on the supposition that there is now a law extant in France (said to be known as the Law of the 3rd Brumaire) which excludes all the connexions of *émigrés* from any right of voting till after the end of the war. The inference is, that the present Directory will not (if they can help it) make any peace till after the new elections in March, as the expiration of the law would give an accession of force to their enemies in choosing the new members, which must end in their ruin. It is very probable that this idea may be without foundation, but I mention it only that you may judge of it. If it appears to deserve a moment's thought, you will let me know what occurs to you on it.

Our accounts from Italy are still so tardy, that I know not how that quarter is likely to influence our Negotiation. Moreau's retreat\* (as far as we yet know the particulars of it) has been less disastrous to the French than might have been expected. But, on the other hand, every thing on the Rhine from Dusseldorf to Strasbourg seems as favourable as possible. Our capture of the Dutch squadron in Saldanha Bay† is not a bad episode, nor a bad lesson to the allies of France; and, above all, the ease and almost unanimity with which (in spite of some violent speeches) we have carried through, in this week, the measures of

\* Before the Archduke Charles.
† On the 17th of August, a Dutch squadron of three 60-gun ships and three frigates lying in Saldanha Bay, near the Cape of Good Hope, surrendered to a greatly superior force under Sir G. Elphinstone. The Dutch ships had 2,000 soldiers on board, intended for the re-conquest of the Cape.

defence for this country, must, I trust, make no small impression. I never saw so much zeal in Parliament, or so much reason to depend upon it in the country.

       Believe me, &c.   W. Pitt.

---

EXTRACTS OF A LETTER FROM MR. CANNING TO LORD MALMESBURY.

Downing Street, Monday, 7th Nov., 1796. Past midnight.

When I promised you in my letter by Mr. Swinburne* (which I trust you will have received) that your messenger should be despatched to you on Sunday, though I was not aware that impediments might arise to the execution of this promise, which it would be wholly out of my power to prevent or remedy, I certainly did not foresee that which has arisen, and which has been the chief cause of the detention of the messenger: I mean, the death of a sister of Lord Grenville's, Mrs. Neville. This event, which took place yesterday, retarded in a considerable degree the completion of the despatches to you, and is perhaps the occasion of their being less full on some points than they might have been made, if Lord Grenville had been able to give them a final consideration. It is the occasion also of Lord Grenville's not answering your private letters, as he desires me to tell you, and to request that you will accept the present state of his mind as a sufficient apology for the omission.

The part of your public instructions which seems to me most particularly to require the supplemental aid that would probably have been afforded to them by Lord Grenville's private letters, or by what he might possibly have added to his despatches, is that which relates to the expectation so confidently held out of a speedy answer from Vienna, upon the subject of the terms that would be accepted there as satisfactory in the event of a general

---

\* Mr. Swinburne was employed by the English Government as agent for the exchange of prisoners. He has published his Memoirs, and describes Lord Malmesbury as an " indolent " man. Lord Malmesbury calls him a *bore*, which may account for the impression he produced upon Mr. Swinburne.

pacification. In this expectation I confess I am not quite so sanguine as your instructor. Nothing has passed since you left England which makes it more certain that Vienna is about to enter into such an explanation—except, indeed, the *time* which has passed, and by which, therefore, the explanation, if it is to come at all, must be so much the nearer.

One thing about which I am pretty certain he could *not* have written, though you professed yourself anxious to hear from him upon it, is the business of the *cockades;* upon which his opinion, as far as I could collect it, appeared to be, that you had better decide for yourself upon your own opinion, as you thought best or might find necessary, but should by no means look for any answer to your reference home. In this opinion, Pitt, I think, seems to concur with him.

What other opinions Pitt entertains respecting your conduct, and the state of your Mission, he will probably have explained to you himself in the letter which I forward to you from him, and which he determined to write on his own mere motion, for the express purpose (as he told me) of letting you see that he was perfectly satisfied with all that you had said and done. He approves, I know, of your having sent to Vienna; he approves of your having passed by, for the moment at least, the irregularity in Lacroix's powers. He would not have disapproved, I am persuaded, of your having taken some short and spirited notice (had you thought it right to do so of your own accord, and on your own responsibility,) of the abusive part of the Mémoire of the Directory. In short, he feels, just as you would have him, the delicacy and difficulty of your situation, and would make you more allowance than you can ever want, and will give you all the support that you can possibly desire. It is a sad anti-climax, but a necessary one, to add, that he has ordered the two thousand pounds that you required, to be put in a certain place. And it would be unnecessary to add further, but that it is an equal though not so useful an indication of his good-will towards you, that his last words to me to-day were, "Pray, write him a comfortable letter."

I know not whether I shall exactly have fulfilled his injunctions; but, if I have not, it is not now the time to repair my neglect. It is now near ten o'clock; your boxes are made up, your messengers wait but for me; and every minute, therefore, that I should add to the length of this letter, would be so much delay in the time of your receiving it, and all that accompanies it. You may, therefore, thank me for bidding you farewell, and you must now believe me, &c. G. C.

---

EXTRACTS OF A DESPATCH FROM LORD GRENVILLE TO LORD MALMESBURY.

Downing Street, 7th Nov., 1796.

HIS Majesty's servants entirely concur in opinion with your Lordship, that no just ground of objection arose from the expression of *Commissaire* used in the powers given to M. Delacroix, as this word is literally translated from that used in His Majesty's full powers to your Lordship, and is indeed more strictly correct than any other that could be used to describe the character and situation of a Plenipotentiary, no otherwise accredited than by the commission which conveys to him the authority to negotiate and conclude; and as it is expressly laid down by writers of the best authority on the subject, that a Commissioner Plenipotentiary in this situation is entitled to all the privileges of a public Minister.

With respect to the powers produced by M. Delacroix, I am concerned to observe, that a difficulty occurs of considerable weight, applying not only to a point of form, but to a matter of much substantial importance. The powers granted to your Lordship contain a full authority "to treat, conclude, and sign," and are not limited by any reference to instructions given, or to be given, to you; and it is this circumstance that properly constitutes them "full powers;" because whatever restraints His Majesty's instructions may have laid upon the exercise of your discretion in *negotiating*, the Treaty, when concluded, derives its full validity and force from your *signature*, by which His Majesty's good faith is bound and concluded. But the powers given to M.

Delacroix do not come under the same description of "full powers;" they contain an express reference to the instructions which he is from time to time to receive: so that, after the signature, his act may be disavowed as being contrary to his instructions, and therefore beyond his ostensible authority conveyed in the instrument communicated to your Lordship.

The extreme importance of every part of this business, and particularly of every circumstance by which the validity of any act signed by the Minister with whom you treat can be in any manner affected, is so great, that His Majesty's servants, however unwilling on such an occasion to start mere difficulties of form, do not feel themselves at liberty wholly to overlook the difference which I have here stated. But, as they are willing to hope that it has not been intentional, they do not judge it necessary that your Lordship should insist on the grant of more ample powers to M. Delacroix in the present stage of the business.

There is indeed a very remarkable circumstance in this business, and one which, while it indicates no very liberal or candid disposition on the part of those with whom you are treating, gives too much reason to apprehend that the point in question cannot have been wholly overlooked by them. What I mean is this,—that immediately after furnishing their own Minister with these defective and insufficient powers, avowedly limiting his authority by a reference to their instructions, and therefore rendering all his acts liable to be disavowed after their signature, they attempted to raise a cavil against the conduct of this Government on the same subject, and presumed to cast some suspicion of bad faith on this Court, because they collected from your Lordship, that, although possessed of such powers as must give undisputed validity to any act to which you affixed your signature, you were restrained in the use of those powers by the orders of your Court; a circumstance which must of necessity occur in every Negotiation conducted by a public Minister out of his own country.

Passing from this point to the substance of the Negotiation itself, it is with very deep concern that I feel myself under the necessity of saying, that the same spirit appears in the whole conduct of the Directory, and especially in the answer returned to the Memorial which you were charged to present. Nothing can be more captious than the pretext for delay which is taken in that answer; and the offensive matter, which is so unnecessarily and improperly introduced into that paper, seems hardly a clearer indication of a wish to set all conciliation at a distance, than the purport of the answer is of a resolution to retard and ultimately to defeat the negotiation. Your Lordship will, however, not fail to observe, from the spirit of the reply which His Majesty has directed that your Lordship should deliver to M. Delacroix, a copy of which I herewith enclose for that purpose, that the King is resolved to suffer no artifice on the part of his enemies so far to succeed as to elude the necessity of coming to the clear and distinct issue on which the business must finally turn. If the negotiation fails, it must be rendered evident to the world that it fails from the hostile determination of those who govern France, and from their resolution to admit of no terms of peace which are consistent with the safety, interests, and honour of the other Powers of Europe.

Whatever may be the answer that is returned to this Note, your Lordship will be careful to take it *ad referendum*, forbearing all reply or comment upon its contents until you shall have consulted with your Court upon them.

But in case the purport of the answer should be (what there is, perhaps, little reason to expect from the present temper and views of the Directory, such as they have been manifested in their conduct at the opening of your Mission) a full acceptance of the proposal contained in this Note, you will then state your expectation of being enabled shortly to enter with more precision and detail into the terms of a provisional negotiation.

It appears highly necessary that His Majesty's servants should be in full possession of all that has passed at Vienna upon so important a point, and should have been enabled to combine and compare it with whatever the ulterior discussions carried on from hence may have produced, before any step is taken, or any communication made at Paris upon the subject.

(MEMORIAL INCLOSED FOR THE DIRECTORY.)

Le Soussigné n'a pas manqué de transmettre à sa Cour la réponse du Directoire aux propositions qu'il a été chargé de faire pour servir d'ouverture à une négociation pacifique.

Quant aux insinuations offensantes et injurieuses que l'on a trouvé dans cette pièce, et qui ne sont propres qu'à mettre de nouveaux obstacles au rapprochement que le Gouvernement François fait profession de désirer, le Roi l'a jugé fort au dessous de sa dignité de permettre qu'il y soit répondu de sa part de quelque manière que ce fut. Le progrès et le résultat de la Négociation mettront assez en évidence les principes sur lesquels elle aura été dirigée, de part et d'autre : et ce n'est ni par des reproches révoltantes et denuées de tout fondement, ni par des injures réciproques, que l'on travaille de bonne foi à l'ouvrage de la Paix.

Le Soussigné passe donc au premier objet de discussion mis en avant dans la réponse du Directoire, celui d'une Négociation séparée, à laquelle on a voulu supposer sans aucune raison que le Soussigné étoit autorizé d'accéder. Ses pleins pouvoirs expédiés dans la forme ordinaire, lui donnent toute l'autorization nécessaire pour négocier, et pour conclure la paix. Mais ces pouvoirs ne lui prescrivent ni la forme, ni la nature, ni les conditions du traité futur. Sur ces objets il doit se conformer, selon l'usage établi et reconnu depuis longtems en Europe, aux instructions qu'il aura reçu de sa Cour ; et il n'a pas manqué en conséquence de prévenir M. Delacroix dès leur première conférence que le Roi son maître lui avoit très expressément enjoint de n'entendre à aucune proposition tendante à séparer les intérêts de Sa Majesté d'avec ceux de ses Alliés.

Il ne peut donc être question que d'une négociation qui combinera les intérêts et les prétensions de toutes les Puissances qui font cause commune avec le Roi dans la présente guerre, dans le cours d'une pareille négociation l'intervention ou du moins la participation de ces puissances deviendra sans doute absolument nécessaires ; et Sa Majesté espère de retrouver en tout tems les mêmes dispositions pour traiter sur une base juste et équitable dont Sa Majesté l'Empereur et

Roi a donné au Gouvernement François une preuve si éclatante au moment même de l'ouverture de cette campagne.

Mais il paroit que ce seroit un délai très inutile que d'attendre une autorization formelle et définitive de la part des Alliés du Roi avant que la Grande Brétagne et la France puissent commencer à discuter même provisoirement les principes de la Négociation. Une marche tout-à-fait différente a été suivie par ces deux Puissances dans presque toutes les occasions semblables. Et Sa Majesté pense que la meilleure preuve qu'elles pourroient donner dans ce moment à toute l'Europe de leur désir mutuel de faire cesser le plutôt possible les calamités de la guerre, seroit de convenir sans délai d'une Base de Négociation combinée, en invitant dès-lors leurs Alliés d'y concourir de la manière la plus propre à accélérer la pacification générale.

C'est dans cette vue que le Soussigné a été chargé de proposer d'abord, et dès le commencement de la Négociation, un principe que la générosité et la bonne foi de Sa Majesté pouvoient seules lui dicter ; celui de *compenser* à la France, par des restitutions proportionnelles, les arrangemens auxquels elle devra consentir pour satisfaire aux justes prétensions des Alliés du Roi, et pour conserver la balance politique de l'Europe. Le Directoire ne s'est pas expliqué d'une manière précise, ni sur l'acceptation de ce principe, ni sur les changemens ou modifications qu'il désireroit d'y apporter, ni enfin sur l'énonciation d'un autre principe quelconque qu'il proposeroit pour servir au même but. Le Soussigné a donc l'ordre de revenir sur cet objet et de demander là dessus une explication franche et précise, afin d'abréger les délais qui devront nécessairement résulter de la difficulté de forme, mise en avant par le Directoire. Il est autorizé d'ajouter à cette demande la déclaration expresse, que Sa Majesté en faisant part à ses augustes Alliés de toutes ses démarches successives relativement à l'objet de la présente Négociation, et en remplissant envers ces Souvérains de la manière la plus efficace tous les devoirs d'un bon et fidèle Allié, n'omettra rien de sa part tant pour les disposer à concourir à cette Négociation par tous les moyens les plus propres à en faciliter la marche et en assurer le succès, que pour les maintenir toujours dans des sentimens conformes aux vœux qu'elle fait pour le retour de la paix générale sur des conditions justes, honorables, et permanentes.

SUNDAY, NOV. 6.—With Perregaux. People dressed, and Boulevards crowded—aux Italiens. Take a box for the month. Place where bodies of the King and Queen were flung after their execution, near la Rue Pépinière.

MONDAY, NOV. 7.—Mrs. Elliot—not seen her since Twickenham. Concert and ballet—Cupid and Psyche, very capital—Madame Millar, married to young Gardel, danced well—full house—women dressed out—nothing striking either in their dress or beauty.

TUESDAY, NOV. 8.—Visited Doctor Gemm dans la Rue Sepulcre. To play—aux Italiens. Buonaparte said to be son of le Général Marbeuf,* by a Corsican woman—well brought up by him at l'Ecole Militaire—clever, desperate Jacobin, even Terrorist—his wife, Madame Beauharnois, whose husband was beheaded—she now called *Notre Dame des Victoires*.

WEDNESDAY, NOV. 9.—Dr. Gemm called. Atheist. *Système de la Nature*, economist, &c.—the cold apathetic scoundrel described by Burke. He came to Paris in 1751 with Lord Albemarle,—described his own life and opinions. Walked. Sandoz with me in the evening, to question, not answer. Gemm was in the same prison and room with Mrs. Elliot.† She told me he cried the whole time, was terrified to death—no candles ever allowed them, or fire after it was dark. Mr. Stevens—a Jacobin, friend of Thomas Payne—he wrote " Les Crimes des Rois d'Angleterre." Corsini—democratic leanings.

* It is almost needless to state that this rumour (current at the time) was perfectly untrue. Madame Buonaparte's supposed partiality for General Marbeuf existed long after the birth of Napoleon. It is equally superfluous to add, that he never was a " Terroriste."

† Mrs. Elliot and Dr. Gemm were imprisoned during the Reign of Terror.

THURSDAY, Nov. 10.—Walked in the Tuileries. To the play, Rue Feydeau—" Le Dissipateur" and " l'Entrevue"—both acted in perfection. At ten, Timms and Wiffen arrived—numberless letters. Dutch fleet taken at the Cape.

FRIDAY, Nov. 11.—Writing—thinking over my new instructions—*cosi, cosi.* Walked—wrote to Delacroix.

EXTRACT OF A DESPATCH FROM LORD MALMESBURY TO MR. PITT.

Paris, 11th Nov., 1796.

I AM most truly sensible of your kindness in writing to me so fully by the last messenger. It is a matter of real satisfaction to me to hear that you do not disapprove the line of conduct I have hitherto observed since I have been here.

I cannot but be of opinion that the Directory consider the duration of their power to its present extent to depend very much on the duration of the war, at the same time that they cannot but perceive the country at large to be much inclined for peace.

It strikes me therefore, that, in order to reconcile their own interests with the temper of the public, they will endeavour to break off the negotiation at some early period, and on some collateral motive; since, if they allowed it to get into a discussion of the conditions, those we should hold out would probably appear so admissible, even in France, that they either must subscribe to them, or consent to incur the odium of prolonging the war. My mind has all along been so impressed with this idea, that it has in a great measure regulated my conduct. I thought I should have played their game, and forwarded their views, had I expressed my indignation as strongly as I felt it, at the offensive insinuations in their answer to the Memorial ; and it appeared to me, that I should have gratified them still more had I given in to the provoking snare they laid for me, and remonstrated loudly against the publication of the papers, or the injurious paragraphs about myself.* Either of these steps would have furnished them with the choice of means of misrepresentation and dispute, and drawn me precisely into the species of altercation they so much wish to engage in, viz. one wholly unconnected with the great question of peace or war. It is to this point I wish to bring them—nothing short of it can in my mind produce the effect we desire. This great question once fairly at issue, the public will be enabled to decide beyond the reach of cavil or subterfuge between us; and we may then, I am sure, safely appeal to their decision. My wish, therefore, would be to bring them fairly into action, to overlook everything that can be overlooked till our *projêt* and *contre-projêt* has passed between us; and, the negotiation engaged thus far, I feel confident it would terminate to our honour. The instructions I have just received seem, in their general tendency, to have this in view; and I trust I have not been to blame in endeavouring, as much as depended on the manner and form of executing them, to avoid every thing which could be laid hold of by the Directory as a pretext for dissatisfaction. I have said thus much, because I wish you to see into the motives of every part of my conduct; and I do it with the most earnest hope that you will give me freely your opinion and advice in consequence of it.

Nov. 13th.

I began this letter before I had seen the French Minister. What has passed between us confirms me in the opinion I expressed in the beginning of this letter; and I now think that if they cannot find a cause for breaking off the negotiation early, they will make one, and I confess I expect every moment to receive a message from the Directory to leave Paris. I hope you do not disapprove the answer I returned to their official Note.† I felt it quite below the dignity of my situation to let it remain unnoticed till I heard from England, besides my being under the full persuasion that this note was meant for *me* only, and by no means as a regular answer to the last Memorial I gave in.

I have written this letter in great haste, and very incor-

* In the " Rédacteur," a French Government newspaper.
† This Note will appear after Lord Malmesbury's despatch of the 13th to Lord Grenville.

rectly; but what the messenger brings will be a proof that I have had a good deal to do, and been exposed to many interruptions. I have sent to Canning several copies of the *décret* which prohibits the sale and use of English manufactures, and he will of course supply you with any you may wish to have.

---

SATURDAY, NOV. 12.—With Delacroix, Montrond,* and Swinburne—these last and Perregaux dined with me. Answer from La Croix at half-past six—replied to it at half-past eight. *Crisis.*

---

SUNDAY, NOV. 13.—Correspondence with Delacroix—many official notes. New mode—bad appearances. Writing all day till nine. Despatched Timms—visited Mrs. Elliot.

---

MONDAY, NOV. 14.—Agreed to send Ellis to London—saw Delacroix on it—very much pleased. Perregaux with me in the evening; proposes me to see Maco or Boncarrer as intermediaries—I express an indifference on the subject—recommends my being well with La Croix. Clavier in the evening with Ellis. Writing till twelve.

---

TUESDAY, NOV. 15.—Ellis went away at eight. Dr. Gemm at breakfast. Called on Sandoz. Nothing very *marquant*. Gemm wanted to go when I did to England—I declined it. At home in the evening.

* M. Montrond was placed about Lord Malmesbury, as he himself said, " pour lui tirer les vers du nez." This person's various but unscrupulous talents dipped him in many unrevealed transactions of the successive revolutions in France. He was much employed by Talleyrand, who particularly patronized him. He had the art, first, to make himself *useful*; secondly, *necessary* to those he served, and then to become *dreaded* by them for what he knew; and this last period was the most profitable to himself. He was both courted and feared in society for his wit, which, although generally agreeable, when it grew insolent, he was ready to back by a quarrel. He attained the longevity which characterizes most of his noted and notorious contemporaries, and died in 1843, at Paris, attended by a servant, who, a short time before that event, replied to an acquaintance of Montrond, who called to ask how he was :—" Monsieur, il est f——; il n'a pas trois semaines de vie dans le ventre. Monsieur pourroit-il me recommander une place ?" The inquirer naturally recalled to mind the vulgar proverb which this answer suggested.

## EXTRACTS OF A DESPATCH FROM LORD MALMESBURY TO LORD GRENVILLE.

Paris, Sunday, Nov. 13th, 1796. 9 at night.

I AM now to give your Lordship an account of the manner in which I have endeavoured to obey the most material part of the instructions conveyed in your last despatches; and it has been attended with such extraordinary circumstances, that I am most anxious to hear that my conduct may have met with His Majesty's approbation.

I used very few words before I delivered into M. Delacroix's hands the reply I had it in command to give to the paper I had received in answer to my first memorial. I contented myself with observing, that it contained the most unequivocal proofs of His Majesty's earnest desire to forward the great work of pacification; and that, if either of the principles laid down in it should be acceded to by the Directory, much time would be saved. M. Delacroix read it aloud. In reading the passage which begins, "Quant aux insinuations offensantes," he paused, and evidently was going to shew some strong symptoms of displeasure, when I stopped him by begging him to recollect that this was only an answer to what was contained in the Memorial I had received from him, and that I had prepared him for it, by saying, when I received it, that it was liable to great and just animadversions, although I myself at the time, from reasons which he could not but approve, abstained from making them. He replied, Your expressions are stronger than ours. (Vous nous surpassez de beaucoup.) I said I was sorry they should have induced the necessity of using such strong language in official papers; but, as no good could result from any altercation on this point, I submitted to him whether it would not be better to let it drop, and to proceed in reading the paper. He went through it, with visible signs of disapprobation, but he made no remarks except a sort of declamation at that part which speaks of the Court of Vienna, and says, "Sa Majesté l'Empereur et Roi a donné une preuve éclatante, &c." I did not think this required notice at the moment, and let it pass apparently unobserved on my part.

When he had finished reading, he said, after a short pause, that he was very sorry to perceive that this paper, containing nothing new, left the matter just where it stood before; and that although he could not speak officially till he had laid it before the Executive Directory, yet he did not foresee that any answer different from what they had already made could be given to it.

I pointed out to him that there was evidently a new and distinct proposal brought forward; that it was stated in the most direct terms, if the French Government would adopt a mode of negotiation which had been so frequently adopted on similar occasions, and enter into *pourparlers* with England as to the basis of the negotiation and outlines of the terms, to be communicated afterwards to their respective allies for their concurrence, much time would necessarily be saved in advancing the great work of a general pacification. I referred him to that passage in the Memorial, beginning, "Mais il parait que cela sera un délai très inutile." I could not, however, prevail on M. Delacroix to admit this mode of reasoning, self-evident as it was; and he persisted in saying, that unless I could explain precisely and clearly what was meant by *compensations*, and, in short, unless I was *now* empowered to treat specifically of terms and conditions, he did not see how any answer different from the last could be given by the Directory. He went on by saying that it certainly was not their wish to keep all their conquests ("Nous ne voulons pas assurément tout garder"); but we want much to know what retrocessions you intend for us and our allies. I said that, till it was known whether the Directory formally accepted the proposal I now made, or whether they would bring forward one which, though different in form, would substantially promote the same end, I was not and could not be empowered by any Court to go the lengths he required; but that, from the face of the proposal itself, it was manifest that these points would be brought into discussion the moment we should be agreed as to the preliminary basis on which they were to rest, and which it was indispensably necessary to establish before we began even a provisional negotiation.

Notwithstanding the apparent clearness of this language,

M. Delacroix persisted in his opinion : he said to me, You acknowledge the integral existence of the French Republic, ("Vous reconnoissez l'intégrité de la République Française,") and surely mean to treat with it as with other powers. I said, my being here was the best answer I could make to this remark ; and I once more resumed all I had said, and urged, that though he might not admit to the whole extent my reasoning, yet that the proposing provisional discussions was really the strongest proof which could be given that we sincerely wished to promote a definitive negotiation. M. Delacroix expressed no doubt on this head ; he did not even hint at the idea of a separate peace ; and on my taking leave of him he said, " C'est avec regret que je vois que votre courier ne vous a apporté que ce que vous venez de me dire."

We parted between twelve and one ; and I certainly was by no means prepared, from anything which passed in our conference, to receive at half-past six P.M. the inclosed Official Note (A). It found me preparing my despatches for your Lordship, and I was on the point of sending Timms to England when it was brought me.

It appeared, that, as it was addressed so pointedly to me, it became me to reply to it directly, and in the same style. I therefore, at half-past eight, returned the inclosed answer (B). I trust, in so doing, I have not exceeded my instructions, and that both in the form and substance it will not be disapproved. To leave them for a moment under the impression that two such captious questions, put so peevishly, required any reference to my Court, or indeed more time in being answered than was necessary to put the answer on paper, struck me as highly unbecoming a Minister representing so great a King, and belonging to so great a Court as I do.

This morning I thought it also incumbent on me to ascertain whether this official Note was the only answer I had to expect. It certainly bore no marks of being one, and looked more like a preliminary step to sending me out of the country, than a reply to a conciliatory Memorial. But, from some expressions used in a private Note I received afterwards from M. Delacroix, I was led to suppose that it was just possible no other would be given me, and for this reason I sent him this morning, at ten A.M., the inclosure (C). At twelve I received the answer (D); and, as it is now avowed to be the only official answer I am to receive to the Note I delivered in yesterday, I shall most carefully forbear all reply and comment upon it, and wait your Lordship's orders how I am to proceed; and if I have failed in adhering literally to my instructions by the reply I made to it, it was from the full persuasion that the Note I received last night from M. Delacroix was framed with a view of procuring from me materials to form the answer to be given to my last Memorial, and by no means the answer to the Memorial itself.

I immediately answered the Note (D) by the inclosure (E). About half an hour afterwards I received from M. Delacroix the inclosure (F), which your Lordship will perceive in the first part is a reply to the answer I gave last night to the Official Note from M. Delacroix, marked (A), and serves as a convincing proof that nothing more will be said on that subject.

In the second part it introduces a question relative to the sending of messengers, never yet brought forward, and in itself perfectly novel. The drift of this question I cannot presume exactly to ascertain; but I have endeavoured to be so guarded in my answer (G), as to make it impossible for them to draw any other conclusion from it, except the general one, that I hold I have a right to despatch messengers whenever I please.

I must confess, my Lord, that the impression which these numberless Notes, all written this morning at the Directory while it was sitting, and under their immediate inspection, have made on my mind is, that they are preparatory to a message to send me out of the country; and the rapidity with which they succeeded each other seems to argue an intention of drawing from me in reply some such hasty and imprudent expression as might furnish a plausible excuse for this act of authority.

Though I flatter myself I have avoided the possibility of incurring this imputation, yet, if it should be their decided purpose to send me away, no conduct of mine can be sufficiently circumspect to prevent their carrying it into effect.

Perhaps they may rather wish that my recall should proceed from home: and that it is their design, at this moment, to break off the negotiation, seems strongly evinced by the whole of their conduct towards me during the last two days.

What new system they may have adopted, or what new event has encouraged them to wish for this measure;— whether they are tempted to believe the King of Prussia will become their active ally, or the Court of Vienna cease to be ours;—or whether they simply presume, that, when the maritime force of Spain and Holland is added to theirs, they may reduce us to their own terms, by a continuation of the war, is impossible for me to guess.

(A.)

Paris, le 22 Brumaire, an 5.

Le Soussigné est chargé par le Directoire Exécutif de vous inviter à désigner dans le plus court délai et nominativement *les objets de compensation réciproques que vous proposez.*

Il est chargé en outre de vous demander quelles sont *les dispositions pour traiter sur une base juste et équitable,* dont Sa Majesté l'Empereur et Roi a donné au Gouvernement Français une preuve si éclatante au moment même de l'ouverture de la campagne. Le Directoire Exécutif l'ignore. C'est l'Empereur et Roi qui a rompu l'armistice.

CH. DELACROIX.

(B.)

A Paris, ce 12 Nov. 1796.

Le Soussigné n'hésite pas un moment à répondre aux deux questions que vous êtes chargé de lui faire de la part du Directoire Exécutif.

Le Mémoire présenté ce matin par le Soussigné propose en termes exprès, de la part de Sa Majesté le Roi de la Grande Brétagne, " de compenser à la France, par des restitutions proportionnelles, les arrangemens auxquels elle devra consentir pour satisfaire aux justes prétentions des Alliés du Roi, et pour conserver la Balance Politique de l'Europe."

Avant l'acceptation formelle de ce principe, ou l'énonciation de la part du Directoire Exécutif d'un autre quelconque, qui puisse également servir de base à la négociation d'une paix générale, le Soussigné ne sauroit être autorisé à désigner *les objets de compensation réciproque*. Quant à la preuve des dispositions pacifiques donnée au Gouvernement Français par Sa Majesté l'Empereur et Roi à l'ouverture de la campagne, le Soussigné se contente de rappeler les paroles suivantes, qui se trouvent dans la Note du Baron D'Engleman du 4 Juin dernier : " Les opérations de la guerre n'empêcheront nullement que Sa Majesté Impériale ne soit toujours portée à concourir d'après telle forme de négociation qui sera adoptée de concert entre les Parties Belligérantes, à la discussion des moyens propres pour mettre fin à l'effusion ultérieure du sang humain."

Cette Note fut présentée *après* la rupture de l'armistice. (Signé) MALMESBURY.

---

(C.)

Paris, 13th Nov., 1796.

Le Ministre Plénipotentiaire de Sa Majesté Britannique s'adresse au Ministre des Relations Extérieures, pour le prier de l'informer s'il doit regarder la Note Officielle qu'il a reçue de sa part, hier au soir, comme la réponse à celle que le Lord Malmesbury a remise hier matin au Ministre des Relations Extérieures par ordre de sa Cour.

Il fait cette démarche pour ne pas retarder inutilement le départ de son courier. (Signé) MALMESBURY.

---

(D.)

Le 23 Brumaire, an 5.

Le Soussigné Ministre des Relations Extérieures déclare au Lord Malmesbury, Plénipotentiaire de Sa Majesté Britannique, qu'il doit regarder la Note Officielle qu'il lui a transmise hier comme la réponse à celle que le Lord Malmesbury lui avoit adressée le matin du même jour.

(Signé) CH. DELACROIX.

(E.)

Paris, ce 13 Nov., 1796.

Le Lord Malmesbury vient de recevoir la réponse du Ministre des Relations Extérieures, dans laquelle il déclare que la Note Officielle qu'il lui a transmise hier doit être regardée comme la réponse à celle que le Lord Malmesbury lui a adressée le matin du même jour. Lord Malmesbury la communiquera dès aujourd'hui à sa Cour.

---

(F.)

Paris, ce 23 Brumaire, an 5.

Le Soussigné, en réponse à votre seconde Note d'hier, est chargé par le Directoire Exécutif de vous déclarer qu'il n'a rien à ajouter à la réponse qui vous a été adressée. Il est chargé également de vous demander, si à chaque communication officielle qui sera faite entre vous et lui, il sera nécessaire que vous envoyiez un courier pour recevoir des instructions spéciales. (Signé) CH. DELACROIX.

---

(G.)

Paris, ce 13 Novembre, 1796.

Le Soussigné ne manquera pas de transmettre à sa Cour la Note qu'il vient de recevoir de la part du Ministre des Relations Extérieures. Il déclare également qu'il sera dans le cas d'expédier des couriers à sa Cour chaque fois que les communications officielles, qui lui seront faites, exigeront des instructions spéciales. (Signé) MALMESBURY.

---

EXTRACT OF A DESPATCH FROM LORD GRENVILLE TO LORD MALMESBURY.

Downing Street, 22nd November, 1796.

I was preparing the answer to your letters, when Mr. Ellis arrived from Paris. The anxiety which I felt to learn from him the various particulars which had fallen under his observation during his residence there, led me to suspend the departure of the messenger till I had an opportunity of conversing with him.

If I had written under the impressions which the perusal of the correspondence between your Lordship and M. Delacroix had created in my mind, I could have considered the letters of that Minister no otherwise than as proceeding from a fixed and deliberate plan to bring to an immediate and abrupt termination the Negotiation with which your Lordship is charged. Even under this impression, no other instructions would have been given to your Lordship than those of proceeding in the same line of temperate but steady conduct which was originally pointed out to you, and which you have followed with so much ability and judgment.

The circumstances which Mr. Ellis has related to me may induce a belief that the unprecedented conduct of the Directory in the whole of this business should be attributed rather to their ignorance of the usual mode of carrying on such negotiations, and to the uncertainty and difficulty under which they act on account of their own precarious situation, than to any settled system of policy.

With respect, however, to the next step to be taken on His Majesty's part, the result is nearly the same; to whatever principle of action the conduct of the French Government is to be attributed, nothing can be done in the present state of the Negotiation, except to adhere to the liberal proposal already made, and to drive the Directory to the necessity of giving to it a plain and direct answer, such as may either forward the progress of the Negotiation, or place their hostile dispositions in the clearest light.

It is in this view that the inclosed paper has been drawn. Whatever answer may be given to it, His Majesty thinks proper to reserve to himself the power of acting upon it according as the state of the Negotiation may appear to require.

It would be very superfluous for me to add anything to the arguments by which your Lordship has already supported the just and candid proposal now made. You will renew them on the occasion of the delivery of this Note, and you will pursue the same line, waiving all other discussion, until the Directory shall have been brought to a clear and distinct answer. upon this point, or to a direct refusal to give any answer upon it.

When the business shall have been brought to this stage in either of those two modes, your Lordship must of necessity again refer it home for further instructions. If the course ultimately taken by the Directory should be that of a positive refusal to explain itself at all as to any principle of negotiation, the necessity of such a reference is so obvious, that it can hardly require to be explained to the Directory, because it must then be for His Majesty to decide, upon a deliberate view of what shall have passed, whether he will take any further step, or consider such refusal so made as a termination of the whole business. If some alteration in the principle now altered by His Majesty, or some principle entirely different from it, shall be proposed, this would also plainly lead to the necessity of a reference home for further instructions on points which could not have been foreseen.

But if the proposal made by His Majesty shall ultimately be accepted, it is probable that your Lordship will be urged to proceed to the detailed discussion of terms; and it is therefore very material that in such case you should apply yourself with particular attention to prove to the Minister with whom you treat, and to the Directory, that the reference for further instructions ought not to be attributed to any desire for delay, but to the nature and necessity of the case itself,—it being absolutely impossible that any precise or detailed proposals should be framed till it has been seen to what extent and in what manner the principle offered as a basis of treaty has been adopted by the enemy. Even if no other difficulty were in the way, (of which there are many,) the situation in which the King stands, as with respect to his Allies, is such as alone to prove the necessity of reference home after the adoption of the general principle, whatever it may be, which may be finally agreed upon.

But you may give the strongest assurances that every practicable endeavour will be used to avoid delay in framing and transmitting such instructions as will enable your Lordship to enter into the detailed discussion of this arduous and complicated business as soon as possible after the general groundwork of it shall have been laid in conformity to the usual practice on similar occasions.

Previously, however, to your receiving such instructions, it may be very material that you should ascertain, and that by the mode of written notes, whether or not it is to be understood that the negotiations which relate to the detail of the conditions of peace are to be rendered public from day to day in the same manner as has taken place with respect to the preliminary discussions. The objections to such a practice, as rendering the success of all negotiation more precarious and difficult, have already been so ably stated by your Lordship to M. Delacroix, that I cannot do better than to desire your Lordship to repeat and enforce the same topics.

I have only to add to this despatch the assurance of His Majesty's perfect and entire approbation of the step taken by your Lordship in returning an immediate answer to the captious questions of the Directory, and of the very proper style and tenour of the different Notes transmitted by your Lordship to M. Delacroix.

---

INCLOSURE TO THE DIRECTORY.

La Cour de Londres, informée de ce qui s'est passé ensuite du dernier Mémoire, remis par son ordre au Ministre des Relations Extérieures, a trouvé qu'il n'y a absolument rien à ajouter à la réponse faite par le Soussigné aux deux questions que le Directoire a jugé à propos de lui adresser.

Elle attend donc encore et avec le plus grand intérêt l'explication des sentimens du Directoire par rapport au principe proposé de sa part pour base de la négociation ; et dont l'adoption a paru le moyen le plus propre pour accélérer le progrès d'une discussion si importante au bonheur de tant de nations.

Le Soussigné a reçu en consequence l'ordre de renouveler la demande d'une réponse franche et précise sur cet objet, afin que sa Cour puisse connoître avec certitude si le Directoire accepte la dite proposition, s'il désire d'y apporter des changemens ou modifications quelconques ; ou enfin s'il voudroit proposer quelqu'autre principe pour servir au même but.

---

LORD MALMESBURY TO LORD GRENVILLE.

Paris, Sunday, Nov. 13th, 1796.

MY LORD,—I have reason to believe from the accounts I have received that there are at Brest eleven sail of the line ready, to a certain extent, for sea, and from fifteen to twenty thousand men. The troops are chiefly at Morlaix ; and it is supposed that an expedition is meditated against Ireland.* In order to encourage the soldiers to embark, the most exaggerated reports are spread of the temper of that country, and of the successful insurrections which have taken place in it. The idea of a descent on the coast of England from Dunkirk, Ostend, and Flushing seems no longer to be a prevalent one, and I understand the embargo is taken off. I have, &c. MALMESBURY.

---

EXTRACT OF A DESPATCH FROM LORD MALMESBURY TO LORD GRENVILLE.

Paris, Sunday, Nov. 13th, 1796.

I REALLY, my Lord, am as yet quite incompetent to speak with any degree of precision on the resources either of men or money which yet remain to be expended in this country. That all the ordinary ones, and those known to regular and well-administered governments have been long exhausted, is evident. But I am inclined to think that the Directory is

* This expedition sailed from Brest December 17th, and consisted of seventeen sail of the line and thirteen frigates, besides small craft and transports, having on board 20,000 men under Hoche, who was ordered to make a descent on the south-west coast of Ireland. This he was unable to effect, owing to continued boisterous weather, which dispersed the fleet, and compelled it to return, with the loss of two ships of the line and two frigates wrecked, and one frigate captured.—(James's Naval History.)

still strong enough, and the Nation still delirious enough, to allow of the practice of revolutionary means; and as these go to take what is wanted, wherever and however it is to be found, they may be considered as a reserve which will last as long as the fever of the Nation can be kept from subsiding. Every week, however, which passes over, without these revolutionary means being employed, renders the exercising them more difficult ; and perhaps as essential a point as can be obtained from my mission in its present state will be, the recovering gradually the minds of the people here from that state of effervescence and frenzy in which they have been for several years past, and placing before their eyes and within their reach a prospect of repose and security.

The change of one-third which must take place at the next elections in the two Councils will probably introduce into them (notwithstanding the law of the 3rd Brumaire still exists) a great number of wealthy persons, (*les nouveaux Riches*, as they are called,) and a large majority will be then composed of men of this description. Their interests will most undoubtedly lead them to adopt a very different system from that which hitherto has been followed. It will not be one of desperate persons, eager by every means to acquire property, but that of men anxious to preserve property already acquired. And this system, whatever their principles may be, or even supposing they have no principles at all, must necessarily lead them to prefer a regular form of government, and one which will not expose their persons and fortunes to the same risks all those possessed with property have run for several years back ; and it is impossible to give a more striking picture of the fluctuating state in which this country has been during this period, than by telling your Lordship that ten thousand laws have been enacted since 1789, and that only seventy of them are now in force.

WEDNESDAY, Nov. 16.—Walked as usual before breakfast. Theophile Barais, bookseller, called on me and Lignereux. Walked to Mousson with Mrs. Elliot. Curious anecdotes of

Duke of Orleans—Lauzun—Louis d'Aremberg—the Queen, &c. Belmote Pignatelli, Neapolitan Minister, called upon me with a letter from Sir W. Hamilton—great professions of confidence, &c.

THURSDAY, Nov. 17.—Called on Neapolitan—saw the powers Delacroix had to treat with him. His plan of a treaty, with the power to suspend everything for a year. Clever and apparently confidential. Went to Barais—bought books. To Lignereux—bought furniture. Perregaux at dinner.

SATURDAY, Nov. 19.—Mde. de Fleury. Wrote to Ellis through Swinburne. Visited Mde. Fleury, who came to the same house where I live. Very pleasant, &c. Leveson ill—sent for Gemm. Supped with Mde. de Fleury.

SUNDAY, Nov. 20.—First Frimaire. Walked. Gemm with Leveson—he much better. Gemm will take no fees. At home in the evening.

TUESDAY, Nov. 22.—Walked to Clichy. Mild day. M. and Madame Montrond and (Madame Fleury) dined. No events. Made a memorial about Sir S. Smith.

WEDNESDAY, Nov. 23.—With Delacroix, &c. Madame Montrond dined with me—Cetto, from Duc de Deuxponts, with me—with a letter from Hardenberg.

FRIDAY, Nov. 25.—Mde. Montrond at dinner—vastly pleasant and friendly. Timms arrived.

SUNDAY, Nov. 27.—Writing in the evening with Delacroix. Carried my point about answer. Singular conversation with him. Bad news from Italy.

EXTRACT OF A LETTER FROM LORD MALMESBURY TO
MR. CANNING.

Paris, 27th Nov., 1796.

ALL the private letters Timms delivered to me on the 25th, and more particularly that from you, were highly gratifying to me. I still persist that I should have roared too soon, and without effect, if I had begun to roar sooner; and on this point we will have a *tête-à-tête* roar over your tea and rolls in Spring Gardens, where I hope to find you established on my return.

I cannot pronounce judgment on the propriety of the last despatch I received till I hear the answer the Directory makes to my Note: I am writing under the expectation of receiving it every moment; and I am inclined to think, from its coming slowly, that it will be at least civil when it comes, as it is a safe logic to infer, that this Government requires more time and reflection to write civilly, than to write as they did during our last conflict of notes. Delacroix observed that we were moving in a *cercle vicieux*, and it is one of the best things he said; we never shall be in a safe and responsible attitude till we have given in a *projêt*. It *may* be such a one as to make my retreat from this country difficult and dangerous, but it *must* make my arrival in England popular and glorious, and this is the great point to look forward to. I shall write fully to Mr. Pitt on this subject, and also to Lord Grenville.

I am no profound jurist, but I think the objections stated to Delacroix's full powers rather frivolous. I hope, after what has passed in the conversation I have had with him about it, it will not be thought necessary for me to press it further; it is on little matters that the *parvenus* are sore; and the great advantage I feel to have here—I should say the only one—is the having lived long and much in this world.

Did I ever tell you that on our arrival, Leveson* was often taken for Lord Grenville, and Ross for G. Rose?†
One of the friendly journalists here, in speaking of the

* Lord Granville Leveson, the present Earl Granville.
† Secretary of the Treasury, and a very able and confidential friend of Pitt.

supposed insurrection in Ireland, says, "*Cela s'est réduit à une levée en masse des pommes de terre.*" Burke's *mot* is too good a one; I fear it will not be forgotten.* Mrs. Crewe wrote to me the other day, and enclosed a letter from the Duc de Nivernois, in which she threatens to send him, through me, a *Cheshire cheese*. I beg you would direct, therefore, your porters at the office to smell all parcels brought for me before they receive them. Mr. Legh the bookseller will send you one, of *books*, which you will be so good as to forward.

Monday, 2 p.m. 28th Nov., 1796.

You will see I was not wrong in my conjectures, and that their having taken near four and twenty hours to write about four and twenty words, has produced a civil and tractable Note. Surely you will not now hesitate to send me a specific *projêt* and broad instructions. If I am again to go on with Notes and Memorials, *I had better be recalled,* as it would only defeat everything good which has been or may be done, and in the end force me to give up the business, and recall myself. I have written freely to Pitt, and clearly to Lord Grenville. Ellis will support me by a statement of facts and arguments, and you, I am certain, will side with me.

The despatch on internal affairs is composed and written by Leveson.

---

### EXTRACTS OF A DESPATCH FROM LORD MALMESBURY TO LORD GRENVILLE.

Paris, Monday, 28th Nov., 1796.

ALTHOUGH I have not, in my last despatches made any mention of that part of my instructions which relates to Sir Sidney Smith, I should be sorry it should be thought I had been unmindful of them, or remiss in my endeavours to liberate that gallant officer from the state of unjust

---

* Burke was strongly opposed to pacific negotiations with France, and taxed the Government with meanness in proposing them. Somebody observing that the badness of the roads had rendered Lord M's. journey to Paris a slow one, he replied, "No wonder, as he went the whole way on his knees."

confinement in which he has so long remained, and in which he is still kept.

But before I went to the whole length of my orders, and held out the menace of reprisals, I was willing to try every other means in my power to procure his liberty and effectuate his exchange.

I have endeavoured by indirect application to the Minister of the Police, and to the Minister for the Marine, and to those who act under them, either to obtain Sir Sidney's release, or to lessen the distress of his situation, by procuring for him leave to see his fellow-prisoner Mr. Wright,* to be allowed to walk in the Court of the Temple, and to receive such small comforts and conveniences as can be admitted within the walls of a prison.

I could not by any means succeed in the first point, but I have reason to hope that I have, to a certain degree, in the second.

I understand from Sir Sidney himself, that he is comfortably lodged, and occupies the same apartments in which the unfortunate royal family of this country were confined.

The most unpleasant circumstance attending his confinement is the character of his fellow-prisoners; not from his ever being in their society, but from an apprehension he is under that they will attempt to force their way out of prison, and expose him equally to imminent danger, whether he acts with them, or refuses to join them. Something of this kind happened to him when the associates of Babœuf † were in the Temple, and Sir Sidney was at that time saved by siding with the keepers, and contributing to suppress the riot.

After, however, having exhausted every means within my reach short of official interference, and having let near a month elapse without receiving any answer to my official Note on this subject, I, on Wednesday last, gave in a Memorial, which is in substance nearly the contents of your Lordship's despatch on this subject.

---

* A brave officer, who distinguished himself greatly at the siege of Acre. He was again taken in 1804, again imprisoned in the Temple, and found dead in his cell under strong appearances of foul play.
† Jacobins who had conspired against the Directory.

On delivering it to M. Delacroix, I accompanied it with all those arguments which so naturally suggest themselves on this occasion, and I spared no pains to impress his mind with the equity of my demand, and with the very unpleasant consequences which would necessarily attend its not being complied with.

The French Minister told me, as he had done before, that this was out of his department; that he was ignorant of the motives which induced the Directory to prolong the confinement of Sir Sidney Smith; that he had laid my last note before them, and would immediately do the same by this. I urged him very strongly to obtain an early answer to it, as it would be quite impossible to delay the execution of the principle of retaliation I held out,—a principle they must be conscious their own conduct compelled us to adopt.

I have as yet no answer to my Memorial, but as Mr. Swinburne is promised leave to see Sir Sidney, I am not without some faint hopes that it will be attended to, and that it will not be necessary to take a step which, from the irritable and jealous complexion of this Government, would, I should fear, tend to a general ill-treatment of all our prisoners, without any benefit resulting from it to Sir Sidney.

I have, &c. MALMESBURY.

DESPATCH FROM LORD MALMESBURY TO LORD GRENVILLE.

Paris, Monday, 28th Nov., 1796.

MY LORD,—The Government of this country being very strongly prepossessed with an opinion, that the real purport of my Mission here was to make observations upon the state of their internal affairs, and, if I found the opportunity, to foment troubles, or at least to encourage existing discontents, has made it peculiarly incumbent upon me to observe such a guarded line of conduct as should remove entirely these suspicions, the continuance of which might be very prejudicial to the attainment of the main object in view. On this account, my means of informing myself with respect to the state of parties, the strength of the Government, and the general sentiments of the people, are much circumscribed; and I must, therefore, still write with great diffidence upon these subjects, and again request your Lordship to consider my observations upon them as not altogether to be relied on.

I have, in a former despatch, endeavoured to give some account of the three different divisions of persons who, at the present moment, are contending for power. It appears that the individuals of each of them may, from personal considerations, be induced to support those who, at the present moment, hold the reins of government; yet, as parties, they are by no means under the influence of the Directory. The Conventionalists have of late evinced strong disapprobation of the measures offered by the Directory for the adoption of the Councils. One message in particular, in which was advised a further restraint upon the liberty of the press, and which was referred to a committee of the Council of Five Hundred, was censured with much asperity in the report made by Daunon, a man of considerable talents, and at the head of the party of the Conventionalists. These are the remnants of the faction of the Gironde. They are sincere friends to the present form of this Constitution; and well knowing that the general enthusiasm in favour of a Republic has evaporated, and that the odium which of late has been attached to Royalism is gradually diminishing, every proposal of moderation and humanity (such, for instance, as the repeal of the law of the 3rd Brumaire) made by Thibaudeau, and the other leaders of *les Honnêtes Gens*, is warmly opposed by them, under the impression that if the people are left with a perfectly free choice at the approaching elections, and that if coercive measures are not rigorously enforced, in order to give solidity to their new-formed constitution, Royalty may again be re-established. The opposition of the Conventionalists, therefore, is chiefly directed against the Modérés or Honnêtes Gens; but the Jacobins inspire them also with considerable alarm, and on that account they very willingly assented in the Council of Five Hundred to the amendment of the *Loi* 3 *Brumaire,* which adds the amnesties to the list of the excluded, and which, if carried in the Council of Ancients, would be a very serious blow to the power of the Jacobin faction. There, however, it will probably be rejected.

Many of the Modéré party, and among them Dupont de Nemours,* have opposed its adoption from a fear of sanctioning the principle of exclusion. In point of numbers the faction of the Jacobins is not formidable, either within or without the Councils; but they compensate, in some degree, for this disadvantage by the concert with which they act, and by the daring courage with which they execute their projects. They, as well as the Royalists, are daily gaining strength from the increasing unpopularity of the Government. That unpopularity may be attributed to the misfortunes that have of late attended all their military operations, to the weight of oppressive taxes that have been imposed, to the total inability of Government to pay even their own functionaries, who, in common with the creditors of the Nation, under the different denominations of Rentiers and Viagers, are actually without the means of subsistence, but whose solicitations for relief are totally disregarded; and to the want of sincerity, which people here in general seem inclined to think the Directory have betrayed in the opening of the negotiation for the restoration of a general peace.

The Directory have, within these two days, subjected themselves to much censure by the wanton cruelty they have exercised towards a M. de Cussy, a poor emigrant; he was tried in the most summary manner, according to a law which, since Robespierre's overthrow, has not been acted upon, and was immediately after the trial conducted to the guillotine. This unusual severity seems, however, to have been very repugnant to the feelings of the people in general. Your Lordship will observe that many of the journalists have reprobated, in the strongest language, this sanguinary measure of the Directory, and the disgust it created may be considered as a further proof of the change that has taken place in the dispositions and opinions of the public.

Of these Mr. Ellis will probably have given your Lordship more detailed accounts; I will therefore content myself with observing, that ever since his departure the dissatisfied venture to shew themselves with still less reserve, that the

* Dupont de Nemours, qui conservoit dans un âge avancé une grande vivacité d'humeur, et montroit l'opposition la plus hardie au Gouvernement actuel. —(Thiers.)

Government is more openly attacked, and that those in power evidently betray how much they feel the embarrassment of the situation in which they are placed. I cannot, however, pretend to foretell which party will at last obtain the superiority; I am inclined to think less favourably of the stability of the present constitution than upon my first arrival. The police of this capital at that moment I had understood to be perfect, but it now appears that they are totally unable to put a stop to the depredations which are nearly every night committed by gangs of robbers, who are said to be more numerous than ever. It is reported that the Fauxbourg St. Antoine, which has always made itself remarkable for its revolutionary spirit, has of late shewn symptoms of much fermentation: that the Jacobins are concentrating their forces at Paris, and are daily introducing their associates from the departments; it appears, therefore, that it is extremely doubtful how long this city may continue to enjoy the same quiet and tranquillity that has reigned ever since my arrival in this country.

It will not be foreign to the subject of this despatch to inform your Lordship that the author of a little pamphlet, addressed to me, and which I forwarded to your Lordship by the last messenger, is a man of the name of Este, son to a well-known clergyman of that name, who is, I believe, editor of a newspaper called the *Telegraph*. He is living here with Lady S * * * *, wife to the notorious Sir R. S * * * *; two more of his brothers, I understand, are lately arrived from England; they are all in close connexion with T. Paine, who at present is very much distressed in circumstances, has little or no influence in the country, and who declares himself to be highly discontented with the new Constitution. I have been informed, also, that an Englishman of the name of Parry is established at Calais, that he is employed by the Minister of Exterior Relations, and keeps up a communication with the *Courier* office in London.

I have, &c.    MALMESBURY.

## DESPATCH FROM LORD MALMESBURY TO LORD GRENVILLE.

Paris, 28 Nov 1796.

My Lord,—A few days ago a M. Clarke, descended from Irish parents, but himself born in France, was sent from hence from the Directory to the army in Italy, with orders, as I have good authority to believe, to proceed after a conference with Buonaparte to Vienna.

M. Clarke was in the regiment of Hussars belonging to the Duke de Chartres, and was in England with the Duke of Orleans in 1789, or 1790. He has now the rank of General; he has not seen any actual service, but has been employed in the War Department under Carnot, whose confidential secretary and adviser he is supposed to be. M. Clarke is about thirty, of good address and manner, as I am told, and perfectly acquainted with all the secrets of the Directory, as far as they are known to Carnot; and, whatever may be the purport of his Mission, it is undertaken on the suggestion of this member of the Directory.

Its avowed motive is to propose an armistice,* and that after having effected this object in Lombardy, he is to go to the armies on the Rhine for the same purpose. But I believe I can venture to say, that he is charged with a special commission to endeavour to engage the Court of Vienna to make a *separate peace,* and that his instructions are so extensive, that it is left almost to his discretion to throw any possible temptation in the way, short of the retrocession of the Low Countries, to effect this object.

I am also told, that the Court of Madrid unites its efforts to those of this Government, and that the most positive orders have been sent to the Spanish Ambassador at Vienna, to use every means in his power to induce the Emperor to separate from the Allies.

I hear no news from the Mediterranean, except that the whole of the Spanish fleet is at Toulon, that it was not well received there, from being under the command of the same

---

* Clarke was also sent by the Directory to report upon Buonaparte's proceedings. It was already jealous of his fame. Buonaparte knew this, and being prepared for the visit, had no difficulty in attaching Clarke to his interest.

Admiral who was there with Lord Hood, that the Spanish sailors are averse to the war, and disinclined to fight, and that many of the officers unite in their opinion, and I know full well that very little confidence is placed here in the operations of this fleet.

The Prussian Minister has lately been frequently with the leading members of this Government, but as he is very much in the habit of seeing them I do not infer anything more from this than that a general confidential intercourse subsists between the two countries, and that no pains are spared by this to make His Prussian Majesty act in conformity to their own interests.

### EXTRACTS OF A DESPATCH FROM LORD MALMESBURY TO LORD GRENVILLE.

Paris, 28th Nov., 1796.

I HAD the honour to receive, on Friday last, the 25th, at 7 P.M., your Lordship's despatch of the 22nd inst. by Timms.

It is with the highest satisfaction that I learn His Majesty is most graciously pleased to approve my conduct hitherto.

The morning after the arrival of the messenger (Saturday the 26th), I was with M. Delacroix, and the conversation which arose on my giving the Note I had your Lordship's instructions to deliver in, was the longest and most interesting that has ever taken place between us.

After expressing his satisfaction at the conciliatory terms in which the Note was drawn up, M. Delacroix lamented that it left the negotiation just where it was; that it contained no new proposals, no appearance of an inclination to comply with their request.

M. Delacroix went on for some time in this strain, and seemed very anxious I should not interrupt him till he had stated all his reasons for asserting, that we were not advanced a single step in the negotiation since the first day of my seeing him. On deducing his arguments to substantiate this, he brought in a great deal of matter widely foreign to the purpose, and talked with much emphasis on the impression our conduct had made on the different Courts of

Europe, who were all inclined to suppose England insincere in its wishes for peace, and that he was afraid the Directory would now undoubtedly think the same.

I thought it by no means necessary to follow him through the very extensive ground that he had gone over; and without admitting or refuting anything he had said, which appeared to me as not directly applicable to the question before us, I brought him closely to the point by asking whether I had ever, either in conversation or in my official Notes, varied my language, or whether the evident object of both was not to know whether the Executive Directory would, or would not, *accept a principle* we had stated to them in very precise and unequivocal terms as the *basis* of a future negotiation. To this no distinct answer had ever yet been given; and till this answer was distinctly made, it could not be expected we should vary our language, unless it was supposed we could vary our system; that the imputation of delay, therefore, did not belong to England, but to France, and that it remained with them to give activity to the negotiation, or to stifle it at once. I said this, I am sure, with temper, and I believe with steadiness; for the immediate answer it produced from M. Delacroix was, that it appeared to him that an acknowledgment of this principle was implied in the answer made by the Directory to the last Memorial I had ever given in. I replied instantly, that if that was really the case, there surely could be no difficulty in expressing now precisely and positively what, if it was conveyed at all in the paper he referred to, was certainly conveyed in obscure and dubious terms.

M. Delacroix, passing over what I said, asked me, as he once had done before, if I acknowledged the integrity of the French Republic. I said, Certainly; as he did that of the British Empire. "And you surely," said he, "would not come here without being perfectly acquainted with the constitution of the Republic." As I saw the drift of his question, I waived a direct answer; but he went on and said, "You knew that by our constitution we cannot, without referring to the primary assemblies, dismember any of the integral parts of the Republic. The Directory is only a *Mandatoire* of the Republic, as I am a *Mandatoire* of the

Directory. We cannot act as sovereigns." I told him that I really was not prepared to discuss with him either the particular principles of this government, or those of governments in general; that we were not yet far enough advanced in our work to make this at all necessary; and I begged leave to bring back his attention to the subject immediately before us, and to request of him to lay my Note, I had just given him, before the Directory, and to transmit to me an early answer. M. Delacroix persevered in repeating, no answer different from those already given could be expected, and that he was persuaded such would be the opinion of the Directory. I said that I could not but suppose that if the Directory agreed in opinion with him, and admitted that, in their former answer, they did intend (though certainly it was not expressed) to accept the principle we had laid down, there could not exist a motive (except it was to be looked for in a total disinclination to enter into a pacific negotiation) to prevent them from their now declaring their intention so to do, in words which could not be misunderstood, particularly as the admission of the principle would not pledge them to anything specific.

M. Delacroix was very eager to convince me of the sincerity of their wish for peace; he went deep into the subject; said the Republic by no means wished to keep all its conquests, and that he was sure he and I should conclude a treaty of peace in five days, provided England did not require anything in contradiction to the principles of its Constitution. I was determined, though I perfectly saw his meaning, not to give in to his views, or to afford him an opportunity of mentioning the Austrian Netherlands, or, as they are called here, the Nine Annexed Departments of Belgium. I therefore always brought him back to the original point, and to the necessity of the Directory choosing (before any further discussion was entered upon) one of the modes proposed in my Note for establishing a basis on which the subsequent treaty was to rest. He promised me to lay it, without loss of time, before the Directory, and thus our conference ended.

Yesterday, at three o'clock, I received the enclosed answer (A), which I immediately acknowledged by the enclosure (B).

Your Lordship will perceive, notwithstanding what M. Delacroix affirmed, that it is an unqualified acceptation on the part of the Directory of the principle we have laid down; and I hope, in having obtained this acceptation in so positive and formal a manner, that I shall have performed a very essential part of my duty, and removed the only obstruction which stood in the way of our coming forward immediately with distinct and specific proposals for a general pacification.

M. Delacroix took a survey of all Europe, and, after speaking of the partition of Poland, the alarming increase of the power of Russia, and the ambition of the Empress, the insignificancy of Sweden, Denmark, and even Holland, said he really did not see how it was possible, without establishing a new order of things, to restore the balance of Europe on its ancient footing, and such as it was settled at the Treaty of Münster. He said it could not be expected that the French Republic should see with indifference the aggrandizement of the other great Powers of Europe, and not for its own security, and that of its Allies, expect also to be aggrandized. The banks of the Rhine, he said, were its natural limits: and on my expressing a mixture of surprise and disapprobation, he said, "England and France have two very different and distinct pursuits. Commerce is your empire. It is to be founded in the Indies and in your Colonies. But as for France," subjoined he, "I should be better pleased with an addition of four villages on the frontiers of the Republic, than by the acquisition of the richest island among the Antilles, and should be even sorry to see Pondicherry and Chandenagore again belonging to France." He then got upon what is one of his favourite topics, and which he always puts in opposition to our conquests in the West Indies, by calling it *la Conquête d'un esprit de liberté,* viz., the affranchisement of the negroes. This, he said, would very soon deprive Europe of its possessions in those parts, and subdue all the Colonies. I said *destroy,* not subdue, appeared to be the proper term; and that the evil resulting from their adoption of this measure had been full, at least, as much felt by them as by any of their enemies.* From

---

* Soon afterwards Jacobin emissaries from France stirred up the blacks of San Domingo (her only remaining colony) to emancipate themselves. They

this point he went to the difficulty of defining *compensations proportionnelles*, how the retrocessions or exchanges were to be made in commensurate quantities, and started numberless obstacles, either because he really considered them as such, or because he wished to make it appear so to me; but I thought it wiser to be a listener than to bear any share in this conversation, and I only said occasionally enough to encourage him to go on.

All this passed in perfect good-humour; and I insert it here, more to give an adequate idea of my fellow Plenipotentiary, than with a view that any inference can or ought to be drawn from it. M. Delacroix was a disciple of Turgot,* one of whose leading principles was, that France would be greater and happier by employing all its industry within its own limits, and that colonial possessions were detrimental both to its interests and power.

I shall conclude this very voluminous despatch with remarking that it is evident, beyond a doubt, that the arrangement relative to the Austrian Netherlands will be the *great* point on which this country will make a stand. On every other, whether it relates to possessions we may have taken from them, or those we have taken or may still take from their Allies, they will be much less difficult to treat, and this because the large majority of the country now think as Turgot taught, and as Delacroix believes.

It is also the Austrian Netherlands (Belgium) that has made them so averse to avow their acceptation of the basis of negotiation we proposed.

To admit, therefore, our principle, would be tacitly admitting an intention of restoring, or, at least, treating about Belgium; and I have no doubt but many of the journalists will attack their answer to me under this supposition. It was to prevent my interpreting it in the same way, and my being led to believe that they had relaxed on this parti-

rose against the white population, laid waste the island, and committed atrocities too horrible for description. Licence, under the mask of liberty, could not generate freedom, and France "*destroyed*" her colony.

* Turgot, Minister of Finance under Louis XVI. He died 1781, aged 54. The virtuous Malesherbes wrote of Turgot and himself, "Nous étions fort honnêtes gens, très instruits, passionnés pour le bien. Cependant nous avons mal administré, ne connoissant les hommes que par les livres; et sans le vouloir, ni le prévoir, nous avons contribué à la Révolution."

cular point, from which they have so repeatedly asserted they cannot and will not deviate, that M. Delacroix so often attempted to induce me to commit myself by drawing me into a conversation on this point, and by talking of the Rhine for the boundary, and the necessity of the aggrandizement of France.

INCLOSURES.

(A.)

M. DELACROIX TO LORD MALMESBURY.

Paris, ce 7 Frimaire, an 5.

EN réponse à la Note remise hier 26 Nov., 6 Frimaire, par le Lord Malmesbury, le Soussigné Ministre des Relations Extérieures est chargé par le Directoire Exécutif d'observer que les réponses faites les 5 et 22 Brumaire dernier renfermoient la reconnoissance du principe de compensation ; et que pour ôter tout prétexte à discussion ultérieure sur ce point, le Soussigné, au nom du Directoire Exécutif, en fait encore la déclaration formelle et positive. En conséquence le Lord Malmesbury est de nouveau invité à donner une réponse prompte et catégorique à la proposition qui lui a été faite le 22 Brumaire dernier, et qui est conçue en ces termes : *Le Soussigné est chargé par le Directoire Exécutif de vous inviter à désigner, dans le plus court délai, et nominativement, les objets de compensation réciproque que vous proposez.* (Signé) CH. DELACROIX.

(B.)

LORD MALMESBURY TO M. DELACROIX.

A Paris, ce 27 Nov., 1796.

LE Soussigné, Ministre Plénipotentiaire de Sa Majesté Britannique, en réponse à la Note en date de ce matin, laquelle lui a été remise de la part du Ministre des Relations Extérieures, s'empresse de lui assurer qu'il ne tardera

pas un moment de la communiquer à sa Cour, dont il doit nécessairement attendre des Ordres Ultérieurs, avant de pouvoir s'expliquer sur les points importants qu'elle renferme.
(Signé) MALMESBURY.

MONDAY, Nov. 28.—Writing. Wiffen went away at 4—sent fruit-trees by him, and books.

THURSDAY, DEC. 1.—Frost began. Walk. Play—au Théatre de la Cité. "Comité révolutionnaire." Singular play. Perregaux told me that 22,000 sacks of flour were consumed daily in Paris, each sack containing 310 lbs. The French pound is to the English as 15 is to 16.

DEC. 2.—Dr. Gemm—breakfast—always harping on his philosophy—told me meat costs 8 French sous per pound, and bread very cheap—a *poularde* 4f. 10s. Madame Philidor* wants a pension for her husband from the Chess Club. Dressins returned from Vienna at 11 P.M.

EXTRACT OF A DESPATCH FROM LORD MALMESBURY TO LORD GRENVILLE.

Paris, 3rd Dec., 1796.

I AM very sorry that the very favourable hopes entertained for several days here on the first successes of the Austrians, as they approached the Adige, have again been frustrated. No other accounts have been received here but by the Directory, and these are stated in the printed official papers I enclose. There can, however, be no doubt but that Buonaparte exaggerates his victory,† even if it deserves that name ; that his loss must have been immense ; and that the

\* Widow of Philidor, the famous chess-player. He died 1795, aged 80.
† Of Arcola, 17th November. Buonaparte defeated General Alvinzi, and prevented his relieving Mantua. The battle of Rivoli, on the 14th January, decided the fate of Italy, and Mantua surrendered to the French on the 2nd February, 1797.

event of this very bloody battle does not so immediately lead to the reduction of Mantua as he asserts.

General Alvinzi is retired no further than Vincenza. General Davidovich still maintains the strong post of the Corona ; and though their plan of junction and getting between Buonaparte's army and Mantua has failed this time, yet, as large reinforcements are daily expected from Austria, and as the French have certainly sent all those they can send to that army, the affairs of Lombardy cannot as yet be considered as quite desperate, although certainly in a much worse condition than I thought them to be, when I began writing by my last messenger.

SUNDAY, DEC. 4.—The play—"Tartuffe and le Cercle"— Fleury acted the Tartuffe moderately—Madlle. Contat the wife inimitably. "Cercle" out of date, and not in the *present* manners.

WEDNESDAY, DEC. 7.—Walk to Pont de Neuilly—Bois de Boulogne, Bagatelle, &c. Bagatelle very pretty. M. de Praslin's house on the Seine at Neuilly. Madlle. Dugazon— "Les Français ne disent plus *ouff*."

EXTRACTS OF A LETTER FROM LORD GRENVILLE TO LORD MALMESBURY.

Cleveland Row, 10th Dec., 1796.

MR. ELLIS, who returns to you to-morrow with the instructions which have been prepared in consequence of your last despatches, will be able to state to you verbally the little which is to be added to them. I flatter myself they will be found so full that nothing can be wanting to forward the negotiation, except a disposition on the part of the Directory, which I am persuaded does not exist, though the public opinion at Paris may force them to go great lengths in appearances. You will observe that we are very strongly impressed with the impossibility of listening to any idea of leaving the Netherlands to France; and, indeed, I must say, that without carrying our point,—at least, to the extent of obliging France to relinquish that possession, I do not see what solid advantage England would gain by a treaty which must contain the sacrifice of so many conquests.

I do not say more to you in my public letter about intelligence, because I do not like to controvert what I strongly feel,—the necessity of great caution in your situation. But, on the other hand, the importance of the object is such, that something must be risked for it; and we should both of us blame ourselves if your Mission should terminate abruptly, without your having established some means of our being better served in that respect than we have hitherto been. I have also desired Mr. Ellis to mention to you very particularly the necessity of frequent communication, (at least, once a week,) in order to keep us informed of what is passing on the Continent now that the Elbe is frozen, and will probably continue so with very short intervals till February or March. Do not forget that Paris may be our only channel of communication, and therefore do not omit anything interesting from any quarter on the supposition that we already know it.

---

EXTRACTS OF A DESPATCH FROM LORD GRENVILLE TO LORD MALMESBURY.

Downing Street, Dec. 11th, 1796.

I SHALL proceed, by His Majesty's commands, to make to your Lordship such observations as now appear necessary.

The restitution of the Emperor's dominions, on the footing of the *status ante bellum*, is stipulated in His Majesty's engagements* with the Emperor as the condition without which His Majesty is not at liberty to make peace, but by the consent of his ally. The existence of this engagement

* In the Treaties of August 30th, 1793, and May 20th, 1795, Austria and Great Britain promise mutual support against a common enemy; and in the event of a peace, reciprocally guarantee the integrity of their dominions.

is public, and the French Government must itself have expected the proposal made by your Lordship in the first instance to be conformable to it.

It may indeed well be doubted whether any other form or arrangement of peace can be so likely to restore and ensure the tranquillity of Europe, as one which should be grounded on the *status ante bellum* with respect to the Netherlands, and to ths Milanese; and on the same general principle, though possibly with more latitude of application as with respect to the affairs of the Empire and Italy at large.

With respect, however, to the Netherlands, His Majesty, though extremely desirous on every account of seeing them restored to the Emperor, would not think it proper to refuse considering any proposals of a different nature that should be made to him, if they were found to be in themselves practicable, to contain an adequate equivalent to the House of Austria, and to afford a reasonable security that those provinces shall not again fall into the hands of France.

Any proposal which should leave those countries annexed to France, would be productive of much greater advantage to that Power, and loss to the Allies, than any just view of the present relative situation of the belligerent Powers could entitle the French Government to expect.

The first object of endeavour must therefore be, to secure the restoration of the Netherlands to the Emperor.

If the demand of the *status quo*, with respect to these provinces and the Milanese, accompanied by a reasonable and suitable arrangement of the other points which must come in question, should be admitted by France, His Majesty is ready to compensate this extent of restitution by that of all which he has conquered from France during the war; and his communications with the Court of Vienna give him, as your Lordship will have seen, and may express to the French Minister, just ground to expect that on that basis, as with respect to his own dominions, His Imperial Majesty will not refuse to proceed to the adjustment of the other points which would remain to be settled, with a view to general pacification.

If, however, the French Minister, persisting in his objections to this proposal, shall bring forward any plan for a different arrangement with respect to those provinces, but such as not to leave them in the power of France,—holding out at the same time to the Emperor a sufficient equivalent for them, the King empowers you to receive such proposal as matter of consideration, and to enter into such discussions as may naturally arise out of it respecting the value of the compensation to be offered to the Emperor, the means of realizing it, and the degree of security in which those provinces may be placed as against France, in order that the whole may be brought as nearly as possible to a distinct issue, in which His Majesty and his Ally may decide. But he cannot proceed to any previous agreement, or authorize your Lordship to express any consent on his part to any such plan, till he has had an opportunity of entering into explanations upon it with his Ally, whose interest is so nearly concerned, and whose just claims His Majesty has so many reasons for enforcing to the utmost of his power.

On this point, therefore, of suffering the Netherlands to remain a part of France, your Lordship must not give the smallest hope that His Majesty will be induced to relax. With respect to the Milanese, much uncertainty still prevails as to the accounts received through France of the alleged successes of the French army in that quarter. If, before the close of this campaign, Mantua should be relieved, it may be hoped that the restitution of the Milanese will not remain to be asked from France. If the contrary should be the case, His Majesty feels himself bound on every account to require that restitution as a part of the price of his conquests which he offers to surrender. Nor can he recede from that demand unless an ample equivalent be offered to the Emperor.

I have now only to add on the general subject of the negotiation, that the short Note accompanying the Memoir now sent to your Lordship has been drawn merely with the view of bringing forward the demand; that if France does not accede *in toto* to the proposals now made, it is incumbent on her to offer a *contre-projêt*, and not abruptly to break off the negotiation. Your Lordship's abilities will enable you to judge how best to follow up this idea.

[This able but very voluminous Despatch from Lord Grenville is much abridged, as the pith of it is to be found in the following Memorials.]

(INCLOSURES.)

NOTE TO M. DELACROIX.

Le Soussigné est chargé de remettre au Ministre des Relations Extérieures le Mémoire confidentiel ci-joint, contenant les propositions de sa Cour sur l'application du principe général déjà établi pour base de la Négociation Pacifique. Il s'empressera d'entrer avec le Ministre dans toutes les explications que l'état et le progrès de la Négociation pourront admettre, et il ne manquera pas d'apporter à la discussion de ces propositions ou de tel contre-projêt qui pourroit lui être remis de la part du Directoire Exécutif, cette franchise et cet esprit de conciliation qui répondent aux sentimens justes et pacifiques de sa Cour.

(A.)

MÉMOIRE CONFIDENTIEL

Sur les objets principaux de Restitution, de Compensation et d'arrangement réciproque.

Le principe actuellement établi pour base de la Négociation par le consentement des deux Gouvernemens, porte sur des Restitutions à faire par Sa Majesté Britannique à la France, en compensation des arrangemens auxquels cette Puissance consentiroit pour satisfaire aux justes prétentions des Alliés du Roi, et pour conserver la balance politique de l'Europe.

Pour remplir ces objets de la manière la plus complète, et pour offrir une nouvelle preuve de la sincérité de ses vœux pour le rétablissement de la tranquillité générale, Sa

Majesté proposeroit qu'il soit donnée à ce principe de part et d'autre toute l'étendue dont il peut être susceptible.

Elle demande donc :—

1. La restitution à Sa Majesté l'Empereur et Roi de tous ses Etats, sur le pied de possession avant la guerre.

2. Le rétablissement de la Paix entre l'Empire Germanique et la France, par un arrangement convenable et conforme aux intérêts respectifs, aussi bien qu'à la sûreté générale de l'Europe. Cet arrangement seroit traité avec Sa Majesté Impériale comme chef Constitutionnel de l'Empire soit par l'intervention du Roi, soit directement, selon que Sa Majesté Imépriale le préférera.

3. L'Evacuation de l'Italie par les troupes françaises avec l'engagement de ne pas intervenir dans les affaires intérieures de ce pays, qui seroit remis en autant que possible sur le pied du *status ante bellum*.

Dans le cours de la Négociation l'on pourroit discuter plus en détail les mesures ultérieures que l'on pourroit adopter sur les objets de ces trois Articles, pour pourvoir plus efficacement à la sûreté future des limites et possessions respectives et au maintien de la tranquillité générale.

1. Quant à ce qui regarde les autres Alliés de Sa Majesté Britannique, elle demande qu'il soit reservé à Sa Majesté l'Impératrice de toutes les Russies, la faculté pleine et illimitée d'intervenir à cette Négociation dès qu'elle le jugera à propos, ou bien d'accéder au traité définitif, et de rentrer par là dans un état de paix avec la France.

2. Sa Majesté demande pareillement que Sa Majesté Très Fidelle puisse aussi être comprise dans la Négociation, et rentrer en paix avec la France, sans qu'il soit question d'aucune cession ou condition onéreuse de part ou d'autre.

3. A ces conditions Sa Majesté offre à la France la restitution entière et sans réserve de tout ce qu'elle a conquis sur cette Puissance dans les deux Indes ; en lui proposant toutefois de s'entendre mutuellement sur les moyens d'assurer pour l'avenir la tranquillité des deux Nations, et de consolider autant que possible les avantages de leurs possessions respectives. Elle offre pareillement la restitution des Iles de St. Pierre et Miquelon, et de la Pêche de Terre Neuve sur le pied du *status ante bellum*.

4. Mais si elle devoit en outre se départir du droit que lui donnent les stipulations expresses du Traité d'Utrecht de s'opposer à ce que la partie Espagnole de St. Domingue puisse être cédée à la France, elle demanderoit alors en retour de cette concession, une compensation qui pourroit assurer au moins en partie le maintien de la balance des possessions respectives dans cette partie du monde.

5. Dans tous les cas des cessions ou des restitutions dont il pourroit être question dans cette Négociation, on accorderoit de part et d'autre la faculté la plus illimitée à tous les particuliers de se retirer avec leurs familles et leurs effets, et de vendre leurs terres et autres biens immeubles. Et on prendroit pareillement dans le cours de la Négociation des arrangemens convenables pour la levée des séquestrations, et pour satisfaire aux justes réclamations que des individus de part et d'autre pourroient avoir à faire sur les Gouvernemens respectifs.

---

(B.)

MÉMOIRE CONFIDENTIEL SUR LA PAIX AVEC L'ESPAGNE ET LA HOLLANDE.

Les Alliés de la France n'ayant témoigné jusqu'ici aucun désir ni disposition pour traiter avec le Roi, Sa Majesté auroit pu se dispenser d'entrer dans aucun détail à leur égard. Mais pour éviter des délais nuisibles au grand objet que le Roi se propose et pour accélérer l'œuvre de la Paix Générale, Sa Majesté ne refusera pas de s'expliquer d'avance sur ce qui regarde ces Puissances.

Si donc le Roi Catholique désireroit d'être compris dans la Négociation ou de pouvoir accéder au Traité Définitif, Sa Majesté Britannique ne s'y refuseroit pas. Aucune conquête n'ayant été faite jusqu'ici par l'un de ces deux Souvérains sur l'autre, il ne seroit question dans ce moment que de rétablir la Paix simplement et sans restitution ou compensation quelconque, excepté ce qui pourrait peut-être résulter de l'application du principe énoncé sur la fin de l'article 4 du Mémoire déjà remis au Ministre des Relations Extérieures ;

mais si pendant la Négociation l'état des choses à cet égard venoit à changer, on devra alors convenir des Restitutions et Compensations à faire de part et d'autre.

Pour ce qui regarde la République des Provinces Unies, Sa Majesté Britannique et les Alliés se trouvent trop directement intéressés à la situation politique de ces Provinces pour pouvoir consentir à rétablir à leur égard le *status ante bellum*, territorial, à moins que la France ne put également les remettre à tous égards dans la même position politique où elles se trouvoient avant la guerre.

Si on pouvoit au moins rétablir dans ces Provinces, conformement à ce que l'on croit être le vœu de la grande majorité des habitans, leur ancienne Constitution et forme de Gouvernement, Sa Majesté Britannique seroit disposée à se relâcher alors en leur faveur sur une partie très considérable des conditions sur lesquelles l'état actuel des choses lui impose la nécessité d'insister. Mais si au contraire c'est avec la République Hollandoise dans son état actuel que leurs Majestés Britannique et Impériale auront à traiter, elles se verront obligées de chercher dans des acquisitions territoriales la compensation et la sûreté que cet état des choses leur rendroit indispensables.

Des restitutions quelconques en faveur de la Hollande ne pourroient alors avoir lieu qu'en autant qu'elles seroient compensées par des arrangemens propres à contribuer à la sûreté des Pays Bas Autrichiens.

Les moyens de remplir cet objet se trouvent dans les cessions que la France a exigées dans son Traité de Paix avec la Hollande, et dont la possession par cette Puissance seroit en tout cas absolument incompatible avec la sûreté des Pays Bas Autrichiens entre les mains de Sa Majesté Impériale.

C'est donc sur ces principes que Sa Majesté Britannique seroit prête à traiter pour le rétablissement de la Paix avec la République Hollandoise dans son état actuel. Les détails d'une pareille discussion ameneroient nécessairement la considération de ce qui seroit dû aux intérêts et aux droits de la Maison d'Orange.

## EXTRACTS OF A DESPATCH FROM LORD MALMESBURY TO LORD GRENVILLE.

Paris, Wednesday, Dec. 14th, 1796.

The internal situation of this country remains nearly the same as when I last had the honour of mentioning the subject to your Lordship.

The amendment to the law of the 3rd of Brumaire, which places the *Amnisties* (as they are called) on the same footing with the relations of emigrants, after several long discussions in the Council of Ancients, was carried a few days ago. It disqualifies at once seven hundred persons from continuing in office.

The moderate party consider the removal of so large a number of their opponents from situations of influence and patronage, as a measure which may prove very favourable to their interest, at the ensuing election — an event towards which all parties turn their thoughts, and look forward to with anxious expectation. Every thing in this country rests on so unsteady a basis; changes can be so little foreseen before they happen, and so little accounted for when they do happen, that it is impossible to venture, from the temper of the day, to say what may take place three months hence. If this continues without any material change, I confess I should almost be led to conjecture that the two Councils, from the character of the *new third* of which they would be composed after the election, would be induced to make a very considerable alteration, both in the power and form of the Directory: that this power would be reduced into a narrower compass, and those entrusted with it charged with a greater degree of responsibility than at present. It is through the two Councils only that a revolution of this sort is likely to be effected. Should any party be inconsiderate or rash enough to attempt it by any other means, or if the people are again to be appealed to, the most horrid anarchy and confusion must ensue, and the dread of this seems too universal for it to be likely to take place.

The prohibitory law relative to English merchandizes has already produced such inconveniences, and so many remonstrances from the trading part of the nation, that the Directory have not only prolonged the time for allowing the re-exportation of English goods, but give daily permission for the sale of them in the country, and these permissions have been hitherto so frequent and so extensive as nearly to do away the effect of the law.

The conduct of this country towards persons vested with public characters is perfectly new. During the short time I have been here, the Ministers of Modena and Geneva have been sent away by the Directory without assigning any reason to justify so unprecedented a measure; and at this moment they are in doubt whether they shall receive, or not, Mr. Pinckney, who is sent from America, in the room of Mr. Munro. M. Delacroix (by order, doubtless, of the Directory) has left the usual message of notification of his arrival, which he sent four days ago without an answer; and I know they have it in contemplation to refuse to receive his credentials, under no other pretence than the inutility, at this particular moment, of any exchange of Ministers between this country and America.* The real reason, however, is, that Mr. Munro was quite in their principles, connected with their friends in America, and devoted to their interests; whereas Mr. Pinckney is reputed to be of a direct contrary character, and not at all disposed to admire them, or be guided by them.†

It was said that Baron de Staël‡ was to return here as Ambassador from Stockholm, but this seems doubtful. It is indeed by no means to be wished he should, as although he also was sent away by the Directory, yet he is in his habits, manners, and principles, fully qualified to reside in this country.

---

WEDNESDAY, DEC. 14.—Called on Pignatelli. Conversation about Russia. Leveson dined with Mrs. Elliot—very

* The French Government had taken great umbrage at a friendly Treaty lately entered into between Great Britain and the United States, one of the last official acts of Washington. This great man had foiled the intrigues of the French emissaries, who endeavoured to propagate their anarchical principles in his country.

† The Directory afterwards refused to acknowledge Mr. Pinckney as Minister, and recalled their own.

‡ The husband of the celebrated Madame de Staël.

good dinner—she *très naïve*. News came of Empress of Russia's death—she died on the 17th of November of an apoplexy, in her closet.

---

THURSDAY, DEC. 15.—With Pignatelli. Walked to several shops—to Madlle. Laurent, who had lived with Lauzun—she attended him to the last—he would not let his hands be tied—he said to the bourreau, " Nous sommes tous les deux Français, nous ferons notre devoir." At five Ellis returned—much conversation with him. The instructions good, but not likely to answer.

---

EXTRACT OF A LETTER FROM LORD MALMESBURY TO MR. CANNING.

Paris, 17th Dec., 1796. 10 P.M.

THE morning of the day after Timms left Paris, news was received here, and inserted officially in the *Rédacteur*, of the death of the Empress of Russia. As her Imperial Majesty was always killed about this time of the year, I did not at first give any credit to it, but since this very important event has come from so many quarters, and is so well authenticated, that I believe there can be no doubt of its being true. It happened on the 6th of November. The Empress was supposed to be writing ; she remained so much longer than she usually did, shut up in her closet, that at last the door was opened. She was found nearly expiring of an apoplexy, her face upwards, and her legs close to the door, which, it was supposed she had attempted to open. Her Majesty continued to breathe for several hours, but no possibility of recovery existed from the beginning.

---

SUNDAY, DEC. 18.—Write. Despatch messengers to England, to Vienna.

---

MONDAY, DEC. 19.—Write—walk. Guiraudet called at 10 P.M.—I not at home—guessed the motive of his visit. It was reported by various persons, and evidently the Directory had been endeavouring to sound the feelings of the two Councils.

Tuesday, Dec. 20.—At 10, Guiraudet, to announce my being sent away—despatch messenger to Vienna, and in the evening to England. Swinburne, Wild, and Gemm, at dinner. Conversation with Sandoz—at Perregaux in the evening. Supper at Mrs. Elliot's.

EXTRACTS OF A DESPATCH FROM LORD MALMESBURY TO LORD GRENVILLE.

Paris, Tuesday, 20th Dec., 1796.

Mr. Ellis returned from London on Thursday last, the 15th inst., at 5 p.m., and delivered to me the Despatches of the 10th and 11th instant with which he was charged by your Lordship.

Although nothing can be clearer, more ably drawn up, or more satisfactory than the instructions they contain, yet, as it was of the last consequence that I should be completely master of the subject before I saw the French Minister, I delayed asking for a conference till late on Friday evening, with a view that it should not take place until Saturday morning.

He appointed the hour of eleven on that day, and it was near one before we parted. Although what is said by M. Delacroix before he has communicated with the Directory cannot be considered as officially binding, and probably may in the event be very different from what I shall hear when he speaks to me in their name; yet, as it is impossible they should not nearly conjecture the nature of the overtures I should make, and of course, be prepared in some degree for them, it is material that your Lordship should be accurately acquainted with the first impressions they appear to make on M. Delacroix.

I prefaced what I had to communicate with saying, that I now came authorized to enter with him into deliberations upon one of the most important subjects that perhaps ever was brought into discussson. That its magnitude forbade all *finesse*, excluded all prevarication, suspended all prejudices ; and that, as I had it in command to speak and act with freedom and truth, I expected that he, on his part, would consider these as the only means which could or ought to be employed, if he wished to see a negotiation, in which the happiness of millions was involved, terminate successfully.

That for greater precision, and with a view to be clearly understood in what I was about to propose, I would give him a confidential Memorial, accompanied with an official Note, both of which, when he had perused them, would speak for themselves.

The Memorial contained the conditions on the accomplishment of which His Majesty considered the restoration of peace to depend. The Note was expressive of His Majesty's readiness to enter into any explanation required by the Directory on the subject, or to receive any *contre-projêt* resting on the same basis which the Directory might be disposed to give in. That, moreover, I did not hesitate declaring to him in conformity to the principles which I had laid down, and from which I certainly never should depart at any period of the negotiation, that I was prepared to answer any questions, explain and elucidate any points on which it was possible to foresee that doubts or misconceptions could arise on the consideration of these papers ; and having said thus much, I had only to remark, that I believed, in no similiar negotiation which had ever taken place, any Minister was authorized in the first instance to go so fully into the discussion as I now was ; that I was sure neither the truth of this remark, nor the manifest conclusion to be drawn from it, would escape M. Delacroix's observation. I then put the two papers into his hands.

He began by reading the Note, on which, of course, he could only express satisfaction. After perusing the Confidential Memorial with all the attention it deserved, he, after a short pause, said that it appeared to him to be liable to insurmountable objections. That it seemed to require much more than it conceded, and in the event not to leave France in a situation of proportional greatness to other powers of

Europe. He said the act of their constitution, according to the manner in *which it was interpreted by the best publicistes*, (and this phrase is worthy of remark,) made it impossible for the Republic to do what we required. The Austrian Netherlands were annexed to it; they could not be disposed of without flinging the nation into all the confusion which must follow a Convocation of the primary assemblies; and he said he was rather surprised that Great Britain should bring this forward as the governing condition of the Treaty; since he thought he had in some of our late conversations fully explained the nature of their constitution to me.

I replied, that everything I had heard from him on this point was perfectly in my recollection, as it probably was in his; that though I had listened to him with that attention I always afforded to everything he said, yet I had never made him any sort of reply, and had neither admitted nor controverted his opinion. That, although I believed I could easily disprove this opinion from the spirit of the French constitution itself, yet the discussion of that constitution was perfectly foreign to the object of my Mission; since, even allowing his two positions, viz. that the retrocession of the Austrian Netherlands was incompatible with their laws, and that we ought to have known that beforehand; yet, that there existed a *droit publique* in Europe, paramount to any *droit publique* they might think proper to establish within their own dominions; and that, if their constitution was publicly known, the Treaties existing between His Majesty and the Emperor were at least equally public. And in these it was clearly and distinctly enounced, that the two contracting parties reciprocally promise not to lay down their arms without the restitution of all the dominions, territories, &c., which may have belonged to either of them *before the war*. That the date of this stipulation was previous to their annexing the Austrian Netherlands to France; and the notoriety of this ought at the very moment when they passed that law to have convinced them, that if adhered to, it must prove an insuperable obstacle to peace. I applied this maxim to the West India islands, and to the settlements in the East Indies; and asked him whether it was expected that we were to waive our right of possession, and be required still to consider these as integral parts of the French Republic, which must be restored, and on which no value was to be set in the balance of compensation. I also stated the possible case of France having lost part of what she deemed her integral dominions, instead of having added to them in the course of the war; and whether then, under the apprehension of still greater losses, the Government, as it was now composed, should consider itself as not vested with powers sufficient to save their country from the impending danger, by making peace on the conditions of sacrificing a portion of their dominions to save the remainder.

M. Delacroix said this was stating a case of necessity, and such a mode of reasoning did not attach to the present circumstances. I readily admitted the first part of this proposition, but contended that if the power existed in a case of necessity, it equally existed in all others, and particularly in the case before us; since he himself had repeatedly told me that peace was what this country and its Government wished for, and even wanted.

M. Delacroix, in reply, shifted his ground, and by a string of arguments founded on premises calculated for his purpose, attempted to prove, that from the relative situation of the adjacent countries, the present Government of France would be reprehensible in the extreme, and deserve impeachment if they ever suffered the Netherlands to be separated from their dominions; that by the partition of Poland, Russia, Austria, and Prussia had increased their power to a most formidable degree; that England by its conquests, and by the activity and judgment with which it governed its colonies, had doubled its strength. Your Indian empire alone, said M. Delacroix with vehemence, has enabled you to subsidize all the Powers of Europe against us, and your monopoly of trade has put you in possession of a fund of inexhaustible wealth. His words were, "Votre empire dans l'Inde vous a fourni les moyens de salarier toutes les Puissances mercenaires de l'Europe contre nous, et vous avez accaparé le commerce de manière que toutes les richesses du monde se versent dans vos coffres."\*

---

\* The reader will have been surprised at the uncommon minuteness with which Lord Malmesbury reported whole conversations to his Principal, espe-

From the necessity that France should keep the Netherlands and the left bank of the Rhine, for the purpose of preserving its relative situation in Europe, he passed to the advantages which he contended would result to the other Powers by such an addition to the French dominions. Belgium (to use his words) by belonging to France, would remove what had been the source of all wars for two centuries past; and the Rhine being the natural boundary of France, would ensure the tranquillity of Europe for two centuries to come. I did not feel it necessary to combat this preposterous doctrine. I contented myself by reminding him of what he had said to me in one of our last conferences, when he made a comparison of the weakness of France under its monarchs, and its strength and vigour under its republican form of government. "Nous ne sommes plus dans la décrépitude de la France Monarchique, mais dans toute la force d'une République adolescente," was his expression; and I inferred from this, according to his own reasoning, that the force and power France had acquired by its change of Government, was much greater than it could derive from any acquisition of territory; and that it followed if France, when under a regal form of government was a very just and constant object of attention, not to say of jealousy to the other Powers of Europe, France (admitting his axiom) was a much more reasonable object of jealousy and attention under its present constitution, than it ever had yet been; and that no addition to its dominions could be seen by its neighbours, but under impressions of alarm for their own future safety, and for the general tranquillity of Europe. M. Delacroix's answer to this was so remarkable, that I must beg leave to insert it in what I believe to be nearly his own words. "Dans le temps révolutionnaire tout ce que vous dites, Milord, était vrai; rien n'égaloit notre puissance. Mais ce tems n'existe plus. Nous ne pouvons plus lever la nation en masse pour voler au secours de la

cially that with the Empress Catherine; but his memory was known to be most remarkable; and Lord Granville has told me, that he used to come from a conference, and repeat to him every word of it, before he wrote it down, almost as each person had spoken. Both Lord Granville and Lord Cowley speak highly of the remarkable clearness and self-possession with which he argued and fought his opponents at the conferences, although he stood *alone* against *three*.

patrie en danger. Nous ne pouvons plus engager nos concitoyens d'ouvrir leurs bourses pour les verser dans le trésor national, et de se priver même du nécéssaire pour le bien de la chose publique." And he ended by saying that the French Republic necessarily must become the most quiet and pacific power in Europe. I only observed that in this case the passage of the Republic from *youth* to *decrepitude* had been very sudden; but that still I never could admit that it could be a matter of indifference to its neighbours, much less one of necessary security to itself, to acquire such a very extensive addition to its frontiers as that he had hinted at.

This led M. Delacroix to talk of offering an equivalent to the Emperor for the Austrian Netherlands; and it was to be found, according to his plan, in the secularization of the three Ecclesiastical Electorates,* and several Bishoprics in Germany and in Italy. He talked upon this subject as one very familiar to him, and on which his thoughts had been frequently employed.

His language and proposals were so like that which used occasionally to be hinted to me at Berlin three years ago, that I can have little doubt that M. Delacroix has obtained most of his ideas on this subject either from M. Sandoz Rollin, Prussian Minister here, or from Mr. Caillard, the French Minister at Berlin.

He talked of making new Electors, and named, probably with a view to render his scheme more palatable, the Stadtholder, and the Dukes of Brunswick and Wertemberg, as persons proper to replace the three Ecclesiastical Electors which were to be reformed.

It would be making an ill use of your Lordship's time, to endeavour to repeat to you all he said on this subject. It went in substance (as he himself confessed) to the total subversion of the present constitution of the Germanic Body; and, as it militated directly against the principle which both His Majesty and the Emperor laid down so distinctly as the basis of the peace to be made for the Empire, I contented myself with reminding him of this circumstance; particularly as it is impossible to discuss this

* Cologne, Mayence, and Trèves.

point with any propriety till His Imperial Majesty becomes a party to the negotiation. I took this opportunity of hinting that, if on all the other points France agreed to the proposals now made, it would not be impossible that some increase of territory might be ceded to her on the German side of her frontiers; and that this, in addition to the Dutchy of Savoy, Nice, and Avignon, would be a very great acquisition of strength and power.

M. Delacroix here again reverted to the Constitution, and said, that these countries were already constitutionally annexed to France. I replied that it was impossible, in the negotiation which we were beginning, for the other Powers to take it up from any period but that which immediately preceded the war; and that any acquisition or diminution of territory which had taken place among the Belligerent Powers since it first broke out, must necessarily become subject-matter for negotiation, and be balanced against each other in the final arrangement of a general peace. "You then persist," said M. Delacroix, " in applying this principle to Belgium." I answered, "Most certainly; and I should not deal fairly with you if I hesitated to declare in the outset of our negotiation, that on this point you must entertain no expectation that His Majesty will relax, or ever consent to see the Netherlands remain part of France."

M. Delacroix replied, he saw no prospect in this case of our ideas ever meeting, and he despaired of the success of our negotiation. He returned again, however, to his idea of a possible equivalent to be found for the Emperor; but as all he proposed was the alienation or dismemberment of countries not belonging to France, even by conquest, (although it is to be remarked, he did not mention Bavaria,) I did not consider it as deserving attention, and it is certainly not worth repeating to your Lordship.

I need not observe, that all the equivalents proposed, however inadequate to the exchange, were offered as a return for our consent that the Netherlands should remain part of France. Of course the admitting them in any shape would have been in direct contradiction to my instructions.

M. Delacroix touched very slightly on Italy; and in the

present uncertain state of the Milanese, I was not very anxious to bring this part of the subject into discussion.

I must add, that whenever I mentioned the restoration of the Netherlands to the Emperor, I always took care it should be understood that these were to be accompanied by such further cessions as should form a competent line of defence, and that France could not be permitted to keep possession of all the intermediate country to the Rhine; and I particularly dwelt on this point when I held out the possibility of admitting an extension of the limits of France on the side of Germany. But as the French Minister no less strenuously opposed the restoration of the Netherlands to the Emperor, than I tenaciously insisted upon it, the farther extension of my claim could not of course become a subject of argument.

It remains with me to inform you what passed between us on the subject of and respecting our Allies.

On the articles reserving a right to the Court of St. Petersburg, and that of Lisbon, to accede to the Treaty of Peace on the strict *status ante bellum*, the French Minister made no other remark, than by mentioning the Allies of the Republic, and by inquiring whether I was prepared to say anything relative to their interests, which certainly the Republic would never abandon. This afforded me the opportunity of giving in the confidential Memoir (B) relative to Spain and Holland, and I prefaced (A) by repeating to him the substance of the first part of your Lordship's, of the 11th instant.

Although I had touched upon the subject of the Spanish part of St. Domingo, when I had been speaking to M. Delacroix on the Peace with France, yet as it did not become a matter of discussion between us till I came to mention the Peace with Spain, I thought it better to place the subject in this part of my despatch. It was the only point on which he entered; but I by no means infer from his not bringing forward some claims for Spain, that we are not to hear of any in the course of the negotiation: on the contrary, I have little doubt that many, and most of them inadmissible, will be made before it can end. He, however, was silent on them at this moment, and confined all he had to say to combating the idea that Spain was bound by the Treaty of Utrecht not to alienate her possessions in America. I had the Article copied in my pocket, and I read it to him. He confessed it was clear and explicit, but that circumstances had so materially altered since the year 1713, that engagements made then ought not to be considered as in force now. I said that the spirit of the Article itself went to provide for distant contingencies, not for what was expected to happen at or near the time when the Treaty was made; and that it was because the alteration of circumstances he alluded to was foreseen as possible, that the clause was inserted; and that if Spain paid any regard to the faith of Treaties, she must consider herself as no less strictly bound by this clause now than at the moment when it was drawn up. I went on by saying, that it did not, however, appear quite impossible that this point might be settled without much difficulty, and that means might be devised that His Catholic Majesty should not break his faith, and both England and France be equally satisfied. I then held out to him, but in vague terms, quite in the shape of a loose proposal, that either Spain might regain her part of St. Domingo by making some considerable cession, both to Great Britain and France, as the price of peace; or that in return for leaving the whole of St. Domingo to France, we should retain either Martinique, or St. Lucia and Tobago. M. Delacroix listened with a degree of attention to these proposals, but he was fearful of committing himself by an expression of approbation; and he dismissed the subject of the Court of Madrid by observing, that France, never would forsake the interests of its Allies. Our conversation on those of its other Ally, Holland, was much longer, as the wording of the Memorial inevitably led at once deep into the subject.

M. Delacroix affected to treat any deviation from the Treaty of Peace concluded between France and that country, or any restoration of territory acquired by it to France, as quite impracticable. He treated as equally impracticable any attempt at restoring the ancient form of government in the Seven United Provinces.

He talked with an air of triumph of the establishment

of a National Convention at the Hague, and with an affectation of feeling, that by it the cause of freedom had extended itself over such a large number of people. He, however, was ready to confess, that from the great losses the Dutch Republic had sustained in its colonies, and particularly from the weak manner in which they had defended them, it could not be expected that His Majesty would consent to a full and complete restitution of them, and that it was reasonable that some should be sacrificed; and he asked me if I could inform him how far our views extended on this point? I said, I had reason to believe that what His Majesty would require, would be possessions and settlements, which would not add either to the power or wealth of our Indian dominions, but only tend to secure to us their safe and unmolested possession. "You mean by this," said M. Delacroix, "the Cape and Trincomalee." I said, "They certainly came under that description, and I saw little prospect of their being restored to the Dutch. M. Delacroix launched forth on this into a most laboured dissertation on the value of the Cape of Good Hope, which he did not consider at all as a *port de relâche*, but as a possession which, in our hands, would become one of the most fertile and most productive colonies in the East; and according to his estimation of it, he did not scruple to assert, that it would ultimately be an acquisition of infinitely greater importance to England than that of the Netherlands to France, and if acquiesced in, should be reckoned as a full and ample compensation for them; he added, "If you are master of the Cape and Trincomalee, we shall hold all our settlements in India and the Islands of France and Bourbon entirely at the tenure of your will and pleasure; they will be ours only as long as you choose we should retain them; you will be sole masters in India, and we shall be entirely dependent upon you." I repeated to him that it was as means of defence, not offence, that those possessions would be insisted on; and if the matter was fairly and dispassionately discussed, he would find that they afforded us a great additional security, but no additional power of attack, even if we were disposed to disturb the peace of that part of the world. If these, and perhaps some few other not very material settlements belonging to the Dutch, were to be insisted on, and if he would be pleased to enumerate all we should still have to restore to them, while they had nothing to restore to England, it was impossible not to consider the terms on which His Majesty proposed peace to Holland as generous and liberal.

M. Delacroix was not at all disposed to agree with me on this point, and said, Holland, stripped of these possessions, would be ruined. He then held out, but as if the idea had just crossed his mind, the possibility of indemnifying the Dutch for their losses in India by giving them a tract of territory towards the Meuse (I could not find out whether he meant Aix la Chapelle, Liége, or the counties of Juliers and Berg), and hinted that if this was not to be done, an additional sugar-island might perhaps be ceded to the Dutch Republic. I told him all this might become a subject of future discussion; and I conceived that if we could agree upon the more essential points, the Treaty would not break off on these secondary considerations.

Our conversation had now been extremely long, and M. Delacroix ended by saying, that although he had taken upon himself to enter with me thus far upon the subject, yet I must not consider anything he said as binding or as pledging the Republic, till such time as he had laid the papers I had given him before the Directory; and in order to do this with more accuracy, he again asked me whether in his Report he was to state the disuniting Belgium from France as a *sine quâ non* from which His Majesty would not depart. I replied, It certainly was a *sine quâ non*, from which His Majesty *would not depart*.

M. Delacroix repeated his concern at the peremptory way in which I made this assertion, and asked me whether it would admit of no modification. I replied, if France could in a *contre-projêt* point out a practicable and adequate one, still keeping in view that the Netherlands must not be French, or likely again to fall into the hands of France, such a proposal might certainly be taken into consideration.

Here our conference ended; and as during the whole course of it I bore in mind, that this, although our first, might be the only favourable opportunity I should ever have of speaking on the general principles on which His Majesty was disposed to treat, I endeavoured, by adverting more or less to almost every point in my instructions, to enable M. Delacroix (if he reports faithfully) to state to the Directory what I said, in such a manner as to put it out of their power to misconceive what were His Majesty's intentions; to remove all possibility of cavil on this side, and to bring them to a clear and distinct answer whether they would agree to open a negotiation on the principle of the *status ante bellum*, or on one differing from it only in form, not in substance.

I have, I believe, given this conference nearly verbatim to your Lordship, and I was particularly anxious to do this correctly and minutely, as well that you may judge on the propriety of what I said myself, as that what M. Delacroix said to me might be accurately known and remain on record.

It must, however, be remembered, (as I observed in the beginning of this despatch) that he spoke from himself, as Minister indeed, but not under the immediate instructions of the Directory; and this consideration will take a little away from the singularity of some of the positions he advanced.

I confess, my Lord, from the civility of his manners, from his apparent readiness to discourse, and even enter upon the subject, the impression which remained on my mind on leaving him, was, that the negotiation would go on, but be liable to so many difficulties, and some of them so nearly insurmountable, that knowing as I do the opinion of the Directory, I saw little prospect of its terminating successfully. But I did not expect the conduct of the Directory would immediately be such as to evince a manifest inclination and even determination to break it off on the first proposals; and I was not a little surprised at receiving on Sunday at 3 P. M., the enclosed letter from M. Delacroix (A). He sent it me by the principal Secretary of his Department (M. Guiraudet), who communicated to me the original of the Arrêté of the Directory, of which this letter, abating the alteration in the forms, is a literal copy.

After perusing it, I asked M. Guiraudet whether he was informed of its contents, and this led to a short conversation on them. I told him that both the demands were so unexpected that I could not reply to them off hand; that as to the last it was quite unusual to sign Memorials which were annexed to a note actually signed; and that I scarcely felt authorized to depart from what was, I believe, an invariable rule. That as to the second demand, made in so peremptory and unprecedented a way, I could without much hesitation say at once that it could not be complied with. M. Guiraudet lamented this very much, and said, that this being the case, he feared our principles of negotiation would never coincide. I agreed with him in my expressions of concern. We conversed together afterwards for some time, but nothing passed at all worthy of remark. I told him I should send my answer the next day. On reflecting more attentively on the request that I would sign the two Memorials which I had given in, it struck me that the complying with it pledged me to nothing, and that it was merely gratifying them on a point of form, insisted on peevishly; and that the doing it would put them still more in the wrong.

As to the strange demand of an *ultimatum*, it was perfectly clear what it became me to say; and I hope that in the enclosed answer (B) (which I sent yesterday morning at twelve o'clock) to M. Delacroix, I shall be found to have adhered as closely as possible to the spirit of my instructions.

Yesterday evening, at half-past nine, M. Guiraudet brought me the note (C), to which I immediately replied by the Note (D). They require no comment; and as I intend leaving Paris to-morrow and travelling with all convenient speed, I shall so soon have it in my power to say the little which remains to say, relative to this sudden, though perhaps unlooked-for close of my Mission, that I need not trespass any further on your Lordship's patience.

I thought it would be proper for His Majesty's Minister at Vienna to receive the earliest intelligence of the negotiation being broken off. I therefore despatched a messenger to Vienna with copies of the several papers which passed between me and M. Delacroix since our conference, and also a succinct account of what passed in it. This messenger left this place to-day at three P.M.

(A.)

Paris, ce 28 Frimaire, an 5.

LE MINISTRE DES RELATIONS EXTÉRIEURES AU LORD MALMESBURY, COMMISSAIRE PLÉNIPOTENTIARE DE SA MAJESTÉ BRITANNIQUE.

Monsieur,—Le Directoire Exécutif a entendu la lecture de la Note Officielle signée de vous, et des deux Mémoires Confidentiels non signés, qui y étoient joints, et que vous m'avez remis hier. Il me charge expressément de vous déclarer qu'il ne peut écouter aucune Note confidentielle non signée, et de vous requérir de me remettre officiellement dans les vingt-quatre heures votre *ultimatum*, signé de vous.

Agréez, &c.     Ch. Delacroix.

---

(B.)

NOTE FROM LORD MALMESBURY TO M. DELACROIX.

Paris, 19 Dec., 1796.

Le Lord Malmesbury en réponse à la lettre que le Ministre des Relations Extérieures a bien voulu lui faire passer hier par les mains du Secrétaire Général de son Département, doit remarquer qu'en signant la Note officielle qu'il a remise à ce Ministre par ordre de sa Cour, il a cru satisfaire à toutes les formalités d'usage et donner l'authenticité nécessaire aux deux Mémoires Confidentiels qui y étoient joints. Cependant pour aplanir toutes les difficultés en autant que cela dépend de lui, il adopte volontiers les formes qui lui sont indiquées par l'arrêté du Directoire Exécutif, et s'empresse d'envoyer au Ministre des Relations Extérieures les deux Mémoires signés de sa main.

Quant à la demande positive d'un *ultimatum*, le Lord Malmesbury observe que c'est vouloir fermer la porte à toute négociation, que d'insister là dessus d'une manière aussi péremptoire, avant que les deux Puissances se soient communiquées leurs prétentions respectives, et que les articles du traité futur aient été soumis aux discussions que demandent nécessairement les différens intérêts qu'il s'agit de concilier. Il ne peut donc rien ajouter aux assurances qu'il a déjà données au Ministre des Relations Extérieures, tant de vive voix que dans sa Note Officielle ; et il réitère " qu'il est prêt à entrer avec ce Ministre dans toutes les explications que l'état et le progrès de la négociation pourront admettre, et qu'il ne manquera pas d'apporter à la discussion des propositions de sa Cour, *ou de tel contre-projêt qui pourroit lui être remis de la part du Directoire Exécutif,* cette franchise et cet esprit de conciliation qui répondent aux sentimens justes et pacifiques de sa Cour."

Le Lord Malmesbury prie le Ministre des Relations Extérieures d'agréer les assurances de sa haute considération.

---

(C.)

Paris, ce 29 Frimaire, an 5 de la République Française une et indivisible.

Le Soussigné Ministre des Relations Extérieures est chargé par le Directoire Exécutif de répondre aux Notes du Lord Malmesbury des 27 et 29 Frimaire (17 et 19 Dec. v.s.), que le Directoire Exécutif n'écoutera aucune proposition contraire à la constitution, aux lois, et aux traités qui lient la République. Et attendu que le Lord Malmesbury annonce à chaque communication qu'il a besoin d'un avis de sa Cour, d'où il résulte qu'il remplit un rôle purement passif dans la négociation, ce qui rend sa présence à Paris inutile et inconvenante, le Soussigné est en outre chargé de lui notifier de se retirer de Paris dans deux fois vingt-quatre heures, avec toutes les personnes qui l'ont accompagné et suivi, et de quitter de suite le territoire de la République. Le Soussigné déclare au surplus, au nom du Directoire Exécutif, que si le Cabinet Britannique désire la paix, le Directoire Exécutif est prêt à suivre les Négociations, d'après les bases indiqués dans la présente Note, par envoi réciproque de couriers.

Ch. Delacroix.

(D.)

Paris, ce 20 Dec., 1796.

Le Lord Malmesbury s'empresse d'accuser la réception de la Note du Ministre des Relations Extérieures en date d'hier. Il se dispose à quitter Paris dès demain, et demande en conséquence les passeports nécessaires pour lui et sa suite.

Il prie le Ministre des Relations Extérieures d'agréer les assurances de sa haute considération.

---

LETTER FROM LORD MALMESBURY TO LORD GRENVILLE.

Paris, Tuesday, 20th Dec., 1796.

My dear Lord,—I am sure you will forgive my not answering fully your kind private letter by Ellis; and allow me to postpone the doing so till we meet, which, although it is perhaps a little sooner than you expected, it would be, is not at all sooner than I wished. I hope I am not mistaken in thinking we have died well; certain I am that I quit *this world* without regret.

The death of the Empress of Russia has, I have the best reasons to believe, very much influenced their conduct here.*

We shall be at Calais on Saturday night, or Sunday morning. Ever, my dear Lord, &c.

MALMESBURY.

P.S. I have sent a messenger to Vienna.

---

LETTER FROM MR. CANNING TO LORD MALMESBURY.

Sunday, 25th Dec., 1796.

My dear Lord Malmesbury,—Brooks insists upon going to meet you at Dover, and I cannot let him go without a line from me to hail your arrival; though I am so busy in preparing for your reception a printed account of your transactions in Paris, that I have scarce a moment to tell you how glad I shall be to see you.

* Her successor, Paul, was at this time in the French interests.

You will find us all in consternation, but I hope many as stout as you can desire.

A Message will be sent to Parliament to-morrow. The Correspondence between you and Delacroix, Notes, Memorials, &c. will be laid before the Houses and published, together with your last despatch, which, by the way, is *admirable*.

Thursday will be fixed for taking the Message into consideration.

I do not conceive it possible that there can be any debate, for never surely was a case so clear as ours. But you must be prepared, and so must George and Leveson, to answer all sorts of questions in your respective Houses. You may con your speeches over upon the road.

Adieu—we have much to talk over when we meet. I will not now begin upon anything.

Ever, &c.     G. C.

---

WEDNESDAY, DEC. 21.—Left Paris at half-past 11—to Chantilly by 4. Dinner at post-house excellent—charge exorbitant. Slept at l'Hôtel d'Angleterre.

---

THURSDAY, DEC. 22.—Left Chantilly at 8—got to Amiens by half-past 6—rain the whole way. Post at Amiens a good inn.

---

FRIDAY, DEC. 23.—Left Amiens at half-past 7—got to Montreuil at half-past 10. Horrid weather. Good inn at Montreuil à la Cour de France.

---

SATURDAY, DEC. 24.—From Montreuil to Calais, eight posts and a half, eleven hours*—roads bad—clear frost. No flag of truce at Dover. Cannot sail.

---

SUNDAY, DEC. 25.—Called on Commissary—he very civil.

* This journey now takes four hours, travelling post.

Osborne arrived at 12. Wind fair all day—but could not get in—changed in the night.

Monday, Dec. 26.—High wind—rough sea—no going. Commissary called in the evening of 25th—complains of Brook's loquaciousness. Osborne brings passengers—wrong —stupid fellow. Wind increases in the evening—no prospect of sailing.

Tuesday, Dec. 27.—High east wind—great sea—no getting out—remained at home. Bookseller Bellegarde — Mouron, Maire of Calais, called on me—very civil. All my Notes in the French papers. No remarks on them in *l'Eclair* —some very proper ones in the *Censeur*.

Wednesday, Dec. 28.—Thaw. Wind S.E. Prospect of going in the evening, or rather night. At bookseller's. The Commissary of the Executive Power called on me — extremely civil and attentive. Lady Rodney comes. The Commissary told me that C——e, formerly with the Duchess of K——, had taken many prizes. Sailed at 1 A.M.—got to Dover by 7—attended to the boat by municipal officers, but all very civil.

Thursday, Dec. 29.—Left Dover at 9—got to London at half-past four. Dined with Pitt.

[The unavoidable failure of this attempt to make a peace with France gave Mr. Fox and the Opposition an opportunity of attacking the Government in both Houses, on the plea that they had degraded the country. The King sent a Message to Parliament with copies of the papers respecting the Negotiation on the 26th of December, and Pitt moved an Address on the 30th, declaring that, as the continuance of the war was entirely attributable to the French, it was incumbent upon Parliament to afford to the Government their most zealous support to meet the emergency. Despite the oratorical efforts of Fox and Erskine, the Address was carried in the Commons by 212 to 37; and in the Lords, where Lord Grenville moved, and Lord Guilford opposed it, by 86 to 8. The overbearing Notes and implacable feeling of the French Directory roused a spirit which thinned the ranks of the Opposition, and left their leaders in unworthy minorities.

Two days before Lord Malmesbury left Paris, Hoche sailed from Brest with Admiral Bouvet's fleet on his fruitless attempt to invade Ireland, and must have received his commands to do so at the same moment, if not before the Directory had sent their last Note to our Ambassador. The war, therefore, continued to rage, proving fatal to the Austrians in Italy, where Buonaparte was running his early course of victory: but glorious upon the sea to us, who gained the battle of St. Vincent, and continually swept the French and Spanish cruisers from the British Channel.]

## LISLE.

[On the 24th of May, 1797, Buonaparte made the Provisional Treaty of Montebello with the Emperor ; and Pitt, still eager for an honourable peace, renewed, on the 1st of June, his overtures to M. Delacroix. They were this time received with courtesy, and Lord Malmesbury was again appointed to conduct the Negotiation. Lord Grenville was decidedly opposed to this step, and long argued it with Pitt; but the latter remained firm, repeatedly declaring that it was his duty as an English Minister and a Christian, to use every effort to stop so bloody and wasting a war.* He sent Lord Malmesbury to Lisle with the assurance that " he (Pitt) would stifle every feeling of pride to the utmost to produce the desired result ;" and Lord Malmesbury himself went upon his Mission, anxious to close his public life by an act which would spare so much misery, and restore so much happiness to mankind.

On the brink of success, it will be seen by what unforeseen events he failed, for Europe was destined to eighteen more years of battles.

From the following letter to Sir Gilbert Elliot, Lord Malmesbury appears to have wished for retirement after his Mission to Paris ; but he probably deceived himself, and mistook physical weakness for a wearied mind, as, when called upon for service, he readily obeyed.]

* This is shewn in several letters from Lord Malmesbury, Mr. Canning, and Mr. Pitt himself, in the Harris Papers.

### LETTER FROM LORD MALMESBURY TO SIR G. ELLIOT.

Paris, Dec. 18th, 1796.

My dear Elliot,—As there is a report in the newspapers of this place that you are at Naples, I shall try to shoot you flying, particularly as I take it for granted you will not be sorry to hear that your wife and children were all well, and at Bath, on the 11th instant. Harriet was also there, and Sir George, and George Cornewall. All our children in high health and spirits, and, what is better, promising all to be an honour and comfort to us whenever we shall be old and quiet enough to feel this blessing.—I am becoming the first very fast, and do not despair that the other will follow; but it is no easy or short task to still the swell which follows necessarily such a storm as has been blowing (and indeed still blows) for such a length of time. I hope, my dear Elliot, that we shall both of us ere long meet in our own country, and there, after the sea of troubles on which we have been so much tossed about, enjoy all the pleasant feelings that a recollection of these things affords.

Mr. and Mrs. Peploe are at Vienna: report, but I do not give it as at all authentic, says, that Pitt is to marry Eleanor Eden. He has behaved with the greatest kindness and attention towards me in the several Missions on which I have been employed since we parted; and I am now as eager to have them end as I was anxious to receive them when we conversed three years ago on the subject.

Ever yours most sincerely and affectionately,

MALMESBURY.

---

### LETTER FROM LORD MALMESBURY TO MR. CANNING.

Park Place, Saturday, 10th June, 1797, 11 a.m.

My dear Canning,—I am very much obliged to Mr. Pitt for the manner in which he has felt and understood what I conveyed to him through you; I can truly say that I do not allow any private or personal considerations, taken simply as such, to influence me on the present occasion.

I held it a duty to state, that it appeared to me possible, that from the publication of my last despatch,* I might be considered as an exceptionable person to resume the negotiation at Paris; if this is not seen in the same light by the Cabinet, I have nothing to add; and it only remains with me to say, that for my own satisfaction, I had much rather meet again Ch. Delacroix face to face, than avoid him. I beg you would repeat to Mr. Pitt that I am ready to be guided implicitly by his opinion on this occasion, and that my sincere desire is to do what is right to be done.

I will not talk of my health; I soon shall not have leisure to be sick, and while I have leisure, I will try to get quite well. I find I must lose G. Ellis; his reasons are good ones, and I ought not to combat them. I wish you could come here with him and Leveson to-morrow.

I am, &c.   MALMESBURY.

LETTER FROM LORD MALMESBURY TO SIR GILBERT ELLIOT.

Park Place, Sunday, 11th June, 1797.

MY DEAR SIR GILBERT,—Many thanks for your letter, and all the kind things it contains. In regard to Lord St. Helens, I have reason to believe that he was never thought of for the Paris Mission, and I am persuaded he never thought of it himself; and I have no doubt, from the footing of intimacy on which we live, and have lived for so long a while, that he would have, previous to any step or order to obtain it, have communicated with me. I know from the best authority, that the cabinet have unanimously decided it should be myself. I held it right to remind them of the publication of my despatches; of the awkwardness this might create between Charles Delacroix and me, if we were to meet again as plenipotentiaries. The Cabinet did not think this a tantamount reason for my not being appointed; *liberavi ani-*

* Lord Grenville had published Lord Malmesbury's last despatch before he was well able to get out of France, which, in the excited state of that country, might have placed his Ambassador in considerable jeopardy. The contents of this paper would naturally be offensive to Delacroix, and render it awkward for him and Lord Malmesbury to meet again.

*mam meam*, and I probably shall go soon after the return of the next messenger. I feel better, and shall, I dare say, be equal to the bodily fatigue of the business; and no great exertions of the mind will be necessary on this occasion. My intention is to be in town on Tuesday, in order to be in readiness. I hope to find you there, since I fear you will not come here, either to-day or to-morrow. It is a very great event indeed—the restoration of order at the Nore :* if it ends right, good instead of mischief will come from the last mutiny. All here well, and join in love.

Ever yours, most truly and affectionately,
MALMESBURY.

---

[On the 17th of June, Lord Grenville informed M. Delacroix, that Lord Malmesbury would be charged with the Negotiation proposed, pointedly declaring that "His Majesty will not abandon the interests of his Ally the Queen of Portugal." To this Note he received the following answer, and it will be observed that the correspondence began by some sparring on both sides.†]

NOTE OFFICIELLE.

Paris, le 2 Messidor, an 5.

Le Soussigné, Ministre des Relations Extérieures, a mis, aussitôt sa réception, sous les yeux du Directoire Exécutif, la Note Officielle, que lui a adressée le Lord Grenville, en date du 17 Juin, 1797. (v. s.) Il s'empresse d'y répondre conformément aux ordres qu'il a reçus.

Le Directoire, partageant bien sincèrement les sentimens pacifiques que témoigne Sa Majesté Britannique, et voulant amener le plus promptement possible les négociations à une heureuse issue, persiste à demander que les Négociateurs respectifs s'occupent, aussitôt leur réunion, d'un Traité Définitif. Il accepte avec satisfaction le consentement de Sa Majesté Britannique, à cet égard, exprimé dans la Note de Lord Grenville.

---

\* The English fleet had been in open mutiny. Some just concessions were made to the seamen's claims, and Parker, the ringleader, was executed. There never was a more critical moment for the country.

† Our staunch fidelity to our allies, during the preceding and present negotiations, reflect great honour on this country, when compared with their abandonment of England.

Le Directoire consent à ce que Sa Majesté Britannique fasse, par son Plénipotentiaire, les propositions ou stipulations qu'il jugera convenables pour Sa Majesté Très Fidèle, comme réciproquement les Plénipotentiaires de la République en feront pour ses Alliés, Sa Majesté Catholique, et la République Batave.

Le Directoire consent à ce que la Négociation soit ouverte avec le Lord Malmesbury ; cependant un autre choix lui eut paru d'un plus heureux augure pour la prompte conclusion de la paix.

Le Directoire demande qu'il soit établi en *principe*\* que chaque paquebot Anglais qui aura transporté le Plénipotentiaire ou un courier, repartira sur le champ, et ne pourra séjourner. Il donnera des ordres pour qu'il soit fourni sans délai un paquebot Français à chacun des couriers que le Plénipotentiaire de Sa Majesté Britannique expédiera. Il désire toutes fois que les couriers ne soient pas trop multipliés ; leur multiplication ayant été une des principales causes de la rupture des négociations précédentes.

D'après les explications ci-dessus, il devient inutile de transmettre au Lord Grenville un nouveau passeport ; les restrictions qu'il craignoit de voir dans celui qui lui a été adressé, se trouvant entièrement levées.

Les Plénipotentiaires Français seront rendus à Lille à l'époque où le Lord Malmesbury pourra y être rendu lui-même.     CH. DELACROIX.

---

NOTE OFFICIELLE.

A Westminster, ce 26 Juin, 1797.

Le Soussigné a mis sous les yeux du Roi la Note Officielle du Gouvernement Français qu'il a reçu le 23 du mois courant.

Sur les deux premiers articles de cette Note, les deux parties sont d'accord. Il n'y a donc rien à ajouter là dessus aux explications précédentes, en conséquence desquelles explications Lord Malmesbury procédera sans délai à Lille, pour entrer en négociation avec les Plénipotentiaires Fran-

---

\* A pedantic expression as relating to packets, afterwards ridiculed by Maret.

çais, pour la confection d'un Traité définitif, la remarque du Directoire sur le choix que Sa Majesté a jugé à propos de faire n'étant certainement pas de nature à exiger aucune réponse.

Le Gouvernement Britannique consent à l'arrangement proposé pour les paquebots ; pourvu qu'il soit fourni régulièrement et sans le moins délai un paquebot Français pour chaque courier que le Plénipotentiaire Britannique se verra dans le cas d'expédier : l'exercice de son droit incontestable à cet égard ne devant et ne pouvant être réglé que par sa discrétion seule, dans la vue d'amener la négociation dont il est chargé à une prompte et heureuse fin.

Pour ce qui est de la rupture de la dernière négociation, les circonstances et les motifs en sont connus à toute l'Europe, et ce n'est pas au moment d'entamer une nouvelle discussion pacifique, que le Gouvernement Britannique pense qu'il peut être utile de les rappeler.

Lord Malmesbury partira de Douvres le 30 de ce mois, et il réglera son départ de Calais selon la notification qu'il y recevra du jour où les Ministres François pourront être rendus à Lille. (Signé) GRENVILLE.

---

EXTRACTS OF A LETTER FROM LORD MALMESBURY TO LORD GRENVILLE.

Spring Garden, 24th June, 1797.

As I understand that there are expressions of dissatisfaction (in the answer received yesterday from Paris) on my being again the person appointed to resume the Negotiations for peace, I should look upon myself as undeserving the confidence which His Majesty has been graciously pleased to place in me, and at the same time be acting in direct contradiction to those principles on which I wish the whole of my conduct to rest, if I were not to intreat your Lordship, that no considerations personal to me, may in any degree influence the determination of His Majesty's confidential servants, as to the propriety or impropriety of my being employed on this occasion.

It is my earnest desire to waive all private feelings, and to do solely what may be deemed the most expedient for the public service. I, after having expressed my own opinion freely and sincerely, leave the decision with those under whose directions I am to act.

N. B.—This letter, which I sent to Lord Grenville while the Cabinet was sitting, was immediately read to them by him—they all unanimously determined that I should be sent on this Negotiation in preference to any other person.*

NOTE OFFICIELLE.

Paris, le 11 Messidor, an 5.

Le Ministre des Relations Extérieures Soussigné s'est empressé de mettre sous les yeux du Directoire Exécutif la Note Officielle, que lui a adressée le Lord Grenville en date du 26 Juin (v. s.) 8 Messidor, présent mois. En réponse à cette Note il a l'honneur de déclarer au Lord Grenville que les Plénipotentiaires chargés par le Directoire de la Négociation, sont déjà réunis à Lille ; et que les conférences pourront être entamées aussitôt que le Plénipotentiaire de Sa Majesté Britannique s'y sera rendu.

Il a été pourvu à ce que les paquebots ne manquassent jamais aux couriers qu'il jugera à propos d'expédier à Londres.

Le Soussigné prévient également le Lord Grenville, qu'une copie de la présente Note sera remise au Lord Malmesbury, à son arrivée à Calais, afin que rien ne s'oppose à son départ immédiat pour Lille.

Pour copie conforme,
Le Ministre des Relations Extérieures,
CH. DELACROIX.

[A copy of this was sent to Lord Malmesbury by M. Delacroix.]

* The truth of this original note is confirmed by letters from Pitt and Canning, in the Harris Papers.

## LETTER FROM LORD MALMESBURY TO M. DELACROIX.

A Calais, ce 3me Juillet, 1797.

Le Lord Malmesbury, qui vient d'arriver dans ce moment à Calais, a l'honneur de remercier le Ministre des Relations Extérieures de la communication de la Note Officielle qu'il a bien voulu lui faire parvenir. Il s'empresse d'en accuser la réception, et se propose de partir aussitôt que ses équipages seront débarqués, pour se rendre au lieu de sa destination.

Le Lord Malmesbury saisit avec empressement cette occasion de renouveler au Ministre des Relations Extérieures les assurances de sa haute considération.

---

EXTRAIT DES RÉGISTRES DES DÉLIBÉRATIONS DU DIRECTOIRE EXÉCUTIF.

Paris, le 25 Prairial, l'an 5, de la République Française, une et indivisible.

Le Directoire Exécutif arrête ce qui suit :—
Les Citoyens Le Tourneur,\* Pléville le Peley,† et Maret,‡ sont nommés Ministres Plénipotentiaires de la République Française pour la Négociation de la Paix avec l'Angleterre.

Le Citoyen Le Tourneur est nommé Président de la Légation.

Le Citoyen Colchen,§ en est nommé Secrétaire.

Le Ministre des Relations Extérieures est chargé de l'ex-

---

\* Le Tourneur had recently vacated his seat at the Directory, and been replaced by Barthelemi.

† Admiral Pléville le Peley was a few days afterwards appointed Minister of Marine.

‡ Maret was created Duc de Bassano by Napoleon, and Minister for Foreign Affairs, 1811. He died in 1839, aged 76.

Hugues Maret—jeune, versé de bonne heure dans le monde diplomatique; il réunissait à beaucoup d'esprit des formes qui étoient devenues rares en France depuis la Révolution. Au contraire des autres qui avoient la sauvagerie révolutionnaire, etc.—(Thiers, vol. vi.)

§ Colchen was afterwards a Préfêt de Département, and Pair de France. He died in 1830, aged 79.

écution du présent arrêté, qui ne sera point imprimé quant à présent.

Pour expédition conforme,
 Le Président du Directoire Exécutif,  CARNOT.
Par le Directoire Exécutif,
 Le Secrétaire Général,  LAGARDE.

---

LETTER FROM LORD MALMESBURY TO MR. PITT.

Lisle, Thursday, July 6th, 1797. 7 P.M.

MY DEAR SIR,—The few days I have passed in France have been so entirely devoted to etiquette and ceremonial, that I might suppose myself at Münster or Nimeguen negotiating with the most formal and oldest Sovereigns of Europe, instead of at Lisle with the Ministers of a new Republic. The attending to these matters of form has furnished, as you will perceive, very few materials for official correspondence, and none for a private letter. I must, however, beg leave to trouble you with one, merely to express to you how much I felt your kindness and confidence on my leaving England. I am now determined not to ask myself a question about my health till I return.

The desire of M. Le Tourneur to delay entering upon business till to-morrow looks as if they were not yet quite ready, which I think may be considered as a good omen. As to their manners and behaviour, although it is widely different from that of Ch. Delacroix, yet it would be very hazardous to draw any conclusion whatever from it.

I fear it will be quite impossible to sign without reference. I only hope that *one* reference will be enough, and that, knowing as I do your wishes and intentions, you will make my second instructions such as may be deemed final: in order to facilitate this, I shall, before I send away another messenger, endeavour to discover, as far as possible, the real intentions of the French.

  I have, &c.  MALMESBURY.

## LETTER FROM LORD MALMESBURY TO LORD GRENVILLE.

Lisle, Thursday, July 6th, 1797. 8 p.m.

My Lord, — My reception upon the present occasion having much exceeded in civility what I experienced upon my former Mission, and the attentions paid to me at Calais, upon my journey here, and since my arrival, having been so marked, I shall not trespass, I hope, unnecessarily on your Lordship's time, if I make this the subject of a separate despatch.

Immediately upon our entering Calais harbour, the Commandant of the place, the President of the Municipality, and the Commissary of the Executive Power, came on board our vessel, and conducted us to the inn; they offered their services in every way in which they could be useful to us, and insisted, as a mark of respect, that I should have two sentinels at my door. I left Calais a little after 6, and about half a mile from St. Omers we were met by an officer and eight chasseurs, who escorted us into the town; some cannon were fired from the ramparts upon our entering the gates. I found waiting at the post-house the Commandant and all the officers of the garrison. I got out of my carriage to thank them for their attention, and continued my journey for the distance of about two miles under the escort of the same detachment. At Armentières, the last post before Lisle, I found an aide-de-camp, sent by M. Liebert, General of the district, who delivered to me a letter. We were visited upon our arrival by the General, accompanied by the commandant and six other officers; his manners were peculiarly gentlemanlike and respectful, and he also desired that I would have sentinels at the door. This honour I at first rather declined, but when he informed me that sentinels were placed at the hotel of the French Embassy, and that he wished the two Embassies might be, with regard to such points, upon an exactly equal footing, I made no farther hesitation about accepting them. Soon after arrived a deputation from the municipality, who, after expressing their earnest wishes for success in settling a peace, told me they had prepared *la Maison de l'Intendance* for our Conferences. I immediately sent

Mr. Ross, my private secretary, to M. Le Tourneur, to inform the French Legation of my arrival, and to desire to know at what hour it would be convenient for him that I should make my first visit of ceremony. Mr. Ross was told by M. Le Tourneur that he would send an answer by his secretary. In a few minutes he arrived with a message, that the Legation would be ready at any hour I should appoint: it was arranged for 12 o'clock on the following day. At the appointed hour, accompanied by the persons who belong to my Mission, I accordingly made this visit. I was placed on the right hand of M. Le Tourneur, and it was then agreed that we should, at 12 this day, exchange our full powers. I was followed home by his private secretary, who desired to know when we should be ready to receive the French Legation; I informed him we would wait at home till they arrived, and they came almost immediately. I observed the same etiquette that they had shewn to me, and placed M. Le Tourneur on my right. He entered the room with a short speech which began by " La Légation Française toujours prête à rendre égard pour égards, &c." He told us that they had waited upon the municipality at the Hôtel de Commune; and I thought it right, therefore, to pay them the same compliment in return, particularly as the municipality had waited on me on my arrival. The President received us with a speech which he read, and of which I asked a copy, which I enclose to your Lordship.

I have mentioned thus particularly the circumstances of my interview with the French Plenipotentiaries, and the general tenor of their expressions, because I think it proves that they have not revolutionized (as M. Delacroix told me they had done) diplomatic forms and ceremonies, but that, on the contrary, they are desirous of adhering to them with the strictest punctuality; and I hope it will not be considered that I deviated at all from my rank, in announcing my arrival to the French Plenipotentiaries; as I have always found it the usual practice in every Court where I have resided, for the Minister who arrives the last, to make the first visit to Ministers of the same rank as himself.

The country through which we passed appeared in a good state of cultivation, and the inhabitants crowded about the carriage to a much greater degree than on my way from Calais to Paris; but, whether this arose from the novelty of a suite of carriages being greater in this country, whether from curiosity being more the characteristic of the Flemish, or whether from the desire of peace being much stronger in the people of France than it was eight months ago, I cannot pretend to decide with any certainty.

I have, &c.      MALMESBURY.

The Conferences held at Lisle between me and the French Plenipotentiaries, Messrs. Le Tourneur, Pléville, Maret, with M. Colchen as Secretary, were held in the Maison de l'Intendance, a fine hotel in la Rue Royale.

After the form of visits, &c., our first conference was held on Thursday, July 6, at noon.—It was confined to the very simple and short ceremony of reading and exchanging our full powers. My private Secretary, Mr. Ross, brought mine and waited in the room.

We adjourned immediately till the next day.

In the morning of Wednesday I sent Brooks to England. He had his passport from the municipality of Lisle.

---

The second Conference was held at noon, Friday, July 7th, 1797. I began by saying that I had no observations to make on the full powers of the French Plenipotentiary—they appeared to me to be in due form and sufficient; but that I had transmitted them to my Court, and reserved to myself the right of communicating any observations or remarks which I might receive.

M. Le Tourneur repeated precisely the same words as to my instructions, and reserved to himself the same right, having made the same communication of them to the Directory, as I had made to my Court.

I remarked that, although the Court of Portugal was named in neither of our full powers, yet it was to be understood that it was to be comprised in the Treaty as Ally of His Majesty, in the same manner as the Court of Spain and the Batavian Republic were to be comprised as Allies of France*

This was assented to without hesitation. I observed on these words, in their full powers, that "*le Citoyen Colchen est admis aux conférences pour prendre note de tout ce qui sera convenu et arrêté*," that I could have no objection to make; that I only wished it to be clearly understood, as I was conversing in their language, and not my own, that no advantage might be taken of this circumstance, and that a copy might be given me of whatever he wrote down. This was of course agreed to.

M. Le Tourneur then began the business by saying,— "Nous nous sommes assemblés ici pour l'ouvrage le plus important qui peut-être a jamais existé. Il sera bien glorieux pour les deux Légations de l'amener à une heureuse fin; et comme nous y porterons autant de bonne foi, de zèle et de franchise, que nous ne doutons retrouver dans vous, Milord, nous avons toute raison de l'espérer."

I returned to this a suitable answer, and went on by inquiring in what manner he expected the business to be opened. By their pressing so strongly for a Definitive Treaty, it was to be presumed he had some plan ready.

He replied, No; that they were prepared to expect proposals from us: "but," continued he, "without delaying this very important negotiation, by standing out on this point of etiquette, tell us at once and fairly on what basis you wish the Treaty to rest; and I will tell you fairly at once, that any proposals you may make not in contradiction to our constitution, our laws, and our existing treaties, [which were the expressions when the last Negotiation failed,] will not only be listened to cordially, but every facility be given consistently with our honour and interests." I replied, that although from His Majesty having a great deal to give, and nothing to ask for back, it was natural to expect a proposal should originate with them; yet, as he spoke so openly and

* At this period England had but one ally, Portugal. France, Spain, and Holland, continued united against her. At sea the British arms were still victorious. The expedition under Hoche, against Ireland, had failed, and Sir John Jervis had gained the battle of St. Vincent, 14th February, over the Spanish fleet, greatly superior in number; but the Court of Vienna, alarmed by the approach of Buonaparte's victorious army, had, on the 18th April, signed the preliminaries of Leoben, by which Austria abandoned Lombardy and the Low Countries.

cordially, I was ready to collect from the materials in my possession what would make a sort of rough *projêt*, and would bring it with me to-morrow—that he must be conscious there must be several articles left in blank, which only could be filled up after our conferences. That I also begged to be understood that, as they set out from the principle that nothing should be proposed in contradiction to their constitution, by which I understood him to mean the integrity of the French Republic, to their laws, and to their treaties (as far as they were known to us—for it was impossible for me to engage any compliance with secret articles; and to this last point they all nodded consent); so I on my part had to stipulate that nothing should be proposed by them contrary to our constitution (to which I attached the same sense, viz., the integrity of the British empire, our laws, and our treaties). To this he seemingly, though not decidedly, assented, appearing to make this point dependent on the terms of the Treaty. On M. Pléville's observing, that the glory of the *two* nations must be consulted, as well as their interests, and that every quarter of an hour lost was lengthening the misfortunes of humanity, I joined issue with him entirely; and added, on M. Le Tourneur's repeating nearly the same sentiment with a handsome compliment to England, that the strongest proofs that this was my Royal Master's wish would appear in the *projêt* I should prepare. That all the Great Powers of Europe being now aggrandized, and France in a greater proportion than any of them, it was but reasonable that Great Britain also should be enabled to hold her rank amongst them; but it would appear by what I had to ask (which from what I had heard must be from the Allies of the Republic, not from the Republic itself), that it was only security for maintaining what we already had, and not additions of territory, that we wished.

M. Le Tourneur by his looks admitted this to be reasonable, but said nothing, except that we would adjourn all further discussion till noon of the next day, when I undertook to be ready with my *projêt*.

Le Tourneur was the only one who spoke, and I only observed that he frequently looked at Maret, as if fearful of not saying all, or saying too much.

Maret said nothing, except a few civil phrases. Pléville talked of *l'humanité souffrante*; and all these repeatedly and strongly expressed their orders to act *avec franchise, loyauté, et d'y mettre toute la facilité possible.*

The difference of their language from that of Delacroix is worthy of remark. The difference of their manner might arise from the difference of their tempers and characters; but the difference of their language, it must be supposed, can only be attributed to a difference in their instructions from the Directory.

At the third Conference, Saturday noon, July 8th, 1797, the French Legation began by explaining about Colchen: that he was simply a Secretary; that it was superfluous and silly to have said in the *arrêté*, " qu'il y étoit pour prendre des notes;" and it was by no means extraordinary I should be surprised at it.

I began by saying that the interests of the allies of France and Great Britain were to be treated of jointly with their own; so it would be necessary, to obtain our end, that their respective possessions should be blended together, and, in the Treaty we were about to begin, that they should be all unitedly considered as the price to be given for the restoration of peace. I said, what would the most facilitate this would be the cession of one of their islands; but as they declared this to be against the letter of their constitution, that now, if the integral parts of the French Republic were not to be meddled with, it was necessary that a compensation for His Majesty should be found in cessions from one or both of the allies of the Republic.

I then gave in my *projêt*,* which M. Le Tourneur read. He began by objecting to the renewal of treaties, but Maret stopped him by saying this was not a material point; Pléville however added, that, as ours was only *une paix maritime*, it was useless to refer to treaties which related

* This *projêt* was again founded on the principle of mutual restitutions; the names of the places left blank for future discussion. Two points were stated in it as indispensable, viz. the restoration of the private property to the Prince of Orange, and the raising the sequestration fines and disabilities of all persons suffering such, in all places mutually restored.

to the affairs of the Continent. I observed, that the three last Treaties, viz. 1748, 1763, and 1783, were all referred to as being *des paix maritimes*. We then went on to Art. VI.,* which I observed, as they would not consent, though I again urged it, to give up any of their possessions, must probably be effaced, and considered as *non avenu*. When we came to Spain, I insisted on Trinidad. This was contested. I argued the necessity of having some one valuable possession in the West Indies, to balance the great acquisition made by France by the having the Spanish part of St. Domingo, which when cultivated would be invaluable. I should have said before, that Le Tourneur sent for the Constitution, and read to me the annexed departments. I took from my pockets such of them as we had conquered. He said, on my coming to St. Domingo, that they had received news that they had retaken the greater part of it, that something must be found; and I mentioned Port Rico, or New Orleans, Demerara, Essequibo, and Berbice: of this Maret took a note.

Trinidad in our hands, Pléville said, would turn to great account; so would New Orleans; and he immediately saw its consequence as to the Americans. On the demands from us, Pléville observed, we asked *all* of the Dutch. I said, No. He said the Cape of Good Hope must be in the hands of an inferior power, that it was of importance both to England and France. The isles of France and Bourbon were supplied from thence. They desired me to send in a note to fill up the blanks, and that they would let me know as soon as they had deliberated on the subject.

---

At the fourth Conference, Monday, July 10th, 1 P.M., I came before they were all assembled, and walked with Le Tourneur in the garden. He talked about Calonne, and attributed the Revolution to him in particular, and in general to the want of morality in the people of an upper class. When M. Maret came, Le Tourneur began by proposing we should renounce the title of King of France.†

---

* In which a blank was left, to be filled up with the places excepted from mutual restitution.

† First claimed by Edward III. in right of female descent, and assumed by each of his successors.

I mentioned the usual Article employed to do away any right belonging to it. It would not do. They persisted in its being renounced.

2nd point.—The restitution of the ships taken or destroyed at Toulon. This I, of course, combated.

3rd.—The idea of our having a mortgage on the Low Countries.

For a more accurate account of this Conference, see the end of my despatch of the 11th July, which I wrote immediately on coming from it.

EXTRACT OF A DESPATCH FROM LORD MALMESBURY TO LORD GRENVILLE.

Lisle, 11th July, 1797.

M. LE TOURNEUR informed me on the subject of the *projêt* which I had given them, and the Note with which I had accompanied it, that, as these papers contain many points on which their instructions did not enable them to answer, they had, after having given them a very serious attention, sent them with such observations as they had thought it their duty to make on them to the Directory, and that the moment they received an answer they would communicate it to me. But that in the mean while, not to delay the progress of the Negotiation, they wished that several points which he termed *insulated*, but which, though not referred to in our *projêt*, were, he said, inseparably connected with the general subject of peace, might be discussed and got rid of now, if I had no objection; and that it was with this view they had requested me to meet them. On my not expressing any disapprobation to this mode of proceeding, M. Le Tourneur began by saying, that in the preamble of the Treaty the title of King of France was used; that *this title* they contended *could no longer be insisted on*—the abolition of it was in a manner essential to the full acknowledgment of the French Republic; and that as it was merely titulary as far as related to His Majesty, but quite otherwise in the sense in which it applied to them, he hoped it would not be considered as an important concession.

I informed him that on all former occasions a separate Article had been agreed to, which appeared to me to answer every purpose they required, and which it was my intention, as the Treaty advanced, to have proposed as proper to make part of this. The Article (the first of the separate ones in the Treaty of 1783) was then read; but they objected to it, as not fully meeting their views. It was to the title itself, as well as to any rights which might be supposed to arise from it, that they objected.

I could scarce allow myself to treat this mode of reasoning seriously. I endeavoured to make them feel that it was cavilling for a mere word; that it was creating difficulties where none have existed; and that, if all the French monarchs in the course of three centuries had allowed this to stand in the preamble of all treaties and transactions between the two countries, I could not conceive, after its having been used for so long a period without any claim or pretension being set forth in consequence of it, how it could now affect either the dignity, security, or importance of the Republic; that, in fact, such titles have ever been considered as indefeasible, and as memorials and records of former greatness, and not as pretensions to present power; and I quoted the titles of the kings of Sardinia, Naples, &c. as examples exactly in point. I argued however in vain; they treated it very gravely, and made so strong a stand upon it, that I could not avoid taking it for reference, which I thought it better to do, than, feeling as I did at the moment, to push the conversation further.

The second insulated point was a very material one indeed, and which, although it has been adverted to as a proposal that might possibly be brought forward, I confess came upon me unexpectedly. It was to ask either a *restitution of the ships taken and destroyed at Toulon, or an equivalent for them.* They grounded this claim on the preliminary declaration made by Lord Hood on his taking possession of Toulon,* and on the Eighth Article of the De-

---

* Lord Hood, on receiving the French ships at Toulon, accepted them as a trust for the Government which we then acknowledged, viz. the Bourbons.

claration of the Committee of the Sections to him. They said, peace, they hoped, was about to be re-established; that His Majesty, in acknowledging the Republic, admitted that a sovereignty existed in the French government, and of course that the ships held only as a deposit by England till this legal authority was admitted, ought now to be restored. I replied that this claim was so perfectly unlooked for, that it was impossible for me to have been provided for it in my instructions; and that I could therefore only convey my own private sentiments on it, which were, that they could not have devised a step more likely to defeat the great end of our Mission. M. Maret said that he sincerely hoped not; that, without a restitution of the ships, an equivalent might be found to effect the purpose desired; since their great object was, that something should appear to prove that this just demand had not been overlooked by them, and was not left unsatisfied by us. I told him fairly I did not see where this equivalent was to be found, or how it could be appreciated; and that, considering the great advantages France had already obtained by the war, and those she was likely to obtain from the act of condescension I had already intimated His Majesty was disposed to make in order to restore peace, I was much surprised and deeply concerned at what I heard. I trusted, therefore, that this very inadmissible proposal would be withdrawn. They said it was not in their power; and M. Le Tourneur, from a written paper before him, which he said was his instructions, read to me words to the effect I have already stated.

The third question was, as to any *mortgage* we might have upon the *Low Countries*, in consequence of money lent to the Emperor by Great Britain. They wished to know if any such existed; since, as they had taken the Low Countries —charged with all their incumbrances, they were to declare that they should not consider themselves bound to answer any mortgage given for money lent to the Emperor for the purpose of carrying on war against them.

I told them that without replying to this question, supposing the case to exist, the exception they required should

The French now claimed them as national property as soon as we recognised the new order of things in France.

have been stated in their Treaty with the Emperor, and could not at all be mixed up in ours; that if they had taken the Low Countries as they stood, charged with all their incumbrances, there could be no doubt what these words meant; and that, if no exception was stated in the first instance, none could be made with a retro-active effect.

The French Plenipotentiaries, however, were as tenacious on this point as on the other two; and, as I found to every argument I used that they constantly opposed their instructions, I had nothing to do but to desire they would give me a written paper stating their three claims, in order that I might immediately transmit it to your Lordship; and, on this being promised, our conference broke up.

Between 4 and 5 P.M. yesterday, I received the inclosed Note,* and I have lost no time since it is in my possession in preparing to send away a messenger, as, independent of the disagreeable subjects brought forward in this last Conference, and which it is material should be communicated without delay, I am anxious His Majesty should be informed of what has passed in general up to this day, as it may perhaps furnish some idea as to the possible event of the Negotiation.

---

EXTRACTS OF A DESPATCH FROM LORD MALMESBURY TO LORD GRENVILLE.

(Separate.) Lisle, 11th July, 1797.

NOTWITHSTANDING the strong declaration of the French Plenipotentiaries, that the three points set forth in their Note of yesterday formed a claim which they were strictly bound by their instructions to insist on, and that they expressed themselves in a style intended to convince me that no modification whatever could be listened to, I cannot bring myself to believe that they will make a determined stand upon any of them, or suffer the Treaty to break off, should these points not ultimately be complied with. I conceive them brought forward rather with a view to become negotiable points, as we proceed in the business, and to be

* Stating the three above-mentioned demands upon England.

employed in order to induce us to make some abatement from the condition stated in our *projêt*.

If I am mistaken, and that the French Government should be so far removed from reason and decency as not only to be in earnest in setting forth these extravagant pretensions, but venture also to reject the reasonable terms His Majesty has condescended to offer, and in their stead substitute others of a direct opposite nature, it will be impossible for any nation of Europe, even their own, not to see through and reprobate their conduct. But I cannot conceive this to be possible; for with the eager disposition for peace which evidently exists in this country, with the utter impracticability of finding means to continue the war, and, above all, with the temper and complexion of the two Councils, the Directory must be wanting in the first principles of common sense and prudence if they dared to reject proposals, the basis of which went to leave France in quiet possession of *nearly all she had conquered* in Europe, and to restore to her *all she has lost* in her colonies; and particularly as it must appear, when stated to the public, that these conditions were rejected on account of points of insignificant form and cavil totally unconnected with either the prosperity or security of the French nation.

I am so strongly impressed with this idea, that I by no means consider these wild proposals (unless they should be followed up by some equally so, on the subjects of the restitution and reservation or cession of territories) as indicating a less favourable issue to the Negotiation than was expected; and it is certainly better, let the event be what it may, that they should be encouraged to come forward with all their exorbitant demands in the outset of the business, in order that an immediate comparison may be made between their conduct and the moderation, equity, and condescension of His Majesty. Such a contrast will be much more striking in the first instance than it would be at a later period of the negotiation, when it might appear to be provoked by previous discussion and altercation.

I certainly had it in my power to combat these demands with many more arguments than those I employed; but I felt that the arguing too strongly on them would give them a degree of credit and consequence they ought not to appear to have. I wished also that the French Plenipotentiaries should suppose that it was impossible for me to have foreseen that proposals of this nature could have been made; that they were such as at once ought to be discarded, and not such as were to be defeated by reasoning; and that the strongest proof I could give of a disposition to continue the negotiation, was the venturing to take them for reference, instead of declaring them at once inadmissible.

---

At the fifth Conference, July 13, 1797, 1 p.m. Le Tourneur said, " Comme vous le jugez bien !" that there was not, neither could there be, any answer yet from the Directory as to the *projêt* itself; but they wished to see me, in order partly not to let too long an interval elapse without seeing me, and partly to speak on some point which might be settled in the mean while. They entered objections against the renewal of the Treaties we had enumerated in Art. II.,* not to the Treaties themselves; but that they thought it would be better to draw up separate articles, and to enumerate everything in them which related to the two countries, and which might contribute to make the Treaty of Peace we were negotiating solid and permanent, and remove all possibility of future disputes, than to put then *all* in a lump, without examining what articles in the Treaties might be useless or exceptionable. I agreed completely with him as to the principle, that, if His Majesty wished that the Treaty we now were making should be as solid and as permanent as possible, every detail which human foresight could advise, should be removed which could produce a contrary effect. That it was with this view, and this only, that the Treaties we had stated were renewed; that they would observe we had selected those which related more immediately to the separate and respective interests of Great Britain and France, and omitted all others that did not relate to them. Le Tourneur agreed with this, and said that

* Of Nimeguen, 1678 and 1679 ; of Ryswick, 1697 ; of Utrecht, 1713 ; of Baden, 1714 ; of the Hague, 1717 ; of London, 1718 ; of Vienna, 1738 ; of Aix la Chapelle, 1748 ; of Paris, 1763, and of Versailles, 1783.

it was because they observed this that they came forward with their present proposal ; he, however, injudiciously enough, talked of their difficulty in renewing them because monarchy was abolished ; that it was an avowal of Kings ; mentioned the Treaty of Pilnitz, &c. To this I replied that these Treaties were become acts of *droit publique;* it was indifferent under what form of government they were made, or by whom signed; that none of them bore any reference to the new form of government established in France, and that the Treaty of Pilnitz was one *we* had nothing to do with.

Maret agreed with me, and rather *persifléd* Le Tourneur for his remark. After a short conversation, carried on in the most civil and even conciliating language on their side, it was agreed that we should peruse these Treaties carefully, and select from them such articles as applied to the two Countries, and endeavour from this to draw up an article that would meet the end both of us wished to obtain. They had, they assured me, employed their minds on this subject, and they wished me to employ mine. We adjourned till the 15th—the 14th being a day of rejoicing in commemoration of the destruction of the Bastille.

This Conference passed off much more cordially, and with a greater appearance of care and desire to please on the part of the French Plenipotentiaries, than any of the preceding ones ; but, whether this is a good or bad omen, I cannot say. It appears evident that they wish to *gain time;* and, on my mentioning to them how important it was not to get into subjects *qui pourroient entrainer des longueurs*, they agreed with me ; but at the same time said, that if these longer discussions tend to settle any doubtful points, and prevent quarrels in future, they were well worth going into. I agreed with them, observing only, that I was sure it was the wish of both Legations that neither of the Governments should reproach either of them with unnecessary delays.

Pléville did not say a word ; his eyes were shut almost the whole time. Le Tourneur spoke very little to the purpose ; Maret very well, and very much like a gentleman. Colchen had no call to speak, but looked consent to all that was said.

MR. CANNING TO THE FAMILY OF THE REV. MR. LEIGH.*

Downing Street, July 12th, 1797.

No messenger yet from Lisle. It is an interval of anxiety and impatience, such as makes it impossible to think, speak, or write, upon any other subject. I get up, go to bed, eat, drink, sleep, walk, ride, with nothing but the messenger in my head, and I hear nothing all day long, but, Well, not come yet ? When will this messenger come, and what will he bring ?—Peace ?

---

EXTRACTS OF A DESPATCH FROM LORD GRENVILLE TO LORD MALMESBURY.

Downing Street, 13th July, 1797.

I HAVE the King's commands to express to your Lordship His Majesty's entire approbation of the zeal and ability which you have hitherto shewn in the execution of the important commission entrusted to you.

With respect to the demands contained in the note transmitted to your Lordship by the French Ministers, they have naturally been received here with great surprise.

On the subject of the Netherlands as connected with the Austrian Loans, it is conceived that any explanation between His Majesty and the French Government is wholly unnecessary. The loans raised in England for the service of the Emperor of Germany, and guaranteed by Act of Parliament here, rest, as your Lordship will perceive by the annexed copy of the Convention on that subject, upon the security of all the revenues of all the hereditary dominions of His Imperial Majesty. They do not seem, in any manner, to come under the description contained in the Sixth Article of the Preliminaries between Austria and France respecting mortgages upon the soil of the Netherlands, on which ground alone France could have any pretence to interfere in the business ; nor is the subject one which appears to be in any

* Mr. Leigh was uncle to Mr. Canning, and resided at Ashbourne, in Derbyshire.

manner a fit point of discussion between His Majesty and the Republic. The King neither forms, nor has any intention of forming, any demand on the French Government for the payment of any part either of the interest or capital of those loans. It is to the Emperor alone that His Majesty looks for the performance of His Imperial Majesty's engagements to him; and it is upon the Austrian Government, and upon its revenues, that individuals concerned in those loans have claims of private right, and means of personal demand secured to them by the Convention.

On the other two points I have nothing to add to the observations which your Lordship has already made upon them; and we can, therefore, only wait with impatience for the answer to the *projêt* delivered by your Lordship, which will enable us to form a judgment on the intentions of the Government with whom you are treating.

I have only further to remark, that the French Ministers were either themselves grossly deceived on the subject of St. Domingo, or desirous of misleading your Lordship. The inclosed statement, on the authority of which you may entirely rely, will prove to your Lordship that, so far from the French having regained possession of the whole of that Island, they have been repulsed with considerable loss in the only important attempt which they have lately made on any of the posts occupied by His Majesty's forces.*

---

LETTER FROM LORD GRENVILLE TO LORD MALMESBURY.

Cleveland Row, July 13th, 1797.

MY DEAR LORD,—I was the more anxious to use expedition in sending the present despatches, in order that you might have a messenger with you, so as to enable you as fast as possible to feed our anxious expectations. I do not think much conclusion can be drawn from what has already passed,

---

* The inclosure contained an official account, that, in their attack on Fort Trois in St. Domingo, the French had been defeated, with the loss of a thousand men, by General Simcoe. Colonel the Hon. Thomas Maitland appears to have deservedly had the honour of this victory.

though the three demands made by France are more unreasonable and unconciliating than was generally expected here.

The negotiations between France and the Emperor were at a stand, and the latter appears by the last letters from Vienna to have insisted on the concluding his Definitive Treaty only at a Congress. How far the knowledge of your Mission, and of the avowed object of it, may change this determination, I cannot say; but, if the Court of Vienna suffers from this separation of interest and conduct, it has only itself to thank for it. Some good may, perhaps, result to our Negotiation from any rub which that Negotiation experiences; but in the end Austria, unsupported by England, must acquiesce in almost any terms that France will give her.

Buonaparte seems to be settling Italy, (if a total subversion of a country can be called *settling* it,) without reference either to the Directory or their Treaties.

Yours, &c.     GRENVILLE.

LETTER FROM MR. PITT TO LORD MALMESBURY.

Downing Street, Thursday Evening, July 13th, 1797.

MY DEAR LORD,—Having been kept in the House of Commons almost from the time our Cabinet broke up to-day, I can hardly do more than thank you for your letter, and say to you very shortly with how much satisfaction I have seen the account of all the steps you have taken in the Negotiation as far as it has yet advanced.

Till we receive a *contre-projêt*, or the result (whatever it may be) of your Conferences after the answer from Paris, I know not how to form anything like a conjecture on the probable issue of the business; and you will perceive, by the despatch sent now, that we think it best to avoid giving any instructions on the *three* separate points urged by the French Plenipotentiaries, (except the explanation respecting the supposed mortgage of the Netherlands,) till we know what they propose or consent to on the principal points in question. I own I am not without some hope that in one way or other difficulties on these separate points will not long retard the Negotiation, if in other respects an agreement is practicable. In the mean time the great object seems to be, not to encourage in them any idea of our relaxing, at the same time taking care not to give them any opportunity (which, however, I do not think they would at present be desirous of seeking) of prematurely breaking off on any ground, before we are in possession of the whole extent and nature of their views.   Believe me, &c.   W. PITT.

---

LETTER FROM MR. CANNING TO MR. ELLIS.*

Downing Street, 13th July, 1797, or rather, 14th, 2 A.M.

MY DEAR GEORGE,—As usual, I have kept you for the last, meaning to write you a very long letter, and to say to you whatever I had left unsaid to other people, and to say over again to you whatever I had said to them ; and now I am so tired and exhausted that it is a wonder to me how much of these fine purposes I shall execute.

I must tell you, because I have yet told nobody, not even " the Lion†" himself, how much his despatch of yesterday is admired and approved, as well as the conduct which he describes. Nothing could be more able and judicious ; the three points in Monday's Conference would have staggered the most practised combatant. But " the Lion" seems to have received them all without flinching, and to have put them by as quietly as you see they have been put by in the despatch to-day, where there is not a word said about them.

With regard to the title of King of France, I am inclined to agree with you, that, if it is to be reasoned upon seriously, we shall be beaten in the argument, and had best look out for the most fanciful and innocent mode of renunciation. The chance in our favour is, I think, that this frivolous question may ultimately be overwhelmed in the greater considerations arising out of the *projêt*, and the commentary upon it ; and that if a Treaty is agreed upon, or nearly so, within

---

\* Mr. Ellis continued to be attached to Lord Malmesbury's embassy.
† " The Lion" was a nickname by which his intimate friends called Lord Malmesbury, since some foreign newspaper had described him as resembling " un lion blanc," from his fine eyes and his profusion of white hair.

a short space of time, you may in the ardour of consummation overleap all matters of form, and then tack on your old apologetical article at the end without much notice being taken. After all, it is a grating thing—God knows, I feel it so ; and which of *us*, that is, of the " Lion," you and me,— we might add Windham, but he is beyond us,—we might add Jenksburg,* I believe, and all told—which of us is there that does not feel it grating to have to contrive modes of concession, instead of enforcing the justice of demands ? And were I writing to you on the 13th of last December, instead of the present 13th of July, could I have thought with patience of renunciation and restitution, unaccompanied by cessions to balance and compensate them ? But we cannot and must not disguise our situation from ourselves. If peace is to be had, we must have it ; I firmly believe we must, and it is a belief that strengthens every day. When Windham says we must not, I ask him, " Can we have war ? " It is out of the question, we have not the means—we have not, what is of all means the most essential, the *mind*. If we are not at peace, we shall be at nothing. It will be a *rixa* between us and our enemy—of *pulsation* on their side, and *vapulation* on ours. For my part, I adjourn my objects of honour and happiness for this country beyond the grave of our military and political consequence, which you are now digging at Lisle. I believe in our resurrection, and find my only comfort in it.

But though I preach peace thus violently, do not imagine that I am ready to take any that you may offer. I think it clear, from the conferences that have yet passed, and from so much of the instructions of the French Plenipotentiaries as has yet been made known to you, that there is no objection on their part to our stripping their Allies, provided we do it with decency and moderation ; and one of the characteristics is, that, so as they get something, they care not much from whom. Give us then something to shew as an acquisition—but remember (this is all that I intended by my shabby declamation two pages ago), that what may be very splendid as an acquisition, would be very insufficient as a cause of quarrel. We can break off upon nothing but what

* A nickname for Jenkinson, afterwards Lord Liverpool, and prime minister.

will rouse us from sleep and stupidity into a new life and action, what "will create a soul under the ribs of death!"—for we are now soul-less and spiritless; and what would, do this, except the defence of Portugal (I believe that would), or the preservation of our integrity (our *entireness*, I would say), I know not. All beyond this we shall like to have, but we never shall fight for it. I am persuaded, however, that we may yet have a good deal without fighting.

I ought now to tell you something of what has been passing here since you left us. There is but one event, but that is an event for the world,—Burke is dead!* How and when the newspapers will tell you. I know the details only from them. Mrs. Crewe, who was at Beaconsfield at the time, wrote only to say that she could not write to me; *for* he had, among all his great qualities, that for which the world did not give him sufficient credit, of creating in those about him very strong attachments and affection, as well as the unbounded admiration which I every day am more and more convinced was his due. It is of a piece with the peddling sense of these days, that it should be determined to be imprudent for the House of Commons to vote him a monument. He is the man that will mark this age, marked as it is in itself by events, to all time.

But it grows very late, and I very tired—my hand, at least, though I have yet much to say, having in truth said nothing. Now for a very few questions, and I have done.

How is " the Lion's" health?

What is your private life and conversation at Lisle?—for I have heard nothing of it from anybody.

Why does not Morpeth write as well as the rest of you in the despatches? Is he idle?—or is " the Lion" delicate?—or is it chance?—or does he do something else for you that does not appear?

And now good night, dear George, and God bless you!

Ever yours, G. C.

---

* Burke died July 8th, aged 68.

### LETTER FROM LORD MALMESBURY TO MR. PITT.

Lisle, Sunday, 5 p.m., July 16th, 1797.

My dear Sir,—It is very satisfactory to hear that my conduct hitherto has been approved, and still more satisfactory to learn it in so kind a manner from you. I am induced to hope from your letter that you will equally approve the steps I have taken since, and not think I acted injudiciously in wishing to come to some explanation with my French opponents before I transmitted officially the Note they sent me yesterday. It is calculated more to perplex than to surprise us, since it was all along to be supposed that the French would begin the negotiation in a tone of high demand and arrogance. I own, however, I draw rather a favourable conclusion from our conference of this morning; besides doing away a great deal of the obnoxious part of the Note, it was carried on with an uncommon degree of good temper and patience on the part of the French Legation, considering the plain and strong language I thought it my duty to employ.

If the Directory mean peace at all, the step they have now taken is only a parade of their intentions to fulfil scrupulously their engagements with their Allies; and from this they will recede to a certain degree, as the Negotiation goes on. On the other hand, if the Directory intend to continue the war on system, they will not only insist on this declaration to its full extent, but even bring forward conditions still more inadmissible. I really have no safe data to enable me to form an opinion which of the two cases is most likely; the Councils, indeed, seem to be gaining strength, and it ought to be inferred from hence that the Directory is losing it; that peace, therefore, would be the result of my Mission; but I know by experience this not to be safe ground to argue upon, and either my conjectures may be erroneous, or my conclusions false. Fortunately we are already in possession of many valuable official testimonies of the exorbitancy of *their* demands, and probably we shall obtain still stronger ones, if the Negotiation is to break off.

It was very evident that when Le Tourneur mentioned

this morning, that some new mode of compensation might be proposed equally advantageous to our interests with that I brought forward, he alluded to Gibraltar; and that Spain would give some one, or perhaps more than one, of her valuable possessions in the West Indies in exchange for it. I do not recollect even hearing your feelings on this particular point. As to the general turn of the Treaty, I am inclined to think, (without, however, anything like strong ground for my opinion,) that, if it proceeds in the way in which it is begun, we shall be able to retain one of the two great Dutch establishments, and this will probably be Ceylon.*

I have in a letter to Canning put down very hastily, and very incorrectly, some ideas as to the title of King of France, and on the renewal of Treaties; they will here be more tenacious on these two points than they deserve. In regard to the last, I really do not see, after having very carefully and attentively perused all the Treaties stated in the second article, why it is important to renew any of them but that of 1763, and that of 1783.

I am, &c.    MALMESBURY.

DESPATCH FROM LORD MALMESBURY TO LORD GRENVILLE.

Lisle, 16th July, 1797.

MY LORD,—Yesterday, at the moment I was preparing to attend the Conference, in which we were to enter into fuller discussions on the litigated subject of the renewal of the Treaties mentioned in the second article of the *projêt*, I received from the French Legation the enclosed papers. In about an hour I returned the enclosed answer (B,) to which I received the enclosed reply (C,) and am this moment come from the conference which has taken place in consequence of it.

Before I attempt to give your Lordship an account of

---

* It will appear in a subsequent Diary, that Mr. Pitt had given Lord Malmesbury private instructions to surrender *Ceylon* or the *Cape* to the French, rather than break off the negotiation, so anxious was he for peace.

what passed in it, I must express my hope that I have not judged improperly, or acted in contradiction to the spirit of my instructions by the step I have taken. To have communicated such a paper as this to my Court, crudely and without any attempt to come to an explanation on its contents, would have left scarce a choice as to the measures to be adopted in consequence of it. And if I had taken upon myself to answer it petulantly and intemperately, it must have produced nearly the same effect on the Directory; and I felt it my duty to avoid both the one and the other, as long as it could be done without committing the dignity and interest of my Royal Master.

The event will also, I hope, justify what I have done.

On meeting the French Plenipotentiaries, I began by saying, that I had solicited this interview from the same motive which would actuate every part of my conduct : that I wished to make my reports not only correct, but conciliatory as far as depended on me ; and I now was come, in order, if possible, to obtain from them such comments and explanations on the Note they sent to me yesterday, as would enable me, when I transmitted it to my Court, to secure the Negotiation from being interrupted, perhaps abruptly terminated, by the perusal of it. If I understood it right, it meant that the Directory requires, as a *sine-quâ-non* preliminary, *that everything the King had conquered from all and each of his enemies should be restored; and that, till this restoration was consented to, the Negotiation was not even to begin.*

M. Le Tourneur was going to interrupt me, but I begged he would hear me a little further. I said, if I was correct in this statement, and the plain sense of the declaration would bear no other interpretation, I must add, that it would not only most certainly prevent the Treaty from beginning, but would leave no room for treating at all, since it deprived His Majesty of every means of negotiation ; for I could not suppose that it was in their thoughts to intimate that the principle of the Treaty, as far as it related to His Majesty, was to be one of all cession and no compensation, and yet that it was precisely the position in which His Majesty was placed by their Note.

M. Le Tourneur, who had let me proceed rather reluctantly, here stopped me, and said, that he and his colleagues were exceedingly happy that I had expressed a wish to see them before I despatched my messenger; that they wished to assure me that they had thought it dealing fairly and honestly to state what they had received from the Directory in the very words in which it came to them; that they felt it, however, necessary to "explain" what must appear to me as a contradiction in their behaviour, viz. their receiving the *projêt* when its terms were in opposition to the *secret* articles of their alliances. They assured me they were perfectly ignorant of these secret articles; and, had they known them, they would, in the first instance, have informed me of the difficulty which stood in the way of the dismissal of the conditions proposed; and he begged I would acquit them of any intention to mislead me on this point.

I received this explanation with civility, and only observed that they must recollect I had expressly stated, when they mentioned their constitution, laws, and treaties, that I only understood it to mean treaties, the articles of which were *public*, and by no means *secret* ones; and that, when I said this, *I* was perfectly aware that no stipulations, such as I now heard of for the first time, existed as avowed and public articles in their treaties of alliance either with Spain or the Dutch. I hinted, that, as M. Le Tourneur was a member of the Directory at the time these treaties were made, it was to be supposed he could not have been unacquainted with these secret articles; but that I presumed he considered them as State secrets, and did not think himself at liberty to communicate them officially to his colleagues, or to act upon them in his character of Plenipotentiary without the leave of the Directory. To this he assented, and proceeded by saying that they should be sorry if the declaration they had been directed to make me should be of a nature to interrupt, much less to break off, the Negotiation; that it was the sincere wish of the Directory, the Negotiation should proceed and end successfully; and that, far from shutting the door to further discussions, they were perfectly ready to hear any proposals we had to make, and only wished that these proposals should be, if possible, such as were compatible with their most sacred engagements. I repeated what I had said, that no door was left open, if His Majesty was, *in limine,* to restore everything; and that a peace, on these conditions, would not be heard of by my country.

M. Le Tourneur then entered, but with great propriety and in very becoming language, on the history of the war, its cause, its progress, and its object. Your Lordship will naturally suppose that he stated all this in a way very different from that in which it would have been stated by me. The conclusion he drew from it was, that France, even aggrandised as it was by its various acquisitions, was, at the end of it, not so great a Power as England would be, if, in addition to what His Majesty now possessed, the places we required by our *projêt* were to remain to us. "But," added he, "though we think that in arguing on your own grounds, viz. the balance of power," (and he referred here to what I said in our first conference,) "we should at least keep pace with you, yet we will tell you here confidentially, we do not mean to lose sight of *all* compensation for the King your Master; we only wish it to be sought for in points *different* from those you mention." I said I saw none such existing; that, if they had any to propose, I entreated him to bring them forward. He turned to his colleagues, who, however, both said it was premature; but they seemed to hint that it related to some arrangement to be made with Spain. Without, however, encouraging this idea, (as I thought I saw it would lead to Gibraltar,) I continued by saying, that this proposal, let it be what it would, must, according to my ideas, render the business more complex and intricate; that I had simplified it by acceding in full to their first proposition; that we required nothing in contradiction to their constitution, by letting all the cessions naturally rest on those Powers in the war who had made the smallest efforts, either as allies to the French Republic, or in defence of their own territories.

M. Le Tourneur took up the defence of Holland on rather odd grounds, by saying they were compelled by France to do what they did. Had the Dutch not been conquered, they would still have been faithful allies to England. I said I readily admitted this argument, but drew a direct contrary inference from it, namely, that the burthen of the cession to be made for the restoration of peace ought to come from them.

M. Le Tourneur observed, that, although we pressed very hard on their Allies, we took very good care of our own, and seemed not disposed to hear of any burthensome conditions being imposed on Portugal. I said the Court of Lisbon had done no harm, had lost nothing, and that it was but reasonable to expect it should be allowed to return to a state of peace without any sacrifice. M. Pléville here observed, the Portuguese troops and ships were at Toulon. I agreed to this, but begged him to recollect that this was in consequence of their alliance with Spain; and that it was impossible for me to avoid remarking, what I was sure must also strike him, that it was peculiarly hard on the Portuguese, that the very country who had made them first take a part in the war, should be the very first to attack them for having borne a share in it. However, we were getting wide from the point, to which I begged leave to recall their attention. That immediately on leaving them I should despatch a messenger; that what that messenger carried would most materially affect the progress and issue of the Negotiation. I therefore desired to know whether, in consequence of what I had heard from them, I might consider the strict and literal meaning of the Declaration not to be a decided negative (which it certainly seemed to imply) on all compensation whatever to be made to His Majesty; but that proposals tending to this effect would still be listened to. M. Le Tourneur answered, " Certainly; and, if they should be found such as it will be impossible for us to admit, we will on our side bring forward others for your Court to deliberate on." Under this assurance, which at least to a certain degree qualifies the declaration of yesterday, I broke up the conference.

I have, &c.

MALMESBURY.

(Inclosure A, Declaratory Note.)

Lille, 27 Messidor, an 5 de la République une et indivisible.

Les Ministres Plénipotentiaires de la République Française ont fait passer à leur Gouvernement le Projêt de Traité et la Note relative qui leur ont été présentés le 20 du présent mois par le Ministre Plénipotentiaire de Sa Majesté Britannique.

Ils viennent de recevoir des communications nouvelles, et des ordres, en conséquence desquels ils doivent faire au Lord Malmesbury la déclaration suivante.

Il existe dans les Traités Patents et Secrets qui tiennent la République Française et ses Alliés, l'Espagne et la République Batave, des Articles portants garantie respective des territoires que les Trois Puissances possédaient avant la guerre. Le Gouvernement Français, ne pouvant pas se défaire des engagemens qu'il a contractés par ces Traités, établit comme préliminaire indispensable de la Négociation pour la Paix avec l'Angleterre, le consentement de Sa Majesté Britannique à la restitution de toutes les possessions qu'elle occupe, non seulement sur la République Française, mais encore et formellement sur l'Espagne et la République Batave.

En conséquence, les Ministres Plénipotentiaires soussignés invitent Lord Malmesbury à s'expliquer sur cette restitution et à y consentir s'il y est suffisamment autorisé. Si non, et dans le cas contraire, à envoyer un courier à sa Cour pour en obtenir les pouvoirs nécessaires.

L'objet de la Conférence qui devait avoir lieu ce jour, se trouvant nécessairement ajourné par l'effet de la déclaration ci-dessus, les Ministres Plénipotentiaires de la République ont à témoigner au Lord Malmesbury le regret qu'ils éprouvent de manquer cette occasion qu'ils avaient recherchée et de s'entretenir avec lui ; au surplus dans le cas où le Lord Malmesbury auroit quelque communication à leur faire, ils le prient de croire qu'ils se montreront toujours empressés de le recevoir, et de l'entendre quand il le jugera à propos.

Ils le prient en même temps d'agréer de nouveau l'assurance, &c.
Le Tourneur.
Pléville Le Pelley.
Hugues B. Maret.

(Inclosure B.)

Lille, ce 15 Juillet, 1797.

Le Ministre Plénipotentiaire de sa Majesté Britannique a prêté l'attention la plus sérieuse à la Note, en date de ce matin, qu'il vient de recevoir de la part des Ministres Plénipotentiaires de la République Française.

Il n'hésite pas à leur déclarer que ses instructions ne l'autorisent nullement à admettre, comme principe préliminaire, celui que leur déclaration parait vouloir établir. Cependant, étant persuadé que son premier devoir est de ne renoncer à l'espoir d'une conciliation que lorsqu'il aura épuisé tous les moyens d'y arriver, et voulant écarter, dans le rapport qu'il aura à faire à sa Cour sur un objet aussi important, la possibilité de toute mésintelligence, il leur demandera pour demain, et à l'heure qui pourra leur convenir, une Conférence, à la suite de laquelle il se propose d'expédier un courier à sa Cour.

Il prie les Ministres Plénipotentiaires, &c.

MALMESBURY.

---

(Inclosure C.)

Lille, le 27 Messidor, an 5 de la République une et indivisible.

Les Ministres Plénipotentiaires de la République Française s'empressent d'accéder au désir que leur témoigne le Ministre Plénipotentiaire de Sa Majesté Britannique de conférer avec eux sur l'objet de la Note qu'ils lui ont adressée ce jour. Ils ont, en conséquence, l'honneur de lui proposer de se rendre demain, à onze heures du matin, au lieu ordinaire des conférences.

Ils le prient, &c.

Le Tourneur.
Pléville Le Pelley.
Hugues B. Maret.

### DESPATCH FROM LORD MALMESBURY TO LORD GRENVILLE.

(Separate.)              Lisle, Sunday, 16th July, 1797.

My Lord,—Before I had seen the French Plenipotentiaries, and had no other ground to go on than their Declaratory Note, I was inclined to think that the Directory were determined to continue the war; and, had I transmitted it to your Lordship yesterday, all my opinions would have leant that way. Since my Conference of this morning, they are somewhat staggered; I do not believe that the Directory are systematically bent on pursuing the war, but I do believe that they feel themselves strong enough in office, and think themselves sufficiently safe with the two Councils, to insist on terms of peace very hard to submit to.

I can have no information here to go upon. Though very civilly and attentively treated, yet I am strictly watched; and, if any persons were inclined to bring me intelligence, it would be very difficult for them, in a town like this, (full of unemployed, inquisitive, prying inhabitants,) to see me without risking a discovery which would be very fatal to them.

It is from this reason that my separate despatches must be very uninteresting.      I have, &c.      Malmesbury.

---

On the 14th of July an Englishman, whose name is Cunningham, who has been for some years resident at Lisle, called on Mr. Wesley,* and said he was come on business of the utmost importance, which he had been desired to communicate to some persons in my suite. He then produced a note, which he said he had received that morning from a M. Pein, a most intimate friend of his, and a near relation of Maret's. The following were the words of the note:—" Il serait peut-être nécessaire que, pour presser la Négociation, Lord Malmesbury eût des

---

* Secretary of Legation to Lord Malmesbury's Mission. He afterwards with the rest of his family changed his name to *Wellesley*, was subsequently created Lord Cowley, and appointed in 1841 Ambassador at Paris.

moyens de s'entendre et préparer les matières avec la personne qui est vraiment la seule en état de conduire l'affaire : dans ce cas on pourrait ménager au Lord Malmesbury un intermédiaire, qui a la confiance entière de la personne en question, et qui, comme elle, n'a d'autre but que l'intérêt de tous, et un arrangement également convenable." As soon as Mr. Wesley had read the note, Mr. Cunningham proceeded to state that his friend (M. Pein) was in possession of the entire confidence of *Maret*, by whom he had been authorized to make the above overture. Mr. Wesley immediately informed me of what had passed between Mr. Cunningham and him, and it was agreed that Mr. Ellis and M. Pein should meet in the evening. At that interview M. Pein repeated nearly what Mr. Cunningham had said in the morning; and added, that Maret's opinions on all political subjects were very different from those of the other Plenipotentiaries—that he was the intimate friend of Barthelemi,* through whose means he had been appointed one of the Ministers to treat for peace with England; that therefore his sentiments could not be doubted, as it was well known Barthelemi was sincerely desirous for the restoration of peace. M. Pein added, that Maret had his suspicions with respect to the intentions of the Directory; but that the cry of the whole Nation was so decidedly for peace, and the majority of the representatives in the two Councils so convinced of the impracticability of carrying on the war for a much longer term, that, if the Negotiation was prudently conducted, the Directory must in the end give way. M. Pein, in the course of this conversation, frequently insisted on the necessity of gaining time, on which he said the success of the whole business chiefly depended.

EXTRACT OF A DESPATCH FROM LORD GRENVILLE TO LORD MALMESBURY.

Downing Street, 20th July, 1797.

I AM much concerned to be under the necessity of remarking, that the claim brought forward in the Note

* Barthelemi was now one of the Directors, and of the moderate party.

transmitted to your Lordship by the French Plenipotentiaries* is in itself so extravagant, and so little to be reconciled either with the former professions of those Ministers, or with their conduct in the previous stages of the Negotiation, that it affords the strongest presumption of a determination to preclude all means of accommodation. If such is really the determination of the Directory, nothing can remain for this country but to persevere in opposing, with an energy and spirit proportioned to the exigency, a system which must tend to perpetuate a state of war and civil tumult in every part of Europe.

The natural step upon the present occasion would therefore have been to direct your Lordship to terminate at once a Negotiation which, on the footing now proposed by the enemy, affords neither the hope nor the means of any favourable conclusion; nothing being left for treaty, where, as a preliminary step, one party is required to concede everything, and all compensation from the other is absolutely and at once precluded.

His Majesty's servants have, however, observed, that, in the conclusion of your Lordship's last Conference with the French Plenipotentiaries on the subject of the Note in question, the President of that Mission informed your Lordship that it was not intended to resist all compensation for the immense extent of restitution demanded from His Majesty, and for the other obvious circumstances of disadvantage to this country in the situation of Europe, as resulting from the war; and even added, that he and his colleagues would eventually bring forward proposals on this head for the deliberation of the King's Government. It appeared possible that some advantage might perhaps arise to the great object of peace from grounding on this declaration a further proceeding, such as might afford to the Directory (if they are so disposed) the means of replacing the Negotiation on a more practicable footing. With the view, therefore, of leaving nothing untried which can contribute to restore peace on any suitable terms, His Majesty has been pleased to direct that your Lordship should, for that purpose, ask another Conference with the

* The Declaratory Note of the 15th July (page 390).

French Plenipotentiaries. In this Conference your Lordship will remark, in such terms as the occasion must necessarily suggest to you, upon the indefensible spirit and tendency of the demand now made by France. You will observe that France, treating in conjunction with her Allies, and in their name, cannot with any pretence of justice or fairness oppose her treaties with them as an obstacle in the way of any reasonable proposal of peace in which they are to be included. In a separate negotiation, to which they were not parties, such a plea might perhaps have been urged; but in that case France would have been bound to offer from her own means that compensation which she did not think herself at liberty to obtain from her Allies. And such was, in fact, as your Lordship must remember, the principle on which His Majesty offered to treat last year, when he was really bound by engagements to Austria similar to those which are now alleged by France. Spain and Holland negotiating jointly for a peace with Great Britain, cannot set up as a bar to our just demands the treaties between themselves, from which they are at once able to release each other whenever they think fit. You will further remark, that even, if contrary to all reason, such a principle could have been for a moment admitted on our part, still even that principle (inadmissible as it is) could only apply to public treaties, known to those who agreed to be governed by them, and not to secret articles unknown even to the French Plenipotentiaries, or concealed by one of them from the knowledge of the others. You will add in explicit, though not in offensive terms, that the whole of this pretence now set up by France is incontestably frivolous and illusory, being grounded on the supposition of a state of things directly contrary to that which is known really to exist; it being perfectly notorious that both Spain and Holland, so far from wishing to continue the war, were compelled by France to engage in it, greatly against their own wishes, and to undertake, without the means of supporting it, a contest in which they had nothing to gain, and everything to lose. It never can, therefore, be allowed to be a question of any possible doubt, but that the Directory, if they really wish it, must already have obtained, or could at any moment obtain, the consent of those Powers to such terms of peace as have been proposed by His Majesty. If, however, France, from any motive of interest or engagement, is in truth desirous to procure for them the restitution of possessions which they were unable to defend, and have no means to reconquer, the *projêt* delivered by your Lordship afforded an opening for this; those articles having been so drawn as to leave it to France to provide a compensation to His Majesty, either out of her own colonies or out of those of her Allies respectively conquered by His Majesty's arms. The choice between these alternatives may be left to the Directory; but to refuse both, is, in other words, to *refuse all compensation.*

This is, nevertheless, expressly declared not to be the intention of those with whom you treat. It is therefore necessary that your Lordship should demand from them a statement of the proposals, which, as they informed you, they have to make in order to do away this apparent contradiction, which the King's servants are wholly unable to reconcile by any suggestion of theirs, even if it were fitting and reasonable for them to bring forward any new proposals immediately after the detailed *projêt* which was delivered on the part of this country at the outset of the Negotiation. Since that *projêt* is not acceded to, we have evidently, and on every ground, a right to expect a *contre-projêt*, equally full and explicit on the part of the enemy. You will therefore state to the French Minister distinctly, that the only hope of bringing this business to a favourable conclusion is *by his stating at once, plainly and without reserve, the whole of what they have to ask,* instead of bringing forward separate points one after the other, not only contrary to the avowed principle of the Negotiation proposed by themselves, but, as it appears, even contrary to the expectations of the Ministers themselves who are employed on the part of France. There can be no pretence for refusing a compliance with this demand, if the Plenipotentiaries of France are disposed to forward the object of peace; and the obtaining such a statement from them is, as I have before stated to your Lordship, a point of so much importance in any course which the Negotiation may take, that it is the King's pleasure that your Lordship should use every possible exertion to prevent them from eluding so just a demand.

After what has passed, it is, I fear, very doubtful whether such a *contre-projêt* would be framed on principles such as would be admitted here; but it would, at all events, place the business on its real issue, and bring distinctly to a question the several points on which the conclusion of peace, or prolongation of war, will really depend.

EXTRACT OF A LETTER FROM LORD GRENVILLE TO LORD MALMESBURY.

Cleveland Row, 20th July, 1797.

THE complexion of your last despatch is certainly much more unfavourable to Peace than I thought the Directory could have ventured to shew under the present circumstances of the country in which you are. My only hope is in firmness, without asperity of tone. We have purposely postponed saying anything on the two points of the King's title and of the Toulon ships, till we see more clearly into the intentions of the French respecting terms; for, in truth, neither those points, nor any other in such a treaty as this, are separate, or can be insulated (as they call it) from the general consideration of the whole. Good terms as to matters of substantial importance might make us more disposed to overlook points of form, which are, however, as you well know, matters of real substance when they relate to the intercourse of two great Powers, whose most valuable possession is national dignity, and a due sense of their own importance and weight.

I think the first point might be arranged (but this is merely my own private opinion) by using *in the Treaty* the style of King of Great Britain only, for which you will see there are precedents enough down to the peace of Utrecht; but retaining the present style in full powers, the ratification, and all other instruments to which this Government is a party. Perhaps the words *Britannic Majesty* would be better than *King of Great Britain*, and these are now very often used even in our latest treaties and conventions. As to the acts of our own Government, the French have no more right to object to any title the King takes, than we have to quarrel with the denominations of their Councils, or any other branch of their Government.

Beyond this we might go so far as to add to the separate article some words not admitting it to be only a *genealogical title*, but declaring that it is not meant to prejudice the King's acknowledgment of a republican form of government in France.

The Toulon question is more difficult, and has more of substance in it. We do not quite understand how far the demand is meant to go, whether to restore those ships which can be restored, or to compensate for those which are burnt; or to restore, and, if not, to compensate for those only which are now in our possession. If the former, it is the question of a fleet of eighteen sail of the line, and as many frigates, the value of which is perhaps fully equal to some of the conquests we restore. I confess I hardly see how we can in any case do more than let some words be inserted in the act of our restitutions, in which they shall be said to be *made in compensation for the ships*, &c. This, however, is also private opinion only, and on a point on which the King's Government think an ultimate decision cannot be taken without some reference to the terms of the peace.

### EXTRACT OF A LETTER FROM MR. CANNING TO LORD MALMESBURY.

*Spring Gardens, 20th July, 1797.*

THERE could be but one answer to the contents of your last despatches, and that I think is well, and firmly, and temperately given in Lord Grenville's despatch of this day. I am lost in conjecture as to what the Directory can possibly mean, and have already so fully detailed my doubts and anxieties to George Ellis, that I will content myself with expressing to you the patient solicitude with which I shall wait for their solution;—patient, because the cheerful manner in which you (and all of you) describe the alteration in your feelings, and the improvement of your prospects, between the time of the receipt of the Note, and the despatching of your messenger, induces me to believe (in contradiction to any judgment I can form for myself from the premises laid down to me) that good will come of it in the end, and that these monstrous demands are but the prelude to some handsome conciliatory accommodation.

I communicated to Lord Grenville, as you will see by his private letter, that which you wrote to me upon the two points of the King's Title, and the Renewal of Treaties. Upon the last point he appears to have said as much as need be said, that is, to have left you entirely to yourself. Upon the first he has added rather more than I expected to the spirit of your proposal. I should think the style of "Britannic Majesty" might get over all objections; but a formal surrender of the title—Are the French aware what it means? that it will go to alter every public instrument in every civil process in the kingdom? that the alteration itself cannot be made but by Act of Parliament? that to make it otherwise would be high treason, and against the Act of Settlement, which is to us what the Constitutional Act is to them, or at least might be represented as such without much exaggeration. I am aware that these arguments cannot be urged without one danger, that of making the thing of so much importance as to render the concession of it (if it ultimately be conceded) a matter of increased difficulty and dishonour, and possibly even to lead them to suppose that we attach more substance to the title than in reality we do, and to be therefore the more anxious to extort it from us. But, on the other hand, if there be the smallest desire to conciliate, and to come to the conclusion of a peace which shall not leave in us more hatred towards each other than we have carried through the bitter parts of the contest, I think the fair representation of the infinite inconveniences that would arise from calling for a Legislative Act of such a nature as to put the people of this country immediately out of humour with the issue of the Negotiation, compared with the very trifling importance to them (the French) of a sacrifice so insignificant, would induce the French Plenipotentiaries to acquiesce in one or other of the compromises that may be proposed to them, if not to let the matter drop altogether.

---

LETTER FROM MR. CANNING TO LORD MALMESBURY.

Spring Gardens, Thursday night, 20th July, 1797.

MY DEAR LORD MALMESBURY.—I have not much matter for my *most private* letter to-night, besides approving (as I do exceedingly) of the invention, and expressing my desire that we may keep to the use of it, throughout the Negotiation, in the manner and for the purposes for which it has been originally designed. I am glad, too, that you kept back (though not expressly desired to do so) from everybody but George Ellis what was said in my last letter about the Cabinet.

You will, I think, have understood the meaning and intent of the resolutions* of the Cabinet mentioned in my other letter of this day, in the manner in which I understand it; which is, that it was devised by Lord Grenville to *tie up Pitt's tongue alone,* whom he suspected of communicating with other persons, and fortifying himself with out-of-door opinions against the opinions which might be brought forward in Council by those with whom he differed in his general view of the Negotiation. I am not sure that he did not suspect him further of sounding the public sentiment through the newspapers as to the terms which it might be proper to accept, and the concessions which it might be excusable to make for the sake of peace.

Upon the last decision of the Cabinet there can have been, and was, but little difference—a difference only with respect to expressions. It is the fault of the French, if they

---

* " In consequence of some circumstances having transpired, a resolution was passed to oblige the members of the Cabinet to secrecy on the subject of Lord Malmesbury's negotiation. Mr. Canning and Mr. Hammond were alone to open the despatches and answer them; and, as the latter wrote an abominable hand, his copies only were to be shewn to the minor members of the Cabinet, who, it was hoped, would not take the trouble to decypher them."—Mr. Canning's Letter.

have not a peace as good as to terms as they can reasonably desire. But if they will not only be stout *in re*, but in mode offensive and insulting, even all the desire for peace which is felt here, and all the difficulty of carrying on war, great and growing as this desire and this difficulty are, must give way to the conviction, that, though to purchase peace at a high price might be a safe disgrace, to submit to the law of the Directory thus insolently laid down, in any one instance however comparatively unimportant, would be to go through disgrace to destruction.

There are very few points, very few indeed, of *acquisition*, perhaps in reality none, upon which, in a negotiation fairly and creditably carried on, much difficulty or much stand would ultimately be made *here*, at the hazard of another campaign. But I think there is no point among them which, urged in the manner in which the Directory seem disposed to urge them, would not make it to be felt here impossible to take any other line than resistance. I hope we shall not come to the necessity of taking that line seriously. At present the demands are so extravagant that I think they can hardly be in earnest. And yet, what can they mean? do tell us truly and speedily. Adieu!

---

EXTRACTS OF A DESPATCH FROM LORD MALMESBURY TO LORD GRENVILLE.

Lisle, 25th July, 1797.

I RECEIVED on the 18th instant, from the French Legation, a notification in form, that M. Pléville Le Pelley* was named to the Ministry of Marine, in the room of M. Trüguet;† and, at the same time, they communicated to me an *arrêté* of the Directory, empowering the two remaining Plenipotentiaries, Messrs. Le Tourneur and Maret, to go on with the Negotiation.

On the 19th I was informed that a further change had

* Pléville Le Pelley, vieux et brave marin, administrateur excellent.—(Thiers.)
† Truguet étoit un homme loyal et à grands moyens, mais n'ayant pas pour les personnes les ménagemens nécessaires à la tête d'une grande administration.—(Id.)

taken place in the French Ministry. That M. Delacroix had been removed from the post of Minister for Foreign Affairs, and was replaced by M. Talleyrand Perigord (formerly Bishop of Autun);* that also the Ministers of the War Department, of Police, of Home Affairs, were to be changed; but I could not learn with certainty that any of these places had been actually given away, excepting those of Messrs. Delacroix, Truguet, and Cochon.†

It appears, not only from the public papers which your Lordship undoubtedly has perused, but also from private information on which I can rely, that this alteration of the Ministry was first determined on in consequence of great discontents which demonstrated themselves at Paris; but that the change, as it has now taken place, has by no means tended to quiet the public mind, since, though the Ministers of Marine and Foreign Affairs have been superseded, it also has displaced some of the most popular Members of Administration, and left Ramel and Merlin, two against whom the general cry was loudest, in possession of their office.

Messrs. Delacroix and Truguet were removed by the unanimous vote of the Directory; the other Ministers were discarded by a majority of only one. Barras, Réveillière Lépaux, and Rewbell, were for their dismission; Carnot and Barthelemi were for their remaining in office.‡ I am told, and I believe I speak from good information, that, when the question of a change in the Ministry was in agitation, it had been previously settled that only Messrs. Delacroix and Truguet should be removed; but Barras, who had affected to agree in opinion with Barthelemi and Carnot, deserted them when the five Directors met; and though he voted with them for the removal of Delacroix and Truguet, he

---

* The universal reputation of Talleyrand renders any notice of him unnecessary in a work of this kind. It is sufficient to remember, that, during a life of eighty-five years, he served the old French Monarchy,—the Directory, Consulate, Empire, Restoration, and Orleans Dynasty. He must be regarded as the most able political pilot on record.

† This was the first step of the Ultra-Republican section of the Directory towards the expulsion of their more moderate colleagues, Carnot and Barthelemi, and of the Peace party.

‡ The first three composed the violent section of the Directory, and were for continuing the war at any price; the two latter were of the moderate party, and for peace with England.

voted also with Rewbell and La Réveillière Lépaux for the removal of the other three : that of Bénézech,* Minister for the Home Department, is not very important ; but the dismissal of Cochon, Minister of Police, and Petiet,† Minister of War, are considered as highly so. They are both reputed to have filled their situations with equal ability and integrity; and their being turned out without any ostensible cause, fixes suspicion of the most serious nature on the three Directors who voted for their dismissal. These suspicions go to the most extreme lengths ; and if your Lordship has attended to what has been said in the Councils, particularly by Thibaudeau,‡ Henri Larivière, and Boissy D'Anglas, (who, although often divided in opinion, are, on this point, strictly united,) you will perceive that it is impossible for the Legislative Authority to call in question the intentions and measures of the Executive Power in more plain or direct terms.

The removal of an upright and incorruptible Minister of Police, it is affirmed by the leaders of the moderate party, is intended with a view to get an entire possession of Paris, in order that the Directory may fill it with their dependents and emissaries. Le Noir La Roche,§ who is appointed to this office, is taken from the club held at the Hôtel de Salm, and he has the reputation of being well fitted for the purpose of the Directory, both on the score of moral character and political opinions.

The removal of Petiet from the War Department is, it is said, done with a similar view. It is to place the uncontrolled disposal of the army in the hands of the Directory, when a breach of constitution is already fixed, by their having ordered a considerable body of troops to approach within twelve leagues of the place where the two Councils are held, without any requisition or authority from those assemblies.

When I mention the Directory, I must be understood to mean only the three Directors, Barras, Rewbell, and La Réveillière Lépaux.

* Bénézech, administrateur excellent, courtisan docile.
† Petiet étoit la créature dévouée de Carnot.
‡ Thibaudeau, chef du parti Constitutionnel.—(Thiers.)
§ Le Noir, homme sage et éclairé.—(Thiers.)

Their object evidently is to maintain their present power by force, to govern by force alone; and this, whether under the denomination of a Jacobin, a Girondiste, or Sectary of any other faction, comes so much to the same, that it is not worth while to investigate which may predominate among them.

It is not difficult to say what would be the consequences of their success; probably a confirmation of almost despotic government in France, and a systematic attempt to introduce a revolutionary one everywhere else, beginning, in the first instance, with Spain, and extending it to Portugal.

It appears, from various circumstances, that Buonaparte professed himself to be acting in concert with the Directory; but it remains to be seen whether he will support them throughout, or whether he will not shake off their authority when he no longer wants their support to complete his wild and gigantic plans in Italy.

A considerable majority in the two Councils, and a still greater one in the country at large, dread the return of "*the system of terror*," watch with the most jealous vigilance every step of the Directory, and declare avowedly their fixed intention to resist it to the utmost. The Directory, on their side, are endeavouring to rally their friends round them, and are using all those means which desperate and daring characters, invested with great authority, venture to employ when restrained by no scruples; and I fear the great expectations and secret means of acting which they derive from their situation will, when the struggle comes, balance for a while the advantages the Councils may derive from their numbers, and from the popularity of their cause.

Both parties, however, seem determined not to postpone this struggle, but to come to a speedy trial of their strength; and a person, whose authority cannot be called in question, and who is deeply interested in the event, describes Paris at this moment as being "*dans une crise abominable.*"\*

The consequence I deduce from it is, that, while this crisis is pending, we cannot expect our negotiations to proceed regularly or smoothly; and, if I may hazard an opinion, I cannot but believe we shall be gainers by delay.

---

\* These words are Barthelemi's, in a letter to Maret.

The present conflict between the Executive and the Legislative branches of this Government has arisen on subjects of internal government only, and is, in its first principle, foreign to the great question of peace or war, though ultimately closely connected with it. If the party in the Directory which preserves the old principles of that body should be in the end victorious, it is probable that they will not be willing, after their victory, (supposing it to be brought about by anything short of what is called "*the system of terror,*") to renew the conflict on grounds which must give considerable advantage to their antagonists : if, on the contrary, the moderate party should prevail, there is little doubt but that Barras would join with Carnot and Barthelemi, who are decidedly friends to peace, and enemies to the late violent determination respecting the interests of the Allies ; and the pacification might then be considered as almost certain,

In either case, therefore, I think the issue of this critical juncture, be it what it will, cannot be very unfavourable. I have only to apprehend Rewbell, who is disposed to run all risks, with a view of supporting and increasing the Directorial authority, and who may, (although it would be a violent step even for him to take,) in the first impulse of passion, order the French Plenipotentiaries to break off the Negotiation, and me to leave Lisle.

It was in contemplation for a moment to send M. Delacroix to this Mission in the place of M. Pléville, but he is now fortunately appointed to Basle ;—I say *fortunately*, as I have very good reason to believe, that, from personal pique against me, he would have employed every means in his power to defeat the Negotiation, and that the extravagant idea set forth in the French Note of the 15th was of his suggesting. I know it was strongly opposed by the two moderate Directors, but violently insisted on by Rewbell ; and this is an additional ground for the apprehension I have expressed concerning the possible consequences of his rashness and intemperance.

I was disposed to think very favourably of M. Pléville ; and the way in which he has expressed himself at Paris, and the impression he has endeavoured to give, prove I was not wrong in the opinion I had formed of him.

It is possible that M. Colchen may be appointed to fill his place in the Mission ; and I confess, if it is to be filled at all, I am desirous it should be by him. He is a friend of M. Barthelemi, and protected by him ; and of the sentiments and wishes of this Director relative to peace, I can have no doubt. It is much to be regretted that he has not acquired an adequate degree of power in the Directory, being supported only by Carnot, and that on some general subjects, and not uniformly and on system.

M. Le Tourneur, from the connection which he still keeps up with his old colleagues, may be considered as acting under their impression, and, of course, I must not expect to find him so practicable as M. Maret, with whom hitherto I have every reason to be satisfied.

I venture to say that I have inserted no doubtful facts in this despatch, and, by placing them at once under your eyes, you will be able to form as just an idea of the present uncertain situation of this country, as it is in my power to give. I believe it to be true and genuine; and, if I see it in its right point of view, the conclusion to be drawn from it is, *that the fate of the Negotiation will depend much less on what passes in our conferences here, than on what may happen very shortly at Paris.*\*

---

EXTRACTS OF A DESPATCH FROM LORD MALMESBURY TO LORD GRENVILLE.

Lisle, 25th July, 1797.

It was impossible that the claim brought forward in the Declaratory Note enclosed in mine of July 17th could have produced on your Lordship's mind any impression different from that which you describe ; and I am happy to find that the conduct I observed when it was first delivered to me, was such as puts it in my power to execute with great consistency the spirited instructions your Lordship now sends me.

Immediately on the arrival of the messenger, I proposed

\* It will be seen, by subsequent events, how correct a channel of private information Lord Malmesbury had established.

an interview with the French Plenipotentiaries, and we met on Sunday, the 23rd, at 1 P. M.

My first object was to state, in as forcible a way as possible, the utter inadmissibility of the pretension set forth in the Note, the frivolous and illusory reasons alleged for bringing it forward : and I observed, that if it was persevered in, it must lead to this necessary conclusion, that there did exist, when it was framed, an intention on the part of the Directory to break off .the Negotiation in the outset. My second object in point of reasoning, though a very primary one in point of importance, was either to prevent the Negotiation from breaking off at all, or, if this was not to be prevented, to endeavour to be so clear and explicit in my language, and to draw the line so distinctly between such sacrifices as His Majesty might be inclined to make, in order to restore so great a blessing as peace, and those to which the dignity of his Crown and interest of his subjects would never allow him to attend, as to make it impossible that by any future cavil or subterfuge the interruption of the Treaty, if unfortunately it should be interrupted, could be imputed to any other cause than the exorbitant demands of the French Government ; and, the better to ensure this purpose, I explained to them that His Majesty having already in a detailed *projêt* stated freely and fully his conditions, and those conditions having been at once rejected by a sweeping claim on the part of the French Government, it was not fitting or reasonable, neither could it be expected, that any new proposals should originate with His Majesty ; and that on every ground the King had a right to expect a *contre-projét* from them, stating at once plainly and without reserve the whole of what they had to ask, instead of bringing forward separate points, one after another.

On the first point, on the inadmissibility of the preliminary conditions as proposed by the French Government, M. Le Tourneur said, it was impossible for them to do more than to take it for reference; that the instructions they had received, when the Directory sent them the Note, were precise and positive, and that they had received none since.

In regard to the second point, he had no hesitation in agreeing with me, that the best method, and, indeed, the only one which could accelerate the whole of the business, was for them to give in a *contre-projêt*; neither did he attempt to disprove our perfect right to expect one from them before we made any new proposals. But he said that it was not necessary for him to observe, that, as long as they were bound by their instructions not to give way on the proposition I had now so decidedly rejected, it was impossible for them to move a step without new orders from the Directory. That they would ask for these orders immediately, and lose no time in acquainting me when they were received.

I observed, that in our last Conference he had intimated to me they were empowered to come to some explanation with me on the subject of *compensation* to be made to His Majesty for the great cessions he was disposed to make; that, at the time, I conceived these explanations were of a nature to qualify the wide claim stated in the Note; and that, if I had abstained from pressing him further at the moment, it was from perceiving a reluctance on their part to bring them forward. That, however, if they really had such proposals to make me, and if they were of a nature to meet in substance and effect the basis laid down in the *projêt* I had given, I should be well disposed to listen to them.

M. Le Tourneur, after some hesitation, and a sort of silent reference to M. Maret, said he thought, as matters now stood, it would be much better to wait their answer from Paris.

I confined myself, in my reply to M. Le Tourneur, by saying I had no objection whatever in giving to the French Plenipotentiaries a paper, stating the strong motives on which His Majesty rejected the proposition made in their Note of the 15th; and that as I, on my part, had considered it a duty to make my reports as conciliatory as was consistent with truth and correctness, so I heard, with great pleasure, the assurances he gave me of their intending to observe the same line of conduct.

That, as we seemed perfectly agreed as to the propriety of their producing a *contre-projêt*, I had nothing to say on that point, except to express my most sincere wish that it would soon appear, and, when it did appear, be such a one as would lead to a speedy and satisfactory conclusion of the Negotiation.

If I did not animadvert on the sort of retraction of M. Le Tourneur from what he said on a former Conference on the subject of *compensation*, and allowed his mode of reasoning to pass by unnoticed, it was in part because I did not see any benefit that would arise from my controverting it at this moment, and much more from reasons which I shall state to your Lordship in a separate despatch.

Although I have not mentioned M. Maret's name, he acquiesced in every thing which passed.

I have the honour to enclose the paper I sent yesterday evening to the French Plenipotentiaries.

The return of the courier from Paris can scarce take place under five days. What he brings must be important, and even conclusive. If the Directory persist in their claim, it may lead to an immediate breaking up of the Negotiation: if they give way, there will, I hope, be reasonable grounds to expect (though many difficulties will still remain) that it will proceed in a way to make its conclusion such as may not be deemed unfavourable.

(ENCLOSURE.)

NOTE FROM LORD MALMESBURY TO THE FRENCH
PLENIPOTENTIAIRES.

A Lille, ce 24 Juillet, 1797.

Le Ministre Plénipotentiaire de Sa Majesté Britannique a fait passer à sa Cour la Note qui lui a été remise le 15 de ce mois par les Ministres Plénipotentiaires de la République Française; et ayant reçu les ordres du Roi son Maître à ce sujet, il s'empresse de leur réitérer par écrit, conformément au désir qu'ils lui en ont témoigné, les réflexions suivantes, qu'il leur a déjà exposées de vive voix d'après ses instructions les plus positives.

Il observe d'abord, que demander, comme préliminaire

indispensable de la Négociation pour la Paix avec l'Angleterre, le consentement de Sa Majesté Britannique à la restitution de toutes les possessions qu'elle occupe, non seulement sur la République Française, mais encore et formellement sur l'Espagne et la République Batave, c'est vouloir établir une condition préalable, qui exclut toute réciprocité, refuse au Roi toute compensation, et ne laisse aucun objet de négociation ultérieure.

Que la République Française, autorisée par ses Alliés à négocier en leur nom et formellement les articles de la paix, ne sauroit opposer ses traités partiels avec eux à des propositions raisonnables, puisqu'il est reconnu que les Parties Contractantes conservent toujours le pouvoir de modifier, d'un consentement mutuel, les conditions auxquelles elles se seront respectivement engagées, toutes les fois que leurs intérêts communs, pourront l'exiger ; par conséquent la proposition faite au Roi d'une restitution générale et gratuite, comme préliminaire indispensable, supposerait nécessairement à Sa Majesté Catholique et à la République Batave des dispositions bien moins pacifiques que celles qui animent la République Française. Que d'ailleurs, d'après ce qui s'est passé dans les premières conférences, le Lord Malmesbury a toujours cru devoir s'attendre à ce que le Roi son Maître fut compensé des sacrifices qu'il était porté à faire pour la paix, par la conservation d'une partie de ses conquêtes ; et il pourroit d'autant moins prévoir quelque obstacle à l'occasion des Articles Secrets des Traités qui lient la République Française ; que le principe de compensation fut reconnu par une déclaration formelle et positive faite au nom du Directoire Exécutif, et communiquée dans une Note Officielle en date du 27 Novembre, 1796, déclaration postérieure à la confection de ces Traités.

C'était donc à fin d'applanir autant que possible toutes les difficultés, que, dans le projet de traité que le Lord Malmesbury a remis aux Ministres Plénipotentiaires de la République Française, on laissa à la France l'alternative d'établir cette compensation sur ses propres possessions, ou sur celles de ses Alliés ; or le refus absolu de cette alternative parait écarter le seul moyen possible de concilier tous les intérêts, et d'arriver à une paix juste, honorable, et permanente.

Le Lord Malmesbury, persuadé que telle ne sauroit être l'intention du Gouvernement Français, espère d'après les raisons qu'il vient de leur exposer, qu'on ne continuera pas à insister sur une condition à laquelle Sa Majesté Britannique ne pourra aucunement se prêter.

Il prie de nouveau les Ministres Plénipotentiaires de la République Française d'agréer, &c. MALMESBURY.

LETTER FROM LORD MALMESBURY TO LORD GRENVILLE.

Lisle, 25th July, 1797.

I COULD have wished to have entered in this private letter into a long and accurate detail of some very material communications and overtures which have within these few days been made me: but as I cannot do it in a way which could satisfy you, without committing the names and opinions of several persons to a very dangerous extent, I shall reserve it to a still safer opportunity than even that of a messenger; and this I think will offer itself in about a week, when the business will be brought probably to such a point as will justify my sending over Lord G. Leveson. I may, perhaps, be over-cautious and prudent; but, besides there having been instances of messengers having been rifled, I am a little influenced by the circumstance of the paragraphs which have lately appeared in our papers; and, although it would be most unfair to say I could fix a shadow of suspicion on the fidelity of any of the King's messengers, yet, on a point where the safety of other persons, not my own, is so materially exposed, I have no right to be rash.

LETTER FROM LORD MALMESBURY TO MR. PITT.

Lisle, Tuesday, 5 P.M., July 25th, 1797.

MY DEAR SIR,—If I were compelled to give an opinion, I should say that the French would give way in the present instance, and that on the return of their messenger from

Paris the Negotiation will be resumed on grounds not very different from those originally proposed; as I myself am fully persuaded that its fate must be determined by the turn things take at Paris, and not by any effect I can produce here. I hope I have not judged improperly in endeavouring to convey strong and decided sentiments in temperate and even civil language. If we are sent away abruptly, the contrast will be the more striking; and, if the business proceeds, it certainly may be brought to account.

I intended to have explained, in this private letter, the manner in which I obtained the materials for my separate despatch; but as the doing it in a way at all satisfactory must necessarily have led me to mention names, &c., I thought it better to delay it for a week, when I shall have a fair plea for sending over Leveson, to whose correct memory I can venture to trust as safely as to a letter. There is indeed little risk of a messenger being stopped and rifled; but such things have happened in France, and it is not quite fair on an occasion when the danger is not mine, but that of another person, to leave anything to chance. I am the more inclined to give way to this motive, since I know you to be already in possession of some information on this subject; that you will receive a little more to-day from the same quarter; and also because I trust you will give me credit for not proceeding on light grounds, or for being likely to listen to the intelligence of idle or officious informers.

I am much obliged to you for what you say about Gibraltar. I have all the old prejudices on this point, and am glad to perceive that you also partake of them. The chief reason for my not resisting longer the admission of the principle of the inviolability of the French Republic was to obtain the same admission with respect to us, and *to place Gibraltar by that means beyond the reach of Negotiation.*

I rather wish than expect that the inferior points of the King's title, and Toulon ships, may be overlooked, when we begin to deliberate on more important ones; and I should be very sorry if, under this expectation, we should neglect to be prepared to meet them.

I will strain every nerve to obtain a *contre-projêt*, and have reason to think I shall succeed, if our Negotiation survives the return of the next messenger from Paris.

I am, &c. MALMESBURY.

---

[Mr. Canning having hinted to Mr. Ellis that Lord Grenville was dissatisfied with Lord Malmesbury's admission of "reciprocal inalienability of territory," &c., Mr. Ellis defends him in the following letter.]

LETTER FROM MR. ELLIS TO MR. CANNING.

Lisle, July 25th, 1797.

MY DEAR CANNING,—I will begin by a very short answer to your few words. 1st. You think, or rather some persons think, that "the reciprocal inalienability of territory was admitted too soon."

Now the first answer to this objection is, that it was *reciprocal*, and that if it excluded on one hand all Negotiation about Martinique, St. Domingo, &c., it on the other hand excluded all question of *Gibraltar*. 2nd. It was *not* a formal admission of a principle, but an agreement for mutual convenience; that it was meant to save trouble and dispute, and that it has done so. It might have been an excellent subject for argument—I dare say the French Legation would have been unable to answer us satisfactorily. But they must have given in their proposals about Toulon and the King's title, because they were ordered to do so by the Directory, who are not at all disposed to listen to our arguments, and not much disposed to be convinced by their own Legation.

The second point is, that "the second messenger was despatched too soon, and brought the proposition of the Directory in a shape in which it was the most difficult to discuss it." But was it not of some importance that you should receive such a Note as soon as possible? Besides, what was there to discuss?

If I understood Mr. Pitt right, you want either a tolerably good peace, or the most unreasonable requisitions. If "the

Lion" can make a good peace, he will do it; and he is not the less likely to do so from having complied with the desire of the French Legation by sending their Note, with all its absurdity and folly on its back.

Why should he wish to send it? In its present shape it will be an excuse for our conduct if circumstances should hereafter enable us to assume a higher tone; if otherwise, by receiving it temperately, we shew our wish for conciliation.

"The Lion" trusted that his instructions would not be altered, and that the Cabinet would not be bullied; but suppose they had wavered—was it his duty to take the responsibility upon himself? But, instead of dwelling any longer on argument, I must now come to my *narration*, for which you are prepared by my last little note.

I then only spoke doubtingly about my informant;[*] but I now am quite sure of his ability and dispositions. I saw him the day after the messenger went away, and he then assured me, on the part of Maret, that the Note of the Directory had appeared no less offensive to the French Legation than to us: that even Le Tourneur had expressed the most violent indignation on the subject, and that they had sent to the Ministre des Relations Extérieures the most pointed remonstrance that they could venture on the subject. His own opinion was, "que c'était une infamie de Charles Delacroix." He added, that the Directory had kept Maret five days at Paris after the departure of Le Tourneur and Pléville, with a view of giving him the fullest private instructions, during which time they never hinted at the Secret Articles of the Spanish or Dutch Treaties. He begged me to state this to Lord Malmesbury, and assure him that the French Legation were by no means accessory to so absurd and childish a measure; that they were perfectly sincere in their wishes for the restoration of peace; that they adjured him to palliate the measure as well as he could to his Court, &c.

I have seen him often since, and will now communicate to you generally what has passed. He told me, that Maret, being personally known to and liked by Barras, was pro-

---

[*] M. Pein.

mised by him, as well as by Carnot and Barthelemi, to be promoted to the place of Minister of Foreign Affairs; but that, knowing Talleyrand (the Bishop of Autun) to be his rival for that place, he had waited on him to say, that his wish was to begin by some foreign Mission, that he should prefer London, for which his appointment to the Legation at Lisle was a natural preparation, and that he would willingly quit his pretensions to the Ministry, if he (Talleyrand) would assist him in his other views. My informant added, that Delacroix could not stay in long; and that his dismissal, and the nomination of the Evêque d'Autun, (both of which have since happened,) would tend very much to further our views. He said, that Le Tourneur was so dull and obstinate, that Maret found it very difficult, with all his address, to guide him right; that he had with some trouble managed Pléville, and through him Le Tourneur; but that Pléville's appointment to the Ministry of the Marine would be very inconvenient to him, unless he could procure the appointment of Colchen in his room. He told me of our escape in not being saddled with Charles Delacroix, who was upon the point of being named to this place, but is now to be sent to the Mission at Basle. From him, too, I learnt the news of the Dutch fleet,—indeed everything you will find in Lord Malmesbury's despatch on the subject of French news, comes from him. He seemed very anxious about the answer to be brought by our courier, and begged to know in time what that answer was, in order that Maret might be prepared to act in concert with us, both by preparing Le Tourneur for the Conference, and by making the earliest favourable impression in Paris. We agreed about a sign of intelligence by which Lord Malmesbury and Maret might understand each other without attracting the attention of Le Tourneur and Colchen.

Immediately after the Conference, he sent to beg to see me, and told me he had two requests to make. One was, that Lord Malmesbury would delay sending his Note to the Legation for twenty-four hours; the other (which I might possibly think indiscreet), that I would communicate the Official Note to Maret before it was delivered. As "the Lion" had by this time ascertained beyond a doubt the truth of his being completely in Maret's confidence, I immediately acceded to both, and received the Official Note back from him this morning. He read to me a few words from Maret to himself, in which he says, after some handsome things about "the Lion," "qu'il n'y aura plus entre eux, d'autre dispute que celle de franchise et de loyauté." He then put into my hands a note for Lord Malmesbury,* in which Maret says, that, in consequence of the temper with which the note is written, it cannot but do good; that, far from wishing to weaken any part of it, he thinks, if Lord Malmesbury had no personal objection to it, he might strengthen it still further by a reference to the *arrêté* of the Directory of 27 November last. You will see that Lord Malmesbury has taken the hint and inserted this argument.

He then said, that, in order to prove to me that he had not insisted without reason on the necessity of delaying our Note, he would read to me a letter which Maret had last night received from Barthelemi. It was expressed very nearly in these words:—

"J'ai parlé hier au nouveau Ministre des Relations Extérieures sur l'affaire de notre ami commun, Colchen, et il m'avoit promis de proposer aujourd'hui au Directoire sa nomination à la place vacante dans votre Légation. Il n'en a cependant rien fait. Je ne sais pourquoi, peut-être le fera-t-il demain.

"J'en aurais fait moi-même la proposition, si je n'avais craint de vous nuire. Pléville, grâces à vos soins, me paroit bien disposé pour la paix, mais j'ai de fortes raisons de croire qu'une *certaine personne* revient, ou se dispose à revenir à l'avis de ses anciens collègues. [The *certaine personne* means Le Tourneur.] J'ai les plus grandes inquiétudes sur l'absurde obstacle qu'on a mis en avant pour retarder la paix, c'est à dire nos liaisons envers nos Alliés. Comment, avec du sens commun, peut-on insister sur un raisonnement aussi absurde, dans un tems où la paix nous est absolument nécessaire, et où nous sommes sûrs de la faire glorieuse? Cependant cela est. Vous ne sauriez vous figurer la jalousie, les sottes préventions de certaines gens." The remainder of the letter was principally on private

* Vide p. 417.

business, so that he did not read it to me; but he quoted towards the end,—" Nous sommes dans une crise abominable, mais avec le tems et la modération on vient à bout de tout. Patientez, je vous prie, et cherchez s'il est possible à gagner du temps." I looked over him while he was reading, and, the subject being so interesting, I can venture to say, that, though I may not have remembered every word, I have not mis-stated the meaning of one phrase. Maret's letter to Barthelemi, and the Evêque d'Autun, will reach Paris to-night, so that they will pave the way for our Note; and, if we have failed in making that Note as conciliatory as a direct negative could be, it is certainly not from want of pains and attention.

Shall we be sent back or not this time? Seriously, the Directory is so strange a body, and this so strange a nation, that I have my doubts, and yet this letter surely contains some reasonable grounds of hope. Be assured we are zealously served. Remember this letter must be kept as secret as the last. Ever, &c. G. ELLIS.

SECRET NOTE FROM M. MARET, SENT THROUGH M. PEIN AND MR. ELLIS TO LORD MALMESBURY.

LA mesure dans laquelle la Note est conçue me parait entièrement favorable aux intérêts communs. Non seulement il ne me parait aucunement nécessaire de l'affoiblir, mais je crois même, que si la position personnelle ne s'y opposait pas, on pourrait tirer quelque avantage de la concession faite dans la Note du 7 Frimaire du principe des compensations. Il est évident que si l'on était lié par des articles secrets, ce principe ne pourrait être admis; et que si l'on a pu se délier, alors on le peut encore aujourd'hui. Il reste à savoir si, traitant séparément avec l'Angleterre, on a pu se disposer à lui offrir en compensation les conquêtes en Italie. Toutes les autres se trouvaient irrestituables d'après la constitution et les lois. Si, comme on peut le penser, les compensations, dont le principe a été convenu le 7 Frimaire, portaient sur d'autres objets, ces objets n'étaient que des possessions maritimes. Donc, &c.

A FEW hours before Mr. Wesley left Lisle, Mr. Ellis had
another interview with M. Pein. M. Pein said, that Maret
had written him word that he had that morning received
private letters from Paris, containing very favourable intelligence. Pein believed these to be answers to the letters
written by Maret to prepare his friends at Paris for my
Note. He said he did not think it likely that the official
answer to my Note would arrive at Lisle before Monday
or Tuesday; but that he had little doubt of its being such
as would enable him to go on with the Negotiation. It
would not be possible for him, he said, to see Maret before
the departure of Mr. Wesley, as he was gone out of town,
and was not to return till the next day. He then told
Mr. Ellis that an article had appeared in one of the French
newspapers, stating that Carnot had had an interview with
La Réveillière Lépaux, for the purpose of endeavouring to
bring him round to the Moderate party. This, he said, was
not true; that it was Pichegru who was the real mediator
between the Modérés and the violent part of the Directory;
and that from the style of Pichegru's Report to the Council
upon the conduct of the Executive Power in having violated
the constitution, which Report is much more moderate than
was expected, it is probable that he has succeeded in bringing about something like a reconciliation. It seems that the
Modéré party in the Council, though generally alarmed
beyond measure at the Jacobins, are now perfectly fearless
under Pichegru; and that, though they cannot easily attack
the authority of the Directory immediately, they can get the
better of them through the medium of the Ministers. They
have driven out Delacroix, Truguet, and very lately Le Noir
La Roche; should they succeed against Merlin, which seems
probable, they will greatly diminish the preponderance of
the Jacobinical part of the Executive Power. A committee
is at this moment framing a Report on the *Compatibilité des
Ministres*, and they are passing a bill for the purpose of
reorganizing the National Guard, which, when under the
influence or control of such men as Pichegru, will become a
most formidable body, entirely devoted to the Moderate
party. It should seem, from all these circumstances, that

the Directory, divided as it now is, must grow weaker every day; and this is certainly an argument in favour of Pein's maxim, that everything depends on gaining time. He told Mr. Ellis, that every day that passed over our heads put us upon surer ground, and that it is impossible for the Directory to hold out much longer against the clamour for peace, when the impracticability of furnishing funds for the continuation of the war is notorious to everybody.

EXTRACTS OF A LETTER FROM MR. CANNING TO LORD MALMESBURY.

Spring Gardens, 27th July, 1797.

This messenger will bring you but very little, but in such a state of things you cannot expect much to be said on this side of the water; we have talked all day in nothing but interjections of impatience, doubt, and anxiety. I thought, however, that it would be a comfort to you to have as quick an acknowledgment (though nothing more) of despatches so interesting, as possible. Lord Grenville agreed without hesitation, because he can with the safer conscience get out of town again (and he is gone); and I, that there may be no unnecessary delay on my part, have sworn not to dine till I have despatched Brooks.

By the way, I must not omit, at a time when secrecy and discretion are so much in request, to tell you that Brooks has conducted himself admirably in this respect. The first intimation that I had of his arrival to-day was to this effect, "that a gentleman was come in a hackney-coach to the next door (Lord Malmesbury's), and the porter wished to know if I could come and speak to him there." I obeyed, went through the garden, and saw Brooks, silent as a ghost, gliding by the bow-window. Our meeting may be better imagined than described; and I assure you, it is from his prudence and management on this occasion, not from any corrupt view to the tributary turbots which he never fails to bring me, that I send him back to you, instead of the messenger next in turn.

Our plans of secrecy here have not been very auspiciously

begun, as you will see in my letter to Morpeth, but I trust we shall be less unlucky another time. They have had one effect, however, not very pleasant personally to *me*, which is the procuring me the reputation of stock-jobbing. I have traced a report of this sort up to Mr. Perry, of the *Morning Chronicle*, and have sent him a civil message in consequence, importing, that, if he should think proper to print what I understand he has not scrupled to say, I shall certainly prosecute him.

I congratulate you upon having escaped the meeting with Ch. Delacroix, which the French papers had promised you. It was a sort of practical epigram, which I thought the Directory would have felt themselves strongly tempted to play off upon you. You say nothing of his successor.

---

LETTER FROM MR. CANNING TO MR. ELLIS.

Spring Gardens, July 27, 1797.

I CRY you mercy, dear George. If I had understood the admission of the " inalienability " to have been given in the way in which you now represent it, or, to speak quite plainly, if " the Lion " had so represented it in his despatch, I should never have lifted up my voice, even in a *most private* letter, against it: an admission, not of the principle itself, but of its result and application only, and a compensation for that admission by a similar forbearance on the part of the enemy with regard to whatever we conceived (rightly or wrongly) to be annexed, *inalienable* with regard to ourselves;—*voilà* the only points which I meant to say should have been contended for and made clear to both parties. You say they were so; I have only to answer, that then I think " the Lion " did not quite do himself justice in the despatch which described what he had been doing in this respect. With regard to the second point, the moment at which the reference was made here, you must be much better judges than we can be; and, till I see the whole chain, I will not pretend to count the links of it. You will, however, have understood, that what I said upon that point belonged rather to the state of things *here* than that at Lisle—to the triumph procured by the particular discussion to those whom I wish not to triumph, over *those* to whom I wish to maintain an *ascendancy*, which they have so recently obtained, and of which I am not yet sure that they have more than a precarious and temporary possession; and, upon my conscience, I believe the safety and welfare of the country hereafter to be involved in their maintenance and exercise of this ascendancy. And, though I am not so unreasonable as to wish or expect that the great work about which you are employed can be squared in the whole, or altogether in any one part, with a view to circumstances of this nature at home, yet I do not think it an inconsiderable object to soften as much as can be done, without hazarding truth and substance, the roughnesses of the work to be done here to those who are determined to go through with it; and to give as little opportunity as can be helped to those who hate the work to revile the master workman.*

If I write enigmatically, you must blame yourself; for all that has come from you to-day is so full of doubt and difficulty, that I hardly venture to speak or think positively upon any one subject connected with it.

"The Lion" mentions slightly his having been indisposed. I hope this is not really so. I think, if it had been, you would, some of you, have mentioned it. Pray do in your next. Adieu! Ever yours, G. C.

---

LETTER FROM MR. CANNING TO MR. ELLIS.

Spring Gardens, 27th July, 1797, ¾ p. 9, P.M.

MY DEAR GEORGE,—Never was so tantalizing a beginning of a letter as that which I received from you to-day. It is well for me that I have fatigued myself as I have done in

---

* Mr. Canning here alludes to the difference of opinion between Mr. Pitt and Lord Grenville on the question of Lord Malmesbury's negotiation for peace. As Lord Grenville believed and argued that it could not be obtained upon terms honourable to England, every hitch at Lisle confirmed this idea, and furnished him with an argument against Pitt; and Mr. Canning, who was devoted to the latter, was anxious to prevent this as much as possible.

preparing matters for Brooks's return. I should else pass a sleepless night in ruminating upon all the impossibilities and extravagances which an imagination thrown loose into such a wilderness of conjecture would conjure up. As it is, being very tired, and having to dine before I sleep, I think I shall contrive to sleep soundly.

You have alarmed me so much by your caution with respect to what you write, that I hardly know whether I can venture to communicate all that I have heard from different quarters which I think might be of use to you; but, as I can quote no authority, I compromise nobody.

I shall therefore tell you without scruple, first, that what I mentioned in my former letter of Barthelemi's speculations in the funds has been confirmed to me since, in a manner that very much persuades me of the truth of that circumstance.

Secondly. That we have what we think here good reason to believe that Maret has a commission separate from his colleagues, (I know not whether from Dutch or French authority,) to treat for the surrender of the Cape *for a sum of money.* Thirdly. That the inclosed is a copy of a letter from Paris to Bobus Smith,* written the day after Talleyrand's nomination, and the first part of the contents of which, but not the letter itself, Bobus has since communicated to me. Talleyrand, you may not know perhaps, has been always a great friend of Bobus's and of mine, since I went to Mr. Pitt some years ago, at Smith's desire, to endeavour to obtain a remission of his sentence of exile. You may guess how I got the copy of the letter, but must not say.

In addition to this information of a foreign kind, I may add with still more safety that we are all well at home; that the mutiny is remembered only by the hangings that are still going on; that Ireland is much better than it has been; that there is a man in the Strand who has written *stump legs* over his door, which I will take Dr. Leg to see when he comes to town; and that the Corresponding Societies are to assemble at different places all over England on Monday next, for the purpose of stirring up sedition, and

* This letter I do not find among the Harris Papers, although a subsequent one from Talleyrand to Bobus Smith is extant.

that the Yeomanry Corps throughout the kingdom are appointed to meet them.

Now, to seal up my letters, and then to dinner!

Ever, my dear George, &c. G. C.

---

LETTER FROM MARET, SENT THROUGH M. PEIN TO LORD MALMESBURY.

Lille, 31 Juillet.

UN courier adressé à une seule personne,* et apportant des dépêches pour *elle seule,* arrive à l'instant. Elles font pressentir que des sentimens d'honneur ne permettront pas de revenir sur la mesure antérieure. Il ne reste donc à cet égard que très peu d'espérance de changement dans l'état présent des choses. Un résultat plus heureux dépendra uniquement des *intérêts moins directs.*† La personne qui a reçu le courier est autorisée à faire par écrit les communications nécessaires pour amener à des dispositions plus faciles sur ces *intérêts moins directs.* Elle se propose d'expédier cette nuit un courier vers les lieux d'où doivent être adressées les intentions des co-intéressés, dont les agents doivent bientôt se rendre à Paris à fin d'influer utilement sur les instructions qui leur seront remises, et auxquelles tient tout espoir d'accommodement. Il serait sans doute précieux de connaître les bornes dans lesquelles pourraient être restreints les prétentions énoncées contre eux. On concevra qu'en sollicitant des indications d'une nature aussi grave, aussi confidentielle, on ne peut avoir d'autre but que de favoriser ce désir réciproque de succès, et d'autres règles de conduite que celles que doit prescrire la plus prudente réserve. Ce qui serait confié servirait uniquement de direction dans les efforts qui vont être faits près des co-intéressés, et aucune personne qu'elle ne serait initiée dans ces détails de pure et d'entière confiance. On réclame également dans les rapports à faire à qui que ce soit, l'oubli absolu de la communication présente offerte comme un témoignage de la plus véritable estime.

\* To Maret. † The Allies of France.

### REPLY FROM LORD MALMESBURY TO M. PEIN.

*Lille, 31 Juillet, 1797.*

On regarde le Billet remis comme une preuve également loyale et obligeante des sentimens de la personne qui l'a écrite, et on se fait un plaisir d'y répondre dans le même sens. On voit avec chagrin dépendre le seul espoir de succès d'un rapprochement d'intérêts aussi difficiles, pour ne pas dire impossibles, à concilier. On assure bien sincèrement que les instructions sont positives. Tout ce qu'on peut faire c'est de promettre d'employer toute son *influence personnelle* pour se procurer la permission de co-opérer avec l'auteur du Billet, en obtenant, s'il est possible, quelques modifications pour les *intérêts moins directs*. En attendant, pour répondre à une confidence dont on ressent tout le prix (et comptant sur le même secret qu'on promet à son tour) on n'hésite pas de dire qu'on recevra sans difficulté toute proposition de cette nature, et même qu'on l'appuyera en autant que cela est compatible avec son devoir.

---

July 31.—Everything in suspense till this day. A courier arrives from Paris—Directory not likely to depart from their strong claim. A *biais* to be found by applying to the Dutch to release the French from their engagements—this communicated confidentially by Maret. It is evident that on one side the Democratic Government, (at least the three governing Directors,) either from pride, from bad policy, or from what they *suppose to be their own interest*, are not *well* inclined to peace; that they think the idea of maintaining good faith with their Allies, and employing strong and high words, will popularize the duration of the war. On the other side, the other two Directors, the new Minister Talleyrand, and many others, wish for peace, perhaps nearly from similar motives; and this will account for such a wide difference between the official language I hear, and that held by Maret and his agents. I did not think it safe to trust a minute detail of this in writing, even by a messenger, and only hinted at it in private letters to

Pitt and Lord Grenville, by Brooks, whom I despatched on the 25th of July, and sent the particulars by Wesley on the 30th.

The result of these secret conferences and communications appears to be a desire on the part of Maret that the business should end well—an appearance of sincerity from his manner and from the nature of his communication. It seems also to be his interest (at least his *personal* interest) to act as he does.

TUESDAY, AUG. 1.—I pressed Ellis, before he saw Pein, to urge the necessity that their public and official conduct should correspond with their private and confidential communications; that, otherwise, they could neither be credited nor made use of. Pein said this was certainly difficult, but that Maret would contrive it.—(N.B. I have my doubts of the sincerity of all this, and suspect they are lying by for events, particularly for the signature of the Definitive Treaty with the Emperor; but, as *we* also may gain by delay, we are, perhaps, only playing off each other.)

Things at Paris appear to be compromised. Pein assured Ellis that the great stumbling-block was Holland; that they could manage Spain, and were indifferent as to Portugal; and gave for reason, the Dutch owed France money, and that this probably would not be paid if the entirety of the Dutch Republic was violated at the peace. He seemed to hint, if we would give up the Cape, peace would be made immediately.

AUG. 2.—Ellis, at my instigation, pressed the necessity of a *contre-projét*—but this not likely. It is evident that the whole depends on getting rid of the Directors, or, at least, on getting *one*[*] of them out.

AUG. 4.—G. Ellis sent for by Pein at 11 A.M., who informed him letters and instructions were arrived—favour-

---

[*] So as to give the casting vote to the Moderate section.

able, particularly one from Talleyrand to Maret—announced a Conference in which I was to hear *officially*, what he had told me ex-officially, about the Allies being applied to, &c. N.B. This did not happen at the Conference, on which, August 5th, Saturday, Ellis met him again. He explained it by saying, that, when he had seen him on the 4th, the public instructions had not been read; that they were not thought sufficient by Le Tourneur to authorize him and them to speak out; and on August 6th, just as I was despatching Lord G. Leveson, a note came from Maret.—N.B. For the details of this, see the private accounts of each conversation between Ellis and Pein.

N.B. Lord G. Leveson carried all this private communication to England on the 6th August. Ellis saw Pein again on the 10th, 12th, and 14th. He communicated the Portuguese Treaty with France.

---

EXTRACT OF A DESPATCH FROM LORD MALMESBURY TO
LORD GRENVILLE.

Lisle, 6th Aug., 1797.

IN the Conference of Friday, M. Maret expressed a desire to obtain the exchange or release of a relation, prisoner in England. This gave me an opportunity to mention Sir Sidney Smith, and to state to the French Plenipotentiaries, that it was because their Government persisted in his detention, that no exchange whatsoever of officers had taken place, and that I was afraid none would be listened to on our part till they thought proper to consent to the release of him. I addressed myself particularly to M. Le Tourneur, who, I observed, must be acquainted with the circumstances of the case, from the several conversations I had held with M. Delacroix, and from the Memorials I had presented, and which certainly had been laid before him in his capacity of Director.

M. Le Tourneur appeared to have a very imperfect recollection of the subject, and said he now heard for the *first time* that it was on the account of Sir Sidney's confinement that the cartel had been stopped. He observed, this was indeed a very serious consideration, and one which deserved the greatest attention. This induced me to enter very fully into Sir Sidney's case, situation, and treatment, and the great inconveniences to which it led; and it made so much impression on M. Le Tourneur, that he promised me he would write immediately to Paris to one of his friends in the Directory, and also to M. Pléville, and that he would endeavour to make them feel how unwise and unjust it was to keep so many persons in confinement on account of a single man, let his conduct even have been such as to call in doubt his right to be treated as a prisoner of war, which he was told was Sir Sidney's case.

EXTRACT OF A DESPATCH FROM LORD MALMESBURY TO LORD GRENVILLE.

Lisle, 6th Aug., 1797.

I FULLY expected, when I received the inclosed note[*] on Friday, that the Conference proposed was to acquaint me with the instructions the French Plenipotentiaries had received from the Directory, on the Note I had given in near a fortnight ago, as an answer to that in which the restitution of the *whole* of His Majesty's conquests from each of his enemies is required as an *indispensable* preliminary to all Negotiation.

I was therefore surprised and disappointed, when I had taken my place at the Conference, to hear from M. Le Tourneur that the letters they had received that morning from Paris did not bring any specific reply to my last Note, but only went to inform them that the Directory had taken the subject into their most serious consideration, and would acquaint them, as soon as possible, with the result.[†]

I could not avoid expressing my concern and surprise that there existed any hesitation whatever in the mind of the

---

[*] Inviting Lord Malmesbury to a Conference on the 4th inst.
[†] This despatch is a decisive proof (if such were wanting) that the charge of wilful procrastination, imputed to us by the Directory and subsequent French historians, is untrue.

Directory on a point which, although very important, was a very simple one—that of allowing it to remain in doubt whether the Directory sincerely meant peace or not; and that, although I was very far from wishing for any improper haste, or not to move in a matter of such magnitude with becoming prudence and deliberation, yet I could not forbear lamenting that more than a month had now elapsed without our having advanced a single step, notwithstanding His Majesty had in the very outset of the Negotiation manifested a moderation and forbearance unprecedented under similar circumstances. That, anxious as I was not to prejudice it by any representations of mine, I must say this delay placed me in a very awkward position, as I really did not perceive how I could account for it in a way at all satisfactory; at the same time, that it was quite impossible for me to suffer a longer space of time to pass over without writing to my Court.

M. Maret expressed his earnest wish that I would write immediately; he was confident this delay would be seen in its true light, and added, "Si nous n'avançons pas à pas de géant, j'espère que nous marchons d'un pas sûr;" and M. Le Tourneur repeated the phrase.

They observed to me that the *contre-projét* would of course be contained (virtually) in their next instructions; and that their only motive for wishing to see me was to convince me that this delay had neither originated with them, nor been occasioned at Paris by any want of attention to this important business, or from any cause not immediately and closely connected with it.

I desired to know from them when they thought it probable they should receive positive and explicit instructions, —whether in three, four, or five days? M. Colchen said it would probably be eight or ten.* On that M. Le Tourneur observed, that, as our not meeting more frequently gave rise to many idle rumours and false reports, he would propose to me, if I had no objection, to meet every other day at 2 o'clock;

* The real causes of this delay were the state of affairs in Paris, and the divided opinions of the Directory.
Carnot et Barthélemi votaient pour qu'on acceptât les conditions de l'Angleterre, les trois autres Directeurs soutenaient l'opinion contraire. — Thiers, tom. vi.

that it was very possible that in our next two or three meetings we might have nothing material to say, but that we should get better acquainted with each other, and in our conversations mutually suggest ideas which might be of use.

I readily consented to this; and we were breaking up, when M. Maret said, that an additional cause for the slowness with which the business had proceeded, arose from the appointment of a new Minister to the Foreign Department; that M. Delacroix had not yet had time to give his papers up to M. Talleyrand; and that the confusion in the office from the change of clerks, &c. was such, that the business did not go on so quickly and so regularly as it ought. He seemed to have introduced this circumstance with a view to speak in terms of high commendation of M. Talleyrand, and to sneer at M. Delacroix.

I had a conference again this morning, as I was very desirous of being enabled to transmit to your Lordship some more satisfactory account as to the motives of this delay. I again pressed the French Plenipotentiaries on this point. They each of them repeated what they had said before, and on my applying particularly to M. Le Tourneur, and endeavouring to make him feel how impossible it was that His Majesty should not be hurt at this demur on so very simple a point, he said, "You ought to augur favourably from it. Your Note was a refusal to agree to what was stated by the Directory in their instructions to us as a *sine quâ non*. If the Directory were determined to persist in this *sine quâ non*, they would have said so at once." "Je vous assure qu'il nous auroit promptement renvoyé le courier," were his words. The time they take to deliberate indicates beyond a doubt that they are looking for some "temperament," and it scarce can be doubted that one will be found. I said I was well pleased to hear him say this, but that still he must be aware that it would not be an easy task for me to make my despatches to-day either interesting or satisfactory.

M. Maret said that he really believed that this would be the only great impediment we should have to encounter, that everything would go on quickly and smoothly, and that I must admit the present to be a very important and difficult point in the Negotiation. I agreed with him entirely as to its importance, but could not acquiesce as to its difficulty.

I am very sorry, my Lord, that in such a moment, and after waiting so long, I should not be able to send you more explicit and decisive assurances; but it is not in my power to compel the French Negotiators to move on faster. All I can do is, by my conduct and language, to take care that no part whatever of the imputation of delay should attach to me. I have at every conference always declared my readiness to proceed, and I shall not fail to repeat this every time we meet.

#### LETTER FROM LORD MALMESBURY TO LORD GRENVILLE.

Lisle, Sunday, Aug. 6th, 1797.

MY DEAR LORD,—Mr. Wesley will have acquainted you with the secret channel of communication that has been opened here, and with such information as I had derived through it, up to the day of his leaving Lisle. Since then still more material intelligence has come to my knowledge; and the same motive which induced me to employ Mr. Wesley, determines me now to send Lord G. Leveson to England. I have no doubt you found Mr. Wesley exact and accurate; you will, I am sure, find Lord Granville equally so; and, besides the advantage this mode of communication has over all others in point of secrecy and safety, you derive from it the power of question and inquiry, which for my own satisfaction and comfort is one that I am very desirous of affording you, since what is now passing *ex-officially*, is so much more important than what passes *officially*, that I do not feel at all justified in acting upon it on my own judgment, and am very anxious to have it stated so correctly, and examined so carefully, that its real value may be ascertained, and Lord Granville bring me back orders in consequence.

Had I no other grounds at this moment to form an opinion but the conduct of the Directory, I should look upon the Negotiation as in a very precarious state, and apprehend its breaking up to be a very near event. But, if what I hear from this secret quarter can be relied on, I must hold a contrary belief. I must suppose the French will contend only for *forms*, and give way in *substance;* and that they will affect to perform their engagements (real or supposed) in *appearance*, but break them in *fact*.

It required no great art to see through the object of Maret's Note of the 31st of July. I hope my answer will be thought sufficiently guarded, and at the same time explicit enough to encourage him to continue his communications; at all events, it is to be recollected that the originals of both our Notes are restored, and that they never can be produced.

It is clear from what Maret writes, that, if the Directory wish to make peace at all, it is at the expense of their Allies; and, from the step they have taken, they probably are in earnest. If this should be the case, (which must shortly appear,) the Negotiation will soon be brought to a discussion of the more or less we are to keep from the Dutch, since (if what is told us could be credited) the interests of Spain and Portugal will not throw any great obstacles in the way of the Treaty; but this is so contrary to the conduct observed by the Directory during their last negotiation with the Court of Lisbon, that I fear, on this particular point, our informant is either not trusted or not sincere.

From every thing you read and hear to-day, you will, I am sure, be confirmed in your opinion, that on the upshot of the present contest at Paris depends the fate of the Treaty; that it cannot possibly be forced on here by any means in my power, and that the best and only line of conduct I can adopt is, by temper and patience to prevent its premature rupture from being imputed to us, and by prudence and caution to let nothing escape me which may betray an overeagerness for its success, or pledge me directly or indirectly to any unbecoming conditions when we really begin to negotiate.

If the delay, which from the confidential channel is accounted for as being purposely managed for good ends, should after all arise from direct contrary motives, and be concerted on the part of the three hostile Directors[*] for the purpose of gaining time, in order that they may the better

---

[*] Barras, Rewbell, and La Réveillière Lépaux.

accomplish their views of power, I do not see, even in that case, (except that every additional day of war is to be regretted,) any particular evil which will result from it. If the Treaty is ultimately to break off, it must be done on the part of the French Government in a more offensive way, after they have allowed it to go on for a length of time, than at its beginning. I have no good grounds to suspect this; but it is possible that the three Directors, who are certainly more daring than able, may, either by reckoning on support from Buonaparte, or by means of the armed force with which they are surrounding Paris, perhaps after the signing of the Definitive Treaty with Austria, think events turn up in their favour, of which they are desirous to take the chance.

I shall conclude this letter by saying, that, with respect to our secret information, Mr. Ellis has been troubled at my request, after each interview, to write down a detailed and circumstantial account of every conversation which passed, in order that I might, by comparing the whole together, be enabled to judge whether it tallied exactly. And, as I cannot discover that his informant has been betrayed into any contradiction, I really do not think there is any internal evidence against his credibility.

I am, &c.     MALMESBURY.

---

EXTRACT OF A LETTER FROM LORD MALMESBURY TO MR. PITT.

Lisle, 6th Aug., 1797.

As in addition to what you will already have heard from Mr. Wesley, I can depend on the correct memory and faithful report of Lord Granville Leveson, and also on the satisfactory manner in which he will answer your questions and explain your doubts, I shall begin this letter under the impression that you are as much master of what has passed here privately and confidentially as we ourselves, and much better able than we can be to estimate its value, and the degree of credit to which it may be entitled.

The intermediary person trusted and employed by Maret,

is a plain, sensible man, who says he is actuated by no other motive than because he considers it to be the interest of France in general, and the advantage of his friend and relation in particular, that the Negotiation should succeed. He has been employed from an early period of his life in different public offices, and has nothing about him which denotes the adventurer. I can have no doubt of his acting under Maret's authority, as, in order to ascertain it, I agreed upon certain signs to be used at the Conference, which were made and understood by us both.* He is known to be a Modéré; he has an office here, (Inspecteur des Postes et Messageries,) which he got by purchase. He is perfectly acquainted with what passed during our last negotiation at Paris, and appears to possess the full confidence of Maret in this.

---

EXTRACT OF A DESPATCH FROM LORD MALMESBURY TO LORD GRENVILLE.

(Separate.) Lisle, 6th August, 1797.

As I derive from a secret and confidential channel the only means I have to throw any light on the present incoherent conduct of this Government, and as the information I receive is so complex and intricate as to leave me no hopes that I should be able to convey it to your Lordship with precision and clearness by letter, I have determined to request Lord G. Leveson to be the bearer of these despatches. His Lordship is fully acquainted with every circumstance of the transaction; he will state the whole of it to your Lordship, and enable you to form a judgment as to the degree of attention proper to be paid to it.

I shall not anticipate any part of what Lord Granville has to say, although it would be, perhaps, necessary that I should, in order to explain some passages of my despatch of this date.

The intention to intimidate, if not to subdue, the Legislative Body by force, comes out on further investigation to

---

* The sign agreed upon was Maret's taking his handkerchief out of one pocket, passing it before his face, and returning it into the other.—*Harris Papers and Lord Granville.*

have been a measure actually resolved on. Considerable bodies of troops were approaching in every direction towards Paris, and the troops still remain but just beyond the circle prescribed by the Constitution.* Your Lordship will perceive from the motions of Willot† and Doulcet, in the Council of Five Hundred, that violent suspicions still exist, and that strong measures are prepared in consequence. But the strongest of all, and one which may ultimately plunge this country into a state of the most bloody civil war, is the plan in contemplation by the Councils of arming a body of national troops for their defence against those of the line.

On the other side, the language of the troops of the line which have entered France clearly betray the intentions for which they are brought. They conduct themselves not as an army marching quietly through its own country, but as if they came for hostile purposes. Violent but most unconstitutional declarations in support of the Directorial authority have been made by divisions of Buonaparte's army; and it is evident that the three Directors have endeavoured to form a strong party amongst the soldiers, and expect effectual support from them. Of this support, however, they will be no longer secure than while they are enabled to pay for their services.

I hear it said that the Moderate party is gaining strength, and that it is becoming every day more numerous and more popular. But I am far from being confident that from these reasons we are to reckon that it will ultimately prevail. A very few regular troops would keep great numbers in awe; and the return of the "system" of terror for a very short time would completely overthrow the two Councils.

Rewbell and Barras are determined characters. Goubert, a friend of the first, told him some time ago, "que s'il ne changeoit pas de conduite, il le verroit dans trois semaines à Vendôme" (where Babœuf was confined). Rewbell an-

---

* Twelve leagues from Paris.
† Willot made a motion that a report be drawn up on the state of affairs, and questions addressed to the Directory respecting the march of the troops. This was adopted, and, in answer, the Directory in bold language justified their conduct.

swered, "Eh bien! en ce cas j'irai, car je ne m'en démordrai pas."\*

From this situation of the two great parties in this country, it might fairly be inferred that Paris would be at this moment in a state of apprehension and alarm. The contrary, however, is the fact; the greatest dissipation prevails: and it should appear to be the policy of the Directory to try to divert the minds of the people from every reflection, by procuring them every sort of amusement which can gratify either their love of pleasure or their curiosity; and the incurable levity of the French assists them powerfully on this occasion.

There reigns, however, a very deep and serious uneasiness amongst the graver monied men and thinking merchants. They dread the continuation of the war, well knowing that the only resource left to this country is a forced loan; and they are almost equally afraid of the ruinous effect that the event of the present struggles between the two parties may have on their credit and property. Indeed, in the present state of party, they seem to have forgotten that they have a foreign enemy; and what I have written will in some measure account for the delay we have been forced to submit to.

---

LETTER FROM MR. CANNING TO MR. ELLIS.

Spring Gardens, 8th Aug., 1797.

MY DEAR GEORGE,—You have done great things, and we expect great things from you. I have no remark to offer upon any part of your communications by Wesley or by Leveson, but only to approve and admire, and wonder what will come next. In the mean time I proceed to answer, as far as I recollect them, all the questions which you have put to me, and the answers to which can be of any use or comfort to you.

I was not quizzing you, but telling a most sober truth,

---

\* The third, La Réveillière Lépaux, was quite in the hands of these two. Pichegru and Lacuée were at this time trying to bring him over to the Restoration party.—*Harris Papers.*

when I gave you the copy of Talleyrand's letter to Smith.
As a proof of its authenticity, I inclose to you the copy of
another, which has been since received, but of which no *communication* has been made to me. It is written, as you see,
in English, and (which you cannot see, but must believe as
I do,) in T.'s hand. You will see the remarkable coinci-
dence of this letter with everything that you have been told:
1st, the date of the receipt of the result; 2nd, *the knowing
them a little before; the much to repair and to do;* the
*taking patience;* the *idea* he may have had, of the determination you all appear to have of being disappointed. I wish
he had written again on the 29th, which I cannot find that
he did. I cannot find either, that the person of confidence
mentioned in his first letter is arrived. When he does, I
shall probably insinuate myself into his secrets, without his
knowing it.

With regard to Barthelemi's gambling in our funds, I do
not think it matters much any way. If you have strong
reasons for disbelieving it, I do not wish to press it. I have
it second-hand from a person who says Charretier told it
him, he (Charretier) being Barthelemi's manager in the business. I know, from incontestable proof, that Barthelemi
and Charretier have correspondence together, but that proves
little. My informant may have belied Charretier, or Charretier his correspondent.

The account of Maret's commission concerning the Cape*
comes through Wickham from Paris, and everything that we
have had through the same channel from the same authority
has turned out so accurately true, especially of late, that I
confess I give great credit to the intelligence. Indeed, I
*think* I see in Maret's conduct strong grounds of confirmation.
By the way, however, I must say that I do not believe one
word of the unwillingness of *the Dutch* to give up the Cape
(in addition to Trincomalee) as the price of peace. We have
information, and very respectable information, directly from
the Hague of a tendency exactly opposite. And, if the
money is wanted at all, I am clear it is not to satisfy the
Dutch, but to enable them to satisfy the French; and that,

* It was said that Maret had a separate commission to leave us the Cape for a sum of money.

contrary to the usual habits of Batavians, they are compelled to offer for sale what they are of themselves ready to give away.

"The Lion" expresses some doubt, both in his Despatch and in his private letter, (to Mr. Pitt, I think,) of the propriety of allowing Dutch and Spanish Plenipotentiaries to come into the Negotiation. I do not know whether he wished to get an answer to this doubt now, or to have it in reserve, as what he might take hereafter *ad referendum* for the sake of gaining time. To take it *ad referendum* will certainly be very proper; but I apprehend (and Pitt, if he writes, will write to the same effect to "the Lion,") that there can be no hesitation as to the admission of the Plenipotentiaries—little doubt, I should imagine, as to the prudence of admitting them—the Dutch especially, with a view to the question last mentioned, of the Cape. And, for the Spaniards, I should like to see "the Lion" try his hand upon Cabarras. The only possible inconvenience that I foresee is, that "the Lion" may be in return encumbered with the assistance of Aranjo. There are few things in your communications that I like so well, and expected so little, as the facilities that are promised about Portugal.

Wesley complains that he has failed in procuring an answer to three points which Lord Malmesbury has been referring again and again to Lord Grenville and to Mr. Pitt for decision—the King's title, the Toulon ships, and the renewal of treaties.

First, I think I can safely tell you that "the Lion" never will get a distinct answer upon either of the *two first* points, until they are formally brought under discussion at Lisle, and *forced* upon the Cabinet for deliberation; the third may, perhaps, be in the same situation. But Pitt seems to have no manner of difficulty in agreeing to renew or omit as many treaties, or as few, as any gentleman pleases, convinced that, in the way in which we are going about this matter, we shall start afresh from the present pacification, and have everything to begin upon a bran new plan adapted to the present occasion. It seems, however, to him, and I should think to everybody, that it would be shorter to renew in a lump than to pick and cull; but be that as it may.

With regard to the King's title, I confess I attach more importance to it in my own mind than I think Pitt is at present inclined to do. Wesley will tell you that I could only get him to make jokes (and those for the most part bad ones) at dinner to-day. But I feel very much persuaded, that, argued as a point of our internal constitution, the unqualified demand of its renunciation may be got over; and that a separate article, worded as strongly as you please in favour (and the more *exclusively* in favour the better) of the French Republic, together with the use of the words " Britannic Majesty," may be made to satisfy all parties.

As to the Toulon ships, surely those which are destroyed cannot come into question. We had them *in trust:* good. What is required of a person who takes a thing in trust— what is the law?—the equity?—the usage in private life? that he should be as careful of it as if it were his own; pay the same attention to its preservation, expose it to no other than the same dangers, and defend it at no less than the same cost. It is *not* required that *more* attention should be paid to it, that it should be *more* carefully guarded, *more* obstinately and laboriously defended. Well, then, supposing ships, incontestably *our own*, to have been in the situation of the Toulon ships at the time of the evacuation, what should we have done? Undoubtedly brought away as many as we could, and destroyed the rest to prevent their falling into the enemy's hands. It is the every-day practice of war. We did so with the ships which we took in trust. We should have been unfaithful to our trust if we had done otherwise; and, having done so, we stand acquitted and discharged of any responsibility concerning *them*. If the question be only with regard to those which we have in our possession, I am clear (are not you?) for *returning* them, not *paying* for them. In God's name, do not let us pay *tribute* in any shape, under any pretence, qualification, or disguise whatever. I think, if the matter be rightly stated, the French Government have the best of the argument, with respect to the property taken in trust for France, and found at the time of our pacification with France in our possession, and in a restorable state. But then it is to the things themselves, as expressed in the bond—" to the pound of flesh, not a drop of blood,"—to the rotten ships,—not a guinea of our money, that the French have a fair pretension. Give them back what we have ; assert our acquittal and discharge as to what we have lost, fairly and *bonâ fide* lost or destroyed, as we would have lost or destroyed our own. And there is one clear, honourable, uniform, principled argument on which we may stand against the world, and there is no meanness in it. But, once admit compromise or equivalent, the principle is gone, the limits can no longer be ascertained between what we owe and what is extorted from us; we are no longer accounting for a trust, but acknowledging and atoning for an injury.

I wish you would think over this and agree with me in it. I talk to Pitt about it; but I do not think he gives this point all the attention it deserves. He hopes it may be staved off, involved in other discussions and views, and decided without distinct consideration. Can this be ? I think not. Is it desirable that it should be ? Indeed I think not too. Adieu! G C.

Wednesday Morning.

P.S.—I have just read over, with Pitt, all that I had written to you. He denies "the bad jokes"—not the *jokes*, I believe, but the *badness* of them; and the want of consideration for the Toulon ships, which I attribute to him at the end of the letter. As a proof to the contrary of this charge, he desires me particularly to add, that, to make my system respecting Toulon complete, we ought, in return for our acknowledgment of the present Government of France, as that with which we virtually made and are bound to keep our bargain, to stipulate for the restoration of those individuals, with whom we treated, to a situation of safety and protection under that Government. This seems quite right and necessary, and I should imagine would not be difficult. Indeed, I apprehend that the Toulonese are already restored. If so, we have only to say, that without that circumstance we would not, &c.

(INCLOSURE.)

SECRET LETTER FROM TALLEYRAND PERIGORD TO ROBERT SMITH, ESQ.

27th July, 1797.

I RECEIVED to-day only, the result of the conferences at Lille since your last despatches—it is true, I knew them a little before.

I am ready, and to-day will be busy about. To-night I shall have an idea, if not a determination. But, as it is not a post to-morrow, I will not write again but on the 29th.

My wish is good, but I have a great deal to repair,* and to do,—must take patience. Adieu!

---

LETTER FROM MR. CANNING TO MR. LEIGH.

Downing Street, 11th August, 1797.

You will have seen in all the newspapers that Granville Leveson arrived here on Tuesday, and, in some of them, that he and I left town together on Wednesday for Dropmore, than which nothing is more true. Granville Leveson *did* arrive on Tuesday morning. Pitt came to town from Hollwood to dine with us at my house (where Leveson is established in W. L.'s room), and to talk over and over all that Leveson had to tell us. On Wednesday morning we set out, Leveson and I, for Dropmore;—staid there that night— very busy, and rather dull; and yesterday morning we proceeded for relaxation to Park Place, where we had a delightful, idle, and pleasant day with Lady Malmesbury, Charles Ellis, Frere, the Lavingtons, &c.; and from Park Place we are just returned to town. I mean to have to-day *tête-à-tête* with Leveson in Spring Gardens, for, except on our journeys, we have scarcely been alone together since his arrival. To-morrow I have promised to carry him to Hollwood, where I think we shall spend to-morrow and Sunday very comfortably.

* Alluding to Delacroix's warlike plans.

EXTRACTS OF A DESPATCH FROM LORD MALMESBURY TO
LORD GRENVILLE.

Lisle, 14th Aug., 1797.

In consequence of the resolution we had come to, to meet on the days of the arrival of the post from Paris, our conferences for this last week have taken place regularly every other morning, except on Thursday the 10th of August, which being the anniversary of one of their festivals, the French Legation could not attend.

On the 8th nothing was said at all worth transmitting, except an intimation flung out by M. Maret, that it would be necessary to take into consideration the rights of Neutral Nations on this occasion.

What passed on the 12th was rather more interesting. The return of M. Wesley afforded me a very natural opportunity of expressing the impatience with which an answer to my last Note was expected by my Court. That *three weeks* had now elapsed since its transmission; and that, although I by no means wished to insinuate that due attention had not been paid to so very important a subject as that on which we were treating, yet I could not but greatly lament that day after day should be allowed to pass away without our proceeding at all in the great business for which we were met. M. Le Tourneur said, that it was impossible I could lament this delay more than he and his colleagues did. That he had already declared to me, that it was occasioned by a wish not to create but to remove difficulties; and he could assure me positively that the French Government had no other object in view, and that I should find, when once we began fairly to negotiate, we should proceed very rapidly.

I replied, "It was indeed very material to make good the time we had lost." "You would not," answered M. Le Tourneur, "call it time lost, if you knew how it was employed." On my expressing by my manner a wish to be informed, he went on by saying, "I will not scruple to tell you, though I feel I ought not yet to do it officially, that we are consulting with our Allies, that we have communicated to them all that has passed here. We have stated, that, unless they mean to continue the war, they must release us from our engagements, and enable us to a certain degree to meet your proposals."

I told him, I heard this with pleasure, as it was a much more satisfactory account for the slowness of their proceedings than any that had yet been alleged; but that I imagined a sufficient portion of time had elapsed to receive answers from Madrid, and much more than sufficient to get them from the Hague. M. Le Tourneur observed, that, in regard to the Court of Spain, M. Del Campo and Count Cabarras having very extensive full powers, it was not necessary to wait for any answer from Madrid; that the difficulty arose from the side of the Batavian Republic. They were divided into so many factions, and were so fully employed with forming their new constitution, that no answer was to be got from them.

The Conference of to-day is this moment over. M. Le Tourneur informs me, that he had received this morning a letter from M. Carnot, President of the Directory, assuring him that in four or five days they would receive their final instructions; and he added of himself, that he trusted these would be such as to enable us to continue our work without any further interruption. I said, I hoped these instructions would be in substance a *contre-projêt*, as I did not see how anything short of one could enable us to proceed so rapidly as he described. He agreed with me entirely, and assured me, that both he and his Colleagues, as well officially as in their private correspondence, had repeatedly stated the necessity of a *contre-projêt* being sent them; and he observed, that he really thought the French Government might have foreseen everything which had passed, and been prepared with one; and that this would have saved a deal of valuable time. As I could not myself have said more, I readily gave a full assent to what I heard.

---

EXTRACT OF A DESPATCH FROM LORD MALMESBURY TO
LORD GRENVILLE.

(Separate.) Lisle, 14th Aug., 1797.

As your Lordship will perceive from my other despatch of to-day, that nothing very material has passed in any of the

Conferences which we have held since I had last the honour of writing to you by Lord Granville Leveson, I should perhaps have deferred a few days longer despatching a messenger, if I had not received an express in the night of the 12th from the Chevalier d'Aranjo, Minister from the Court of Lisbon at Paris, with an account that he signed, the preceding evening, a Treaty of Peace between Her Most Faithful Majesty and the French Republic.*

It is necessary to remark that he had not given me any previous notice either of his return to Paris or of the Negotiation having been resumed between him and M. Delacroix; and the whole of the transaction would have taken me entirely by surprise, if I had not been informed by M. Maret, some time before the arrival of the express, that the telegraph had conveyed to the French Legation the news that this peace was on the point of being concluded.

The French Plenipotentiaries were evidently pleased with this event, but, in speaking to me, they accounted for their satisfaction by saying, that they looked upon it as a good omen for a general peace; that it indicates clearly the pacific dispositions of the Directory; and much more to this effect.

M. Le Tourneur observed, that, as our greatest difficulties arose from our being bound to have an attention to the situation and interest of our Allies, he thought one great obstacle was now removed; and he spoke of the probable success of our Negotiation with a great degree of confidence. As it was not, however, quite clear to me what mode of reasoning he had adopted on this occasion, or on what new principle, arising out of the Portuguese Peace, he grounded this confidence, I did not think it necessary either to agree with him, or dissent from him.

* This Treaty of Peace was concluded by M. Aranjo, not only without the *authority* of his Court, but absolutely *against its commands*. It was immediately disowned by M. Pinto, the Portuguese Prime Minister, and the Prince of Brazil. Although signed by Delacroix, it was the handiwork of Talleyrand. By its articles, a mutual restitution of all territorial possessions gained by either party during the war was agreed on. Portugal was to remain absolutely neutral between France and England, and never to admit more than six ships of either nation in her ports during the war. By this hostile and treacherous act of M. Aranjo, we lost (for the moment) an ally, and it gave the French some advantage at this period of the Negotiation.

## EXTRACTS OF A DESPATCH FROM LORD MALMESBURY TO LORD GRENVILLE.

(Separate.) Lisle, 14th Aug., 1797.

THE message and answer from the Directory to the two Councils on their inquiry relative to the unconstitutional march of part of the army* of the Sambre and Meuse, which was delivered to them on Thursday last, appear to have excited a very considerable degree of alarm at Paris, and to have renewed all those apprehensions which for a few days have subsided.

General Bournonville passed through here on the 8th, and it is rumoured that he is intrusted with some secret commission by the Directory relative to the troops.

There is, indeed, no doubt that the Directory has not yet given up all hopes of asserting their authority, either by really employing force, or by threatening to do it. It is generally thought they will not venture beyond the latter; and that, if the two Councils do not allow themselves to be intimidated, the Directory will ultimately give up the attempt, and be well satisfied to come to a reasonable compromise. I still, however, think Barras and Rewbell desperate enough to go any lengths, and do not feel quite so secure of this compromise as many, who, however, are certainly more competent to form an opinion as to its probability than I can possibly be.

It appears that General Hoche was recalled from the army so long ago as the 29th of June, in order to be sent on a new expedition against Ireland.

---

## EXTRACTS OF A LETTER FROM LORD MALMESBURY TO LORD GRENVILLE.

Lisle, Aug. 14th, 1797.

I AM very sorry that my official letters of to-day will tend so little to remove the state of suspense in which we have

* Ordered by the three Directors of the War Party to march upon Paris, to overawe the Councils, &c., preparatory to their final struggle with them.

been kept so long. The French Plenipotentiaries themselves appear to think this delay unreasonable, and endeavour, in our Conferences, to make up by personal attentions and civilities the deficiency in their ministerial communications. Whatever may be my private opinion as to the effects of this delay, you will perceive, that, in my conversation with them, I always complain of it, and represent it as calculated to create uneasiness, and give rise to the most unpleasant suspicions. Everything, however, that I hear and observe, convinces me no real evil will result from it, provided it is not carried too far; and I am glad to find that your opinion coincides with mine on this point.

The person who is alluded to in my separate despatch is M. St. Simon, who (though of a very great family) has lived through the whole of the Revolutions of Paris, and increased very considerably his family property by the purchase of Church Lands. He is a shrewd, sensible, strong-headed man; and there can be little doubt but that he spoke his own genuine sentiments, and those of the public in general. But you must consider what he says as the consequence more of opinion and observation than of positive information, and make allowances accordingly.*

It tallies exceedingly well with what we have heard from Pein, though certainly no communication subsists between them; and one of the great inducements I had in being so accurate in stating the conversation between Ellis and his friend was, that it may serve to convey a great deal of what Pein has told us, without being under the necessity of committing either him or Maret. I could wish you would be so good (unless it be absolutely necessary) not to mention M. St. Simon's name to any one but Mr. Pitt.

It was perfectly evident to me, and I really thought I had mentioned it in one of my private letters, that the question of money, when connected with the Dutch Cessions, was precisely what you say.—The French were to have had

---

* M. St. Simon, who saw Mr. Ellis in secret, affirmed that peace would eventually be granted, and on fair terms, as the Directors dared not oppose the general wish of the nation on this point; but that the Directors were at this moment more engaged with their own personal danger than with the Negotiation, and that hence arose the delays. He was of the Moderate party, and spoke as he wished.

about five millions from the Dutch. They have received about two, and would certainly be very glad to get the remainder from us, as the price of the Cape.

---

EXTRACTS OF A LETTER FROM LORD MALMESBURY TO MR. CANNING.

Lisle, 14th Aug., 1797.

It gave me very great pleasure to hear Wesley and Leveson were so clear and satisfactory in their accounts; I was sure they would be so, but I am particularly glad that Leveson has had this opportunity of making his merits known, and that he has done it with such good effect. I am not without my apprehensions that you infer *too much* from what we transmit to you; that you get *too* sanguine, or at least sanguine *too soon*, and will be more disappointed than you ought to be, when you find that numberless and great difficulties will still arise, and that the event (though I am ready to confess the prospect is tolerably fair) is far from being ascertained. Pray check this *too eager hope;* it is not to be justified. We may, and probably shall, have peace, but *not soon, not on our own terms,* (I mean original terms,) and it will be a work of labour and altercation to obtain some, not very different from them.

Do not, in return for my taxing you with being too sanguine, retort upon me by saying that I am despondent. It is not so; I also am sanguine, but without the *too.* Still less suppose me shrinking from the business, fearful of being plagued and perplexed, and disposed, for the sake of finishing the business soon, to finish it ill. On the contrary, I pledge myself to fight desperately every inch in the East and West; *to cavil at the ninth part of a hair;* to wrangle till I am hoarse for titles, dignity, treaties, ships, and what not; nay, to live on patiently at Lisle for the sake of maintaining the smallest portion of either of these. I only wish for my own sake not to indulge the false hope, that a very difficult task, as it first presented itself, is now likely to become a smooth and easy one; and you will readily suppose, I am on every account anxious that this should not be admitted on your side the water as a likely contingency.

I laboured, with the help of G. Ellis, my separate despatch of to-day, in hopes that it may serve as a diversion to all our private and confidential intelligence, and be brought forward as sufficient to explain what has appeared mysterious to those who have a right to read my official correspondence; at all events, this messenger will not, I think, carry over any materials for a Cabinet discussion.*

The Portuguese peace is a very sufficient reason for my sending him, and no other reason *need* be alleged. I hope, (observe here, *I hope,*) that soon I shall have something *officially* decisive, and then, if it squares tolerably with what I have heard ex-officially, *I see no reason why as much of this ex-official intelligence should not be communicated to the Cabinet, as is wanted for fair deliberation.* The great things to be concealed are *names,* and such *facts* as may lead to the prejudice or danger of individuals, either now or at any future period, without being essentially necessary for the public advantage, and *I am sure this consideration will never be lost sight of.*

Nothing would vex me so much, because I think nothing would be more unwise or more undignified, as our involving ourselves and our interests again with Austria.† We have done even more than our duty towards Austria, while Austria has totally forgotten what she owed to us. We have now the most respectable story to tell; but, if we again commit ourselves with the Court of Vienna, we shall be like an old Dutch ambassador with whom I was acquainted, who, after having divorced his wife for the most notorious misbehaviour, intrigued with her and ruined his constitution. I am sure you will agree with me, particularly after what we have heard of Thugut this morning. In regard to the other Imperial Court, I think we cannot be

---

* All the Cabinet, excepting Pitt and Lord Grenville, were kept in ignorance of Lord Malmesbury's most important despatches, and he was obliged to write one for the whole Cabinet, and another for Lord Grenville. Canning complains often of the difficulty he had in keeping up this game.—*Harris Papers.*

† Mr. Canning wrote to Lord Malmesbury that at this time Thugut (Prime Minister at Vienna) began to perceive that his Court had the worst of it, and hinted to ours that he should be glad to see Austria assisting our Negotiation.

too attentive to it, as we may have to want its assistance, or at least interference.

I scarce know whether to be glad or sorry for the peace with Portugal. D'Aranjo seems to have given a great latitude to his instructions. Conversing last night on this peace with Le Tourneur in their box at the play, (you see we now begin to associate,) he said, " Qu'il me félicitait de cet évènement, puisqu'il nous débarrassoit de nos Alliés, et qu'il voudrait pouvoir se débarrasser des leurs." I said, " Donnez les nous, nous en aurons soin." On returning to the charge, and saying seriously that he thought this event a favourable one for our Negotiation, I said, " Que de mon naturel je voyois assez volontiers couleur de rose." His answer was very odd, " Ma foi! si vous étiez François dans ce moment, vous auriez bien de la peine à en trouver de tel côté que vous regardassiez." He went on by saying, " A croire M. Thugut, nous aurons bientôt la paix avec l'Autriche. *L'Empereur n'insiste plus sur un Congrès.* Il laisse aux petits Princes de l'Europe les soins de démêler leurs intérêts après et comme ils pourront ; et j'espère," added he, " ne pas sortir des portes de Lille que la paix générale ne soit faite." You may guess my answer; but perhaps you cannot guess why my next question to him was, How far it was from Paris to Madrid? He replied, " Ah! je vous vois venir ; vous croyez que nous attendions le retour d'un courier d'Espagne,—point du tout. Les difficultés ne viendront pas de ce côté là ; ce sont ces maudits Hollandois qui font les revêches." I said, " Mais mettez les à la raison." " Aussi le ferons nous," answered Sir Gregory,* " s'ils ne veulent pas l'entendre tous seuls." Maret was near us, and heard all he said without contradicting it. This, you will say, was odd conversation during a play in a box with twenty people, but we were not overheard ; and as it was the first time I had visited them and their ladies in the box, and as it was a crowded night, being Sunday, and as I had my large star on, and as our intercourse appeared familiar and cordial, you cannot conceive how much

---

* *Sir Gregory* was the nickname given to Le Tourneur when mentioned in the English official correspondence. Pein was called *Henry*, Maret *William*, Talleyrand *Edward*, &c. I have restored their real names, to prevent confusion.

it struck the whole house, and I am much mistaken if you do not see a very fine article about it in the papers.

You will perceive, as I do not write to Mr. Pitt, that I take it for granted this letter will be shewn to him. I should have written precisely the same, although perhaps with a little more care and attention to him. G. Ellis has shewn me his letter to you. We never compare what we mean to say before it is actually said and put on paper, and I am glad to find that we always jump as great wits ought to do.

---

MR. ELLIS'S ACCOUNT OF HIS INTERVIEWS WITH M. PEIN.

DRAWN UP BY HIM FOR LORD MALMESBURY.

MONDAY, 31st JULY, 1797.—I had this afternoon a message from Pein, desiring to see me as soon as possible, and we met at half-past six. He told me that his friend[*] had received a very important letter from Paris, which he had been very anxious to discuss with me as soon as possible; but that having been obliged to dine with Le Tourneur, whom it was necessary to keep completely in the dark, and whose jealousy was extremely watchful, he had not ventured to send to me at three o'clock, when the letter arrived. The news it contained, he said, would disappoint me, as it had disappointed him: the Directory refused to give way; but, while they did so, shewed their anxiety not to break off the Negotiation entirely, since they had recourse to an expedient,—a very shabby one, indeed; but such an expedient might, if we thought fit, still leave some hopes of peace. They were too proud to retract, but at the same time had invited the Dutch to send immediately some Plenipotentiaries to Paris, in hopes that these Ministers would advise them to make such concessions on the part of Holland as should be absolutely necessary. That the Bishop of Autun had written on this subject to his *friend only*, informing him that he would keep back the messenger to the Legation for twenty-four hours, in order to give him a chance of making use of the communication; that in this interval he might

[*] Maret.

consult with us, and then despatch to Noel, the French Minister at the Hague, (who was directed to pay the greatest attention to his *advice*,) to urge him to procure, if possible, such instructions for the Plenipotentiaries as might ultimately lead to peace. He said, his friend had written a note on this subject to Lord Malmesbury, which he would first read to me, and then put into my hands, desiring me to copy and return it to him ;* and he begged me to give him a written answer from myself, after consulting with Lord Malmesbury, which he would in the same manner return after communicating it to his friend. That the letter to Noel† must be written during the night, and sent off at five o'clock this morning, when the gates would be open, and consequently a messenger might depart without notice, which was necessary in order to avoid giving umbrage to Le Tourneur.

When he came to that part of the note which requests a communication in confidence of our ultimatum, he said, "Je vous prie de croire que mon ami sent comme vous la délicatesse d'une pareille demande. Mais enfin, on ne croit pas que votre premier projêt soit votre dernier mot. J'avoue que quand cela seroit, on ne sauroit trouver vos prétentions exaggerées—mais si cela n'est pas, s'il vous est permis de vous relâcher un peu, d'accorder quelques facilités; il s'agit de savoir si vous avez assez de confiance dans la probité de mon ami‡ pour lui confier votre secret, afin qu'il puisse de son côté prendre les mesures les plus propres à faciliter votre marche."

After he had told me all he had to say without any interruption, I answered him that I would willingly take the note to Lord Malmesbury, and would promise a written answer on the same terms; but that I could tell him beforehand, this answer could not possibly quite meet the wishes of his friend. "You must consider," I said, "our present situation; this is not our first offer of peace. Your Directory affected to believe our first offers insincere; they would willingly persuade the world that we do not now wish for peace; but you know this is impossible,—you know that, if we now broke off the Negotiation, they would

---

\* This note has been given, page 423.
† Noel was French Ambassador at the Hague.     ‡ Maret.

incur in the eyes of Europe the whole responsibility. They wished us to admit, as a principle, the inalienability of all that they chose to call a part of their empire: we did not, and could not do this,—not because this was humiliating, but because it was absurd; but we did what was better for them, we consented to take no notice of the folly of the principle, and acquiesced in the inference. They admitted the principle of *compensation;* they now deny it. You know they are not, and cannot be bound, even by secret articles, to demand the restitution of our conquests from the Dutch. But having advanced an assertion in the face of all Europe, which all Europe knows not to be true, they will not recede. What is to be the consequence if we break off the Negotiation? Will the French Legislature and the French nation consider the cause of the Directory as a just cause? Will they devote their lives and fortunes in the prosecution of a war which has no longer a national object? You admit that this is not very certain; you admit it is certain that France would incur much more than her natural share of misery from the continuation of the war—nay, you urge this as a plea to induce us to make further sacrifices. But surely this argument ought to weigh a little with your own Directory?"

He said all this was very true; but convinced that we, too, were sincerely desirous of peace, he wished to know whether we would make any further sacrifice in order to obtain it. "You know," said he, "that the Legislative Body gains ground every day; that the majority of the Directory (and it is only to that majority that your reasoning applies) grow weaker in the same proportion: consequently, every day that the Negotiation continues advances your cause. You best know how far you have any confidence in my friend; you know how far you wish, and how far it is in your power, to co-operate with him. The Directory have, in their distress for money, very meanly, very foolishly, perhaps very unconstitutionally, *pledged* themselves to the Dutch to procure the restitution of *all* your conquests. Perhaps this money transaction cannot be defended under the terms of the Constitution as a *secret article of a treaty.* Of this you are certain, that they will not break off immediately, nor *force* you to break off immediately. Judge for yourselves; tell me your decision. What passes between us is not binding—it is not public or avowed, it is nothing till it is avowed by your Cabinet, till Lord Malmesbury receives orders to act in consequence at his conferences with the French Legation."

I told him that Lord Malmesbury's instructions were positive; that our *first* object had been to evince our sincerity by the reasonableness of our proposals; that, as to Ceylon, any definitive demand of that island would shew a determination of depriving us of all means of defence in the East Indies, where we have no other port; and that such a demand could only be dictated by the previous desire of re-commencing the war in that country as soon as the finances of France should enable her to send a fleet there. That the Cape, I was very sure, was not an object of profit to any nation; that it was necessary, like Ceylon, for the preservation of our territory; and that, from the little I had heard on the subject, I saw no reason for believing that we attached such importance to it as to let it stand in the way of the attainment of any great national object, but that it was ours at present, and I had not yet heard a shadow of reason why we should part with it. Lastly, that our demand of Cochin was only in return for Negapatam, which was, I conceived, of much higher value to the Dutch. Here he said, with much eagerness, "Vous m'étonnez beaucoup. Oh! si vous vouliez rendre le Cap, je suis persuadé qu'il ne tiendrait qu'à vous de signer la paix dans quinze jours." I told him that Lord Malmesbury *could* not consent to any such thing—that he was to remember I had only spoken my private opinion; that his proposal to me was, in three words, only a proposal to gain time, to which I was persuaded Lord Malmesbury, from his confidence in his friend, would consent, and that I would go immediately and bring him a written answer to his note. "But," said he, "if we put the answer, which will come from the Directory to-morrow, into civil words, will you answer it civilly, and wait?" I said, "Certainly." "But your Cabinet will think we are doing nothing. Will you send over a confidential person (for we must intreat you not to write) who will explain verbally, *dans le tuyau de l'oreille de votre Ministre*, that Lord Malmesbury and my friend are jointly labouring on the same subject, and that, unpromising as the Negotiation now appears, we have still great hopes of concluding it by an honourable peace? I told him I did not see the present state of things in so flattering a light as he seemed to do, but that Lord Malmesbury *would* send over a confidential person. I then left him, and at ten o'clock at night returned to him with Lord Malmesbury's note, which I delivered to him, and which he is to restore to me this morning. Nothing new passed between us during the few minutes that I walked with him on the *esplanade*.

Tuesday, Aug. 1.—I called on Pein this morning, when he returned my note. He said that his friend had written to Noel in conformity to what we had agreed on, stating that he was desired by Talleyrand to insist on the necessity of some complaisance on the part of Holland; to remark that it was probable no future opportunity of making peace would be so favourable as the present; that the penury of the French finances was notorious; that it was impossible for the Directory to look forward to the formation of such a marine as, with the fullest assistance from Spain, aided by the navy of the Batavian Republic, could face that of England; that the whole navy of Holland, being now blocked up by a small English squadron, and that of Spain by a fleet far inferior in number—the Brest squadron, whatever might be its spirit of enterprise, could do nothing; that the remainder of the Dutch colonies must probably soon fall. That the Directory was ready to go all lengths for the purpose of fulfilling its treaties, but that the Dutch must feel the difficulty of continuing a war which must henceforward become a naval war, without money or ships, or effective allies, and contrary to the decided wishes of all Europe and the French nation.

I told him all this was very good sense, and I trusted it would be listened to with attention; but that it was impossible seriously to suppose for a moment that the

Directory, if truly desirous of peace, were unable to force the Dutch to compliance. That in his conversation of yesterday he had stated a circumstance to which I had not at that moment time enough to make any reply, being so much pressed by the necessity of procuring the quickest possible answer to his friend's note; but that certainly the Directory were not bound to the performance of the secret articles by which they pretended to be confined, since it was absurd to suppose that any such money transactions as he had alluded to could have been kept secret in Holland. He said, "You certainly misunderstood me. The sum of money to which I alluded is mentioned in the public articles. Great part of it has not been paid, and in our distress we want that money extremely. It was stipulated in a secret article, that we should compensate for the large sum demanded by obtaining from you the restitution of all you had taken or might take from them. How can we now press for payment on one side, and refuse the condition to which we had bound ourselves? It is for this reason that address is necessary. If the Plenipotentiaries were now at Paris, invested with full powers, it would be easy for Talleyrand to carry his point with them. But the Dutch are aware of this, and it is therefore that Noel's commission is so difficult. I answered, "In this case, why did the Directory, in November last, agree to the principle of mutual compensation, and why did they lately propose to treat in the name and on the part of their Allies, since it appears by what you now say, if I understand you right, that you had not, and have not, full powers? His answer was rather extraordinary: "Je pourrais vous remarquer en général que le Directoire ne sait ce qu'il dit. D'ailleurs, pour répondre à votre première question, le Directoire ne voulait pas la paix, il voulait savoir votre dernier mot, découvrir où se bornaient vos prétentions; vous faire une querelle d'Allemand, et vous renvoyer. Quant à la seconde, il a encore agi sottement. Il espérait dominer les circonstances, et il se trouve dominé par elles. Vos objections sont sans réplique. Mais que voulez-vous? la paix? Je vous avais déjà dit dès notre premier entretien, que le *biais* qu'on vient d'imaginer pourroit nous y mener, et je le crois encore, pourvu que vous y consentiez. Le moyen que nous employons nous fait peu d'honneur, il est vrai, mais que vous importe s'il vous mène où vous voulez arriver ?"

I thought that nothing could be added to these remarks, and therefore, changing the subject, I observed to him, that his friend's note of yesterday requested, and indeed stipulated, perfect secrecy on the part of Lord Malmesbury; and that this secrecy would, I was afraid, defeat the whole object that his friend had in view. That, while the Directory insisted on keeping such untenable ground, I could not guess how his friend could frame an ostensible answer, that should at all convey the spirit of his private assurances. That Lord Malmesbury, acting under orders which had been submitted to the confidential servants of His Majesty, must satisfy the Cabinet that he was not so far hurried away by his private wishes for peace, as to act in opposition to those orders. He interrupted me here, and said, " Certainly ; we will take care that the communication which we shall make to you will not put you under the necessity of breaking off the Negotiation ; it shall express that the Directory will consult with our Allies ; and this will give Lord Malmesbury an opportunity of taking our answer, if he pleases, *ad referendum*. If Noel should succeed in his commission, which we shall know in a few hours, it will then be for your Cabinet to determine what instructions they will give you on the subject, and to relax or desist in their present demands. You are hitherto bound to nothing. If this cause were pleaded before a jury of Frenchmen, before the whole French nation, they would certainly think your present demands very fair, because it is certainly just that your gains by the war should be in some measure proportionate to ours. I have already explained to you that the Directory are perfectly unlike such a jury, but you can lose nothing by a little delay. The strength of the Directory sinks every hour." I said this might be true, but that I could conceive the Directory might in some respects be great gainers by delay ; that the signature of the Definitive Treaty with Austria, for instance —He interrupted me and said, " The mere approach of peace has given strength to the Councils, and every additional step towards it must add to their strength. The wish for peace is, as you know, universal in France, and has long been so; but the many complicated interests which it would have been necessary to reconcile, had we negotiated when we had Austria and all Germany for our enemies, would have eternally offered new subterfuges to the Directory. The question is now become so plain, that they will very soon have no means of evading it." I replied, that, though this did not quite satisfy my mind, it was not necessary for *me* to make any more remarks on the subject. "But," said I, "why should you give in any written declaration at all? why not ask for a Conference? You must feel that your note, word it as you will, cannot meet all the objections stated to you in our last. It is notorious that you did invite us to treat with you as Plenipotentiaries for your Allies; you now say you are not so. Why put this proof of your evasion on paper? Besides, this want of notes is ridiculous. It would be better that our Court should correspond with yours, as you proposed last year, by couriers. *We* at least should be so much better amused in London than at Lisle. Cannot your friend explain to Le Tourneur that he is making himself the most ridiculous of all ex-directors, and that part of the business of a negotiator is to negotiate?" He answered that he would not fail to convey the proposal to Maret, and that he agreed in opinion with me. I then said, "You have hitherto taken no notice either of Spain or Portugal, and yet the last instructions of the Directory relate to the interests of Spain as well as those of Holland." He replied, "C'est vrai; mais ne vous inquiétez pas sur l'Espagne, nous saurons bien la mener où nous voulons. Ce n'est pas qu'elle ne soit honnêtement déraisonnable, ce n'est pas l'embarras! Cabarras a bien remis au Directoire des pretentions excessives, et Del Campo s'évertue depuis quelque temps pour qu'on y fasse un peu d'attention; mais on trouve tout cela si absurde qu'on ne songe seulement pas à y répondre. Non, vous pouvez être tranquille là dessus." In faith, I did not think it necessary to make any comment on this whimsical and laconic answer, but again pressed him on the subject of Portugal; observing to him that the integrity of the Portuguese possessions was so much a *sine quâ non*, that, if he foresaw any difficulty on that subject, he had better save himself and me any further trouble by stating it, as that would certainly compel us to put an end to the Negotiation. He said, "Non, Le Portugal ne sera jamais un accroc ; si les intérêts des Bataves s'arrangent, vous pouvez compter que nous arriverons sans difficultés considérables à la paix." Our conversation ended by his telling me, that, the courier not being yet arrived, we should do well to meet to-morrow at the same hour ; and that he would not fail to communicate to me in time the substance of the instructions that should arrive, in order that the two Plenipotentiaries might perfectly understand each other before the Conference.

WEDNESDAY, AUG. 2.—I met Pein this day at the usual hour, when he told me the despatches from the Directory were not yet arrived, and that they would not arrive till Friday, because they were to come by the common post, and not by a special courier. He said, Maret and Le Tourneur had received private letters from Carnot and from Guiraudet, but that these letters contained nothing beyond what we knew, except that the present delay had been owing to the ceremonies and forms of the reception of the Turkish Ambassador, which had prevented the Directory and Minister for Foreign Affairs from meeting in time to sign the despatches. I told him that such an excuse was not very honourable to any of the persons concerned, because it did not evince the impatient desire of putting a stop, at the first possible moment, to the calamities of Europe, which the French Government were so much in the habit of proclaiming. "But," said I, "since this delay, which I regret for many reasons, is unavoidable, I wish you would endeavour to turn it to some advantage. You have assured me repeatedly, and I hope with truth, that the interests of Holland are the only serious obstacles to the conclusion of peace ; that it is the only point on which the full powers of your Legation

are incompetent, the only point which necessarily requires
a reference to the Directory. Now, I am perfectly satisfied
that you do not wish to deceive me ; I hope you do me
the same justice : but this conviction on your part, and on
mine, can in no way satisfy the English Cabinet ; they will
and ought to require proof, and this proof it is in your
power to furnish. I wish you to press this on your friend
Maret, and you will now have full leisure to do it. If
the present difficulty were at this moment removed, it is
evident that the remaining articles will require some discussion, some time before they can be arranged. I will
suppose that the interests of Spain and of Portugal, the
articles respecting the renewal of treaties, the King's titles,
the Toulon ships, &c. are all subaltern objects; still it is
evident that they are not without difficulty, because your
Legation began by making difficulties about them. There
are also many points of detail to be arranged, particularly
those respecting the West Indies, which will require much
patient and deliberate investigation. You are sensible
that the wild spirit of innovation and revolutions has
created in the colonies numberless evils, which the whole
power of our two Governments, employed in its fullest
extent and directed with the utmost wisdom, will with
difficulty remove. Let the respective Legations, therefore,
occupy themselves, provisionally at least, with these articles.
If, as you say, these points are easily settled, are you not
sensible of the immense advantages that would attend the
settling them as soon as possible ? Is it not evident that
the two Legations would, in the course of these discussions,
necessarily get rid of that jealousy and distrust which must
necessarily subsist at first between the representatives of rival
powers ? Is it not evident that they would become mutually
anxious for the completion of a work in which they were
far advanced ? Would they not suggest mutual facilities,
and assist each other in making the most favourable impressions on their respective Governments ? Besides, the
question would stand very differently from what it now
does, if you could say to the friends of peace in both
countries, 'All difficulties but one are now removed, a
single step on either side will enable you to sign the

peace.' It is no longer a haughty Directory advancing an absurd and inadmissible claim as a preliminary to all negotiation, stating the most absurd pretensions in the most offensive form, but a Government expressing its desire of peace, while it alleges the stipulations of treaties as an excuse for not going all lengths in order to obtain it." He listened to this very attentively, and promised to communicate it to his friend, and then said, after some hesitation, "Why does not Lord Malmesbury make this proposal?" I said, "He wished to do so; but it is essential that he should first secure your friend's co-operation. If your Legation should reject so just and reasonable a proposal, would it not operate as a fresh affront? Would it not shew that your friend, however zealous in his wishes for peace, is perfectly unable to promote it? Would it not effectually destroy the weight of every argument that Lord Malmesbury can urge to dissuade our Cabinet from breaking off the Negotiation?" He acquiesced in this, and again promised to urge this point with all his power.

I then reverted to the strange conduct of the Directory, and expressed my apprehension that Lord Malmesbury would be unable to state the matter at home in such a way as to convince any part of the Cabinet that there remained even that slight hope of success which his friend had admitted in his note to be the only hope. He immediately said with great eagerness, " I feel this as strongly as you do, and it is my greatest cause of anxiety. Certainly, if the Directory sincerely wished for peace, they would force the Dutch to withdraw all opposition, promising to indemnify them for the sums already paid to France, as soon as the state of our finances should permit it. The inhabitants of France would gladly pay for peace almost any contributions,—indeed they know that much higher contribution must be exacted from them if the war should continue. But the Directory are not sincere. It was proposed to them to compel the Dutch to come to terms; the proposal was rejected. My friend proposed to them to order the Dutch Commissaries to this place, where *he* hoped to bring them to terms; this too was rejected. Talleyrand proposed to appoint a special Minister at the Hague for the same purpose, and we hoped to fix the

choice on Simonville. In this, too, he failed. All he could
obtain after the Directory had ordered the Dutch Ministers
to repair to Paris, was the permission to send some fresh instructions to Noel, alleging as a reason for it, that the Directory would only make themselves ridiculous by affecting to
consult their Allies, if those Allies should afterwards appear
to pay no regard to their remonstrances. He has written to
Noel, who is very well disposed; he has referred him to my
friend for further instructions, and we too have written.
Noel, I am sure, will exert himself to the utmost; Talleyrand
will not be inactive at Paris. We may expect an answer in
eight days from the Hague, and shall then be able to judge
whether our hopes are well or ill founded. I trust we shall
not be disappointed; but if we should—" and here he hesitated—" il faudra nous remettre à guerroyer." As I wanted
to know exactly what his ultimate expectation was, I pretended not to have heard this last phrase distinctly, and
said to him " Comment? vous voulez encore continuer la
guerre?" He replied, " No, certainly; we have still means
of success in our power, means which the Directory seem
not aware of; it will be very disagreeable to employ them,
but they must be tried if all others fail. The moment of
the return of peace and dismission of the armies must be the
moment of confusion and civil discord if we have not a strong
and well regulated Government, if we cannot put an end to
that unfortunate and disgraceful struggle which the *majority
in the Directory so foolishly and wickedly desire to provoke*
between the constituted authorities; but even at this risk
we must defend the Constitution. The Directory have a
right to conclude secret articles without the immediate participation of the Councils; but the Councils have a subsequent right to demand the communication of such articles,
and finally to break them if they appear incompatible with
the happiness of the people. Were it otherwise, it would
be in the power of the Directory to plunge us into war, which
they might render endless by means of secret articles.
Sooner than submit to the further continuance of the present
war, the Council of Five Hundred will certainly try this
desperate remedy; but they will not try it till every other
attempt has failed. Souvenez vous," he added, " que je

vous parle à cœur ouvert et sous le sçeau du plus profond secret ? Les longueurs de cette Négociation font désespérer, mais tâchez de ne pas perdre patience. Elles sont accablantes pour nous aussi, et—" As I found he had nothing more of importance to tell me, I interrupted him here by remarking, that what he had just said proved most forcibly the necessity of the measure I had recommended ; and that if he could shew to the Councils and the nation a treaty depending for its completion on the removal of one single difficulty, and that difficulty grounded solely on the obstinacy of the Directory, the friends of peace and the Constitution could not fail of success. We now parted, after agreeing to meet again on Friday, and to take care reciprocally that no point should be brought forward for litigation at any conference till his friend and Lord Malmesbury should have had an opportunity of concerting the means that might be necessary to remove any opposition on the part of Le Tourneur.

FRIDAY, AUG. 4.—I was sent for this morning to meet Pein ; he told me the Despatches were arrived, and that the French Legation had sent to propose a Conference with Lord Malmesbury to-day at one or two o'clock, when they would declare to him officially what I had so often heard privately. He said that he had communicated to his friend the proposals which I mentioned in my last number ; that he felt as strongly as we could do the disagreeable effects that might be produced by the total interruption of the public conferences; and that it would be proposed to Lord Malmesbury to-day to meet on every post-day, in order that, although neither party should have anything to communicate, they might not let the public into the secret of their inactivity. But he said, his friend did not see the possibility of forming at this moment any *contre-projêt*, or of discussing particular articles in that transmitted by Lord Malmesbury ; indeed, the very arguments he had used would shew the danger of attempting it, since the Directory would never suffer us to bring the whole Negotiation to one point, and thereby shew that the continuance of the war, if it should be continued, was owing solely to an obstacle which they had unconstitutionally thrown in the way of peace. I did not press this any further; and he continued, " Maret has received to-day a private letter from Talleyrand, which gives us great hopes of success. He writes word, that Lestevenon is arrived at Paris; that he has seen him, and is perfectly satisfied from his conversation that he may be easily brought to hear reason. I have no doubt, that in consequence of Noel's efforts the other Commissioners from Holland will be equally reasonable. And, in the mean time, my friend has been, I hope, usefully employed. You asked me the other day about Cabarras: do you know him?" I said, No, but he had seen Lord Malmesbury; and I gave him an account of so much of their conversation as I had been desired to communicate to him. He continued, " He is a vain, talkative man, without abilities, but possessed of considerable influence through his daughter, (Madame Tallien,) who is the mistress of Barras, and he has it in his power to be of use to us; he arrived here in his way to Amsterdam, where he is appointed to transact some money business. He received, a few hours after his arrival here, a Note from Del Campo, by a courier, stating that our Government had just communicated to him the present state of the Negotiation; that, with a view to shew their respect for the engagements contracted with their Allies, they had for the present suspended all discussion on the articles of the British *projét*; but that they hoped their Allies would, on their part, consider the fatal consequences likely to arise to all parties from the continuance of the war, and that they would not render such a continuance necessary by the exorbitancy of their pretensions. Cabarras immediately transmitted this Note to our Legation; and Maret waited on him about twelve o'clock yesterday. Knowing the vanity of the man, he immediately made his application to it. He wrote to the Commandant of the citadel to say he should probably have in the course of the day an opportunity of introducing to him Count Cabarras, the Plenipotentiary of a friendly Power, and a person highly esteemed by the Directory; and that it would be proper to receive him with all possible honour. He told Cabarras that the French Legation had received orders to direct their whole attention to the interests of the Allies; that, indeed, but for these interests, the peace between France and England would have been already signed; that he had, in addition to what was the duty of every Frenchman, particular reasons for wishing to merit the esteem of the Spanish Court and nation, as the Embassy to Madrid would be in future one of his principal objects of ambition. That, from his anxiety for their welfare, he thought it his duty to submit to him (Cabarras) his private opinion on the probable event of another campaign. That the superiority of the English navy was irresistible; that the distant colonies of Spain were consequently in great measure at its mercy; that, whatever might be the distress of the English finances, that of the French and Spanish treasury was much greater; and that in Spain this distress and weakness of Government might possibly lead to the most fatal consequences; that Spain had a right to insist, if she thought fit, on the continuation of the war, but that he wished him to consider, whether it would not be for the real interest of that country to be contented with the best terms that could be secured at present in the way of negotiation, without trying so formidable an experiment. Cabarras was very tractable; my friend never lost sight of him during the day, and having found an opportunity of proposing to him, without affectation, a visit to the citadel, where he was received with all the honours of war, (a circumstance which my friend represented as naturally due to a person of his merit,) he seemed to treat him with the most perfect confidence, and this morning shewed him the answer he had written to Del Campo, which was conceived in terms of the most perfect conformity to his advice. My friend then said to him, "It is in your power to do us a most essential service. An application similar to that which you have received has been made to the Dutch, and Noel has orders to second it as well as he can; but if you, whose influence on our Government is so well known, and who are the representative of another power in alliance with the Batavian Republic, would have the goodness to enforce all his arguments, there can be little doubt of your success. I am afraid it may be very inconvenient to you to be stopped at the Hague, instead of immediately pursuing your business in

Amsterdam ; but you must feel how much your Court is interested in this event, since the whole burthen of the war, if it should be continued, must fall on Spain and France,— the impotence of the Batavian Republic being sufficiently evident." This, too, Cabarras readily promised; and his assistance, though not of such importance as my friend affected to consider it, is very well worth having.

He then told me that he trusted Lord Malmesbury would find the French Legation very generally civil and cordial; and that, being sure of the co-operation of his friend, he would use all his address to gain over Le Tourneur. I said he might be easy on this head ; that the important point was to satisfy our Cabinet that the French Government was in earnest, and for this purpose it was necessary that Lord Malmesbury should be assured officially that the Allies had been applied to. He again repeated that this would certainly be done ; that indeed he had not seen the official despatches, because Le Tourneur was not up when he came away ; but that Talleyrand's letter was so precise, that he could have no apprehensions on that score ; and besides that, his friend, knowing he was not to see me till eleven, must have had since nine o'clock time enough to give him notice of any alteration if any had taken place.

The rest of our conversation was perhaps not worth repeating. I asked him if he was acquainted with La Réveillière Lépaux, of whom when I was last at Paris I had heard a more favourable character than he seemed to deserve. He said he was an irresolute, but not a bad man, and at present a mere agent in the hands of Rewbell, whose violence overpowered him ; that on the mere question of peace, if it stood clearly as an insulated question, Carnot would be nearly sure of gaining him over to their side, but that at present he conceived it to be implicated with the diminution of the Directorial authority.

I then asked him about these new Ministers. He said that their characters were indifferent to us, and that he was personally acquainted with only one of them, François de Neufchâteau, who was not deficient in talents, but probably little fitted for administration, particularly in troublesome times ; that of *Sotin* he knew nothing ; that Scherer was a friend of Pichegru,* and directed by him; that on Pichegru's resigning his command, the Directory had displaced Scherer, who was then at the head of a division of the Italian army; and that his late appointment to the Ministry was meant as a civility to Pichegru.

SATURDAY, 5.—Lord Malmesbury not having received at yesterday's Conference the official communication expected, I this day called on Pein to inquire into the reason of this change. He told me that, in fact, the despatches had not been exactly such as he had expected from Talleyrand's private letter; that indeed they communicated what had been done, but referred them to a future letter for instructions; and that Le Tourneur had not thought himself authorized under such orders to communicate the step which the Directory had taken, but had contented himself with assuring Lord Malmesbury that the delay augured well for the final success of the Negotiation; that the two Commissioners had hinted at the truth as plainly as they could venture to do; that, if Lord Malmesbury had pressed Le Tourneur with questions, he would quickly have divulged the secret, and that one of them had even been much alarmed at the facility with which he thought Lord Malmesbury appeared to understand them, but apprehensive that a person of common sagacity (which fortunately Le Tourneur is not) would have seen in that facility the proof that he had, through some secret channel, acquired a perfect knowledge of the truth.

I said, "This is, perhaps, all very true; but you should consider that it is not official, and therefore not satisfactory." "That I admit (replied he), and when I received your note, announcing your intended visit, I called on my friend, and suggested this to him as the probable cause of your uneasiness. He bade me assure you that it was not his fault, and observed, it cannot after all be of very great importance; if at to-morrow's meeting Lord Malmesbury will return to the

---

* Pichegru, at the head of the Republican armies, had conquered Holland and the Low Countries. His correspondence with Condé being discovered, he was banished in 1797. He entered into a conspiracy against Napoleon, 1804; was arrested, and found strangled in prison.

charge, and question Le Tourneur pretty closely, he will soon satisfy himself, and acquire the right of announcing in his public despatch the real cause of our delay. For the rest, if the Directory had made this application to their Allies with a mere view to gain time, they would of course have been ready enough to announce the measure as an excuse. He knows, too, that they would be capable of using it as a pretext, even if it were false; if he believes us at all, he must have more confidence in our assurances than he can have in the official assurances of the Directory; but I wish him, for many reasons, to resume the subject. My colleague will be sure to tell him enough, probably more than he ought—but that is no business of mine. The conduct of our Government is certainly very unsatisfactory; but if it is not such as to force the British Cabinet to break off the Negotiation (and, even if Lord Malmesbury were ignorant of all that we have communicated to him, I cannot think they would feel this necessity at present), I trust we shall yet bring matters to a favourable conclusion." Here our interview ended.

SATURDAY, 12.—Pein told me that he had only wished to see me in order to inquire whether D'Aranjo in his communication with Lord Malmesbury had inclosed a copy of the Treaty, and, if not, whether we thought it important to procure one. He then said, that Maret had received a sketch of it from Talleyrand containing all the articles, excepting those which consisted solely of forms; and that he would immediately fetch it, provided I would promise to get it copied within an hour, because it was essential that Le Tourneur should not suspect its communication.* He then added, that he had seen a letter from Talleyrand that morning, stating that he was promised some important and pleasing intelligence from the Hague by the next post; but that, as the acceptance of the Constitution would probably put it out of the power of Noel to communicate such intelligence so very soon, he could not venture to expect it in less than four or five days. He told me, also, that Noel had written to Maret in such terms as to make him very con-

* This Mr. Ellis did, and Lord Malmesbury sent it to England.

fident of success. He observed, that Talleyrand's letter contained one circumstance which he hoped augured very well for our ultimate success, viz. "that his last accounts from Thugut contained assurances that the Court of Vienna were as little disposed as the Directory to delay the work of peace by the unnecessary forms of a Congress, and that they were determined to conclude it separately, and as speedily as possible."

On the 22nd Pein told me, that, if Aranjo had possessed common honesty, he might have made a very different Treaty for Portugal; that Thugut's letters were explicit on the subject of peace with the Emperor, which would immediately be signed; and that the Directory was equally anxious to make one with England, and popularize themselves.

LORD MALMESBURY'S DIARY RESUMED.

AUG. 11.—Maret came, for the first time, into my box. He said he had been thirty months in close confinement (*au secret*); that St. Estevenon had given in his resignation; that he had *un procès criminel* in Holland. Said the Spaniards did not appear so well disposed as he expected. (N.B. This explained by Pein.)

AUG. 15.—At the *Spectacle de la Société Dramatique*, led by the inhabitants of Lisle. Conversed with Maret, Le Tourneur, M. and Mde. Ducos. Maret said the *Gouvernement Provisoire* in Holland were timid and cautious. In about five days they ought to have an answer. Ducos apparently clever.

AUG. 16.—Thirteenth Conference.—Nothing of any sort passed but common conversation; the same on the 14th, and on the 18th instant. Talking of the late Negotiation,* Le Tourneur said, that I saw very little of the Minister; that all the negotiation passed in Notes; he said, "Votre

* At Paris, in the preceding year.

rapport étoit très bien fait." I replied, "I had made it as exact as possible." "It certainly was so," said Maret, " puisqu'on n'en a pas fait la moindre réclamation." Le Tourneur said, " et je vous assure nous en étions très contents au Directoire." We talked about an article in the French papers which gave a very exact account of what we were doing. I said, it was certainly written in France, though dated London. Le Tourneur seemed to admit it, and that the *Eclair* had a correspondent here.

They said they hoped things were going on well at Paris; that *universal tranquillity* depended on it. " Si on tire un coup de canon à Paris, il sera senti par toute l'Europe. C'est le repos qu'il nous faut," said Le Tourneur, " un long repos après une si cruelle guerre." I inquired what was passing in Holland. " The primary assembly refuse the Constitution," said Le Tourneur, and added, " cela augmente l'embarras; en vérité nous avons mal fait de ne pas leur avoir envoyé une Constitution toute faite, et de leur avoir dit, Tenez, voilà la Constitution telle qu'il nous la faudroit; acceptez la." I agreed with him entirely.

Le Tourneur called the play written by Fabre Eglan, " *du vrai et bon Molière.*"

---

August 17.—Maret and all *his* dependents, viz. Colchen, De L'Orme, &c., came into my box, and remained during the whole of the two last acts of the play. No politics. They said the innkeeper of Venice (the play was " Le Roi Théodore à Venise") when in his uniform was like General Santerre. On this and every other occasion Maret took an opportunity of expressing his dislike to revolutionary principles, and always said, " *du temps de la révolution,*" or " *maintenant que la révolution est finie.*"

---

August 18.—In the box of the French Legation at the play. Conversation with Madame Ducos about English novels. Maret said he had no news. De L'Orme a quick, sensible man. Ducos a ———. These two, Secretaries. A third called *Isidore*, who seems less trusted. Poullin, Secretary to Le Tourneur, has a wife. Le Tourneur himself recently married. Maret said he was " un homme très casanier, bon père, bon mari."

EXTRACTS OF A LETTER FROM LORD GRENVILLE TO LORD MALMESBURY.

Cleveland Row, 18th Aug., 1797.

THIS Portuguese business is of bad omen for what is to come from Talleyrand. You may be assured that the whole has been settled entirely by him and D'Aranjo, and the Court of Lisbon* is no party to it, as indeed the inclosed despatch to him, sent here under flying seal, sufficiently demonstrates. If the Directory refuses to listen to any discussion upon the subject, our Negotiations must break off. If the business is referred to Lisle, it will much embarrass your proceedings; because it will be of course more difficult to make them recede from an advantage gained, and which they have made matter of triumph at Paris, than it would have been to have stood firm upon this point, which they have no pretence to insist upon. The best expedient that I can devise is, that (supposing the two parties agreed on all other points) the Directory should declare, for which the words would afford me grounds, that these stipulations had reference only to the present war, and expire with its termination. This, if coupled with the signature of peace, and made a part of it, we might accept; but not otherwise, as in any other case it would afford to the enemy both a motive and a means of continuing the war. But I greatly doubt whether the period of peace is yet arrived. There seems so much insolence, and such an overbearing opinion of their own consequence and power, even among those who profess themselves the best disposed, that I fear it will be impossible yet to obtain such terms as we must require. Our best chance is in patience and firmness; but these are no security against such dispositions as we have to contend with.

* Eventually the Court of Lisbon, refusing to ratify the terms of the Treaty signed by Mons. D'Aranjo on the 10th August at Paris, the Directory, on the 26th October, declared it null and void.

We have no other account than through you, of the Emperor's resolution to treat for definitive peace at Udine; but I have no doubt of the fact.

DESPATCH FROM LORD GRENVILLE TO LORD MALMESBURY.

Downing Street, 19th Aug., 1797.

My Lord,—His Majesty has learnt with the deepest concern the particulars of the transaction concluded by M. D'Aranjo at Paris, both because the clandestine and precipitate manner in which the business has been conducted affords indisputable proofs of the total absence of a sincere and candid disposition for peace on the part of His Majesty's enemies, and because the nature of the terms contained in the Treaty signed by M. D'Aranjo must very much embarrass the future progress of the Negotiation in which your Lordship is engaged.

From the whole tenour of the communications received by His Majesty from the Court of Lisbon, and, most of all, from those which M. D'Almeida has made here within these few days, in consequence of orders dated at two different periods subsequent to the date of the alleged full powers of M. D'Aranjo, there cannot be the smallest doubt that this Minister, in treating separately for peace with France, has not only exceeded, but *positively disobeyed* the instructions of his Court; the terms to which he has agreed are so directly in contradiction to the subsisting treaties between His Majesty and the Court of Lisbon, and to the whole system on which the political union between Great Britain and Portugal is founded, (particularly in the refusal of supplies to His Majesty's Navy, and the exclusion of his vessels, beyond a limited number, from the Portuguese ports,) that His Majesty cannot possibly consent to, or even acquiesce in, this sacrifice of his unquestionable rights, made without his knowledge or consent, and by the unauthorized act of the Minister of his Ally. Mr. Walpole has therefore been instructed to require, that the Court of Lisbon shall, in conformity to its repeated assurances and engagements, *decline to ratify this Treaty*, or at least give only a conditional and qualified ratification of it; reserving for discussion between the Ministers of the Three Powers at Lisle all those parts of the fourth and fifth articles in which the rights or interests of Great Britain are in any way affected : and he is expressly ordered, if necessary, to enforce this demand by the most explicit declaration, that any attempt on the part of Portugal to obstruct the accustomed resort of His Majesty's ships to the Portuguese ports will be considered as an act of hostility, and acted upon by them as such.

The only other remark with which I have to trouble your Lordship by this messenger relates to an expression in the late message of the Directory to the Council of Five Hundred, which, if literally taken, conveys an accusation against His Majesty's Government that some delay has arisen on the part of this country in the negotiation at Lisle. This is so avowedly contrary to the fact, that it must be considered as impossible that such a charge could be intended to be made by a Government which had at that moment delayed for three weeks making any answer to His Majesty's distinct and liberal proposals of peace, and whose Plenipotentiaries were daily apologizing to your Lordship for this unbecoming, and, as they almost confess, unaccountable delay. But, as the point is too important to be left unnoticed, it is the King's pleasure that your Lordship should present a Note, remarking upon the sense to which these words are liable, expressing your persuasion that such cannot be the intention with which they were used, but asking, on the part of your Court, an explanation to that effect, and which cannot be refused without a violation of every thing which truth and justice require on such an occasion.

LETTER FROM MR. PITT TO LORD MALMESBURY.

Downing Street, 19th Aug., 1797.

My dear Lord,—You will see, by the public instructions, the impression made here by the manner of concluding the Portuguese peace, and still more by the terms as contained in the fourth and fifth Articles. They are certainly directly contrary to the express provisions of our Treaty with Portugal in 1703, and such as that Court could not justly agree to without our consent at any time, much less after the repeated and recent assurances given us on this very subject. The preventing us from the full and free use of the Portuguese ports, is also in itself a point of the utmost practical importance. The facility, if not the possibility, of blocking or watching Cadiz during a great part of the year, depends, in a great measure, on the use of those ports; and with it the means of obstructing the junction of the French and Spanish fleets, or the detaching the latter to the West Indies or other remote parts of our dominions. Our means would, therefore, be crippled by this concession in every future naval war; and in the present (if it continues) we should sacrifice one of the proudest, or rather one of the few proud parts of our situation, the blockade of Cadiz, and with it impair materially the security of the Irish, if not our own coasts, and of our Colonies. The prospect of such a change in our means of war might (if we acquiesced in it) be perhaps more likely than anything else to encourage a perseverance in the war, or in unreasonable terms of peace. On these grounds I feel strongly the necessity of our making a stand; but I own I do not feel as much discouraged by the circumstance as some others.* I think it is a *natural*, though an *unworthy* game in those we are treating with; but I do not much expect that, if other points could be settled, this would stand in the way of peace. The expedient Lord Grenville has mentioned is, I think, a very good one; and, either in that shape or some other, the same mixture of firmness, conciliation, and address, by which you have already smoothed so many obstacles, will, I trust, be as successful when applied to this. I rather hope we shall hear from you again on Monday or Tuesday. We are as impatient for a *contre-projêt* as if we were at Lisle. Canning will have told you how much we were gratified by the communications from Lord Granville and Wesley. I have had the good fortune to see a good deal of Lord Granville since his arrival, and

---

* Alluding to Lord Grenville.

of course am more and more pleased with him. Your last separate letter put the secret intelligence into an excellent form for communication; and Mr. Ellis's friend has the merit of furnishing one of the most *interesting*, and certainly the most entertaining dialogues that ever made part of a negotiation. Such episodes must be not a little wanting to enliven Lisle. Believe me, &c. (Signed) W. PITT.

AUG. 19.—A Mr. Melville, of Boston, in America, makes the same offer as to Barras.* He declares he made the peace with Portugal by means of money (ten or twelve millions of livres) given to the Directory. He proposes to us fifteen millions. Of course his offer was rejected. I would not see him, and he conveyed it through Ellis. He was about twenty-six, reserved and vulgar—says he knew Perrégeaux intimately. Ellis saw him twice in the morning and afternoon. He said Réveillière Lépaux would not take money, but Barras and Rewbell would. I suspect him to be the same person who was mentioned to me at Paris by D'Aranjo, as one who had officiously interfered in his business, and done mischief. He has been at Boston.

AUG. 20, SUNDAY. — Sent Ellis to inform Pein of what Melville had said. He not at home.† Play at the Société Dramatique. Maret there without his colleagues. He told me, an answer very unsatisfactory, and drawn up in a high tone, had been received from Holland; but that M. Talleyrand had taken on himself to send it back, and required another. This, he said, proved how much Talleyrand wished to promote peace.

On resuming the subject of my last negotiation, Le Tourneur said, " Vous et Charles Delacroix n'ont jamais pu vous

* A person named Potter came to Lord Malmesbury at the beginning of the negotiation, stating, that he was sent by Barras to say, that if the English Government would pay that Director 500,000*l.* he would ensure the Peace. Lord Malmesbury, believing the offer to be unauthorized by Barras, or only a trap laid for him by the Directory, paid no attention to it.—*Harris' Papers.*

† When he told Pein, the latter knew nothing of it, and advised him to refer to Perrégeaux for Mr. Melville's character.

rapprocher." I said, "Que j'avais été content de lui;" and mentioned an account which had just appeared of the whole of this business. They expressed a curiosity to see it, and Le Tourneur said, "Si jamais on publie l'histoire de celle-ci, j'espère que l'on rendra justice à la loyauté que nous y avons tous mis de part et d'autre." In conversing again on Holland, he said, "Le Gouvernement Provisoire est trop foible; il n'ose rien prendre sur lui."

15TH CONFERENCE this day.—Nothing remarkable.—Delay still on the part of the French Legation.

16TH CONFERENCE, TUESDAY, 22.—See despatches.

17TH CONFERENCE, THURSDAY, AUG. 24.—Still no news from the Directory. Le Tourneur said, "Qu'il en étoit bien aise." So said also both Maret and Colchen. It was a certain proof that things were going on well. We conversed for a quarter of an hour on common subjects.

No Conference on Saturday, the 26th, as Maret was at Dunkirk.

18TH CONFERENCE, MONDAY, AUG. 28.—Further delays. Answer from Holland sent back by the Directory. Le Tourneur called it "complexe et louche."

EXTRACTS OF A DESPATCH FROM LORD MALMESBURY TO LORD GRENVILLE.

Lisle, 22nd Aug., 1797.

IN my conference of this morning I took an opportunity of remarking to the French Plenipotentiaries on the very unfair and extraordinary assertion which had appeared in the message of the 9th instant from the Directory to the Council of Five Hundred, viz. "*Que les puissances coalisées ont mis autant de lenteur dans les Négociations, qu'Elles avaient montrée de l'ardeur pour les terminer.*" I observed to them that I had orders from my Court to ask a precise explanation whether this accusation of delay was meant to apply to the manner in which His Majesty had conducted the negotiation at Lisle; and if it was meant so to declare, no accusation was ever more destitute of foundation, nor a wider deviation from the real fact. I observed, I was perfectly ready to abide by their determination on this point, convinced that it was impossible for them not to acknowledge that the delay (if there had been any blamable delay) rested with the French Government, and not with His Majesty.

The French Plenipotentiaries admitted this to be most strictly true; that the phrase I had quoted was an ill-judged one, and *mal rédigé*, but that it could not in any point of view whatever be construed as applying to England; and they were ready to say, that, when it was written, the Directory alluded solely to the Court of Vienna. That they could assure me they had been very faithful, and that, when they said this, it was saying in other words that I had carried on the negotiation with as much expedition as possible; that, if it had proceeded slowly for this last month, the slowness arose on their side, and not on mine.

M. Le Tourneur, with very strong expressions, assured me the Directory certainly did think and feel like them, that no unfair or invidious allusion was meant; and added, "*Que ce message était fait pour stimuler les Conseils.*" I went on by observing it was very essential to me to have this fully explained, and that I should give them in a Note to this effect.

They requested I would not; it would lead to disagreeable discussions, and it would not answer the end I proposed. They would take upon themselves *now* to assure me, in the name of the Directory, that nothing at all similar to the construction I put on the phrase was intended, and that, as soon as they could receive an answer to the report they should make of to-day's conversation, they would say the same from the Directory itself.

I hope, my Lord, I have therefore, by obtaining this very precise and formal disavowal of an intention to fix any imputation of delay on His Majesty's Government, fulfilled the object of my instructions on this particular point.

EXTRACT OF A DESPATCH FROM LORD MALMESBURY TO LORD
GRENVILLE.

Lisle, 22nd Aug., 1797.

I HEAR from good authority that letters were received by M. Talleyrand on Friday last, with accounts from Baron Thugut and M. Gallo, so explicit on the subject of peace, that every difficulty relative to the conclusion of the definitive treaty with Austria is removed, and that we may expect in a very few days to receive news of its being actually signed. An Austrian agent, it is said, is already at Paris.

In regard to the peace with Portugal, I am told that the Directory were so anxious to conclude this treaty, that, if the Chevalier D'Aranjo had been either a very able or very faithful Minister, he might have made very nearly his own conditions. My informant* admits that one of the objects was to insulate England, and separate her from all her allies; but insists that the great motive which induced the Directory to proceed on this occasion with so much precipitation was to gain popularity with the public and the army, and to give an air of probability to their pacific assurances.

An answer arrived about a week ago from Holland, drawn up in a high and discontented tone: a full performance of all the engagements France has entered into with the Batavian Republic was insisted on. The Dutch enumerate the great sacrifices they have already made for France, and allege them as a fair plea for their not consenting to any cession of territory. This answer M. Talleyrand took upon himself to send back to the Hague, saying it was not such a one as he could venture to shew to the Directory; that the Dutch *must* consent to enter into a negotiation for some cession of territory, or risk the loss of the friendship of France. And he went so far as to say, that the form of answer they were expected to return would be explained to them by M. Noel. It will arrive at Paris to-morrow or next day, and of course at this place about the time that M. Le Tourneur mentioned he expected it. My informant pointed out to me that I was to infer from this, that the pacific party was gaining ground, since M. Talleyrand could not have ventured

* M. Pein.

to take so strong a step as that of sending back the letter from the Dutch without communicating it to his employers, and of insisting on a different answer, if he were not sure of very sufficient support; and, if the premises laid down are not false, the conclusion is certainly a very reasonable one to draw.

EXTRACTS OF A LETTER FROM LORD MALMESBURY TO MR. CANNING.

Lisle, 22nd Aug., 1797.

LET G. Ellis's long letter tell for us both to-day.* I promise you faithfully by the next messenger one as long on the same cursed subject.

You will see my private letters to Lord Grenville; they will speak for themselves. I felt all the horrors of Aranjo's rascality when it first was made known to me; but I wished somehow or other that you would not feel it at home, and leave to Providence the care of repairing this work of the devil, which, unless Providence does, I do not know who can.

Surely it was a hasty measure, the ordering me to give *in a note* on those foolish expressions in the Message from the Directory;† and I trust, as you had time to cool, the line of conduct I have adopted will not be disapproved, or deemed inadequate to the end proposed. You may, however, if you please, recall me for *disobedience* of orders, and try me by a *Court Cabinet;* I will bow down with submission to the sentence.

I knew Walpole very well some five and twenty years ago: he is not a bright man, but with a plain strong understanding, and I think will not execute ill the orders he is to receive. What is to be done if Her Most Faithful Majesty has already ratified? Go mad, like her!

* Giving an account of the secret negotiations.
† On the message of the Directory to the Councils, attributing the delays of the Negotiation to the English Cabinet. Lord Malmesbury did not present it, contenting himself with a strong verbal condemnation of the message by the Plenipotentiaries. He saw by this time that peace was safe if Maret's party remained in power, and impossible if they lost it.

THURSDAY, AUG. 24.—Le Tourneur came into my box with Poullin, his secretary. Le Tourneur very communicative. He said that the first answer which came from Holland was a refusal to give up anything. This was sent back by Talleyrand. The second was little better: it was *très entortillé*. This the Directory sent back angrily on the 21st, and dictated a third to them, counselling them to consent to reasonable sacrifices. "It would be better," said Le Tourneur, very *naïvement*, "if the *usages diplomatiques* allowed us to be sincere at once, and to declare our last word at first. But this cannot be, we must go through the necessary forms of negotiation; but we shall end well." He said Spain would be as tractable as Holland at last. I led him to talk of this country, and I chose to agree with him to induce him to talk; and said that the Councils were now in a quite opposite system, and seemed to think all imposts wrong. Le Tourneur flew out against the Councils, and betrayed all his Directorial leanings. I encouraged him in his feelings, and he ended by expressing himself as clearly and distinctly as if he had been conversing with a brother Director. He complained, however, bitterly, of being left here without information, and of the limitation of his full powers; and said, what I believe is really true, that, if the Negotiation succeeds, it will be principally owing to the conduct of the two Legations; "for," said he, "our *principals* have not helped us much,—at least," added he, "les nôtres nous ont abandonnés bien cruellement." Ellis, who had seen Moulin this morning, heard from him all that Le Tourneur had told me; and the consequence is, that some days must yet pass before our negotiation will be afloat again.

AUG. 25.—At the play Maret told me he had postponed his intended journey to Dunkirk till the next day, in order to write by Poullin to Paris; that he wished also to receive letters he expected from Talleyrand; the accounts he had hitherto received of the last step taken relative to the Dutch not having come immediately from him (Talleyrand), but from another member of the Government. I asked him when he thought, really and seriously, this long-expected answer would arrive, and he calculated the time. The second answer (that which Le Tourneur called *entortillé*) got to Paris on the 19th of August, and was communicated on the 20th to the Directory. It was deliberated on the 21st, returned on the 22nd to the Dutch Plenipotentiary, with a strong note and *injunction* to demand a more explicit answer, and one more conformable to the intentions of the Directory. This the Dutch Plenipotentiaries could not take on themselves to do. Their express left Paris for the Hague early on the 23rd. I observed, that at least a week must elapse before an answer could arrive here ; that it would not be before the first week in September that any could be expected, unless Noel was authorized to transmit it to them here, and they authorized to act upon it. This was not the case, he said. He added, that he was puzzled about letting the Dutch Ministers come here. They wished it. He thought it might do good if he and I were to see them *separately*, but not at the Conference. I said I had thought over this circumstance, and was not prepared with an opinion on it. We then fell into common conversation, and he said they meant to take a short excursion on the sea when at Dunkirk. I desired him to be careful not to be taken prisoner. Lord Morpeth, Wesley, and Ellis visited the Colonel of Hussars this morning, Monsieur Dudevant, and found him at home and extremely civil. I walked round the whole ramparts, about four miles.

SATURDAY, AUG. 26.—De L'Orme, one of Maret's secretaries, called upon me to say, that, as no letters of any importance had come from Paris, and as Maret was desirous of going to Dunkirk, he wished the intended Conference of to-day not to take place.

Le Colonel Dudevant called ; a native of Bordeaux—not a *ci-devant:* he brought two aides-de-camp with him—one of the name of Robert, who had been in Bengal, and served under Suffrein.

SUNDAY, AUG. 27.—Called on Dudevant and De L'Orme. Adjutant-General Paulet visited us in the evening—an ex-noble—talkative—rather vulgar—was aide-de-camp to

Biron,* native of St. Quentin—had been in England with the Duke of Cumberland—talks English—served against Spain—fond of talking of his exploits. Le Tourneur came into my box.

MONDAY, AUG. 28.—Writing—Conference—great civility—expressing a wish for our more frequent meetings—propose that we should belong to their society; went into Maret's box at the play—applause from the audience—De L'Orme and Isidore in my box. Maret told me, that, when the Directors drew in April, the two which remained last in the vase were Le Tourneur and Rewbell. Le Tourneur was to draw first; he took up one of the two remaining balls, but on reflection dropped it; took the other, in which was written "*Directeur sortant.*" Thus, said Maret, "le sort de la France a pensé dépendre d'un battement de pouls." Le Tourneur went on by saying, that he hoped it was now the same; that everything would go right; that he felt more easy than he was a fortnight ago. He talked of Dunkirk, of the beauty of the road, and said that they should very soon propose to us *une partie de campagne.*

TUESDAY, AUG. 29.—Visited Paulet with Ellis; some anecdotes from him about the death of Theobald Dillon,† who was killed by the people of this town near the Port St. Maurice, and about Biron. He praised Pichegru. Drove with Wesley; in the evening visited the French Legation—first visit; many people there; amongst others, General Vandamme.

WEDNESDAY, 30.—Wesley set out at 5 A.M. General Vandamme visited me at an early hour—very civil and conversable. Talked of his Dutch and German campaigns—much about Stutgardt, and the ruined state of the Duchy of

---

* Biron, better known as the *roué* Lauzun. His connection with the Duke of Orleans (Egalité) proved his ruin. Having at the age of forty-six commanded the Republican armies unsuccessfully, he was guillotined in 1793. He and Lord Malmesbury were companions at Berlin in 1773, and each speaks of the other in his Memoirs at that time.
† Surnamed Le Beau Dillon.

Wurtemberg, and the pride and etiquette of the Duke. Spoke of Count Walmoden, General Harcourt, Fox, Abercromby, &c. His chief object seemed to be, to declare himself a partisan of Moreau and Pichegru. He returned to Cassel, where his family live; he is about twenty-seven, and looks like a Dutchman. Conference—nothing passed. Maret and Ducos called after dinner. Long conversation with Maret: he said that General Vandamme was a suspicious character; that his visit to me was an insidious one; that he would spread false reports of our conversation; and Maret said he was sorry he had not let me know his character yesterday. I told him the substance of what passed between us, and the apparent nature of his visit. He said Vandamme was "un brave militaire, mais sa morale n'étoit pas sans reproche;" that he was always in motion, and was *sent* by the adverse party from one place to another, to collect news and give dangerous impressions. Maret then went very confidentially into the Dutch business; he read me the extract of a letter from Guiraudet (first secretary to Talleyrand); it says, "Nos amis dans les marais font les revêches d'une manière inconcevable;—Je ne conçois rien à leur conduite; ils nous parlent sans ménagement, et nous manquent dans les formes; ainsi le Directoire les traitent à l'avenant, et a *exigé* une réponse catégorique et conforme à ses vœux." Maret commented on this: he said he believed their obstinacy came from the expression employed in one of my memorials last year, in which I stated, that, if the Stadtholderian form of government was re-established, the King would not insist on such great cessions; that this expression was taken up by the partisans of the Prince of Orange, and used successfully in the Batavian Republic in general, to induce them to resist the proposals of the Directory. I treated this as a very *far-fetched* conjecture, and void of foundation; that it was idle to refer to what had been said under circumstances so very different from the present; that the Dutch must be aware of this, and that *he* and the Directory knew what our present idea about Holland was; and that it could not be supposed, either in wisdom or good faith, that we could encourage (for Maret seemed to have a suspicion of this sort) a conduct equally in contradiction to both. He said he was pleased to hear this, and did away his apparent doubts by the strongest professions of belief. I went on by saying it was much more natural to account for this inconsiderate conduct in the Dutch from the internal state of their own country—from "l'exaltation de leurs têtes, surtout des têtes gouvernantes, et probablement des avis que ces Messieurs continueroient à recevoir d'ici du parti auquel ils tenoient." Maret said, certainly not; that on this point the Directory were unanimous, and that he found the Dutch plenipotentiaries at Paris to be prejudiced and insufficient men.

I said "que cette affaire languissoit trop longtemps; que si les Hollandois ne vouloient pas entendre raison, qu'il faudroit leur forcer la main et déclarer qu'on feroit la paix sans eux." Maret assented to this; and I quoted the last peace as a sort of precedent. In regard to Spain, he continued in the same language. He added, "Il y a une communication du reste établie entre le Prince* de la Paix et le Ministre des Relations Extérieures, et nous sommes maîtres de la conduite de la Cour de Madrid."

It struck me, as he read a short letter from Guiraudet, that he put a much larger one in his pocket, which he had drawn out of it at the same time, saying, with a melancholy air, "Ceci regarde mes affaires particulières, qui sont très derangées par des vols qu'on m'a fait, tant chez l'Etranger, qu'en France." I said, "I trusted que L'Ambassade d'Angleterre réparerait tout cela;" and, without waiting for his answer, I went on by dwelling on the extreme importance of having a well-disposed and cool-headed person for that Embassy—one who, like him, had "les usages du grand monde, l'habitude des affaires, et aussi étoit sans préjugés." This I saw pleased him: he affected modesty and diffidence —mentioned Talleyrand and Chauvelin as proper persons. I said, Talleyrand would not surely quit the office he now held, and that *Chauvelin n'étoit pas en mesure.* Maret assented, and intimated, that if he was asked for, it would forward his nomination. He then told all the story of his two journeys to England, in 1792 and 1793; his connexion

---

* Godoy, the all-powerful favourite of Charles IV., and also of his Queen.

with Le Brun.* He said Mr. Pitt had received him very well, and that the failure of his negotiation could be attributed to the then French Government, who were bent on that war; that the great and decisive cause of the war was "quelques vingtaines d'individus marquans et en place qui avoient joués à la baisse dans les fonds, et là ils avaient porté la Nation à nous déclarer la guerre. Ainsi," said he, "nous devons tous nos malheurs à un principe *d'agiotage*." He said, on his return to France he was informed of this, and was considered as in possession of so dangerous a secret, that they wanted first to send him to Portugal, which he refused; then to Naples, which he was *forced to accept;* and that he had every reason to believe that his arrest and confinement were settled and concerted at Paris before he left. He said he spent thirty months in prison, partly at Mantua, (where, if he had staid, he must have died,) and partly in the Tyrol; that the academicians in Mantua, out of regard to the memory and character of his father, interested themselves about him, and that he believed he owed his change of prison to them; that, after all, his long confinement saved his life, as he certainly should have been guillotined had he remained in France, under the government of Robespierre. I inquired whether La Réveillière Lépaux being President instead of Barthelemi was of consequence. He said, inasmuch as declamatory and inflammatory speeches can do harm, but no farther;—that *four* Directors must be present at all deliberations, and that the President cannot conceal any measure resolved on from any member of the Directory. Maret said it was indolence, and perhaps timidity, which had induced Barthelemi not to have pushed for it. The Presidency was his right by turn, and it was very foolish of him to have given way. We then talked over the preliminary Notes which had passed on the opening of this negotiation. I said I was mentioned so disagreeably in one of them as to be very near declining the commission. He said it was very natural; but they were

* Maret's first mission related to the domestic concerns of the Duke of Orleans. He had an interview with Mr. Pitt, and gave a favourable account of it to the Convention, who sent him over again in January, 1793, with a conciliatory mission, which was rendered nugatory by the murder of Louis XVI. Le Brun, French Minister for Foreign Affairs in 1792-93.

drawn by Charles Delacroix, "qui n'entendoit rien aux devoirs de sa place et aux bienséances;" and he told me that he and his colleagues, from whom these Notes had been withheld until they were setting out, declared unanimously that the advantage was all on our side, both as to the matter and style. He ridiculed the absurd stipulations about packet-boats, and the pompous expression of "établir un principe," when applicable to packet-boats. He also strongly reprobated the form in which my passport was drawn up, which after all, however, he said, operated more against them than against us; and he applauded and admired our forbearance and temper on this occasion. In regard to my nomination, he said, the day it was known, he, Talleyrand, and several others, were at dinner with Barras, to whom Barthelemi mentioned it. They all agreed that it was a favourable omen for peace; that *the Mission would not have been offered to me, or I accepted it, had the intentions not been sincere and admissible;* and that the *words**\** used in the note were Charles Delacroix's own, and the note was sent before he communicated it to any one. He said, they really were ashamed of the idle aspersions which had been allowed to be propagated about me when I was at Paris, and still more for the brutal manners of Charles Delacroix. I said, that, as to the aspersions, I forgave them heartily; that, as for Charles Delacroix, "Je commençois à croire qu'il se *vantoit* de m'avoir mal traité; puisque dans le fond il a toujours eu vis-à-vis de moi des manières très honnêtes." Maret smiled. I said I spoke strictly true; that he was very observant of everything I did, and always did the same; that now and then he tried *terrification*, by letting out some strong Jacobin phrases; but, when he found this kind of declamation did not affect me, he left it off.

Maret brought a letter from Talleyrand to Huskisson. We went together at a late hour to the play, and afterwards walked round the town. Colchen came into my box, and we had a very pleasant and reasonable conversation.

\* Carping at Lord Malmesbury being the person appointed.

[The following despatch deserves attention, as it is a good recapitulation and explanation of the events at Lisle to the present date.]

EXTRACTS OF A DESPATCH FROM LORD MALMESBURY TO LORD GRENVILLE.

Lisle, 29th Aug., 1797.

It is so important to ascertain with precision whether the reasons alleged by the French Plenipotentiaries for delaying the Negotiation are really founded in truth, that I have spared no pains to investigate this very essential circumstance; and although, from its nature, it is impossible to get at anything like demonstration, yet I consider it as my duty to submit to your Lordship the result of my researches, rather in the hopes of enabling His Majesty's Government to form a safe opinion, than from the wish of suggesting one of my own.

I see no better mode of discovering the degree of credit which ought to be attached to the language of the French Legation, than by a summary recapitulation of what has passed, examining whether their assurances have hitherto been contradicted by facts, and whether from the whole (when seen at once) we shall have reasons to conclude that their professions have been sincere, or that their conduct has been contrived with a view of concealing some secret and treacherous purpose.

If we connect the very unsatisfactory result of our Conferences with what we hear from every quarter, there is reason to suppose, that, when the Directory agreed to a renewal of a pacific negotiation with His Majesty, it was done much more with a view of avoiding a direct opposition to the universal wishes of this nation, than with a sincere intention to negotiate. They, however, were studious to assume every appearance of being in earnest; and their Legation was sent here surrounded with more diplomatic appendages than ever were employed on a similar occasion. I, too, had my share in this *parade*, and was received on the road, and on my arrival, with a very unusual and affected degree of attention and ceremony.

The most formal civility subsisted between myself and

the French Plenipotentiaries during our first interviews; not a word irrelevant to the great subject in discussion was pronounced on either side, and we were perfect strangers to each other except at the moment of our Conferences; and there is little doubt that the majority of the Directory, when, on the 16th of July, they set forth their extravagant claim of a general restitution of all His Majesty's conquests, expected, and probably hoped, that the Negotiation would be broken off, either by my immediate act, or by that of His Majesty's Government.

In the mean time, however, enough of the reasonableness and moderation of His Majesty's proposals transpired to create a strong *peace party* in the Councils, and to make the Directory hesitate as to the safety of abruptly ending the Negotiation. The able and temperate instructions I received from your Lordship, and from which I formed the Note I gave in on the 24th of July, further contributed to defeat the object of the ill-intentioned Directors, and to assist those who wished to see the Negotiation terminate successfully. This Note is a great period in the Negotiation: everything which has passed since bears reference to it, or arises out of it; and the event, whatever it may be, will be determined by it.

Your Lordship will recollect, that, immediately after the reception of the hostile answer to our *projêt*, an overture was made to me on the part of the pacific party in this country, that the conduct which they meant to pursue was at the same time communicated to me, and that they professed to found all their hopes of peace on delay, and on the suggestion of such an expedient to the Directory, as, without forcing them to a direct and open renunciation of the principle on which they founded their haughty message, should still leave the door open to further negotiation. The channel through which this communication was made to me was certainly liable to suspicion; but when it is considered that Charles Delacroix was at that time Minister, and that consequently the proposal made to me was attended with extreme hazard to those from whom it came, while *I was in no shape committed*, and that the success of the parties concerned in their future prospects was apparently staked on the event, it was very difficult not to afford it a considerable degree of credit. I dwell the more on this, because most of what I am about to say rests *principally* on this authority—principally, but not wholly; since your Lordship knows it has been nearly *all* confirmed through two other sources of intelligence, quite distinct from this, and each of them in their way as well entitled to belief as any information of this sort can be.

Almost immediately after the dismission of Ch. Delacroix, and very soon after the arrival of my Note at Paris, I was told that the Directory were disposed to depart from their extravagant claim ; that they had brought it forward because it was a duty imposed upon them by their engagements with their Allies, and that, this duty performed, they were now prepared to try all means of persuasion with their Allies to induce them, for the sake of peace, so necessary to all parties, to release France from its engagements, and consent on their part to some such cession of territory as went to meet the proposals made by His Majesty ; and this, which was communicated to me through my secret channel, was confirmed fully to me officially in some of the subsequent Conferences.

Holland, I was told, was much more difficult to manage than Spain, and my informant gave me a detailed account of the steps which had been taken with a view to reconcile the Dutch to the terms proposed. He acquainted me with the order sent to M. Noel ; the journey of Count Cabarras to the Hague ; and your Lordship may recollect about this time the dexterity with which he endeavoured to draw from me an avowal, whether we were disposed to give way or not in our demands on the Dutch. All this passed between the 25th July and the 6th August, when Lord G. Leveson went to England. From that time my informant has continued to give me regular accounts of what has passed between the French and Dutch Governments. M. Noel's first letters written to this place, and dated the 5th, appeared to be encouraging ; but he represented Holland as in such a state of confusion, and the *Batavian* Directory so timid, as not to speak with confidence as to their final answer ; and, in fact, the new Dutch Plenipotentiaries, who arrived at Paris about the 8th instant, gave one on the 10th, which contained in substance a refusal to agree to any cession, and insisted strongly that the French Government should fulfil the stipulations of their Treaty. This answer M. Talleyrand took upon himself to send back as insufficient, improper, and not likely to be attended to by the Directory; and my informant explained this bold measure by saying, although it was done without the knowledge of the Directory, yet it had the previous *consent* of the *two friendly* Directors and some other members of the Government, who were determined to support him in case he should be called to account. On the 19th instant a second answer was delivered by the Dutch Ministers, which M. Talleyrand, although he was dissatisfied with it, could not venture to suppress. The Directory, however, found it so puzzled and obscure (i. e. *entortillé*), and so little answering their expectations, that they immediately ordered it to be returned to the Dutch Ministers, and instructed M. Talleyrand to say, in their name, that nothing short of an unqualified compliance with their request could be admitted. The Dutch Ministers were not empowered to take this upon themselves, but on the 23rd they referred it by express to their Government. I am told it will require about ten days before the answer can be known here; of course a further delay is incurred, and it will not be till the end of this week or the beginning of the next that we may expect to resume the negotiations.

Such is the manner, my Lord, in which the slowness of our proceedings is accounted for.

You will observe, my Lord, that the cause of this delay is attributed solely to the Dutch; and that, although I very frequently have mentioned the Court of Madrid, it never was alleged that any great difficulty would come from that quarter.

In regard to Holland, I could not avoid observing, when I heard from my informant so much about the difficulty of getting a satisfactory answer from thence, that this circumstance appeared to me as somewhat extraordinary, and not quite compatible with the pacific intentions he assured me belonged to the French Government, for I considered that the Batavian Republic was little more than a state dependent on France.

To this I received the following answer:—That I could not be unacquainted with the internal situation of this country, of the struggle between the Councils and the Directory, of the different opinions, not only in the Directory, but amongst some of the leading members of the Government, and that one of the most material points on which they disagreed was as to *the question of war or peace with England.* That two months ago the war party was certainly the most prevalent; that now it was hoped the greater weight was in the other scale; but still, that the question was by no means so far determined as to leave it in their power to employ strong measures, or such as might furnish their antagonists with a pretence for arraigning their conduct; that great *ménagemens* and skill were still necessary, and that any attempts to force matters would still risk the loss of the vantage-ground on which they stood. That it was, indeed, notorious that France governed Holland; and if, when the negotiation first was set on foot, the Directory had thought proper to prepare the Dutch, and to tell them what would be ultimately expected of them, and what they *must* submit to, all these delays would have been spared: but the Directory then were not disposed to take any steps preparatory to peace; and now, when they were induced to promote this measure, it was much less from their own choice than from the management of the Minister for Foreign Affairs, and from the sentiments which prevailed in the public. However ready, therefore, they might be to dictate to Holland on any other occasion, on this they certainly would affect to treat her as a free and independent state, and to omit none of the forms used towards one; and the authoritative tone the Directory had assumed in their last Message to the Dutch Plenipotentiaries might be considered as a great point gained.

I appeared satisfied with what I heard. I only adverted to what was said as to the good disposition of M. Talleyrand. I questioned seriously *his* being really *desirous* of peace; and, above all, I supposed in him a rooted dislike to England. I was answered by one short word, that it was his *interest* to make peace; that he could not retain his office if war continued, but would be dismissed from it probably with disgrace, because he was not liked or cordially trusted by the three Directors; whereas, if peace with England was made under his directions, it would give him such a degree of popularity and consequence, that it would fix him in office, and probably give him a greater share of power than any head of a Ministerial Department had possessed since the Revolution.

After having obtained this sort of explanation, which, as far as it goes, seems to shew that the delay produced by the Dutch was neither wished for, nor likely to prove advantageous to the Directory, it remained with me to endeavour to procure some means of judging whether, in any other point of view, this delay of the negotiation would appear more suitable to their interests.

I remarked, that it was perhaps resolved on by the Directory to wait for the signing of the definitive treaty with the Emperor before they proceeded on that with England; and that this measure might be adopted either to gratify a little national pride, by having it to say that England was left the last, and alone in the war, or from an idea of bringing Buonaparte and his Italian army into France, to be employed on a general attack on our coasts.

My informant treated these as very ill-founded conjectures. He said everything was so far settled between the French Republic and the Emperor, that what remained to be done was purely matter of form; and that, if the insulating England was the great object of the Directory, it was already as effectually done as if they had received the news of the signature of the Treaty at Udine.

That, as to the idea of bringing Buonaparte back to France, he himself was not at all disposed to listen to such a proposal; and if he did, his return, with the temper and spirit which belonged to his army, would cause infinitely more alarm to the nation than we should feel by the menace of an attack on our coasts under his direction; and this led me to the last point on which I wished to push my inquiries, viz. whether the apprehension of *the return of the numerous armies* into the country did not make the Directory, and perhaps the nation in general, *less eager in their wishes for peace* than they would otherwise be.

My informant admitted my remarks to be very just; but added, that, accustomed as these troops were to live on free quarters, it was almost equally dangerous to reform them, or to keep them collected. But, continued he, you will recollect that this danger is nearly the same, whether we have peace with England or not; since, the moment we cease hostilities on the Continent, these armies must retire from their present situation into this country, and remain in it nearly without employment; for, as to the idea of an invasion of England, it will very soon be found to be chimerical: and, indeed, were it to be seriously resolved upon, it could, from the state of our marine, only employ a small number of these troops; and the tedious preparations attendant on every maritime expedition would be such as these soldiers, used to rapid and decided operations, would not submit to, and they would either mutiny or desert before the expedition could be got ready.

I have now, my Lord, related, to the best of my memory, everything I have heard which can contribute to throw any light on the question which induced me to trouble your Lordship with this very long despatch. With these materials, I hope His Majesty's Ministers will be empowered to judge with tolerable safety whether the French Government are sincere in the intention of making peace, and whether the obstacles which retard the progress of the Negotiation are genuine or feigned; and in either case it will still remain, perhaps, a matter of doubt whether this delay is to be regretted by us, and whether, should it be the effect of design, the French are not overreaching themselves by their own cunning.

---

LETTER FROM LORD MALMESBURY TO MR. CANNING.

Lisle, Thursday, Aug. 29th, 1797.

My dear Canning,—I consider the Portuguese peace, from the manner in which it has been taken up,* as an event

* The English Government insisted on the Queen of Portugal refusing to

very likely to break off the Negotiation, and, I much fear, in a way that will not leave us any favourable appeal to make to this nation on our departure, nor any which will be satisfactory or intelligible to our own on our return.

I was not more explicit on this subject in my last private letters, because so many ideas crowded into my mind at once that I could not methodize them. I was vexed and out of humour, and felt it necessary to commune quietly with myself before I ventured giving a serious opinion to you upon it.

As to my official letters, they were answers to instructions—to instructions so forcibly inculcated as to produce rather unpleasant sensations; and, in replying to such, you know there is no medium between a resignation of opinion and resignation of office.

D'Aranjo and Ch. Delacroix, to whom the drawing up of the articles was left, *meant* that they should be as injurious to us as possible, and produce on our minds *precisely* the impression they have. A little pique in both of them against me, and a rooted hatred to England, actuated their conduct. D'Aranjo knew he exceeded his powers, foresaw the danger he ran of disgrace and confiscation of his property, but he also saw the cruel dilemma in which he placed his Court if it refused to ratify. He depended a little on the word *peace* to popularize him in his own country, and, at all events, he is sure of an asylum in this.

Their object, I repeat, was to perplex and anger us. They have done both, and the latter so effectually, that it will, I fear, in its consequences, greatly add to the former. It will plunge us into a *sea of troubles*.

It will make us deviate from our straight-forward line of conduct, and fix upon us the imputation (from which we could not easily exculpate ourselves) of being the aggressors in breaking off the Negotiation.

Do not suppose me ignorant of, or insensible to, the immense detriment that this Treaty must cause to England. I see it in as strong a point of view as it can be seen by those who

---

ratify the Peace with France made by Aranjo without authority. Her Faithful Majesty had no right to do so without our consent.

apprehend such serious consequences from it; but when I compare these consequences, which may be *distant* ones (and which, therefore, we may have time to correct and palliate), with those which appear to be the *immediate* ones we bring on ourselves and Portugal by insisting on the non-ratification of this Treaty, I do not hesitate, in this option of evils, as to that which we should choose.

The question of peace or war must in a short time be decided. If we have peace, the effects of this Treaty are suspended, and we shall have time to amend, or perhaps to annul it. There are, I conceive, no articles very materially injurious to us except the fourth and fifth, which are war articles; and I would set out by taking it for granted, that those two articles are binding only during the present war. The words " pendant le cours de la présente guerre" are to be found in the fourth article; and the engagements entered into by the fifth, without any very forced construction, may be considered as under the same limitation. I would say this *quietly* and *gently* at Lisbon. I would obtain some written acknowledgment from Her Most Faithful Majesty that such was her intention, and such the sense in which she understood the Treaty. With this paper to produce at the beginning of another war, we may use the Portuguese ports as we have done hitherto, provided the French (as it is reasonable to expect) should be less powerful than at present. Should they be more, or equally so, no treaties, no engagements, no precautions will avail, and force alone must determine the sense of these articles. And one of my chief arguments for temporizing rests on the conviction I have in my own mind, that peace will debilitate France, and check in its progress the destructive system it has hitherto pursued so successfully; while the events of another year's war may (as I shall state presently), even exhausted as France is, still give it the means of persevering in it, to a degree that may be fatal to us all. But supposing the other case, viz. that our Lisle Treaty breaks off, and the war is prolonged, with these engagements existing between France and Portugal, all cause of invasion of that country will, of course, be at an end. Portugal may protest against the violation of its ports (for they must be violated), and she may state to France her disposition, but at the same time her inability, to perform her engagements. Should France not be contented with this declaration, but quarrel with the Court of Lisbon, England will have the choice (Portugal having so manifestly broken faith with her by this recent transaction of Aranjo's) to afford it assistance or not, and time will be gained to put that country into a better state of defence than at present; and you may be certain that Spain, once relieved from the dread and anxiety of seeing a French army march through her provinces, will be much more averse to it than ever; and Spain alone, I will be bold to say, cannot conquer Portugal. Remember, I am only lessening, not removing difficulties and dangers. Many and great ones belong to the two cases I have just put; but it remains to be seen whether the third case (that of our forcing Portugal to annul the Treaty now) will not lead to difficulties and dangers incomparably greater.

1st. As the most essential. Is the spirit—or, if you please, are the spirits—of the country so much mended since I left England, as to consent to pursue the war with alacrity and vigour, after they are told that on all material points of discussion and compensation England and France were agreed, and that the Treaty of peace broke off solely on account of stipulations Portugal had entered into with France; stipulations which, they may say, an independent country has a right to make? An assertion, by the way, not very easy to disprove, since I do not think the 19th article of the Methuen Treaty meets the question fully, and there is no other immediately applicable, unless it be the 14th; and what is said there has been so much more forcibly expressed by everything that has recently passed between England and Portugal, that it cannot be worth adverting to.

2nd. This Treaty of D'Aranjo's has been ratified by the Councils, and apparently much approved by them. Our oversetting it, therefore, will, at least on the question of war with England (which, after all, is now one of the great points of dissension), reunite the Councils and the Directory; and their acting in concert on an object of this magnitude will probably tend to bring them together on inferior ones.

Their union will operate powerfully on the nation, and the continuance of war with us will become as popular as it is now the contrary. Pause here, for a moment, and reflect on England and France fighting under so different dispositions. Is it fear or prudence that makes me shrink from the idea?

Should we not be exposed to an hostile attack much more dangerous than the wild ones hitherto projected by the Directory alone, against the judgment and inclinations of the country at large? And, what I dread infinitely more, would not Government, by pursuing this line of conduct, so greatly unpopularize itself, as to risk the overthrow, not only of administration, but with it, I sincerely believe, of all government whatever?

Portugal and its ports we should indisputably lose; for what have we just now to oppose for the defence of that country, equal to what our enemies can bring to the attack of it? And by its being annexed to Spain, or, what is worse, revolutionized, should we not lose irrecoverably those advantages which seem now only to have escaped us for a while—advantages which patience, dexterity, and the chapter of accidents may restore to us, but of which precipitation would deprive us for ever?

As I have admitted that our interests are materially injured by this measure, so I am equally ready to allow that it gratifies the *amour propre* of our enemies, and hurts our own nearly in the same proportion: even our national dignity may be said to be slightly wounded. I do not mean to extenuate any part of the mischief; I only mean to contend, that *this is not the moment* for attempting to repair it. I may be wrong, and I must suppose myself so after the judgment pronounced by the Cabinet; but I cannot alter my feelings, and I need not suppress them when writing to you. I end, therefore, as I began, by regretting the measure we have adopted, and by looking to its effects with an uncommon degree of apprehension. I am, &c.

(Signed)    MALMESBURY.

[Mr. Canning, in his reply to this letter, regrets equally the course taken by Government, and laments that it did not confine itself to demanding the erasure of those articles most mischievous to us, and the use of the Portuguese ports as before.]

[As I have before stated, Lord Grenville was, from the beginning, opposed to the Negotiation for Peace, but gave way to Pitt, who saw how much England required rest, and how much he strengthened himself in public opinion by tendering Peace to France, and leaving to *her* the odium of a refusal or a rupture. Mr. Pitt has always been held up to the present generation as fond of war; but the Harris Papers could furnish the most continued and certain evidence of the contrary, and that he often suffered all the agony of a pious man who is forced to fight a duel. The cold and haughty temper of Lord Grenville was less sensitive; our overtures were to him synonymous with degradation, and he could not now brook the delays of the Directory.

Lord Malmesbury entirely agreed with Pitt, and at this time saw a fair chance of obtaining an honourable peace. This will explain the two following letters.]

EXTRACT OF A LETTER FROM LORD MALMESBURY TO
MR. CANNING.

Lisle, 29th Aug., 1797.

I WANT to say a few private words to you on my own personal feelings.

You must have perceived that the instructions and opinions I get from the Minister under *whose orders I am bound to act*, accord so little with the sentiments and intentions I heard expressed by the Minister *with whom I wish to act*, that I am placed in a very disagreeable dilemma.

If I do not conform to my instructions, I am guilty of diplomatic mutiny; if I do strictly and up to the letter of them, I am guilty of what is worse, by lending myself to promote a measure I think essentially wrong. It was under this impression that I brought forward in my other private letter to you, the alternative of resignation of office or resignation of opinion. Let me now explain these words: I will abandon, readily and cheerfully, my opinion, as long as we are all travelling to the same place, and not quarrel about which is the best road ; but if we turn back, or alter the object in view, the case changes. I ought to give way, and I certainly will, on every point which does not materially affect the principle on which we started, but I cannot give up the principle itself ; so long as peace—to be procured on the terms and in the way it was so kindly and confidentially explained to me—is our end, I will shrink from no difficulties, repine at no privations, but steadily persevere in pursuit of my object, till either it is attained or demonstrated to be unattainable. But if another opinion has been allowed to prevail—if the *real* end is to differ from the *ostensible* one — and if I am only to remain here, *in order to break off the Negotiation creditably, and not to terminate it successfully*, I then, instead of resigning my opinion, must resign my office. I should do it most reluctantly, because I am well aware it would create embarrassment where I truly wish to give every proof of regard, attention, and deference ; *but I must do it*, since it is impossible for me to become instrumental to a measure I should condemn and reprobate from the bottom of my conscience. I hope, after all, I may be wrong in my misgivings, and that the war party in the Cabinet have not *surprised the religion* of the pacific one ;—that I may not be called upon to make a painful exertion, but continue to proceed in this Negotiation with the same comfort and confidence I have always felt when I was acting under the directions of Mr. Pitt. I should, however, think I dealt unfairly if I did not explain myself, and declare my resolution on it. I leave, therefore, to your judgment to employ what I now communicate to you as my private friend, according as circumstances may require, and at a time, and in a way, to exempt me from any imputation of having acted hastily, or taken Government by surprise.

EXTRACT OF A LETTER FROM LORD MALMESBURY TO
MR. CANNING.

Lisle, 29th Aug., 1797.

You will be tired with my private letters; but, besides the degree of importance we all attach here to the subject on which they dwell, they are made the longer from the leisure I have had for these last three or four days.

For Heaven's sake, do not let the only person* in England, perhaps in Europe, who seeing right can act with effect, be seduced to wander from the principle he laid down two months ago; do not let *him* be misled by false reports of a change in the situation and sentiments of this country. If any change has taken place, it is only just such a one as will admit here the discussion of peace on this principle; if the demands are raised, (and I fear I must in justice to truth add) if they are not a little abated in the *ultimatum*, a relapse will take place, and this country return to the same unpacific disposition it was in when we arrived. Patience and temper on our part, and, above all, events, have since operated a change; but I repeat that this change, at most, makes the principle on which we set out practicable, and by no means whatever justifies our rising in price.

You will understand, from every word I write to-day, both official and private, that I am somewhat uneasy: it arises from my feelings that peace is within our reach on most respectable terms, and from my apprehensions that we shall lose it when it is within our grasp. I am the more anxious for peace, because, in addition to all the commonplace reasons, I am convinced that *peace will palsy this country* most completely; that all the violent means they have employed for war will return upon them like a humour driven in, and overset entirely their weak and baseless constitution. This consequence of peace is so much more to be prized than the very best condition we could insert in the Treaty, that I had rather incur the disgrace of signing one in conformity to the strict *status*

* Mr. Pitt.

*ante bellum,* than let France take the favourable chances, and England run the risks, of another campaign.

I shall regret Wesley, who gains upon my good opinion and affection every day. Be merciful to me, and send me no successor to him; or, if you do, let it be William Elliot (if he will come). Let Leveson return immediately. G. Ellis *says* he must go in a week or ten days; try to dissuade him; I shall do my best.

I hope you understand that you are to act entirely according to your own discretion with my *most private letter.* I never object to anything being shewn to *Pitt,* because I am vastly in his debt on the score of confidence, and because I am sure he will not mistake my meaning; and I do not write to him, because I could say nothing I have not said to you.

---

EXTRACTS OF A LETTER FROM MR. CANNING TO LORD MALMESBURY.

Spring Gardens, 29th Aug., 1797.

THE only point in your last despatches to which it strikes me that you might have expected and desired to receive an official answer, whenever they were acknowledged, is that respecting the Note which you properly omitted to present, though instructed to do so.*

If I had been quite sure myself, or if the one person† with whom I consulted upon the subject could have answered it to me, that a thorough approbation of this omission would be given, I certainly should not have failed at the time when I suggested the sending a messenger to you, to suggest (in the draft which I sent for approval) a distinct commendation of the latitude which you had given to your instructions in this instance; but I vehemently feared, and so did my opposite neighbour, that the warlike spirit was too strong in that quarter‡ to expect a perfect acquiescence, and that the suggestion might possibly raise an exertion of a directly contrary

---

\* Refuting the charge of wanton delays on the part of England.
† Mr. Pitt.     ‡ Lord Grenville.

sort to that which it would have been my object to produce. I hope you will think this a satisfactory reason for the compromise which we made in asking nothing, where by asking we might have got what we did not want.

I do not know what to make of your Mr. Melville.

I have heard nothing more from Talleyrand by the former channel. Letters of his continually pass through our hands, which prove him to be stock-jobbing here to an enormous amount.

THURSDAY, AUG. 31.—Went to Hamilton's house to dinner, with Conyngham—pleasant situation, and well contrived house. Hamilton very odd—Lady Mary, his wife, equally so. Two daughters married to French General officers—one to Thiébaud, the other to Jouy; a daughter by him called Sophie, a great favourite.

Maret came up to my box; he seemed not so confident as to the issue of the negotiations at Udine—thought a Congress still possible—held for the Conservation of the German Empire—talked of animosities between Prussians and Austrians. In our negotiation, he said, since Charles Delacroix had been dismissed, their instructions had been changed—those they received from *him* were such " qu'ils n'auroient pas osé me les proposer ;" those from Talleyrand much more reasonable. Charles Delacroix, he said, was more the tool than a leading member of a party; he was a rank Jacobin—" *un Jacobin effréné*"—the principle of such a one is " de tout révolutionner à coups de canons sans examiner le pourquoi." He said, that, till his coming into office, all the ancient " chefs de bureau" had remained in their offices in the foreign department throughout the whole system of terror; that Guiraudet was the only good man left ; that, for some time before Charles Delacroix went out, he had also withdrawn his confidence from him ; that Talleyrand meant to replace some of the old " Commis," Rayneval and others ; to put in a person of the name of Otto,[*] who had been employed in Ame-

---

[*] Otto was afterwards a distinguished Diplomatist. He signed the preliminaries of the Peace of Amiens, and negotiated the marriage of Napoleon with Marie Louise. He died in 1817, aged 63.

rica as Secretary of Legation. Maret talked of Lafayette; seemed to think we were the cause of his being kept in prison. I assured him we did not care the least about him. On speaking of the interests of the Prince of Orange, he said they ought and would be attended to, but he did not see how they could be introduced as an article in a public treaty. In regard to the collateral points on which I questioned him, he was not disposed to speak; he, however, said it was their intention to give in a formal *contre-projêt* as soon as they had the materials.

FRIDAY, SEPT. 1.—Walked with Ellis; dissuaded him from going. Conversation on Pitt's weakness in regard to Lord Grenville. Conference. Play,—in the French box; nothing remarkable passed, except that Délille, author of the words and music of the Marseilloise, was there.

SATURDAY, SEPT. 2.—Called on Le Tourneur at noon: he very conversable; talked of Buonaparte and his successes; he had on going out to his command only 30,000 men, half naked. Berthier is to write his campaign. Le Tourneur was, or affected to be, angry with the Dutch; said " qu'il fallait qu'ils fissent des sacrifices pour la paix—nous le voulons absolument," added he, " car je vous assure que notre Gouvernement désire cette paix bien sincèrement. Lemoyne's concert—bad music—bad execution; sat by Madame Ducos—nothing remarkable. Larrey returned from Paris with the commissions he was to execute.

SUNDAY, SEPT. 3.—Walk—Conference. Maret at the play; said Charles Delacroix was likely to be named to Lisbon, although Bourgoin had been in a manner promised; that Tallien's apology looked as if *his* party was not the strongest; by his apology, he meant a speech he made in answer to Thibeaudeau, who had flung out some strong accusations against him. He said, La Réveillière's speech had done harm; it had rekindled the spirit of animosity between the parties; Réveillière an unhealthy, peevish man. He hinted to Ellis that they had a right to break off the Treaty at Udine. A Count de Salis—a friend of Maret. Hamilton drunk and absurd.

[Barras, Rewbell, and La Réveillière Lépaux, the three Directors who represented the violent and war party, had now determined to try their strength with the Councils, and maintain their authority by force. Augereau and Hoche had been ordered to approach Paris with troops within the distance marked by the Constitution. The terror which pervaded Paris at the eve of the 18th Fructidor is described in the following letters of Lord Malmesbury's agents, preparing him for this Revolution.]

EXTRACT OF A DESPATCH FROM LORD MALMESBURY TO LORD GRENVILLE.

Lisle, 5th Sept., 1797.

THE most recent and best information I can transmit to your Lordship on the present very critical situation of this country is to be found in the inclosed papers, which are copies of letters I have received from Paris since Mr. Wesley's departure on the 30th ultimo.

ANONYMOUS LETTER FROM PARIS TO M. PEIN, SENT TO LORD MALMESBURY.

Paris, 5 heures du Soir, 17 Fructidor, Dimanche, le 3° Septembre.

Je viens à l'instant d'apprendre de la part sûre et authentique ce que portent les Réponses de la Hollande. Le Comité des Relations Bataves y déclare de la manière la plus positive, qu'il ne peut jamais consentir à céder à l'Angleterre Ceylon ni Trinquemale, qu'il regarde comme la source des richesses du pays et la clef des autres possessions; que ce seroit rendre l'Angleterre Maîtresse de l'Inde. Il fait entendre, au milieu d'un langage très obscure, qu'il pourroit tout au plus consentir à la neutralité, c'est-à-dire à la Communauté du Cap entre les trois Nations, mais jamais y renoncer en entier. Quant à Cochin et à ses dépendances, il déclare qu'il consent volontiers à les livrer. Il indique ensuite quelques comptoirs sur la Côte de Coromandel qu'il pourroit joindre à ces cessions. Le ton de la dépêche est ferme, tranchant aussi, et ils annoncent que jamais ils ne prendront sur eux de renoncer à autre chose. Ils paroissent croire que la France ne peut pas, pour son propre intérêt, consentir à les abandonner et à traiter sans eux. Ils insistent surtout beaucoup sur le vœu d'être admis par un Plénipotentiaire au Congrès de Lille, pour y discuter, et y soutenir leurs prétensions et leurs intérêts. On peut compter sur ces détails que je donne pour sûrs. Le Ministre n'en est pas satisfait, parcequ'il craint que le Directoire ne veuille pas prendre sur lui de céder plus que ne fait la Hollande. Le Directoire n'a pas encore eu lecture publique de ces dépêches ; et ce n'est que demain ou après qu'un rapport pourra lui être fait à ce sujet pour qu'il prenne un parti.

J'ai écrit pour vous donner ces détails aujourd'hui, afin de n'avoir pas à vous écrire de quelques jours à moins de quelque chose d'important, car les craintes pour la nuit prochaine sont encore plus vives de la part des Conseils qu'elles ne l'ont été pour la dernière. On dit que les Rassemblements commencent à devenir inquiétans en ce moment dans les Fauxbourgs. Je viens de rencontrer des Députés influans qui s'attendent à être attaqués cette nuit. Si cela est, ils conviennent qu'ils sont sans aucun moyen probable de défense et surtout de succès. S'il y avoit une crise, je ne pourrois plus vous écrire de quelque tems, à moins que vous ne m'envoyassiez quelqu'un ici ; il y auroit trop de danger.

---

ANONYMOUS LETTER TO LORD MALMESBURY.

*Paris, 17 Fructidor (3 Sept., 1797).*

Le Courier de Hollande vient d'arriver aujourd'hui à trois heures avec la réponse aux dépêches si importantes et tranchantes du Directoire. Elle est adressée aux trois Commissaires Bataves qui remplacent ici l'Ambassadeur Meyer; elle ne sera communiquée que dans la soirée au Ministre des relations extérieures, et je ne pourrai par conséquent vous en rien dire que demain. Tout ce que je sais aujourd'hui c'est que les Commissaires Bataves ont dit que cette réponse de leur Gouvernement étoit *décisive;* ils ne se sont pas expliqués davantage. Est-ce décisive dans le sens où le vouloit le Directoire, et par conséquent favorable aux Cessions demandées ? Ou est-ce *décisive* contre ? La première interprétation est la plus vraisemblable, cependant une personne qui a causé avec les Ministres Bataves me dit à l'instant qu'elle croit la réponse des Hollandois négative sur les cessions, qu'ils disent qu'ils auroient mieux aimé s'exposer à tout que de signer eux-mêmes leur ruine. En ce cas nous verrons si le Directoire tiendroit la menace qu'il leur a faite de traiter sans eux. A demain du certain là dessus.

Talleyrand est toujours persuadé que le Directoire fera la paix avec l'Angleterre, à peu près aux conditions déjà énoncées, pourvu que nous n'ayons pas ici auparavant une *explosion.* Car s'il y en avoit une, comme, vu le dénuement des forces des deux Conseils et la nonformation de la Garde Nationale, la victoire resteroit presque certainement au Directoire, qui a pour lui les nombreuses troupes de Paris et des environs, les dispositions actuelles du Directoire changeroient presqu'infailliblement relativement à la paix avec l'Angleterre. Une fois les maîtres dans Paris et débarrassés des entraves des Conseils, ils repousseroient par des conditions exagérées la paix avec l'Angleterre, dans l'espoir d'y porter une Révolution, de l'essayer du moins, au moyen de quelque descente confiée à Buonaparte. Quoique cela soit fou, on y reviendroit, et on se flatteroit de réussir par quelque surprise. Je vous donne pour certain que Rewbell et Barras se sont, il y a deux jours, presque formellement déclarés à cet égard. Je tiens de part sûre qu'ils ont dit que, sans les tracasseries des Conseils, ils ne se montreroient pas si faciles pour la paix avec l'Angleterre : que si les Patriotes l'emportoient à tems, il faudroit à tout prix faire la paix avec l'Autriche, même en lui cédant sans difficulté la Bavière ou plutôt en lui promettant de l'aide à l'envahir ; mais qu'alors ils romproient les Négociations de Lille, et ils développoient ainsi leur plan, mais seulement (observez le bien) dans le cas d'une défaite de la majorité des Conseils. La paix avec l'Autriche derechef n'importe à quelles conditions : rappeller l'armée d'Italie et Buonaparte dans l'intérieur, et l'approcher de Paris sous prétexte de se rendre sur les Côtes pour une descente en Angleterre : destiner en effet à cette descente, lorsque le moment s'en présenteroit, cent mille hommes, pris moitié dans l'armée d'Italie, moitié dans celle de Hoche : ôter à Moreau (intime ami de Pichegru, et par conséquent très suspect au Directoire) le commandement de l'armée, et vaincre les résistances qu'on pourroit rencontrer dans l'intérieur ; et enfin avec la partie disponible de l'armée de Hoche, et quelques corps des autres armées, se rendre de nouveau maîtres de la Hollande entière, et la réunir à la France, pour la punir de n'avoir pas accepté la constitution. On prétend savoir que les Révolutionnaires Hollandois, qui ne sont pas très rassurés sur leurs destinées, consentiroient volontiers à nous aider encore à convertir leur pays en Département François, et à se joindre à nous comme la Belgique, sous la condition d'avoir des Députés au prochain corps législatif en France ; toute folle que peut paroître cette conversation, soyez certain qu'elle a eu lieu. Barras et Rewbell ne croyent pas cela plus difficile à faire en Hollande que cela n'a été en Italie, surtout lorsqu'ils en chargeroient Buonaparte. Mais ne perdez pas de vue que ce n'est qu'une hypothèse dans le cas où il y auroit *combat et triomphe pour eux*, car tant qu'il y aura lutte, ils persistent à croire que les deux paix valent mieux pour eux, afin de s'entourer des armées rentrées, et parceque le Corps Législatif ne leur donne pas d'argent, et ils continuent à vouloir les deux paix, comme il a été dit. La Réveillière d'ailleurs les y forceroit, comme il l'a fait pour Mantoue en se joignant à Carnot et à Barthelemi pour ce seul objet—car lui, il croit la paix nécessaire avec l'Angleterre et l'Autriche. Il préfère des cessions à la guerre. Vous n'avez pas d'idée à quel point il est jaloux de l'honneur de mettre son nom comme Président du Directoire au bas de la Paix Générale. Ces petits calculs d'amour propre influent souvent beaucoup sur la destinée des Etats. Rewbell et Barras haïssent l'Angleterre comme un ennemi personnel, parceque l'orgueil Anglais est le seul qui n'ait pas ployé devant le leur ; les Jacobins ont tous le même sentiment contre une puissance qui les a toujours molestés et tourmentés. On peut juger de ce qu'ils exigeroient du Directoire, s'ils étoient devenus les maîtres dans un choc, par les cris de fureur qu'ils poussent déjà, depuis qu'ils soupçonnent le projet de céder Ceylon, le Cap, et Mantoue. En cela ils sont très bien secondés, comme vous avez pu le voir dans la *Quotidienne*, qui trouve aussi horrible qu'on abandonne Mantoue et le Cap. Ce concert des deux partis extrêmes à déclamer contre les conditions de la Paix ne laisse pas que d'inquiéter un peu l'Evêque d'Autun, et influeroit bien plus sur le Directoire, s'il n'étoit occupé de considérations en ce moment plus pressantes pour lui. Quant à moi, je suis intimement convaincu que les embarras actuels du Directoire ne contribueront pas peu à faire obtenir à l'Angleterre les conditions qu'elle désire : *qu'elle ne peut pas traiter et conclure dans un moment plus favorable pour elle :* qu'elle n'a nulle espèce d'intérêt d'attendre pour finir, le résultat de la crise actuelle, qui, si on en vient aux mains, ou si la violence est tentée, ne peut que fortifier le Directoire et le mettre à portée de reprendre ses projets gigantesques ; parceque toutes les chances du succès intérieur sont pour lui. On suppose dans le Directoire une toute autre opinion au Lord Malmesbury et au Gouvernement Anglois. On y est persuadé qu'ils désirent que le combat s'engage dans l'idée qu'ils pourront avoir après de meilleures conditions : ou que du moins ils veulent attendre l'issue, avant de terminer. Les Plénipotentiaires Français leur soupçonnent aussi la même intention et la transmettent à Paris ; il seroit utile de les détromper, lorsque l'occasion s'en présente dans les Conférences. Au reste, voici la situation intérieure. Peu d'union entre les deux Conseils, parceque les Cinq Cents s'irritent du rejet de plusieurs de leurs résolutions, parcequ'ils se voyent avec humeur plus accusés et menacés par le Directoire que les Anciens. Ils accusent les Anciens d'être cause de leurs dangers actuels, en les ayant arrêtés lorsqu'ils croyoient pouvoir frapper le Directoire. Ils les soupçonnent aussi toujours un peu de chercher à négocier avec le Directoire, quoique je sois certain qu'il n'en est rien, et que nul Député n'aille même plus au Luxembourg ; très rarement même chez Barthelemi et Carnot, qui se tiennent toujours bien, mais qui sont sans aucune espèce d'influence sur toute la Direction intérieure, parceque les trois autres ont tout concerté d'avance. La peur ou la prudence a beaucoup gagné les Conseils. Ils ne songent plus du tout à mettre le Directoire ni aucun Directeur en accusation, parcequ'ils savent qu'on leur résisteroit et qu'ils n'auroient pas assez de force pour faire exécuter leur décret, quand on leur laisseroit le tems de le rendre, au milieu des interminables formalités que la constitution exige pour cet acte ; et si ces formalités n'étoient pas épuisées, le Directoire s'insurgeroit en déclarant la constitution violée, et le décret rendu contre lui nul. Le hors de la loi n'est pas dans la constitution.

Les Députés ont tellement peur, depuis qu'ils voyent les armées prononcées contre eux, que la moitié d'entre eux ne couchent plus chez eux ; parcequ'on leur fait croire toutes les nuits qu'ils seront attaqués. Soit qu'on y songe réellement, soit que le Directoire espère trouver son compte à répandre ces sortes d'alarmes pour rendre les Conseils plus complaisans.

Pendant que les Conseils baissent leur ton, le Directoire en prend un plus audacieux que jamais. Il parle avec une assurance qui annonce qu'il croit la victoire certaine, s'il est attaqué, ou s'il le décide à attaquer. Et en effet les trois Directeurs Gouvernans n'ont plus la moindre inquiétude sur le moment actuel. Ils defient tout ; ils bravent et provoquent partout ; ils ne placent que des hommes dévoués ; ils destituent, dans le militaire comme dans les Administrations, tous ceux sur lesquels ils ne comptent pas absolument ; ils se sont déterminés à ne faire aucun cas de toute opinion qui n'est pas celle de leur parti ; ils redoutent bien les journaux, qui sont presque tous contre eux et pour les Conseils. Mais ils ne laissent pas pénétrer les journaux jusqu'aux armées, qui sont aujourd'hui à leurs yeux tout le peuple Français ; et pour tâcher de contrebalancer cette influence des journaux, ils commencent à multiplier aussi les écrits et surtout les placards en sens contraire, et mis à la portée du vulgaire. Ils voudroient bien réchauffer dans la multitude le fanatisme révolutionnaire ; mais jusqu'ici dans Paris (car c'est de là que tout dépend et a dépendu depuis la Révolution) la multitude sans appeler l'ancien régime, comme on le suppose à tort, reste inerte et indifférente entre tous les partis.

Nous sommes, en un mot, dans une situation, sous plusieurs rapports, pareille à celle qui précéda et suivit le 31$^e$ Mai, lorsque le parti qui avait pour lui l'immense majorité nationale fut vaincu par la minorité détestée, mais active, fanatique, et resolue à tout. S'il y avoit un combat, le résultat seroit le même, après des résistances qui ne seroient pas plus efficaces que l'insurrection départementale d'alors ; la différence est, qu'au lieu d'un régime révolutionnaire, nous aurions le régime militaire, qui seroit aussi dur, mais moins sanglant, jusqu'à ce que la guerre civile ne vint à éclater entre les généraux divisés.

---

MONDAY, SEPT. 4.—Called on Pein ; note from him to Ellis. Called on Maret and Colchen ; not at home. Writing private letters. Play.

---

TUESDAY, SEPT. 5.—Walked with Ellis. Conference. Maret, Colchen, and Isidore visited ; a word on Portugal. Maret announced that Le Tourneur intended to call on me on the next day, and to propose a dinner on Friday. Colchen reasoned well : he said, (and it is worth remark,) after talking over the absurd conduct of the Dutch, and on my mentioning Spain, " Nos engagements ne sont pas si positifs à l'égard de cette Cour ; nous avons les idées plus grandies." He conversed like one long used to business. Writing ; Play. News arrived of a *great commotion at Paris*, by the telegraph ; no particulars. Rumour that the Directory had attacked the Members of the Council adverse to them—great uneasiness and consternation. Cumberland told this to George Ellis. Sent away Brooks at half-past eleven ; doubts of his being allowed to cross over.

---

WEDNESDAY.—No papers from Paris. Pein called to confirm what we suspected. Twenty-two members of the Councils were arrested at five on the morning of Monday the 4th, with two Directors, and Ramel, head of the Legislative Guards, who made no resistance. The twenty-two members arrested were Camille Jourdan, Thibeaudeau, Boisset, Coudnoir, Rovéré, Masset, Vauvilliers, Henri Larivière, et Alphonse Delarue, Imbert, Colinges, Pichegru, Bourdon de L'Oise, Dumolard, Willot, Dumas, Perrée, Rambureaud, Debonnières, Boissey d'Anglas, Gilbert Des Moulins, and one more, whose name was forgotten.*

The barriers at Paris all shut. In the evening the Telegraph said, that "Paris étoit tranquille, et que le Directoire et les deux Conseils réunissoient leurs efforts pour découvrir la conspiration des Royalistes." Great marks of consternation in the opposite box. Michen acted in Felix, and Madame Chevalier acted incomparably. I sate by Madame Ducos; her behaviour gentle and charming, just as it ought to be; no affectation or any assumed indifference. Deep, but calm anxiety. Maret less master of himself; he looked absent and *consterné*; so did the others.

---

SEPT. 7.—No post or letters from Paris. Ellis with Pein. At the Play; Maret with me; he said they knew no more than would appear in a newspaper Venacken was going to reprint from *one* he had received from Paris; that sixty-three or sixty-four, chiefly Deputies, were condemned to banishment; about one half to Cayenne, the other "hors de la République;" that he heard Pichegru and Barthelemi were among the first; that the word of alarm was "Conspiration Royale;" and that papers had been taken, from which that was to be proved. Pichegru was said to have been in correspondence with the Prince de Condé, and the commander of the Austrian army in 1794, to deliver up some of the French fortresses. D'Entraigue's papers, he supposed, would be produced in evidence, and the declaration of Duverne.†

---

\* This list was very short of the number. Sixty-two were banished; among whom were the two Directors Carnot and Barthelemi; they were judged by the Councils, and sentenced to *deportation*.

† Duverne denounced a Royalist conspiracy in which he said he had himself

All Wickham's* attempts to produce a counter-revolution would come out in the latter. He thought Garat and François Neufchâteau likely to be the new Directors; that the first had been in England with Chauvelin; was rather a weak than dangerous man. He did not know much of the other; both of them were Conventionalists, and it was on these principles that the present Government was formed. The liberty of the press was taken away, by all journalists being obliged to submit their journals to the censure of the police (or Minister for the Home Department) before they were printed. The emigrants were to be sent out of the country in fifteen days; the law relative to them commuted from death to deportation. The law of the 3d Brumaire † re-established, till four years after peace. The line of constitutional demarkation for the troops abolished; the place where the Councils met removed. In short, it appears that, under pretence of preserving the Constitution, they have violated it in various very essential points, and established the most complete despotism that ever belonged to an executive power. No change yet amongst the Ministers; fifty-three departments to have new elections — amongst them, that of the north; the primary assembly to be held at Douay. Moreau supposed to be arrested. In regard to our immediate object, he was apprehensive it might be much affected by this revolution, unless the new governors thought they could popularize themselves by making peace; that, as to himself, he expected to be recalled; that he would not remain if his instructions were altered, but at least derive the only possible good which could spring from this event, and, by remaining steady to his principles, establish his character for firmness; from this he declared no threats or fears should drive him. He said Le Tourneur was affected

---

been two years engaged.—D'Entraigue's papers were seized at Venice, and sent by Buonaparte to the Directory. They professed to implicate Pichegru as the chief of the Royalist conspiracy, who was to receive, as the price of a restoration, the *Baton* of Marshal, the governorship of Alsace, the Château de Chambord, 40,000*l.* in money, and 8000*l.* a-year.

\* English Minister in Switzerland, who corresponded with Pichegru and Condé. Moreau intercepted the correspondence, but did not betray them, and consequently incurred very reasonable suspicions.

† By which the relations and connexions of emigrants were incapacitated from holding office.

on account of Carnot; but, as he was very *sensible à la liberté,* he thought he was saved by what had passed. He said Colchen was deeply affected, but with great calmness and good sense. He was certain a third Plenipotentiary would be sent here, and he believed it would be Gourlade, who had been talked of to succeed Pléville in the Marine Department. He did not doubt peace would be made with Austria on any terms; but that they would remain at war with us, in order to have a pretence to keep up their armies, and also existing means of forging compensations. Lamarque, the new President, an able and bold man; he was delivered up to the Austrians at the same time with Bournonville. He ended by saying, the principle now was the same as on the 13th Vendémiaire (4th Oct.) 1795, when the Sections of Paris rose. They were suppressed exactly on the same grounds, and by the same means, as the Directory had now employed to produce this very extraordinary event. Barras then at the head of the *Force Armée.*

FRIDAY, SEPT. 8.—No letters or papers from Paris. Great consternation in the appearance of the people in the streets; groups assemble to talk politics and collect information. Several of the military, who never came there before, visited my box at the play, and expressed their sentiments very strongly. Walked between the acts with Le Tourneur; he persevered in the idea that this change would not affect our Negotiation, but rather hasten its successful conclusion. He was of the side of the Directory, and pleased with what had passed. He talked of Duverne's declaration—of Wickham being quoted in it. This he said he knew when he was Director, but it could not have any effect on what we were doing; it was a long time ago, and a thing over. He was very civil, and more courteous than usual. I spoke to Maret and Madame Ducos on coming out of my box at the play; Madame Torcy in my box.

SATURDAY, SEPT. 9.—George Ellis with Pein. Charles Delacroix coming here. Merlin de Douay one of the new

Directors; he reasons as if peace would still be made; these reasons all appear in my despatch of this date. I only omitted by forgetfulness that L'Abbé Sieyes* is again come forward, and that it is probable the forty resolutions voted by the Councils are drawn up by him. Conference. Writing. Le Tourneur called on me in the evening; unusually civil; made his excuses for not bringing me a paper he had promised (Duverne's declaration); still assured that we should conclude peace; called Vandamme *par fois trop républicain*; said François Neufchâteau (Ministre de l'Intérieur) was the second new Director; he was quite silent as to Charles Delacroix. Colchen was with him, and apparently in better spirits. I consider Colchen as an honest and worthy man.

---

EXTRACT OF A LETTER FROM LORD MALMESBURY TO LORD GRENVILLE.

Lisle, 9th Sept., 1797.

SOME papers, (which I inclose,) published under the immediate eye of the Directory, have arrived to-day, and a few imperfect accounts have been received by indirect means; and it is from these very barren sources, with a little help from the conversation of the French Plenipotentiaries, who are, however, without any official accounts, that I principally derive my information. It will, therefore, be far from being such as I could wish, at this very interesting moment, to be able to transmit.

The inclosure in my last separate despatch has, by the events which have since taken place, been rendered much more important and interesting than I could venture to think it at the time I had the honour of transmitting it to your Lordship, since it describes very minutely, and, as it now appears, very correctly, the hopes, and fears, and views, of the different parties, and the general state of the public

---

* Sieyes at this time had a great reputation as a statesman, but he was only a theoretical politician. Napoleon saw through him, used him, and laid him by. It being remarked to Talleyrand, "L'Abbé Sieyes est un homme profond, très profond,"—"C'est creux, très creux que vous voulez dire," replied Talleyrand.

mind, a few hours preceding the great explosion on the 4th. It shews that the secret of the Directory had transpired; that the public were in hourly expectation of some terrible event, and that the Councils were aware of their danger; but that, acting with little concert, feeling the impossibility of resisting the armed force, (which, as it now appears, amounted to between twenty and thirty thousand men,) and, perhaps, trusting that the Directory would not choose openly to violate a Constitution from which they derived their only right to power, they confided their safety to the forms of that Constitution, and neglected every other precaution. Still, however, it must appear rather extraordinary that the whole transaction passed over as if they had been taken by surprise, and totally unprepared to meet it; for, between the hours of 5 and 7 A.M. on Monday morning, the greatest number of them were taken into custody without the smallest resistance, and, in the course of that day, sentence of banishment pronounced upon them. The people of Paris, (by whom many of them were beloved,) either from apathy or astonishment, did not shew the least disposition to move in their favour; and the Guards of the Legislative Councils appear to have sided with those of the Directory, without shewing the least disposition to take up arms in defence of their arrested members.

The whole proceeding rested on a vague and general accusation of a conspiracy in favour of Royalism; and under this specious pretext, and as if the charge was substantiated by the most incontestible evidence, the Directory have accomplished their ends with a degree of effrontery, and, I must add, intrepidity, almost unparalleled in the annals of history.

The documents tending to prove this conspiracy are deduced from papers said to be found on M. d'Entraigues when he was taken by General Buonaparte at Venice, and from the declaration made in the end of February last by the Chevalier Duverne, who evidently put into it every thing he thought likely to save his life. Both of these papers are amongst the inclosures; and I need not remark how liable everything they contain is to suspicion, and, even if true, how little they justify so violent a measure as that of passing sentence on the persons accused without allowing them to make any defence.

While the Directory are loud in their cry of having acted solely to preserve the present form of Government, they have violated the Constitution in all its branches, not only by the most hasty repeal of some of the most salutary laws, but in defiance of many of the original and fundamental principles on which it was formed.

The accused Deputies have been condemned without any trial, without being heard, and in express contradiction to the forms prescribed by law. The deposing and punishing abruptly two Directors, is, from the nature of their high situation, a still more manifest breach of the Constitution; and it is difficult to suppose a case in which the means employed operate so directly against the intention professed. The real intention, however, is very different: it is not to maintain the present Constitution; but, by altering some of its laws, and abrogating others, to reduce it to the principles and system of the Conventionalists, to make the Executive power as strong and as unlimited as that of any of their most despotic Monarchs, or their most despotic Committees of Public Safety, and leave the Councils with as little or less authority than, during the Monarchy, the Parliaments were allowed to assume.

It may not be improper to remark, that the vengeance of the Directory has, in this instance, been principally, if not solely, directed against that class of the Moderate party who were known to be true Republicans. The Royalists have almost universally escaped, and continue to form a considerable though an inert and passive body in the Councils. The more active part is composed of those who distinguished themselves in maintaining the power of the Convention against the Sections of Paris during the insurrection of the 13th Vendémiaire (4th October, 1795), and who, in that instance as well as in the present, obtained a victory over the country by the assistance of the army. They are attached to the Directory, because they share its power, and act the same part in the Councils as the Commissaries of the Executive Power perform in the Provisional and Municipal administrations.

They profess a hatred to the Jacobins and Anarchists, from whom they differ in wishing to establish a tyrannical government by means of an army instead of a mob. They are, like the Jacobins, partisans of requisitions and forced loans; and, like them too, they have a system of terror, which they call La "*demi-terreur.*" Their vengeance is gratified by perpetual banishment, not by death; and they have extended this clemency to the emigrants, who, if they attempt to return to France, are no longer subject to a capital punishment, but are to be immediately driven out of the country.

The army, as I have already observed, is the great instrument with which they hope to acquire and secure their power. Your Lordship will observe the court that is paid to it, and that the *milliard* to be given to the soldiery at the peace is now actually voted, though the means of raising any considerable part of it are known to be perfectly impracticable. Conscious that inability to perform this engagement, or even to make good the deficit of the present expenses, must soon appear, and dreading that the nation should rouse from the state of stupor into which this violent convulsion has thrown them, the language of the Directory recommends the greatest rapidity: "*Frappez sur-le-champ; si vous hésitez, ç'en est fait; demain il ne sera plus tems.*" Such are the expressions employed in their message of the 5th of Sept. (19 Fructidor), and the whole of it betrays the greatest apprehension from delay, and the dread of a reaction.

Paris is represented as in a state of silent consternation, and wears the appearance as if a return of the reign of terror and all its miseries was expected. This town, not excepting even the military, evidently betrays the same feelings, and I should conceive they were universal: but I much doubt whether, strong and just as they are, they will be such as to call forth resistance; and whether the spirit of the whole country is not so exhausted and depressed by repeated acts of persecution and tyranny, and by the failure of every exertion which has been made to oppose them, that it will submit quietly to this new act of oppression, and patiently bend under the yoke of the Directory.

P.S.—SATURDAY, 2 P.M.—I have this moment learnt two very important circumstances—that Merlin de Douay (Minister of Justice) was elected yesterday to the office of Director, and that M. Chas. Delacroix is named the third Plenipotentiary here,* in the room of M. Pléville, and is expected to arrive to-day or to-morrow. The other new Director, it is thought, will be Garat.

It appears, by further information I have obtained, that the Directory have on this occasion conducted themselves with more art, forethought, and circumspection than they have usually employed. It comes out, beyond a doubt, that the bold measure they have now carried into execution has been preparing for some time; that they and General Buonaparte have understood each other from the beginning; that he has not only remitted sums of money to them for the purpose of carrying this plan into effect, but consented that a considerable part of his army should march into the south of France, to direct the new elections; that 30,000 men are near Lyons, under General Massena, and 20,000 men under another officer devoted to his interest, but whose name I cannot learn,† near Marseilles, besides which the Directory have in and near Bourdeaux a corps of about equal force; and that every precaution is taken in the fifty-three departments, where the primary assemblies are to be convened, in order that the elections may proceed in perfect conformity to their wishes.

This department is one of the number. The primary assemblies are to be held at Douay, and 3,000 men are soon to march into Cambray. General Joubert, who commands this division, and who is a very respectable man and much attached to General Pichegru, will probably be dismissed from his command, which will be given to General Vandamme. All the municipality of this town are in daily expectation of being removed, and I shall severely feel their loss, as they are attentive and civil to a degree. The only public functionary who is likely to remain in office here is the Commissary of the Executive Power, whose principles are in perfect conformity to those of the persons by whom he is immediately employed.

* This report proved incorrect. † Joubert.—Orig. note.

M. Barthelemi is still at Paris—not in prison, but under arrest in his own apartment. He is said to behave with great coolness, and to observe a strict silence on everything that has passed.

M. Carnot has certainly escaped, and it is supposed he will attempt to join the army of the Rhine and Moselle, where he is very popular; and if General Moreau (who is not yet taken up) should be able to do the same, it is possible that that corps may be disposed to oppose the despotic authority usurped by the Directory; but, as they are well aware of this, great precautions have been taken to keep all the avenues on that side France strictly guarded.

I understand that, in return for this assistance from General Buonaparte, the Directory, besides pledging themselves to return the money he has lent them, engage to give him their full support and concurrence in prosecution of all his plans, whatever they may be.

HALF-PAST SEVEN, P.M.—M. Le Tourneur has this moment called upon me, to say, that the telegraph has brought information that François Neufchâteau (late Minister of the Home Department) was elected this morning the second new Director; and that Paris, at five o'clock this afternoon, was perfectly quiet.

EXTRACT OF A DESPATCH FROM LORD MALMESBURY TO LORD GRENVILLE.

Lisle, 9th Sept., 1797.

As it may possibly be expected that I should give some opinion as to the manner in which the negotiation I am carrying on here is likely to be affected by this violent convulsion in the French Government, I shall put in this separate despatch whatever relates more directly to this particular point, entreating your Lordship to read it with that indulgence a letter of this nature necessarily requires.

I confess, before this extraordinary event had taken place, I was very sanguine in my hopes of success; and from what I have observed since it has happened, from the behaviour and language of MM. Maret and Colchen, I am confident they were equally so; and it now comes out, beyond a doubt, that they were perfectly true and sincere in everything they said on this subject. I collect, from a person who enjoys their most intimate confidence, that they still entertain hopes, and that even the appointment of M. Delacroix does not discourage in them the idea that our Treaty may still be signed. They contend that the Directory must make peace, to ensure by popularity the power they have acquired by force; that one of the heaviest charges which they brought against the Councils was, that they prevented, by their factious opposition, the possibility of peace being made; and this charge may, without the power of reply, be retorted on the Directory, if they, in their present situation of unmolested authority, refuse to consent to such conditions as it is understood we are ready to grant.

But, notwithstanding the deference I have for their judgment, and that their opinion is so very analogous to my wishes, I am free to confess that I cannot subscribe to it; for, although I admit the truth of their facts, and great plausibility of their arguments, yet their being true and plausible does not appear to me sufficient grounds for the inference they draw, when we consider the character and disposition of the Directory. It is to this we must look as the only test by which we can determine their probable conduct; and, if we are to be directed by it, I much fear we either must not expect peace at all, or expect it on conditions the most intolerable.

It is, I think, proved to demonstration, that the Negotiation was begun on the part of the French Government with an intention of breaking it off on the first favourable opportunity; and that it has been protracted to the present day, because the majority in the Councils would have reprobated such a step, in a way which might have very materially affected, if not entirely prevented, the execution of the vast design the Directory have since accomplished. It is known that the original instructions given to the French Plenipotentiaries were drawn up by M. Chas. Delacroix, under the advice of MM. Barras and Rewbell; that they appeared extravagant even to M. Le Tourneur; and it is scarce to be credited that M. Delacroix himself would now come to act under the more reasonable and moderate instructions sent to the French Plenipotentiaries by his successor, M. Talleyrand, and on which all hopes of peace were grounded.

Besides, whatever may be the language of placards and journals, there are some expressions in the Directorial Messages which by no means look pacific. "*Dicter la paix*" is used in one of them; and, in another, "*une paix digne du triomphe du Peuple Français et de sa générosité;*" which last phrase, I presume, applies to their allies, rather than to their enemies, although in either case it is the language of haughty and imperious demagogues.

In short, my Lord, unless they depart entirely from their character and system, I scarcely can be brought to hope for a favourable termination to our Mission; and they hitherto appear to have acted but too systematically; for, to what we have now seen happen, I impute the dilatory answer repeatedly sent from Holland, and the sudden cessation of correspondence between Count Cabarras and M. Maret, (a circumstance I omitted to mention at the proper time,) and all the delays, real or imaginary, which have succeeded each other, and stopped the progress of the Negotiation since the middle of July; and, if we want a more recent instance of the views and intentions of the Directory, it is to be found in M. La Réveillière Lépaux superseding M. Barthelemi in the presidence of the Directory, and in beginning his office by a speech which, though not in opposition, perhaps, to his general political sentiments, was certainly very unlike the natural phlegm and tranquillity of his character.

The arrival of M. Delacroix will, however, very shortly determine the question; and although it will be impossible for me not to carry to the first conference I shall have with him the opinion I have just expressed, yet I shall be most happy to acknowledge my mistake, and to find there is a probability of my going on as smoothly with him as I am confident I should have done with the others, had not this extraordinary revolution taken place at Paris.

EXTRACTS OF A LETTER FROM LORD MALMESBURY TO
MR. PITT.

Lisle, 9th Sept., 1797.

I* I do not write to you by every messenger, it is because my letters could be only a repetition of what I say to Canning, or of my official Correspondence, and the reading of them would be giving you useless trouble.

The violent revolution which has taken place at Paris has overset all our hopes, and defeated all our reasonings. I consider it as the *most unlucky event that could have happened.* We were certainly very near obtaining the great object of our wishes, and I fear we are now more driven out to sea again than ever. I have given my sentiments so freely and so fully (as I considered it my duty to do), in my despatches by this messenger, that there is nothing left for me to say in a private letter. My apprehensions that the Negotiation may now fail, shall not affect my conduct; I will strain every nerve to weather the storm, and the arrival of Ch. Delacroix will operate upon me like a *stimulant.* I am not sorry that, this time, we shall converse before witnesses.

There can be no doubt whatever that we shall begin business in earnest on Monday next; and I think I may safely take upon me to say, that before the end of the week I shall send over George Ellis, if what I have to transmit is worthy of such a messenger. In the mean time I wish Lord G. Leveson would return, as I shall, when Ellis goes, be in want of his society and his assistance, although Morpeth is of great comfort to me in both these respects.

I am, &c.

———

Sunday, Sept. 10.—Le Tourneur at home; nothing new; walk by the side of the river to Marquette; Maret and Ducos came at half-past three; Delacroix's coming very doubtful; the letters directed to him here were probably sent by mistake. Maret reasons still in favour of peace, and that, if Charles Delacroix had come, it certainly would have been with pacific instructions. He would have asked for this nomination, in order to be appointed afterwards to England. He was more attached to his interest than his political principles; and although, if he had remained in office, he might have gratified his hatred to England, and spleen against us, yet he would scarcely take a journey of one hundred and fifty miles, with his infirmities, merely for that purpose. Maret again here; mentioned their *original* instructions drawn up by *him*, and which he said were such as could not be produced, so very intolerable were the conditions stated in them. Le Tourneur certainly wishes peace, and hopes for no alteration, either in the Legation or the instructions. On my asking Maret about Holland, he said Noel had written him word that the Dutch began to be more tractable, but it was not to a very great degree. General ———, Inspector of this Division, who came here a day or two ago, said Colonel Cabarras had left Brussels on the 5th inst., and he understood that he was coming here. He probably had some advice of what was likely to happen from his daughter, Madame Tallien,* and is gone to Paris, or keeps aloof.—At the play; Isidore and Ducos came into my box; then Colchen, and also Maret. Isidore said he believed Delacroix would not come: it would be singular if he were appointed: he had dismissed him, Ducos, and Colchen from his office, on being appointed to the Relations Extérieures, and it would be hard if he was to follow them here for the same purpose. After all, if the Negotiation was to break off, he had rather it should be done by any one than by themselves. He talked of the weakness of the evidence to be deduced from D'Entraigue's papers against Pichegru, and that great part of them were manifestly forged.

Colchen entered into a very long discussion on the times with infinite good sense and calmness, and in the language of a man accustomed to think seriously on public events. What he said was nearly this—That, from his private attachment

---

* Tallien was a violent Jacobin, scarcely less bloodthirsty in his career than Robespierre, whom he overthrew. He followed Napoleon to Egypt, and, being taken by the English on his return, came to London, and was *fêté* by the Whig Club, and at Devonshire House. He lived unnoticed under Napoleon, and died in extreme want in 1820.—(Biog. Univ.)

Madame Tallien, celebrated for her beauty and wit, exercised a favourable influence over her husband, in restraining him amidst his cruelties. She was divorced from him, and afterwards married the Prince de Chimay.

to several of the individuals comprised in the proscription, he was deeply affected by it, particularly by the sentence passed on Barthelemi, with whom he was connected by the sincerest friendship; that this friendship would never be impaired by false accusations; and he was the more hurt, because he was the principal cause of Barthelemi's accepting the post of Director. But he thought now, as he did at the time, that it was his duty to accept, and he could not repent the advice he had given, although it had produced such fatal effects to his friend; that Barthelemi was prepared for the event; that he foresaw what might happen; but, tired of revolutions and their consequences, which had been so fatal to his family, he was determined to accept the office of Director, *et de se dévouer à la chose publique*. His object never was any other than to support and strengthen the present form of constitution. Colchen then mentioned the circumstances of his (Barthelemi's) uncle's death, and the firmness he shewed on this occasion. He was eighty years of age. He furnished all the materials of '*Le Jeune Anarcharsis;*' but Barthelemi's brother, who was employed in the King's library, was the *redacteur* of these materials. He went on to say, that all the persons arrested are the most estimable and most able men in the Republic. It is for this reason, and not from any principles of Royalism, (for such principles do not belong to them,) that they are sentenced to banishment. *They* would have supported the Constitution; but, in doing this, they would have circumscribed the authority of the executive power, and have taken from the Directory the means of acquiring and of exercising undue authority: that the seeing this Constitution so easily overthrown was painful to him, because it contradicted his opinions as to the wisdom and fairness of the basis on which it stood; and that its being abolished, and a dictatorial authority instituted in its place, destroyed in him, for the moment, every hope of quiet at home and peace abroad: that in regard to himself he certainly would fall with his friend, and expected every hour to be dismissed. These, he said, were serious causes for being deeply afflicted; but that he had lived long enough in the world, and acquired a sufficient degree of experience, to bear them with resignation, and not to be surprised at their happening. He then went on by saying, that it was quite impossible that the struggle *(la lutte)* between the two great authorities should not be renewed; that he had much confidence in the spirit and disposition of the Council of Ancients: that it consisted of two hundred and fifty; that, of these, eighty only were Montagnards, and amongst these several were Terrorists, and, of course, anti-directorial; that only twelve or thirteen of this Council had been banished, and that of course there remained a very great majority, with Dupont de Nemours at their head; that they would certainly, when the first moment of fermentation was over, see the great violation that had been exercised on the Constitution. They would set an inquiry on foot to know " *Why* the place of meeting of the Councils had been altered; *why* laws had been repealed in four days, when the Constitution required a year for so doing; *why* others had been enacted, in direct breach of its fundamental principles; *why*, when, by the constitutional act, a regular form of proceeding was provided for the impeachment and trial of members of either Council, these had all been set aside, and the most arbitrary proceeding adopted in their place; *why*, in equal violation of the fundamental laws, two Directors had been banished out of the Republic; and *why* all this had been done without any regular trial, on the most imperfect evidence, on supposed or real facts which had happened a long time back, which were all known to have happened for many months, and before the last elections, not only by the Directory, but in a manner by the public; and *why*, instead of bringing the persons accused to justice, if they were guilty, at the moment these facts came to their knowledge, they waited so long, and now thought them such strong proofs of guilt as to authorize them to punish without hearing any defence, and to break through the Constitution in all its most sacred points." That with such very powerful reasons, which no argument or assertion could overthrow, he was in hopes the Council of Ancients would again return to its former conduct, and that it would be followed in time by that of the Five Hundred was little to be doubted; a new contention would then be opened between them and the Directory, in which they would stand on the constitutional

ground; they would be supported at least by the opinion
and wishes of the nation (for he was fully convinced, that
their minds were so worn out and disgusted with revolutions, and so cowed by persecution, that nothing short
of self defence could induce them to move or act); and,
besides the next to impossibility that the Directory could
venture on a second measure of deportation, there could be
no mock conspiracy to allege, or any fresh papers, real or
fabricated, to produce, on a point where they were the party
attacked, not the attacking party. That the great object to
look at with attention was the armies; that, if they entered
France for the purpose of supporting the Directory, no other
government than martial law could exist, and this return of
the armies was the only case he reserved for the people acting. They would act for their own self-defence in such a
case; and a civil war become inevitable. But when he considered the characters of the two Directorial generals, Buonaparte and Hoche, he did not think this likely. The first,
whose reputation was made, would not risk it by joining in
a civil commotion; and besides, it was known almost to a
certainty, that he had views for himself in Italy, and perhaps even in Greece: that, as for Hoche,* he had not yet
*fait ses preuves, et qu'il brûloit d'avoir l'occasion.* That he
therefore would be very unwilling to be employed merely for
the police of the country, and would encourage foreign war—
more likely with Germany, where he was almost as much his
own master as Buonaparte was in Italy. He therefore did
not think the armies would lend themselves for this purpose;
since, besides the views of their commanders, the soldiery
were divided in opinion, and would not be pushed into the
heart of France. The result of his reasoning was, that the
supreme authorities would go on contending till one completely subdued the other; and that in his opinion (which
however he confessed might be biassed by his wishes) he
thought it more probable that the Councils would prevail;
but it might be a long struggle, and while it lasted be

---

* The brave Hoche was near his end. He died this same year, by poison,
aged 29. He was Buonaparte's rival in military fame, having commanded the
army of the Moselle at 24, and gained repeated victories over the Austrians and
Prussians. His attempt upon Ireland, when his fleet was partly dispersed by
storms and partly destroyed by ours, is well known to the reader.

attended with every kind of public evil and misfortune. On collateral grounds, he said, that the two new Directors, Merlin de Douay and François Neufchâteau, were well known to him. He had seen a great deal of the first when he belonged to the Committee of Public Safety, where he himself was employed, with the rest of the clerks in the Foreign Office, as a secretary. That Merlin was a very laborious, indefatigable man, with great courage and firmness of character, and with sufficient abilities ; that he was not a Modéré ; but still that he was inclined to peace, and by no means *un enragé*. That it was Merlin who had ventured first to propose the Prussian, and afterwards the Spanish Peace, at a time when it was dangerous to pronounce the word *peace;* and that he fancied (though he was far from asserting it as a fact), that he was inclined to make peace with England.

Neufchâteau was a *demi-savant.* Voltaire had spoiled him. He was a poet and a *bel-esprit*—not used to business, though thinking himself a statesman ; that he was an honest man, but *qu'il avait l'esprit extrêmement faux.* Both of them were the favourites and dependents of Rewbell ; but that it did not follow from this, that the Directory would be for *war. All* that had hitherto passed, and he could assure me that it was pacific, had been approved by Rewbell ; and it would have been perhaps still more approved, if it had not been too strongly supported by Carnot and Barthelemi ; and, *if* Rewbell meant peace, it was much more likely to happen when the Directory were agreed than before. That Rewbell was ignorant and vain, with the most vulgar prejudices of an uneducated and illiterate mind ; but that he was easily led by those who knew him : that the great secret was not to let him perceive that his ignorance was discovered—by giving him ideas, and then receiving and executing them as his own ; that Merlin understood this perfectly ; and when, in addition to it, by his fondness for business and facility in doing it, he would be able to take almost the whole share of it to himself, and leave Rewbell and Barras time to pursue their enjoyments, (for they were both voluptuaries,) he did not doubt that, in a short time, Merlin must be the leading Director.

The Austrian Peace not yet signed. No letters from Udine

for the last fortnight, although every person seems to say that that Negotiation is now on the point of being concluded.

Maret said nothing new this evening; that he considered the nomination of Charles Delacroix as very doubtful; but, if he did come, it certainly would be with pacific instructions. His reasonings like those of the others. I should give them more credit, if the people with whom we have to deal were like others; but they are not governed by the same rules and principles, and the causes and effects do not agree when applied to them, as they would were they like the rest of mankind.

MONDAY, SEPT. 11.—Colchen called to say, that the post of this morning had brought the recall of the whole French Legation, and that Treilhard* and Bonnier d'Alco† were appointed in their stead. He added, that they were required to say, that this would make no alteration in the principles of the Negotiation, or in the sentiments of the French Government. Treilhard, originally a very famous advocate at Paris, was of the Constituent Assembly, du Coté Gauche, and behaved well; afterwards of the Convention, where he became of the Mountain. He voted the King's death, and was at the head of a revolutionary committee. When the present Constitution was formed, the Directory appointed him Consul at Naples. Colchen called him "un homme qui avoit de la loyauté et de la franchise, avec de la bonhommie;" at the same time, he described him as *un emporté*, but was sure he would be attentive in observing all the forms of civility and good manners. Bonnier d'Alco, a Languedocian, was one of the members *qui étoit au haut de la Montagne*. He was cried up extremely before he appeared in the Constituent Assembly, where he was sent to be an equal to Mirabeau, but he never opened his mouth, and retired in order to get round (*pour accaparer*) Rewbell; and it was this D'Alco who assisted him in drawing up all the papers

---

* Treilhard was employed in several missions by the Republican Government, and was made Councillor of State by Napoleon. He died in 1810.

† Bonnier d'Alco in the ensuing year was sent to the Congress of Radstadt as Plenipotentiary. On his way to Strasburg, after the rupture of the Negotiations, he and his colleague, Robergot, were killed by a detachment of Austrian Hussars.—(Biog. Univ.)

when he directed the Department of Foreign Affairs, for Charles Delacroix was trusted with nothing. Since Barthelemi's election, all those departments in the Directory have been suppressed, and D'Alco was without employment. He is a rank Jacobin; he was very "aimable," but is now quite the reverse. They are to choose their own secretary.

Colchen observed, that he was, in his own mind, persuaded the Directory meant peace; and that, if they had intended a rupture, they would have left to them the *désagrément* of transacting it. "*On n'aime pas les amis de ses ennemis*," and it was very natural that the *successful* termination of the Negotiation should not be left to them. Many, and I believe sincere, regrets on their recall, as far as it related to us personally. Le Tourneur seemed particularly to feel these. He very angry and mortified. Maret bears it well and *gaiement*. I am heartily sorry on every account to lose them. They have acted openly and fairly by me; more so than I ever experienced from any French negotiators with whom I have had to do.

Pein at twelve, to announce what we had already heard. Cheerful note from Maret. Agree that Maret, from his intimacy with Talleyrand, may still be of use, and that he would be so when at Paris. Pein abused the two new negotiators; said they were rank Jacobins; but, like all the others, contended we should have peace. He said, the Directory would name to the vacancies in the Councils, and call the primary assemblies together before the time fixed, viz. 1st of Germinal next.

Conference. Writing.—Play—My box filled with the French Legation—Mesdames Pascal and Jouÿ. The Commissary of Executive Power called Le Tourneur out to say, that he had discovered that Carnot was here, and that I was going to send him away with a passport, disguised as a courier (Vanscheick[*] being taken for Carnot); it was very amusing. Le Tourneur in a rage—abused the Commissary. "Tant qu'il étoit ici, c'étoit à lui de régler les ordres pour mes

[*] A very faithful old servant, who had been with Lord Malmesbury in Russia, and was always employed by him to carry important despatches. He was of gigantic stature and strength; and, as he could never be persuaded that his master's life was safe in France, he always insisted on sleeping across the outside of his door.

couriers ; et s'il étoit nécessaire d'y veiller, que l'intervention du Commissaire étoit preuve de sa bêtise et de sa malveillance." Maret apologised to me. I said it was much more a matter of laughter than of anger, and by no means worthy of notice. Vanscheick started at midnight.

SATURDAY, SEPT. 9, 24TH CONFERENCE.—Le Tourneur began by saying he had no letters, and went on by assuring me, that he could, with certainty, promise me the Negotiation would go on on Monday. I did not remark the impossibility of his affirming this so positively if he had received *no* letters. Maret said he had received a letter from the Hague (from Noel), which was a little more satisfactory than the answers hitherto made by the Dutch. Colchen was silent.

MONDAY, SEPT. 11, 25TH CONFERENCE.—Le Tourneur announced to me his recall, and that of the whole Legation. Treilhard and Bonnier named to succeed them. He had orders to say, that this was to produce no change as to the dispositions of the Directory. Very much hurt. Maret said, " Nous sommes victimes de l'amitié ; Le Tourneur a été sacrifié à cause de son attachement pour Carnot, moi à cause du mien pour Barthelemi." Colchen silent. I begged them to give me an official Note of what they said, and it was sent me before dinner.

EXTRACTS OF A DESPATCH FROM LORD MALMESBURY TO LORD GRENVILLE.

Lisle, 11th Sept., 1797.

M. COLCHEN called on me this morning, immediately after the arrival of the letters from Paris, to acquaint me with the recall of the whole French Mission, and to prepare me for what I was to hear at the Conference.

I was very sincere when I expressed to him my concern at what he told me ; and I should be highly unjust if I was not to declare that, under the circumstances for which we are met, it is impossible to have conducted themselves with more cordiality, good-humour, and good faith, than the whole of the French Legation, as well in their official capacity as when we have met (as we have daily of late) under the more familiar and intimate intercourse of private society.

M. Treilhard was, before the Revolution, an advocate of distinction at Paris, and was chosen a member of the Constituent Assembly, where his conduct met with very general approbation : but, during the progress of the Revolution, he became more and more exaggerated in his ideas of liberty, and, being returned to the Convention, gave his vote for the King's death ; and, during the Reign of Terror, distinguished himself in the Revolutionary Committee as an active and zealous, though not a cruel, partisan of the Mountain. On account of these principles, though his character in point of probity is unimpeached, he became generally odious to the nation ; and, when the Directory had appointed him as Consul to the Court of Naples, they were forced, by the indignation which was excited by the indecency of sending one of the King's judges to a Court where his sister-in-law was on the throne, to revoke the nomination. Though his temper is passionate and violent, his manners are said to be decent and proper, his behaviour frank and open, and his talents respectable.

M. Bonnier d'Alco was a President de la Cour des Aides at Montpellier, a man of letters, and possessing the sort of talents which, during the Monarchy, were admired in society. He was returned to the Legislative Assembly, and, from the reputation he carried with him, he was expected to become the rival of Mirabeau in eloquence ; but he never opened his mouth, and has never distinguished himself, except by the Jacobinical violence of his principles during the course of the Revolution. He was a member of the Convention and of the Legislative Councils, but went out on the first third. During the time that the Directory had a separate office distinct from the several ministerial departments, Rewbell, who had assumed to himself the management of Foreign Affairs, and who was at a loss for a person who should have sufficient talents for the office, and who should, at the same time, be so obscure as to leave him in possession of all the credit arising from it, made choice of Bonnier ; and he was the person who really drew up all the diplomatic papers that were submitted to the Directory while Ch. Delacroix (who never enjoyed any confidence) was in office. He is said to have adopted, in lieu of the elegant manners for which he was once distinguished, the Jacobinical arrogance of his party, and to be haughty and impracticable in business. His general character is as bad as possible.

It is the unanimous opinion of the French Mission, and I do not doubt that they were perfectly sincere when they gave it me, that this new appointment will make no difference whatever in the event of the Negotiation, and that it will proceed precisely as it would have done if it had been left in their hands.

M. Le Tourneur, who is not the least hurt by this abrupt dismissal, was even stronger in his assurances on this point than his colleagues; and he went so far as to say, "*Qu'on lui avoit arraché la douceur de faire la Paix.*"

In regard to my own opinion, I confess it remains nearly the same. The new Plenipotentiaries may perhaps bring what they may term a pacific *contre-projêt;* but, till I find it really deserves that character, I cannot admit expectations and hopes into my mind which to me seem to rest on no solid foundation, and which the tried character of this Government by no means authorizes.

---

EXTRACTS OF A LETTER FROM LORD MALMESBURY TO MR. CANNING.

Lisle, 11th Sept., 1797.

IF you do not intend that I should remain here alone, and in my shirt, (for I shall be compelled to pawn my clothes if you do not supply me with the means of going on,) send me *messengers and boxes.* I should not have parted with so necessary a servant as the man I now send, if I did not think it material that the names, characters, and dispositions of my new antagonists should be known, and time given for reflection in consequence. It is not fair to bring in *fresh* men after I have been so long in the field; and it is seriously a matter of very great concern to me to lose those with whom I have acted hitherto : their whole conduct and behaviour has been as straight-forward and as honourable as possible; and I have little, I will say no doubt, but that, if this ill-timed mischief had not burst forth at Paris, we should have ended our Negotiation in a very satisfactory way to our respective Governments and to ourselves. As it is, the most I can do is, to begin this fresh encounter with no unfavourable impressions ; for, however just and probable the reasonings I hear may be why it should terminate to my advantage, I cannot give them admission, or allow myself to retain a particle of those sanguine hopes I entertained (and I believe so justly) at the time of Wesley's last departure. But remember, there is a broad line between hope and despondency; that I shall carry none of this last to the Conferences I may hold, but act as if I was persuaded that moderate and just propositions ought to prevail over arrogant and ridiculous pretensions.

George Ellis writes : pray, when he comes to England, do not let him coax you into the propriety of his remaining there, and that there is no necessity for his returning to Lisle. The fact is, there is no reason at all, everything considered, that makes his being in England an hour beyond that belonging to the business, even a justifiable measure *for a man like him, in times like these.*

Pray send Leveson back; he will not be in at the death else.

LETTER FROM MR. PITT TO LORD MALMESBURY.

Downing Street, 11th Sept., 1797.

MY DEAR LORD,—If Lord Granville had been the bearer of the despatch now sent you, I would have written to you all that occurs to me (vague and conjectural as it must be) on the late extraordinary events. Deferring that for the present, I need now only say, that on the main points in question in the Negotiation my opinions remain *unalterably* what I stated to you in our last *conversation;* that, on that line, I shall *at all events* act; and that *collateral* difficulties may, I think, always be overcome by a mixture of firmness and temper. I rather incline both to believe and hope that the party now predominant will think the enjoyment of their triumph more likely to be both complete and secure in peace than in war. Yours, &c. W. PITT.

---

TUESDAY, SEPT. 12.—Sent my answer to the French Note announcing the recall. Called on Madame Ducos. She very well-bred, gentle, and *naïve;* very unreserved in her public sentiments, and very sorry and angry at the recall. Play— in the French box nothing new, vague reports; general belief that the present state of things would not last; that it was not even over; that all the public papers we saw concealed the real truth, and that in some of them they appeared to confess they did so from fear; that it was extraordinary no one had arrived here from Paris; that it looked as if things were not settled, and this idea confirmed by the great eagerness the Directory expressed to proceed with rapidity. But all these are conjectures, and although they may be founded on probability, yet are certainly not such as to be acted on. *My* belief is, that this event may produce an *immediate* evil by breaking off the public negotiation with which I am charged; but that, in the end, it may tend to create such a confusion and disorder here, that more essential advantages may arise from it than any which would follow the conclusion of peace at this moment. The only consideration to be attended to (and it is one that overrules all others) is the way in which it will be understood and felt in England; and whether it will be possible to impress this very probable chance so forcibly on the minds of the public at large as to prevent the effects of their disappointment at the breaking off a Treaty they had reason (and with great truth) to think on the point of being concluded, and to raise in them a spirit and disposition to carry on the war with vigour for one or two more campaigns. Were this certain, I should not consider the event of the 4th September as one at all to be lamented; for here it is, *I really* believe, impossible by any means, even by force, to get at money equal to pursue the war in a way dangerous to us. The war too is become most unpopular; and its duration will be more so, when it is made evident to the French that the terms proposed by us were such as this Government could not have repelled if they sincerely meant either the advantage of the country or the good of the people.

WEDNESDAY, SEPT. 13.—On getting up, it was said the new Plenipotentiaries had arrived in the night; at eleven they went to the Municipality, and from thence sent their Secretary to me, to ask when I would receive them. I said, Immediately. They came accompanied by their predecessors. Treilhard spoke: he said he had orders to declare the pacific intentions of the French Government; and that he and his colleague were, from their own personal feelings, strongly disposed to act up to them. He then talked, and talked well, and like a man " qui a l'usage du monde." His countenance is a good one, his manners easy and well-bred. Bonnier said little: his countenance vile; his dress and address affectedly Jacobin, and his whole accoutrement in the same character; he looked like a *proselyte* to those principles, and rather ashamed to be in good company, to which he had once belonged. The Secretary, Monsieur Derché, also of a Jacobin appearance. On leaving me, Le Tourneur in a very well turned phrase, and with a good manner, said, " Nous ne pouvons, Milord, terminer notre Mission, et nous éloigner de vous, sans vous témoigner la satisfaction que nous avons eue de traiter avec un négotiateur qui s'est conduit avec autant de loyauté et de franchise. Nous n'en perdrons jamais le souvenir, et nous espérons conserver une place dans votre estime comme vous en aurez toujours dans la nôtre." I made a suitable reply to this very civil, and (if we consider that his successors were present) very manly and handsome speech. As soon as they were gone, I sent Ross to inquire their hour, and when I might return the visit. The answer was " Immediately, if I chose it." I went. The old Legation did not come into the room. I presented Ellis and Morpeth. Treilhard again took the lead in the conversation, repeated his instructions were pacific, and his disposition equally so. " Qu'il désiroit faire la paix avec tout le monde." Bonnier rather more communicative. He repeated what Treilhard said, and seemed to have more sense than his countenance and outward manners announce. On entering the room I said, " Que j'étois empressé de rendre égards pour égards," and repeated what Le Tourneur had said to me on my first coming. We agreed to hold no Conference to-day, and perhaps not to-morrow. They attended me to the door.

From them we called on our old friends, whom we found assembled in Madame Ducos's room. We vied with each other in assurances of regret, &c., and were equally sincere; for I must repeat, nothing can have been more straightforward, more liberal, and more confidential than the whole of the behaviour of them all. Le Tourneur took uncommon pains to express his concern at leaving me. He gave me his direction, and we made a kind of promise to correspond. Madame Ducos had tears in her eyes, and the most amiable confiding freedom possible in her manners and expressions. Le Tourneur, whom I whispered as we went down stairs, said that he believed their instructions were really pacific, and that Peace would be made. He spoke well of Treilhard, as did Colchen. Certainly the first impression is in his favour, as much as it is against Bonnier. In the evening walked by the side of the Canal de Douay with Monsieur and Madame Ducos and Maret. The latter said they had been giving an account, and a very exact one, to their successors, of all that had passed in the course of the negotiation up to this day; and from the way in which they received it, and particularly from their having expressed their approbation of declining to bring forward the extravagant instructions drawn up by Charles Delacroix, he was inclined to think their orders were pacific, and that they would *bonâ fide* go on with the negotiation in the same manner, and with the same object, as it had proceeded hitherto. He said, on his arrival at Paris he should be able to know the precise truth of this, and would take care to keep me informed—*his idea of two seals*—that if the Bishop of Autun stayed on, he should have it in his power to do this, and with great utility. He said he believed we should be able to get from the Dutch Trincomalee, and all the towns and military establishments in

Ceylon, if we would consent to carry on the trade in common with the Dutch, and not monopolize the commerce; that some means might be devised for making the Cape neutral, under all circumstances of peace or war. He wished to know of me whether these conditions would be sufficient. I hesitated as to the Cape; but believed some arrangements, like that he proposed, might be made for Ceylon. He said that Spain wanted a great deal, and would bring forth extravagant proposals, but that she would give nothing; perhaps France would consent to increase our settlements near Senegal, if we restored Trinidad. That in regard to the claim of France, the Toulon ships would not be a great difficulty, nor the mortgage on the Low Countries; but that a stand would be made on the King's title, and not easily got rid of. That they wanted also something more at Newfoundland, but to a small extent. That I should find Treilhard disposed to please and be civil. The other, Bonnier, was become *farouche.* That, however, they wished to live familiarly and on an easy footing with us, and were very particular in their inquiries about those with us. He told them I had sent one of my suite to England when anything extraordinary occurred, and he prepared them for my doing so again. Speaking of them, he said, they appeared embarrassed and awkward. He thought the business would last much longer, as no answer was yet arrived from Holland. In speaking of Paris, he said, " *L'affaire paroissoit s'affermir et prendre racine.*" He believed in Moreau's letter about Pichegru. We walked till it was dark. At half-past eight, Maret and Colchen called to take leave of me; very friendly and kind behaviour. The new ministers have for their Secrétaire Général Monsieur Derché, Chef de la troisième division politique dans le Bureau des Affaires Etrangères. He talks English. He was a teacher of French in London, and was sent away under the Alien Bill in the beginning of the war. Each of them has also a private secretary. Pein told Ellis, that Treilhard was "*faux comme un jeton, avec des manières assez séduisantes.*"

THURSDAY, SEPT. 14.—Le Tourneur left Lisle early: Maret and his friends at noon.* I received in the night accounts, brought back by Vanscheick from Calais, of the messengers Brooks and Magister being drowned as they were landing in a boat from the Diana packet, Captain Osborne, off Calais; one out of the two sailors was saved, and all the boxes but one, in which there was nothing material. I heard since from the messenger J. Panter, that Brooks held by the boat three-quarters of an hour; that then his strength failed him,—in about twenty minutes afterwards relief came.† Nothing was brought by this messenger except very comfortable private letters from Pitt. I had just time to communicate this to Maret, &c., before they went away. Drove with Morpeth and Ellis by the Douay canal, and walked to some distance; the sides of it, about five miles from Lisle, very pleasant. An Abbé Dumontel, who said he was connected with Drake,‡ wrote me a letter in the evening, expressing a wish to see me, and that he had important things to communicate. I sent Ross to him: it appeared that he was connected closely with Montgaillard,§ and one of the useless agents employed by our duped Ministers in Italy. I refused to see him, and recommended his instant departure from Lisle.‖

* Maret always retained a high opinion of Lord Malmesbury, and it is probable from the following anecdote that he had expressed it to Napoleon.
Extract of a letter from the Dowager Princess of Orange to the Greffier Fagel, dated Berlin, 1809:—
"Je ne vous parle pas politique, car je ne saurois qu'en dire que vous ne sachiez comme moi; car avant que le voile tombe entièrement, on ne peut encore s'en former une idée juste. La plupart de ce que l'on sçait des plans de celui qui dispose des destinées de l'Europe ne sont encore que des conjectures. Parmi les anecdotes curieuses que M Alopeus m'a raconté de la présentation à Paris, il y en a une qu'il auroit voulu pouvoir faire connaitre, s'il lui fut permis d'écrire de vos côtés; c'est le grand éloge que Buonaparte a fait de Lord Malmesbury. Il dépend de vous de le lui dire, si vous croyez que cela puisse l'intéresser. Buonaparte est revenu plusieurs fois sur ce chapitre. Quel en a été l'apropos ou le but, voilà ce que j'ignore."
† Lord Granville Leveson, in spite of his earnest request to be allowed to return to Lisle, as he had promised, with these messengers, was detained by Mr. Pitt for a few days, and saved his life by this delay. He would otherwise have shared the fate of poor Brooks, whose name has often recurred in these volumes.
‡ British Minister at Stuttgart.
§ A political intriguer attached to the army of Prince Condé. He had been banished from London under the Alien Act in 1794.
‖ Lord Malmesbury afterwards discovered that this Dumontel was sent to

Friday, Sept. 15.—Visit from Hamilton and Jouÿ; first conference with Treilhard and Bonnier: Ellis with Pein in the evening. Pein said the note given me by the new Plenipotentiaries was *Ch. Delacroix tout craché;* augured ill from it; did not understand it; saw there was something behind. At the play; no one in the French box but their secretaries, most ill-looking fellows. Two officers of the *Troupes de Ligne* were with them, but no one of those who used to frequent the box went near them.

Saturday, Sept. 16.— Walked. Evident dissatisfaction in everybody's face on the change in the French Legation. Vanacker, the bookseller, concealed all such books as were anti-revolutionary; and the dread of a return of the System of Terror seemed to prevail universally.—A Note from the Plenipotentiaries, sending me home in twenty-four hours.

Sunday, Sept. 17.—Last Conference at twelve. Writing; Play; Consternation on my going away very general. The conduct of the French Government quite unintelligible. The Plenipotentiaries as civil in their manners as possible, and *outrés* in pacific professions, as well in their own name as in that of the Directory; yet their conduct is more violent and absurd than was ever heard of. It was a matter of very interesting curiosity to me to see the *real Jacobin's* manner and costume, which Bonnier had assumed; insolent, with an air and affectation of protecting civility: Treilhard was more open and frank. It was also a very curious circumstance to see the horror that prevailed everywhere, lest the System of Terror should be revived. People looked as if some *Exterminating Spirit* was approaching: this fear *must in the end* create resistance, although, perhaps, at a

entrap him into an interview, and enable the Directory to hold up Lord Malmesbury as conspiring against the State, and they would have founded their rupture of the negotiations upon this plea. Adolphus's account of this circumstance is incorrectly told, as he states that Lord Malmesbury met the traitor in person. It is the only error I have discovered in his work which I have been able to test from the internal evidence of the Harris Papers. Both as to facts and *motives*, Adolphus is singularly exact.

distant period. At the play, the actors partook of the sensation. The Directeur called Paris said to Ross, on his paying him, "*Nous allons actuellement être Vandalisés.*" Madame Chevalier, who learnt it in the middle of the play, was so affected as not to be able to sing as usual. She and her sister (Madame Fabrassart) came to me after the play, and expressed their concern and apprehensions in the strongest degree. Ellis with Pein; the latter astonished, and very angry; said that they were *les plus méchants des sots*, &c.

### LETTER FROM MR. PITT TO LORD MALMESBURY.

Hollwood, Thursday, 14th Sept., 1797.

MY DEAR LORD,—I have this moment learned from Canning, that the equinox has been fatal to two of our messengers, and that it is doubtful whether our packet will have reached you in a legible state. I do not like to detain the messenger who is to go to-night, by writing at any length, but I wish you extremely to know that I think the business of Portugal cannot be an unsurmountable obstacle; that what has been done at Lisbon before our remonstrance was received, puts it in the best state for any line we may ultimately adopt; and that, on all material points in the whole of your negotiation, my opinion will remain unaltered (though my hopes are rather more sanguine), and my ultimate determination will be what I think you know. I believe, however, all will end in what I shall reckon more than well.    Yours, &c.    W. PITT.

P. S.—I know not what to expect from the underplot of the Revolution in changing the faces of all the French Negotiators. It will be strange if we come to regret Sir Gregory.

[The preceding events described in the Diary were of course officially communicated to Lord Grenville and Mr. Pitt; but, as Lord Malmesbury writes to them almost in the same words as in his Journal, I have omitted the Despatches.]

DESPATCH FROM LORD MALMESBURY TO LORD GRENVILLE.

Lisle, Sunday, 17th Sept., 1797, at Midnight.

My Lord,—I shall endeavour in this despatch to give your Lordship as circumstantial an account as my memory will allow me to do, of what has passed in the two Conferences I have held with the new French Plenipotentiaries.

In that of Friday the 14th, after communicating to me the *arrêté* of the Directory appointing them to succeed Messieurs Le Tourneur and Maret, and empowering them to continue the Negotiation with me, M. Treilhard began by making the strongest assurances of the sincere desire entertained by the Directory for peace. He observed, that, if this desire had manifested itself so strongly at a moment when the two great authorities of the country were at variance, it must naturally become stronger and be exerted with more effect when all spirit of division was suppressed, and when the Government was strengthened by the perfect concord which now reigns between all its branches. That the first and most material point to be ascertained in every negotiation was the extent of the full powers with which the Negotiators are vested; that I should find theirs to be very ample, and that, as it was necessary to the success of our discussions that mine should be equally so, they had it in command to present a Note, the object of which was to inquire whether I was authorized to treat on the principle of a *general restitution of every possession remaining in His Majesty's hands, not only belonging to them, but to their Allies;* that I was not unacquainted with their laws and with their treaties; that a great country could not on any occasion act in contradiction to them; and that, aware, as I must be, of this, I could not but expect the question contained in the Note, neither could I consider the requisition of an explicit answer previous to entering upon the negotiation as arising from any other motive than that of the most perfect wish on the part of the Directory to bring it to a successful, and, above all, to a speedy conclusion.

I replied that, if, after what I heard, I could allow myself to hope for such an event as he seemed to think probable, or give any credit to the pacific dispositions he announced on the part of the French Government, such hope must arise solely from the confidence I might place in his assurances, since the measure itself now adopted by the Directory was certainly calculated to make a directly *contrary impression* on my mind; that I could not conceal from him, that, far from expecting such a question, it being now put surprised me beyond measure; and still more so, when, from his comment upon it, I was to infer that he wished me to consider it as tending to promote a speedy pacification; that the question expressed in the Note he had delivered (for he had given it to me, and I had read it over as he ended his speech) was word for word the same as that put to me by his predecessors so long ago as the 14th July; that on the 15th, I had, from my own authority, given an answer, and that this answer I confirmed fully and distinctly, by order of my Court, on the 24th July; that these Notes had to the present hour remained *unnoticed*, and a delay of *two months* had occurred; that the reasons assigned for this delay were, as I was repeatedly told, a decided resolution on the part of the French Government to listen to the reasonable proposals made by His Majesty; but that being bound by their engagements with the Court of Madrid and the Batavian Republic, and wishing to treat their Allies with due consideration, they were desirous of consulting with them previous to any positive declaration, and obtaining from them a voluntary release from those engagements sufficient to enable the French Plenipotentiaries here to admit the basis His Majesty had established, and to ground on it all future discussions which might arise in the course of the Negotiation; that, if he had read over the papers left undoubtedly in his possession by his predecessors, he would find what I stated to be strictly true; and that of course it could not be difficult to account for my surprise, when, after being told that he and his colleagues were to take up the Negotiation precisely where they found it, it now became evident that it was to be flung back to the very point from which we started, and flung back in a way which seemed to threaten a conclusion very different from that he foretold.

I shall not attempt to follow M. Bonnier through the very elaborate and certainly able speech he made in reply, with a view to convince me that the inquiry into the extent of my full powers was the strongest proof the Directory could furnish of their pacific intention, and the shortest road they could take to accomplish the desired end. It was in order to give activity to the Negotiation (*activer* was his word), and to prevent its stagnating, that this demand was made so specifically; and he intimated to me, that it was impossible for the Directory to proceed till a full and satisfactory answer had been given to it. I interrupted him here by saying their manner of acting appeared to me calculated to decide the Negotiation at once, not to give it activity ("de décider d'abord, et non d'activer la Négociation"), since it must be known I could not have powers of the description he alluded to; and, even supposing I had, the admitting it would be in fact neither more nor less than a complete avowal of the principle itself, which once agreed on, *nothing would be left to negotiate about.* Mr. Treilhard interposed here, by saying, *that would not be the case; many articles would still remain to be proposed, and many points for important discussion.* I said every word I heard seemed to present fresh difficulties. Without replying to me, M. Bonnier went on by endeavouring to prove that the avowal of having powers to a certain extent did not imply the necessity of exercising them; that it was the avowal alone for which they contended, in order to determine at once the form the Negotiation was to take; that the Note, and the time prescribed in it, were in consequence of the most positive orders from the Directory; and that, if I drew from it a conclusion different from the assurances they had made me in the name of the Directory, I did not make the true inference. I replied, that although the prescribing the day on which the question was put to me as the term within which I was to give my answer to it was both a very unusual and abrupt mode of proceeding, yet, as a day was much *more* than sufficient for the purpose, I should forbear making any particular remark on this circumstance. That, as to the inference to be drawn from the positive manner in which they appeared to maintain the question put to me, I really could not make it different from that I had already expressed; that the reverting, after an interval of two months, to a question already answered, and which question involved the fate of the Negotiation, certainly could not be considered as wearing a very conciliatory appearance; that, in regard to my answer, it could not be different from that I had given before. That my full powers, which were in their hands, were as extensive as any could be, and it did not depend on me to give them more or less latitude; but that in fact their question went not to the extent of my *full powers*, but to require of me to deliver the nature of my *instructions*; and on this point they certainly would forgive me, if I did not speak out till such time as the circumstances of the Negotiation called upon me to do it.

M. Bonnier strove to prove to me, what he had before attempted, that the claiming a right of inquiry into the nature of the discretionary authority confided in a Minister by no means implied an intention of requiring of him to act up to its utmost limits. I observed, if no such intention existed, why institute the inquiry? And, if it did not exist, why not say so at once? M. Bonnier said, "What we now ask is little more than a matter of form; when you have given us your answer, we shall follow it up by another step, which we are ordered to take." I said, my answer was given two months ago; that although I was ready to give it them again, and in writing, as one to their note, yet, as it could not be different, I did not see why they should not proceed immediately to the "*other step*," by which I was told the question was to be followed up. "It would be premature," said M. Bonnier. "But, in drawing up your answer, do not forget the force of the arguments I have used; or, in your report to your Court, the assurances we have given of the earnest wish of the Directory to terminate the war."

I replied, that I still must maintain, that, from the manner in which they thought proper to define full powers, I could see no distinction between acknowledging the power and admitting the principle, and that the question itself could not be put with any other intention; (your Lordship will observe, from the subsequent Notes which passed between us, that I was perfectly grounded in this assertion;) that in my reports they might be fully assured I should act up to that conciliatory spirit which, from the earliest period of the Negotiation, had always decided my conduct; and that, inauspicious as appearances were, I certainly would be careful not to make them look *hostile*. At the word "*hostile*," both the French Plenipotentiaries were most warm in their protestations that nothing could be less so; that the idea of the Negotiation breaking off, was as far from their thoughts as from their wishes. I said, that, although I heard this with pleasure, yet I could not avoid adverting to facts; and that when, instead of an answer, and the favourable answer which I had every reason to expect, I received only the repetition of a demand which had been already satisfied two months ago, I certainly could not think this a good omen. If it did not bode an immediate rupture of the Treaty, it assuredly did not announce a near and successful termination of it. M. Bonnier persisted I was mistaken; that the business would end speedily; that speed was their wish, and speed with peace for its object.

On breaking up our Conference, I said, that I took it for granted we should meet again at the usual hour on Sunday. M. Bonnier said, *that it perhaps might not be necessary, but that they certainly would let me know in time;* and this conveyed to me the first idea of what has since taken place.

I inclose your Lordship the Note A, I received in this Conference from the French Plenipotentiaries, and the answer B, which I made to it yesterday morning.

At six P.M. the Note C was transmitted to me, to which, at 8 P.M., I returned the answer D by Mr. Ross, whom I sent in order that he might bring me the passports I asked for. But at a quarter before 10 P.M., M. Derché, Secretary of the French Legation, delivered to me the paper marked E; and this morning, at 9 A.M., I replied by the note F, which immediately produced that marked G.

The Notes sent by the French Plenipotentiaries speak

for themselves; and it is unnecessary to enter into any reflections on them. I am willing to hope that the answers I have made were such as became the situation in which I stand, the importance of the cause entrusted to me, and the steady but temperate conduct which the spirit of my instructions enjoins me to hold.

It was my wish to give every opening to the French Plenipotentiaries to *recall* the violent step they had taken, and, if possible, to convince them of its extreme impropriety; and it was with this view, and with a most anxious desire not to exclude all hope of the restoration of peace, that I determined on suggesting the idea of our meeting before I left Lisle.

This meeting took place to-day at noon. I opened it by observing, that the several Notes they had received from me since the preceding evening had been too expressive of the surprise I felt at the measure the Directory had thought proper to adopt, to make it necessary for me to enlarge upon it in this Conference; and, indeed, my sole motive for suggesting that it might be for our mutual satisfaction that it should be held, was because this measure appeared to me to be in such direct contradiction to the very strong assurances I had so constantly and repeatedly heard from them, and to the pacific intentions with which they declared they were sent, that it was my earnest wish (before I considered their conduct as forcing me to a step which must so materially affect the success of the Negotiation) to be perfectly certain that I understood clearly and distinctly the precise meaning of their official notes. On their admitting that nothing could be more reasonable than that I should on so important a point require explanation, or more satisfactory to them than to give it me (as far as lay in their power), I proceeded by saying, that it appeared to me that I was called upon to produce immediately my full powers, or rather, my instructions; (for, however different these were in themselves, in their demand they seemed constantly blended;) and that, if either I refused to consent to this, or if, on consenting to it, it was found I was not authorized to treat on the principle they laid down, I was then, in the space of twenty-four hours, to leave Lisle, and to return to my Court; and that I was required to obtain full authority to admit this principle, if it was wished the Negotiation should proceed. This, I said, appeared to me to be the evident sense of the Notes, and I begged to know whether I had mistaken it or not. M. Treilhard said, "You have understood it exactly; I hope you equally understand the intention of the French Government, which is to accelerate peace, by removing every obstacle which stands in its way."

I replied, that having now no doubt left on my mind as to their exact meaning, and being quite sure, that, notwithstanding the observation they had made *que je n'avais pas saisi le véritable intention de leur Note*, it would, I feared, be a very unprofitable employment of our time to argue either on the *nature* of the *principle* they announced as a *sine quâ non* to even a preliminary discussion, or on the extreme difficulty of reconciling the peremptory demand with which they opened their Mission, to the pacific professions that accompanied it; that, if they were determined to persist in this demand, it was much better to avoid all useless altercation; and nothing in that case remained for me to do but to ask for my passports, and to signify to them my intention of leaving France at an early hour the next morning.

They said they had their hands tied by an *Arrêté* of the Directory, and were bound to observe the conduct they had followed by the most positive Orders; and, although we remained together some time longer, not a hint dropped from them expressive of a wish that, instead of going myself for new instructions, I should either write for them by a Messenger, or obtain them by sending to England one of the Gentlemen who are with me. I endeavoured by every indirect means to suggest to them the necessity of adopting some such modification, if they meant that their wishes for peace, in the expression of which they were this morning more eager than ever, should meet with the slightest degree of credit. I again brought to their recollection that I was authorized to receive any proposal, any *Contre-Projêt*, they tendered to me; but that they must be aware that it was not possible for me to alter the orders I had received, or to assume an authority with which I was not invested. I dwelt particularly and repeatedly on my being competent to take anything they said for reference; but this availed nothing, except drawing from M. Treilhard a remark, that the full powers which authorized a Minister to hear proposals were widely different from those which would enable him to accede to them, and that it was such full powers that the Directory required me to solicit.

An easy answer presented itself to this mode of reasoning, but I saw no advantage to be derived from prolonging a conversation which, after the positive declaration they had made, could lead to nothing. I therefore ended the Conference by declaring my resolution to begin my journey at a very early hour the next morning, and by saying that immediately on my arrival in England I would make an exact report of everything that had passed since their arrival.

I trust, my Lord, I shall not incur censure for having declined to offer in distinct terms to wait at Lisle till I could know His Majesty's pleasure on the peremptory proposal made to me. But when I considered the nature of the proposal itself, the avowal *that this would not be the last* nor perhaps the most *humiliating* condition required of us, and the *imperious* style with which I was enjoined to depart in twenty-four hours, *it was utterly impossible for me to assume a language, or affect a manner, that could be interpreted into solicitation or entreaty.* I felt myself called upon to treat the whole of this extraordinary proceeding with calmness and temper; and, notwithstanding the deep and poignant concern I must feel at an event which I fear will remove all probability of an immediate pacification, I trust that, in the expression of this sentiment, I have not used a language unbecoming the character with which I am invested, or the greatness of the Sovereign and Country whose dignity and interests it is my primary duty to consult and to maintain.

I have, &c.

(Signed) MALMESBURY.

Calais, 18th September, 10 P.M.

P.S.—In consequence of what passed between me and the French Plenipotentiaries, I left Lisle at a very early hour this morning, and expect to be in London either to-morrow or on Wednesday.

INCLOSURES REFERRED TO IN LAST DESPATCH.

(A.)

Les Soussignés, Ministres Plénipotentiaires de la République Française, chargés de traiter de la Paix avec l'Angleterre, ont l'honneur d'assurer le Lord Malmesbury, Ministre Plénipotentiaire de Sa Majesté Britannique, que le Gouvernement Français veut aussi sincèrement, aussi fortement que jamais, une paix désirée par les deux nations ; mais ne pouvant conclure qu'une Paix basée sur les Lois et les Traités qui tiennent la République Française, persuadé que pour parvenir à ce but il faut s'expliquer avec une entière franchise, et voulant imprimer à la Négociation la plus grande activité, le Directoire Exécutif a expressément chargé les Soussignés de demander au Lord Malmesbury s'il a des pouvoirs suffisans pour, dans le Traité qui seroit conclu, restituer à la République Française et à ses Alliés toutes les possessions qui depuis le commencement de la guerre ont passé dans les mains des Anglais.

Les Soussignés sont également chargés par le Directoire Exécutif de demander au Lord Malmesbury une réponse dans le jour. Ils le prient d'agréer, &c. (Signé)  TREILHARD,
BONNIER.
Par les Ministres Plénipotentiaires ;
Le Secrétaire de la Légation,
DERCHÉ.

Lille, le 29 Fructidor,
An 5 de la République.

. (B.)

Le Soussigné, Ministre Plénipotentiaire de Sa Majesté Britannique, reçoit avec beaucoup de satisfaction l'expression du désir sincère pour la Paix que les Ministres Plénipotentiaires de la République Française lui ont annoncé hier au nom de leur Gouvernement. Il a l'honneur de les assurer que le Roi son Maître est animé du même désir, et n'a rien de plus à cœur que de mettre fin aux malheurs de la guerre. Quant à la question que les Ministres Plénipotentiaires de la République Française adressent au Lord Malmesbury sur l'étendue de ses pleins pouvoirs, il croit déjà avoir fait à ce sujet la réponse la moins équivoque dans les deux Notes qu'il a remises à leurs prédécesseurs le 15 et le 24 du mois de Juillet. Cependant, pour éviter toute mésentendue, il renouvelle la déclaration qu'il a faite hier, savoir qu'il ne peut et ne doit traiter que d'après le principe des *compensations ;* principe qui a été formellement reconnu comme Base d'un Traité de Paix également juste, honorable, et avantageux aux deux Puissances.

Le Lord Malmesbury prie les Ministres, &c.

(Signé) MALMESBURY.

A Lille, ce Samedi,
16 Septembre, à 10 A.M., 1797.

---

(C.)

LES Ministres Plénipotentiaires de la République Française, chargés de traiter de la Paix avec l'Angleterre, ont l'honneur d'accuser la réception de la réponse du Lord Malmesbury à la Note qui lui a été remise dans la Conférence d'hier ; il résulte de cette réponse, et des deux Notes des 15 et 29 Juillet auxquelles elle les réfère, que le Lord Malmesbury n'a pas de pouvoirs pour consentir à *la restitution de toutes les possessions* que Sa Majesté Britannique occupe, soit sur la République Française, soit sur ses Alliés ; en conséquence, en réitérant au Lord Malmesbury les assurances les plus positives des sentimens du Gouvernement Français, les Soussignés lui donnent connoissance d'un arrêté du Directoire Exécutif, portant que dans le cas où Lord Malmesbury déclarera n'avoir pas les pouvoirs nécessaires pour consentir à toutes les restitutions que les loix et les traités qui lient la République Française rendent *indispensables,* il aura à se retirer dans les vingt-quatre heures vers sa Cour pour demander les pouvoirs suffisans. Le Lord Malmesbury ne peut voir dans cette détermination du Directoire Exécutif qu'une intention de hâter l'instant où les Négociations pourront être suivies avec la certitude d'une prompte conclusion.

Les Ministres Plénipotentiaires de la République Française prient, &c. (Signé) TREILHARD,
BONNIER.
Par les Ministres Plénipotentiaires ;
Le Secrétaire Général de la Légation,
DERCHÉ.

Lille, 30 Fructidor,
An 5 de la République Française.

---

(D.)

LE Soussigné, Ministre Plénipotentiaire de Sa Majesté Britannique, a l'honneur d'accuser la réception de la Note en date d'aujourd'hui, qui lui a été remise de la part des Ministres Plénipotentiaires de la République Française.

Quelque chagrin qu'il éprouve à voir s'évanouir l'espoir d'une prompte conciliation, il ne peut répondre à un refus aussi absolu de continuer les Négociations sur les bases qui lui paraissaient déjà arrêtées qu'en demandant les passeports nécessaires pour lui et pour sa suite, afin de pouvoir dans les vingt-quatre heures se mettre en route, et se rendre de suite en Angleterre.

Il prie les Ministres Plénipotentiaires de la République Française d'agréer, &c. (Signé) MALMESBURY.

A Lille, ce Samedi, 16 Septre., à 8 P.M.

---

(E.)

LES Soussignés, Ministres Plénipotentiaires de la République Française, chargés de traiter de la Paix avec l'Angleterre, ont l'honneur d'accuser la réception de la réponse de Lord Malmesbury à la Note qu'ils lui ont adressé aujourd'hui. Ils croient devoir lui observer qu'il ne paroit pas en avoir saisi la véritable intention ; qu'elle ne contient nullement un refus de continuer les Négociations, mais, au contraire, un moyen de les activer et de les suivre avec un succès aussi désirable pour les deux nations qu'il seroit flatteur pour les

Ministres chargés de négocier. Le Gouvernement Français, est si éloigné des intentions que semble supposer la Note du Lord Malmesbury, que les Ministres Plénipotentiaires de la République Française n'ont reçu aucun ordre de quitter le lieu des Conférences après le départ du Ministre Plénipotentiaire de Sa Majesté Britannique.

    Les Ministres Plénipotentiaires, &c.

              (Signé)     Treilhard,
                        Bonnier.

        Par les Ministres Plénipotentiaires ;
           Le Secrétaire Général de la Légation,
              (Signé)     Derché.

Lille, ce 30 Fructidor,
  An 5 de la République Française.

---

## (F.)

Le Soussigné, Ministre Plénipotentiaire de Sa Majesté Britannique, a l'honneur d'accuser la réception de la Note que les Ministres Plénipotentiaires de la République Française lui ont transmise hier au soir, par les mains du Secrétaire Général de leur Légation. Il croit ne pas pouvoir mieux répondre qu'en leur soumettant à son tour les observations suivantes. Qu'ayant déjà fait par sa Note du 24ᵉ Juillet, et d'après les ordres exprès de sa Cour, une réponse à la question qui vient d'être si inopinément renouvelée, question qui ne portant en apparence que sur les limites de ses *pleins pouvoirs* (qui sont des plus amples) exige en effet la déclaration de toute l'étendue de ses *instructions;* et ne pouvant être autorisé en aucun cas, hormis celui de la rupture des Négociations, de quitter le lieu de sa destination sans les ordres exprès du Roi son Maître, il n'a pu regarder une Note portant d'après un arrêté du Directoire Exécutif, " qu'il avait à se retourner dans les vingt-quatre heures vers sa Cour," que comme une démarche peu propre à accélérer la confection de la Paix.

Cependant, pour répondre aux assurances des Ministres Plénipotentiaires de la République Française, et pour témoigner son désir de saisir bien leur véritable intention, sur laquelle il serait très fâché de se méprendre, il croit qu'il pourrait être plus satisfaisant de se réunir encore une fois ; et dans le cas où les Ministres Plénipotentiaires de la République Française se trouvassent du même avis, le Lord Malmesbury leur proposerait que cette réunion eût lieu de meilleure heure que de coutume, afin qu'il se trouve à temps de prendre le parti que pourra exiger le résultat de leur Conférence.

Il prie les Ministres Plénipotentiaires, &c.

(Signé)   MALMESBURY.

A Lille, ce Dimanche,
17 Septre., à 9 A.M., 1797.

(G.)

LES Soussignés, Ministres Plénipotentiaires de la République Française, chargés de traiter de la Paix avec l'Angleterre, ont l'honneur d'accuser la réception de la note que le Ministre Plénipotentiaire de Sa Majesté Britannique leur a transmise ce matin, en se référant aux Notes adressées à Lord Malmesbury le 29 et 30 Fructidor, et notamment à la première du jour d'hier. Ils acceptent la réunion que le Lord Malmesbury paroit désirer, et lui proposent l'heure de midi.

Ils prient, &c.   (Signé)   TREILHARD,
BONNIER.

Par les Ministres Plénipotentiaires ;
Le Secrétaire Général de la Légation,
(Signé)   DERCHÉ.

Lille, le 1 jour complémentaire
de l'an 5 de la République Française.

LETTER FROM MR. CANNING TO LORD MALMESBURY.

Spring Gardens, Sunday, 17th Sept., 1797.

MY DEAR LORD MALMESBURY,—I keep my promise in despatching a second messenger to you, though I have heard enough since that promise was made to make me doubt whether his arrival at Lisle is likely to be of that use and comfort to you which I intended, or if he is likely to arrive at Lisle at all. I send him nevertheless. I have, indeed, detained him twelve hours, from last night till this morning, in expectation of hearing from you,—an expectation founded on calculations of time and place, which I now suppose must have been erroneous. I wish I could suppose that the report of facts which set me upon making these calculations was erroneous also.

In this state of fearful apprehensions as to the issue of the business, I know not what I can have to say upon the state in which it was when last I heard from you, however much I felt I had to say upon it when I mentioned to you, on Thursday, my intention of writing again in a day or two. It is a moment rather for looking back than looking forward; and in doing so I find (as you, I am sure, will find it) a great consolation, whatever the issue may be, in seeing that *no step has been omitted*, and (what is more) *no step hazarded on your part* that could reasonably be expected to lead to any other than a satisfactory conclusion. It is a consolation too, but not unmixed with feelings of a less pleasant nature, with disappointment and regret, that the hopes which you had entertained yourself, and the prospect which you held out to us, were such as to justify the idea that such a conclusion could not be far off, and that it will not have been altered by any event that human foresight or prudence could have anticipated and prevented. It is a consolation to me to know, and to you to have collected, as I think you must have done from two letters,—the first (if it were legible) by the last conveyance but one; the other written in part to supply its place if it should have missed you, and to enforce its meaning if you should have received it,—that in *one* quarter,\* at least, no obstacles would have arisen to the progress which you had apparently marked out for your proceedings; and that it required, on the part of our adversary, not only that too much should be asked, but should be asked in such a manner as that much, or anything, could

\* Alluding to Pitt.

not possibly be granted, to defeat the *settled purpose* of your Mission.

I wait with more impatience than I can describe for the first news from you.

Poor Brooks!—The sort of news that I expect reminds me of him and his fate. Two more unpleasant events could not be brought together. I have sent the Captain of the packet-boat who brought me the intelligence of the misfortune, Captain Sutton, a very decent, sensible, good man (as he appears to be), to bring over (if they can be found) the bodies of Brooks and his companion, for interment at Dover.

Adieu, &c.    G. CANNING.

---

MONDAY, SEPT. 18.—We left Lisle at half-past six A.M., and arrived at Calais at a quarter past six P.M. No adventure on the road. The President Bailleul at Calais, the Commissary of the Executive Power, and all our old friends, called on us. Pegou the Commissary said, " Quoique nous vous voyons, Milord, toujours avec plaisir, cependant nous regrettons beaucoup votre retour, bien que nous sommes sûrs *que ce n'est pas votre faute.*" This was a strong expression in the mouth of a person who is immediately employed by the Directory. Despatched the messengers on to England in a neutral vessel.

---

LETTER FROM LORD MALMESBURY TO MR. PITT.

Calais, Sept. 18th, 1797.

MY DEAR SIR,—Although I shall in a very few hours have the pleasure of seeing you, I cannot delay till then thanking you most sincerely for your two last very comfortable private letters.* No consolation could ever come at a moment when it is more wanted. I almost feel guilty of ingratitude in making so ill a return to it as that of leaving Lisle so

---

\* These letters, written just as Pitt heard of the Revolution at Paris, reiterated his "unaltered determination" to obtain peace if possible, and to give Lord Malmesbury every facility for that object.

rapidly, notwithstanding, God knows, my will by no means consented to this act. I trust this will appear in everything I have said and done, and that nothing has been omitted on my part to obtain what I know to be *your first wish*, and which I can safely say was also *mine*. The having failed in it hurts me still the more, as we infallibly should have succeeded had not the *political earthquake* of the 4th of September taken place. But, success being impossible, the next best comfort is, the having failed without discredit to myself; and if, when I have the pleasure to meet you, I should be assured of it, I shall feel comfort fully equal to that in which I began this letter by thanking you.

  I am, &c.     (Signed)   MALMESBURY.

---

LETTER FROM LORD MALMESBURY TO MR. CANNING.

          Calais, Monday, 9 P.M., Sept. 18th, 1797.

MY DEAR CANNING,—If the date of the place from whence this letter is written surprises you, let me refer you to my public despatch for all the wholesale reasons, and desire you to wait for the more detailed one till to-morrow evening, or probably Wednesday morning, when I hope we shall meet. Your private letter to me by Herslet, although on an uncomfortable subject, afforded me very great consolation; since I not only perceive you are prepared for my return, but prepared for it in a way which totally disperses the few apprehensions I had, lest my conduct, under the present circumstances, might not in every respect have met every approbation.

From what you say, I am now certain it will; and it gives me the more pleasure, from a consciousness that I never in my life acted more rightly.

I am too fatigued to go on to-night with the messengers, but we sail to-morrow at nine A.M.; and, on the whole, I had rather you should read my story than hear it told by me. I have much to say to you, and to some others, but I should not like to hold forth before a Cabinet.

I am infinitely obliged to you (in the strict sense of the word) for your very friendly and attentive goodness in endeavouring to replace all that I lost by the cruel accident which has happened to poor Brooks. Your principal does not partake of this sort of feeling ; and he has as few of this species of human *imperfections* as any being called *human* can pretend to.

Let us hear from you on our arrival. I shall drive at once to my own house, and, if possible, before twelve o'clock on Wednesday.

    I am, &c.   (Signed)  MALMESBURY.

---

EXTRACT OF A DESPATCH FROM LORD MALMESBURY TO LORD GRENVILLE.

Calais, 19th Sept., 1797.

THERE can be little doubt, from the language and manner of the French Plenipotentiaries, that there is a fixed determination on the part of the French Government to continue war with England ; and that if in any part of their behaviour or conversation with me there appeared a contrary intention, it was solely with a view to avoid, if possible, that the odium of breaking off the Negotiation should be imputed entirely to them. They, however, have managed this with so very little ability—what they have done has been so positive, and what they have said so vague—that it is difficult even for the most prejudiced minds to entertain a doubt on this subject.

The whole of my official Correspondence since the event of the 4th of September will, I trust, have so far prepared your Lordship for what has now happened, that, although it may very justly cause concern, it will not create surprise. Disposed as I was to pay attention to whatever I heard from the late members of the French Legation, as well from their knowledge of their own country, as from my having on every important point always found their information correct, I could never allow my opinion to go with them on this particular point ; and although the satisfaction of having judged rightly cannot, on an occasion like this, be very great, yet the not having misled your Lordship diminishes, to a certain degree, the regret I feel on having failed in the great end of my Mission.

It would be vain to search for any rational motive for such conduct as the Directory have thought proper to adopt, or to endeavour to explain on what grounds they can prefer a hazardous and unpromising continuation of a war, become extremely unpopular, to an advantageous and honourable peace, and one which, I am confident, would have had the approbation of the whole French nation. The solution of this difficulty cannot be found either in the internal situation of France, or in its present relative position to other powers, but must be sought for in the daring and inconsiderate character of the two governing members of the Directory, Barras and Rewbell. The success which has attended their late very bold undertaking appears to have given them the most implicit confidence in their own abilities, and in the strength of their party; and they never at any time appeared to have any fixed system, or to look forward beyond the circumstances of the moment.

---

LETTER FROM MR. CANNING TO MR. LEIGH.

Spring Gardens, 19th Sept., 1797.

Do you like to know bad news before anybody else, and under the penalty of saying nothing about it for a whole day?

Know, then, that I have this morning heard that Lord Malmesbury and his companions are on their way home. This cursed Revolution has baffled our good intentions for this time. It cannot finally defeat them.

---

TUESDAY, SEPT. 19.—I gave twenty louis to the sailors who had saved the boxes when Brooks was drowned. No passports were asked of me at Calais, or given me on going away. I sailed at half-past ten A.M.; a very smooth but rainy passage. Wrote to Pitt and Lord Grenville. Got to Dover at half-past four; some people, but not many, on the shore. Dined at Payne's, and slept at Sittingbourne.

WEDNESDAY, SEPT. 20.—Got to London at one A.M. Hammond came from Canning's, and Canning was with me immediately.—With Lord Grenville at his own house; he expressed great satisfaction with all that had been done; confirmed what I had already heard from Canning, that secret communication had been made of the *arrêté* of the Directory for sending me away before my despatches arrived. It was dated Monday the 11th. This came through a secret channel to Pitt. O'Drusse (*Grand Vicaire* to the Bishop d'Autun) also here. Both of them offer peace, on our terms, for money. O'Drusse (the most reasonable) says, the Bishop can undertake (if he remains in power) to get us one of the Dutch settlements (Ceylon, probably,) for 200,000*l.*, and without any *conditions onéreuses*. Lord Grenville says, what was proposed by the other was Pitt's secret, and I should probably hear it from him. Lord Grenville seemed to doubt the necessity of any further Note; I strongly for it; that I had left the business *unfinished*, and had left it so on purpose; that, if we said nothing, it would be giving an advantage to our enemies, who would have it to say, we had left them at Lisle, and refused to go on with a negotiation they never intended to break off. Lord Grenville admitted my reasoning, and said he would mention it to the Cabinet. Duke of Portland called on me; just come from the King, who is highly satisfied with me. Duke himself seems glad that the Negotiation seems likely to be at an end. He expressed his surprise at my getting such true and accurate intelligence at Lisle. (N.B. He was not in the secret of Pein or La Garde.\*) Dined with Canning; note from Pitt, who had lost his brother-in-law, Mr. Elliot, in the morning. He first fixed the evening for seeing me, then put me off, being unwell. Canning and myself agreed as to the great advantage of making a judicious answer to the Note sending me from Lisle. We wrote on this subject a letter to Pitt. It appears from Canning that Pitt's informant comes *from Barras*; that his offers are like those of Melville and Potter;

---

\* La Garde was Secretary-General to the Directory, and communicated the discussions and correspondence of the Government to Maret, to whose party he belonged.

any terms we choose for *money*, but this asked for to a great amount. It would seem that Rewbell is not in the secret, and a degree of mystery hangs over the whole, which makes it suspicious, and it ought in my mind to be scouted.

THURSDAY, SEPT. 21.—Breakfast with Canning; continue our conversation of the preceding night; at eleven with Pitt. He confirms all I heard from Canning and Lord Grenville; read me the *arrêté* of the Directory of the 11th; stronger than the terms used in their Note. The words, " Il (Lord M.) aura à déclarer ses pleins pouvoirs suffisants (that is to say, sufficient for the restitution of the King's conquests), et à les exhiber d'abord; et, en cas qu'il ne les a pas, d'aller en Angleterre dans les vingt-quatre heures les chercher lui-même." Treilhard and Bonnier softened this; they gave " *un jour*" to declare whether I had these full powers or not, and twenty-four hours " pour *m'inviter* à mon retour à ma Cour." Pitt said this *arrêté* was communicated to him on the 15th by a person he was not at liberty to name (N.B. It was Boyd, the banker), but of whose authority he could not doubt; and he then told me all I had heard from Canning. I much recommended sending such an answer as would strengthen even the strong ground we now stood on (if war was to be the event), and, if these secret offers meant anything, to afford the Directory an opening to renew the Negotiation. Dundas came in with some old news from France; then Lord Grenville and I went to the office. Dined with George Ellis, and at Lord Grenville's at half-past eight; he had sent me the draft of the answer he meant to be given by Canning, with a request that I should alter or amend it, as I thought proper. I carried it back to him; and although I could have wished to have shortened it in several places, yet I contented myself with proposing only a few verbal corrections, and altering some phrases not quite *French*. We talked over the business, and its probable success; he doubtful; cannot comprehend the intention of the new Government, or how to connect the *secret offers* (which evidently appear to be authorized) with the strange behaviour of the Ministers at Lisle, a behaviour which they were ordered to hold by the Directory; the only solution of it was, that it was meant to shew what they dared to do if we refused to acquiesce in their pecuniary demands. I observed, that it appeared as if their *secret offers* were made, not *solidairement*, and by the whole firm, but *only by Barras and his set;* that Rewbell was as corrupt as Barras, and still more violent, and that war was his passion; that it was possible he would send the Dutch fleet out,* and take the chance of their success; but, if they were beat, he would accuse them of treachery, and avail himself of it as a pretence to *annex* Holland to the French Republic; that his entire conduct relative to the Dutch seemed to bear a reference to such an intention. Lord Grenville agreed in this: returned tŏ George Ellis's, where Canning was; read over the Note; proposed more alterations; consulted with those who were with me at Lisle, who happened all to be at G. Ellis's, and all agreed with me.that there were expressions in the Note which committed the late Plenipotentiaries, and I was most anxious on every account to avoid this.

FRIDAY, SEPT. 22.—Private business; at half-past eleven with Pitt, at his request; the Note altered as we wished. He said I was quite right as to judging it was right to continue the Negotiation; his informant said it was necessary to the plan of the Directory; he (Pitt) had informed him of our intentions; he was actually gone to Paris to prepare the way for proper instructions being sent to Lisle. I said I trusted he (Pitt) had been very explicit both as to the terms and the price; that *no cure no pay* should be stipulated—not a penny to be given till after the ratifications, and every article valued and paid for *ad valorem;* that I should never return to Lisle for any other purpose but to *sign* a *Treaty;* and that before I left England we should see an *arrêté* of the Directory, fixing

* Lord Malmesbury was right in his conjecture. Urged by repeated messages from the Directory, Admiral Winter put to sea on the 9th of October. On the 11th, after a very hard-fought action with the British fleet of equal force, under Admiral Duncan, off Camperdown, he was captured with almost all his line-of-battle ships.

the terms and instructions given by them to Treilhard
and Bonnier in consequence. This Pitt said was actually
done, and agreed with me that nothing short of it was
worth attending to. Lords Grenville and Dundas came:
I went to the office; they sent for me in half an hour.
Lord Grenville then read to me the Note as he meant it
should be signed by me, and a very handsome despatch
with which he accompanied it, strongly expressive of the
King's approbation; the King, he said, approved the measure.
When alone with Pitt, we entered into a long discourse
of conjectures and speculations, which turned nearly
on what has been already said; observed the great advantage
of keeping Opposition in the dark; Pitt sanguine,
*more* sanguine than I am. I see doubts and dangers in all
this *secret* intelligence. I admit the *desire* of getting the
money, but I question the *power* of delivering the thing
purchased. *Barras confessedly the only one in the secret;*
he and his expect to persuade Rewbell, and to prevail on
him to take his share of the bribe. *Thence* my apprehensions;
and it clearly appears that the two informants
(O'Drusse's and Pitt's) act separately. It is to be remarked
that Huskisson is in the whole secret; but it is enjoined
that he is not to say so to Pitt, or Pitt to him. I dislike
Huskisson, both as to his principles and the turn of his
understanding; he wants to make money by this peace,
and dares not apply to me to act with him; the whole
secret was known in the City the day it was told Pitt,
and acted on by the stock-jobbers; *stock-jobbing is at the
bottom of the whole*, I fear. The Chancellor, Lord Loughborough,
walked home with me from Pitt's: he not in the
whole secret, and, as usual, questioning, and apparently
sanguine.—Electrified for my arm; dinner at G. Ellis's;
concerted means to get at Pein.

SATURDAY, 23.—Breakfast early with Canning; Wyck
the messenger who goes to Lisle; I desire him to ask
Cunningham whether *our friend* has got the *seal* ready
I desired him to get for me; this will make Pein understand
what I mean, and we shall hear from him; Wyck

clever. At half-past nine set out for Park Place; got there by two; found all well.

---

DESPATCH FROM LORD GRENVILLE TO LORD MALMESBURY.

Downing Street, 22nd Sept., 1797.

My Lord,—I have had the honour of laying before His Majesty your Lordship's despatches, in which you have given the account of the extraordinary conduct of the new Plenipotentiaries of the French Republic, and of the answers given by your Lordship to their unjustifiable demand, and of your consequent departure from Lisle.

I have the satisfaction to be able to assure your Lordship, that His Majesty has been pleased to express his entire approbation of your Lordship's judicious and temperate conduct in the *unprecedented* situation in which you were placed, and of the manner in which you expressed yourself both in your official Notes and in your conversations with the French Plenipotentiaries, as well as of the manner in which you have conducted yourself during the whole course of the Negotiation, which seems too likely to be now brought to its close.

As it appears, however, that some further answer will probably be expected by the French Government to their late extraordinary demand, notwithstanding the full and conclusive reply given in your Lordship's Notes, I have received the King's commands to transmit to you the inclosed draft of a Note, which it is His Majesty's pleasure that your Lordship should transmit to the Plenipotentiaries at Lisle by a messenger, whom I shall direct to be in readiness for that purpose.

I have, &c.  (Signed)  GRENVILLE.

## NOTE TO THE FRENCH PLENIPOTENTIARIES.

A Londres, ce 23e Septembre, 1797.

Le Soussigné, Ministre Plénipotentiaire de Sa Majesté Britannique, a rendu à sa Cour un compte fidèle des circonstances qui ont interrompu l'exercise des fonctions importantes qu'il avait plu au Roi son maître de lui confier. Sa Majesté a daigné honorer de son approbation entière les réponses que le Soussigné a déjà faites à la demande extraordinaire et inattendue que les nouveaux Plénipotentiaires de la République Française lui ont adressée dès leur arrivée à Lille. Mais pour ne laisser aucun doute sur la nature et l'objet de cette demande, le Soussigné a reçu l'ordre exprès de déclarer au nom de sa Cour :

1°. Que les pleins pouvoirs que Sa Majesté a jugé à propos de lui accorder pour traiter et conclure la Paix, sont conçus et rédigés dans la forme la plus ample, autorisant le Soussigné pleinement et sans réserve à signer tout Traité de quelle nature et sous quelles conditions que ce fut, dont il pourroit convenir avec les Plénipotentiaires Français, en se conformant toujours aux instructions qu'il auroit reçues de la part de sa Cour.

2°. Que ces pleins pouvoirs *ont été réçus et reconnus* pour suffisans, tant par les Plénipotentiaires avec lesquels il a traité jusqu'ici, que par le Directoire lui-même. Et qu'il ne peut en conséquence y avoir lieu à aucune nouvelle discussion sur cet objet déjà terminé par un commun accord, et qui d'ailleurs n'est susceptible d'aucune difficulté ou doute quelconque; tout ce qui a été fait à cet égard étant entièrement conforme aux usages établis depuis long-tems, et reconnus par toutes les nations de l'Europe.

3°. Que la demande du Directoire se rapporte donc réellement non pas aux pleins pouvoirs du Soussigné, mais à l'étendue de ses instructions, dont le Directoire ne pouvoit en aucun cas lui demander la communication, qu'en autant que le Soussigné pourroit la juger utile au succès de la Négociation. Et que bien loin d'être dans le cas de donner des nouvelles explications quelconques, le Soussigné avoit tout lieu de croire, d'après les communications réitérées qui lui ont été faites par les Plénipotentiaires Français, qu'il recevroit incessamment un contre-projêt de nature à faciliter la marche ultérieure de la Négociation suspendue depuis plus de deux mois.

4º· Que la Cour de Londres a dû être bien plus étonnée encore du contenu de la nouvelle demande faite au Soussigné, cette demande portant sur des conditions préliminaires qui avoient déjà été rejetées dès le commencement de la Négociation, et dont les Plénipotentiaires Français s'étaient en effêt départis par l'annonce formelle des mesures dont le Directoire s'occupoit pour s'arranger en conséquence avec ses Alliés.

5º· Que ce n'est donc qu'en consentant à traiter sur la base du projêt détaillé avec tant de franchise, que le Soussigné a remis dès les premiers jours de son séjour à Lille, ou bien en lui faisant passer un contre-projêt d'une nature conciliatoire, conformément aux assurances qu'il en a reçues depuis si long-tems qu'il paroit possible de continuer la Négociation, dont les Plénipotentiaires l'ont si fortement assuré que le Directoire ne désiroit pas la rupture malgré la démarche adoptée à son égard—démarche que le Soussigné s'abstient de qualifier, mais qui n'a pu manquer de produire ici l'impression des dispositions les moins pacifiques de la part du Directoire.

Le Soussigné est chargé d'ajouter que Sa Majesté verroit avec un vrai regret la certitude de ces dispositions si peu compatibles avec le désir ardent qui l'anime de pouvoir rendre la paix aux deux nations. Mais que si, sans y avoir contribué de sa part, Sa Majesté doit encore se trouver dans la nécessité de continuer la guerre, elle se conduira dans toutes les occasions d'après les mêmes principes, en faisant tout ce qui peut dépendre d'elle pour le rétablissement de la paix, mais en persistant toujours à défendre avec une fermeté inébranlable la dignité de sa Couronne, et les intérêts de son Peuple.

Le Ministre Plénipotentiaire de Sa Majesté Britannique prie les Ministres Plénipotentiaires, &c.

(Signé) MALMESBURY.

### REPLIES OF THE FRENCH PLENIPOTENTIARIES.

Lille, le 4 Vendémiaire, an 5 de la République.

Les Ministres Plénipotentiaires de la République Française, chargés de traiter de la paix avec l'Angleterre, ont reçu la note datée de Londres, qui leur a été apportée par un Courier Extraordinaire de la part de Lord Malmesbury. Ils ont l'honneur de lui répondre que leur Note de 29 Fructidor, à laquelle ils se réfèrent, présentoit la double assurance de l'intention formelle du Gouvernement Français de continuer les Negociations de la Paix, et de sa détermination constante de n'accéder qu'à des conventions compatibles avec la dignité de la République Française ; une paix dont la base seroit contraire aux loix, ou aux engagemens pris avec les Alliées, ne sauroit remplir l'espoir de la nation ; c'est un point dont le Directoire Exécutif ne s'est jamais départi, et sur lequel ses sentimens n'ont jamais varié.

Le Lord Malmesbury ayant formellement déclaré dans ses Notes du 15 et 29 Juillet, et, en dernier lieu, de 17 Septembre qu'il n'avoit pas les pouvoirs nécessaires pour restituer les possessions Hollandaises et Espagnoles occupées par les troupes de Sa Majesté Britannique, le Directoire Exécutif a donné une nouvelle preuve de sa loyale franchise, et de son désir d'accélérer la conclusion, en invitant le Lord Malmesbury à se retirer vers sa Cour pour obtenir des autorisations, sans lesquelles il ne peut pas conclure ; démarche nécessitée par les déclarations du Ministre Plénipotentiaire de Sa Majesté Britannique, et sur laquelle il est impossible de faire prendre le change à tout esprit juste.

Les Ministres, &c.     (Signé)     Treilhard,
Bonnier.

Par les Ministres Plénipotentiaires :
Le Secrétaire Général de la Legation,
(Signé)     Derché.

---

Lille, le 10 Vendémiaire, an 6 de la République Française.

Les Ministres Plénipotentiaires de la République Française, chargés de traiter de la paix avec l'Angleterre, ont l'honneur de faire savoir au Lord Malmesbury, qu'ayant adressé copie de sa dernière Note à leur Gouvernement, le Directoire Exécutif leur a prescrit de déclarer en son nom, qu'il n'a pas cessé de vouloir la paix, qu'il a donné une preuve non équivoque du sentiment qui l'anime, lorsqu'il a ordonné aux Ministres Plénipotentiaires de la République de réclamer une explication catégorique sur les pouvoirs donnés par le Gouvernement Anglais à son Ministre Plénipotentiaire ; que cette demande n'avoit et ne pouvoit avoir d'autre objet que d'amener enfin la Négociation à une issue prompte et heureuse.

Que l'ordre donné aux Ministres Plénipotentiaires de la République de rester à Lille après le départ du Lord Malmesbury, est une nouvelle preuve que le Directoire avoit désiré et prévu son retour avec des pouvoirs qui ne seroient pas illusoires, et dont la limitation ne seroit plus un prétexte pour retarder la conclusion de la paix.

Que telles sont toujours les intentions et les espérances du Directoire Exécutif, qui enjoint aux Ministres Plénipotentiaires de la République de ne quitter Lille qu'au moment où l'absence prolongée du Négociateur ne laissera plus de doute sur l'intention de Sa Majesté Britannique de rompre toute Négociation.

Qu'en conséquence le vingt-cinq Vendémiaire courant (16 Octobre, vieux style) est le terme fixé pour le rappel des Ministres Plénipotentiaires de la République Française, dans le cas où à cette époque le Ministre Plénipotentiaire de Sa Majesté Britannique ne seroit pas rendu à Lille.

Le Directoire Exécutif éprouvera un vif regret qu'un rapprochement déjà entamé deux fois, n'ait pu être consommé ; mais sa conscience et l'Europe entière lui rendront ce témoignage, que le Gouvernement Anglais seul aura fait peser le fleau de la guerre sur les deux nations.

 Les Ministres, &c. (Signé) TREILHARD,
             BONNIER.

 Par les Ministres Plénipotentiaires :
  Le Sécrétaire Général de la Légation,
    (Signé) DERCHÉ.

### REPLY TO THE FRENCH PLENIPOTENTIARIES.

A Londres, ce 5 Octobre, 1797.

Le Soussigné ayant remis au Ministre du Roi la Note des Plénipotentiaires de la République Française, a l'ordre de leur observer—Que ce n'est qu'en conséquence de l'injonction formelle et positive du Directoire qu'il a quitté Lille. Que ses pouvoirs n'étoient ni illusoires ni limités, et que rien n'a été omis de sa part pour accélérer la Négociation, qui n'a été retardée que par les délais du Directoire, et qui n'est aujourd'hui suspendue que par son acte.

Pour ce qui regarde la reprise des Conférences, le Soussigné ne peut que se référer à sa dernière Note où il a désigné avec franchise et précision les *seuls moyens* qui restent pour continuer la Négociation, observant en même tems que le Roi ne pourroit plus traiter en païs Ennemi, sans avoir la certitude de voir respecter pour l'avenir, dans la personne de son Plénipotentiaire, les usages établis parmi toutes les nations civilisées à l'égard des Ministres publics, et principalement de ceux chargés de travailler au rétablissement de la Paix.

Le Lord Malmesbury prie, &c.

(Signé) MALMESBURY.

---

Park Place, Sunday, Sept. 24.—Windham here. Walk with him; tell him the outlines of the Negotiation. He adverse to the measure from the beginning, but very fair and reasonable in his opposition to it. He now croaks, and thinks France must be master of Europe. He stated his reasons, and several are good ones. I oppose to them, first, the probability of Buonaparte's erecting Italy into a kingdom for himself; secondly, a civil war in France; thirdly, the renewal of that with the Emperor. In talking of Pitt, he agreed he was not sufficiently acquainted with mankind; had not mixed enough in the world; "went on by concessions, and lived in office by *tiding it over*," was Windham's expression. He doubted much whether his friends would stick by him, if a popular cry was raised against him; and whether most of them who support him in the House of Commons would not leave him if he was attacked by a more serious and active Opposition. He said, on my suggestion, that *quizzing* was made a vile part of the present system; and that, when any thing could be *quizzed away*, it was considered as completely got rid of. Of Lord Grenville he said, he was well-informed, and high-minded; more ideas of national dignity than Pitt, but so reserved and *caché* that it was impossible for him to be a great Minister. *He knew nobody, and was known by nobody.* Of the Government in general, he said it was a *Scotch one.* Dundas ruled despotically. Sir G. Elliot had been sacrificed by him; and, from personal dislike to him, the worst of all measures had been adopted, viz. the abandoning of Corsica,* and with it the loss of Italy. Windham is uncommonly and classically clever, but has the very fault he attributes to Pitt—no real knowledge of mankind; not from not living in the world, but from not being endowed with those qualities (inferior in themselves) which would enable him to judge of their real designs and character. From this reason he was the dupe of every emigrant who called on him; and he still persists in the idea of the *Bellum internecinum,* and the invading of France. Burke spoilt him, and his genius still rules him. He is withal the most honourable and most sensible of the Cabinet, and with many very great and amiable private virtues—a first-rate scholar, and quite of the right school—not the Etonians.†

WEDNESDAY, SEPT. 27.—Left Park Place half-past six; in London a quarter past ten; breakfast with Canning. Arthur Paget called on me. Saw the Duke of York for a moment at his own house. Levee; all of us except G. Ellis presented. At three, Pitt came; he, to my great surprise, told me, Wyck was returned, and with such an answer as left little

* In October, 1796, the British Cabinet ordered Corsica to be evacuated, in opposition to the remonstrances of Sir Gilbert Elliot the viceroy, and Commodore Nelson, who had undertaken to defend it.

† The Etonians were looked upon as better versed in classical poetry than prose, philosophy, and grammar; and yet no public nursery of learning has ever produced so many accomplished and great men as Eton. If she does not foster accurate Grecians, she produces neither purists nor pedants; and sends forth her manly children not the less ready to wrestle with the present century because versed in the lore of two thousand years ago.

chance of any good coming from the interposition of their *secret* agents; one of them was detained at Dover a day, in endeavouring to cross to Calais. Pitt in spirits; had provided supplies for two more campaigns. Talk of publishing extracts of my correspondence: not quite determined as to the manner. Intends now to propose a separate Peace to Spain—this suggested from Lisbon, by Pinto. Lord Grenville informed me soon after of the return of Wyck. Went with him to his house, to see the answer; ill drawn up, and impertinent. He seemed to think some immediate publication proper. Various conversations with most of the Cabinet, on this and other points. In the closet with the King; extremely gracious; highly satisfied; most right in his opinions, and dignified in his sentiments. Dined *tête-à-tête* with Canning; conversation about himself. Pitt has made him an offer of Clerk of the Alienations, worth 700*l.* a year, and a sinecure. Canning more out of sorts with Lord Grenville than ever; talks of taking a place at the India Board; I dissuade him. Conversation on the Ministry. He agrees with Windham, Dundas is more active and more diligent than any other, but also selfish and Scotch. Pillage and Patronage—pillage by conquest, patronage at home. Lord Grenville hates him, and *vice versâ*. Lord Grenville seems to have made up his mind to retreat. Canning thinks he *must* resign—I do not. Wyck allowed to go no farther than Calais; his letters sent on to Lisle by an express. He brought several for me. Mrs. Elliot coming.

---

THURSDAY, SEPT. 28.—Wrote private letters till half-past ten. Duke of York breakfasted with me; read him my correspondence; he very kind and most friendly; stayed till half-past twelve. Drawing-room; Queen very gracious —*contre l'usage*. Death of Hoche. Vague reports of insurrections in the southern departments. Spoke to Lord Grenville about Ross. Dine with Pitt; small dinner— pleasant; Lords Chatham and Mornington, Windham and Canning; little or no politics. Cabinet after dinner.

Obtain Barnier's* pension for Ross, 200*l.* a year. Return home and write.

---

FRIDAY, SEPT. 29.—Lord Grenville sends for my correspondence, to select extracts proper for publication. I wish that only what passed since the arrival of Treilhard and Bonnier at Lisle should be published *now*, and the first part of the negotiation, which promised so favourably, kept till the meeting of Parliament. I also was very anxious not to publish anything which might bring Le Tourneur,† Maret, or Colchen into a scrape. Lord Grenville not absolutely inattentive to this, but bent on *not weakening our case*, as he termed it, on any consideration. I think our case too strong to need such an unlimited publication; I also think, that if we should by it draw down any punishment on the heads of the first Plenipotentiaries, besides the cruelty of such conduct, it will, from the effect it necessarily must produce, do the very thing Lord Grenville fears—*it will weaken our case.* I conversed much on this point with Canning and with Lord Spencer, with whom I dined. They both (particularly Canning) agree with me. I write to Pitt in the evening to this effect. I had then seen the extracts Lord Grenville had made, and besides considered them as uselessly long, and many of them likely from their nature to furnish Opposition with a handle for cavil, instead of strengthening the hands of Government.

---

LETTER FROM MR. CANNING TO MR. LEIGH.

Downing Street, 29th Sept., 1797.

I AM very busy indeed. There is all Lord Malmesbury's Correspondence to be prepared for the press, to convince all mankind how little it is his fault or ours that we have not at this moment a peace. We were within a hair's breadth

---

\* Barnier was Lord Malmesbury's old Secretary during his Missions to Berlin and Russia, and had lately died.

† It is necessary to observe, for the sake of historical accuracy, that Le Tourneur had been kept throughout in ignorance of the secret Negotiation between Maret, Talleyrand, the moderate Directors, and Lord Malmesbury.

of it. Nothing but that cursed Revolution at Paris, and the sanguinary, insolent, implacable, and ignorant arrogance of the Triumvirate, could have prevented us. Had the moderate party triumphed, all would have been well; not for us only, but for France, for Europe, and for the world. As it is, if there be any comfort in comparison, it is worse for the world in general, for all Europe, and for France above all, than it is for us. I am persuaded there would be but one sentiment in this country upon this occasion. Pray do not let your Sir B. B.'s or anybody else mislead you for a moment with talking about *terms*. It was not any question of *terms*, of giving up this or retaining that—it was a settled determination to get rid of the chance of Peace, on the part of the three scoundrelly Directors, that put an end to the Negotiation. Nothing else could have done so. I write this in the midst of a hubbub of clerks; all of whom I am taking home from their work to dine with me, that they may work again the more readily and actively after dinner.

### EXTRACTS OF A LETTER FROM LORD MALMESBURY TO MR. PITT.

Spring Gardens, 29th Sept., 1797.

In the selection of extracts made from my correspondence for publication, I am apprehensive that in several places it exposes my first French colleagues, in the present state of things in France, to imminent danger; and it appears to me that these parts might either be wholly suppressed, or at least softened, without at all weakening our case. The never naming them *separately*, but calling them everywhere *the French Plenipotentiaries*, would equally convey to the Republic what it is requisite for them to know, and deprive the Directory of the means of gratifying any personal ill-will against any particular member of the French Legation.

I waited in town to-day, that I might be in the way in case I was to be consulted; but as I understand from Canning he is to shew me the despatches, *in the course of circulation*, I do not see well how I can venture to state my opinion officially; but *I feel it so strongly*, and am so convinced that you will understand my motive, that I cannot forbear mentioning it to you before I return to Park Place. I hope, however, to see you in London on Wednesday, but I am afraid it would then have been too late to state what I now write.

SATURDAY, SEPT. 30.—Received at nine o'clock a letter from Lord Grenville. From the tone, I find him aware of my sentiments, and that his by no means agree with them in respect to using more caution and more delicacy towards my first colleagues. I wrote to him to state my opinion, and to press strongly the substituting everywhere the words "French Plenipotentiaries" for "Le Tourneur, Maret, or Colchen." I send my letter by Ross. Lord Grenville admits him, and, after perusing my letter, consents to the alteration: he says he even thinks it "more *dignified!*"

SUNDAY, OCT. 1.—A letter from Pitt; agrees with me as to substituting the general expression of French Plenipotentiaries for the naming of Ministers, inasmuch as it can be done without "*violating the accuracy of quotation.*"

TUESDAY, OCT. 3.—Went to London with G. Ellis; find a French courier addressed to me from Lisle; the Note he brings a repetition of the last, but in the name of the Directory. I was sorry and angry he was not stopped at Dover; lodge him at Schau's, who has orders to attend and watch him. Canning informs me all idea of immediate publication is laid aside; he believes the Cabinet were against it, and particularly Lord Liverpool. A declaration to be made, but that delayed by the arrival of their courier. Huskisson and Hammond at Canning's. No secret information from Paris, either through O'Drusse or Boyd. This, in my mind, proves all their information to be calculated for stock-jobbing. No Minister in town. Dinner at Canning's —Windham, William Elliot, &c.

WEDNESDAY, OCT. 4.—Lord Pembroke at breakfast; prepare a sketch for an answer; send it by Canning to Pitt. N.B. It was adopted only in substance, and much shortened by Lord Grenville. Levee; Duke of Portland; Lord Chatham. Conversation with them on the style of the answer; they apparently not very much prepared on the subject. The King told me he had been at Park Place the day before; said my ricks were very fine; that I was a good farmer; that I made as good ricks as I wrote despatches, &c. Lord Grenville shewed me his *projét* for an answer to the Note; like mine, but less pacific. He cannot account for this behaviour of the Directory; he believes they mean *war*, yet want to gain *time*. *Lord Grenville invariably against peace from the beginning;* considers the secret information as a mere trick to serve the purpose of stock-jobbing. Pitt objects to that part of my intended answer where I suppose the French may mean to establish a principle in the outset, and give way on it as the Negotiation goes on; says, the saying it would look churlish. I agreed with him; but that it would be *they*, not *we*, that would appear so. He went in to the King before he could end our discussion. Duke of Portland tells me Sir G. Elliot is to be created a peer;* dinner at the Admiralty; Lord Spencer inclined to be warlike; Lady Spencer (who is very free-spoken, and at times imprudent) said to me in a half-whisper, "Take care they don't turn the tables on us." She meant, I believe, but am not sure, Pitt and Dundas; she never liked the joining them. Windham and the Duke of Portland dined there; as did Sir G. Elliot, William Elliot, and Canning.

---

THURSDAY, OCT. 4.—Batt at breakfast; W. Elliot, about Ireland, says there is a numerous and safe army, but that there is great disaffection in the north, and constant intercourse with France. Forster† about Brooks's‡ will; a very benevolent and kind one to his friends and relations. Can-

* He was created Lord Minto.     † Mr. Forster, the Solicitor.
‡ Brooks, the messenger, who was drowned. Lord Malmesbury and Mr. Canning gave themselves much trouble in arranging his affairs for his family. It is but one of many kind acts of this nature, the traces of which I find in my papers, quietly, but effectually, performed by these amiable men.

ning; answer ready; sign it, and despatch the French courier at two. Go to Oatlands; Duke of York always right and always kind. Colonel Wynyard there; a good-humoured man; conversation as usual—military and horses: Duke of York assures me the King is highly pleased with all I have done.

---

EXTRACTS OF A LETTER FROM LORD MALMESBURY TO MR. CANNING.

Bath, 20th October, 1797.

It was great satisfaction to me to hear that the private communication has in the event come out to be nothing. The relative situation of England and France is such, that, at this moment, I should be sorry either for a continuance, or even for a speedy renewal, of a pacific Negotiation. Security without peace is better than peace without security. The country at large may be taught this very plain truth now better than at any other period of the war; and, if they can be brought to admit it, we can be only gainers by delay. I have no doubt, even from the perusal of the papers printed under the authority of the French Government, that there is a general rising in the southern provinces, and that (if we do not interfere, through Royalists and Emigrants) a civil war will be the consequence; if we do employ those fatal means, we shall strengthen the Directory in their power, and palsy all those who are disposed to dispute it with them.

I am glad such a Declaration as you describe is to appear soon.

I hope to be able to remain here quietly for some time longer. I am told that ease and quiet are necessary to reinstate me, to put me in the same situation of health I was in before I went to Lisle, and I am desirous of obtaining the strict *status ante bellum*. I have been cupped this morning, and advised to abstain from the waters for a few days. What is good for my stomach is, they say, bad for my head; and with this principle they may keep me in their hands as long as they please.

If you are at Walmer, remember me kindly to Mr. Pitt.

## EXTRACTS OF A LETTER FROM LORD MALMESBURY TO LORD GRENVILLE.

*Park Place, 27th October, 1797.*

I HAVE many thanks to return you for the obliging communication of the Declaration which is intended to be published by His Majesty on the breaking off the Negotiation at Lisle. It appears to me to state with great truth, fairness, and precision the whole of the transaction. The new paragraph which has been added in consequence of our victory on the coast of Holland* is admirably well conceived, and calculated to produce the best possible effect both at Paris and at the Hague. I confess I am not sorry to hear that you pause as to the propriety of the publication of the Correspondence. There certainly could be no harm in trusting the public with the extracts from it which you had marked out; but it is impossible that it should not appear to persons accustomed to Negotiations that much is concealed, and from this, both Opposition here, and the present prevailing party in France, might derive great advantage. The nomination of Ch. Delacroix to the Dutch Embassy, and that of Truguet to Spain, look as if the Directory had views on those countries.

I need not say, that, if my personal attendance in Parliament is considered as absolutely necessary, I shall most certainly be present; but, if it is not absolutely necessary, I should hope to be dispensed with.

---

[The reader will, I think, be convinced by the foregoing papers that Pitt was not only sincere in his overtures for peace, but anxiously eager to obtain it on almost any conditions short of dishonour. The last fruitless attempt made by Lord M., in proposing to the French Ministers *another meeting*, after he had been rudely ordered to leave Lisle, is a public proof, which his private correspondence confirms, of his own zeal in the same cause. After being thus twice cavalierly turned out of France with his pacific proposals,

* Battle of Camperdown.

it is only the insolence of Ultra-Jacobin Directors, and of their contemporaneous historians, which could presume to assert that England never was sincere in her wish to make peace.*

There can be no doubt but that Lord M. would have succeeded, had Carnot and the Moderate party obtained the ascendancy. A vast portion of the French nation were eager for rest; and it has been seen that Maret, (whose character and services were afterwards so justly appreciated by Napoleon,) acting in the present Negotiation with the most patriotic and humane motives, and in concert with two of the Directors, was on the point of smoothing every difficulty, when the Revolution of the 18th Fructidor destroyed his means and all possibility of success.

With this second Mission to the French Republic, Lord Malmesbury closed his public life. From the age of twenty-four, he had held responsible situations, and had been employed in the most difficult and honourable Negotiations of his time; and at fifty he had obtained the first position in his line, and the highest reward from the Crown. At this comparatively early age he was forced to stop, and, in consequence of increasing deafness, to refuse all future employment. He continued in the intimate confidence of Pitt, the Duke of Portland, Canning, and other eminent men of that party; and was consulted by them, and later by Lord Liverpool, whenever our Foreign Policy (which, at the beginning of this century, was so difficult a subject) became the matter for discussion.

In 1800 he was created an Earl, and Viscount Fitzharris.]

* Thiers, who, with the exception of his character of persons, is a fair historian, says, " Jamais la France et l'Angleterre n'avaient été plus près de se concilier" (tom. vi. p. 22).

Since the above note was written in my first edition, M. Thiers' "Hist. of the Consulate" has appeared. Few books contain so many inaccurate accounts of men and events as this work, which, scarcely giving a single reference in support of its statements, cannot easily survive the short-lived enjoyment which the agreeable style of the writer affords to his readers of the present generation.

END OF THE THIRD VOLUME.

LONDON:
Printed by S. & J. BENTLEY, WILSON, and FLEY,
Bangor House, Shoe Lane.